The
Challenge
of
Development

The Challenge of Development

THEORY AND PRACTICE

A sourcebook edited by RICHARD J. WARD

ALDINE PUBLISHING COMPANY/*Chicago*

First published 1967 by
ALDINE Publishing Company
320 West Adams Street
Chicago, Illinois 60606

Library of Congress Catalog Card Number 66-28315
Printed in the United States of America

Preface

Books of readings in the rapidly expanding field of economic development are often limited in the areas they cover. This volume includes six basic subject areas and forty-five articles on the theory and practice of economic development. The advantage of this collection is that it represents a cross-section of the theory and practice of development as demonstrated by well-known scholars and technical experts concerned with solutions to problems at the planning and operations levels. Its emphasis is upon a pragmatic approach to development problems in countries and areas of different structural character.

Such a comprehensive selection of readings on development will have considerable value in the undergraduate course, the graduate seminar, and in development institutes. It will serve the interested general reader as well as students in both aid-giving and aid-receiving countries.

The articles derive originally from an effort to promote the United Nations Decade of Development. Delegations from all member countries were invited to Geneva in February 1963 for a conference on "The Application of Science and Technology for the Benefit of the Less Developed Areas." Participating countries were also invited to submit papers on subjects related to development, ranging from economic model building to creating coated fertilizers for controlled plant cultivation. The United Nations also encouraged joint authorship between American technicians and their counterparts working with them in the underdeveloped countries. Some of the articles, therefore, exhibit a unique venture in cooperative probing of development problems, between American advisers and technicians abroad and the host country technicians and planners only recently caught up in the practical operations of development. I had the opportunity of supervising the preparation of some of the papers from the vantage point of Jordan, where I served as economist for the United States Agency for International Development.

While contributions to the Geneva Conference came from many countries, the authors of each of these articles were associated in some way with American universities, foundations, business concerns, and government agencies concerned with economic development. Many of them have had long experience carrying out phases of this work in the developing countries around the world.

From the hundreds of contributions to the United Nations conference, these forty-five articles have been selected as the most useful for educational and practical purposes. The criterion for inclusion was the general applicability of the subject matter to problems of development in any country or region of the world, rather than to any particular problem or place. However, specific case histories are frequently used to provide focus and concrete meaning. Duplication of themes, some repetition of introductory remarks, and articles with narrow or esoteric technical appeal were avoided, and some pictures and illustrative materials included in the original articles have been omitted for reasons of space and cost, since they were not essential to the message.

The wide range of topics covered can readily be grasped from the table of contents. Almost every phase of economic development is represented. Part One, "The Challenge in Development Planning," deals with methodology, strategy, and decision-making criteria. What should be the roles of government and of the private sector in helping the less-developed nations realize more of their potential? How far should regional planning take precedence over national aspirations with respect to specific development goals? How does the planner in underdeveloped lands objectively determine the capital requirements of development? What tools can be applied to stimulate and guide economic planning toward genuine rather than artificial self-sufficiency in underdeveloped economies?

Experienced and highly qualified men—such as Gerhard Colm and Theodore Geiger of the National Planning Association, Hollis Chenery, Howard Ellis and P. N. Rosenstein-Rodan—address themselves to these questions.

Part Two takes up "The Challenge in Developing Human Resources," including labor force and manpower needs and projections, the entrepreneurial function, the needs in science and technology, public management, and education. What emphasis on manpower improvement is best calculated to provide the foundations for effective short- and long-run growth in the underdeveloped economy? What role should health and medical programs play in enhancing the productivity of the human element in development?

Part Three, "The Challenge in Developing Natural Resources," deals with the importance of the intrinsic value of the land, including its agricultural potential as it relates to a development plan. What are the conditions for rapid and sustained progress in resource development? How does the use of hydrological data facilitate the search for an efficient use of water? What part should government take in resource development? Several articles deal with methods of organizing resources in the agricultural sector to increase productivity. What relationship should this sector, including forestry and fisheries, have with industry in the structure of the developing economy?

Part Four, "The Challenge in Developing Industry," provides a cross-section of essays on the strategy and practical problems involved in promoting the industrial sector. What criteria should be used in establishing small, medium, or large industry? This section also uses specific industry areas—steel, textiles, food processing, and others—to demonstrate the problems involved in establishing new enterprises in underdeveloped countries.

Part Five deals with the development of infrastructure: power, transportation, and communications. One article evaluates power technologies from a theoretical approach. Another uses case histories and practical criteria for examining the problems developing countries face in extending the use of electricity and other power supplies, and in providing roads, marine facilities, and railroads. Some new vistas are gained in the field of communications through the realization of the awesome silence prevailing between vast rural areas of the world and modernized sectors. The dual society is partly a problem in communications.

Finally, Part Six poses answers to intriguing questions about social problems created by modern growth trends. What happens when new classes assume leadership roles in hitherto tradition-bound societies? How can the flow of rural workers into urban centers, with all the attendant personal and social problems, be accommodated? And, in Dyckman's words, "What is the optimum allocation of capital to social overhead for achieving the objectives of the society?" This part also provides a fitting conclusion to these readings by dealing with some international aspects of the worldwide spirit of development. How can the advanced nations inspire in the underdeveloped cultures a desire for technological advance? How far will the "emerging international culture," in Lasswell's phrase, suffice in setting common goals leading to "a more perfect system of universal public order"?

Taken together, these selections encompass a broad spectrum and illustrate the need for an eclectic and interdisciplinary approach to worldwide problems of economic development.

CONTENTS

PART ONE

The Challenge in Development Planning

MUCH of the practice of economic development these days evolves out of the planner's blueprint. At the same time, many of today's theories about development have been formulated out of past experience. These essays reflect some of the methodology and practice that make up the challenge of modern development. The first five articles are concerned with techniques of development planning, while the second four are concerned with international aspects of development planning.

The role of the public versus the private sector in development is always a lively subject. Colm and Geiger describe tasks the government might well undertake more effectively and those where the private sector could more efficiently spur the development process.

Model building has not been neglected in development economics, as the next three articles demonstrate. Holland opts for simulation techniques, which he believes can have more realism and flexibility than mathematical or econometric models. On the other hand, Chenery, who has figured importantly in the programming techniques used in the Agency for International Development, shows how econometric models can be used to experiment with alternative policies and programs, with a view to promoting consistency in the overall development program.

Without the use of basic theoretical concepts, planning could be frustrated in a confusing day-to-day reaction to immediate pressures. The planner needs theoretical anchors to keep him from drifting. Accounting prices represent one such anchor, used to gauge the divergence of prevailing privately determined market prices from those that would reflect actual scarcities, marginal productivities, or social values of goods or services. Papanek and Qureshi describe how accounting prices may help divert resources into activities more beneficial to development.

The growing role of development banks, especially created to cater to the special needs of development rather than to strict commercial criteria, is the subject of Checchi's article.

In the next series of four articles, various problems, multinational in character, are discussed. The advantages of regional economic planning, already proven in western experience, are applied to underdeveloped regions in the Ellis essay. Similar efforts to avoid duplication and to promote regional strength in the Alliance for Progress are ably covered by Perloff and Saez. Aubrey reviews the problem of the limited commodity markets, to which so many underdeveloped countries have been bound, and proposes means for breaking away from this dependency.

Finally, P. N. Rosenstein-Rodan provides a veritable treasure of useful maxims for the economic developer in his treatment of the volume of aid required from the few who are rich to the many who are poor, if the latter are to have some hope of achieving, not comparable living standards—for that is out of the question for most—but at least steady economic growth.

A. PLANNING TECHNIQUES

Public Planning and Private Decision-Making in Economic and Social Development

GERHARD COLM

Chief Economist, National Planning Association, Washington, D.C.

THEODORE GEIGER

Chief of International Studies, National Planning Association, Washington, D.C.

Regardless of its name, every modern form of economic system combines some measure of public planning with some latitude for private decision-making. Even in the freest of market economies, the government's own expenditures are planned in accordance with annual requirements and with the anticipated longer-range needs for those services considered appropriate for it to provide, and many large private enterprises plan their investment and market development programs for five or ten years ahead. Even in the most centralized socialist economies, the planning and administering authorities must take into account the probable responses of individuals and of local institutions to central government directives regarding production, consumption, saving, and investment. Hence, the task of harmonizing public and private decision-making confronts every modern economic system, though in different forms and in different degrees.

The less developed countries of Latin America, Asia, and Africa are in the process of working out reconciliations of public and private decision-making which are relevant to the character of their economies, consistent with their social values, and more or less effective in achieving their chosen goals. The variation is very wide, ranging from such countries as Mexico, Brazil, and Argentina, in which private decision-making in the free market plays the major role, to countries like Niger and Chad, in which the modern sector of the economy consists of a few government-owned or foreign-owned enterprises of various kinds. In consequence, it is impossible to discuss public and private decision-making in a way which is equally valid for all less developed countries. While our aim is to present some guidelines and suggestions, the analysis which follows is necessarily cast in the form of a generalized discussion of the subject and is not to be construed as descriptive of any particular country.

Functions of Government Planning and Private Decision-Making in Less Developed Countries

To a greater or lesser degree, the countries of Latin America, Asia and

5

Africa are faced with common difficulties in seeking to accelerate their economic and social advancement. Among the problems relevant to the subject of this paper are: (a) the inadequacy of the existing infrastructure (transportation and communication, energy, and power facilities, etc.) and social capital (education, health, and housing facilities, etc.), (b) the shortage of investment capital, (c) the limited supply of managerial and technical skills, (d) the inadequate incentives and institutions for stimulating productive investment and increasing productivity, and (e) the heavy dependence upon foreign trade and external aid for obtaining the capital funds and the capital goods required for economic and social development. In such circumstances, governments have had to assume responsibility for discharging three types of functions in order to insure that economic and social development would actually occur in their countries.

The first function is that of national development planning. Broadly speaking, this function consists of defining the goals of the national development effort, estimating and mobilizing the necessary domestic and foreign resources of money and skills, and allocating or guiding them to those specific uses which seem likely to make the greatest contributions to achieving the national goals. This function may be carried out by explicit preparation of a long-range national development plan, as has been done in India and Pakistan, and is now beginning in several Latin American countries. Or, it may be done implicitly and unsystematically, as was customary in many less developed countries until recently. Today, most countries have recognized that, to be effective, national development planning

must be carried on in a deliberate and systematic way.

The second function of government in economic and social development is to initiate those investments and manage those activities which comprise the public sector of the economy. In every economic system, there are certain essential services which only governments can perform (national defense, maintenance of law and order, etc.). In addition, there are certain types of investments which are so large or so pervasive in their importance to the economy as a whole that it is necessary or desirable for the government to undertake them. These generally include certain kinds of infrastructural and social overhead capital.

However, the public sector may cover a much broader range of economic activities either by deliberate preference, as in socialist countries, or because there are no practical or acceptable alternative ways of conducting them. For example, in some less developed countries, significant accumulations of capital exist in private hands, but these are often not invested in ways which directly and immediately contribute to economic growth. Traditional habits or present uncertainties may cause such private funds to flow into real estate, commodity transactions, money-lending, and other activities promising quick or large returns, which may eventually result in luxury consumption or investment abroad, usually in Western Europe or the United States. In other countries, there is no private capital or private sector of the economy in the modern sense of the term. In default of government initiative, too few private entrepreneurs would come forward to take advantage of such economic opportunities as may exist. Hence, for a variety of different reasons, the governments of many less-developed countries not only invest in essential services and infrastructure but also establish and operate, at least initially, some or all of the new economic activities that are envisaged under the national development plan.

The third function of government in economic and social development is to stimulate, guide, and assist private initiative and activities so that they contribute to achievement of the national development goals. Virtually all the less-developed countries are explicitly or implicitly committed to a significant measure of private economic decision-making as an essential complement to the economic functions of the central government. This results not only from deliberate choosing of the social values served by decentralized, nongovernmental decision-making in economic life. Paradoxically, it is necessitated by the same scarcities of capital and skills as have impelled governments to assume the national development planning function and the entrepreneurial and managerial functions comprised in the public sector of the economy. In most less developed countries, neither the governments nor the ruling political parties possess the trained supervisory personnel, the technical skills, and the funds necessary to replace all significant privately conducted activities by central planning and government operation of the economy. Determination of the output and consumption of certain types of activities and products—especially those in services and consumer-goods industries—seems to defy the detailed directives of central planners. Moreover, there are always potential sources of capital, talents, and initiative that are unavailable to governments, particularly when they operate by compul-

sion, but which can be stimulated to manifest themselves voluntarily by appropriate incentives and encouragements. The less developed a country, the less it can afford to neglect the potential resources that could be activated only voluntarily and in decentralized, nongovernmental forms.

In addition, the more numerous and detailed the entrepreneurial and managerial decisions that have to be made by the central government authorities, the slower, more cumbersome, and less flexible the operation of the economy becomes. Most less developed countries have found that the market mechanism is a much less wasteful way of making many kinds of economic decisions and for getting many kinds of economic tasks accomplished. A system of centralized direction of production, investment, and consumption is also susceptible to political pressures and the ponderous inflexibility of bureaucratic control. Some of the socialist countries have recognized this deficiency of a large, centralized public sector, and have tried to solve their problems by decentralizing many economic decisions and activities, and providing market-type incentives and pressures for guiding them. Yugoslavia is the leading example of such a country.

Also, many less developed countries have concluded that there are substantial benefits to be derived from attracting responsible private investment from the more developed countries. Continuing, well-conducted enterprises established by foreign companies and businessmen in less developed countries significantly increase the amount of capital available for productive investment; disseminate much needed managerial and technical skills among the local population; and create opportunities for—and often provide financial and technical assistance to—indigenous enterprises to get started as suppliers of the materials, components, and services required for their own operations.

There is a wide variety of different ways by which the government carries out its third function of stimulating and channelling private economic initiative and activity. Thus, it is able to select the particular combination of policy measures that seems best adapted to achieving national development goals in socially acceptable ways.

The question, then, which each less-developed country must answer for itself is which economic decisions and activities can best be undertaken by the government and which by private institutions and individuals. This choice is sometimes deliberate, but more often it grows out of the historical background and existing socio-political structure of the country.

The Participants in Public Planning and Private Decision-Making

In order to clarify the interplay between public planning and private decision-making, the actors or participants have to be defined.

In the Public Sector. Though we usually speak of the government, it must be remembered that the term covers a multitude of ministries, departments, and agencies, each engaged in planning its own activities. These include not only the several ministries or departments of the central government, but also those of provincial and local governments, as well as quasi-governmental agencies, such as social security funds, central banks, de-velopment banks and corporations, port authorities, railroad administrations, public utilities, highway commissions, government-owned and managed manufacturing enterprises, and so on. The planning of each of these governmental institutions has a greater or lesser effect on consumers, workers, and private enterprises. Each of these units of government is interested in specific policies and often subject to pressures from various groups in the population.

The multitude of activities and effects of the various parts and levels of government can themselves be planned only if there is some central planning agency which coordinates and directs planning for the government as a whole. Such a body is, in effect, responsible for the national development plan, as distinct from the different sectoral, functional, and regional programs, which deal in greater detail with the separable parts of the national economy.

The central planning agency has different locations in various countries. In some, it is located under the jurisdiction of one of the ministries (economics or finance); in others, it is organized as a ministry of its own; and in still others, it is an agency under the jurisdiction of a planning council in the office of the country's Chief Executive. National development planning is not a separate activity isolated from the other functions of government. Like budget-making, it is intimately related to all functions. Therefore, it can be effectively carried out only if, regardless of the location of the planning agency, it has the full backing of the country's Chief Executive, who is responsible for all official policies. This dependence on the highest governmental authority is best symbolized when the national development planning function is performed by an agency in the office of the Chief Executive, or the Prime Minister, and when he is directly involved in the planning process as head of a planning council.

Generally, the sectoral and functional programs contained in the national development plan can best be prepared and implemented in a decentralized manner by the individual ministries, departments, and agencies concerned. However, in some less developed countries with a scarcity of government planning personnel, the central agency may have to take on the additional functions of guiding the programing activities and training the programing personnel of the individual governmental and quasi-governmental agencies of the central administration and of provincial and local authorities.

In the Private Sector. While the participants in the public sector can be readily identified as units of the central and local governments, there is no simple way of defining the many different kinds of non-governmental enterprises and activities that play significant roles in national development efforts. A definition by enumeration will be clearer than a definition by characterization.

In some less-developed countries, non-governmental activities in commerce and industry may take the form of corporate enterprises similar to the business corporations of the United States and Western Europe. In many other less-developed countries, the most important commercial, industrial, and financial activities in the private sector are individual and family proprietorships, like those that predominated in the highly industrialized nations at earlier stages of their development. However, in most parts of Africa, Asia, and Latin America, the numerically largest portion of private economic activity is in agriculture and takes the form of large estates and of small peasant farms, the latter producing either cash crops, or subsistence crops, or a mixture of both.

In recent years, other forms of non-governmental economic activity have been established in less developed countries and have been assuming increasing importance. These include producers and marketing cooperatives, predominantly in agriculture; credit unions and other types of cooperative saving and lending institutions; productive enterprises financed or managed by trade unions, political parties, kinship groups, etc.; and similar institutions. In addition, there are various kinds of local community projects and village organizations. Though many of them may be officially sponsored or government financed, their operations largely depend upon the voluntary initiative and labor of their members, and they may be properly classified as part of the private sector.

Less numerous, but economically more significant, are various forms of joint government/private ventures, involving the participation of local entrepreneurs, and often of foreign companies, which contribute capital and managerial and technical "know-how". When, as is most often the case, the private participants in such joint enterprises are responsible for management, these activities, too, may be considered part of the private sector.

These many and diverse forms of private economic activity play different roles in the national development effort through people's decisions regarding what and when they will produce, consume, save, and invest. In the traditional forms of private economic activity (e.g. peasant farming, latifundia, moneylending, shopkeeping, etc.) these decisions tend to be based upon short-run calculations and on the assumption of static economic conditions, not of dynamic growth. Indeed, by definition, the less-developed and more traditionalist a country, the more private economic activities will be of a subsistence nature in agriculture and characterized by a static outlook in commerce, banking, and industry. If these traditionalist and static enterprises are to contribute more effectively to economic growth, their motivation and decision-making have to be reoriented toward the prospects for future expansion and growth. One essential element in bringing about such a dynamic transformation is to enlist the active participation of the numerous, smaller types of private enterprises in the national planning effort.

Generally, it is only the larger, more modern, and more productive private enterprises, including the subsidiaries of North American and West European companies, that are oriented toward longer-term growth expectations. Some follow the practice, increasingly prevalent in the developed countries, of undertaking their own long-range planning of investment and market development within the framework of the national development plan. Such private planning plays a most important role in ensuring that the private sector will make the fullest possible contribution to achieving the goals of the national development effort.

The Character of Planning in Less Developed Countries

The publication of a plan is merely one stage in national development planning. The process as a whole consists not only of preparing the plan, but also of debating and adopting it, implementing it, and then comparing actual performance with the plan and revising it periodically on the basis of experience.

A national development plan always should have a long-range perspective covering general goals for at least ten years ahead, and more details of specific objectives for an intermediate period of four or five years. It should be an operational tool, closely related to the annual government budget, particularly for the short-run period of the next year or two. Operational shorter-term and perspective longer-term planning should be in fluid interrelationship, particularly through the "feed-back" effect made possible by effective progress reporting and evaluation, and periodic revisions.

In an economy in which private decision-making plays the major role, the national development plan establishes goals for social and economic development; determines the programs in the public sector; presents forecasts of agricultural, industrial, and commercial investments in the private sector; and estimates the international transactions needed to realize the objectives. These estimates of investments in the private sector and of international transactions are of a different character and significance from the detailed investment programs prepared for the public sector.

In the public sector, the government can determine the specific programs needed and can then direct the execution of these programs. However, even in the public sector, there is an important qualification. These programs are financed either by voluntary private savings and taxation, or by forced savings of various kinds, such as inflation, restriction of consumption, compulsory labor, etc. While the programs are determined in part on the basis of estimates of the productive facilities, manpower, and skills needed to achieve the national development objectives, the expected growth in turn is the most important factor determining the financial resources which will become available.

In the private sector there is the additional task of estimating the likelihood that private domestic and foreign decision-makers will in fact engage in the activities postulated by the plan. In addition, it is important to know the amounts and kinds of consumption which would be compatible with the national development goals and with the public programs subject to government direction. For this purpose, the plan has to contain consistent relationships among investments in public undertakings (infrastructure); in social capital (education, health, housing); in directly productive enterprises (public and private); and among government and private savings, consumption, and the other major components of the national domestic and external accounts. For the private sector, the estimates have not only to be consistent with the public sector and with the plan as a whole; they must also be realistic—that is, they must represent realistic forecasts of consumer actions, personal and private institutional savings, etc.

The government can influence consumption by price, tax, wage, and other policies and by a number of other devices discussed in the next section. For the determination of these policies, the plan has to serve as a guide. Thus, the estimates of the sectors in the economy which are not under direct government control commonly consist of forecasts of actions of private decision-makers as they are likely to behave under the influence of government policies specifically designed to affect their behavior. The realism of the forecast depends in part on the degree of influence the government can and intends to exert over the behavior of the private sector.

The uncertainty is inevitably greater with regard to the estimates of international transactions embodied in the plan. A country that depends largely on exports of a few primary products traded on world markets can usually exert little influence on the prices and quantities of these exports. Hence, this item in the plan will always be purely a forecast, and it must be treated as independently given data. In contrast, other variables in the plan are subject to a greater or lesser degree of direct or indirect control (e.g. imports), and can be so adjusted as to be compatible with the independent factors. Because forecasts of the more or less independent factors may turn out to be erroneous and because these factors themselves cannot be significantly influenced by government policies, it is always prudent to provide contingency measures for adjustment in the other, controllable sectors in case adverse developments occur; for example, if export earnings are less than expected.

In forecasting investments in the private sector, an important distinction needs to be made between what may be called "strategic" investments and "collateral" investments. The former relate to increases in capacity in key industries which are essential for the fulfillment of other parts of the plan. These private investments are often projected on the basis of actual negotiations between the planning agency and the private enterprises concerned. As to the collateral investments, they may be estimated on the basis of surveys of the intentions of private enterprises, taking into account the fact that new investment opportunities arise with expanding markets. Thus, the collateral investment decisions will generally be made automatically as the economy expands in the course of economic development. Inclusion of a projection of collateral investment in the plan is necessary in order to estimate the total demand for funds and the total increase in productive capacity which are likely to be forthcoming. These estimates are, however, less firm than those for the strategic investments and are subject to a considerable margin of error.

It has not been possible in the short space available to indicate more than a few of the many ways in which goal setting, program determination, forecasting, and choice of implementation policies interact with one another in the complex process of planning for economic and social development. The essential role which the forecasting, or projection, of the main components of the national accounts and balance of payments plays in the planning process is not always sufficiently recognized. Conversely, it is sometimes denied that any process which relies so heavily upon forecasting can legitimately be called planning. Those who hold this view maintain that national development planning is only possible if the government has, and is willing to use, the power of directly determining all significant decisions in the economy concerning production, consumption, saving, and investment.

Such a narrow definition of planning is neither accurate nor useful. It is not accurate because all national economic plans, even those of the most centralized and authoritarian socialist coun-

tries, contain an important element of forecasting the probable future behavior of individuals and organizations. The level and composition of consumer demand as specified in the plans of centralized socialist economies are essentially estimates of the likely behavior of consumers under certain conditions fixed by the government, rather than directives that will inevitably be obeyed, or which could be exactly enforced. The production goals fixed by central socialist planners, particularly in agriculture, contain a large measure of uncertainty—and to that extent are forecasts—because they are based upon assumptions about the effects on productivity not only of the weather and other natural phenomena but, more importantly, of the attitudes and motivations of farmers and other producers. The external transactions posited in the plans of socialist economies also contain a large element of forecasting. Their inability to control the behavior of world markets and of other governments is one reason why these countries strive to minimize their dependence upon imports—especially from noncommunist economies—despite the higher costs often involved in such autarkic policies.

Indeed, planners of all ideological persuasions have to recognize the fact that governments have only a limited capacity to influence or offset the effects of certain developments, such as a drop in the world prices of primary products, natural catastrophes, the initiative and conscientiousness of the individual citizen, and the variability of producer and consumer responses. Also, a country cannot enjoy the advantages of vigorous innovation and enterprise without giving the managers of private and public enterprises a high degree of freedom from bureaucratic regulations and political interference. However, no country pursuing a determined policy of social and economic development could expect that all required adjustments in the plan would be made only in the public sector. A successful economic and social development plan depends on the ability to work out a constructive relationship between government planning and private decision-making, particularly with respect to strategic investments.

Techniques for Harmonizing Public Planning and Private Decision-Making

For each country, the major elements in its national development plan can be ranged from those which are most independent of control, such as foreign trade and the weather, to those which are susceptible of control by the government, such as public expenditure programs. In between, are the many factors in which private decision-making predominates but is subject to more or less influence by government policies. Thus, every plan implies some combination of direct implementation through government action, and indirect implementation through the guidance provided by government policies and by the planning process itself for the actions of private decision-makers.

While public and private economic activities should be conducive to realization of the goals of the national development effort, they do not always have this character. In the public sector, governments may not make the necessary decisions or may not carry them out effectively, for a variety of political and social reasons. Similarly, the results of

private decision-making may not always contribute to economic and social advancement, and in some cases may be counter to it, again for a variety of reasons. Insofar as the causes are accessible to remedial action—and this is not always possible at any given stage of a country's political and social evolution—there is a variety of techniques for harmonizing public planning and private decision-making with one another and with the goals of the national development effort.

The Announcement Effect of the Plan. A national economic development plan will generally specify the amounts of investments in the different branches of industry in the private sector which are consistent with the other elements of the plan and are required for the increase in production posited as a goal for a future year. The problem is to maximize the probability that private decision-makers will actually undertake the investments proposed in the plan.

A major factor working toward this result is what has been called the "announcement effect" of the plan. If the managers of private enterprises are convinced that the government is determined to execute the programs and actions required of it in the public sector and, hence, that there is a good chance that the development goals could be achieved, then the plan for the private sector represents not only what is required of private enterprises but also reveals the opportunities for expansion likely to occur in various industries. In effect, it becomes a matter of self-interest on the part of entrepreneurs to increase productive capacity in line with the opportunities highlighted in the plan. This result depends, of course, on the conviction that the plan is feasible and that the government and other private decision-makers will play their respective roles. Success breeds success, and the "announcement effect" can be a continuing one rather than a one-time event.

It is particularly important for the success of the "announcement effect" that the investments be made which provide the transportation and energy facilities and other elements of infrastructure required for expansion of the private sector. Public educational and training programs, and housing for additions to the work force, are often required for labor mobility and industrial expansion. Confidence in the plan can also be strengthened if representatives of private enterprises are consulted in the planning process so that they have a sense of participation and have an opportunity to explain the kinds, locations, and timing of the infrastructure and social capital investments they believe are needed for the success of their own efforts. Such private participation in national development planning is discussed below.

Government Policies in Support of Private Investments. Important as it can be, the announcement effect of the plan is not sufficient by itself to induce the required investments by the private sector. Assuming that the reasons for the lag are not primarily deficiencies in infrastructure or social capital, they are usually caused by a lack of capital available to the private sector; by absence of the required technology, skills, or manpower; or by attitudes and motivations which are not conducive to increased investment or increased productivity. There is a variety of government policies which can help to fill these gaps, and provide incentives and pressures for more productively oriented behavior by private individuals and organizations.

Fiscal and monetary policies of various kinds are important means by which governments can support the private sector. The government's budgetary policy has a major influence on the activities of the private sector through the size and timing of a surplus or deficit. Special tax benefits can be provided for stimulating productive investments, and differential rates may be used to discourage traditional kinds of investments which make little or no direct contribution to the national development goals. In providing such tax incentives, however, care must be taken to prevent possible misuse of them as tax "loopholes." Sometimes, the entire tax system needs to be reformed in order to ensure that all groups in the population contribute equitably to the national development effort.

Through its ability to influence long- and short-term interest rates, the government can ease the shortage of investment or operating capital available to the private sector from the commercial banks and other private lending institutions. More important in many less-developed countries than interest rate policy are the ways in which the government exercises direct control over credit availability, investment licensing, construction permits, rationing of capital obtained as foreign aid, etc.

Governmental policies relating to prices and wages can help to maintain the profitability of efficient enterprises within a framework of reasonable price stability. In addition, price policies for public enterprises can be designed which will improve the performance and prospects of private enterprises. Import and foreign-exchange policies can help the private sector to obtain the quantities and kinds of capital goods, materials and components, and operating supplies which can only be purchased abroad; and they can also provide protection against foreign competition for "infant" industries.

43. Agricultural policy is particularly important in less developed countries, for the agricultural sector often provides the major source of domestic savings for investments in infrastructure, social capital, and new industries; of the foreign-exchange earnings needed to import capital goods; of labor for new factories and service trades; of food to feed the growing population of the towns; and perhaps also of some of the raw materials required for manufacturing. The capacity of the agricultural sector to fulfill these functions exercises a major influence on the development of industry and other new activities. Hence, it is generally necessary to undertake extensive and continuing programs of technical assistance and vocational training in the countryside; to provide adequate credit facilities for agricultural improvement; to encourage the development of producers' and marketing cooperatives and other new forms of cooperation among small farmers; to build farm-to-market roads, irrigation systems, and other installations; and to institute other measures required to increase agricultural productivity. In some countries, basic reform of the whole agrarian system is required before agriculture can begin to play its proper role in the national development effort.

Often, however, more direct measures of specific assistance to the private sector are needed. Development banks—sometimes operating through industrial development corporations—serve as important instruments for extending loans, and in some cases equity capital, to enterprises wishing to expand, or to new ventures which lack the financial resources required for investment in accordance with the plan. Government subsidies have also been used, either in the form of low-interest loans or of outright grants to cover the initial deficits of new enterprises, public and private. Whether institutionalized in development banks and corporations or administered by regular government agencies (e.g. ministries of finance or industry), such government loans and grants form an important link between the public planning process, on the one hand, and the decisions of private enterprises, on the other. Their effectiveness is increased when development banks and corporations provide not only funds but also managerial advice, particularly to new enterprises.

A major contribution to the development of the private sector is made by government policies and measures for mobilizing external resources of funds, commodities, and technical assistance, and making them available by various devices to private enterprises. These external resources may take the form of aid from international organizations and the governments of other countries, or they may be obtained through private foreign investment and the nonprofit activities of educational, research, and philanthropic institutions, trade unions, cooperative societies, and other voluntary private groups in the developed countries.

There is also a regulatory or restrictive group of government policies, in addition to the measures of positive stimulation and assistance just outlined. It may sometimes happen that enterprises will invest faster than envisaged in the plan in order to gain an advantage over competitors or for other reasons. This may be beneficial except where, as in countries with a basic shortage of capital, it may divert resources from higher priority purposes. In such cases, funds for financing "excess" expansion may have to be restricted.

Alternatively, it more often happens that, despite the government's incentives and subsidies, traditionally oriented enterprises—indigenous and foreign—may not invest in the expansion or modernization of their facilities, which may play a strategic role in achieving the objectives of the plan. In this case, new entrepreneurs may be encouraged by the government, or it may itself have to make and initially operate the investments which the private sector is unwilling or unable to undertake.

Other types of limitations on the freedom of action of the private sector imposed by governments include the regulation of the monopolistic and restrictive practices of private—and sometimes public—enterprises, the protection of labor and consumers, the maintenance of public health and safety, and the elimination of other activities and conditions considered socially undesirable.

Governments have to consider not only the impact of restrictive or compulsory measures on the specific enterprises that have provoked them but also the broader effects on attitudes and motivations in the private sector as a whole, as well as the implications for achievement of the national development plan. Since inconsistencies between the objectives of the plan and private decisions are bound to arise from time to time, it is essential that machinery be provided for resolving those conflicts that are of strategic importance in a manner which is just to the individual enterprises involved and is in the best interest of the national development effort as a whole.

In this brief space, it has been possible only to list the main kinds of policy instruments at the disposal of governments for stimulating the private sector to grow and to contribute as effectively as possible to the national development effort and for harmonizing private activities with those of public authorities. In many ways, this is the crucial portion of the strategy of economic and social development. Selecting the proper combination of policy measures and direct subsidy programs is an exceedingly difficult task in most less developed countries not only because of the scarcity of the required financial resources and administrative skills but, more fundamentally, because of social and political obstacles. As already explained, national economic projections or forecasts are most useful tools for helping governments to determine the particular combination of public policies and programs needed to assist the private sector to perform its functions more effectively. But, whether these policies and programs will actually be carried out depends upon the willingness and ability of the government to overcome the political and social resistances to change, the weaknesses in its own administrative capabilities, the resentment of influential special interest groups, and sometimes even the apathy of the people themselves. However, all of these difficulties can be significantly eased to the extent to which the private sector and the people generally become voluntary participants and partners in the national development effort.

Private Planning and Participation in Public Planning. The harmonization of public planning and private decision-making is not a one-sided process involving only policy choices and actions by the government. It also requires appropriate measures by private decision-makers.

In order to contribute most effectively to the national development effort, private enterprises need to engage in their own long-range planning, particularly of their investments in plant and equipment. It is desirable for large enterprises of all types to calculate the productive capacity, manpower, import, and financial resources they are likely to require during the planning period. These private plans should then be made available on a confidential basis to the government planning agency and revised periodically. This applies particularly to what we have called strategic investments in the private sector. Mention has already been made of the desirability of meetings between government planners and the managers of such strategic private enterprises. These negotiations are important not only to ensure consistency in the requirements of the public and private sectors but also to foster constructive attitudes on both sides and mutual understanding.

If the private sector is to make the greatest possible contribution to the national development effort, the many different kinds of private decision-makers, large and small, have to be permitted and encouraged to participate actively in the public planning process so that they can acquire a sense of voluntary commitment to achieving the objectives of the national development plan. One method used in a number of countries is for the planning agency to establish advisory committees composed of representatives of industries, the farmers, the trade unions, and other significant private groups. In addition to such direct participation of the private sector in the planning process, each country will, of course, officially review and legally adopt its national development plan in accordance with its constitutional and political procedures.

Ultimately, the success of a national development plan depends upon the basic attitude toward it. To the extent that both public planners and private decision-makers recognize that the planning process is a tool, not an end in itself, the task of harmonizing public planning and private decision-making will be less difficult in practice and more fruitful in results. Successful fulfillment of this task will make a most important contribution to social and economic progress within a framework of democratically developing institutions.

Principles of Simulation*

Edward P. Holland

Director, National Economic System Studies
The Simulmatics Corporation
New York City

Science and technology may be applied for the benefit of the less developed areas in several different ways. One way is through the introduction of new or improved goods and services which contribute to a higher level of welfare. Another way is through the introduction of more reliable or more economical techniques for constructing facilities, producing goods, and providing services of kinds that are already in use. Another, less obvious, sort of application, which also may be beneficial, is the adaptation of engineering and scientific techniques of analysis to the understanding and handling of economic problems that impede development. In this last context, the engineering technique of using a computer program to simulate a system and make experiments on it has been adapted to the study of economic systems and the design of development policy.

The idea of simulation is like the concept of making a model of an airplane and testing it in a wind tunnel to study its behavior and to see what happens when various changes in it are tried. Of course we cannot make a physical model of an economy or an industry or a firm. But in economics it is not the physical geometry of factories or oil fields that is important; it is relations—technological relations like production functions, accounting relations like balance-of-payments accounts, and behavioral relations like consumers' demand functions. So, instead of a physical model, an abstract model composed of mathematical equations and rules of decision serves our purpose. In the kind of simulation to be described here a large number of such relations are incorporated in a computer program, which also includes a complex sequence of instructions for using the relations to work out the evolution, step by step through time, of the many interdependent variables that make up the system.

What distinguishes simulation from other techniques, and what are the unique features of a simulation model? In simulation we abandon the idea of finding a general solution in algebraic form, and at the same time we abandon the idea of finding the optimal program. This seems like giving up some very worthwhile objectives. But in return for giving up these, we gain the possibility of working with a far more realis-

*With permission of the editor, the author has taken material for this paper from an article which he prepared for publication in *La Revista de Economia Latinoamericana,* of Caracas, Venezuela.

tic model, and of working with it in a much more satisfactory way. The process of simulation (as done on a digital computer) is a step-by-step process of working out particular numerical time paths of variables, starting from a given set of conditions. This removes many limitations from the formulation of the model. The equations need not be linear. They may include products or ratios of variables, powers, roots, logarithms, or relations so arbitrary they must be tabulated. There may be alternative formulae for the same variable with a rule which specifies the conditions for choosing one or the other. There may be abrupt discontinuities. And there may be time delays, which may be sharp or distributed in any of various ways, so that past history as well as the present situation enters into the relations. Almost anything that can be described without ambiguity can be a part of the model.

It is not necessary, of course, to throw away the valid features of other formulations. A simulation model will generally be a synthesis of many kinds of relations including some which are derived from econometric studies and from input-output analyses as well as others inferred from qualitative observation of dynamic processes.

In using a simulation, we do not seek for one optimal solution within a set of fixed constraints and *ceteris paribus* assumptions. Rather, we try a great variety of programs and policies and observe their consequences through time in terms of a whole array of criteria. A simulation study will start with the production of a group of time histories each representing the outcome of a particular set of assumptions, exogenous variables, and policies. Once these have been examined and compared, the study is likely to proceed as a series of experiments designed to answer questions that start, "What difference would it make if . . .?"

Problems of Economic Development Policy

The need for more powerful methods of analyzing the problems of economic development should not be underestimated. In spite of the great progress that has been achieved in mathematical economics in the past generation, the techniques available to the designer of development policy are still inadequate, requiring him to distort reality badly in his formulation of the problem, and allowing too little flexibility for studying the dynamics of his policy instruments. Engineers designing a satellite-launching system would not put up with the limitations of such methods. Yet an economic system starting to develop is far more complex and nonlinear than the combination of rockets, controls, communications, and other mechanisms used with a satellite—complex and nonlinear though that is—and the criteria of performance of the economy are more complex, as well.

In actual countries which are pursuing the goal of economic development, the design of policy is made especially difficult by two factors: first, by the conflict that may exist between the immediate impact and the longer range effects of any action and, second, by the degree to which policies aimed at one set of economic phenomena may have unintended side effects on other aspects of the economy. A further complication is that any nation has a variety of goals, all of which must be considered in evaluating each policy action.

It is not only raising the level of national income that is important.

Typically, a government's policies are intended to contribute toward the following list of objectives, or one very similar:

(a) Income and product:
　(i) Increase total per-capita product.
　(ii) Increase especially the per-capita income of poor groups, such as farm workers, and unskilled labor.
　(iii) Reduce unemployment.
　(iv) Establish structure for continued development.

(b) Financial stability:
　(i) Avoid, or hold down, inflation.
　(ii) Maintain balance-of-payments equilibrium.

(c) General welfare and environment:
　(i) Provide adequate defense and police.
　(ii) Assure adequate education, health services, housing, sanitation, etc.

(d) Social and political conditions:
　(i) Maintain or establish desirable levels of freedom and justice.
　(ii) Maintain or establish political stability.
　(iii) Encourage cultural, artistic, and scientific development.

Some day it will be possible to estimate the effects of economic factors (such as, for instance, income distribution) on the noneconomic goals like cultural development and political stability. That day has not yet come. The best that can be done today by analysts is to estimate the comparative economic effects of alternative policies and leave it to the policy makers to exercise judgment about those other effects that are beyond analysis but are just as vitally important.

For pursuit of the various national goals a variety of instruments are available. The principal instruments considered here are:

(a) Investment policy:
　(i) Allocation of government investment.
　(ii) Incentives and obstacles to private investment.

(b) Fiscal policy:
　(i) Level and structure of tax rates.
　(ii) Expenditures (level and allocation).

(c) Credit and interest-rate policy.

(d) Foreign trade policy:
　(i) Tariff and quota structure.
　(ii) Exchange rates.

(e) Price, rent, and wage controls.

It would be most convenient if each of the instruments of policy could be identified with a particular objective and assumed to have no effects on the attainment of other objectives in the set. Then certain policies could be used to promote the desired pattern of growth, while others could be addressed independently to the control of inflation and still others to stabilization of the balance of payments. A national economic system is not that simple, however. Almost any action, addressed to the solution of a particular problem or to the attainment of a particular objective, will have repercussions or side effects, some of which may take place indirectly and after some delay and which are therefore difficult to foresee.

The experiences of less developed countries in recent years have clearly demonstrated the need not only for sound planning of long-range investment programs, but also for coordinating such programs with fiscal, monetary, foreign-trade, and other policies. Although economists may often theorize about these aspects of economic policy as separate problems, successful policy making demands that their interdependence be understood and taken into account.

Sheer growth of national income tends to upset the balance of trade, stimulating the demand for imported consumer goods, intermediate goods, and capital goods, without necessarily helping exports. This problem can be made less severe for some time by focusing a plan in its early years on the development of import-competing industries. Later, a limit to such possibilities will be approached, and this must be anticipated by planning development of a diversity of export industries.

Attempting to make foreign exchange available for machinery and capital goods by restricting consumers' imports might seem to be a straightforward matter. However, one of the effects of such restriction is likely to be increased inflation. Inflation, in turn, will increase the cost of producing import substitutes and goods for export, thus not only making competition in world markets more difficult but also discouraging private investment in those industries which are needed for long-run improvement of the balance of payments.

The design of anti-inflationary measures is complicated by demonstration effects and time lags in the dynamics of consumers' and investors' behavior and by the gestation time that must elapse while investment is being transformed into new productive capacity. An increase in capacity for manufacturing consumer goods should help relieve inflationary pressure—after the new plants are in production. In the meantime, however, the investment expenditure will tend to make the inflation worse. Monetary policy works against inflation by inhibiting investment and, in so doing, may interfere with needed investment and distort the pattern of development.

Because of such indirect repercussions as these, and because of the time delays in the processes by which some of the effects take place, it is not practical for the makers or executors of policy to act on the basis of trial and error. Whether their decisions are actually effective toward any particular goals, they cannot tell by watching the immediate consequences, which often take the form of crises in the balance of payments, inflation, and distortions in the goods and factor price patterns. What to do in such circumstances must be decided on the basis of some sort of theory (explicit or intuitive), for policies based solely on alleviating the short-run difficulties will probably not lead to long-run progress.

The problem clearly calls for a multi-sectoral model, with flexible prices, capacity limits, capital formation, consumers' behavior, foreign commerce, and various instruments of policy. In the real economy time-delays and time-spreads are basic to the physical processes of capital-formation and capital attrition; output in various sectors is limited by past capital formation; supply prices at capacity are determined differently than below capacity; and there is continuous interaction between production of various sectors, income, demand, prices, foreign commerce, and the balance of payments. These interactions are too significant to allow reaching valid conclusions from analyzing parts of the system separately with all else assumed constant; the non-linearities invalidate linearized analysis; and the time-spreads and irreversibilities in the system, together with the dynamic character of the forces applied to it, make comparative statics of little use. Let us then see what features can be incorporated in a simulation model to make it suitable for dealing with these problems.

Simulation of a National Economy

Many of the interactions, nonlinearities, and dynamic phenomena described above were included in an experimental simulation which was directed by the present author in the Center for International Studies at the Massachusetts Institute of Technology (1). Still more of these processes will be included in simulations designed for studying actual problems of specific countries, according to plans now being made by The Simulmatics Corporation.

The model which was simulated at M.I.T. was first formulated in abstract terms and was later made concrete on the basis of data on the economy of India. (A simulation, of course, has to be in terms of specific numbers, whether actual or hypothetical; an unquantified abstraction cannot be simulated.) The experiments which were done on the model, however, were purely hypothetical and did not have any relation to actual problems or plans of the Indian government. These experiments, although they were somewhat limited by restrictions of time and money, demonstrated the feasibility and some of the uses of the technique. Also, of course, many ideas were generated for improving the model formulation and the procedures of the operation.

There follows a description of a simulation model which is planned for a future project. It is similar in basic design to the one which was simulated at M.I.T., but includes improvements which are planned to make it more applicable to the actual problems in less developed countries.

The model will be composed of many equations and instructions corresponding to the many different processes that take place in an economic system and to the interrelations among the different parts of the system. These will not be long-run equilibrium relations, of course, but a mixture including partial-equilibrium type relations for adjustments which take place quickly, and, for other processes, equations for the mechanisms of adjustment. Thus, none of the relations described below are to be thought of as static, but are in general to be seen as continually shifting. In the M.I.T. simulation, the computations progressed in steps of one-twentieth of a year. These increments yield a fair approximation to a continuous process when we are concerned with over-all periods of from 5 to 25 years. Steps of about the same duration will probably be used in the future.

Some of the different kinds of economic activity that will be represented in the simulation are the following:

(a) Production of goods and services.

(b) Formation and attrition of capital.

(c) Determination of prices and wages.

(d) Determination of income and its distribution.

(e) Consumers' decisions.

(f) Decisions of private entrepreneurs.

(g) Exports, imports, and foreign payments.

(h) The effects of various instruments of economic policy.

The interactions among these activities are suggested in the schematic diagram of figure I. Within each of these categories of activity various subdivisions and many detailed functional relations will be specified. The most important of these are briefly described in the following paragraphs:

Production of Goods and Services. In macro-economic analysis two or three categories of products are generally distinguished. For input-output analysis thirty to fifty are frequently used. This model will probably have ten or twelve sectors; the exact number will be determined on the basis of the various production functions, decision functions, and marketing situations that it seems desirable to distinguish. Some of the categories that will be distinguished are:

Agricultural crops

Livestock

Processed food

Other consumer goods (will probably be subdivided)

Basic materials and intermediate goods (will probably be subdivided)

Petroleum

Power, transportation, and communication

Education and public health services

Other services

For each sector, corresponding to a category of products, a production function will be specified. In some sectors this will be a simple relation between capital and output with fixed coefficients determining inputs of intermediate goods and labor. In other sectors, provision will be made for such refinements as changing technology and some degree of factor substitutibility. Relations will also be included for determining production costs from the prices of intermediate goods and labor.

Formation and Attrition of Capital. For most sectors the process of capital formation will be accounted for. Capital is defined as a quasi-physical concept indicative of physical production capacity. In any sector the creation of each new unit of capital is a reflection of an investment decision, which may be part of a development program or a response to profit expectations. The creation of physical capital takes time and involves a flow of expenditures for equipment, materials, and labor. This gestation period and the inputs into the process will all be accounted for. Productive capacity of each sector may change continuously as new capital comes forth from the gestation process and old capital wears out in accordance with an actuarial life-expectancy function.

Determination of Prices and Wages. Prices will be determined differently in different sectors. In some there will be an interplay of supply and demand, adjusting continuously as in a competitive market, perfect or imperfect. Production costs and limits of capacity will be suitably reflected in the supply functions. Demands from other industries and from foreigners will be added to consumer demands (determined by a function described below). In other sectors prices may be fixed by government regulation, or administered as in monopolistic or oligopolistic industries. Wages in industrial sectors will be determined by an approximation to a bargaining process. For agricultural and other sectors appropriate relations will be formulated after further study.

Determination of Income and Its Distribution. The current values of the production and capital formation activities in the economy at any time will determine the Gross National Income. In addition the distribution of income among various classes or groups in the population will be determined from their roles in production in the various sectors. Such categories may be distinguished as the following:

Rural laborers and tenants
Landlords, proprietors, and executives of large enterprises
Professional people and proprietors of small enterprises
Skilled workers
Unskilled workers

Consumers' Decisions. For each group in the population there will be a demand function which determines the consumers' budgets on the basis of income and the prices of the various items available for purchase. Income elasticities will be high for some classes of goods and low for others, and will vary with the level of income. On a relative-price basis, some pairs of product groups will be relatively substitutable, others much less so.

Decisions of Private Entrepreneurs. In certain sectors, capital formation decisions will be made continuously on the basis of profitability expectations and replacement needs. Expected profitability will be based on current profit rates adjusted to reflect the newest technology and the current cost of capital and adjusted for optimism, uncertainty, or pessimism on the part of the investors concerning future cost increases, demand shifts, etc. Under some conditions, a "tight money" policy may inhibit the undertaking of capital projects that are otherwise attractive. Development policy may call for government participation or the use of incentives to achieve certain minimum capital formation targets when profit expectations are otherwise too weak.

Exports, Imports, and Foreign Payments. The prices of goods available for import will be programmed exogenously, either as constant values or as time profiles. Export market prices will be similarly treated, but may also be affected by quantities supplied.

The availability of foreign private finance may be sensitive to profit opportunities. Intergovernmental finance may be exogenously programmed or may, at least for some runs, be determined as a dependent variable, assuming a hypothetical elastic source of funds.

The Effect of Various Instruments of Economic Policy. To the economic system defined by the relations outlined above, various policy measures can be applied. The simulation will provide for policy-directed action through the following instruments:

Direct government investments
Patterns of incentives to and restrictions of private investment
Tax structure
Tariff structure (and import quotas)
Exchange rates
Price and wage controls
Control of money and credit.

The operation of any of these instruments may be programmed in advance according to an arbitrary time schedule, or may be made endogenous, on the basis of appropriate feedback signals. An example of the former option would be the establishment of a rigid investment program to be followed throughout a particular run. The other approach would be illustrated by a specification that import duties will be raised *x* percent if and when the balance-of-payments deficit exceeds *y* dollars per year. Various combinations of these two approaches will be used in the course of an investigation.

Simulation as a Guide to National Policy

After a model has been put into the form of a computer program, some preliminary experiments are performed and adjustments are made until the simulated system exhibits realistic dynamic behavior under appropriate test conditions. Then a series of trials and comparisons are made, testing alternative programs, strategies, and policies, with various assumptions about the time paths of variables that are determined outside of the system. Some experiments might be run, for example, with programs that stress early development of industries to produce substitutes for imports—perhaps consumer goods industries first and capital goods industries later, or vice versa. Other trials might include greater emphasis on the development of new export products. Variations would be tried, not only in the relative emphasis on expansion of different sectors, but also in the ways that the relative emphasis shifts as time proceeds.

Other experiments, instead of comparing investment programs, would explore the effectiveness of different tactics for coping with particular kinds of problems that might arise, such as an excessive balance of payments deficit. One researcher in the M.I.T. project set up an investment program which generated a growing deficit and then tried out various combinations of tariff, quota, and exchange rate manipulation, and compared the effectiveness of each combination for different elasticities of demand for imports and exports (2). (His study, incidentally, showed that the resistance of the economy to inflation was much more important than demand elasticities in making a devaluation effective.)

The results of each individual simulation experiment (or "run") are in the form of time histories of an array of variables which are chosen to indicate the performance of the economy. As an example, figures II and III are part of the results of one run with the M.I.T. simulation (3) (with a somewhat simpler model than that which is described above).

Figure II shows how the gross national product—both in current prices and in real units—grew throughout a simulated 20-year period in response to a specified investment program, and what happened to the rate of inflation and the balance of foreign payments. For three of the five sectors of the economy in which physical capital is accumulated, definite programs of real investment were specified. These were sectors 2, 4, and 5 (agriculture, non-power-using manufacture of consumer goods, and public overhead services). For sectors 1 and 3 (powered manufacture of consumer goods, and capital and intermediate goods), minimum programs were specified, but provision was also made for spontaneous, profit-motivated investment in excess of the minimum. The resulting time histories of real investment in each sector are shown at the bottom of figure II. Since some investment was spontaneous, and since Gross National Product evolved as a dependent variable, the percentage of GNP invested—also shown in figure II—was a dependent variable as well.

Figure III shows some of the components of the overall performance variables. The rate of inflation, for instance, is derived from the behavior of the price indexes in separate sectors, which are closely interrelated with the respective wage rates as well as with the pattern of consumption shown in the middle of figure III. (The Q's represent real quantity flows; the C's represent value flows. CP is expenditure for services not included in the five capital sectors, and C6 and Q6 relate to imported goods.) At the bottom of figure III are the various components of the balance of payments on current account.

One run, like that summarized in these figures, is of no value alone, because there are too many uncertainties about external events and about some of the information that goes into the model. Conclusions are drawn, from a simulation study, on the basis of comparing large numbers of runs—perhaps several hundred—in which assumptions as well as programs are varied.

The question is often raised: "If the economic data are incomplete and the behavioral relationships among variables have not been fully established, how can a simulation give the right answers?" This depends on what is meant by "right answers." It should be obvious at the outset that neither simulation nor any other technique could yield absolute forecasts with any useful degree of accuracy for a period twenty-odd years in the future, even if perfectly complete data on the present state of the economy were available. Too many unpredictable decisions and external events will have major effects on the long-run course of economic affairs.

On the other hand it is quite reasonable to expect that some strategies will effectively promote development under any of a variety of contingencies without being critically sensitive to errors in the data. Similarly, it should be possible to devise policies to cope with potential problems, without knowing precisely whether or when they are going to arise. Experiments with the simulation will show how much the comparisons are affected by changes in various assumptions. This may show the need for better data at some points. However, if the aim is not

perfection but only better plans and policies than can be devised with current methods and the same data, then there is no reason to doubt that simulation can produce them.

The study of development programs with the aid of simulation can include more of the dynamics of the entire economic system and more testing of the effects of alterations in the assumptions than are feasible with other methods. Many more alternative programs can be tried and compared. Furthermore, different anti-inflationary measures, patterns of taxation, wage or price controls, and balance-of-payments policies can be tried out, so that policy-makers can gain some of their insight from studying results of experiments on a computer instead of having to get it all the hard way—from uncontrolled experiments in the real world, with irreversible effects.

With simulation the results of a variety of assumptions and programs are compared in terms of the time profiles of separate economic variables such as those shown in figures II and III. One advantage of this is that it is far easier and more reliable to choose between alternative results than to specify an abstract preference or welfare function. Furthermore, comparing such results from different runs, policy makers can make their own estimates of the intangible social and political side effects and can use their own judgment in weighing the relative importance of total income, income distribution, unemployment, inflation, and so on. Since different people will have different estimates about the intangible factors and will also have different sets of values, it is better that such judgments be made by those who are responsible for making the final decisions rather than by the technicians analyzing the economic part of the problem.

With more formal techniques of investigation the questions that are to be studied must be formulated in relatively narrow terms, whereas with simulation we can more easily investigate those ideas that suggest themselves during the study in the form "What difference would it make if we did so-and-so?" Simulation, thus, is a more flexible way of exploring complicated systems and of devising practical policies with a minimum of limitations on the formulation of the model or on the form of questions that may be asked.

REFERENCES

(1) Holland, E. P., B. Tencer, and R. W. Gillespie, *A Model for Simulating Dynamic Problems of Economic Development,* M.I.T. Center for International Studies, report C/60-10, Cambridge, Mass. (1960); also Holland, *Simulation of an Economy With Development and Trade Problems,* American Economic Review, 52, 408–430 (1962).

(2) Gillespie, R. W., *Simulation of Economic Growth With Alternative Balance of Payments Policies,* Ph. D. thesis, M.I.T. Department of Economics and Social Sciences, Cambridge, Mass. (1961).

(3) Holland, *Simulation of an Economy, op. cit.*

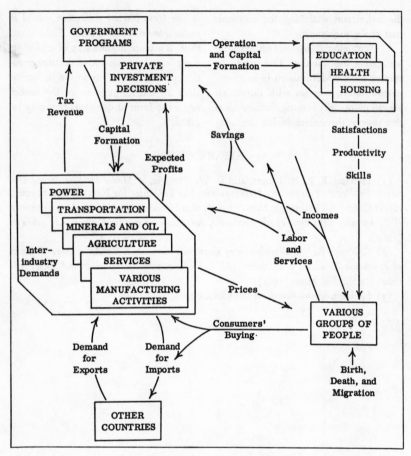

Figure I. Dynamic economic system model.

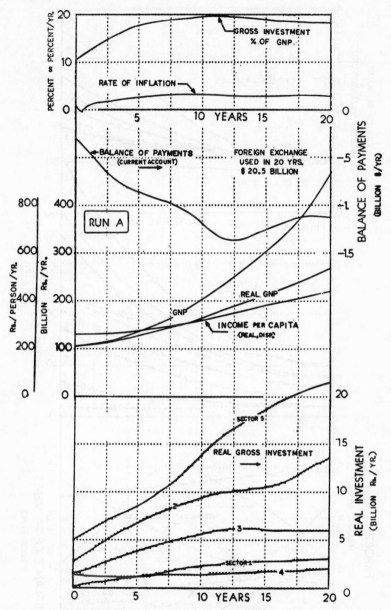

FIGURE II. A sample history: Part of results from Run A.

The editor of the *American Economic Review* has permitted use of the above figure, which appeared originally in volume II of the Review, June 1962.

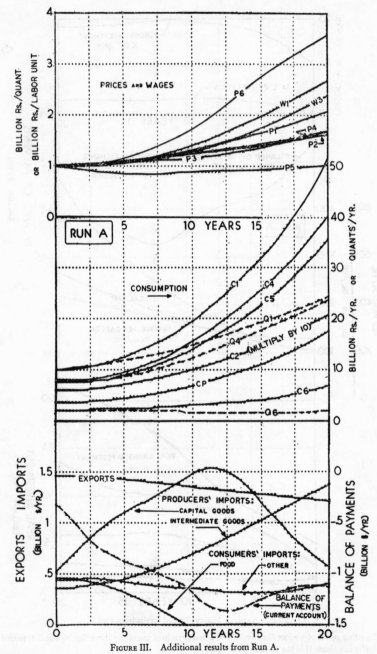

FIGURE III. Additional results from Run A.

The editor of the *American Economic Review* has permitted use of the above figure, which appeared originally in volume II of the Review, June 1962.

A Model of Development Alternatives

HOLLIS B. CHENERY

Assistant Administrator for Program
U.S. Agency for International Development
Washington, D.C.

In drawing up a development program it is not sufficient to prepare a single set of economic projections. It is necessary to consider alternatives, both for the program as a whole and for its separate parts. The analysis of alternatives is needed to clarify the relative urgency of the social objectives as well as the means to achieve them.

Formal economic models find their main application to development planning in this type of study. The quantitative significance of various kinds of economic interdependence can only be adequately analyzed by means of a comprehensive model. Although overall models must be supplemented by qualitative as well as quantitative analyses of specific parts of the economy, the model provides an indispensable element in the study of alternative sets of policies.

Work in this field derives largely from two sources. The first is the postwar development and application of policy models by Tinbergen (10), Theil (9), Sandee (7), and other economists associated with The Netherlands Central Planning Bureau [1]. Second is the general approach of operations research,

in which the testing of alternative programs by means of formal models has
been highly developed for a range of military and industrial applications.

The present paper summarizes the
main features of a method for studying
alternative development policies which
has been tested by the present author and
his collaborators in exploratory studies of
Southern Italy (1), Argentina (2) and
Israel (3). In the brief space available,
I shall give the principal elements of the
aggregate model that was used and the
nature of the results achieved. Since attention will be focussed on the strategic
choices to be made in a development program, the relation between the aggregate
model and more detailed sectoral analyses
will be indicated only briefly.

Elements of Policy Analysis

General Scope. A policy model is
designed to determine whether proposed
economic policies are mutually consistent
and to facilitate the choice among them.
To fulfill these functions the model must:
(a) incorporate the principal limits to
achieving social objectives and (b) contain variables that indicate the nature of
the policies implied by a given solution.
To avoid becoming unwieldy, the model
may omit variables which do not significantly affect the type of problem being
considered or which can be handled in a
separate analysis.

These considerations suggest that
models designed to analyze long-run
policy in the less developed countries
should be significantly different from the
models now used for the analysis of
primarily short-run policies in the advanced countries. Certain features will
be emphasized, for example:

(a) Long-term supply limitations, both

in the aggregate and by sector, should be
specified.

(b) Since the less-developed country is
typically quite dependent on foreign
trade, exports and imports must be explicitly included.

(c) The model should allow for the
inflow of foreign capital as a significant
element of development policy.

Objectives. The objectives of economic development are not adequately
described as the maximization of any
single measure of welfare, such as per
capita output or consumption. All societies recognize the need to take account
of a number of other social objectives,
such as reduced unemployment, greater
equality of income, and reduced economic instability. Some of these objectives can properly be taken as limitations
on the economic system by assigning a
given value or target to the appropriate
variable. In most cases, however, it will
be desirable to consider a range of alternative values in order to discover the
opportunity cost or "trade off" between
this and other objectives.

Variables. In his pioneering work
on policy models, Tinbergen [10] divides
all variables into four categories.

(a) *Objectives,* which reflect the aims
of policy;

(b) *Instruments,* which measure the
direct effects of policy;

(c) *Exogenous variables (data),* which
are taken as given;

(d) *Other endogenous (irrelevant)
variables,* which do not directly affect
either the choice of policy or the social
welfare.

The first two types of variable—objectives and instruments—are the main
concern of policy analysis, and I shall
call them *policy variables.* Formally, the
analyst's task is to maximize some (un-

known) function of the objective variables. As Theil (9) has emphasized, the social welfare is also affected by the values assumed by some of the instrument variables, such as taxes or income distribution, which thus take on some of the welfare characteristics of the objectives. Although a few policy variables, such as the exchange rate, are "pure" instruments which have no welfare implications *per se,* it will be convenient to assume that the desirability of a given type of policy is determined by the values of all the policy variables. A set of values for the policy variables may be called a *program.*

The Choice of Programs. In order to arrive at a political decision on the nature of the development policies to be followed, it is useful to focus attention on a few strategic variables having wide economic and social implications. These variables are primarily those which apply to large segments of the economy and occur in aggregate models, although a few sector decisions may be of the same degree of importance.

The formal model contributes to the choice of policy by determining *alternative feasible programs*—i.e., combinations of the strategic policy variables that are consistent with the social and economic structure of the economy. A feasible program is determined primarily by a solution to an aggregate model, supplemented by whatever elements of sector or inter-industry analysis may be necessary.

The range of programs to be considered should cover values of the policy variables that are politically as well as technically attainable. The solutions produced by the planners should indicate the possibility of achieving the several social objectives in varying degrees. In the absence of prior knowledge of the relative valuation of these objectives, the economist cannot determine an *optimum program.* At best, he can present the alternatives in such a way as to focus political attention on the problem of determining a social choice among a limited number of relevant alternatives. This is likely to be much easier than solving the larger problem of describing social preferences in general terms.

Structure of the Model

A policy model should specify the various factors limiting growth and the ways in which they can be modified by the instruments of government policy. The limits to be included depend on the present structure of the economy, the extent of the possible changes in the structure, and the data available for estimating economic relationships.

Since the economic structure may change rapidly in an underdeveloped economy, even a general planning model must pay some attention to the sector composition of demand and supply, which will affect both trade patterns and capital requirements. Once sector analyses have been made, however, their results can be incorporated into an aggregate model, which can then be used to study variations from the initial solution. This procedure will be followed here.[2]

In designing econometric models for less developed economies, it is useful to start from the experience in advanced countries, making allowance for the differences noted above. An examination of aggregate models by Chenery and Goldberger (2) concluded that the long-term model developed for the Netherlands by the Central Planning Bureau,[3] came closest to fitting the needs of the less developed economies. Features of this model that are particularly relevant to the choice of development policy are:

(a) The inclusion of a number of policy instruments: the savings rate, import substitution, the relation of domestic to foreign prices, migration.

(b) Explicit analysis of foreign trade.

(c) Incorporation of the results of inter-industry analysis into the aggregate model by an iterative procedure.

16. These elements are utilized in the policy model designed by Goldberger (2) to analyze existing data available for Argentina. The model was further developed by Chenery and Bruno (3) to determine development alternatives in Israel. These models explicitly recognize four limits to growth:

(a) The supply of capital

(b) The supply of labor

(c) The supply of foreign exchange

(d) The composition of internal and external demand.

The first three limits are reflected in the basic equations of the aggregate model. The composition of demand at different income levels, together with the possibilities for imports and exports, determines the capital requirements and import demands.

The principal equations in the aggregate models for Argentina and Israel are shown in figure II. The variables used in the two models, revised slightly to make them consistent with each other, are contained in figures I and II. Omitted from figure II are equations for the depreciation or replacement of capital and the terms-of-trade effect, which are needed to complete the models. Comments on the forms of the equations chosen are given under *"Determination of Alternative Policies."*

A policy model is characterized by having more variables than equations.

For Argentina, the model initially consisted of 15 equations in 17 variables, while for Israel 12 equations in 16 variables were used. This excess of variables constitutes the number of degrees of freedom of the model—two for Argentina and four for Israel. To solve the model, the values of a number of variables equal to the number of degrees of freedom must be fixed in advance. In general, the planner can assign consistent values to any combination of policy variables—objectives or instruments—equal to the number of degrees of freedom and then solve for the values of the remaining variables.

The process of solution is facilitated by first eliminating some or all of the irrelevant endogenous variables—i.e., those that are not selected to represent policy objectives. In the Israel case, for example, it was found convenient to reduce the model to four equations in eight variables, of which five are instruments and three are objectives.

These two models both allow for the anticipated composition of demand in estimating import requirements. The coefficients μ_c, μ_g, μ_i, μ_e, represent the total import requirements per unit increase in the four components of final demand: private consumption, government consumption, investment, and exports. The differences in the coefficients show the importance of allowing for changes in the composition of final demand. (In the solutions shown below, a fixed composition is assumed.)

In designing the model, the analyst has a considerable choice of variables to represent government policy. It is sometimes feasible to use a variable that directly reflects the effects of government actions, such as the exchange rate. More often there will be several intermediate links between the actual policy measures, which may affect individual sectors of the economy, and the summary measure that it is convenient to use in the general model.

The range of choice is illustrated by the alternatives proposed for the analysis of savings in Argentina. On theoretical grounds, the following set of equations was suggested:

(a) *Net Domestic Saving*
$$S = \alpha_1 W + \alpha_2 R + T - G$$

(b) *Taxation*
$$T = tY$$

(c) *Income distribution*
$$W = w(R + W)$$

Where W = Disposable wage income

R = Disposable non-wage income

T = Taxes

G = Government current expenditure

t = Tax rate

w = Share of wages in disposable income

This formulation shows the several effects of government policy on savings by using three instruments: government expenditure (G), the tax rate (t), and the share of wages (w). Since information was not available to estimate the parameters in the savings and tax functions, the formulation was first simplified to:

(d) $S = \alpha^* Y - G$
and finally to:

(e) $S = \alpha Y$

In the last form, α reflects all the government policies that influence the rate of savings. A similar range of alternatives could be shown for other instrument variables which are less directly connected to the actions of the government.

The Determination of Alternative Policies

Procedures. The greatest value of a formal model is its ability to determine consistent sets of alternative policies. The weakness of the model approach is its oversimplification of many of the individual features of the economy in order to bring out their interrelations. This drawback can be minimized by starting from a trial program in which additional elements of detailed analysis and judgment have been introduced. The model structure should be adjusted to be consistent with these added elements.[4]

Given a realistic starting point, the model can then be used to explore a range of solutions in which the policy variables vary within predetermined limits. This range, which I shall call the *feasible area of choice,* should cover all the consistent programs that might be of interest to policy makers.

The specified limits for each policy variable must be determined from outside sources. For example, the limits to increased saving may be set by feasible improvements in the tax structure and administration and the probable distribution of income. An optimistic estimate of these factors would set an upper limit to the savings rate that it is worth considering.

This approach demands less precision and detail in the model than would a mechanical application of a formal optimizing procedure. Additional information is used both in establishing the starting point for the analysis and in setting the range over which the equations in the model must hold. The use of linear approximations to non-linear functions can be quite accurate for a limited range when it would not be acceptable for the whole range of values.

Having specified the starting point and the allowable range for each policy variable, the analyst's next step is to fix values for a number of policy variables equal to the number of degrees of freedom in the model. If it is desired to determine the limits to the feasible area of choice, this can be done by setting the instrument variables and the objective variables alternately at their minima or maxima. A set of solutions will determine the range of values that is consistent with all the restrictions. This procedure will be illustrated in the application of the model to Israel.

The last step in the analytical procedure is to narrow the range of choice and finally to present a few of the leading alternative programs to the political authorities for decision. Some comments on this problem are given later under *Conclusions*.

Application to Israel. The model for Israel given in figure II can conveniently be reduced to the following four equations in eight policy variables by eliminating all of the irrelevant (non-policy) variables. The first three equations correspond to the three limits to growth specified in the aggregate model.

Savings—Investment Equilibrium

$$(12i) \quad V_n = \frac{\left[\frac{\rho}{\beta} + S_o - R_n\right] - sV_o + F_n}{\frac{\rho}{\beta} - s}$$

Policy Variables

$$V_n, s, F_n$$

Where ρ is the ratio $\left(\dfrac{I_n}{K_n - K_o}\right)$

Balance of Payments Equilibrium

$$(13i) \quad V_n = \frac{(1-\mu_e)E_n + (1-\mu_c)F_n + (\mu_c - \mu_g)G_n + \left[(\mu - \mu_c)\left(\frac{\rho}{\beta}V_0 - R_n\right)\right]}{\mu_c + (\mu_i - \mu_c)\rho/\beta}$$

Employment Equilibrium

$$(14i) \quad \left[V_n = \frac{N_0(1+\gamma)^n}{\lambda_0}\right]\frac{(1-u)}{(1-l)^n}$$

$$V_n, E_n, F_n, G_n$$

$$V_n, u, l$$

Total Consumption

$$(15i) \quad C_n + G_n = (1-s)V_n + (s - \alpha_0)V_0$$

$$C_n, G_n, V_n$$

Of the eight policy variables, five—exports (E),[5] foreign capital (F), government expenditures (G), the increase in labor productivity (l), and the marginal savings rate (s)—represent the instruments of government policy. The other three policy variables—GNP (V), consumption (C), and the rate of unemployment (u)—represent social objectives.

The predetermined limits for the

policy variables are assumed to be as follows: [6]

	Upper	Lower
Unemployment rate (u)...	......	.05
Marginal savings rate (s).	.30	.16
Foreign capital (F) (million dollars)............	285	0
Government expenditures (G) (million pounds).........	1010	1010
Export growth (annual rate).................	20%	13%
Annual growth in labor productivity...........	5%	3%

In this simple model it is possible to determine the whole range of feasible combinations of policies fairly easily. A graphical procedure for determining the feasible range of solutions is to choose two variables as axes and then to plot each upper and lower boundary as a line. For this purpose, two of the seven variables in equations (12i), (13i), and (14i) are fixed; in the Israel case, it is appropriate to assume values for G and l (or u)[7]. Setting any one of the remaining five variables at a given value gives a system of three equations in four variables, whose solution gives a line or curve in the dimensions chosen.

This procedure is followed in constructing figure III. Here savings and the foreign capital inflow at the end of the plan are chosen as axes; they are transformed by taking them as ratios to GNP to give the resulting graph a more useful interpretation. G and l are held constant at their respective limits of 1010 and .05. The line SS is then derived by fixing s at its upper limit of .30 and solving the model for consistent values of $F, U, V, S,$ and E. The upper boundaries for exports (EE), labor productivity (LL), and foreign capital inflow (FF) can be determined in the same way.

The variables $\frac{S}{V}$ and $\frac{F}{V}$ were selected as axes [8] because their total is the

rate of investment, $\frac{I}{V}$, which determines the growth of GNP: $\frac{\Delta V}{V} = \beta\left(\frac{S}{V} + \frac{F}{V}\right)$. Isoquants of constant values of V (shown as percentage growth rates) therefore appear as straight lines at 45° to the two axes. In the present model, an increase in GNP and a reduction in unemployment always go together; both are represented by a movement away from the origin.

Assuming that investment is financed in a given proportion from S and F, the maximum achievable value of V is found by proceeding outward from the origin until one of the four potential limits is reached. Each of the four is effective over some range. The upper boundary to the feasible range of choice is found in this way to be *abcde*. The lower boundary *efa* is set by the minimum values of F and E, indicated by E_oE_o and F_oF_o.

It is interesting to note that the savings limit is more restrictive than the export limit for high growth rates (above 7.7 percent), but that the export limit is much more restrictive at low growth rates. The full employment limit, LL, is only effective over a narrow range, *cd*.

There are two reasons for determining a feasible range of programs rather than a single optimum program. One is uncertainty as to the ability of the government to raise savings, expand exports, secure foreign aid, etc. The range shows what will happen to the whole program if there is a shortfall in any of these instruments. The second reason is inability to express social preferences with any precision. Since most of the instruments involve some social cost, this cost must be weighed against the gain in GNP or other objectives.

Maximum GNP and employment

are only reached along the boundary *cd*, with a narrow range of choice for F and s. The selection of the optimum combination of foreign assistance and domestic savings within this range requires a balancing of the reduced cost of foreign capital against the loss in current consumption that occurs in moving from d to c.[9]

This flexible approach to development programming is particularly useful when there is a change in the underlying assumptions from which the program is drawn up. Suppose, for example, that the anticipated rate of population growth increases from 3.4 percent to 4.4 percent per year (as actually happened in the course of Israeli planning). This would have the effect of raising the full employment boundary from LL to $L'L'$, which corresponds to a growth in GNP of 10 percent. The range of feasible programs that will achieve this maximum rate of growth is now reduced to $c'd'$.

Application to Argentina. Unlike the Israel study, the Argentine analysis was undertaken for purely experimental purposes, unrelated to any actual planning effort. Its main object was to evaluate the adequacy of different types of aggregate model for use in less developed economies. Argentina was selected because of the large United Nations study (12) that had just been completed.

Although they are otherwise quite similar, there are two significant differences between the models used in Argentina and Israel:

(a) The exchange rate is explicitly introduced in the Argentine model as a determinant of both imports and exports, while in the Israeli case it is only one of several determinants of imports and exports. In this respect, the Argentine formulation is theoretically more

satisfactory, although the demand elasticities used are purely illustrative.

(b) The greatest difference is in the form of the production function. The Argentine function results from experiments with different forms in an attempt to separate the effects of increases in labor and capital, and of technological change. Although the underlying time-series data extend over 55 years, this effort met with the well-known statistical difficulties found in other countries, which led to the treatment of labor as complementary to capital, as in Israel.

The form in which technological change is introduced assumes that existing capital becomes more efficient with time, regardless of the rate of investment. While a good statistical fit is achieved on this assumption, the results cannot be applied to estimate the marginal effects of varying investment rates, which is the central policy question. A better basis for time series analysis would be provided by more sophisticated models of the Solow-Johansen type (8)(5), in which technological improvement depends on the rate of capital formation. Barring this possibility, the cruder Harrod-Domar assumption used in the Israel model is a better approximation than the production function given in equation (1a). While the Israel equation (11) overestimates the productivity of additional investment, the form (1a) used for Argentina greatly underestimates it.[10]

In figure IV, the solutions to the Argentine model are plotted in a form similar to the Israel results. A better estimate of the productivity of investment would show larger increases in growth for a given rise in investment, but the isoquants would otherwise be unchanged.

The principal addition to the analysis is the explicit treatment of the exchange rate r. The amount of devaluation (rise in r) needed increases somewhat with the rate of growth but decreases substantially with an increase in foreign capital inflow. For a given growth rate and foreign capital inflow, the proper exchange rate can be directly determined from the graph. For example, if foreign capital inflow were raised to 5 percent of GNP with domestic savings of 18 percent, point A shows that an exchange rate of .75 compared to the base year would be appropriate. The relation between the foreign capital inflow (F), the exchange rate (r), and the level of GNP (V) is as follows:

$$F_t = r\mu_1[\mu_0 V_t - \overline{E}_t V_t^{-(1+\mu_1+\epsilon)}]$$

Which in the Argentine model becomes [11]

$$F_t = \frac{.07 V_t}{r} - \overline{E}_t r^{1.5}$$

$$\text{since } \mu_1 = -1, \ \epsilon = -1.5$$

In other respects, the Argentine model would yield results similar to those derived above for the Israeli case.[12]

Conclusions

This paper has been concerned with several experiments in using econometric models to improve planning techniques in less developed countries. In addition to the aggregate models discussed here, reference may be made to applications of mathematical programming to France by Massé (6), to India by Sandee (7), and to Southern Italy by Chenery (1), which are mainly concerned with sector and inter-industry aspects of planning. In those cases, the effects of

parametric variation on the results were also studied.

The principal conclusions that I would draw from these experiments are the following:

(a) The main purpose served by the use of formal models is to ensure consistency among the various parts of a development program. A secondary purpose of increasing importance is to facilitate the calculation of trial programs.

(b) The simplified assumptions required by comprehensive models can be offset to a considerable extent by the use of judgment in deciding on the range of variation to which the analysis should apply and in choosing among feasible solutions.

(c) The most important conclusion to emerge from the two studies discussed here is the value of systematically computing a number of alternative solutions. The range of parametric variation should be determined in large part by the needs of policy makers to know more accurately the implications of alternative policies. (Political discussion would be more useful if it were focused on consistent alternatives rather than on partial proposals that are often mutually inconsistent.)

(d) As a result of exploring development alternatives in a number of countries, it should in the future be possible to identify more clearly the key policy variables and the extent to which they can be varied in different situations. In this way, it may be possible to describe alternative development strategies much more clearly than has yet been the case.

FOOTNOTES

[1] Also relevant is the work of Frisch (4) and of the Commissariat au Plan; a good summary of the current methodology of the latter group is given by Massé (6).

[2] A similar procedure is suggested by P. Massé (6).

[3] An early version is described by Verdoorn (13).

[4] This point is elaborated by Massé (6).

[5] Exports is used as an instrument variable instead of the exchange rate in the Israel model because it also incorporates other policy elements, such as trade promotion.

[6] These assumptions are taken from Chenery and Bruno (3) except for Emax=20 percent and Fmin=0.

[7] Here l is fixed at its maximum of .05 and u is allowed to vary. In the original article, u was fixed and l varied. Equation (15i) is omitted because it only serves to determine c.

[8] This representation is chosen for comparison to the Argentine model. Other graphs on the $E-V$, $S-V$, and $F-V$ axes are given in the original article.

[9] This aspect is elaborated in the original article.

[10] The marginal productivity of investment in the Argentine estimates is only .07, as compared to an average productivity of about .28 in recent years. For planning purposes, the question is not one of varying capital alone but of increasing education and other resource improvements at the same time.

[11] The elasticity of $\mu = -1$ assumed for imports is unrealistically low for downward changes in the exchange rate, and consequently the inflow of foreign capital could probably be increased with much less decrease in the price of imports than is shown here.

[12] A number of solutions to the model are given in the original paper.

REFERENCES

(1) Chenery, H. B., *The role of industrialization in development programs*, American Economic Review, Proceedings (May 1955).

(2) Chenery, H. B., A. S. Goldberger, *The use of models for development policy*, Research Center in Economic Growth, Stanford University, 1961 (mimeographed); published (in Spanish) in Trimestre Economico (1962).

(3) Chenery, H. B., M. Bruno, *Development alternatives in an open economy: The case of Israel*, Economic Journal (March 1962).

(4) Frisch, R., *A Method of Working Out a Main Economic Plan Frame With Particular Reference to the Evaluation of Development Projects, Foreign Trade and Employment* (1962), mimeographed.

(5) Johansen, L., *A method for separating the effects of capital accumulation and shifts in production functions upon growth in labor productivity*, Economic Journal (December 1961).

(6) Massé, P., *Discretionary or Formalised Planning*, paper presented to the International Congress on Economic Development, Vienna, Austria (30 August–6 September 1962).

(7) Sandee, J., *A Long-Term Planning Model for India*, United Nations (1959).

(8) Solow, R. M., *Investment and Technical Progress,* in Arrow, Karlin and Suppes, eds., Mathematical Methods in the Social Sciences, Stanford (1960).

(9) Theiel, H., *Economic Forecasts and Policy,* Amsterdam (1958).

(10) Tinbergen, J., *Economic Policy: Principles and Design,* Amsterdam (1956).

(11) Tinbergen, J., H. C. Bos, *Mathematical Models of Economic Growth,* New York (1962).

(12) United Nations, *Analyses and Projections of Economic Development: V, the Economic Development of Argentina,* Economic Commission for Latin America, Mexico City (1960).

(13) Verdoorn, P. S., *Complementarity and long-range projection,* Econometrica (October 1956).

Variables

Endogenous Variables

*V	Gross National Product
*C	Private Consumption (Israel)
I	Net Investment
R	Replacement (Israel)
D	Depreciation (Argentina)
E	Exports (Argentina)
M	Imports
S	Gross Domestic Savings
K	Capital Stock
*u	Unemployment Rate

Exogenous Variables

t	Time
Pe	Export Price Index
Pm	Import Price Index
E_t	Exports in time t at present prices (Argentina)

Instrument Variables

G	Government Current Expenditure (Israel)
F	Foreign Capital Inflow
s	Gross Marginal Propensity To Save (Israel)
α	Net Average Savings Rate (Argentina)
r	Exchange Rate (Argentina)
E	Exports (Israel)
l	Annual Increase in Labor Productivity (Israel)

*Also objectives of policy. Policy variables include objectives and instruments.

FIGURE I. Variables.

Basic Equations of Models*

	Israel	Argentina
1. Production function.	(1i) $V_t = V_o + \beta(K_n - K_o)$ where $\beta = .364$	(1a) $V_t = V_o \left(\dfrac{K_n}{K_o}\right)^{\beta_1} (1 + \beta_2)^t$ where $\beta_1 = .224$ $\beta_2 = .027$
2. Savings function.	(2i) $S_t = S_o + s(V_t - V_o)$	(2a) $S_t - D_t = \alpha_t Y_t$
3. Capital functions	(3i) $I_n = \rho(K_n - K_o)$	(3a) $K_t = K_o + (t-1)$ $[\bar{\alpha}\sqrt{Y_t Y_o} + F]$
4. Export demand	(4i) $E_n = E_n(r, n)$	(4a) $E_t = \bar{E}_t \left(\dfrac{P_{et}}{r}\right)^\epsilon$ where $P_{et} = 1$ (assumed) $\epsilon = -1.5$ (assumed)
5. Import demand	(5i) $M_t = \mu_c C_t + \mu_g G_t$ $+ M_i(I_t + R_t) + \mu_e E_t$ where $\mu_c = .13 \mu_i = .30$ $\mu_g - .22 \mu_e = .38$	(5a) $M_t = \bar{M}_{it}(r P_m)^\mu$ $\bar{M} = \mu_c(C_t + G_t) + \mu_i(I_t + D_t)$ $+ \mu_e E_t$ where $\mu_c = .056$, $\mu_e = .040$ $\mu_i = .151$
6. Labor supply	(6i) $N_t = N_o(1 + \gamma)^t$ where $\gamma = .034$	(6a) $N_t = N_o(1 + \gamma)^t$ where $\gamma = .023$
7. Labor demand	(7i) $L_t = \lambda_o(1 - l)^t V_t$	(7a) $L_t = \lambda_o(1 - l)^t V_t^{\lambda_1}$
8. Savings investment equilibrium.	(8i) $S_t + F_t = I_t + R_t$	(8a) $S_t + F_t = I_t + D_t$
9. Employment equilibrium.	(9i) $L_t = (1 - u)N_t$	
10. Balance of payments equilibrium.	(10i) $M_t = E_t + F_t$	(10a) $M_t = \left(\dfrac{P_e}{P_{mr}}\right) E_t + F$
11. Gross national product.	(11i) $V_t = C_t + G_t + I_t$ $+ R_t + E_t - M_t$	(11a) $V_t = Y_t - D_t$

*The subscripts o and n refer to the beginning and end of the plan period. Equations for the Israel case are identified as (1i), (2i), (3i), etc., and for the Argentina case as (1a), (2a), (3a), etc.

FIGURE II. Basic equations of models.

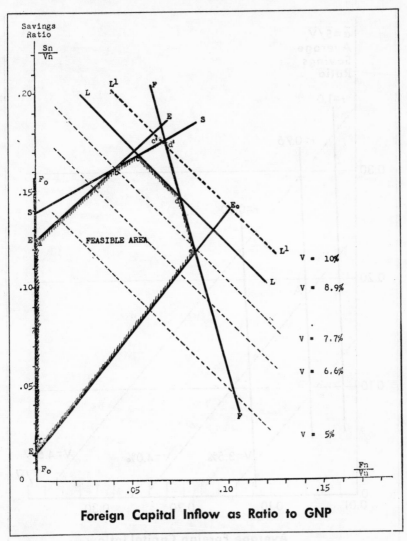

FIGURE III.   Limits to growth: Israel.

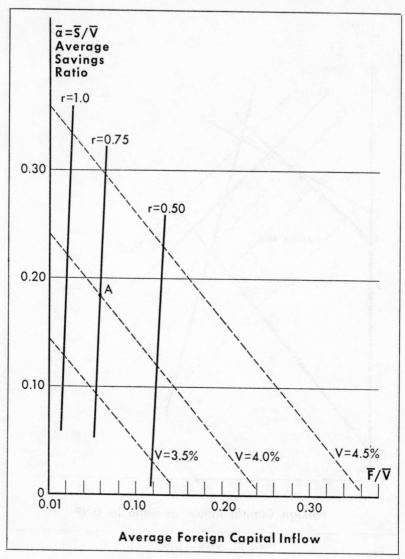

Figure IV. Limits to growth: Argentina.

The Use of Accounting Prices in Planning

GUSTAV F. PAPANEK

Deputy Director
Development Advisory Service, Center for International Affairs
Harvard University, Cambridge, Massachusetts

MOEEN A. QURESHI

Adviser, African Department
International Monetary Fund
Washington, D.C.

"Accounting prices" or "shadow prices" are among the most popular subjects in the recent literature of planning methodology. This is not unrelated to the fact that, unlike most other concepts in economic development, they can be rigorously defined and quantified, are derived from economic theory and, at least in the abstract, can be calculated and applied by the use of sophisticated techniques attractive to the economist. Yet actual, empirical calculations of such prices have been few in number and they have hardly been used in planning. This paper is concerned with their operational use and significance.

Concept and Purpose

"Accounting prices" are prices used in economic calculations, as distinct from the prices used in actual transactions. They serve a useful purpose when the prevailing prices of factors or goods are not appropriate for calculations which underlie some allocation decisions. Usually this means that the price of labor, or capital, or imported goods, or of some products, which prevails in the market is not the appropriate price for planning decisions. The market prices may not correctly · reflect the current scarcity of goods, or productivity of factors of production; or the market prices may reflect current scarcities/productivities quite well, but not take into account that these will change sharply as the result of development; or finally, the market may not reflect social values of goods, where these differ from the sum of individual private values.

Differences between prevailing market prices of factors of production and their marginal productivity are widespread in rapidly changing economies. They lead to the inefficient allocation of factors, leaving shortages and surpluses and reducing output below what is possible with the same factors efficiently employed. Accounting prices aim at eliminating this discrepancy and represent a set of equilibrium prices associated with an efficient allocation and maximum output. They can also be used to express social values that differ from market values.

Problems in Calculation and Use

Despite the greater potential efficiency of planning decisions made by the use of accounting prices, they have rarely been calculated and Pakistan is one of the very few countries where they have actually been used in planning. There are a number of reasons for this. First of all, the concept of accounting prices is difficult to make plausible and acceptable to non-economists. It is difficult to justify the use of accounting prices in planning decisions while different market prices govern actual transactions. Secondly, accounting prices are not easy to calculate. Data are inadequate and acquiring them is costly and time-consuming. Furthermore, there are disagreements on the basis and approach to be used for calculations. Finally, decisions based on accounting prices are difficult to implement. Not only is there a reluctance on the part of both privately owned enterprises and public officials to accept plans based on accounting prices, but the implementation of these plans can create difficult problems of financial administration.

Calculating Accounting Prices in Practice

Calculating accounting prices presents serious methodological problems. The only theoretically efficient solution is a general equilibrium solution using factor supply schedules, alternative production functions, and final demand schedules to derive simultaneously all factor and product prices and quantities,

as well as desirable production functions. Neither data nor techniques are adequate at present to make this a practical solution. The alternative is partial solutions, that is to derive in the first instance each set of accounting prices separately.

In calculating an *accounting price of capital,* that is, a rate of interest, one should take into account the effect of interest rates on both the supply of and demand for capital. However, it is difficult to establish empirically a relationship between interest rates and the supply of capital or savings especially in economically less developed countries with their poorly developed institutional framework. It is therefore a useful, and not too dangerous, simplifying assumption to ignore the effect of the rate of interest on savings. The accounting price of capital can then be set equal to the marginal productivity of capital. This has the added advantage that it reflects also the social time preference. Since the choice between consumption and investment depends on the social time preference, and since the magnitude of investment affects its marginal productivity, the marginal productivity of capital can be taken as indirectly reflecting social time preference.

The marginal productivity of capital, and therefore the accounting rate of interest can be derived by obtaining the rate of return—earnings minus costs—for the marginal project in a field where cost-benefit calculations are feasible. Availability and manageability of data for industrial projects usually dictates that the analysis be largely confined to them but, where feasible, the results can be checked against projects in fields like power, irrigation, or transport, where some reasonably reliable cost-benefit calculations may be made.

Generally, information will be most readily available on proposed government investments and these will also involve fewer problems with deliberate distortion. In addition, government projects are more likely to include some with returns that are marginal or close to it, since private enterprise will seek high profits while government will undertake some projects it considers desirable, though less profitable. Finally, in the case of private business substantial returns to entrepreneurship will be mixed in with returns to capital and be difficult to separate.

The marginal productivity of capital then can be approached by obtaining the rate of return on the proposed government industrial project with the lowest return among those included in the development program (ignoring any projects included largely for non-economic reasons). In these calculations, the prevailing interest rate can be used in calculating investment costs and in discounting future cost and benefit streams. The result is a first approximation to a rate of interest which can then be used to recalculate the rate of return for a few industrial projects to find a new marginal rate of return. This more refined rate of return on capital employed in industry can then be checked by similar calculations for projects in other fields and for private industrial projects on which reasonably reliable information is available.

Calculations of the simple rate of return on capital, charging no interest during construction and without discounting future income streams, were made for proposed government industrial projects in Pakistan's first Five-Year Plan. The rate of return on the projects that could be included in the development plan ranged around 12–15 percent, including some important private investments. No more sophisticated calculations were made, since the industrial projects being compared had rather similar gestation periods and expected lengths of life, and application of the accounting interest rate was therefore not expected to affect their relative priority sufficiently to warrant the additional time and effort. Attempts were made to compare the results for industrial projects to the rate of return on power and irrigation projects. This proved disappointing since data were inadequate and in many cases clearly unreliable.

The accounting interest rate derived from marginal productivity of capital can be checked against the market interest rate, if a market can be found where institutional and other distortions are largely absent. Generally, the central bank discount rate and the rates applied to government transactions are established with little regard to the productivity of capital and tend to be too low. On the other hand, interest rates outside the organized money market tend to be too high because of monopoly elements, high administrative costs and high risk premiums. It might be possible, however, to find market interest rates that are least affected by institutional factors such as the highest rates charged by banks or similar institutions to medium-size commercial and industrial borrowers, or the lowest rates charged by large scale individual lenders to the same type of borrower. In Pakistan the discount rate has been around 3–4 percent, the interest rate charged by commercial banks ranges from 4–10 percent, and money lenders may charge 25–40 percent or more. However, it appears that at times industrialists and businessmen obtain funds from each other at rates ranging from 10–15 percent.

A major difficulty in calculating the

accounting price of labor stems from the fact that labor is a much less homogeneous and mobile factor than capital, and institutional considerations are an even more important source of imperfection in the labor than in the capital market. First of all, there are various categories of unskilled, semi-skilled, and highly skilled labor and their supply varies. Second, although unskilled labor might be an abundant resource for the economy as a whole, this does not necessarily hold true of particular occupations, or of particular areas, or at particular times of the year. The only correct procedure would be to calculate the accounting price of labor separately for each set of circumstances. However, this is clearly not feasible, and approximate adjustments in the accounting price to take account of broad differences in areas, occupations, or seasonal factors, may prove quite adequate.

As in the case of the price of capital, the accounting price of labor should be calculated taking into account both the supply schedule and productivity or demand for labor. However, it is doubtful that in most less developed countries with abundant manpower there is a very direct and stable relationship between wages and the supply of unskilled labor. In these countries there is a floor, close to the minimum subsistence level, below which real wages do not fall. Concurrently, above this level the unskilled labor supply may be almost perfectly elastic, depending more on employment opportunities than wages.

A first approximation then to the accounting price of unskilled labor involves the estimation of its marginal productivity. This usually means labor productivity in agriculture. In a particular country it is usually possible to discover whether there are a substantial number of persons on land who have only a few hours of work a day during most of the year. Could they engage in other work without a reduction in agricultural production as long as the remaining workers increased their effort correspondingly? If so, the marginal productivity of labor can be assumed to be zero or close to zero, and the accounting price of unskilled labor on land for most of the year can be set at this level. However, this is not the same as saying that the accounting price for all labor is zero-seasonal, locational, and skill factors have also to be taken into account.

Since agriculture is highly seasonal, there may be unusually large demands on the available manpower at particular times of the year, especially in a relatively undiversified agriculture. Thus, the social cost or productivity of labor during the harvesting or planting period may be quite high, and if the labor is to be employed year-round, a positive accounting price must be fixed. This can most easily be set with reference to the cost of capital required to free labor during the busy period. That is, the accounting price of labor would be equal to the accounting interest rate plus depreciation on the capital (e.g. tractors) required to free one worker during the months of peak labor demand in agriculture.

The accounting price for labor must also cover its transfer costs if it is to be employed away from home. These costs include not only transportation and housing as such, but also the cost of the additional facilities required—water supply, roads, sewage, etc. Finally, only some labor is completely unskilled. Many investment decisions involve workers in industry where some skills, and therefore some training, is involved.

Training costs also need to be included in accounting prices.

Although the labor market is undoubtedly imperfect, actual wages for unskilled and semi-skilled workers will to a considerable extent reflect differing circumstances with respect to training, seasonality of work and the cost of social overhead facilities. For unskilled and semi-skilled labor it may then be best not to fix a uniform accounting wage rate but rather to establish a uniform accounting wage percentage. A fixed percentage of the market wage prevailing for a particular group at a particular time would be its accounting wage.

As regards skilled and professional labor, the divergence between market wages and equilibrium wages is in the opposite direction from unskilled labor—market wages tend to be below equilibrium wages. Normally, it is too difficult to calculate accounting wages for these workers because there are too many disparate groups. Since most allocation decisions are in any case not very sensitive to accounting prices for very specialized and scarce manpower, it is sufficient to calculate accounting wage rates for unskilled and semi-skilled labor.

In preparing Pakistan's first Five-Year Plan, data and time were not available to calculate a separate accounting wage rate or percentage. Most cost-benefit calculations were therefore made on two bases. One used the current market wages. The other calculation showed a project's "contribution to national income" as the benefit and therefore excluded wage and salary expenditures from costs; this implied an accounting rate of zero for all wages and salaries. Clearly, this underestimated the opportunity cost for labor just as using the market wages overestimated it. By comparing the two measures of return, it was possible to obtain an indication of the effects of a low accounting wage, but not to derive a single priority listing of projects according to a reasonably rigorous set of criteria. Given additional data since collected, it should now not be difficult to make the somewhat more sophisticated calculations outlined above.

The *Accounting Price for Foreign Exchange,* that is, an accounting foreign exchange rate, can be conceived of as the rate that would achieve an equilibrium in the country's balance of payments without reliance on restrictions. One problem in calculating the equilibrium rate arises from the existence of various extraordinary foreign exchange transfers such as intergovernmental or international loans and grants which, in recent years, have become an important element in the balance of payments of several countries. These transfers can be assumed to be exogenous and unrelated to exchange rates. There is, however, a different equilibrium rate of foreign exchange at each level of such transfers. As a starting point, therefore, one can estimate a single level of such transfers and calculate the accounting rate while taking the level of extraordinary transfers as fixed.

The less the direct controls over foreign exchange, the easier it is to calculate accounting prices. In an exchange system which relies exclusively upon multiple exchange rates to maintain balance of payments equilibrium, the weighted average effective rate should give an approximate indication of the accounting exchange rate. Similarly, in a system with a unitary exchange rate but with reliance upon tariffs and subsidies, the total amount of customs duties collected, plus subsidies paid out as a proportion of total imports plus exports, should indicate the undervaluation of foreign exchange. (In both cases, the assumption is made that there are no long-run gains or losses in exchange reserves.) These approaches remain useful so long as direct controls are not an important means of achieving a balance in foreign accounts. The more important the direct controls, the more these calculations become a check on other methods rather than the primary method for calculating the accounting foreign exchange rate.

A second approach is based on the application of the purchasing power parity theory. This involves the calculation of the accounting exchange rate from a comparison of the variation in the country's prices, over some reasonable period of time, with that in some other country which has approximate equilibrium in its balance of payments and no reliance on restrictions. According to this approach, the relative variation in the price levels in the two countries should be proportional to the relative variations in their exchange rates. The main limitations of this approach are: (a) it is difficult to find a suitable period for purposes of comparison since one must start with a certain "normal" stage in the country's balance of payments; (b) price data are frequently neither adequately comprehensive nor sufficiently comparable, and (c) it takes no account of the fact that over a period of time, economic growth and other changes can profoundly alter the structure of demand and of imports and exports of a country.

A variant of the above approach is to compare prices in the country and in the world market for the major domestically produced and consumed commodity or commodities and derive the exchange rate from their relationship. That is, if the country primarily produces and consumes rice, and the price of rice is 1,000 monetary units per ton while it is $200 per ton on the world market (c.i.f.) one would conclude that the accounting exchange rate should be five units to the dollar. A comparison of goods that are largely imported or exported is not of much use for this purpose since their international price and the official exchange rate are the main determinants of their domestic price. This method is therefore useful only when (a) the country produces and consumes itself one or a few commodities that make up a substantial part of the GNP, (b) these commodities are traded internationally but are not major imports or exports for the particular country, and (c) there are no serious problems in comparing quality. Even so, the method has substantial weaknesses since the prices of domestically produced and consumed commodities are often strongly influenced by institutional and other domestic factors which introduce price distortions.

Third, some idea of the adjustment necessary in the exchange rate can also be obtained by looking at the profitability of exports and imports, especially the former. Although there is usually a time lag in wage adjustments in the agricultural sector, a squeeze on the profitability of exports is frequently an early sign of the undervaluation of foreign exchange. On the import side the situation is, of course, the reverse; profits tend to be excessive particularly if direct controls are applied, and the extent of profits on imports is one rough indication of the undervaluation of foreign exchange.

Finally, the international free market rate of a currency is of some use in indicating its accounting price. Usually, however, this market is a narrow one and is greatly influenced by the risk involved, since it normally relies on illegal transactions. The wider and more legal the market, the more useful its rate.

To obtain the equilibrium exchange rate the most practical approach involves looking at a whole range of relevant factors including monetary and other developments. Which of the above approaches, or which combination, is most useful depends upon the circumstances of a country. In a country which relies essentially on cost restrictions (e.g. tariffs) the calculation of the weighted average effective rate may give the best indication, checked perhaps against the free market rate. When greater reliance is placed on direct controls, the other approaches may provide a more appropriate guide.

In Pakistan, the undervaluation of foreign exchange presented one of the clearest and most compelling problems for the planners. Accounting prices were used for calculations underlying the First Plan wherever possible. They were set at 66.6 percent higher than the official rate. This was a rather arbitrary rate, derived from three sources. First, it was assumed that Pakistan's foreign exchange disequilibrium was worse than that of some neighboring countries and its rate should therefore be somewhat higher than theirs. Secondly, that the free market was narrow and had a high risk premium, and that therefore the accounting rate should be somewhat lower than the free market rate. Thirdly, some approximate indication of the accounting rate was obtained by looking at the profitability of imports and exports. Use of the accounting rate for foreign exchange for both the cost and return side, substantially changed the relative priority of some projects. The effect was less than might be expected, since nearly all projects

finally included in the Plan had substantial foreign exchange benefits, either import saving or export earning.

Interrelationships

The discussion so far has been in terms of calculating the accounting price of each factor of production separately. Clearly these calculations are not independent. Calculating the accounting interest rate requires some price for labor and foreign exchange, and similarly calculating either accounting wages or exchange rates requires prior calculation of the other two factor prices. Since each calculation assumes the prior calculation of the other two accounting prices, the only practical solution is a series of successive approximations. It will usually be easiest to start with the calculation of the accounting rate for foreign exchange if this differs from the prevailing rate. The accounting exchange rate can then be used for the calculation of the accounting interest rate, using either the market price or the best guess of a suitable accounting price for labor. Using the accounting interest rate and the accounting exchange rate, the accounting wage rate can then be calculated. Using these rates in turn, one can derive a second approximation of the accounting interest rate. In this way, the calculation can be progressively refined.

Time Horizon

The discussion has also ignored the time horizon. It has been suggested that accounting prices should approach equilibrium prices, prices at which all factors are fully employed and yield maximum output, without specifying at what period in time. Should accounting prices be set in terms of equilibrium prices at present, at a given time in the future, or continuously? If they are set to achieve equilibrium at present, this will lead to an efficient allocation of resources at present, but since factor supplies will change in the future, it will lead to increasing inefficiencies over time. On the other hand, setting accounting prices to achieve equilibrium at some future date would mean inefficiencies now. Theoretically, it should be possible to have a time profile of accounting rates, with separate rates for each year, calculated in terms of equilibrium prices in that year. Taking into account the current state of availability of information and other problems in calculating accounting prices, this alternative is impractical at present. Moreover, it would greatly complicate the problem of administering accounting prices. The most practical compromise will usually be to take the last year of the period planned for as the time horizon. That is, accounting prices should approach what are expected to be the equilibrium prices four or five or six years in the future. Detailed information is not likely to be available beyond the last year of this Plan period. Moreover, if a suitably high discount rate is used, inefficiencies that are more than five or ten years in the future lose much of their quantitative significance. At the same time, using a future year as the relevant time horizon will force some consideration of changes in factor proportions, though it is difficult to forecast in this field with any degree of confidence.

Accounting Prices for Products

Market prices for products are often as inappropriate for efficient decisions as market prices for factors. In part they tend to reflect the basic divergence between the prevailing market prices of factors and their marginal productivity and in part they are affected by official controls, prices, taxes, and subsidies which cause variations in the selling price unrelated to the real cost of production. The former effect is not too important in countries where foreign trade is unrestricted and would be corrected if accounting prices come into wider use. For the latter effect a correction has to be made. This correction is relatively easy when it is limited to the direct effect of the taxes. It is not difficult to subtract customs and sales taxes from relevant product prices but it is much more complex to take account of the indirect effect of these taxes such as, for example, the effect of a customs duty on coffee on the price of tea. In such cases the best course is to check prices against those prevailing in the international market and to assume a value for the product equal to the cost of importing it.

There are two further adjustments that can and sometimes should be made. First, a particular investment decision may involve external economies or diseconomies. These, if they can be estimated, should be added to or substracted to get the accounting prices. If, for instance, a steel mill provides training as well as steel, the estimated annual value of the training can be added to the value of the steel to get the product accounting price. Second, some products may have a higher or lower social than economic value and this again can be expressed in the product accounting price. If, for instance, it is considered desirable for social reasons to speed up the development of a region, a certain percentage could be added to the value of any good product in that region. Alternatively, if the main purpose is to increase employment, this can be better accomplished by reducing the accounting wage rate in that region. Regional development goals were taken into account in making cost-benefit calculations in Pakistan's First Plan. This took the form of including projects for East Pakistan in the Plan with rates of return lower than those of rejected projects in West Pakistan. This is essentially identical to adding a fixed amount to the returns from projects in East Pakistan.

Implementing Accounting Prices

While accounting prices can be calculated and used in formulating plans, it is not easy to induce government officials and private entrepreneurs to base their decisions on them and shift to alternative projects and techniques which, at prevailing market prices, do not seem equally profitable. There is resistance to the use of accounting prices because of their abstract nature as well as some deliberate opposition to them because enterpreneurs and managers do not want to see their profits reduced. However, a number of steps can be taken to make accounting prices more effective guides in decision making.

Direct Controls and Instructions. It is conceivable, though not likely, that in a fully planned economy the state could fix all prices to approach the equilibrium level, but such a policy would be completely impractical in a mixed economy. Some reliance can, however, be placed on direct controls and instructions for implementing accounting prices. Government officials concerned with investment or management decisions can be instructed to use accounting prices and all proposals submitted to the central planning or other reviewing agency, drawn up in terms of both market and accounting prices.

Private entrepreneurs can also be induced to use accounting prices to some extent if the Government announces that these prices will determine its own decisions with respect to private firms such as, for example, those involving the issue of import licenses and other permits. However, these measures cannot be fully effective since the returns of private firms will continue to depend on market prices. In order, therefore, to make accounting prices effective for the private sector, greater reliance must be placed on indirect measures, such as monetary and fiscal policies, aimed at bringing effective factor costs closer to their accounting prices.

Indirect Measures. The Government can influence the price for capital and foreign exchange more easily than that for labor. One effective method of increasing the cost of capital is to levy a tax on credit provided by the organized banking sector. A proportional tax on all outstanding loans can be added on to the interest charge and would be an efficient tax to administer and collect. The structure of market interest rates can also be influenced to approach the accounting interest rate by gradually adjusting central bank discount rates, and the interest rates of government credit institutions, to more appropriate levels.

When the prevailing foreign exchange rate is overvalued in relation to the equilibrium rate and a devaluation is ruled out due to political or other considerations, the next best alternative may be to apply a uniform rate of surcharge on imports and apply the proceeds to a subsidy for exports. A differentiated application of import taxes or export subsidies, unless based on clearly defined protective or other economically justifiable considerations, will itself create further distortions in the economy.

To influence the effective cost of employing labor, it might be practicable in certain situations to provide a subsidy for wages, although in general this presents very difficult administrative problems. First of all, to fulfill its purpose, the subsidy must be applied mainly to new investments, and particularly those which offer some technological alternatives. There would be little gain in providing the subsidy to existing plants which employ techniques based on market prices and have little room for flexibility in factor use, or to those new investments where no technological alternatives exist. Secondly, the subsidy must be applied to encourage the effective employment of labor in production rather than to subsidize the hiring of "surplus" workers, a common occurrence in less developed countries reflecting traditional employment patterns and inefficient management. Finally, since accounting wages for labor should not be uniform, though they could be a uniform percentage of the market wages of unskilled and semi-skilled workers, the subsidy too should not be uniform. An attempt to provide a different subsidy to different types of undertakings according to different criteria would present formidable administrative problems.

Despite these shortcomings, it may prove possible to use a direct subsidy in countries where there are only a few enterprises. In others, indirect subsidies to labor in the form of government subsidization of social overhead capital—to an even greater extent than is now the case—would seem more desirable. Gov-

ernments can subsidize particular worker groups by subsidizing their housing, their transport and their water. However, this type of subsidy would be effective only if it did, in fact, reduce wages below the level that would otherwise have been established, or otherwise reduce costs that the employer would have to bear.

The policies discussed above have clearly wider implications than the question as to whether or not they promote the most efficient allocation of resources. For example, an upward adjustment in interest rates may create problems for holders of financial assets and may also have an unfavorable effect on investment. An adverse effect on investment might also be produced by the higher cost of imports resulting from an exchange rate adjustment. Any decisions on the adoption of these policies must obviously be based on an over-all assessment of their economic effects. However, it should be possible to encourage investments by techniques other than artificially low interest rates and import costs. In Pakistan the demand for permission to invest both from private and public units, has continued to exceed the supply of foreign exchange available, despite increasing government interest rates and increases in the cost of imports.

One of the most important problems in implementing accounting prices arises from their *financial implications.* The Government can disregard the profitability of projects and base its decision strictly on their economic return, calculated in terms of accounting prices, but it would need to raise additional taxes to meet the financial loss implied by such a policy. The dimensions of the financial problem are much greater if, in addition, employment is encouraged through wage subsidies. In practice there is a limit to the desire and ability of governments to raise additional taxes even though in theory a more efficient allocation of resources means a greater total product and therefore an opportunity to increase taxes without reducing the absolute consumption of any part of the population. If taxes are not, in fact, raised to meet the financial burden of accounting prices, the way could be open for inflation which may distort prices seriously.

Conclusions

Experience with the calculation and use of accounting prices in Pakistan shows that even where statistical and other data are extremely inadequate, a beginning can usefully be made in deriving accounting prices and using them operationally. In the absence of necessary statistical data the calculation of accounting prices has to be attempted through alternative approaches and by a process of successive approximations. The problem can, however, be simplified by confining the analysis to a few key factors and products.

The implementation of accounting prices presents both administrative and financial problems. In the beginning their main usefulness will be to provide a sounder basis for allocation decisions in the public sector. It is more difficult to make them effective in the private sector but, in various ways, government actions can influence the effective cost of factors of production to move closer to their accounting price.

Finally, the effects of implementing accounting prices will tend to accrue in the long run. In the short run, the choice of technology, particularly in large scale production, is quite limited but, over a period of time, the country's productive system will gradually tend towards a more efficient technology based on increasingly fuller utilization of all factors.

Development Banks

VINCENT CHECCHI*

President, Checchi and Company, Washington, D.C.

Introduction

The purpose of this paper is to examine the circumstances in which development banks are created, their potential as an instrument for accelerating economic change, and the factors affecting success in utilizing this potential. As used in this paper, development banks are autonomous financing institutions organized in developing countries with assistance from foreign lending agencies for the purpose of lending to or otherwise investing in economically desirable projects in the private sector.

The number of such institutions has increased steadily in the past several years, encouraged by financial and technical assistance from U.S. Government and international lending agencies. As of June 30, 1962, the World Bank and its affiliates, the Inter-American Development Bank, the U.S. Export-Import Bank and the U.S. Agency for International Development had made 105 loans to 50 development banks in the less developed nations totaling $738 million. Of the 50 banks, some 20 were created with the technical advice of international agencies or as a direct result of loans from these

agencies. Private American and other banking firms have also invested in development banks.

Development banks provide attractive features to an international lending agency. They constitute "projects" and can thus receive loans which the lending agency is happy to make. Such loans are relatively safe in the sense that they are reloaned or "retailed" by the development bank to a number of projects, diversifying the risk. In addition, the lending agency bears no risk on the individual projects. The development bank is obliged to repay the whole amount of the loan made by the lending agency regardless of what happens to individual projects. Through the development bank channel, the international lending agency is relieved of the task of finding sound projects in the private sector.

The development bank, as an autonomous financial institution, is more amenable than government agencies to technical advice from the lending agency and to the selection of competent professional management. Development banks, with sufficient independence, broad enough powers, and imaginative enough management, could serve as a powerful financial force for encouraging economic change and new attitudes toward business. Each bank in each coun-

---

* Mr. Checchi has directed a number of studies on this subject conducted by his firm in various developing countries.

try provides a mechanism for focusing attention on opportunities to encourage private local and foreign investment in the bank itself and in projects financed by the bank.

Development banks thus represent an institutional arrangement ideally suited to the policies and operational procedures of foreign sources of financing. They are in a good position to receive foreign assistance which is convenient for both the lending and the borrowing country.

As an additional and sometimes the sole source of medium- and long-term credit for industrial enterprise, development banks can be a powerful stimulant for new investment and for new jobs. In fact, the very process of creating such an institution stimulates new projects and creates a favorable climate for risk-taking.

Adequately conceived and operated, they can help create a vigorous class of local entrepreneurs and investors. They can help gather and channel local savings. They can serve as a training ground for professional personnel such as economists, accountants, and engineers as well as for private entrepreneurs and managers. They can influence public attitudes toward business and can have an important effect on business organization, law, and the related apparatus of conducting business. They can become self-supporting institutions performing functions so important in the economy that they become points of stability in the society because their valuable work must continue despite changes in government.

This paper will cover some of the varied considerations relating to development banks: the need for them, their form, their scope, their relation to other institutions, and some special problems which they face and which they generate.

The Need

A development bank or a similar development institution is essentially a device to fill a gap in the existing financial structure of a country. (The inducements offered by the Government to encourage the creation of small business investment companies in the United States was an effort to fill what was considered to be a gap in the credit system of that country.) Most development banks which now exist were designed to meet a need for medium and long-term credit on reasonable terms for new industrial enterprises. However, some of them have made few loans, not because of a lack of funds but because of shortcomings such as inadequate management simply failing to carry out the function of the bank or a lack of applications sufficiently well prepared to justify a loan. The problem of need therefore is usually broader than the problem of adequate credit availability.

Even a cursory examination of the experience of development banks and of U.S. Government and other international loans to these banks suggests that there is more money available for industrial development than there are projects in satisfactory condition to qualify for loans under normal banking criteria.

The shortage of projects is, in part, a result of the shortage of skills needed in preparing projects for financing. This problem can be met by providing, through a development bank or through a separate institution, technical services to help potential borrowers identify, investigate, and organize specific projects for financing.

But in many of the smaller developing countries, the shortage of projects is even more a result of a shortage of entrepreneurs—of individuals and groups willing and able to spend their time, effort and money to identify and develop projects. In these areas, the need is perhaps for institutions which help create a market for development banks and related institutions.

There thus appear to be needs for several kinds of development banks—broadly defined. One kind consists of those sponsored by the World Bank and other official lending agencies in countries where entrepreneurs and investors exist in sufficient numbers and kind to respond actively when financing and technical assistance are made available on reasonable terms.

A second group would include an institution fitting a situation where there are few entrepreneurs, where the market is small, and where there is not likely to be any significant short-term response to increased credit availability. This kind of institution is perhaps more nearly an investment company than a lending institution, fills the function of the entrepreneur and acts as the "self-starter." Such institutions would tend to rely heavily on government for initial capital, would at first seek to attract local investors in enterprises initiated by the institution alone or in association with foreign groups, and eventually would attract local initiators of new enterprises.

The diagnosis of the problem is as important in prescribing financial institutions as in medicine. While every economy probably has entrepreneurs, the problem is one of accurately gauging the nature and extent of entrepreneurial potential. It is a questionable use of resources to create a development bank to make loans where the effective demand for credit does not exist. Where the absence of entrepreneurs is a problem, a source of credit alone or even in conjunction with technical assistance is not the solution.

All development banks to a greater or lesser degree attempt to undertake some entrepreneurial or promotional functions. By and large, however, development banks by circumstances or by choice are operated as lending agencies. When they take equity, they do so usually to maximize profit, rather than because such action is necessary to spark the creation of the particular enterprise.

Some development banks will tend to become increasingly conservative as time goes on. The responsibility of management to avoid losses will soon outweigh its responsibilities to pioneer. Once the institution is created, needs will change. The financial structure is an evolving one and circumstance may require other financial institutions to fulfill other needs, such as insurance companies, savings and loan associations, and housing banks. There is even the happy prospect that the development banks can help create specialized institutions to fill the need for specialized kinds of financing. The development bank may thus work itself out of a job.

There are other needs bearing on a development bank—its potential role in creating an organized securities market, its role in linking local and foreign investment in projects, and others. The needs must be determined with care because the institution—whether conventional development bank, investment corporation or other—must be carefully designed to meet that need.

The Form

There can be no such thing as the standard model, ready-made, all-purpose development bank which can be utilized effectively in any country. The needs vary country by country and the form must be tailored to each situation. Should the development bank be government-owned, privately-owned, or have a mixed ownership? Whatever the ownership, experience suggests that the institution must have independence of decision if it is to grow and to command respect and resources in the money markets at home and abroad.

Private organizations are likely to have greater flexibility and may result in more stable institutions in the long run, since the management of the private bank will be more insulated from political pressures and political changes than is possible in a government-owned and controlled institution. Where government can appropriately mobilize private resources and energies to take over the job, it is certainly to its advantage to do so.

There are situations in which the government must assume this burden either because of the lack of a local entrepreneurial or investor class, or because there is need for a pace-setter to enter into projects which are either too large, too risky, or too oriented towards a particular government objective but nonetheless important for speeding the pace of industrial development.

In many countries the ideal set of development financing institutions might include both a government-owned and a privately-owned development bank which can complement each other's activities. Other circumstances favor the mixed institution in which the government participates financially, but which is controlled by private ownership. There are distinct advantages in early government financial support which may be necessary to the viability of the institution and which may provide some restraint on private management to protect the institution from becoming a tool of special private financial interests.

In some countries, this problem demands a form of organization which reflects some of the features of a privately-owned public utility.

The form of the bank must often take into account important local political or regional considerations. For example, the interests of the Greek and Turkish communities in Cyprus must be satisfactorily represented in any board of directors of a development bank in that country. Similarly, the *sierra* and *costa* areas of Ecuador are likely to demand specific acknowledgment by a development bank of their interests.

Relations With Other Institutions

One of the most important initial tasks for a new development bank will be to establish satisfactory relations with other important agencies with which it must work. The bank must be responsive to a number of masters, some within the country and some outside.

Perhaps the simplest of the bank's relations are those with the international assistance agencies. These agencies will expect the bank to be aggressive in utilizing the funds committed to it, but at the same time will expect the bank to follow sound financing practices to protect the funds with which it has been entrusted. Beyond these fairly obvious points, the bank will be expected to keep the agencies adequately informed on changes in scope of operations and to discuss any additional indebtedness which the bank may decide to undertake beyond the loans it has already received. The development bank must also begin the process of building relations with foreign private capital sources which may become the major source of the bank's foreign borrowings.

Domestically, the bank will have to work closely with the country's planning groups, the local technical assistance agency, local business organizations, and local banks and others in the local business and financial community. All of these organizations could be of valuable assistance to the bank's management in establishing policies and in evaluating applications for financing.

Scope

The local needs determine the scope as well as the form of the development bank. There is a wide range of possible functions which a development bank can undertake.

Even in small economies, it may be desirable to have separate organizations for agricultural financing and for industrial financing. These require entirely different types of management attitudes and abilities and involve different administrative problems. In some instances where a development bank has been authorized to carry out both types of activities, it has frequently had to concentrate so extensively on needed agricultural financing that it failed to achieve any significant record in the industrial financing field.

In addition to lending and other financial services, development banks can provide technical assistance services, entrepreneurial services, and financial agency services.

Technical assistance services can be particularly important and include re-

search and consulting functions covering the identification of business possibilities, assistance in developing the facts relating to technical and financial feasibility of projects, and technical and managerial advice to borrowers. The entrepreneurial services which a bank might provide involve the promotion, organization, and possibly direct management of enterprise. The agency services of a bank are such activities as trusteeships, investment management, placement of insurance and bonding, and acting as loan administrator for other organizations.

In one situation the primary need may be for a bank simply to administer loans. Elsewhere the need may be to provide its technical assistance services linked to credit to make the credit effective. In another situation, the entrepreneurial services of the bank linked to credit may be of vital importance.

The bank will probably begin by obtaining loans from the foreign assistance agencies. As the bank grows its record of performance may warrant its successful entry into the private capital markets of the world. At home the bank may borrow from the general public by placing its bonds and also in some instances by accepting demand or time deposits. The bank, however, may also do its borrowing from domestic institutions with whom it may negotiate loans, place its bonds, lay off loan participations or rediscount its portfolio.

A bank's discretion in borrowing from foreign lending agencies is rather limited in that all of the agencies maintain debt-equity ratio standards within a fairly narrow range. The bank must consider to what extent its entry into the domestic capital market to raise its own capital may divert local capital which might otherwise flow into equity financing of the projects to which the bank hopes to extend loan assistance.

A bank's loans may be in several fields and in a variety of forms. For instance, the bank can make medium- and long-term secured and unsecured loans to projects and business enterprises. The bank might make loans or extend guarantees to other financial institutions. The skill of the bank's management determines the degree to which the bank becomes successful in achieving its potential as a development institution. Conventional commercial banking standards may be too restrictive for developmental lending purposes. A loan commitment by a development bank may make it possible for the applicant to attract additional risk capital to the project.

A bank might invest directly in shares of stock either in existing or in new enterprises or it might buy shares by exercising conversion rights on its loans. The bank could also sell new issues of existing or new enterprises, perhaps as part of an underwriting arrangement; the bank could spin off older securities; the bank might sell its own stock in order to acquire and expand its investment resources and its borrowing capacity. These buying and selling activities are part of the way in which the bank can stimulate a securities market in an economy where none has existed heretofore. Through these activities the bank can supplement equity capital required by an individual entrepreneur which might not otherwise be available to him; acquire it; hold new issues for seasoning and then place them on the market when they are salable. It can increase the supply of securities and thus broaden the market which might otherwise be dominated by a few investment groups; and it can educate the general public on the purchase of

equity instruments and the taking of risks. Equally important, a well managed bank which exercises appropriate control on the enterprises it finances to protect the interests of minority stockholders will generate the kind of public confidence in equity securities which might otherwise be impossible to achieve.

By providing its guarantee for foreign borrowing by other enterprises, the bank can also act as a mobilizer of foreign credit substantially in excess of its own borrowed funds. Most foreign lending institutions find it difficult to administer international loans directly from abroad and require a local institution to assume the risk and sometimes the administration of such credit. This requirement of a local bank guarantor is even more indispensable in the case of foreign suppliers of capital goods who extend credit directly. Where domestic borrowers find it difficult to obtain such guarantees in adequate volume from local banking institutions, the development bank fulfills a vital need.

Special Problems

A most difficult problem facing development banks in many countries is the viability of the bank in its early years of operation. Normally, a bank requires a number of years of loss operations before it can reach a breakeven point. Aside from its lending operations, the bank is usually pioneering in introducing new forms of financial operations in the country and cannot expect to look forward to substantial non-interest income for some years after it commences operations. The bank's early income is tied to its lending volume. But at the same time, most banks are faced with a heavy initial investment in operating personnel and thus high operating costs relative to lending volume.

From its inception a bank can try to alleviate partially this problem by seeking a maximum of borrowed funds in relation to its capital to make up the total resources it needs to supply its market. However, the bank's international creditors, by the conditions they impose on their loans to the bank, fix the bank's maximum possible income from capital lending activities by applying standards of debt-equity ratio and interest spread (the amount the lending agency charges the bank and the amount of additional interest the lending agency permits the bank to charge its customers).

Some of the foreign assistance agencies have recognized this problem as have many governments of the countries in which such banks are established. They have provided various forms of subsidies to enable a development bank to weather the difficult early years and establish itself as a generator of capital and an energizing force for a growing economy.

Foreign assistance has served to subsidize the cost of management and technical personnel by paying the costs of technical assistance contracts providing foreign personnel for the bank's operations. United States Government agencies have also been of substantial assistance in some cases by making such banks agents for the lending of aid-generated local currency funds (with consent of local government). By so doing, they have enabled the development bank to increase the volume of resources which it can lend with the same equity capital base at commissions which are higher than the interest spread on borrowed funds and with no risk to the bank. Local governments have also supported the opera-

tions of their development banks (in addition to concurring in the bank's being a lending agent for aid-generated local currency funds) by subsidizing operating costs and in some instances through local logistical support; by giving the bank additional agency business; by providing the bank with additional capital funds in the form of long-term low-interest loans or the purchase of preferred stock; by guaranteeing dividend payments by the bank to the bank's investors; and by providing the bank and its investors with tax exemptions.

A second major problem area which faces the international lending agencies which sponsor development banks involves the dangers of monopoly. The development bank is likely to be the sole practical source of credit, medium- and long-term, that is, other than short-term. It may also be the only channel through which equity capital can be raised from the general public.

The dangers inherent in a single development bank is that it may fall under the control of a special interest group. In addition, its management, free from any of the influences of competition in a country, may acquire that kind of arrogance which makes it impossible for it to recognize a mistake. Such an institution, controlling as it does vast economic power relative to the economy in which it operates, might (due to ill-considered policies or mismanagement) come to be a deterrent rather than an accelerator of economic progress in its country. An over-emphasis on the part of such a bank on over-directing private enterprise rather than to support, stimulate and serve it would fall short of the purposes for which such banks are intended.

A third, and perhaps the most important problem is the shortage of skill and experience in the field of development lending. Unfortunately, we have yet to develop a direct means of measuring the effectiveness of a development bank's management in terms of its success as a "developer" rather than as an income earner. Lacking such a means, banks tend to be judged on their financial records and balance sheets, but this is at best an imperfect basis. Thus, there is every pressure on a bank's management to seek maximum profitability as its goal, rather than maximum development. Such a management is likely, for instance, to make equity investments only in situations where it desires to maximize profit for the bank, rather than in situations where its equity would permit a project to come into being. Such managements are not likely to welcome competition from other financial agencies and are more likely to short-circuit the growth of other needed financial institutions, such as investment banks, stock exchanges, savings banks, insurance companies, finance companies, and others.

National Development Planning and Regional Economic Integration

HOWARD S. ELLIS

Professor of Economics
University of California
Berkeley, California

The present analysis is divided into two parts. In Part I, the advantages of regional economic integration are examined with the purpose of discovering which of them largely depend upon national development planning and which do not. The examination in this part is in terms of the more highly developed, generally industrial, nations. Part II considers the different conclusions which are to be drawn if the scene is shifted from the more developed to the less developed countries of the world. In order to economize effort in this paper, Tibor Scitovsky's treatment of the general theoretical presumptions as to the gains of integra-

tion is followed. The choice of this framework is amply justified by the excellence of this work (1). What I attempt to add is—to repeat—first, the dependence of certain gains of integration upon national planning, and second, the peculiarities of underdeveloped economies.

Following Scitovsky's organization, the effects of regional economic integration are considered, first, upon *employment* and, secondly, upon *productivity*. The latter is approached under three main headings: (a) methods of production, (b) allocation of production and resources among producers, and (c) the direction of investment. Part II of the paper considers each of these subjects again, with particular reference to less developed areas. The first part of the paper is thus relevant to the European Common Market and to trade between the U.S.S.R. and some of its more industrial neighbors, while the second part is applicable to the LAFTA and Central American tariff unions, and certain other organizations proposed for Asia and Africa.

In Industrially Advanced Countries

A. Employment

Wherever full employment has come to be a major objective of national governments, the realization of this objective depends upon international trade conditions and the balance of payments. If the mutual reduction of barriers to trade among the participating countries has a strong positive effect on national output, the employment problem—as in most of the members of the European Common Market—recedes, and the pressure upon government employment measures and planning is correspondingly reduced. Aggregate employment within the common market can probably be more easily maximized if wage levels, "fringe benefits" and social security programs are not too disparate among member nations. This implies, as a second qualification to the importance of national development planning for employment, the necessity of co-ordination of national employment policies, i.e. some measures of international planning.

Although "employment policy" may be conceived in somewhat narrower terms as pertaining to public measures to relieve unemployment, it has come to embrace fiscal and monetary policy also. Terminological differences should not be allowed to impede recognition of the fact that customs unions imply intensified competition within the union, and that this in itself would be expected to restrain fiscal and monetary behavior of an inflationary character. In some cases, the force of competition on individual firms might be a sufficient restraint; but the strength of modern labor unions and of producers' monopolies is such that price stability requires conscious national policy; and the effectiveness of national policies could be enhanced by the coordination of national measures. Such indeed seems to have been the general influence of the OEEC and of European payment systems.

A third aspect of the subject of unemployment is that the erection of a common market would be expected to reduce bottlenecks and shortages in the productive process and thus to reduce seasonal and episodic unemployment.

(a) It is important, however, to distinguish seasonal and episodic unemployment from structural or chronic unemployment. It is the expectation of free traders, "freer traders", and advocates of customs unions, that aggregate output within the union will rise and will be paralleled by reduced unemployment in the aggregate. But the advocates of lowered barriers to trade have never denied that, even within a regionally integrated area, a particular country might be adversely affected. Hence the necessity of national development planning in order to cope with unemployment within a particular country which might arise as a consequence of regional integration where no such necessity existed before.

(b) Furthermore, while regional integration should, aside from such presumably exceptional circumstances, increase employment as a national aggregate, it is not written that unemployment would disappear. Many industrial nations face difficult problems of "depressed areas"; and in less developed countries almost all areas are "depressed." Here "development planning" assumes the aspect of a necessity.

B. Productive Efficiency

Methods of Production. An analysis of the gains to be expected from regional economic integration under the heading of methods of production shows that there are marked differences in the degree to which national planning would be a necessary component. Possibly the least amenable to planning and the least dependent upon planning are certain quite important improvements in production methods. These are the improvements which could follow upon the reduction of "cultural" differences with the opening up of trade through customs unions. Labor discipline and entrepreneurial drive would improve; neither would be primarily the result of national planning but would follow mostly from what the anthropologists like to call "acculturation" or the economists, the "demonstration effect."

A straightforward conclusion cannot be reached with regard to the effects of regional economic integration through price and competitiveness but it seems justifiable to say that here again substantial gains might be made without national development planning. As a general basis one could take the strong presumption that freer trade within the integrated area would reduce prices and profit margins. The mere exposure of firms under capitalism, or of state enterprises under socialism, to foreign competition would promise much. Furthermore, a tendency toward greater uniformity is likely from the standpoint of what consumers spontaneously demand and what productive units are prepared to throw upon the market. This, at least, has been the experience of such large economically integrated areas as the United States of America and U.S.S.R., and the tendency would probably prevail for newly created integrated areas. From greater uniformity would spring two powerful tendencies toward lower prices: technical standardization (of screws, gauges and "parts" in general) and the standardization of consumers' goods. Both of these contribute to mass production, mass consumption, and greater popular participation in material comforts.

On the other hand there may be obstacles which can only be removed by national development planning. For example, the expansion of consumers' markets may be held up by limitations upon consumers' credit facilities. Consumers' credit is largely an institutional arrangement of the more developed countries. In some countries, such as the United Kingdom, the development of hire purchase in the last few years will have largely removed this particular obstacle to the expansion of consumers' goods markets. In some cases state intervention may be desirable but the capacity of "free enterprise" to provide this sort of credit does not appear too limited.

Another limitation of the so-called free market mechanism to extend to the mass of consumers the potential gains which could accrue from tariff unions is said to be the conservatism of the entrepreneurial classes. A policy of small turnover with large profit margins does indeed seem to have characterized the business strategy of European producers. There is no denying that this policy is extraordinarily unfavorable to economic development. Consumers' goods, both durable and semi-durable, remain too expensive for mass consumption, and consequently for mass production. In the low-income economies which we call "less developed" this phenomenon is still more in evidence. Planning devices for the encouragement of mass consumption and mass production can increase the real income of labor in the more developed economic areas. In the less developed areas, such measures may benefit still larger fractions of the nation's population.

A review of the gains accruing from the effects of regional economic integration upon methods of production reveals the following: Gains which depend upon the spread of the economically advantageous personal characteristics of labor, such as industriousness, frugality, and the desire to rise in the economic scale, as well as the aggressiveness of the business and entrepreneurial classes—elements which may be classified in general as "cultural"—do not depend in conspicuous degree upon national development planning. But there are factors, such as the limitation of consumers' credit, and the character of entrepreneurship represented by some European countries which would warrant, and indeed require, government measures for the encouragement of competition, whether under private or state auspices.

Allocation of Resources. To proceed now to the effects of integration upon the allocation of resources and output, pursuing Scitovsky's very perspicacious analysis, we may refer the gains of international specialization, which must certainly be increased by tariff unions, to three principal sources: (a) differences in transportation costs; (b) differences in natural endowments; and (c) differences in productivity. Scitovsky is inclined to

attribute to all these factors a somewhat limited role in the setting of Western Europe, and I am inclined to agree. With regard to the third factor specifically, he argues that, while differences between firms within an industry are in general very great, the differences in national averages are much smaller. The persistence of low-cost excess capacity and, by the same token, the persistence of the high-cost producer, is explained by four factors: (a) cartel agreements; (b) the less aggressive character of European entrepreneurship; (c) small business units as a "way of life"; and (d) government protection to small business. In the United States, these same elements are present, though perhaps in lesser degree. But the implication that national (and indeed international) development planning has a potentially positive role here, is quite strong. The success of the European Steel and Iron Community is an instructive example.

Direction of Investment. Another of the major influences of regional economic integration upon productive efficiency is exercised through the nature and pattern of investment. To what degree does this depend upon deliberate planning? A common market increases confidence in the stability of the area. But for the old settled regions of Western Europe, new investment is only a small fraction of the total of invested capital, and so this factor is not very prepossessing. What is decisive for the foreigner is the possibility of obtaining in free exchange the profits and interest on his capital, and, in limited cases, the rapidity with which the capital sum itself can be repatriated. This possibility is obviously a matter of the exchange control and currency regulations. Economic union or integration is generally regarded as a separate matter from currency unions; and yet the two are, in spirit, rather closely akin. In any event, economic integration is favorable to currency unions; and the latter may be regarded as national economic planning coordinated through international means.

In connection with the nature and pattern of investment as influenced by regional economic integration, it is worth observing that such schemes of integration may involve concentration of output in countries which are too small to finance plants of new optimum size. In such cases, international financing becomes indispensable; but since national monopolies would be intolerable under these circumstances, international control seems to be clearly implied. This is said to be the situation for Norway and Austria with regard to hydro-electric projects and aluminum production, both for the European market.

In Less Developed Countries

A. Employment

Herewith we arrive at the second question posed: What differences in the analysis of integration and planning are involved with the low per-capita income countries of the world? In some aspects of the problem, the difference seems to be very great. Thus in the high-income industrial nations, unemployment is mostly a cyclical or episodic phenomenon, whereas in the less developed regions it is a structural matter predominantly. Being structural or chronic, it is very much more predictable than in the industrial nations. Furthermore, regional economic integration in the less developed world confronts countries of differing degrees of structural unemployment with the necessity of working out tolerable

conditions of competition and rational lines of specialization. This puts a greater stress upon national planning for full employment, and upon the international coordination of these plans, than is the case in the more developed nations, where average unemployment is neither as chronic nor as severe. Indeed, the contrast might be described as follows: whereas the industrial nations may proceed on the general presumption that the increase of efficiency through regional integration is the sole purpose of the union, less developed nations will have to put employment very nearly on a par with efficiency. Economic integration thus involves, besides the reduction of trade barriers, some deliberate plans for more effective use of labor within the region. In the very long run, of course, what is good for productive efficiency is also good for employment. But in the short run the contrast may be very great and involve a legitimate concern for public policy.

B. Productive Efficiency

Methods of Production. With regard to methods of production, one factor is labor discipline and economic motivations in general. In the setting of the less developed countries, this factor takes on very much greater significance than in the industrial world. It embraces not only those subjective or "cultural" matters touched upon briefly by Scitovsky, but also the transmission of productive techniques and includes the whole area of technological backwardness, technical aid, etc., etc. Indeed, this category comes very close to covering the chief causes of the lack of development, including perhaps even the ubiquitous scarcity of capital. But while the terrain is immense, the present analysis is concerned with it only as far as economic integration and national planning are involved.

(a) The conclusion reached by Scitovsky for Western Europe may be extended to the less developed countries—namely, that one of the chief gains of integration is the furtherance of productive techniques and economic motivation, rather than the fact of a common market *per se*. In other words, we have to do here with economic effects which flow from the exposure of one economy or one culture to another through competition—competition of goods, of ideas, and of men. Undoubtedly, this is to some degree a function of the magnitude of international trade. But it is in large measure independent, both in volume and in character, because this category of gain has to do with changes in the very constitution and nature of the economy. It is not to be identified with the per unit saving in the purchase of imports or the per unit gain upon the sale of exports although, of course, these gains will also accrue in the larger run.

(b) National development planning can expedite the adoption of new and improved techniques. In less developed countries this is particularly important for agriculture. But there would appear to be little difference between purely national and integrated areas so far as the role of government planning is concerned. This also seems true of the spread of attitudes conducive to economic development on the part of labor.

There is another aspect of production methods which has a potentially strong influence flowing from integration. It is the breaking down of producer inclinations toward high profit margins and small turnover. Scitovsky attributes to this factor the leading advantage of Western European integration. For the larger part of the economically less developed world—but particularly for most of Latin America—conservatism of producers is a formidable barrier to progress. One of the chief gains of arrangements such as LAFTA promises to be the invasion of previously monopolized territories by foreign wares, with the consequent reduction of price and profit margins. It was Ragnar Nurkse who, under the caption of "balanced development", emphasized the critical role which could be played by the expansion of domestic markets. For these to develop, however, requires the reduction of price and that many consumers' goods now regarded as luxuries or semi-luxuries become articles of mass consumption. Gains of this category accrue through the opening up of competition and not through national development planning, unless the organization of the integrated area is itself to be regarded as planning.

Allocation of Resources. A second set of gains in productive efficiency from integration are the advantages of *specialization,* which classical theory attributes to free trade, and which a general theory might suppose to be the chief gains of economic integration. Scitovsky's conclusion for Western Europe that savings from integration in certain respects would not be great, it is believed, would also hold for integrated areas of less developed countries. Trade among less developed countries is only a small fraction of the trade of such countries with the economically developed world, and a still smaller fraction of the trade of the more developed countries *inter se*.

(a) Many factors are responsible for the lack of trade among the less developed countries, including currency difficulties, exchange controls, and high tariffs. But there are two factors not so easily subject to reform through economic integration. In the first place, international trade is small because of the low purchasing power of the large mass of people. In the second place, *as matters now stand,* there is a lower degree of economic complementarity among the less developed countries than among the industrial countries. This need not always remain so. The customs union aspect of economic integration would not have a very broad base upon which to operate at first, simply because the volume of trade of the less developed countries is itself relatively small. National development planning can indeed change this but it cannot do so on the basis of the economy as it stands. It must be on the basis of new investment.

Direction of Investment. The third aspect of productive efficiency is the effect of economic integration upon new investment. In part one would expect that favorable effects on the volume of foreign investment would flow from the larger domestic markets and greater stability of an integrated area. Greater gains can be realized over the long run, however, by what might be called "contrived" specialization of the various countries through national (possibly complemented by international) development planning of new investment.

(a) For Western Europe, with its impressive complement of fixed capital equipment, the economic gains to be realized by the rationalization of *new* investment are doubtless relatively small. For the newly developing nations, however, the matter is quite the reverse. Most of the investment lies in the future; nearly all of it will be new and will therefore be subject to rationalization.

(b) Much of the present day national specialization is not the result of natural endowment, but the result of the "early start". Probably the Swiss watch industry, the Swedish fine steel industry and the German chemical industry illustrate this kind of evolution. In cases of this sort, in the new countries with virtually no capital equipment, an almost unlimited field is open for the determination of investment by national development policy. But even if natural endowment imposes certain limits on the freedom of choice for new investment, concerted policy can press these natural advantages to the full. Thus in the case of an integrated Latin American Market, the manufacture of steel can be concentrated in two or three most advantageous centers. Or the manufacture of some rather highly specialized item such as light bulbs might be concentrated in one place. National development planning can play a very large role; but for its best functioning, a co-ordination of the national development plans in an advisory central investment agency of the integrated area would be highly desirable. This type of activity could be the greatest gain of integration in the presently less developed world.

Conclusion

The gains of integration in the less developed areas differ although, both for them and for the industrial countries, a very substantial part of the gain comes, not from the quantitative increase of trade, but from salutary effects of increased competition from foreign sources of supply. This is probably the chief similarity for both types of countries and for these gains economic development planning plays a rather subordinate role.

The chief difference is that for newly developed countries new investment is important, and this implies that the deliberate rationalization of investment to secure national specialization is correspondingly promising.

REFERENCE

(1) Scitovsky, T., *Economic Theory and Western European Integration*. George Allen and Unwin, Ltd., London (1958).

National Planning and Multinational Planning Under the Alliance for Progress

HARVEY S. PERLOFF AND RAÚL SAEZ

Committee of Nine—Alliance for Progress
Washington, D.C.

Introduction

The possibilities of achievement of high level self-sustained economic growth by the less developed countries of the world has taken on a new dimension in the past generation with the emergence of three powerful forces. First, widespread desire on the part of the people of these countries to rapidly raise their standards of living and a belief that this is a feasible goal. Second, the provision of substantial financial and technical assistance by the more developed nations. Third, the forging of regional institutions to advance economic growth.

These elements have come powerfully to the forefront in the Western Hemisphere and have been given form and substance through the cooperative system called the Alliance for Progress— La Alianza para el Progreso. While the Alliance is quite young, having been proposed in March, 1961, and organized in August of that year, it provides certain general features which should be of interest to persons concerned with the problems of development.

Although the Alliance as a formal arrangement is recent, the ideas and forces behind it have been developing over many years. Thus, over the past few decades the countries of Latin America have increasingly devoted themselves to the goal of economic development. The joining of forces for the achievement of common goals through the inter-American regional system is an idea of long standing—which was given a new form in the Alliance. The emphasis on internal structural reforms to ensure that all the people of a nation benefit equitably from economic improvement—a key feature of the Alliance—is a natural outgrowth of the far-reaching ideas of reform stemming from the various popular movements in Latin America.

Formal planning as a valuable tool for designing and implementing an effective, consistent development effort has increasingly come to be accepted as a result of successful experience with planning in the Western Hemisphere, as well as in other parts of the world. Western Hemisphere scholars, many of them associated with the United Nations Economic Commission for Latin America, as well as other scholars and practitioners, had over a long period of time devoted themselves to strengthening planning and programming techniques. The know-how and technical skills thus developed could be drawn on by the Alliance program.

Far-seeing individuals from universities, government and business, over the years saw the need and developed ideas for commodity stabilization and for regional economic integration, and movements to foster both of these ideas preceded the establishment of the Alliance program.

In addition, the experience with the Marshall Plan in Europe, with a full awareness of the great differences involved, provided a valuable background for the design of an assistance program in Latin America. Among the pertinent aspects of the European experience was the use of country programs as a basis for external financial assistance, the review of country programs by an international body, and the general multilateral approach to assistance programs. The idea of what came to be known as "confrontation" within the framework of the Organization for European Economic Cooperation not only helped strengthen the forces of regional cooperation, but provided a truly suggestive plan of action that could be drawn upon.

So the key elements for a far-reaching cooperative hemispheric effort had been maturing over the years. It was evident, finally, that for implementing such an effort an adequate base of financial support for Latin American development programs would be required and that all potential sources of external financing would have to be tapped.

Certain present features of the Alliance for Progress program, and even more, its potentialities in the future are, we believe, highly suggestive, and of direct significance for development efforts in every part of the world.

The Strategy of the Alliance

The Alliance for Progress seeks to accelerate the economic and social development of the participating countries in Latin America. The Charter of Punta del Este,[1] looking toward the achievement, within a reasonable time, of self-sustaining development, has set a goal of per capita income increases in each nation of not less than 2.5 percent annually. With population increasing on the average at an annual rate of some 2.6 percent, the minimum per capita goal requires an average rate of increase in national income of at least 5.1 percent per year. Relatively few Latin American countries have maintained such a level of growth over the past decade.[2] At the time of the Charter, it was estimated that the achievement of these growth rates would require over the decade about $100 billion in capital funds, of which at least $20 billion would have to come from sources outside Latin America. These figures are on the low side and now it seems likely that larger sums will have to be made available to achieve the goals set.

Country planning has been given a large role in the Alliance program. Each nation is to formulate plans to provide (a) a firm direction to its development effort by establishing goals, priorities, and a general development strategy, (b) guidelines for carrying out needed structural and social changes, (c) a general framework within which to develop specific sector programs and projects (as well as the priority programs and projects), and (d) a rational basis for estimating required internal and external financing (assuming a "maximum" effort to mobilize internal resources). Planning has been emphasized because of the contribution it can make to a more effective and disciplined channeling of resources into developmental purposes. Given the ambitious growth goals on the one side and the severely limited internal resources on the other, there is need to ensure that an adequate volume of both public and private savings are generated and are invested in an optimum fashion in the development of the natural, human, capital, and organizational resources. The programming of needed investments of specified categories encourages appropriate production scale and production linkage, while the projection of the flow of funds provides a strong weapon in the achievement of monetary stability. Country plans can also help highlight conflicts with plans of other nations and thus provide a basic framework for working out continent-wide policies geared to common objectives.

A highly significant feature of the Alliance is the emphasis placed on basic social reforms, particularly land and tax reforms. All the signatory nations of the Charter of Punta del Este have agreed to carry out "programs of comprehensive agrarian reform leading to the effective transformation, where required, of unjust structures and systems of land tenure and use . . ." Similarly, all the nations have agreed to promote tax reform where necessary both to provide for the effective mobilization of internal resources and to bring about a more equitable distribution of income. Since such, among other reforms, are deemed essential to lay a foundation for sustained economic and social advance within the countries of Latin America, their implementation is considered a key requirement for the extension of long-term plan-related financial assistance under the Alliance. The dual function of structural reforms—the increase in productivity and the mobilization of resources on the one side and the satisfaction of equity requirements on the other—is critical to rapid development under current conditions in democratic countries. The optimum use of natural resources (and particularly the land) and the tapping of the great potential energies of the human resources (which requires widespread involvement in development by the people of a nation) are at the very foundations of economic advance. People who have relatively little cannot be expected to work hard and accept the discipline of a development effort, unless they feel that they are receiving and will continue to receive a fair share of the total returns.

The reforms are matters of extreme complexity, compounded by the great variations in national situations and institutions. There are important groups within each of the Latin American countries who are strongly opposed to social reforms and such groups can be expected to resist the implementation of such reforms with all means available to them. At the same time, the formal acceptance of the concept of reforms by all the participating countries, plus the pressures involved in the tying of reforms to long-term financial assistance, provide a foundation for meaningful progress along these lines.

A central feature of the Alliance is the provision of long-term United States and international financial assistance based on country plans comprising all the above-mentioned elements. The idea of foreign assistance being provided to finance a development plan rather than isolated projects was first utilized in the case of India's Third Five-Year Plan. This approach is currently in the process of being adapted to the specific factors involved in the Latin American situation.

Evaluation of Country Plans and the "Committee of Nine"

The evaluation of national development programs has been given a pivotal role in the execution of the development strategy under the Alliance. The evaluation mechanism has been established for three interrelated purposes. First, it provides the nations submitting plans with expert judgment on the adequacy of the policies and methods proposed for achieving the national development goals and targets which the country has set. Secondly, this serves as a means of advising the signatories of the Charter of Punta del Este on matters related to their obligations under the Charter. The evaluation covers the extent of consistency with the Charter. Thirdly, and as a direct counterpart of the other two, it serves as a technique for helping to bring national plans up to a qualitative level where the possibilities of obtaining an adequate amount of public and private external financial assistance is maximized.

Any Latin American government, if it so wishes, may present its plan for evaluation of an *Ad-Hoc* Committee composed of three or less members from a panel of nine experts [3] together with an equal number of experts not on the panel.[4] The *Ad-Hoc* Committee studies the development program, exchanges opinions with the government and, with the consent of the government, reports its conclusions to other governments and institutions that may be willing to extend external financial and technical assistance.

The *Ad-Hoc* Committee, in examining a national plan, is concerned with a number of key elements. Thus, it will test the realism and consistency of the goals and targets set, in terms of the rate at which programs can be implemented, the distribution between economic and social projects, the provision of adequate overhead facilities to make the production targets feasible, and the like. It will evaluate the plan, as well as the means of implementation, in terms of the specific criteria set forth in the Charter of Punta del Este. This includes a review of the social investments and structural reforms. The Committee will analyze in great detail the provisions made in the plan concerning the achievement of an equilibrium in the balance of payments, as well as the provisions made for the mobilization of internal resources. On the basis of such an analysis, the requirements for external financing can be evaluated. In addition, the Committee studies carefully the major policy proposals—with regard to such matters as prices, wages, imports, subsidies, and the like—to decide whether these are consistent with the development objectives set forth in the country's development plan.

The *Ad-Hoc* Committee, of course, has at its disposal the reports of national, foreign, and international agencies on various aspects of the economy under study and may commission special reports in areas where it feels they are required.

The *Ad Hoc* Committee is, among other things, a technique of confrontation which gives the country under study the opportunity to discuss recommendations informally and make changes in its plan before it is presented for financing. The significant element here is the support provided by an independent international group, without any special-interest motive, to a government to adopt and carry out sound economic and social policies. Aside from the general prestige of the Committee, the backing of the U.S. Government and international financial agencies gives substantial weight to the "confrontation" of the Committee.

The Committee's findings are presented in a report addressed to the nation which has submitted the plan for evaluation and, with its approval, to financial institutions and governments that may be prepared to extend external financial and technical assistance in connection with the execution of the nation's development program.

While the experience with this mechanism is quite limited—as of September, 1962, it had been applied to only three country development plans—it seems to be fulfilling its central purposes. In each of these cases, the recommendations of the *Ad-Hoc* Committee have provided a stimulus for the introduction of important policy changes and new measures by the governments and have provided terms of reference for international financial arrangements.

This is not to suggest that an ideal mechanism has been invented. There are many problems yet to be overcome before there can be assurance that this is a truly viable mechanism, working as an integral part of a well-functioning scheme. Thus, for example, since the scheme depends on the ability of the Latin American countries to chart and carry out important economic and social changes, the fact that the Alliance concepts are not yet generally understood by the public means that the planning cannot yet be deeply rooted. In addition, given the importance of a high quality of national planning and execution of

plans, there are problems stemming from the inexperience of the planning agencies, the lack of adequate planning personnel, the inadequacy of statistics and economic information, and the inadequacies of institutional arrangements for plan execution. Also, it is evident that there are serious problems of scale since the key objectives of regional integration and commodity stabilization cannot be achieved until a large share of all the Latin American countries have come into the scheme and taken the necessary steps to promote region-wide progress. Finally, there is the problem of adequate international financing of national investment programs, which is something of a chicken-and-egg proposition, since assurance of such financing is needed in many cases to generate truly significant self-help efforts, while such efforts are themselves the best assurance of adequate international financing.

However, with improvements that can be anticipated over time on the basis of experience, and a strong start in a few of the countries that are ready to move ahead, the scheme described above may well turn out to be one of the most important of the levers in Latin America's economic and social development.

Multinational Planning

The evaluation of national programs on the basis of formally-established criteria is in effect a beginning of multinational planning. Programs and policies within national plans are, as indicated above, tested by the evaluating committees for consistency with what other Latin American countries are doing, or propose to do, and potential conflicts are brought to the forefront. Thus, for example, a country seeking to diversify its exports might be proposing greatly to increase the production of a crop, which in its own country in the past has been minor, but which is the chief earner of foreign exchange in another Latin American country and already tending toward world oversupply—for example, coffee or sugar. In such a case, the *Ad-Hoc* Committee could be expected to highlight this fact and discuss with the government the possibility of introducing alternative crops or livestock. Potentialities of greatly increasing trade, particularly among nearby neighbors—where transportation bottlenecks can be overcome—will be carefully reviewed. And, of course, the potential role of the nation's economy in the evolving regional common market would be a matter of special interest. Clearly, the value of such a review increases progressively as more countries prepare their plans and submit them for evaluation.

The force of such evaluation stems from the fact that it is rooted in the core principles of the Alliance for Progress. The search for effective means to promote the stabilization of income derived from exports both by stabilizing the income from present exports and by encouraging diversification to reduce dependence on a limited number of primary export products is, as mentioned earlier, a central feature of the hemispheric strategy for development. Diversification is an aim of development planning in each of the Latin American countries in which the present commodity exports provide a limited and unstable base for economic expansion. In addition, the problem of commodity stabilization, being worldwide in scope, requires multilateral solutions through international agreements and arrangement. The member nations associated with the Alliance have established study groups, such as the Coffee Study group, focusing specifically on the particular commodity problems of Latin America. In the case of coffee, extensive preparations preceded the working out of an International Coffee Agreement, signed in August, 1962, which provided for export quotas and production controls. Special attention is also being devoted to the possibility of creating a compensatory financial mechanism designed to reduce fluctuations in annual export earnings from commodity transactions on an international or on a hemispheric basis.

The same principle is true of the effort to strengthen region-wide economic integration. The broadening of markets in Latin America is deemed essential to accelerate the process of economic development in the hemisphere; it is seen as an important means for obtaining greater productivity through specialized and complementary industrial production.

In general, then, the conception of the Alliance for Progress, as a simultaneous, cooperative and multilateral development effort, provides an initial base for multinational planning.

It will undoubtedly take a number of years to implement completely the elaborate framework outlined by the Charter of Punta del Este. However, already over three-quarters of the countries of Latin America are in the process of preparing national development programs. The Central American Common Market—covering five countries—is almost an accomplished fact, while the Latin American Free Trade Area—covering nine countries—is going through the slow, tedious process of working out product-by-product trade arrangements. In addition, a significant start has been made toward the solution of the coffee problem, while stabilization arrangements for other basic products are being discussed.

This progress, as much as the great problems yet to be overcome, highlights the need for an additional tool which can strengthen the present efforts and mechanisms. A regional approach to development calls for relatively extensive direct region-wide planning. The key objectives of the Alliance for Progress and the mechanisms which have been set up to implement them would be strengthened significantly through more extensive region-wide planning—what might be called "framework" planning—viewing *all* of Latin America in relation to the changing "rest of the world" situation.

What is meant by framework planning here is: (a) the preparation of analyses of economic and social trends on a region-wide basis and projection of key series to reveal the interregional implications of the evolving situation. Such projections would be broken down by economic sub-regions as well as by sectors. This would call for a central institution to provide detailed information far beyond anything now available; (b) Analyses and projections of regional markets within and outside Latin America for major products and services, as well as production, exports and imports within each commodity category, prepared within the context of analyses of world market developments; [5] (c) Analyses of capital flows, terms of trade, balance of payments, and requirements of external financial assistance; and (d) The detailing of the developmental potentialities of the region, seen as a single cooperating unit, in terms of complementary industries, increased trade, and development of region-wide infrastructure facilities, such as transportation and communication.

This type of multinational planning would furnish extremely useful specific terms of reference for the preparation of country plans and of expansion plans by private firms. It would, at the same time, provide a key element in the strengthening of Latin American economic integration. The major objective of such integration is the speeding of *new* economic development, particularly in manufactures, rather than merely the freeing of current trade. The basic need is to encourage internal (within-region) investment in productive enterprises as well as to attract investment from outside. As Europe is now demonstrating, broad planning can help reduce certain kinds of risks and encourage productive expansion.

The question of economic integration among lesser developed countries is, of course, quite different from what it is in the case of an economically more advanced region, such as Europe. In the latter, inter-country trade accounts for a large part of their total trade; by contrast, inter-Latin American trade is only a minor share—amounting on the average to some 10 percent of the total external trade of the countries concerned. While there are sizeable variations from country to country, it is evident that Latin American countries have separately geared their economy to complementarity with the outside world, predominantly the United States and Europe. It is noteworthy that there is a practical absence of any exports of manufactures from one Latin American country to another, suggesting the lack of competition and excessive protection under which these industries have evolved. Even more important, however, is the fact that the process of industrialization has still a long way to go in the region. Thus, for Latin America, integration is not so much a question of competition among already existing industries—with all the extensive adjustments that are involved—as an opportunity to promote and plan the development of new industries collectively, avoid unnecessary duplication or uneconomic location and ensure from the beginning the most appropriate scale of production for the industries to be started. This does not mean, of course, that the appropriate route to development is the establishment of vast multi-product cartels, for these can be just as stultifying on an international as on a national basis. The key question is one of markets and scale, but within a context of lively competition for sales in a rapidly growing regional market, reinforced by international competition.

Multinational planning is also required to arrive at some basic decisions as to the degree of autonomy and types of external trade that the region should seek in a world which is increasingly becoming regionalized. Such a decision requires cooperation among regions. It would not be wise to develop product surpluses which were not exportable to other regional markets; nor to encourage dependence on external sources of capital goods and raw materials without seeing to it that the corresponding means of finance were available. It is to be hoped that Latin American regional economic development can take place in a world economy increasingly geared to extensive and relatively free international and interregional trade.

The evolving multilateralism and planning of the Alliance for Progress suggests that a foundation for region-wide planning is being laid stage by stage. In the not-too-distant future, a point may well be reached where the merging of national and multinational planning will be a key element in, as well as a symbol of, a high level of economic and social development throughout the whole of Latin America.

FOOTNOTES

[1] Named after the small resort outside Montevideo (Uruguay) where the Alliance was organized.

[2] During the period 1950–1961 the annual average increase in the gross national income for Latin America was 4.3 percent.

[3] The Inter-American Economic and Social Council of the Organization of American States has selected a panel of experts, the so-called "Committee of Nine", organized in such a way as to enjoy "complete autonomy in the performance of their duties". Seven of the nine members are Latin Americans.

[4] Thus far, there has emerged a certain pattern in the composition of the *Ad-Hoc* Committee. The membership has been predominantly Latin American; in each case there have been four members from Latin America, one from the United States, and one from Europe or elsewhere outside the Western Hemisphere.

[5] It is assumed that such data would be used with extreme care in practice. Forecasts for commodity markets are often wrong. Furthermore, there are at times reasons for a low-cost producer to expand in spite of a relatively unfavorable world market "outlook."

International Commodity Markets as a Factor in Development Planning

Henry G. Aubrey

Research Fellow
Council on Foreign Relations
New York City

Economic planning requires assessment of available resources so that they can be productively and optimally deployed. Future resource flows should be predictable, dependable, and rising over time in order to supply the greater inputs that a rising output demands. In a closed economy, or one little influenced by foreign trade, the many variables entering into planning are within the policy maker's grasp and—at least potentially—subject to his influence or control. To the extent he is dependent on developments beyond the national borders this is not so; and the larger the foreign sector in the economy, the greater this dependence.

Trade is the most important foreign element in the economic reality of less developed areas, the range of domestic production being limited and the need to import a broad range of goods great. For development their imports will have to include most of the capital goods, intermediate materials and at least a part of the raw materials the growth process requires. Apart from whatever capital they can obtain from abroad these imports must be paid for by exports. Inevitably, less developed economies offer chiefly primary commodities—food, raw materials and fuels; and major markets

for these products are industrial countries. Hence, exports provide a vital resource—foreign exchange needed to buy development and consumer goods basic to further economic advance.

Foreign trade considerations are thus essential in planning calculations. Moreover, in all but the largest countries of the less developed world, production for export is a sizable component of national income, partly because the economy has not yet benefited from the diversification that development promises. Consequently export income bears directly, usually heavily, on savings, capacity to invest, and capital formation—the foundation of future progress. Furthermore, in the reality of many primary producing countries the "tone" of the entire economy is influenced by exports, whose fluctuations thus have indirectly magnified effects.

Thus, as a determinant of income, savings and investment, and of import capacity, exports are a strategic variable in economic development; and these two aspects are closely related, for the conversion of savings into real investment, i.e., imported capital goods, is a vital element that raises productivity of the available resources—along with greater inputs, the backbone of economic growth. Instability of export receipts thus disrupts the planner's effort to project the volume and origin of total resources. Moreover, unless exports grow commensurately with mounting import needs for development, growth will be retarded.

Both short-run stability and long-term export growth are, therefore, essential developmental prerequisites. And as external instability disrupts internal continuity and discourages investment, the interaction of these two aspects—cyclical and secular—is intimate, especially in the institutional-political framework of a less developed economy. The planner's task is doubly difficult if instability prevails while exports grow slowly; for it is always easier to make adjustments within a buoyant than in a sluggish trend.

Unfortunately, the realities of world trade have often not been favorable on both counts. Fluctuations in export receipts of non-industrial countries have been frequent and wide. On the whole, export values have risen significantly, but to very different extents, depending on the fortunes of various products. Moreover, it is likely that price instability of some commodities has encouraged substitution, thus reducing long-term demand—another instance of interaction of cyclical fluctuations with secular trends. Most important, however, the export rise of primary commodities has tended to lag behind two strategic variables in world economic development: the rise of national income in the industrial countries, the decisive determinant of world demand; and import needs of developing countries. And these two factors are most unhappily combined in the early stages of development; for initially an acceleration of economic development usu-

ally requires disproportionally large imports of capital goods to generate faster growth.

The planner's task is consequently a difficult one indeed, consisting partly in planning for essentially unpredictable developments and optimizing the utilization of doubtful resources. The scope for policy here is plainly limited. It is difficult enough to combine economic growth with domestic stability—as some developed countries have recently also become more painfully aware. In an underdeveloped institutional environment, not only is the task even more forbidding, but the effects of external instability are superimposed on the domestic difficulty, aggravating internal imbalance and impinging upon growth.

Problems of external origin with world-wide implications obviously cannot be solved by the policy maker's efforts in the producing countries alone. The global character of the issues calls for international approaches. What an individual primary producing country can plan for itself in the foreign field is circumscribed by what the rest of the world does. Likewise, planning for domestic growth and stability needs to be complemented by international support of both stability and growth in the world economy.

In this broader sense a national development program and international coordination are dependent upon each other; and coordination will have to be supplemented by international cooperation and finance. Whether this takes the form of commodity agreements, market guarantees, compensatory payments, trade liberalization or more development aid, barring more dependable export receipts planning may well become tangled up in external constraints beyond redress. Thus, for most primary-producing countries commodity markets are a vital factor in development planning or perhaps fatal, unless external and internal elements can somehow be kept in harness.

Trade Dependence and Instability of Export Receipts

The planner's difficulty due to overdependence on foreign trade is basically twofold: (a) Policy scope is limited by an uncontrollable foreign element; this limits his autonomy in defining the pace and character of the economy as internal needs would dictate. (b) As external demand bears heavily on one sector of the economy, yet indirectly affects others, a restructuring in the direction of greater balance is the harder to achieve the more unstable this foreign element due to the great dependence on a narrow range of commodities. No less than thirty less developed countries rely on a single product for half or more of export receipts (1). And more than four-fifths of the primary producers' exports consist of three of these commodities (2).

The wide price fluctuations of primary commodities are well known. Yet, export volumes have sometimes fluctuated even more. Since it is not necessary for the purpose of this paper to present much detail, it is preferable to concentrate on the export values of primary producing countries and their purchasing power over imports. On the average, the export proceeds of a number of countries displayed year-to-year changes of about 10 percent before the First World War, 18 percent in the interwar period and 13 percent in the post-war decade beginning in 1948. Averaging, of course, conceals substantial country variability, ranging from 1948 to 1958 from a minimum

of about 5 percent in Venezuela to nearly 21 percent in the Sudan and 20 percent in Malaya. In terms of the importing power of exports, considering not only export earnings but other receipts including capital, the incidence of instability was wider. For 38 countries the year-to-year percentage change of importing power averaged 13 percent (compared with only 12 percent for exports alone) and ranged from a low of nearly 8 percent in Ceylon to about 21 percent in Burma, Pakistan, and the Sudan (3).

Shortfalls in external receipts usually prompt attempts at cutting imports, with a frequent "assist" (in a somewhat morbid sense) by the income drop induced by lower exports. This import reduction includes some luxury goods, and otherwise consists of the least essential of the consumer goods. But for the development planner the issue assumes particular significance when retrenchment in capital goods imports follows. Where capital goods production is still small, this means reduced fixed investment and inevitably a slower growth. As a panel of UN experts has observed, there is a tendency "to place a large part of the burden of restrictions on imports of capital equipment", and "total domestic investment has been quite closely related to available supplies of imported capital equipment; and partly through this relationship the year-to-year changes in total investment have tended to reflect the instability in export proceeds or in importing power of exports" (4).

Cutting imports if export receipts fall is, naturally, not the only measure of adjustment. Already slender exchange reserves fall still further. This effect is difficult to measure but the UN Secretariat has attempted it for 1953–60. Cumulative shortfalls in export earnings from a three-year average amounted to about 16 percent of primary exporting countries' foreign exchange reserves at the end of 1960. Averages are again deceptive and the impact on some countries was much heavier. "In about a fifth of the primary exporting countries the average shortfall on the basis of 1953–60 experience might be expected to drain away in any one year more than a fourth of the total gold and foreign currency holdings. Inasmuch as declines in exports are not always limited to a single year, this ratio tends to underestimate the potential strain on reserves" (5).

A country's reserves are its last bastion against an excessive cut of imports and, once depleted, leave it near-defenseless against the next adversity. And in absolute terms, these shortfalls were very large indeed. During 1953–60, the cumulative annual shortfall from a three-year trend in 99 primary exporting countries totalled over $9 billion, or about $1.1 billion yearly on the average (6). And in individual countries the cumulative shortfall exceeded $400 million each in eight countries (7). These are very sizable amounts by any measure, even for large countries; yet much lower figures may spell more substantial dislocation in smaller countries for which export-dependence and hence vulnerability are often greatest.

Such data help explain the grievance voiced by certain countries that their trade "losses" offset aid receipts. While this contention is hardly valid in the aggregate at present in view of the steep aid increase in recent years, it may well have been true in certain countries at certain time periods, much depending on the base period selected for comparison and on a country's short-term trade fortunes. Yet, the seriousness of the problem

is plainly evident; it is quite evident that precipitous declines in the price of specific commodities such as coffee are bound to have a severe impact. Thus it has been said that price drops of coffee "since 1956 have cost producing countries more than $2 billion in exports, with Latin America accounting for $1.2 billion of these losses (8). And it has been estimated that a fall of one cent in the price of green coffee means a $50 million loss to Latin American producers (9).

This instability, however defined or measured, has a number of indirect effects spreading outward from the export sector. Abrupt income declines prompt governments to adopt policies designed to counteract the economic and social impact. To the extent these measures sustain income, imports will fall less than they might otherwise, thus aggravating the payments imbalance. The manner of public support has also a bearing on the future, due to fiscal rigidity in many less developed countries. Public revenue is promptly and severely affected by reduced exports and imports—an important part of the tax base. As incomes fall so do other taxes. Public expenditures to shore up the sagging economy increase the mounting budget deficit. Borrowing to raise the necessary revenue—usually from banks, since at times of depression funds are even harder than usually to raise publicly—create an inflationary potential against which measures taken in a subsequent boom are rarely effective.

In depression or boom, political pressures tend to favor expenditure patterns intensifying, rather than mitigating, the effects of instability. The planner, moreover, is easily caught up in the maelstrom: in the downswing shortage of both revenue and foreign exchange is a handicap and in the boom the very plenty is his enemy. At that time luxury imports syphon off part of the export proceeds; an inflation-begotten pattern of investment favors unproductive uses; and in a boom psychology, controls, always unpopular, appear unnecessary while the usually short-lived prosperity lasts.

Certainly fluctuations do not all originate in developed areas. Crop and other supply variations can also initiate oscillations, and policies in the primary producing countries are rarely free from blame; wrong anticipations of trends and attempts to influence prices in a monopolistic fashion but with unsuitable means have sometimes aggravated the trouble. Yet, the scope for action is limited, and the planner's task complicated, by the difficulty of anticipating the sustainable level of export production and realizable earnings.

Long-Term Problems

The effects of fluctuations do not necessarily exhaust themselves in short-order but frequently have effects extending over several years or permanently. For instance, if a change in demand does not meet with a quick response in supply, disproportionate price swings can occur. The response in most agricultural commodities is delayed by at least a growing season, to the extent stocks cannot take care of the variation; and in the case of tree crops the delay extends over several years, by which time the market situation may have reversed itself. In minerals the short-term response is more elastic up to a point, but not if new facilities have to be brought into operation; and, since the economic size of new mines and processing plants is usually very large, the sudden supply increase can easily upset the market. Meanwhile, if demand rises

while supply lags, high prices may encourage substitution by materials that are not imported and import demand would thereby be permanently reduced; protracted instability of supply and prices tends to encourage this process of displacement that has indeed become one of the gravest long-term problems for the primary producers.

These difficulties are aggravated if the long-term trend of demand for these export products is sluggish, though this is not the case for all products or to the same extent; also, an individual country may be able to improve its market through increasing productivity and proper policies. Yet, it operates within a given world demand and, at least for the primary producers as a group, the prevailing long-term trends constitute a limiting factor.

Broadly, these secular trends have not benefited primary producing countries as they would have, had imports of industrial countries risen proportionately to output. This is indeed the core of the long-term problem facing development planners; and this situation prevails not only in foods but also in raw materials.

Comparing the averages of 1948/52 with 1958/60, money incomes in industrial countries increased by 78 percent and real income by 42 percent in this period. Yet, while the consumption of 13 major foods (excluding wheat) in these areas rose by 35 percent the volume of imports increased by 28 percent and the value by only 19 percent. A number of reasons can be found for this lag. Food consumption generally trails rising incomes and this has particularly affected beverage crops. Further, the industrial countries produced an increasing share of their food. And as these factors depressed the growth of import volume, prices fell by 7 percent while the general price level in industrial countries rose by 25 percent. "If the value of primary producing countries' exports of these commodities had risen in line with money incomes in the industrial countries, they would have been worth $8.5 billion a year in 1958/60, instead of the estimated figure of $5.7 billion—a gap of $2.8 billion" (10).

A similar computation for raw materials (covering a shorter time period) shows a 38 percent increase in the consumption in industrial areas from 1950/52 to 1955/57 while the value of imports increased by only 4 percent. Again price developments played a role, but in volume terms the lag between consumption growth of 27 percent and that of imports of 19 percent is no less revealing. And this is not a recent trend, for the world-export volume of primary products has been lagging behind world-manufacturing production for a long time. From 1913 to 1957/59 manufacturing grew nearly fourfold, but export volume of primary products less than twofold (11).

To see this lag in bolder relief, we may compare the growth of manufacturing production in North America, Western Europe and Japan with the volume of exports of primary commodities after excluding advanced areas that are also major exporters of such products. From 1928 to 1955/57 manufacturing production in the former countries grew by 145 percent, exports of 34 primary commodities from the primary producing countries by 53 percent. And excluding petroleum—specially favored by circumstances, yet produced in few countries— they increased only by 23 percent in these 28 years. In fact, petroleum was the only commodity group outstripping world manufacturing growth in this period. "The expansion in volume of primary commodity exports of the less developed regions, exclusive of petroleum, amounted to no more than one-sixth of the advance in world manufacturing production" (12).

The reason for this lag stems from three related elements. By a number of technological developments, including the use of material-saving methods and greater recovery from scrap, the input of materials per unit of output has been declining. Moreover, the use of natural raw materials—more often imported than the synthetics replacing them—has been declining relatively. Consequently the volume of imports has been lagging far behind that of consumption. For instance, by a rough estimate for the U.S. in the first half of this century manufacturing production grew more than three times as fast as raw materials consumption (13). For all industrial countries, between 1938 and 1954 total production of commodities increased 77 percent, input of natural raw materials into manufacturing by 33 percent and net imports of natural raw materials (in value terms) not at all (14). Particularly illustrative of the lag of imports behind consumption in the two main industrial areas, U.S. and Europe, seen separately, is this comparison: U.S. consumption of primary commodities, exclusive of petroleum, from 1927/29 to 1955/57 grew 35 percent, the value of their imports only by 17 percent. In Western Europe while consumption advanced also by 35 percent, imports increased by only 9 percent. Thus, the trend towards more self-sufficiency was greater in Europe than in the U.S.; and since Western Europe is also the larger importer, the combined lag-effect for both areas is that much more significant—11 percent import growth compared with a 35 percent increase in consumption (15).

Price developments have played some part in this, particularly in the last part of this period. From 1953 to 1960, a period of slow deterioration of the purchasing power of primary commodity exports, the volume of such exports to the United States, Canada, and Western Europe grew by 45 percent, their purchasing power only by 38 percent. Interestingly, the hypothetical "price gap" implied in these figures amounted to about $1.25 billion. In this recent period, too, import of raw materials continued to trail manufacturing production. While the latter grew 31 percent in these industrial areas, consumption of raw materials increased only by 25 percent. In the same period the volume of imports rose only by 20 percent, indicating further advances towards self-sufficiency (16).

The Outlook for the Commodity Markets

Though the preceding data suggest generally sluggish growth, this implies only a relative lag, not an absolute one— relative to rates of income growth in advanced areas and to aspirations and needs of developing countries. Still, in absolute terms, export growth will remain the mainstay of import capacity among primary producers; and while rates of increase may not be ideal they are still significant. To illustrate, 1 percent annual growth in North America and Western Europe is likely to mean an increase in import demand from the outside world in the order of $300 to $400 million (17); and if that area can achieve its 50 percent growth target in a decade, related import growth is obviously significant.

The persistent problem then, is not that the past and expected rise of primary

product exports is small, but that it is insufficient for a world in which accelerated and planned development has become a permanent feature.

It is difficult to quantify these observations, and it is hazardous because anticipation of future developments requires arbitrary assumptions. The resulting "gaps", therefore, represent rough and illustrative orders of magnitude. With this caution, it may be useful to mention some examples.

The future of agricultural exports is particularly worrisome—due to sluggish demand and a growing trend towards self-sufficiency in some products in industrial regions. Even projecting income growth in North America, Western Europe and Japan at an optimistic 5 percent annual rate, the combined net import volume of sugar, oils, tropical beverages, citrus and agricultural raw materials is expected to grow only by 20–25 percent from 1957/59 to 1970 (18).

An attempt to project both the import needs of the developing countries and their export prospects on given assumptions, has been made by the United Nations Economic Commission for Europe. If non-industrialized countries were to achieve a rise in per capita income of 3 percent annually—clearly an optimistic assumption—their imports (c.i.f.) would need to grow from about $29 billion in 1957/59 to over $79 billion in 1980. By contrast—extrapolating rather conservative 20-year growth assumptions, made earlier for 1975, until 1980—imports (f.o.b.) of primary commodities into Western Europe, North America and Japan are expected to increase only from about $17 to $33 billion (19).

Imports of the developing areas from the industrial countries of the West would thus have to grow about twice as fast as their expected exports (7 percent vs. 3.4 percent). Yet, debatable assumptions apart, the exercise suggests a sizable gap between anticipated earnings and export growth needed for development. And this is the key issue in this paper.

The Scope for Policy

Facing uncertain and insufficiently dynamic prospects, how can policy makers approach the two major problems of instability and export growth? And the compatibility of policies for stabilization and growth necessarily cannot be assumed, since export-sector investment is likely to be lower if stabilization eliminates the stimulus and boom-induced profits, and it is possible that investment may be less over a cycle with stabilization than without (20); much depends on price levels and producers' incomes established by stabilization policy, and on the link, or absence, of stabilization with development. It may help to view this relationship in both national and international policies.

National policies. Though instability may originate abroad, this does not preclude the primary producer from trying to counter its effects. National action has the advantage of independence from outside consent, though it cannot easily anticipate the consequences on others (21). Since the war many countries have attempted internal measures for stabilization, including marketing boards, export taxes or duties, or multiple exchange rates. Their purpose is generally to stabilize prices and thereby incomes of the export sector by syphoning off a part when prices are high while sustaining its purchasing power when they are low.

While this smoothing effect was the announced objective, export incomes have, in effect, often been kept low and sizable funds accumulated by marketing boards or other institutions, including the government. Whether it is equitable or efficient (a different criterion) to draw on the export sector in this manner and use the funds for development is debatable (22). But the link to economic development is directly relevant.

Such efforts can evidently minimize the impact of instability on certain sectors and, through fiscal measures, on the economy at large, but only by concentrating the impact on the public sector; for if export producers receive stabler (though lower average) income, marketing boards and/or government absorb the peaks and troughs of fluctuating (though higher average) revenue. This may make the consequences more manageable by enlarging the potential scope for policy; it does not eliminate the overall impact.

Still, this broader scope for planning policy may be important; what does it involve? Theoretically, it should be possible to equalize receipts over a cycle by excess revenue in the boom and excess spending in the slump. Unfortunately, fiscal efficiency and flexibility in less developed countries (and not only there!) are rarely adequate for this task, especially when the upswing is sudden and unpredictable; and social policy inclines to softness in a recession. Hence, from the development angle, it is as unfeasible to check rising consumption in the boom as it is impractical to avoid investment cuts in slumps, thus yielding a ratchet-like deterioration in investment-fund availability, quite apart from perverse expectations and investment incentives. "Equalization over the cycle" proves illusory in practice.

Were it possible to save excess proceeds in boom time, would it even be wise to? They could, e.g., be invested in foreign securities until needed. But this sacrifices immediate development for future security; for plainly marginal productivity of safe and liquid assets in industrial countries is less than in a capital-scarce country (23). Idle or low yielding savings withheld from development thus represent an economic loss, apart from the temptation of pushing development at a maximum rate as long as possible. Yet, even this is not just political myopia. At any point of the "cycle" it is usually impossible to foresee its duration and amplitude; one may not even be able to distinguish in advance cyclical from secular trends. Uncertain diagnosis frustrates the best planner's intent.

International policies. Limitations of national policy make it imperative to review potential international arrangements among countries comprising the world market as producers and consumers. And while policy cannot do much to counteract the relative lag in world demand, international measures for both stabilization and support to development imports are conceivable.

Attempts at commodity price stabilization have been many but their success limited (24). Apart from difficulties of agreement between producers and consumers, it is frequently unclear whether primary exporters really want more stable, rather than higher, prices; and whether price stabilization, or income and exchange receipts, is the real need. The question in the present context is what matters most for development planning. In this respect prices are only one component—not necessarily the most important—of income and exchange proceeds;

and what is at stake is not just stability, but growth, over time.

From this narrow focus stabilization is not desirable *per se* (though it may well be that) but it is desirable, first, to limit the aggravation of technological substitution that excessive fluctuations promote—"a means of slowing down technological progress in one of its more unwelcome aspects" (25). Second, as instability usually hinders optimal use of development resources, action is required; and as this cannot be achieved by producing countries alone, international measures are necessary. Third, this demands better operation of world markets—also beneficial to industrial countries, though commodity fluctuations hurt them less than primary producers. Fourth, as economic development amidst political stability has been recognized as a policy objective in advanced countries too, cooperative international action for commodity stabilization is indicated and progressing on a rising scale.

The functioning of price as a regulator of supply and hence of production must not be ignored, for stabilization at an excessive price in the face of lagging demand encourages substitution and causes surpluses. In such instances, a system of "deficiency payments" may be preferable. Such counter-cyclical payments to keep development moving (26) deliberately link aid with commodity stabilization; and rightly so, as "pure" stabilization involves too harsh a discipline to be bearable without assistance. This does not demand a rigid calculation of gains and losses from the terms of trade (27)—impractical statistically and otherwise; and a tax on price differentials to be used for economic development, besides the difficulty of deciding on a fair price, would require a highly administered system. Rather, partial compensation for deviations of export receipts from a trend may be adopted which, by using a moving average, combines a smoothing effect with automatic availability of compensatory finance. This has the additional advantage of moving away from the single-commodity approach and, through internationalization, permitting rises in some commodities to offset declines in others, at least partially.

Two such proposals are now being discussed internationally, one comprising two alternatives devised by a group of United Nations experts, the other by a panel of the Organization of American States (28). The United Nations schemes deliberately introduce a social insurance element providing a transfer of resources by calling for higher contributions by developed and greater benefits by developing countries.

This mixture of trade with an element of aid is perhaps awkward administratively and therefore opposed by some. Yet, it is precisely this combination that recognizes the effects of instability on economic development and attempts to counter them by tying assistance into commodity schemes. Moreover, a conditional repayment of loans (United Nations scheme type II) takes into account the impossibility of determining in advance whether a downward movement is cylical or manifests a trend. A loan that is to be repaid only if export proceeds rise again is realistic. In the absence of such a provision, if earnings continue to be depressed, repayment may become impossible and just lead to defaults and recrimination; or to avoid them more credit would have to be provided, thus adding to an excessive debt burden.

It would seem more practical to acknowledge that foreign exchange not earned by trade will lead to demands for more credit if development imports are to be maintained. The development planner must know what he can count on by way of compensatory payments receipts and realistic repayment obligations. Other international devices suggest themselves: assistance to national stabilization schemes, say, by finance for buffer stocks or buffer funds in order to reduce the amount of domestic savings that need to be kept idle for this purpose. Mostly, however, industrial countries should be expected to promote imports from less developed areas rather than obstruct them through import quotas, tariffs and internal taxes whose abolition could increase the exports of primary products very sizably (29). Further, as more countries turn to production of labor intensive products, such as textiles and light engineering goods, attempts to limit their sale in industrial countries further inhibit trade expansion with the gap left by insufficient trade only to be filled by capital transfers. "Trade or aid" is more than a slogan.

Conclusion: Problems for Planning

Planners face two difficulties specifically related to the foreign trade sector. They must estimate income, savings and investment, yet trade income is uncertain and volatile. The same obstacle affects foreign exchange allocation for essential consumer and development goods. In the face of this instability and uncertainty policy must seek to (a) reduce the extent of instability, (b) minimize the effects of instability, (c) plan flexibly to adjust to unforeseen fluctuations with a minimum loss of forward momentum.

If instability originates in demand abroad there is little exporters can do alone to reduce it. However, in conjunction with others they can press for international cooperation aiming at greater stability. As supplier, the exporting country may have to accept restrictions and it should be encouraged to adjust not only exports, but also production. It befits economic growth that surplus resources be transferred to other lines of production, for development calls for diversification; by the same token, a broader foundation reduces dependence on a notoriously unstable export sector. This is a task for planning, possibly requiring outside finance for both stabilization and growth. International assistance, in the form of compensatory payments or otherwise, should therefore serve diversification as part of the development program.

Further, to reduce the impact of instability, domestic counter-cyclical measures are needed. Here, strengthening of fiscal administration—a prime development prerequisite too—is essential. Buffer stocks, marketing boards, variable export taxes and even (despite obvious monetary drawbacks) differential exchange rates, may be used. Ideally, purchasing power diverted in upswings could be released in recessions; but diagnosis and implementation are difficult. Moreover, funds put aside in the boom would be withheld from development. Planners must weigh liquid investment yields and benefits of greater programming continuity against sacrificed fixed investment in terms of growth; decision models may provide useful approximations to solving this dilemma.

Planning techniques are thus involved in all phases of the commodity problem. More directly, a dilemma

arises in the over-all approach: is it safer to estimate export receipts conservatively and risk temporarily unused resources; or to estimate optimistically and chance disruption of the plan through shortfalls that may cause cumulative distortions with time? It may be more desirable, and possible, to build alternative assumptions into long-range plans from the outset, either by pre-planning contingency-cuts in a fairly high plan, or by programming optional expenditures as additions to a modest plan. To assign alternative scarcity values to foreign exchange using shadow exchange rates may be useful. Flexibility is the key, introduced with full attention to internal consistency in all sectors, and made operative by annual reviews, or whenever a decisive cyclical turn appears.

Instability, however, is not the only issue in development planning. To pay for rising import needs requires steady export growth. Based on past experience, the outlook for growth of primary product markets is not sufficiently dynamic though significant in absolute terms, depending on the product in question. In this respect, progress towards greater stability may slow the noticeable tendency towards substitution. Elimination of import restrictions and of outdated internal taxes, and a progressive reduction of tariffs by the developed countries would go a long way towards a higher rate of trade growth in the impending phase of accelerated world economic development. Accommodating labor-intensive light manufactures from developing countries is equally imperative and would optimize use of the industrial countries' own resources as well. This is politically difficult and hard to undertake by individual nations alone. But given the fundamental common interest to producers and consumers in more orderly commodity markets, and that of advanced and less developed countries in greater welfare through faster world development, international cooperation must—and can—progress in this direction, thereby also easing the national planner's task.

REFERENCES

(1) cf. Cairncross, A., *International trade and economic development*, Economica, 28 (August 1961).

(2) *International Compensation for Fluctuation in Commodity Trade*, U.N., N.Y., p. 4. (1961).

(3) 1900–1913; 17 countries; 1920–1939: 42 countries; 1948–1958: 48 countries. *Fund Policies and Procedures in Relation to the Compensatory Financing of Commodity Fluctuations*, International Monetary Fund, Staff Papers (November 1960).

(4) *International Compensation* . . . pp. 10 f. U.N.

(5) *Stabilization of Export Proceeds Through a Development Insurance Fund*, U.N., N.Y., Document E/CN. 13/43 p. 32 (18 January 1962), mimeographed.

(6) *Ibid.*, pp. 146 and 151.

(7) Iran, Malaya, Singapore, Cuba, Indonesia, Brazil, India, Australia. *Ibid.*, table 39.

(8) *Business Week,* (May 19, 1962), p. 88.

(9) Szulc, T., *Latin need for trade*, The New York Times, (April 29, 1962).

(10) *The demand for food in the industrial countries 1948–1960*, National Institute Economic Review, pp. 40 f. (May 1962).

(11) Maizels, A., *Recent Trends in World Trade*, paper presented at the International Economic Association Conference in Brissago, tables 1 and 5 (September 1961), mimeographed.

(12) *World Economic Survey 1958*, U.N., N.Y., p. 18 and table 1 (1959).

(13) cf. Nurkse, R., *Patterns of Trade and Development*, Stockholm, p. 25 (1959).

(14) *Trends in International Trade*, GATT, Geneva, p. 40 (October 1958).

(15) *World Economic Survey*, p. 25 (1958).

(16) Data obtained from OECD.

(17) *Ibid.*

(18) "Net imports" implies an offset by exports which in the case of the U.S. cotton in this computation means net exports of raw cotton minus net imports of cotton textiles in terms of raw cotton (assumed to remain constant over the period). *Agricultural Commodities-Projections for 1970*, FAO, Rome (1962), table 17.

(19) *Economic Survey of Europe in 1960*, U.N. Economic Commission for Europe, Geneva, tables 4 and 5 (1961).

(20) e.g. H. W. Singer in *Stabilization and Development of Primary Producing Countries*, Kyklos, 12, Fasc. 3, p. 281 (1959).

(21) Lerdau, E., *Estabilizacion de los productos basicos*, El Trimestre Economico, 28, No. 2, p. 269 (April–June 1961).

(22) e.g. Reubens, E. P., *Commodity trade, export taxes and economic development*, Political Science Quarterly (March 1956); P. T. Bauer and F. W. Paish, *The reduction of fluctuations in the income of primary producers*, Economic Journal (December

1952), and discussion in subsequent issues in 1953 and 1954; Ragnar Nurkse in *The quest for a stabilization policy in primary producing countries*, Kyklos, 11, Fasc. 2, pp. 141 ff. and 244 ff. (1958).

(23) Lerdau, *op. cit.*, pp. 270 f.

(24) Summary discussions may be found e.g. in *Commodity Trade and Economic Development*, U.N., N.Y. (1954); *World Economic Survey 1958*, Chapter 3; *Trends in International Trade*, Chapter IV.

(25) Hirschman, A. O., in *Stabilization and Development of Primary Producing Countries*, loc. cit., pp. 354 f.

(26) Wallich, H. C., *Stabilization of Proceeds From Raw Material Exports*, in Economic Development for Latin America, Ellis and Wallich eds., New York (1961).

(27) As suggested in *Commodity Trade and Economic Development*, especially Appendix D.

(28) *International Compensation for Fluctuations in Commodity Trade*, cited earlier, and *Proposed Articles of Agreement of the International Fund for Stabilization of Export Receipts*, OAS, Doc. 64, Rev. 4, Washington (3 April 1962), mimeographed.

(29) See, e.g., *Trends in International Trade*, pp. 80–122. In a forthcoming volume for the Twentieth Century Fund, Professor Jan Tinbergen also shows that the cost of abolition of such impediments is fairly small compared to the benefits for the exporting countries.

Determining the Need for and Planning the Use of External Resources

P. N. ROSENSTEIN-RODAN

Professor of Economics
Massachusetts Institute of Technology
Cambridge, Massachusetts

Foreign exchange in less developed countries is a specific factor of production. It can buy external resources (notably machines and raw materials) which either could not be produced at home at all, or only at vastly higher costs and after a long time.

The need for external resources increases sharply with growing investment in developing countries while their ability to accumulate capital and to earn additional foreign exchange for that purpose may be limited not only by poverty, i.e., inability to save enough ("the resources gap" which should really be called the "savings gap"), but also by deteriorating terms of trade as the volume of non-diversified exports increases ("the foreign exchange gap").

In most less developed countries the foreign exchange gap is at the start of development even greater than the resources gap. A considerable amount of external resources in the form of foreign capital inflow including aid is needed to supplement low domestic savings, i.e., to fill the resources gap. A great deal more is needed in all those numerous cases in which additional domestic savings could not be transferred to buy additional foreign resources, i.e., to fill the foreign exchange gap. In the past three years aid amounted to 25–30 percent of investment in the less developed countries of the noncommunist world and to about 20 percent of their export earnings.

The scarcity of foreign exchange—which may be even greater than the scarcity of other resources—explains the need for planning their use. An estimate of the necessary imports of machinery and spare parts for maintenance and replacement, of raw materials, intermediate products, and consumer goods for current account purposes and of the same items for the purpose of increasing productive capacity (net investment) will determine the need for them. Such an estimate is however the end result of a development program not a simple summation of independent projections. The scarcity of foreign exchange should be reflected in a relatively high, real, or "shadow" price (accounting price) (1), of foreign exchange. That price is an instrument both of optimizing (minimizing) the use of external resources and of delegating such rationing decisions.

Dynamic programming can determine the optimum distribution of investments and allocation of both national and external resources (including notably the relative emphasis on export gaining and import saving) once the objectives and the availability of resources are given. If foreign aid were assumed to be available permanently or for a very long period, a given amount of resources could yield a higher sustained growth. If the objective is, however, to become independent of foreign aid after a period of (10–15) years, that is, to achieve self-sustained growth, then the same given amount of resources may yield a lower rate of growth since the need for import substitution will raise the capital-output ratio. More aid in the first decade will reduce the need for aid in the second decade. More aid in the first decade will give the necessary time to restructure the economy. Without this time export gaining and import saving could not be realized to anything like the same extent. The value of aid is therefore very much greater than its share in national investment might suggest. The rate of growth in less developed countries would fall by very much more than 25–30 percent, if aid of that amount (equal to 25–30 percent of total investment) were not forthcoming.

National resources will rise if higher investment is undertaken which is only possible in practice if more external resources become available for that purpose. The availability of external resources depends on the one hand on projected export receipts and projected private foreign investment, and on the other hand on available international aid. The amount of aid should depend on the development program—but the program itself will also depend on the assumed amount of foreign aid. To estimate its availability is unavoidable. It can be done best by assess-

ing and describing the philosophy and the principles of international aid for less developed countries.

The following may be said to be the basic principles of international aid for less developed countries (2):

(a) The purpose of aid is to accelerate the economic development of these countries up to a point where a satisfactory rate of growth can be achieved on a self-sustaining basis. The over-all aim of development aid is not to equalize incomes in different countries but to provide every country with an opportunity to achieve steady growth. Aid should continue not until a certain income level is reached in less developed countries but only until those countries can mobilize a level of capital formation sufficient for self-sustaining growth.

(b) The criterion of aid is achievement of a maximum catalytic effect of mobilizing additional national effort, not to maximize income created per dollar of aid. If this last were the aim, dollars invested in developed countries might easily show better results. Nor would a criterion of maximum increase in income suffice even if only less developed countries were considered. In different stages and different phases of economic development more investment may be required to produce a unit of additional income than in others. This is invariably the case where, for instance, social overhead capital has to be built up first. Such investment yields directly only small increases in income. It creates, however, a framework necessary to the profitability of more immediately lucrative subsequent investments. Direct increase in income in the short run is less important here than the increase in investment opportunities. Income created per dollar of aid may, therefore, at first be low; far from being an argument for *less* aid, there are circumstances in which this might well be an argument for *more*.

(c) Continuity of aid over a period of five or ten, or in some cases more, years is essential for good planning. Knowledge that capital will be available over a decade or more will act in many cases as an incentive to greater effort. Private investment may not be stimulated by sporadic short-run injections of external resources. Assurance of continuity of aid is, therefore, as important as the amount of aid.

(d) The amount of aid ideally should come up to the country's limits of *absorptive capacity* if the internal national effort is sufficient. Absorptive capacity relates to the ability to use capital productively. There are narrow limits to the pace and extent at which a country's absorptive capacity can be expanded. Education in the long run and revolution of habits in the short run may widen the scope. But it is not true to say that absorptive capacity depends entirely on the amount of effort one is willing to put into massive technical assistance. Foreign experts and managers may best be used without compromising domestic control and without stifling the growth of domestic entrepreneurs. The real bottlenecks moreover do not occur so much out of the scarcity of generals or colonels (i.e. high powered engineers and specialists) but out of scarcity of sergeant majors or corporals (semiskilled foremen). Outside skills and knowledge may well supplement but cannot entirely substitute for domestic abilities to organize and to administer. While the capacity to absorb capital is a limiting factor, it can, within a few years, be stepped up considerably in many less developed countries.

(i) Additional national effort should be considered as part of a country's absorptive capacity. Its most important expression is the difference between the *average* and the *marginal rate of savings*. Domestic investment supplemented by additional resources and know-how provided by foreign capital inflow produces an additional product. The proportion that can be saved out of this additional product can be very much higher than average savings at the pre-existing income level. While the *average* rate of savings is, for instance, 7 percent in Asia, the *marginal* rate of savings can be stepped up to 20–25 percent. A marginal rate which is much higher than the average rate of savings is the main lever of a development program and a good measure of the adequacy or inadequacy of a country's national effort.

(ii) If a country's additional effort (sufficient or deficient) and absorptive capacity could not be measured, it could not be the basic criterion of aid. Fortunately no exact measurement is needed, and three indexes can be used to estimate absorptive capacity. The first two refer to "objective" verifiable facts, while the third relies on rough common-sense rules of thumb which may indicate a ranking order of magnitudes.

(iii) We may ascertain by how much a country has succeeded in increasing its volume of investment during the past five or more years. If a rate of increase of investment could be realized in the past, then a slightly higher rate made possible by technical assistance can plausibly be projected for the future.

(iv) We may also ascertain whether a country has succeeded in the recent past in raising its savings, notably in maintaining or in widening the deviation between the *average* and the *marginal* rates of savings. A similar spread for the next five-year period may constitute the lower limit of a possible savings effort. Judgment on the country's ability to mobilize additional taxes when incomes are rising may justify a projection above the recently realized lower limit of the country's ability to save. A changing composition of output (more industry with high marginal rates of savings) will lead in many cases to foreseeably higher savings rates for the country as a whole.

(v) Finally a judgment on a country's over-all administrative and developmental organization is by no means as "arbitrary" as it may seem. There is not much difference of opinion on the relative "push" or "potential" of, say, India, Ceylon, Indonesia, or Brazil, Guatemala, Paraguay, among businessmen, economists, or even average tourists, although unforeseeable shake-ups, positive or negative, may either lower it or raise it. The longer the time period the less certain is the judgment. On the assumption of historical continuity, however, agreement can be obtained on a ranking order of magnitudes (3).

(e) The form of aid: While the amount of aid depends on absorptive capacity, its form, i.e., the method of financing it should be determined by the country's *capacity to repay*. Where the capacity to repay in low-income less developed countries is below their absorptive capacity, a proportion of aid will have to be given in grants, or "soft loans," 40–99 year loans with a 10–20 year grace period and a low rate of interest, or loans repayable in local currency which will be re-loaned for subsequent investment. The capacity to repay should not be assessed

by a static projection of the present situation but should take into account the increase in income and the increase in the rate of savings which will result from the adoption of a soundly conceived development program. Nor is it sensible to assume that the whole ("hard") foreign debt of each country should be amortized within twenty or thirty years. It is by no means rational for each country to reduce its foreign indebtedness to zero. The rational question to ask is: "How much foreign indebtedness can a country maintain in the long run?" After ten to twenty years of aid the net capital inflow to less developed countries will come to a stop. The gross capital inflow, however, will continue, while at the same time old loans will be repaid. Just as any national debt (or corporate debt) need not be reduced if it is within sound limits, the ("hard") foreign debt of debtor countries need not be amortized to zero in a sound world economy.

(f) The definition of aid: "Foreign capital inflow" and "aid" are not synonymous. Aid, properly speaking, refers only to those parts of capital inflow which normal market incentives do not provide. It consists of:

(i) Long-term loans (20 years or more) repayable in foreign currency.

(ii) Grants and "soft loans," including loans "repayable in local currency".

(iii) Sale of surplus products for "local currency" payments (P.L. 480 in the United States). Not only capital (equipment) goods but also consumption goods can constitute capital. In fact agricultural products can form an important part of a capital in its original sense of a subsistence fund. If sufficient foodstuffs could not be supplied in a country to meet the demand from the additional workers employed on construction or other investments, then either more investment capital ("circulating") would have to be spent for imports, or the amount of additional investment would have to be reduced. It cannot be said in reality, however, that the whole of imported surplus products will be used for additional investment. A good economic development policy can see to it that a major part is used for raising investment, but a part will merely bolster domestic consumption. In practice, therefore, a withdrawal of surplus product sales would lead to a reduction in both consumption and investment. As a rule of thumb it may be assumed that two-thirds of surplus product sales (at world market prices) can be considered investment aid, while one-third goes into increased consumption. Even on that basis up to one-fifth of total aid to less developed countries can usefully be rendered in this form.

(iv) In addition technical assistance is undoubtedly a most important part of aid to less developed countries. It is merely a matter of terminology—variously used in development literature—whether it should or should not be included as part of the "foreign capital inflow."

(g) What is not "economic aid"? Economic aid was defined above as that part of capital inflow which normal market incentives do not provide. Accordingly, neither short- or medium-term loans nor private foreign investment should be counted as aid. They are "trade not aid." Short- and medium-term loans are mostly selling devices for (tied) exports of equipment goods. They are not tools of an international aid policy. Private foreign investment is undertaken in response to normal market incentives.

In this sense it is not "aid," but it is an important part of the foreign capital inflow required for less developed countries.

(h) The measure of the volume of aid cannot be meaningfully expressed in arithmetical figures or sums of millions of dollars transferred to less developed countries. Such capital sums would be equivalent to an addition of numbers of chickens and elephants irrespective of their weight. The obvious need is to reduce all types of aid to a single standard for measuring their relative value. There are, of course, no "right" or "wrong" definitions only definitions adequate or inadequate for certain purposes. The appropriate standard of measurement of aid depends therefore on what one wants to measure. There are two different aspects of aid in this connection: (1) costs of aid (sacrifices involved in aid) to creditor countries; and (2) benefits received through aid by less developed countries. An international aid cost-benefit ratio is still, however, a partly non-operational concept, quite apart from the much greater difficulty of meaningfully measuring all the benefit aspects of aid. The second (benefit) aspect of aid need not therefore be examined in the present context, apart from stressing the obvious point that the longer the maturity of the loan and the lower the rate of interest the greater is the benefit received by the less developed countries. The first (cost or sacrifice) aspect is, however, operationally useful for discussions of adequacy or inadequacy of the international aid effort by developed countries and of general principles of sharing the burden of international aid.

(i) The appropriate standard of measuring the relative burdens of aid is the sacrifice of real resources made by the country providing the aid. The burden of aid can be defined as the present value of aid disbursements minus the present value of (future) repayments, discounted at an appropriate rate of interest. While the appropriate rate of interest for calculating the present value of aid disbursements may be different in various creditor countries, reflecting the domestic opportunity costs of capital, such differences can be disregarded in the first approximation and for practical purposes the discounting rate of interest may be assumed at, say, 5 percent. The discounting rate for calculating the present value of repayments should include, in addition, a premium for the risk of default. Since the private international bond market for less developed countries has shrunk to insignificant proportions, it is not possible to refer to a "free market" interest rate; only a rough approximation may be agreed upon. The longer the maturity of an international loan, the greater may be the risk of default. The discounting rate for repayments may therefore be assumed to be, say, 5.5 percent for loans from 10–15 years maturity, 6 percent for loans of 15–20 years maturity and 6.5 percent or 7 percent for loans of still longer maturities. Loans for less than ten years could only be counted as aid if they were given at rates of interest below the market rate. This does not seem to be the practice at present, so that such loans should not be counted as aid. Buying at market rates of interest bonds of international bank institutions like the International Bank for Reconstruction and Development or the Inter-American Bank whose repayment is amply guaranteed in convertible currencies is "trade not aid."

(ii) The difference between the present value of aid disbursements and the present value of repayments represents the "true" aid component of international loans and grants to less developed countries. Only if the aid components are expressed in that manner can we have a single compatible weighting for all forms of aid and a meaningful measure of the burden of aid. It is unfortunate that a procedure of that kind has not been adopted yet at D.A.C. (Development Assistance Committee) and that in consequence the available statistical information about the international aid effort is incomplete and inexact. Even so, it is clear that the aid efforts of France, the United States, and Great Britain (in that order) relative to that of other countries tend to be underestimated. General principles of how the burden of international aid should be divided among developed countries have not yet been agreed upon. The social philosophy of the present generation provides nonetheless some clear indications. The problem of burden-sharing falls, however, outside the scope of the present paper.

The total capital inflow required for less developed countries for, say, a five-year period is determined by each country's gross national product (Y_o), its rate of growth (r)—estimated according to its absorptive capacity—its initial average savings rate (S_o/Y_o), its marginal rate of savings during each year period, (b), which determines the initial average savings rate for the subsequent five-year period, and the capital-output ratio (k). The formula (4) for calculating the foreign capital inflow requirement is:

$$F = (kr - b)\Sigma Y + 5Y_0 \left(b - \frac{S_0}{Y_0} \right).$$

The marginal savings rate depends on each country's: (a) capacity to organize development, (b) income level, (c) composition of investment (for instance, the marginal savings rate is higher when industry absorbs a higher proportion of investment). In the majority of cases the marginal savings rate may be assumed as roughly twice as high as the average rate. The capital-output ratio may be assumed in the first approximation as 3:1 or 2.8:1. It may well vary in different five-year periods for different countries, so that a projection for many particular periods may have a considerable margin of error. Where the existing railway capacity, as for instance in the case of Indonesia, is not fully utilized, railway investment for another five years may be very small and the capital-output ratio in such cases of excess capacity can be easily 2.5:1 or even slightly lower. The capital-output ratio obviously also depends on each country's capacity to earn foreign exchange. Where this is limited so that the foreign exchange gap is larger than the resource gap, recourse must be had to import-saving investments which are costly and which raise the capital-output ratio. In large markets like India or even Brazil, the increase in the capital-output ratio may not be very large. For small countries it would be very large if each were to substitute imports individually. It may be assumed, however, that institutions like the Latin American Common Market will provide for some international coordination of investments. It is only on such an assumption that a capital-output ratio of 3 or 2.8:1 can be assumed for the smaller Latin American countries. The margin of error can be reduced only by more detailed specific country studies. It is felt, however, that

for a longer run the assumed capital-output ratio will not be far off the mark.

The total capital inflow required consists of: (a) aid (including technical assistance), (b) private foreign investment. Tentative estimates for each less developed country for three 5-year periods of 1961–66, 1966–71, and 1971–76, have been worked out according to the method described above in "International Aid for Underdeveloped Countries" (5).

The foreign capital inflow into the less developed countries in recent years has been estimated in four studies:

A. *The Flow of Financial Resources to Countries in Course of Economic Development 1956–1959,* OEEC, Paris (1961)   \$6.8 billion

B. *United Nations, International Flow of Long Term Capital and Official Donations, 1951–1959,* New York, (1961)   \$3.9 billion

C. Paul N. Rosenstein-Rodan, "International Aid for Underdeveloped Countries," *The Review of Economics and Statistics,* Cambridge, Mass. (May 1961)
    1960   \$4.1 billion

D. *Development Assistance Efforts and Policies in 1961,* OEC, Paris (1962)
    1960   \$7.4 billion
    1961   \$8.7 billion

These estimates are made, however, on quite different and mutually incompatible concepts of capital flow. A includes all short- and medium-term loans above one-year maturity and such items as reparation payments and guaranteed private export credits. If loans under ten years' maturity (which are vaguely estimated at \$2 billion per annum) were excluded, the estimate would amount to \$4.8 billion. Exclusion of other items would lower it below \$4.5 billion. D excludes loans of less than five years' maturity. The volume of loans between five–ten years' maturity in 1960–61 is not known but it may well have amounted to \$1.4–\$1.7 billion per annum so that the D estimate without them would amount to \$6 billion for 1960 and \$7 billion for 1961. The B estimate is based on a different method using balance-of-payments data conforming to the IMF definitions of long-term capital and official grants. Short-term transactions are excluded. The B estimate gives therefore a more useful basis for estimating the developmental capital inflow. The C estimate uses a concept of aid as described in 7(f). Under private foreign investment oil investments are included only to the extent of 50 percent. If technical assistance and emergency funds are added, the capital inflow in 1960 would amount to \$4.1 billion divided into Aid = \$3.0 billion and private investment = \$1.1 billion. If the whole of oil investments, all P.L. 480 surplus products (not merely two-thirds) and the U.S.S.R. economic aid were added, the total foreign capital inflow into less developed countries in 1960 would amount to roughly \$5 billion.

These calculations, however, cannot constitute a good measure of the volume of aid (see 7(h)) since they do not take into account and weigh the different financial conditions on which various parts of aid are offered.

The recognition that substantial additional external resources are needed to raise the rate of growth of less developed countries led during the last decade to several attempts to estimate the amount of foreign capital inflow (including aid) required for this purpose. All such estimates involve in the nature of things oversimplifications accounting at best very slightly for those human, institutional, structural and social variables which have a preponderant influence on absorptive

capacity and the rate of growth. Even the purely "economic" data (for instance, on the stock of fixed capital, on savings rates, on distribution of income, etc.) suffer from high margins of error. Before presenting the survey of such quantitative estimates of aid and capital inflow requirements, it must be pointed out that all they intend to provide is an indication of a rough order of magnitudes rather than a precise figure.

In five studies, attempts have been made to estimate capital aid requirements of less developed countries; they will be referred to as A, B, C, D and E (6):

A. United Nations, *Measures for the Economic Development of Underdeveloped Countries,* New York (1951)

B. Max F. Millikan and W. W. Rostow, *A Proposal: Key to an Effective Foreign Policy,* Harper and Brothers, New York (1957)

C. J. Tinbergen and Centre de Documentation du Comite D'Action pour Les Etats Unis D' Europe, *La Communaute Europeenne et les Pays Sous-Developpes* (May 1959)

D. Paul G. Hoffman, *One Hundred Countries, One and One Quarter Billion People,* Washington, D.C. (1960)

E. P. N. Rosenstein-Rodan, *"International Aid for Underdeveloped Countries,"* The Review of Economics and Statistics, Cambridge, Mass. (1961)

The methods, assumptions, and conclusions of these studies are presented in Tables 1 and 2. It may be noted that the amount of aid required per annum amounts to around 0.5–0.6 percent of the GNP of developed countries rather than 1 percent.

TABLE 1. *Summary of global estimates of foreign capital requirements of less developed countries*

Source	Reference data — Reference year (1)	National income (billions of dollars) (2)	Per capita annual growth in national income (percent) (3)	Inflow of capital (billions of dollars) (4)	Projection targets — Period of projection	Per capita annual growth in national income (percent) (5)	Capital output ratio (6)	Annual foreign capital required (billions of dollars) (7)	Annul additional foreign capital required (col. 7 minus col. 4) (8)
A (a) Measures for economic dev. of less developed countries	1949	97	0.75	[1]1.0	1950–60	2.0	5.8:1	[2]4.0	[3]13.0
A (b) Measures for economic dev. of less dev. countries, excluding China (mainland) and Mongolia[5]	1949	77	.....	1.0	1950–60	2.0	5.8:1	8.5	[4]10.0
									[5]7.5
									[6]6.0
B A proposal	1953	110	.....	3.0		2.0	3:1	6.5	[6]3.5
C La Communaute Europeenne et les Pays Sous-Developpes	1959	128	.....	4.0		2.0	3:1	7.5	3.5
D Proposal for a cruical decade—the nineteen sixties	1959	100	1.00	4.0	1960–69	2.0	3:1	7.0	3.0
E International aid for less developed countries[7]	1961	[8]192		4.0	1962–66	1.8	2.8:1	6.4	2.1
	1966	[8]232	1.80	6.4	1967–71	2.2	2.8:1	6.4	....
	1971	[8]285	2.20	5.0	1972–76	2.5	2.8:1	5.0	[9]1.4

Table 1. FOOTNOTES

¹ The inflow of capital is assumed to be between $1 and $1.5 billion, but probably nearer to $1 billion.

² Even if allowance were made for a probable rise in domestic savings, the external capital required is expected to be well in excess of $10 billion per annum.

³ On the assumption of present level of national savings.

⁴ On the assumption of an increased level of national savings.

⁵ Estimated by the Division of General Economic Research and Policies of the United Nations Secretariat.

⁶ This is the upper limit of additional capital requirement, the lower limit is assumed at $2.5 billion.

⁷ Including Greece, Portugal, Spain and Yugoslavia in Europe, not covered in A, B, D.

⁸ Gross national product.

⁹ Under Alternative II computation. According to Alternative I computation for this period, the additional capital requirements in 1972–76 would be about $2 billion less per annum than in the period 1967–71.

TABLE 2. *Assumptions and methodology for the summary of global estimates of foreign capital requirements of less developed countries*

Source	Assumptions and Methodology
A..........	(1) Annual transfer of 1 percent of working population from agriculture to non-agricultural employment.
	(2) Annual expenditure of 4 percent of national income on agricultural development.
B..........	(1) Estimates of additional capital requirements are based on "absorptive capacity" and on the stage of development of countries; they are assumed for Latin America at 14 percent and for the other underdeveloped areas at 35 percent of gross capital formation in 1953.
	(2) Estimates of income growth are based on the assumption of a capital-output ratio of 3:1.
C..........	(1) Target rate of growth of 2 percent per head per annum.
	(2) Carpital-output ratio 3:1.
D..........	(1) Target rate of an annual growth of 2 percent in per capita national income.
	(2) Capital-output ratio of 3:1; capital refers to "development capital" only.
E..........	(1) Estimates of additional capital requirements are based on "absorptive capacity."
	(2) Capital-output ratio of 2.8:1; capital refers to "development capital" only.
	(3) It is assumed that marginal savings rate will be appreciably higher than the average savings rate; for most countries the former is taken as roughly twice as high as the average saving rate.

The difference in the estimates of capital requirements in B, C, D, E is slight and greater in appearance than in reality. They result mainly from two causes: (a) a different base year assumed in each study, and (b) different definitions of "developmental capital," B, D and E excluding short- and medium-term loans while C includes them. If 1961 were taken as a base year, if short- and medium-term loans (under ten years maturity) were excluded, while technical assistance were included, if only two-thirds of surplus products under P.L. 480 were counted as developmental capital, and if the less developed countries of Eastern Europe were included in B and D, the total capital inflow required per annum for 1961–1971 would amount roughtly to:

$$B = \$7.5 \text{ billion}$$
$$C = \$6.2 \text{ ”}$$
$$D = \$7.3 \text{ ”}$$
$$E = \$6.4 \text{ ”}$$

C which appears to present the highest estimate of capital inflow required for a 2 percent per annum increase in income

per head, but which seems to include medium-term loans in its capital concept would in fact become the lowest estimate if the "developmental capital" concept used in the other studies were accepted. B is higher than E for three reasons: First, (difference $500 million per annum) because the estimates are made globally for five regions (South Central Asia, rest of Asia, Middle East, Latin America, and Africa) while E has disaggregated estimates for each of the less developed countries, some of which are assumed to have at first a lower absorptive capacity and lower growth potential (increase in income per head of only 1–1.5 percent per annum) while a few others (like Kuwait) do not require aid. Second, including only two-thirds of surplus products in the concept of aid in E accounts for another $300 million per annum difference. Third, excluding the less developed countries of Europe (Greece, Portugal, Spain and Yugoslavia) accounts for another difference of $300 million per annum. As far as D is concerned, the "developmental capital" concept is practically the same as in B and E but its national income estimate for 1959 ($100 billion) is very much lower (by about $50 billion) than that in other estimates. The GNP of the less developed countries in 1961 is estimated in E at $192 billion, corresponding to a national income of around $165 billion; the four countries of Eastern Europe have a GNP of around $21 billion in 1961. Since the method of computing capital inflow requirements is different in D, it is impossible to "translate" its estimate into an equivalent compatible with assumptions in B and E.

A arrives at a quite different order of magnitude ($10 billion per annum) largely because of a different method of estimation (see 16). If China and Mongolia were excluded its estimate for 1949 would amount to around $6 billion per annum. Applied to the 1961 National Income and Savings figures, the A estimate (without China and Mongolia) would amount to $9–10 billion per annum.

Three different methods have been used in A, B, C, D and E. The first one called the "capital-labor" approach (used in A) estimates capital per head required for workers to be additionally employed outside agriculture—assumed in A at $2500 per head—plus capital required for raising agricultural output, which add up to total investment required. Social overhead capital should still be added to this total, which would then "greatly exceed" $19 billion. Deducting national savings from this total gives the foreign capital inflow required.

The second method—used in B, C and E—may be called the "capital-output" approach. It assumes that net investment over a period of five years bears a relatively stable relation to in-

crease in output. Given a target increase in income the amount of total investment required can be calculated. Deducting national savings from this total gives the foreign capital inflow required. Absorptive capacity was the base for the increase in income in B and E, while a target increase in income has been assumed in C.

A third method has been used in D based on an assumed target rate of growth, a capital output ratio and projections of foreign trade over a ten year period. D provides a "general reconciliation" between total investment required (=target increase in income x capital output ratio) and foreign exchange requirements. It is estimated that total merchandise import requirements of the less developed countries would amount to $440 billion in 1961–70 to which $8 billion have to be added for other costs (debt service, transportation and other services) while the foreign exchange earnings would amount to $378 billion over the same period. The foreign exchange deficit of $7 billion per annum has to be covered by the foreign capital inflow.

Methods of determining the need for external resources have been described above. Planning the use of external resources should proceed—like the estimating of the need for them—according to the program, and not the "single project approach." While not every single investment project need be self-liquidating, total investment must not only cover its costs but must also yield a reasonable increase in income. The various projects comprising a development program are interrelated and reinforce each other. This balance depends on whether complementary activities have been planned on the required scale. It is therefore practically impossible to judge the soundness of any particular project without knowledge of the whole program of which it is a part. A program approach, not a project approach, must determine the criteria of productive use of aid capital. Foreign aid capital increases the range of the program as a whole.

Since this may require a reshuffle and changes in several projects, a single loan cannot with any exactness be said to have been given to one specific project only—it should be considered as a contribution to the whole program.

REFERENCES

(1) For the literature on the concept and use of shadow rates see G. F. Papanek and M. A. Qureshi, *The Use of Accounting Prices in Planning*, in paper prepared for UN Conference on Application of Science and Technology (February 1963).

(2) The arguments presented here and in paragraphs 8 and 9 follow the author's *International aid for underdeveloped countries*, The Review of Economics and Statistics, 43 (May 1961).

(3) For a fuller elaboration, see M. F. Millikan and W. W. Rostow, *A Proposal: Key to an Effective Foreign Policy*, Harper and Brothers, New York, 1957, Ch. V and VI; and *The Objectives of U.S. Economic Assistance Programs*, Section VI, a study prepared at the request of the Special Committee To Study the Foreign Aid Program, U.S. Senate, by CENIS, M.I.T. (January 1957).

(4) For the method of calculating capital inflow requirements see Rosenstein-Rodan, *op. cit.*, p. 135.

(5) Rosenstein-Rodan, *op. cit.*

(6) A, B, D and E have been summarized in *The Capital Development Needs of Less Developed Countries*, United Nations, New York (1962).

PART TWO

The Challenge in Developing Human Resources

UNLESS the human resources are adequate to the required technical tasks, economic development cannot produce self-sustaining growth. Many specialists believe that manpower and motivational problems in newly emerging countries are the most intractable problems, yet these are the most in need of resolution. Part Two includes three articles on labor force and managerial problems in development and two on the role of health programs in furthering the productivity of labor.

Normally, urbanization problems are regarded as a special concern of the more industrialized countries. Hauser's article, however, stresses the often overlooked drag of the urban complex in the underdeveloped country, where it is more an indication of the push of people from the overcrowded countryside than of the attractions of urban life. In fact, Hauser believes the urban syndrome, with its debilitating effect on manpower, is the underdeveloped country's "major economic problem."

Hoselitz shifts the focus to the role of the entrepreneur in development—not Schumpeter's "innovator," because through historical accident he is nonexistent in these areas. The need is rather for the industrial manager, who must be recruited from a populace hitherto barren of talent of this kind, as a result of the foreign managers who came along with the foreign capital.

Public management, too, is a critical need in the underdeveloped area, and Toulmin, Chandram, and Chandradhat stress how it should be geared to the development goals of the country striving for self-generated growth.

To supplement the managerial force, a program to provide a supply of vocational and professional skills must be organized. Skapski stresses this and describes how such a program was mobilized in Africa.

Finally, the critical need to adapt health measures to the special requirements of underdeveloped regions and to particular manpower problems is forcefully illustrated in the Vintinner, Vallenas, and Landry article, which uses pointed lessons learned from experience with Peruvian miners.

Population and Labor Force Resources As Factors in Economic Development

PHILIP M. HAUSER
University of Chicago
Chicago, Illinois

Economic development has as its objective the raising of the level of living of a people. The population of a nation, however, not only reaps the gains of economic development through increased per capita income but, as the human resource, also plays a vital role in its achievement. In the contemporary situation, four aspects of population in the less developed areas are operating to retard economic development. These are the relatively high rate of population growth, unfavorable age structure, unbalanced population distribution, and inadequately educated and trained manpower. All of these obstructions to economic development are amenable to control. But they cannot be controlled unless the ways in which they hamper efforts to raise levels of living are fully understood, relevant policies are formulated, and necessary programs put into operation. The relation between each of these population factors and economic development is briefly discussed in the materials which follow.

High Rates of Population Growth

The standard of living cannot be raised unless aggregate output increases more rapidly than total population. This relationship is shown in the following over-simplified equation: $L = \dfrac{O}{P}$, where "L" equals levels of living, "O" equals aggregate output and "P" equals population.[1] It is clear from this equation that an increase in aggregate output does not result in any increase in level of living if, simultaneously, there is a corresponding increase in total population. The greater the rate of population increase, then, the higher must be the rate of economic growth to effect any increase in per capita income.

The implications of this equation may be readily seen in examining the population and income data for the world, as a whole, and for its continental regions. During the second half of this century, according to the United Nations "medium" population projections, world population will increase about 2½-fold to reach a total of 6.3 billion by the year 2000 (table 1). Drawing also on the United Nations data for aggregate income for the world and its regions (table 2) the interrelationships between population increase and income increase may be ob-

TABLE I. *Estimated population and population increases, by continent, 1900 to 2000*

Area	Population (million)					Av. annual increase (%)*			
	1900	1925	1950	1975	2000	1900–1925	1925–1950	1950–1975	1975–2000
World..................	1550	1907	2497	3828	6267	0.9	1.2	2.1	2.6
Africa.................	120	147	199	303	517	0.9	1.4	2.1	2.8
Northern America........	81	126	168	240	312	2.2	1.3	1.7	1.2
Latin America...........	63	99	163	303	592	2.3	2.6	3.4	3.8
Asia...................	857	1020	1380	2210	3870	0.8	1.4	2.4	3.0
Europe (including U.S.S.R.).....	423	505	574	751	947	0.8	0.6	1.2	1.0
Oceania................	6	10	13	21	29	2.3	1.4	2.4	1.6

*Arithmetic mean of percentage of increase for 25-year periods.

Source: *The Future Growth of World Population*, United Nations, New York (1958).

TABLE 2. *Population and income, by continent, about 1950*

Area	Total population		Aggregate income		Per capita income ($)
	No. (thousands)	(%)	Dollars* (millions)	(%)	
World..................	2497	100.0	556	100.0	223
Africa.................	199	8.0	15	2.7	75
North America..........	219	8.8	241	43.3	1100
South America..........	112	4.5	19	3.4	170
Asia...................	1380	55.3	69	12.4	50
Europe (exclusive of U.S.S.R.)...........	393	15.7	149	26.8	380
U.S.S.R.................	181	7.2	56	10.1	310
Oceania................	13	0.5	7	1.3	560

*The calculations were made by using United Nations per capita income figures for each continent applied to revised United Nations estimates of 1950 population of continents to obtain revised aggregate income by continent and for the world. A new world per capita figure of $223 was obtained, as compared with the published figure of $230.

Source: *National and Per Capita Income of 70 Countries in 1949*, U.N. Statist. Papers, Ser. E, No. 1, United Nations, New York (1950).

served. For example, considering the world as a whole, aggregate income between 1950 and 2000, must be increased 4-fold to match the 1950 per capita income of Europe, and by 12-fold to match the 1950 per capita income of North America. A decrease in world population growth to 0.5 percent per year, the rate actually experienced between 1800 and 1850, would diminish the task of raising the aggregate product of goods and services by some 75 to 80 percent.

A similar analysis is possible by regions. Latin America, whose population is projected by the UN to increase more than 3½-fold during the second half of the century, would have to increase her aggregate product 8-fold to match the 1950 European level of living by the year 2000, and 23-fold to match the 1950 North American level of living. Africa, which may increase her population some 2½-fold during the second half of this century, would require a 13-fold increase in continental income to match the 1950 European level of living by the end of the century, and something like a 38-fold to match the North American level of living. Finally, Asia, which according to the United Nations projections may experience a population increase during the second half of this century as great as the population of the entire world in 1950, an increase of some 2.5 billion, would have to increase her aggregate income by a factor of 21 to match the 1950 European level of living by the year 2000, and by a factor of 62 to match the 1950 North American level of living by the same date.[2] Calculations of this type, over-simplified as they may be, nevertheless demonstrate that contemporary and projected rates of population increase in the economically less developed areas impose stupendous burdens upon them in their efforts to raise their living levels. Yet, ironically enough, there is an inverse relationship between the level of living of a region and its current and projected rate of population increase to the end of the century. (Compare tables 1 and 2.)

Rapid population growth also adversely affects investment to achieve economic growth. To effect an increase in output, investment increments must be great enough to produce income incre-

ments adequate to raise per capita income. Capital-income ratios indicate that to achieve an increment of one unit of income approximately three units of capital are required.[3] Populations increasing at a rate of 3 percent per year, already approximated by Latin America and other parts of the world and in prospect for most of the less developed areas in this century, must therefore achieve a savings of approximately 9 percent per annum, merely to maintain their present low levels of per capita income. Yet many of the economically less developed societies find it difficult to achieve a savings rate of more than 4 to 5 percent. It is doubtful that India, even with her prodigious efforts towards economic development, has as yet achieved a savings rate in excess of 10 percent. Thus, even with outside capital, she has been barely able to keep ahead of her 2 percent per annum increase in population.[4] This is why India has so much increased her effort to control population growth as an important factor in planning economic development.

Rapid population increase, however, is not necessarily a barrier to economic development. There can be little doubt that in the history of the present economically advanced nations rapid population growth may actually have contributed to increased product per head and to higher levels of living. But the man-resources ratio in the present economically advanced nations was, on the whole, much more favorable at their initial stages of economic growth than is true of the less developed areas today. In North America during the 19th century, for example, a resource-rich unexploited continent, rapid population increase undoubtedly contributed to increased levels of living. For with its low man-resources ratio, rapid population growth contributed to economies of scale. In the less developed areas today where there is already a high man-resources ratio rapid population growth contributes not to economies of scale but to diminishing returns.[5]

Finally, it may be observed that rapid population increase serves as a barrier to economic development not only in the manner indicated above but, also, in the way it may contribute to an unfavorable age structure, to excessive urbanization, and to retardation of effective investment in human resources.

Unfavorable Age Structure

High fertility areas have larger proportions of young persons than do low fertility areas. (table 3) In Asia, Latin America and Africa in 1950, 40 percent or more of the total population was under 15 years of age. In contrast, in Europe and in North America, 26 and 27 percent of the total population, respectively, were under 15 years of age. By 1975, according to the United Nations "medium" projections, the age structures of the economically less developed, as compared with the economically advanced areas of the world, will not have appreciably changed. Because of their anticipated higher fertility rates they will still have larger proportions of their total population under 15 years of age.

The relatively large proportions of persons under 15 years of age in the high fertility, less developed regions of the world, may be interpreted as "unfavorable" to economic development for at least two reasons. First, the relatively high proportion of young persons below working age tends to reduce labor input per capita and, all other things being equal, tends therefore to reduce income per capita. Second, the larger proportion of young persons in the population requires that a greater part of limited resources be allocated to "social" investment

TABLE 3. *Estimated age composition of the population of the world and continents, 1950 and 1975*

Continent	Percent distribution					
	1950			1975		
	Under 15	15–59	60 & Over	Under 15	15–59	60 & Over
World......................	37	56	7	38	54	8
Africa......................	42	54	4	41	54	5
Northern America..........	27	61	12	28	56	16
Latin America.............	40	54	6	42	52	6
Asia......................	40	55	5	41	54	5
Europe....................	26	62	12	24	59	17
Oceania...................	30	59	11	31	55	14
U.S.S.R..................	33	59	8	30	59	11

Source: United Nations, *The Future Growth of World Population*, United Nations, New York, p. 35 (1958).

rather than to "economic" investment. That is, the more youthful the population the greater is the proportion of total savings that must be devoted to the rearing of the young, and the smaller is the proportion of total savings that is available for investment in agricultural or industrial projects designed to increase per capita production.

The adverse effects on economic development of the age structure of a high fertility society may be readily documented. Changes in age structure are the result of changes in fertility and mortality. Reductions in the death rate occur first of all and disproportionately among infants and youth. In consequence, re-

duced mortality tends to increase greatly the proportions of young persons in a population. On the contrary, reductions in the birth rate tend to decrease the proportion of young persons in a population. Over time, a population ages more rapidly by reason of a reduced birth rate than as the result of a decreased death rate.[6] The effect of reductions in fertility and mortality on the proportion of workers in a population and on "needs" per worker resulting from changes in age structure are presented in table 4.

It may be observed that as mortality decreases, while fertility remains constant, there is a decrease in the proportion of "active" males, that is workers,

TABLE 4. *Estimated active males per 1000 population and estimated needs per 1000 active males at different levels of expectation of life at birth and of gross reproduction rate*

Activity rates in less developed countries*

Gross reproduction rate	Expectation of life at birth		
	30 years	50 years	70 years
	Active males per 1000 population		
4.0	255	240	226
3.0	286	271	257
2.0	328	315	301
1.0	392	382	369
	Needs** per 1000 active males		
4.0	3,323	3,489	3,672
3.0	3,016	3,146	3,288
2.0	2,699	2,766	2,870
1.0	2,283	2,309	2,373

*For effects assuming developed countries activity rates, see source.
**Needs of one adult = 1.0.

Source: U.N. Population Studies, No. 26, *The Aging of Populations and Its Economic and Social Implications*, United Nations, New York, p. 62 (1956).

in a population. For example, if the gross reproduction rate remains at a level of 3.0, the number of active males per 1000 population decreases from 286 when expectation of life at birth is 30 years, to 257 when expectation of life reaches 70 years, a decrease of 10 percent in the proportion of workers in a population. In contrast, as the birth rate declines while the death rate remains constant, an increase in the proportion of workers takes place. Thus, when expectation of life at birth is 30 years, a decline in re-production rate from a level of 4.0 to 2.0 results in an increase in active males per 1000 population from 255 to 328, an increase of almost 30 percent. The joint effect of decreasing mortality and decreas-ing fertility may also be measured. A death rate that has decreased to achieve an expectation of life of 50 years from a level of 30 years while the gross repro-duction rate declines from 4.0 to 2.0, effects an increase in active males per 1000 population from 255 to 315, an in-crease of almost 25 percent.

Since many of the less developed areas of the world are in the process of achieving an increase in expectation of life at birth from approximately 30 years to 50 years, the entries under these two levels of expectation of life in table 4 point to what may be the actual experi-ence of such areas if reductions in fertility are effected.

The "needs" of a population are to some extent a function of its age struc-ture; that is, consumption varies with age, for both children and elderly people have different needs from those of adults of intermediate age. The United Na-tions has estimated the changes in the needs of a population with changing age structure, expressing the needs of an adult as unity, 1.0, and the needs of a child or an

aged person by 0.7 of a unit. The chang-ing needs per 1000 active males in the population under the impact of changing fertility and mortality are shown in the lower panel of table 4.

It is readily seen that as the death rate declines and expectation of life at birth increases, needs per 1000 active males increase. Thus, with a gross re-production rate of 4.0, needs per 1000 active males would rise from 3,323 units to 3,672 units as expectation of life in-creases from 30 years to 70 years, an in-crease of over 10 percent. Contrariwise, a decrease in the birth rate while mortal-ity remains constant has the effect of de-creasing needs per 1000 active males. Thus, if expectation of life remains fixed at 30 years a decline in the gross repro-duction rate from 4.0 to 2.0 would reduce needs per 1000 active males from 3,323 units to 2,699 units, or by almost a fifth. The joint effect of decreasing fertility and mortality may also be traced. Thus, if a gross reproduction rate declines from 4.0 to 2.0 while expectation of life in-creases from 30 years to 50 years, needs per 1000 active males decline from 3,323 units to 2,766 units, a decrease of about 17 percent. A decrease in the birth rate brings about a decrease in the needs of a population per 1000 workers as the net effect of an increase in the proportion of workers and of a decrease in young per-sons below working age.

The decline in the proportion of young persons contributes to economic development in still another significant way. For the smaller the proportion of persons below working age, the smaller is the proportion of total savings that must be allocated to the rearing of the young, and the greater is the proportion of total savings that may be allocated to productive investment. Hence, a decrease in the proportion of persons below working age simultaneously decreases the dependency burdens of workers and increases the proportion of total savings which may be placed in productive channels.

High fertility, then, under conditions of declining mortality, has the effect of retarding economic development not only in being responsible for high rates of total population growth but, also, in producing an age structure which adversely affects economic growth.

Imbalance in Population Distribution

High urbanization generally is identified with economically advanced areas and the advent of industrialization. Yet despite their relatively low rate of industrialization, the less advanced areas in Asia, Latin America and Africa, because they have such a vast total population, have more people living in cities of 20,000 or more, or cities of 100,000 or more, than do the economically advanced

nations of Europe and North America combined. In 1950, Asia, Latin America and Africa, contained over 45 percent of the world's residents of cities of 20,000 or more; whereas, Europe (excluding the USSR) and North America contained but 41 percent of the world population living in cities of this size.[7] (See table 5) Moreover, during the 20th century the rate of urbanization of Asia, Latin America and Africa has exceeded that of Europe and North America.

The degree of urbanization has quite different implications for economic development in the advanced than in the less developed areas. In the economically advanced nations, urbanization is both an antecedent and a consequent of high levels of living. It makes possible and advances the division of labor and specialization, the application of non-human energy to production, improved technology, economies of scale, external economies, minimization of the frictions of space and communication, and, in general, higher per capita income. In the economically less developed areas, how-

TABLE 5. *Distribution of urban population of the world, by continents, 1950*

Continent	Total population %	Population living in cities of 20,000 and more %	Population living in cities of 100,000 and more %
World	100	100	100
Asia	53.2	33.8	33.7
Europe	16.4	27.5	26.5
North America	6.8	13.9	15.2
U.S.S.R.	8.1	12.0	11.2
South America	4.6	5.8	6.5
Africa	8.2	3.7	3.2
Central America	2.1	2.1	2.0
Oceania	0.5	1.2	1.6

Source: Philip M. Hauser (ed.), *Urbanization in Asia and the Far East*, UNESCO, Calcutta, p. 99 (1957).

ever, urbanization tends to be the product of quite different factors and is not accompanied by corresponding increases in productivity and levels of living. In the less developed areas of the world today, urbanization is less the result of indigenous economic development and more the product of economic development of an historical imperial system focused largely on a "mother" country. Urban agglomerations in the less developed areas are more the product of the push of population from over-populated rural areas than the pull of population to urban centers by reason of greater economic opportunity. Furthermore, the recent acceleration in the rate of urbanization in many of the less developed areas reflects the disruption and disorganization produced by the war and post-war political instability creating a troubled countryside and large refugee populations. By reason of the above considerations, the less developed areas of the world may be said to be "over-urbanized" in the sense that larger proportions of their population live in urban places than is justified by their degree of economic development. More specifically, compared with the economically advanced nations at comparable levels of urbanization, a much smaller proportion of the labor force in the less developed areas is engaged in nonagricultural and especially mechanized industrial occupations.

In consequence, the relatively large urban populations in the less developed areas serve as a barrier rather than as an accelerant to economic development. To state that a less developed area is over-urbanized is to pose its major economic problem because what is meant is that it does not have an adequate economic base to support its urban population by the standards of the economically advanced nations. Such areas are faced with the problem of achieving higher levels of economic devolpment to support their present, let alone their prospective urban populations. The accelerating rates of urbanization which confront the less developed areas are likely to worsen rather than to ameliorate their poverty and distress. Asia, for example, is faced with the prospect of tripling her urban population in the quarter of a century between 1950 and 1975, assuming the population increase that is projected by the United Nations and the continuation of her 20th century rate of urbanization; [8] and the prospects for Latin America and Africa are approximately the same. The fundamental economic problem of the less developed areas is that of achieving increased productivity. The many difficulties which obstruct the attainment of this objective are likely to be exacerbated rather than ameliorated by the present and prospective rates or urbanization.

Given the present levels of productivity and limited savings in the less developed areas, a major common problem relates to the allocation of resources for the improvement of agriculture, on the one hand, and the development of industrial sectors of the economy, on the other. In many nations improvement in the productivity of the agricultural sector of the economy may contribute more to rising levels of living than efforts to induce industrialization. The claims of large and growing urban populations and their growing political importance may require disproportionate allocations of limited resources to the development of the urban, rather than the agricultural, sectors of the economy, at the expense of a net increase in product per head.

The achievement of adequate balance between agricultural and urban industrial development is complicated by difficult problems of dividing limited savings between "social" and "productive" investment. This problem, although it is manifest both in the urban and in the rural sectors, finds its most acute form in the city. Urban areas in the less developed nations are characterized by inadequate infra-structure development which precludes the usual amenities of urban existence found in advanced nations. There is a great need and much temptation to allocate resources to social purposes such as the elimination of shanty towns, piped water, sewerage, better housing and social services for in-migrants. Social investment of this type, badly needed as it may be can be made only at the expense of decreased investment in agricultural and industrial productive facilities—investment designed to increase productivity as in tractors and fertilizers or in power plants, factories and transport.

The already acute problems of the urban areas in the less developed areas, social and political, as well as economic, are intensified by the large internal migratory flows of population from rural to urban areas. This fact has been recognized by a number of nations which are making efforts to decelerate rural to urban migration by means of programs designed to raise levels of living of the rural population. It may well be that the quickest way to increase the levels of living of urban population may lie in agrarian reforms, including modification of outmoded land tenure systems, which would give the agricultural population a stake in the land, produce higher productivity, and induce the rural population to remain in rural areas.

Imbalance in the distribution of population between urban and rural areas,

considered in relation to industrial and general economic development, may, then, operate to retard economic growth. Needless to say, such a maldistribution of population is worsened by excessively high rates of total population increase. The dampening of total population growth rates would undoubtedly bring about a sharp decline in the rate of urbanization and make a more balanced population distribution possible.

Quality of Human Resources

The three aspects of population which tend to retard economic development discussed above are each concerned with problems of quantity of population—total population, an unfavorable age structure, and imbalance in urban-rural distribution. Also operating as a barrier to economic development, is the low quality of population in the less developed areas, that is, the low general educational level and low skill of the population and most importantly of the labor force. High levels of illiteracy and the absence of a skilled labor force serve as major barriers to economic growth, particularly in the urban and industrial sectors of the economy.

It is becoming recognized that perhaps the most important single type of investment for achieving economic development is investment in human resources. In fact it is being argued that "investment in the human factor may well have a higher payoff in terms of increased output than does any other input".[9] Moreover, evidence is mounting that only a relatively small share of increased output is the result of increases in the conventionally regarded inputs of labor, land and capital combined. For example, recent studies suggest that for the period

1899–1953 in the United States, only a third of increased output may be accounted for by increased input of labor, land and capital. The remaining two-thirds of the increase in output seems to be the result of the combination of technology, organization, and human capital together with all other factors.[10] Moreover, the data suggest that of these latter four types of input, human capital may be the most important. Investment in human resources is essentially investment in the improved quality of population, as it may be achieved through increased education and training.

There is little need for elaborating the importance of increasing the level of education of a population as an important element in achieving economic development. A major barrier to raising the educational level of a nation, however, may be found in high fertility. This can be readily demonstrated. (table 6) It is apparent that as mortality decreases while the birth rate remains fixed, total school construction needs may increase from a doubling to more than a quadrupling. Thus, with a gross reproduction rate of 3.0 an increase in expectation of life from 30 years to 70 years, would result in a 2½-fold increase in school construction needs, an increase from 10 units to 25 units. Contrariwise, a decrease in birth rate produces a substantial decrease in school construction needs when mortality is held constant. Thus, for an expectation of life of 50 years, a decrease of more than two-thirds is effected in school construction needs when the gross reproduction rate declines from 4.0 to 2.0. That is, annual school construction needs declines from 29 to 8 units. If the birth rate is decreased along with declines in the death rate, appreciable decreases in school construction needs may be effected. For example, if the gross reproduction rate is decreased from 4.0 to 2.0 while expectation of life increases from 30 to 50 years, school construction needs are de-

TABLE 6. *Estimate of total annual school construction needs per 1,000 active males at different mortality and fertility levels**

Activity rates in less developed countries**

Gross reproduction rate	Expectation of life at birth		
	30 years	50 years	70 years
4.0	19	29	38
3.0	10	19	25
2.0	***3	8	13

*Construction required for one male pupil = 1.0

**"It has been assumed that, between the ages of 10 and 24, school attendance rates were equal to the difference between the male activity rates and 1 in the five-year age groups and that all children of from five to nine years of age attended school."

***The difference between the rate of replacement needs (2.9 per 1,000) and the rate of vacancies occurring.

Source: U.N. Population Studies, No. 26, *The Aging of Populations and Its Economic and Social Implications*, United Nations, New York, 1956, p. 69.

creased by more than 50 percent—from 19 to 8 units.

The gains that may be achieved from a reduction in birth rate in decreasing the investment necessary for educational construction may, of course, also be gained in decreasing the investment necessary for increasing teachers and educational facilities. Similar savings may be achieved on training programs, that is, the teaching of occupational skills.

Concluding Observations

Economic development policies and programs must take into account the role of population factors, in general, and specifically the four aspects of population which have been discussed above. To eliminate the adverse effects of population factors on economic development it is necessary to dampen rates of total population increase, to effect a more favorable age structure, to achieve a more balanced urban-rural population distribution, and to raise the quality of the population by attaining higher levels of education and training. Each of these goals is attainable, and, significantly enough, all may be achieved by the same means—namely, through a decrease in the birth rate.

In the contemporary world situation, given the great declines in mortality achieved and in prospect, a decrease in the birth rate would simultaneously reduce rates of population increase, favorably alter the age structure, help to effect better balance between urban and rural population distribution, and permit more adequate and effective investment in human resources.

A decrease in birth rate seems a simple enough solution. But it is not easy of attainment. The hard fact is that in most of the less developed areas there is neither incentive nor motivation for regulating family size. Moreover, it is not clear that the techniques for controlling fertility are as yet available which can be effectively employed in these areas. In the contemporary world there are no economically advanced nations which do not employ both death control and birth control. But, there is no guarantee that the methods that have proved to be effective in the economically advanced areas will automatically prove to be effective in the less developed areas.

There is a great need, therefore, for increased research both in the social sciences and in the natural sciences. Social science research is needed to learn more about how to increase motivation and incentive for the regulation of the family size. Natural science research is needed to learn more about human reproduction so that more effective methods for controlling fertility may be developed. Programs for the development and application of science and technology for the benefit of the less developed areas must necessarily embrace these needs.

FOOTNOTES

[1] For fuller discussion of relation of population growth to economic development see: United Nations, *The Determinants and Consequences of Population Trends,* United Nations, New York, 1953, especially Part III, 181–288; Lewis, W. Arthur, *The Theory of Economic Growth,* Richard D. Irwin, Inc., Homewood, Illinois, 1955, Chapter VI, especially 304–330; Kuznets, Simon, *Quantitative aspects of the economic growth of nations: I, levels and variability of rates of growth,* Eco-

nomic Development and Cultural Change, 5, 1, October, 1956, 5–94; Coale, Ansley J. and Hoover, Edgar M., *Population Growth and Economic Development in Low Income Countries,* Princeton, N.J., Princeton University Press, 1958, especially Part Four.

[2] Hauser, P. M., *Population Perspectives,* Rutgers University Press, New Brunswick, New Jersey, 16–20, (1960).

[3] United Nations, op. cit., pp. 277 ff. Also Ward, Barbara, *The Rich Nations and The Poor Nations,* W. W. Norton and Company, Inc., New York, 1962, p. 91. Kuznets, Simon, *Quantitative Aspects of the Economic Growth of Nations: V, Capital Formation Proportions: International Comparisons for Recent Years,* loc. cit., 8, 4, Part II, July 1960, 1–96; and *VI, Long Term Trends in Capital Formation Proportions,* loc. cit., 9, 4, Part II, 3–124, July 1961.

[4] Ward, B., op. cit., p. 92.

[5] Lewis, W. A., op. cit., pp. 323 ff.; also PEP, *World Population and Resources,* Political and Economic Planning, London, 1955, pp. 90 ff. and also Part II, Chapter 4.

[6] United Nations, *The Aging of Populations and Its Economic and Social Implications,* United Nations, Chapter II. (New York, 1956).

[7] The materials in paragraphs 17 to 23 are drawn largely from proceedings of UNESCO/United Nations seminars on urbanization and United Nations Seminar on Regional Planning published as follows:
Hauser, P. M. (ed.), *Urbanization in Asia and the Far East,* UNESCO, Calcutta, (1957).
Hauser, P. M. (ed.), *Urbanization in Latin America,* UNESCO, Belgium, (1961).
United Nations, *United Nations Seminar on Regional Planning,* United Nations, New York.

[8] Hauser, P. M., *Implications of population trends for regional and urban planning in Asia and the Far East.* Regional Planning: Housing, Building and Planning, Numbers 12 and 13, United Nations, New York, 21–31 (1960).

[9] Frank, Andrew Gunder, *"Human Capital and Economic Growth,"* Economic Development and Cultural Change, 8, 2, p. 170 (Jan. 1960).

[10] Ibid., pp. 170 ff.

The Entrepreneurial Element in Economic Development

BERT F. HOSELITZ

Professor of Economics and Social Sciences
University of Chicago
Chicago, Illinois

Much has been written on entrepreneurship in the literature concerning economic growth, and this variable customarily is designated as a pertinent factor in economic development. Although there have been case studies of the emergence of entrepreneurship in several developing countries, generalizations on entrepreneurial roles and contributions have been rare; there is even some uncertainty as to the proper definition of the concept. This paper suggests some general principles relating to the performance of entrepreneurial functions in the process of economic growth, in general, and in the developing countries, in particular.

The definition of entrepreneurship, as of many other concepts in economics, does not lend itself to uniformity. Entrepreneurs are classed by some primarily as innovators; others regard them as managers of enterprises, and bearers of risks; some place major emphasis on their functions as mobilizers and allocators of capital. Joseph Schumpeter, in 1912, expressed the view that the specific role of entrepreneurs is in the carrying out of innovations. Schumpeter wrote at a time when most entrepreneurial performance was in the hands of private individuals, and government and private bureaucracies still played a relatively limited part in the running of economically significant enterprises. In the past 50 years, however, the corporation and other highly structured public units perform more and more of the main entrepreneurial function in countries whose economy is traditionally based on free enterprise. In socialist countries public officials working in government enterprises or government-controlled corporations may carry the entrepreneurial function; in the developing countries government officials may control some important branches of production. Hence, the individual, "irrational", visionary enterpreneur whom Schumpeter saw as the main carrier of economic progress has been largely replaced by a private or public "business leader" whose action may be based on known and predictable principles, whose risk has been greatly reduced, and whose activities are supported by a large corporation or a governmental agency. These functions have become so routine that the performance of the typical entrepreneurial functions stipulated by Schumpeter has become either impossible or superfluous.

The concept of entrepreneurship as advanced by Schumpeter has been modified in light of the developments in the last few decades, especially in Asian and African countries. Most of the business leadership in these countries is, or may be, carried out by managers of large private or public enterprises, or by small or medium-scale entrepreneurs. Scarcely any of these are innovators in the Schumpeter sense. The technology applied is usually borrowed from abroad. The legal and marketing practices are generally adaptations from more economically advanced countries. Often the commodities produced are imitations of the consumer goods of the more advanced nations.

In view of these considerations, it is necessary to modify Schumpeter's description of entrepreneurship and entrepreneurial functions. The person who typically performs this function in developing countries today may be either a manager or one who adapts the experience of others in production methods, sources of supply, and markets to conditions prevailing in newly developing countries. In the subsequent discussion, we will be concerned primarily with individuals who are active as business leaders in the private sector. The facts of economic development in Asia and Africa seem to indicate that an important role in this process may be played by private entrepreneurs in small and medium-scale plants, provided a private enterprise sector is at all in existence. In addition, there must be within the framework of government plans for economic development some intention to develop "mixed economies" in which business and private enterprise combine for the improvement of the economic welfare.

In short, we are concerned with private entrepreneurs who are active in the small and medium-size industrial, commercial, and financial enterprises which are appearing or will appear in the economically less developed nations. Many of the entrepreneurial characteristics will also apply to persons in positions of business leadership in the public sector. In some cases the differences that result from the different responses of the private and public business leaders will be pointed up.

It may be useful to cite a few figures indicating the general significance of small and medium-scale private entrepreneurs in the process of industrialization and general economic growth in developing countries. If we classify industrial establishments in terms of the number of workers employed and assign enterprises employing fewer than 50 persons to the class of small and medium-scale plants, we find the following data from the economic experiences of some Western European countries: in Austria, in 1930, 57.7 percent of the total labor force in secondary production (manufacturing, mining, and construction) worked in firms employing fewer than 50 workers. The corresponding figures for other countries were as follows: in France, in 1906, the percentage was 70.6; in Germany, in 1907, it was 54.5; in Switzerland, in 1955, it was 43.7; and in Norway, in 1953, it was 51.3. From these figures it becomes apparent that small and medium-sized plants have played an important part in industrial countries, and that even long after the onset of the industrialization process the majority of workers in secondary production were employed in these "small" firms. The corresponding proportions for commercial activities, especially retail trade, and for financial activities, except investment banking and modern types of insurance, are probably much higher than those in secondary industries. In brief, the small and medium-scale firm can be said to have played an important part in the more highly developed countries and may be expected to play an important part in the process of economic growth in the development countries.

But there are still other reasons emphasizing these enterprises in developing countries, especially those with dense populations and large labor supply. It is quite customary, when we think of industrial development in the new nations, to evoke the picture of a large scale industrial plant; e.g., in steel or cement production. But the existing markets, demand patterns, and conditions of comparative advantage in developing countries are such as to make the establishment of small plants, mainly producing light consumers' goods, most attractive. Hence, industrialization must be thought of in the next two or three decades not in terms of new Pittsburghs or Birminghams in the developing nations of Asia and Africa, but rather as a process in which small capital is allocated in various industrial and commercial fields. Although these units may increase in size, they will remain—from a world point of view—fairly small, or at best medium-sized, in their fields of economic activity. The reason for this stems from the very different relative supply of labor and capital, and particularly from the fact that capital to be invested on a long-term basis is in very short supply and often unavailable through the ordinary chan-

nels. In other words, banks will ration credit to small entrepreneurs who wish to grow rapidly. Many enterprises may have to begin with meager capital funds and grow only to the extent to which they can reinvest their profits. In the industrial field the certainty that small and medium-scale enterprises in the developing countries will persist must be taken into account. In the light of Western Europe's historical experience entrepreneurs on the small and medium scale will have important roles for several decades.

Up to this point no distinction has been drawn between the different areas of economic activity in which entrepreneurship is exercised. Moreover, in the literature of entrepreneurship little or no distinction has been made usually among the fields of entrepreneurship. Yet, a superficial study of business leaders in many developing countries shows that industrial entrepreneurship falls far short of the degree to which commercial and financial entrepreneurship flourishes. Why do we find in so many developing countries no dearth of moneylenders and traders but so few indigenous industrialists? For example, in almost all the new Nations of West Africa, there are extended networks of trade in which Africans, persons of Middle Eastern origin, and other Mediterranean people participate. Yet few of these persons engage in industrial pursuits. A similar situation is noticeable in several East African countries and in various parts of Southeastern Asia. Various arguments have been raised to explain this phenomenon. Foremost is the fact that local industrialists, especially in former colonial areas, were unable to compete with the powerful enterprises set up by Europeans. A similar argument may be made for those developing countries which were politically independent but whose potential entrepreneurs faced the overwhelming competition of foreign investors. Most European foreign investments were concentrated in such basic industries as mining, transport, and power, and only small proportions of private foreign capital flowed into manufacturing. A look at the kind of enterprises which entrepreneurs established in trading and moneylending fields shows that they were often supplementary to the similar activities of European firms. The small indigenous traders and moneylenders had to find their places in the unoccupied interstices of the economic system. They mediated between the urban centers and the countryside; they provisioned small retailers; they serviced the financial needs of rural and semi-rural populations unable to offer bankable securities; and they distributed commodities on a scale that would have been uneconomical for the large foreign enterprises.

Why do we not witness similar developments in the industrial field? Clearly we should not expect that the small indigenous entrepreneurs would have competed with the large foreign mining or transport companies. There were and are, however, numerous industrial branches in which ample opportunities exist for the establishment of small and medium scale plants providing for the role of trader and moneylender with regard to the foreign import houses, wholesalers and bankers. This difference in behavior in different economic fields by indigenous entrepreneurs stems from the fact that economic development everywhere is tied, to a substantial degree, to the growth of industry. In mixed economies industrial growth is confined to a few large establishments, mainly in the field of heavy industry. However, highly

significant is the rapid growth of many small and medium-scale firms producing consumer goods and offering services. Hence, the gaining of a clearer insight into the different conditions under which industrial, as against commercial and financial, entrepreneurship may flourish in a developing country may be an important guide for over-all economic policies.

A reason advanced for the sluggishness of industrial entrepreneurship in developing countries turns on the talents required to guide an industrial enterprise. These talents differ from those needed for most successful commercial or financial dealings. A small trader or moneylender can operate successfully with only a few, and often without any, permanently employed assistants, but the industrial entrepreneur—provided he is more than a craftsman or artisan—usually must hire men or women whose work he must organize and guide. In short, we may presume that an industrial entrepreneur must have a broader range of abilities than a moneylender or trader. He must be a person who can lead others in a common enterprise and he must have technical knowledge in his branch of production.

Another distinction between industrial entrepreneurs and financial or commercial entrepreneurs is found in the commitment of assets in the production process. A trader may carry on his operation without ever attaining property rights to the object he deals with; if he is a broker or commercial agent, he may merely lose his earnings from a transaction but not the capital invested in it. In addition, the capital that a trader, or moneylender, does invest has a faster turnover normally than that invested in an industrial establishment. Moreover, a moneylender or banker deals in a commodity that has the widest currency, that is accepted by everyone, and that can be easily transported, hidden, or converted into other assets. On the other hand, an industrial entrepreneur usually has a much larger proportion of his assets tied up in fixed capital. He often depends on an imperfect market for the sale of his output; his profit is exposed to dangers which moneylenders or traders sometimes escape. Other things being equal, the risk of transforming a given amount of capital into industrial assets is much greater than in trading or financial operations. A commitment of one's property to investment in industry normally implies a longer-term commitment, and this increases the uncertainty. There is less flexibility in an operation once capital has taken the form of fixed assets, and the prospective profitability of an enterprise is more directly influenced by changes in taste and fluctuations in demand than is true for capital invested in commerce or finance.

Thus, entrepreneurship depends partly upon the appearance of persons with a psychological make-up for entrepreneurial activity, and partly on the social and economic environment that would make it an attractive venture to such individuals. Since many developing nations wish to create a climate favorable for the rapid development of entrepreneurship, especially industrial entrepreneurship, a detailed discussion of the ways in which these personal and environmental conditions can be enhanced may be helpful. The significance of the psychological dispositions for entrepreneurial activity is quite clear from the preceding discussion. Some writers have made these personality factors the fully determining conditions of economic innovations and economic growth, but this appears perhaps too extreme a position. There is little doubt that features in the environment can be manipulated with much more predictable outcomes than can the shaping of personality development. In brief, we may consider that certain conditions in the economy will make possible the successful exercise of entrepreneurial functions regardless of the relative abundance or scarcity of certain personality types.

These conditions of the economy may be classified as consisting, on the one hand, of certain forms of social and economic overhead capital, and, on the other, of certain governmental services which are placed at the disposal of entrepreneurs. One such condition is the maintenance of law and order. Involved here are the distribution of status and political power, the manner in which power affects entrepreneurial functions and the business community's part in the making of political decisions. A system of private enterprise can exist only if the following basic conditions in the legal-political field are met:

(a) Governmental action short of complete non-intervention but so designed that it does not deny to private persons, explicitly or implicitly, any kind of autonomy in decision-making in the economic field.

(b) A minimum provision of legal, and legally enforceable, institutional rules according to which private economic decisions can be made and implemented.

(c) Protection of the assets owned by an enterprise against expropriation by others, and protection of the contractual relationships entered into by business leaders with one another or with outsiders.

These conditions in some historical situations have been forced upon governments by the political action of business leaders and their political allies. The Industrial Revolution, whether it arose gradually through a process of legal and political reform, as in Britain, or was strongly supported by a political revolution, as in France in 1789, generally altered the prevailing legal and political system—a lessening of arbitrary privileges in the economic area for the aristocracy, no more special treatment of certain privileged groups, wider access to the elite from the ranks of the business community, and a forum (Parliament or some less visible arena) in which pressures by business leaders for legislation in support of their most important needs could be exercised. In other countries the processes by which this greater participation and protection of the entrepreneurial community were achieved differed. In Germany a political alliance was concluded between the aristocratic junkers and the interests of industrial enterprise. In many of the ex-colonial countries the development of entrepreneurship—the pattern which Max Weber called "pariah entrepreneurship" was based largely on a European system of legal security and predictability imposed upon these countries. In Japan, finally, this system was attained with a minimum modification of the social structure, primarily because the elite were persuaded to realization of the nation's needs and to the wisdom of adopting Western technology and economic organization.

The crucial lesson of these instances teaches that private entrepreneurship will develop only if the legal order provides the necessary accommodation for the needs and protection of entrepreneurial activity. Accommodation must include not merely the promulgation of a "neutral" system of laws, but also the shaping of institutions through which entrepreneurs can exert pressure on actions of the state and especially upon legislation. In the change, entrepreneurial performance may rise to a level where it can provide not wealth alone but also social status and some form of political influence. But if those favorable conditions are not created, other outcomes are possible. One is socialization of all enterprise, the government assuming all decisions in the economic realm, the establishment, in short, of a fully planned economy after abolition of private enterprise. A second possibility is the establishment of a system of statism, such as existed in Turkey in the inter-War period, in which private enterprise nominally exists but actually functions under the full direction of the Government. A third is the neglect of enterprise altogether and subsequent stagnation of the economy. Thus, the creation of a "climate of entrepreneurship" has not only economic and social dimensions, but also a political one.

In the establishment of a social structure conducive to the development of entrepreneurship, the feature of economic overhead capital must not be overlooked, since provision of this capital influences the development of entrepreneurship in a positive direction. Most important is provision of power for industry and of transport facilities. These two are perhaps the most significant items in the vast variety of economic overhead capital whose presence in abundance encourages the growth of industrial and commercial enterprise. It is not necessary to enlarge on the importance of power; without it modern productive processes are impossible. Nor is it necessary to expand on transport facilities, since their lack has severely limited markets and prevented establishment of some industries. But it is paramount to state that the less developed a region is, the greater the need for a good transport network.

In this discussion of socio-economic environment we have moved from the most difficult features to the less difficult. The most significant and most difficult is the creation of an appropriate psychological and political structure for entrepreneurial effort. Slightly less important and easier to provide, given the necessary financial resources, are facilities for power and transport. Easier still is the establishment of various government agencies to offer, either without charge or at low cost, services of importance to an entrepreneurial community. Among these services are information on markets, sources of supply, technical innovation, internal organization of plants, innovations in design, and other technical matters which the small and medium-scale entrepreneur in a devolping country finds difficult to obtain on his own. Markets in most developing countries are too small and too confined to make the publication of technical and marketing journals attractive. Thus, business leaders must and often do rely upon government for this information.

In addition to the technical information of use to entrepreneurs, the government may offer other services at low cost or as a subsidy. These services may include assistance with accounting, long-term credit, and the provision of various types of technical education. The need for such services has been widely recognized and, in several developing countries, appropriate institutions have been created to supply them. The agencies charged with providing the services bear different names, but have been designated collec-

tively as development banks or development corporations. Common to all these development corporations is the function of providing credit to entrepreneurs, particularly for long-term needs. In addition to the credit-financing function, the development corporations should provide technical and economic information useful to new enterprises in the earliest stages of their activity.

The development bank should have facilities to find out where the most suitable machinery can be purchased; to supply information on industrialists' markets, freight charges, insurance costs, and other expenses incurred in establishing new business. It will have better information than most traders. Its staff, after examination of production processes, can develop a system of accounting which will be relatively simple and accurate and will meet the needs of the entrepreneur at each stage of his operation. It may even establish a department to acquire machinery to sell to new firms on a hire-purchase plan. Finally, it may cooperate with new firms to find suitable locations and design work procedures and related patterns of practical operations which make for sound production and at the same time reduce the cost of productive operations.

In many developing countries in which industrial development banks have been established, financing activities are largely confined to larger-scale enterprises. This is understandable. The technical assistance these firms need is proportionately less than that needed by smaller firms. In most larger establishments the chief assistance needed by entrepreneurs is long-term credit. In smaller firms the chief requirement is advisory services of various kinds, in addition to credit. Also, the manpower training required, although it may be more extensive than training of managers of large private or public corporations, is oriented toward the economic, organizational and technological processes on which their enterprises are likely to concentrate. This suggests that the development of commercial, financial, and especially industrial entrepreneurship on a wider basis requires not only different approaches by banks and government information services but also by educational services.

Successful entrepreneurship, this paper has argued, implies the exercise of leadership, maturity of character, a sense of security and knowledge of, or familiarity with, the skills related to the entrepreneur's undertakings. The entrepreneur is a man with the broad view, as distinguished from the technical or economic specialist, but familiarity with technical aspects of production is helpful where it is not imperative. Here he differs from the expert of a large enterprise who is employed for his specialized or technical knowledge of production, purchasing, labor relations or other limited and well-defined spheres of action. The entrepreneur in a small or medium-size plant must be more than a man with some knowledge of the production techniques employed in the plant; he must be also a person who makes the chief decision relating to sales, supplies, production processes, relations with workers and numerous elements of business. Primarily he must display characteristics of personality and leadership, the willingness to take some risks and the desire to perform his role successfully.

Because of the basic personality characteristics essential to leadership, the training of the entrepreneur is of major significance. This is especially true in industry—as has already been pointed out—where the entrepreneur must be informed on matters relating to the technical processes. Education and on-the-job training in a growing establishment are prime sources for the acquisition of this information. For example, an entrepreneur who wishes to start a foundry should be able to obtain access to an enterprise at home, if foundries are already in operation there. Otherwise, he should visit nearby developing countries which have foundries.

Up to this point we have been concerned with the analysis of external factors which may influence the growth and encouragement of entrepreneurship in developing countries. In the last resort, the appearance of entrepreneurs is a matter of changing human effort and human action. However, we must also consider certain aspects of recruiting and promoting a corps of entrepreneurs in developing countries. In dealing with this problem we are in one of the most disputed and uncertain areas of social research relating to developing countries. Opinions concerning the human factor in entrepreneurship range all the way from sheer resignation from the impossible task of dealing with this factor meaningfully, to the other extreme of prescribing elaborate schooling and training programs.

The psychological aspects of entrepreneurship have been treated principally by E. E. Hagen and D. C. McClelland, each stressing somewhat different characteristics. In brief, the generally accepted viewpoint on the psychological dimension in entrepreneurial action may be summarized as follows: The industrial entrepreneur, and in fact, the innovating entrepreneur in general, is a distinct personality type. He must be persuaded that change can occur and that it can be brought about by individual action. He also must be motivated to bring about this change by his own activity. This is why—as we have maintained earlier— the general standards of a society must allow persons with newly acquired wealth some access to power or prestige. If overwhelming social obstacles shut these rewards off from entrepreneurial action, persons with the appropriate personality disposition will fail to function successfully, will seek other careers or quit the country.

This sketch of the psychological conditions of entrepreneurship has followed largely in the footsteps of Schumpeter and those influenced by his views on the role of innovating entrepreneurs in economic development. The argument raised by Hagen and McClelland turns on the view that economic growth will occur only if individuals with characteristic entrepreneurial personalities appear in sufficient number; that is, if the appropriate motivations affect not merely a few persons, but penetrate deeply into all layers of society. According to this theory, the appearance of entrepreneurship on a mass basis can be explained as the result of two factors. First, it flows from a special historical situation in which new paths to higher social status are sought through economic achievement. Second, it is the result of the appearance in a society, with more than ordinary frequency, of persons with special personality traits; i.e., persons with unusually high achievement motivation.

McClelland and his students have shown that such persons existed at various periods in history when societies did undergo rapid economic development, and that not only these persons but the whole value system of the societies adopted a more intensive preoccupation with achievement. This group of scholars also has shown that the drive of these persons is a result of their family rearing. But the very fact that a substantial number of entrepreneurs appeared in societies in which a short time ago little or no such talent seemed to be available, makes one suspect that individuals with the required ambitious drive exist in all human societies, though they may not always make their impact felt with the same intensity. If economic development and industrialization are planned as goals of a society as a whole, would-be entrepreneurs will step into a very different environment from that which prevailed in the historical epochs which McClelland and his students, Hagen, and even Schumpeter have investigated.

In the developing countries we meet nations which have written the slogan of economic growth on their banners and are prepared to provide the most extensive accommodation to persons who wish and who can step into positions of entrepreneurship. Moreover, from the great number of traders scattered about the urban and rural areas of almost all developing countries, we may deduce that individuals who exhibit achievement-oriented personalities are available in developing societies. What is required is not so much the creation of new personality types, but rather the opening up of opportunities in the social, economic, and political environment, in the scale and impact of government services, and in the intellectual equipment and training of the persons concerned.

The application of rational principles of planning to the fostering of economic growth will usually be reflected in a mixed-economy; i.e., one in which both government and private enterprise undertake parallel and combined efforts for the over-all economic growth of the nation. This pattern of cooperation and division of functions is appropriate to developing countries, because an underdeveloped economy cannot afford to be doctrinaire. It faces serious shortages of all kinds and it must, in order to experience economic growth, confront the serious business of getting things done—getting capital accumulated and invested in the most useful directions for economic growth. Given widespread backwardness among large masses of the population and urgent desire for economic development, the leadership of the government is essential to an economy which otherwise might remain almost completely stationary. This cooperation between public and private interests may have two results: on the one hand, all available means must be employed to encourage and enhance the rate and amount of savings in the economy, and, on the other, the most efficient channels must be used to allocate these savings among those branches of production in which the over-all net return to the economy will be greatest. It is within this context that a centrally prepared plan has manifold uses, and if such a plan is well conceived and based upon the existing moral and political rules of the society, it may have a crucial influence in the growth of the economy. But if the general moral and political rules of a nation recognize the right and, in fact, the necessity of private enterprise, the plan will be successful only if it makes due allowance for the exercise of private initiative in all or a large number of fields of economic action.

That it is possible to combine an over-all economic development program with the simultaneous encouragement of private enterprise and the fostering of an entrepreneurial class is abundantly demonstrated in the many cases on record in both developed and less developed nations. This does not mean that frictions will not arise between the business community and the planners. There will be conflicts over the merits of short-term gains as against maximum long-term growth rates; the division of decision-making functions between public and private agencies; the precise limits of what industrial functions should be reserved to the government. Though—as was pointed out earlier—the business leaders will want and must get some access to the realm of political decision-making, they must learn, on their part, that a governmental development plan is not an instrument which robs them of all freedom of action. It merely designates, from the point of view of over-all economic considerations embracing the society as a whole, the paths of progress and the primary patterns of investments which are considered most conducive to progress in the economic performance of a society. This will imply regulations and even restrictions on the free exercise of entrepreneurship but may nevertheless conform to the long-run interest of many entrepreneurs, since in many developing countries the differences between social costs and benefits, on the one hand, and private costs and benefits, on the other, are often substantial.

These remarks are intended to reconfirm the fact that entrepreneurship can play a vital role in a planned economy of a developing country, provided the development plan is drawn up in such a way as to provide room for the operations of private entrepreneurs, and provided these entrepreneurs are not dismayed or frightened from making independent decisions even though many decisions relating to production and investment are reserved for, or regulated by, government. It is quite conceivable that the mixed economy as it takes shape in many developing countries, may grow gradually into a new form of "economic system" with its own distinctive characteristics, one of which would be collaboration between public officials and private entrepreneurs in the development of the economy. The ultimate outcome most highly prized by both public officials and business leaders in a developing nation is economic development. Growth and improvement in the performance of the public sector stimulate demand for the output of private entrepreneurs. Also increase in output and improvement in the quality of goods and services supplied by private firms adds to the standard of living and the material welfare of the population at large. Hence, from a secular viewpoint the interests of government, of the newly emerging entrepreneurial class, and of the mass of the population in a developing nation are closely parallel. The main problem is to find a formula by means of which this parallelism of interests can be put into effect with least friction and greatest likelihood of success.

Improving Public Management in Newly Developing Countries

Harry T. Toulmin
Public Administration Service, Chicago, Illinois
Chief of PAS Contract Group in Thailand

M. R. Chandram
Chief of Organization and Methods Division

S. Chandradhat
Budget Bureau,
Thailand

The importance of public management to national development is less generally appreciated than some other developmental prerequisites. Good public management, nevertheless, is vital to development. If other prerequisites are present to a sufficient degree, and if public management is generally good, then there will be developmental progress. If, however, other prerequisites are present but public management is poor, there will be appreciably less progress and perhaps none at all.

Public management is concerned with the way in which government is organized, staffed, equipped, and supplied; the manner in which programs are planned, financed, executed, and reviewed; and with the procedures, systems, and methods employed in accomplishing work.

Good public management would be characterized by a governmental establishment in which appropriate functions of government were fully represented and systematically arranged in the structure of government. Functional assignments to governmental agencies would recognize the importance of the private sector of the economy and provide for its stimulation and control. Enterprises that could be effectively developed under private ownership and management would be excluded from the governmental structure. Lines of authority and responsibility would be clearly delineated throughout the governmental organization; and means of executive communication and coordination would be well developed. Staff services to management and facilitative services for line operations, including financial administration and accounting, planning, budgeting, personnel administration, and procurement and supply services would also be well developed. Continuing attention would be given to work procedures, systems, and methods in order that public business could be performed expeditiously and economically by well-trained public servants. An effective field organization and local governmental institutions for carrying governmental services and activities to the grass roots of the country and population would exist.

Few governments can boast excellence in all of these areas, particularly governments of less developed countries. Public management capacity of such countries ranges widely: from some of the newborn nations that inherited little. from their prior status in terms of public management experience to countries that, by virtue of their own history and devices or prior colonial status, attained a more sophisticated public establishment.

An approach to public management improvement in a developing country should be tailored to fit the prevailing situation. A comprehensive approach would be indicated for countries where public institutions were poorly defined and developed, while dealing with special, identifiable problems might suffice for more highly developed governments. It is important, however, that management improvement be undertaken with sufficient vigor and on a sufficiently broad base; otherwise, there may be no management improvement, with consequent weakening of national developmental efforts.

A comprehensive approach to management improvement would be characterized by the following. With full political backing, the highest executive authority of a country would order a broad administrative survey of the entire executive establishment. This survey, undertaken with expert assistance, would be similar in its purposes to the studies undertaken in Puerto Rico during the 1940's with such notable subse-

quent effect. The survey would ascertain the structure of government as it exists and, broadly, its proficiencies and deficiencies. In consonance with anticipated governmental requirements the survey report would recommend improved functional alignments, the establishment of needed new agencies and as desirable, the consolidation or elimination of some existing agencies. If staff and service functions were poorly developed, the survey report would endeavor to place such activities in perspective as aids to good management and to seek to institutionalize means for their coordination and control. It should also seek to institutionalize, at an appropriately high governmental level, a unit to provide continuing attention, leadership, and stimulation to management improvement.

The initial administrative survey should be related to appropriate elements of the nation's developmental plan, if any, or to any planning studies and projections made, especially those related to public finance, education, manpower development, and training. If such studies had not been originated, they might constitute companion inquiries to the administrative management survey. To the extent possible, the survey report and recommendations should be realistic and realizable in terms of the government's future financial and staffing capabilities.

The report should be accorded executive and political attention consistent with its importance. Some of its more fundamental elements would require legislative action for effectuation; other parts should be permitted the flexibility inherent in installation pursuant to executive order. For example, the broad new framework of government would probably be prescribed in law; but details of internal organization and administration should be reserved to executive direction. Implementing orders should be accompanied by realistic timetables for accomplishment, and executive machinery should be established to assist, facilitate, and review progress toward stated objectives. A prime requisite to a successful program would be the selection of capable key officials to direct major organizational units. The chief executive should exercise much care in this selection process. Should it be necessary to appoint individuals of insufficient professional background for some posts, it might be desirable to backstop them by engaging professional caliber advisors. An intensive executive training program at this level in the governmental heirarchy should be undertaken leading to early sufficiency in terms of managerial capacity on the part of key officials.

The assignment of a portfolio to each key official should be accompanied by an outline program for management improvement in his assigned area. Over the years, but with review of accomplishments as aforementioned, the key executive and his staff would be expected to bring substance and vigor to the assigned management improvement outline.

Operating agencies might occasionally or frequently need technical assistance in matters associated with their operational programs. Such assistance should be directed principally toward institution building and training within the developing organization, and less toward performing operational work for the agency. It would be entirely proper for outside technicians to work side by side with local technicians as a means of training; and some demonstration projects would also be desirable. But wholesale reliance upon outside technicians to perform work that is properly the host

government's would not contribute to institution building.

Some priority in the management improvement program should attach to developing staff and facilitative service functions within the government. These functions, including planning, budgeting, financial administration and accounting, personnel administration, and procurement and supply administration affect and involve all governmental elements. Each requires effective central coordination if the government is to function smoothly; but each also requires adequate technical performance on the part of operating departments in work related to the particular staff or facilitative service function. It would be well to develop at an early date capable central agencies to coordinate activities in each of the named specialized functional areas. These central agencies would then be able to provide stimulation, leadership, and guidance to operating departments in matters related to their specialty. Also, as these central agencies matured they could make available, through transfer, trained planners, budget analysts, accountants, personnel technicians, and procurement specialists to serve in operating departments.

Management improvement and attention to administrative problems and their solution, is a never ending task of good government. It is not sufficient to develop a plan for governmental reorganization and management improvement. The planning process must be superseded by continuing administrative analysis and action if the planned program is to become a reality.

The central staff agencies mentioned above, when organized, could do much to bring about orderly processes within their respective spheres of technical competence. Operating agencies, too, as they developed, and as their staffs became better trained and more proficient, would be better able to cope with and solve management problems. But both staff and line agencies would require stimulation, counsel, and support in relation to management improvement. In short, the management improvement program should have leadership, coordination, and a central reservoir of expert assistance.

For these purposes many governments have found it desirable to establish still another kind of staff unit. Such units may be called by a variety of names: Office of Administrative Management, Organization and Methods Division, or Office of Administrative Research. Regardless of the name, the unit should be located organizationally at an appropriately high governmental level, perhaps in the central budget bureau or in the office of the government's chief executive. Its functions would be: to coordinate and oversee installation of the broad reorganization and management improvement plan; to keep such plan current with governmental growth and changing needs; to perform detailed administrative planning supplementary to the broad improvement program; to conduct organization and methods studies; and especially, to foster, promote, and facilitate the development of a growing competence on the part of all governmental departments to attack and solve their own administrative problems.

It would be well if such a unit could be organized in conjunction with the original management survey of the government—its staff working with or as members of the management survey team. This would afford excellent training for the unit's staff, which would probably be, at first, inexperienced in administrative management. Whenever it is

organized, be it at this early stage or later, the unit should seek to secure the best qualified personnel obtainable as management analysts. Prior training in public administration would be highly desirable if not essential, and supplementary training in accounting and statistics would also be beneficial.

Upon the unit's organization, original staff members should be given intensive training in organization and methods work; and this course should be updated and repeated for subsequent staff acquisitions. Courses covering details related to organization and methods techniques should also be given from time to time. This more formalized training should be supplemented by practical field experience on studies conducted by the central management unit. As operating departments acquire organization and methods technicians of their own, they should be encouraged to participate in the training program of the central management unit. The endeavor should be to develop not only a cadre of capable technicians for the central management unit, but also to develop the capacity of line departments to perform organization and methods work of their own. Some interchange of technical personnel between the central unit and line departments could have a beneficial effect.

It is important that the central management unit establish a good library as a resource of the management improvement program and for training purposes. The unit might also find it desirable to publish a bulletin for general circulation in the government, which would have as its objective stimulation of interest, on the part of executives, supervisors, and public employees, in management improvement and in modern administrative methods, systems, procedures, and techniques. An adequate filing system should be developed for the custody of materials relating to the organization and administration of all government departments and for the projects which it conducts.

It is not necessary here to discuss the management unit's survey program or the mechanics of Organization and Methods surveys. A wealth of information is available on these subjects. Competence in its survey and installation efforts, however, will be the unit's best guarantee of success.

The central management unit can be most effective if it can achieve a position of prestige and stature in the power structure of government. It should seek to reserve, establish, and maintain such a position, and it should use its influence wisely and strategically for the advancement of good administration and good government.

Specialized Training for Developing Basic Scientific and Technological Cadres in Developing Countries of Africa

ADAM S. SKAPSKI

U.S. Agency for International Development, Lagos, Nigeria

Support of Specialized Training by General Education

Trained manpower is customarily classified into three levels:

Vocational—semiskilled and skilled [1] workers

Intermediate—factory and laboratory technicians, non-graduate technical instructors

Senior—graduate scientists and engineers, managerial personnel

The Vocational Level. Industrialists and educators in most countries consider 2 to 3 years of post-primary education as the minimum necessary for efficient specialized training at this level. In French speaking African countries, the 2 years of post-primary education previous to craftsmen training are automatically included as "le tronc commun" which consists of "la 6e" and "la 5e" and leads to further studies for the Certificat d'Aptitude Professionelle (CAP). In English-speaking African countries, this approach is now gaining strength (1). Thus, on the recommendation of this author (2), the Western Nigeria Ministry

of Education is presently reforming the so-called Secondary Modern School (a 3-year course following the 6 years of primary school) by introducing general science and workshops (metal and wood) as obligatory for all students in the first 2 years of this school, and has requested support for this purpose from the U.S. Agency for International Development. Observation and testing of students during these 2 years—which thus correspond to *le tronc commun*—will be used to channel them in the third year into different groups according to their abilities and aptitudes. One of these groups will be "pre-vocational", and will get one more (terminal) year of general education with a strong practical bias consisting of applied science (elementary technology), technical drawing and workshops. Those who leave the terminal class will either enter vocational schools (Trade Training Centers) or take up employment with industry; in the latter case they can be, thanks to their pre-vocational background, easily trained "on the job" as semi-skilled workers (factory operatives, artisans). Pre-vocational bias will also permit reduction of the length of craftsmen training.

The Intermediate Level. In English-speaking Africa, the W.A. School Certificate, (normally taken after 5 years of secondary school and equivalent to the Ordinary Level of the British General Certificate of Education) with passes in English, mathematics, and appropriate sciences, is considered necessary as a prerequisite for normal entry to a technical college for training technicians. The Western Nigeria Ministry of Education is now introducing in the grammar school (3) pre-technical streams in which advanced workshops, technical design and engineering science will be taught besides normal general education subjects. This again will facilitate the training of technicians and leave room for enriching the curriculum of the technical college. In French speaking Africa, specialized training of technicians takes place in lycees techniques and colleges techniques and is thus automatically based on general education included in their programs.

The Senior Level. In French-speaking territories the Baccalaureat, which is the prerequisite for training scientists and graduate engineers in universities, provides a broad enough base of liberal arts (including philosophy) for advanced specialized training. In English speaking territories the Sixth Forms emphasize specialization too much. At least in Western Nigeria, it is felt that the specialization beginning in the Sixth Forms would be more effective if it were accompanied by considerable broadening of general education. The Western Nigeria Ministry of Education, with the support of the Agency for International Development, is expanding the program of the Sixth Forms in its Ayetoro School (see below) by adding 14 periods a week of obligatory general subjects to the 21 periods a week devoted to specialization. These general subjects are: History of Philosophy and Science, History of Art, Introduction to Logic and Psychology, Political Science, and African Problems (sociological, economic etc.). After the Sixth Forms the students may enter the first year of a British-type university; or they will have grounds for requesting "advanced placement" in an American-type university, since several subjects they have taken would have been at the same instructional level as that prevailing in the first two years of an American university.

The Comprehensive School and Technical Training. The Comprehensive School, with its combination of general education and elective biases is the best preparation for specialized training at any level. The Western Nigeria Government, with support of the Agency for International Development, has established a Demonstration Comprehensive Secondary School at Ayetoro, and the Graduate School of Education, Harvard University, is operating it under an AID contract. The Ayetoro Demonstration School, planned by Chief Inspector of Education Mr. Somade and this author (4) is meant to serve as an experimental "laboratory" for the educational reforms in Western Nigeria. Its main characteristics are: (a) a three step structure, each of the steps providing general education with elective biases for specialized training at each of the manpower levels quoted in paragraph 1; (b) introduction of new course content, particularly in mathematics and the sciences, based on the materials prepared in the United States under the auspices of the National Science Foundation but revised and adapted by special writing groups composed of Nigerians and Americans; (c) inclusion of vocational education in the program of the school to foster the status of the craftsman in the society. Yearly conferences on the progress of the school will be held with specialists invited from abroad (United States, United Kingdom, Sweden, etc.) to profit from their constructive criticism.

Planning for Training Schools

When "big" industry starts or expands a plant in a developing country, the first operational stage is directed and supervised by the company's own experienced graduate engineers and technicians. Only when plant operations are well under control, does the company seek to replace its own staff by local engineers and technicians. Semi-skilled and skilled local workers, are, however, needed at once. The former (operatives, artisans) can be trained in the factory "on the job" (see above). But training of fully competent craftsmen requires a minimum of two years and special facilities, which industry may be unable or unwilling to provide; the Government must thus plan for Technical (Craftsmen) Training Centers well ahead. Surveys of anticipated manpower needs should be therefore held as frequently as possible and their results (numbers, fields) communicated to the Ministry of Education. In the absence of such survey data, the number of training places needed can be roughly estimated from the capital investment planned for industrial development. For instance, investment of about £3,000 in "big" (highly mechanized) industry usually opens one job at the vocational level, while in the case of small private industrial or servicing enterprises such a job may require only about £200 capital

investment. In this employment aspect lies the value of small private enterprises for developing countries.

From the numbers of trainees at the vocational level one can roughly estimate the needed number of technicians (one for every ten vocational trainees) and of graduate engineers (one for every five technicians). The above ratios are only a rough approximation and they do not apply to the sector of small private enterprises, since technicians are not needed to supervise small independent entrepreneurs. Also in the important construction industry, because of the way it is operated in Africa, far fewer technicans and craftsmen are needed than indicated by the above ratio. Using the above ratio indiscriminately for estimates of numbers of the needed technicians and vocational personnel from an estimated output of graduate engineers must therefore lead to unrealistically high figures (5).

In Craftsmen Training Schools, one instructor per maximum of 20 trainees and, in Technician Training Schools, one instructor per 10 trainees should be anticipated in planning. Under these circumstances the yearly current expenditure per one craftsman-trainee amounts, in English speaking territories to about £200, and that per one technician-trainee to about £500. Capital investment depends on fields of training and on presence or absence of boarding facilities, the order of magnitude being that of £1,000 per craftsman-trainee.

Content (Syllabi) of Specialized Training

The Present Situation. Most semi-skilled workers are trained "on the job" either in factories or with private "masters" and acquire only manual skills without much understanding of the underlying technology. Short upgrading courses are occasionally arranged for them by the Government agencies and industries, but this is far from being widely spread or systematic.

The training of craftsmen takes place in Government Technical Schools (Centres d'Apprentissage or Trade Training Centers, respectively) in Government agencies (public works, railways, etc.) and in organized training schemes operated by some big industrial firms. Most craftsmen aim at Certificat d'Aptitude Professionaelle (CAP) or at the CGLI (Intermediate) Craftsman Certificate, respectively, as their formal qualifications. Apprenticeship schemes are patterned on those of the respective ex-colonial countries and are, in general, of 5 years duration. The formal training syllabi, particularly in English speaking countries are often unrealistic. For example, a painter-decorator in Nigeria must acquire skill in wallpaper hanging, although wallpaper is not used in Nigeria: it mildews; a bricklayer in Nigeria must learn to lay complex variants of brick bonding and build several kinds of fireplaces, although none of these skills is in demand on Nigeria's labor market.

The training at the intermediate level is geared either to the Brevet d'Enseignement Industriel or to the CGLI Ordinary (seldom Higher) National Certificate and takes place in the Lycees (Colleges) Techniques or in Technical Institutes (Colleges), respectively. The need for trainees at this level is particularly acute in all African countries.

At the senior level there are, at present, only about 13,000 African graduates in the 27 countries south of the Sahara which obtained their independence (or are in the process of obtaining

it) since 1954 and which represent a joint population of over 140 million. The distribution of these graduates is very uneven, about 9,500 of them being concentrated in Ghana and Nigeria. African universities—hardly over a dozen of them in the territories referred to above, and most of them in an early stage of their development—follow in the content of their studies and in the structure of their degrees the pattern of their respective ex-colonial countries, with the exception of the University of Nigeria, at Nsukka, which attempts to set up a new pattern based rather on the American than on the British approach. In recent planning, special attention is given to training of scientists and engineers, but the facilities are still very scarce. The majority of the senior staff is composed of expatriates.

Suggested Measures. The training of semi-skilled workers depends largely on the type of skills required in the industries which are to employ them, and it is therefore difficult to organize it effectively in government-operated technical schools. The opinion is markedly growing that training at this level should be organized by the industries themselves, mainly on the "in plant" training principle, with the Governments giving whatever help they can particularly by introducing pre-vocational subjects (workshops, technical design, science) in general education which precedes specialized training (6). This new approach, besides being practically sound, relieves the Governments of considerable financial burden (the semiskilled workers forming the most numerous layer of trained manpower) of providing student places in technical schools and should be generally accepted. More detailed recommendations appear below.

The training of craftsmen should be the responsibility of the Governments, but the latter should make all efforts to encourage the big industries not only to continue their existing craftsmen training schemes but to expand them and set up new ones. This encouragement should take the form of financial incentives (by allowing industries to write off as current expenses the cost of equipment, of buildings and of instructors used for this purpose) and even by direct subsidies per industrial trainee. Even a subsidy of £150 a year per industrial craftsman trainee would, in effect, save the Governments the respective capital investment and a part of the current expenditures (7).

(a) All training syllabi at the sub-professional level should be revised and adapted to the actual labor market needs. New trades (skills) required by local conditions (agricultural products processing, rubber processing etc.) should be given a formal status and their programs of training should be designed by local professionals, technicians and craftsmen. While some changes of syllabi are possible even under the present dependence from Overseas Institutions (such as CGLI) and while the respective proposals should be formulated as soon as possible by committees composed of the respective technical instructors who have had experience in Africa and should be forwarded to the overseas institutions for their approval—the only permanent solution is the creation of Regional African Technical Examination Boards (Councils). Because of the lack of senior technical African personnel, these Boards would have to, for some time to come, rely to a great extent on the help of the existing Over-

seas Examination Boards and should discontinue this dependence only gradually, as their own personnel strength and experience increase. The West African Examination Council, with headquarters in Accra, is a good example of such a development in general education and should be imitated in specialized training at all sub-professional levels.

(b) All sub-professional syllabi should include the teaching of management, particularly that of small industrial and servicing enterprises.

Senior level training and research could get additional support by the creation of:

(a) *Institutes of Applied Science and Technology,* organized on a geographical basis (arid zone, tropical zone, coastal zone), should explore new fields of development in the fields of agricultural products (and their local processing), of sea and coastal resources, of industrial products particularly suited for Africa, of hydrological and geophysical research, etc. In cooperation with African universities and big industries, they should help train specialized senior research cadres. In the first stage of their activities, these institutes would have to be heavily supported by foreign financial assistance and draw upon the specialist resources of consortia of foreign universities, learned bodies (Academies of Science) and research institutions.

(b) *Educational Research Institutes (Councils),* preferably organized on a politically regional basis, should study the process of teaching and learning of African children, work out more suitable selection and testing procedures (in the latter field they should join the CCTA programs) and explore the best ways and means of fostering Anglo-French bilingualism, particularly among the school children. In Nigeria, such a Council is presently being organized at the federal level with the participation of all Regional Nigerian Ministries of Education and all Nigerian universities.

Both above named institutions should maintain close liaison and cooperation with the African Technical Examination Boards (Councils) so that the latter might profit from the new findings in designing special training syllabi that would be sound and realistic in their content as well as in their pedagogical approach.

Government-Supported On-the-Job Training

As indicated previously, the training of semi-skilled workers is, at present, only too often restricted to learning manual skills without any understanding of underlying technological principles. This is true particularly in the case of apprentices employed by private "masters" and by smaller industrial plants.

For these apprentices, the Government Technical Schools (Centres d'Apprentissage, Trade Training Centers) should operate special courses aiming at: (a) complementing manual skills by theoretical background (principles of the related technology, related technical drawing, related mathematics), (b) improving the apprentices' mastery of the official language of their country, particularly within the requirements of their trade, but also for the sake of encouraging general reading, (c) demonstrating the use of modern machinery which the apprentices might not have encountered in their own practice, and (d) teaching them elements of management of small private business enterprises.

Although for some time to come these courses will have to be operated in the evening, the African Governments, as soon as their Technical Training Schools have been sufficiently expanded, should press for the passing of legislation that would compel employers to release their apprentices during their legal working hours and on their usual pay, so that they might attend the "improvement courses" to the extent of 150 hours a year during at least 3 years.

For workers in small industries which are grouped far from the established technical schools, special demonstration mobile workshop vans, manned by competent instructors, should be used for conducting such courses by travelling from place to place. The vans and their instructors would be normally based in the nearest technical school; but special industrial development centers could be established for this purpose. Such Centers are now being built in Nigeria by the Agency for International Development under an agreement with the Government and will serve, at the same time, to improve techniques (and management methods) of existing small indigenous enterprises.

For craftsmen already well established in their trades and for the intermediate personnel, refresher courses, upgrading courses, and courses in new techniques should be operated in the government technical colleges in the evening.

For the Senior Staff, the Institutes of Applied Science and Technology should arrange special refresher and new techniques courses; also, from time to time, a symposium, arranged on a regional basis, should acquaint the senior scientific and technical staff of the Nigerian universities, the industrial firms and government corporations and agencies with the progress made in selected fields of the Institute's activities.

Training of Technical Instructors

It has been indicated several times previously, that an adequate pre-vocational and pre-technical preparation of the secondary school students plays an important role in increasing the efficiency and reducing the cost (time) of their further specialized training. This preparation includes teaching workshops (wood and metal), elements of technology (particularly that of metals) and technical design. To provide teachers of the above subjects, it is proposed to establish special Workshop Instructors' Training Centers. These would take entrants holding the GCE (Ord.), or the Brevet d'Enseignement du Premier Cycle who have had passes in sciences (physics and chemistry) and give them a 2-year (after GCE) or a 3-year (after B.E.P.C.) course in woodwork, metalwork, technical design and principles of technology, plus another year in pedagogics and methodology of technical instruction. These instructors should be treated as Grade 1 teachers, as far as their salaries are concerned. Nigeria has recently applied to the Scandinavian countries for support of such a teachers training center.

African technical instructors for trade training centers (Centres d'Apprentissage) are now being predominantly trained abroad. For the sound development of African technical education it is necessary that higher levels of craftsmen training (e.g. those corresponding to the CGLI Final and Full Certificate) be operated locally. It is this level that is required as qualification for technical instructors in craftsmen training schools. Extensive industrial practice should also be required of future technical instructors. The course for training of technical instructors in their trade should be of two years duration followed by an additional year of pedagogical training. Pedagogical training of all technical instructors should be mandatory. The instructors who have not yet acquired such training should take it in a technical teachers training college, of which one should be sufficient for each African country. If such a college is not available (or the country is too small to afford one) technical instructors should take a year's pedagogical course in an ordinary teacher training college or in a university-operated scheme for pedagogical training of technical instructors (University of Nigeria, at Nsukka, plans to operate such a scheme).

Lecturers in technical college (forming technicians) should also possess additional pedagogical training. Since such lecturers must be university graduates or otherwise have "professional standing" in the English speaking countries by being active members of respective professional institutions, their pedagogical training should be arranged in the universities as a 1-year course. The latter could be divided into a series of vacation courses with a cumulative effect leading to a diploma in Education.

The sound progress of both general and technical education in Africa seems hardly possible without introducing substantial changes in the content of the present syllabi (8). While the African Examination Councils (both general and technical) will have to decide, eventually, as to the acceptability of the new syllabi, the work on the improvement of the syllabi should be initiated as soon as possible, and should become a "grass roots" movement. To achieve this, African teachers should become acquainted with new developments abroad in course content. With such aim in mind the Government of Nigeria has organized, with the financial help of the Agency for International Development, vacation seminars (of 6 weeks duration), in which American lecturers, selected by the National Science Foundation in Washington, presented the content of new American-developed courses for secondary schools in physics, chemistry and mathematics to qualified Nigerian secondary school teachers, and received their suggestions as to the necessary amendments that would make these courses applicable for Africa.

Such courses should be held annually in all African countries, both French and English speaking. Out of them writing groups should emerge, composed of the Africans and expatriates, who would outline new text books and teachers' manuals for use in schools on an experimental basis. After sufficient experience has been gained, the Examination Councils should be approached for recognizing the new course content and allowing the schools to set up the corresponding examinations.

The National Science Foundation and Educational Services Incorporated have considerable experience in the domain of creating new course content, and should put their resources at the disposal of African countries. The courses, mostly to be operated during vacation, might be supported by the Agency for International Development, or the American foundations.

FOOTNOTE

[1] Craftsmen (skilled workers) are, by definition adopted by the Nigerian Employers Consultative Association, capable of performing their work without direct supervision; artisans (semi-skilled workers) require direct supervision by a craftsman.

REFERENCES

(1) Nigerian Employers Consultative Association: *Reports of Conferences on Training,* Lagos (21–26 Nov. 1960; and 9–13 Apr., 1962).

(2) Skapski, A. S.: *The Development of Technical Education and Its Relationship to the Educational System in Western Nigeria,* a report commissioned by the Government of Western Nigeria (May 1962).

(3) *Ibid.*

(4) Skapski, A. S., and B. Somade: *A demonstration comprehensive school for Western Nigeria,* West African Journal of Education, V. 6, No. 2, 1962.

(5) See e.g. W. L. Cottier and F. Caunce: *Report on the Development of Technical and Commercial Education in the Federation of Nigeria,* a report commissioned by the Federal Government of Nigeria (October 1961).

(6) Nigerian Employers Consultative Association: op. cit.

(7) Skapski, A. S.: op. cit.

(8) Zacharias, J. L., and S. White: The Requirements of Major Curriculum Revision, a paper submitted to the U.N. Conference on Application of Science and Technology for Less Developed Countries (Session K).

Occupational Health, the Development of a New Public Health Discipline in Peru

FREDERICK J. VINTINNER
Chief, Health Adviser, Latin American Bureau, Agency for International Development, Washington, D.C.

RAMON VALLENAS
Director, Institute of Occupational Health, Lima, Peru

A. S. LANDRY
Occupational Health Adviser, U.S. Agency for International Development, Bolivia

Peru, the magnet of gold which attracted the "conquistadores," had, according to Prescott (1), the most extensively organized "social polity" that existed in the pre-Colombian world of South America. Each individual occupied an assigned niche in this society according to the caste into which he had been born and no one suffered from want due to illness and/or incapacity resulting from old age or any other cause.

Actually, an unrecognized interest in occupational health existed at that time since the Incan government regulations "were so discreetly arranged that the most wearing and unwholesome labors, as those of the mines, occasioned no detriment to the health of the laborer; a striking contrast to his subsequent condition under Spanish rule (2).

Nevertheless, there must have been some degree of exposure to quartz among the artisans of ancient Peru, especially among those who spent their lives carving the prolific stone idols or the fabulous granite citadels of Macchu Picchu and Sacsahuaman. Such a premise cannot be proven since these people possessed no written language, and furthermore, the effects of silicosis cannot be depicted, as were so vividly the public health scourges of syphilis and smallpox (3), on the amazing "huacos." The latter are fascinating ceramic sherds, deposited with mummified remains in all epochs of Peruvian pre-history, which serve as documentary evidence of prevailing social customs, religious beliefs, and medical or other practices.

However, it may well be that the as yet undeciphered "quipus" (or Peruvian knotted-string mnemonic system) could hold the key to this missing information, but since the "industrial" processes involved were hand operations, the quantitative aspect of silicosis, for example, cannot be significant as was the case in 1940.

At that time the ever-increasing use of mechanization for the mining of strategic minerals in the presence of quartz and the associated smelting of metals with emphasis on lead resulted in a high incidence of related occupational diseases. The consequences were especially critical since the mining and smelting operations were effected at high altitude, i.e., at heights ranging from 10,000 to 14,000 feet above sea level.

A direct corollary of the situation mentioned above is a unique, practically non-migratory and highly irreplaceable pool of available miners—people who are born, live, and die in one community. These miners have barrel chests, 6-liter or more lung capacities, and 50 percent greater erythrocyte concentration in their blood; or in other words, they are born with a high altitude adaptation for hard physical work. If this group of laborers is decimated by occupational diseases, it becomes virtually impossible to replace them, and further, a psychological pattern develops whereby the offspring of an incapacitated miner is discouraged from following the father's trade or occupation.

Farsighted Peruvian leaders, being desirous of avoiding such a dilemma and concerned with the humanitarian aspects of the problem, had enacted advanced legislation related to occupational risks and issued a "supreme governmental decree" in 1940 which created the National Department of Industrial Hygiene. The general objective was to eliminate occupational diseases but with specific emphasis to be given to the reduction of "pneumoconiosis" among the miners of Peru. It was expected that these actions would have a direct impact on the basic economy of this country and would result in increased productivity decreased compensation costs, and reduced labor turnover. This should have resulted in a general improvement of the political stability and social development of the Peruvian laboring class.

However, inadequate financial and technical resources, and lack of experience in coordinating diverse scientific activities, all necessary to effect the proper evaluation, control, and elimination of the existing occupational health hazards, inhibited fulfillment of these expectations.

The magnitude of the latter was evaluated by Bloomfield in 1947 (4). This study demonstrated that of the 2,475,339 persons gainfully employed in Peru, about a half-million were engaged in industries known to present major health hazards. These hazards were of various nature and in the mines included exposures to silica dust, sulfur dioxide, heat, high humidity, and fumes from blasting powder. Mechanical ventilation was virtually nonexistent and natural ventilation was insufficient to cope with the dust generated by dry drilling—or the handling of dry minerals in the milling operations. At the time of the study, no reliable, nationwide health statistics existed. Therefore, the true incidence of silicosis could not be established, but an educated "guesstimate" placed the figure in the vicinity of 20 percent—a truly appalling picture.

The legislation mentioned above included compulsory sickness insurance and workmen's compensation for occupational diseases but the Peruvian Congress did not establish any legislation for the prevention of industrial diseases until March 12, 1947. At that time, Public Law 10833 was enacted. This authorized the creation of a Department of Industrial Hygiene in the Ministry of Public Health and Social Welfare with the following responsibilities: (a) periodic pre-employment and follow-up examinations of a clinical and radiographic nature for miners; (b) the inspection of mines and related processing plants on a periodic basis for dust control purposes involving the sampling and analysis of dusts in suspension, smoke, gases, acids, and other noxious substances; (c) the design of ventilating systems for mines and working places, as well as the carrying out of investigations to determine the effectiveness of the installation for control; and (d) the promotion of health education among the administrative and labor staff of mining companies to demonstrate the usefulness of preventative measures.

As is evident from the foregoing bill of particulars, the emphasis was oriented towards the silicosis problem, and rightfully so in view of the estimated incidence for this disease. However, the scope of the operation was limited, in the original law, to six major political departments, namely: Huanuco, Huancavelica, Ica, Junin, Lima, and Pasco, which contained the principal mining areas. The Department of Industrial Hygiene was supported financially by a levy of 1.8 percent on the payrolls of companies employing more than 30 workers in the dusty trades, located in the areas mentioned. In other words, the tax applied to companies, "which perform work or make use of mineral substances and soils, rocks, clays, sands, gravel, cements, as well as industrial processes related to the preparation and use of the above substances."

The organization of the new Department of Industrial Hygiene was entrusted, at the request of the then Minister of Health and Social Welfare, to the Institute of Inter-American Affairs. The latter, which was an agency of the U.S. Government, was at that time carrying out technical programs in various Latin American countries in cooperation with the host government. The objective of these cooperative programs was to develop jointly certain needed technical and administrative services to train national personnel and to show how such services could be incorporated into the regular governmental operation as a continuing activity. The cooperative organizations in the host countries were known as "servicios," and were utilized in various sectors including health, education, and agriculture.

In health, SCISP, or the Servicio Cooperativo Inter-Americano de Salud Publica (Inter-American Cooperative Public Health Service) in Peru was the entity that was charged with the responsibility for organizing and administering the recently authorized industrial hygiene service. Such action had a two-fold objective: a) to utilize the administrative, legal, and technical know-how of an existing organization in the interest of rapid action and efficiency; and, perhaps even more importantly at that time, b) to take advantage of the non-political nature of the organization which would facilitate the selection of personnel on a strictly merit basis as determined by competitive examinations.

As a result of the Bloomfield report previously mentioned, two consultants in industrial hygiene were assigned in 1948 by the Institute of Inter-American Affairs to the U.S. Field Mission in Peru. One was an engineer who was responsible for the overall program development, and the other was the junior author of this paper, whose work was related to the chemical phase of the program. The activity in the latter sphere is described in detail in a companion paper by Landry and Ochoa (5).

The initial action was to procure essential facilities and equipment and to train Peruvian personnel by the in-service training technique. The latter action was crucial because no personnel experienced in coordinated public health activities were available. Industrial hygiene is essentially a team-work operation which involves the closest cooperation and collaboration of members from various specialized disciplines in the field of public health. Basically, the group includes physicians, engineers, and chemists supported by other technical personnel, among whom are nurses, statisticians, sanitary engineers, and laboratory technicians—all of whom must have had some training in the general field of public health, since the objective of the unit is to effect the correct evaluation and eventual control or reduction of any occupational hazards wherever they exist.

In 1948, occupational health was a virgin field of endeavor in Peru (and in the remainder of Latin America, for that matter). Consequently, great effort was invested in attracting competent, professionally trained or oriented personnel into this new discipline.

Despite the fact that many capable people were unwilling to risk their future in a relatively unknown career in industrial hygiene, recruitment was successful and early in 1949 sufficient staff and equipment were available to start the first field study in a Peruvian mine.

Initially, the Department was organized as shown in the organogram depicted in figure I. The salient features are self-evident but two facets deserve further mention, namely the Economic Control Board and the Compensation Section.

The former was formed from functionaries of the executive power and from representatives of the industries contributing to the support of the program. The Board consisted, therefore, of the Director General of the Ministry of Labor, the Director General of the Ministry of Public Health and Social Welfare, a member of the National Mining Society, a member of the society representing the small mines, a representative from the Institute of Andean Biology, and the Director of the Department of Industrial Hygiene. This group met on an annual basis to approve the proposed budget and review the projected industrial hygiene program. The Board was a strong stabilizing factor in the development of the Department. This was true because all mining, economic, and political areas related to the industrial hygiene service were represented on the Board, which guided the overall policy of the Department.

The Compensation Section encountered some difficulties at the onset. Decisions and findings of the experienced diagnosticians attached by the Department of Industrial Hygiene were disputed by physicians less experienced and competent in this relatively new area of health activity. However, by a diplomatic approach and patience, the differences were ironed out and the physicians of the Department were soon recognized by the local courts as the only qualified personnel in the aspect of medical examinations for basing adjudications to workers claiming compensation for an occupational disease.

Progress since 1948 has been steady, if not spectacular; the organization has expanded considerably as may be observed from figure II. Law 10833 was amended to apply to all departments in the country. In 1957, the Department was changed to the Institute of Occupational Health. The Institute is organized along functional lines—because any activity depending on a variety of professional personnel (as is especially true of industrial hygiene or, more broadly speaking, occupational health) operates more efficiently in this way. In other words, the function is more important than a given professional contribution. Further, this approach has proven to be very applicable in Peru as the following material will demonstrate.

The Worker's Health Division is headed by a physician as are the three subdivisions, including compensation, which in 1961 examined 789 workers claiming indemnization for occupational diseases, principally silicosis.

The Environmental Health Division has a chemical engineer as its chief, as is also the case for the respective subdivisions. A resume indicating the scope of the operation by one of the latter, wherein 114 scattered field evaluation studies were carried out between 1949–1960, shows that the number of workers examined during the period mentioned reached about 30,000.

At present, the Institute of Occupational Health has a staff of 95 persons. Thirty-six employees are professionally trained and have received post-graduate training in the United States. The staff includes 19 full-time physicians, plus three part-time Peruvian medical consultants—one in dermatology, one in occupational allergy, and the other in opthalmology. There are nine engineers (including a sanitary engineer), seven chemists, one nurse, a pharmacist employed in the clinical laboratory, an anthropologist, two statisticians, and one part-time attorney. The balance is composed of an administrator, laboratory and field aids, administrative assistants, secretaries, chauffeurs, and janitors.

The Institute is financed entirely from the income derived from Tax Law No. 10833 (paid by various mines in 11 political departments.) In 1961 the income amounted to 7.5 million Soles or approximately U.S. $2.5 million. Of this amount approximately 75 percent was spent for salaries. This included the maintenance of a modern two-story building especially designed for the program, as well as the upkeep of the very latest instrumentation. Among the latter are: five high amperage X-ray apparatus for fluoroscopic chest examinations and/or taking large size chest X-ray films, a treadmill and supporting equipment, infra-red and other spectrophotometers, recording polarographs, gas-vapor chromatograph, automatic balances, and other pertinent laboratory equipment. The observation has been made by authorities in the field that there are very few occupational health programs in the United States and in Europe which have as good or complete facilities as those utilized by the Institute of Occupational Health in Peru.

Similarly, the three regional offices are well equipped and staffed to the extent that they can operate autonomously with a minimum of supervision from the central office in Lima. An index to their stage of development may be obtained from table 1, wherein it is evident that the Arequipa field station effected 16 percent of the total number of chemical analyses made during 1961, and the Trujillo or northern regional office made 58 percent of the diagnostic laboratory analyses.

However, insofar as achievements are concerned, the major accomplishment is the reduction in the incidence of silicosis. This, we feel, can be attributed in a large measure to the work of the Institute of Occupational Health. The

TABLE 1. *Activities of the Institute of Occupational Health during 1961*

Description of work studies, plant visits, reports	Lima	Trujillo	LaOroya	Arequipa	Total
Field studies	8	6	9	7	30
Periodic control studies	5	3	6	1	15
Environmental evaluation	1			1	2
Preliminary plant visits	23	13	1	187	224
Inspection and control visits	9	21		18	48
Reports prepared	79	50	13	19	161
Field study physical examinations	794	371	2, 270	1, 462	4, 897
Periodic control physical examinations	369	1, 883	1, 215	67	3, 780
Claimants examined for compensation	593	74	55	67	789
Preemployment and control examinations	265	7	11	130	413
Tuberculosis case finding		10, 262	974	70	11, 306
Electrocardiograms	54				54
Laboratory work physiopathology examinations	991				991
Diagnostic laboratory tests	9, 507	25, 321	3, 414	5, 681	43, 923
Environmental health evaluations samples collected	518	210		114	242
Measurements in field	1, 845	162		62	2, 069
Analyses	1, 143	189		114	1, 446
Determination by instrumentation	117	30		24	171
Chemical analyses	1, 903			363	2, 266
Atmospheric samples	89			38	127
Biological samples	701			110	811
Others	1, 113			215	1, 328

trend is illustrated in that the average dropped from 9.2 to 5.9 percent in six years. Progress, although necessarily slow since the cooperation of the mining companies is involved, has been steady but much remains to be done—as is also evident from the drawing mentioned. The 4 percent incidence of silicosis rate is based on 80 mine studies, involving 23,480 workers. The average age of the latter without silicosis was 29.5 years as compared to 38.3 years for those with this occupational disease. This represents a net productive life span for an average miner of 8.8 years with the obvious economic implication for the industrial growth of Peru.

A function of importance is the medical examination of claimants for the adjudication of cases related to compensation for disability due to occupational diseases. Such physical examinations are very comprehensive and include electrocardiograms, lung function (involving the use of a treadmill), and basic metabolism measurements if required. The results obtained are referred to the courts for final action—with possible appellation to a Board of Experts on Pneumoconiosis, if a dispute should develop. From table 1, it may be noted that 789 miners were examined in 1961, of whom 593 were processed in Lima.

As mentioned in the Landry-Ochoa companion paper, the Institute of Occupational Health of Peru and its predecessor, the Department of Industrial Hygiene, has served since 1952 as a training center for 22 Latin Americans. Although the major effort was in the field of chemistry, other disciplines were also represented. In 1961 alone, six international trainees were processed: two Chileans, one Venezuelan, two Bolivians, and one Brazilian doctor.

The scope of the present operation may be deduced from the fact that in 1961, the Institute personnel made 27 field studies. Of these, 16 were in new industrial centers, whereas 11 were re-evaluations of previously studied locales. This involved the examination of 7,170 workers, 4,528 field measurements, 2,266 atmospheric and biological samples, 991 pulmonary physiopathological examinations and 43,923 diagnostic laboratory tests—an increase of 73 percent over the previous year's work.

The trend toward "total health" for the workers and their families is striking. In the early years of the program, or between 1949-1952, the emphasis was directed exclusively to mine studies (as stipulated implicitly by Law No. 10388) followed by a shift toward industries beginning in 1954. The attention to the families began in earnest during 1957 with the initiation of mass chest X-ray programs for the detection of tuberculosis among the families, immunizations against the common communicable diseases, environmental sanitation, health education and other public health programs in mining and industrial communities. The implication of these activities is greater political, social, and economic stability within the industrial milieu.

As mentioned previously, the law was and continues to be very explicit insofar as the orientation of the industrial hygiene program is concerned, i.e., to improve mining conditions for the workers by eliminating occupational health hazards. Simultaneously, the mining industry has borne the brunt of the tax load. However, with the development, at an astronomical rate, of new compounds, and advanced technical processes for agriculture, and industry—as well as new techniques in the field of ionizing radiations, it is evident that the field of activity will of necessity have to be expanded considerably. As of 1961, such action was initiated by the Institute of Occupational Health. The mining industry still receives the bulk of the attention and benefits. Of the 3,795,500 gainfully employed persons in Peru during 1961, 2,421,000 were in agriculture, 749,000 in manufacturing, and 524,500 in diverse industries. Future activities will obviously have to be along lines that are cognizant of the industrial population trend but legislative modification of the present law is also a must—to distribute the taxation load more equitably.

In conclusion, the impact of technical assistance to a program in an emerging nation, such as was the case of Peru in 1948, is now distinctly evident. This action was possible because of adequate financial self-help, plus a receptive attitude on the part of Peruvian authorities in respect to the implementation of the necessary technical innovations proposed by U.S. personnel. Consequently, a highly developed cadre of professional personnel in a variety of health disciplines is now operating an Institute that is recognized as extremely competent, forward thinking, and constantly expanding.

The need to emulate this success in neighboring Latin American countries is well recognized—and, in one instance, a similar project is underway.

REFERENCES

(1) Prescott, W. H., *The Conquest of Peru*, p. 61, Mentor.

(2) *Ibid*, p. 64.

(3) Doering, *Ancient Arts of Peru*.

(4) Bloomfield, J. J., *Industrial Hygiene Problems in Peru*, IIAA, Washington, D.C. (1947).

(5) Landry, A. S. and Romulo, O. *The Development of Latin American Specialists in the Chemistry of Occupational Health*. In press.

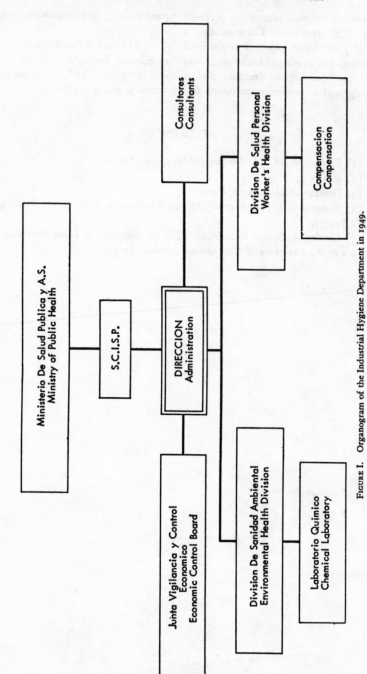

FIGURE I. Organogram of the Industrial Hygiene Department in 1949.

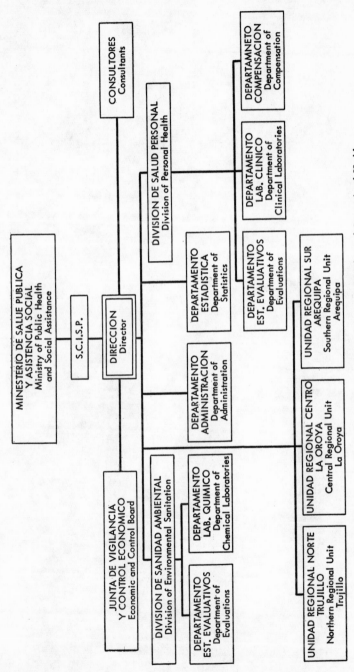

FIGURE II. Functional organizational pattern of the present Institute of Occupational Health.

PART THREE

The Challenge in Developing Natural Resources

MANY underdeveloped countries have natural resources that exist only as potential. Unlike areas where resources are abundant and their exploitation uncomplicated, those seeking to develop regions of sparse or inadequate resources must apply ingenuity and resourcefulness. This part provides a representative group of essays covering resource development in water and minerals and in agriculture, including soil, plant, forest, and fishery resources in the poorer countries.

Todd and Greenman each stress that whether the underdeveloped country is wet or dry, locating and charging of ground water is the key to conservation and to long-range economic progress. Greenman dramatizes the danger by pointing out that, through improper use of water sources, 50,000 acres are withdrawn annually from production in West Pakistan.

Mineral development in backward areas also has great potential. Kelley in his article tells how the government may help to promote maximum use of mining resources, while Khan and Reinemund provide a specific country case of how a cooperative mineral program can diminish heavy reliance upon mineral imports.

In view of the growing and, in some cases, urgent food demands in the underdeveloped world, the techniques of modern science and technology should be utilized fully in irrigated farming, in·shifting of factor proportions into more effective combinations, and in adapting plant and animal breeds to specific environments. In the second section of this part, Hill and Mosher tell why they believe farm research must be geared closely to the specific job and place.

Toward a more efficient use of the factors in backward areas, Johnson and Christensen come up with a scheme for overcoming resistance to change, which they label "K I M": knowledge, incentives, means.

Hagan describes a process, vividly demonstrated in the Middle East, of converting the ancient art of irrigation into a modern science, without costly imports or complicated methods, thereby producing sharp advances in farm output.

Similarly, modern but simple scientific applications to plant and animal breeding can produce startling increases in product yield. The "net merit" system of assigning points to desired breeding criteria, as proposed by Lush and Alba, is particularly interesting.

The history of numerous regions of the world attests to the importance of forestry, as stressed by Gill in the preservation of soils and long-range farm potential.

Finally, Butler, Allen, and Alverson remind us that the unlimited food potential of the oceans should not and cannot be left untapped. Here again, the underdeveloped countries can, without elaborate preliminaries, launch certain fundamental uplift programs.

Advances in Techniques of Ground Water Resources Development

DAVID K. TODD

Professor of Civil Engineering, University of California, Berkeley, California

Introduction

Ground water represents a major water supply source throughout the world. Historically the use of shallow dug wells for domestic and irrigation supplies dates from ancient times. Within recent decades, however, technological advances have enabled ground water at great depths to be utilized. These advances include new methods for investigating ground water, new drilling techniques for water-well construction, and new pumps for lifting water (1). Thus, larger and more dependable water supplies are now available in arid and semi-arid parts of the world.

There are several advantages to development of ground water resources. Ground water reservoirs are available without cost and provide a natural distribution system. Further, ground waters are free from contamination, are not subject to evapotranspiration losses, and possess nearly uniform temperatures. Underground water storage, therefore, with proper development and management can provide efficient and economic water supplies (2).

The purpose of this paper is to describe a few of the recent techniques for developing and managing ground water resources. Emphasis will be placed upon practical applications and examples from field experiences. References are included to facilitate more detailed study of specific topics.

Ground Water Basin Management

The concept of ground water basin management (3) presupposes that a ground water reservoir will be controlled in terms of inputs and outputs of water. First, this implies some basin-wide type of control over pumping in order to insure that extraction of ground water from the basin approximates the average annual replenishment to the basin. Second, control must be exercised over the areal pattern of extraction or recharge. And finally, legal control is involved in that prescribed water rights of users are established. In the past, most ground water basin management has been on a trial-and-error basis. Thus, ground water levels were depressed by excessive pumping, then reduced in order to allow them to rise, and finally depressed again by subsequent pumping. Unfortunately, ground water basins are three-dimensional and nonhomogeneous. It is often difficult to ascertain on an annual basis the amount of water that can be removed or recharged simply by observation of ground water level. A ground water reservoir is entirely analogous to a surface water reservoir; it is useless if the level is maintained at the top of the dam at all times. On the other hand, if this water is stored and released so that fluctuations in water levels occur on an annual basis, maximum benefits in terms of water supply, power, flood control, and recreational benefits can be achieved simultaneously. The same applies to ground water reservoirs. These must be pumped during periods of water need and then recharged during periods when needs are less and additional supplies are available from other sources.

Ideally, ground water reservoirs should be managed in conjunction with surface water supplies. The interrelation is often referred to as conjunctive use. Essentially, conjunctive use means that ground water reservoirs will be pumped during periods when surface water supplies are limited. At other times, when additional surface water supplies are available, ground water reservoirs will be pumped less or not at all and will be recharged both naturally and artificially. This combined water supply source system usually provides a larger, firmer and more economic water supply than would be available from either source individually. Operationally, conjunctive use requires that the surface and ground water resources be properly managed in order to have adequate water supplies at all times. It must also be recognized that ground water levels will fluctuate both seasonally and over a period of years. For example, during an extended drought running for a period of several years, surface water supplies would be limited so that ground water pumping would be at a maximum. Following this, however, in a period of several wet years, ground water levels will have an opportunity to recover.

An important new tool for analysis of ground water basin management is the electronic analog computer. This instrument has recently been put to work in studies of large, complex, ground water basins. Development and application of techniques suggested by this computer can materially assist water resource managers in preventing ground water basin exhaustion and in providing for the most beneficial pattern of extraction of ground water.

An excellent example of the application of the analog computer is the study of ground water conditions in Southern California. Recent work by the California Department of Water Resources has indicated that this tool is a valuable means for preparing ground water basin operational programs for future decades (4). Studies have been carried out on basins which have been subject to withdrawals of water exceeding combined natural and artificial replenishment. As a result, a state of overdraft now exists.

Use of an analog computer for ground water studies is based upon the fact that laws governing the flow of electricity are similar to those for the flow of ground water. This analogy becomes the basis, therefore, for solving complex mathematical equations involved in evaluating the dynamics of a ground water basin flow system. The physical characteristics of a ground water basin can be represented by various electronic components, making the computer a basin model. For example, the permeability of an aquifer is analogous to the reciprocal of the resistance, the specific yield or storage coefficient of the basin is analogous to the capacitance, and the difference in hydraulic head of ground water levels is analogous to the voltage drop in an electrical current.

The general continuity equation of ground water flow, namely that inflow minus outflow equals change in storage, and Darcy's law governing ground water flow are the basic relations involved. Darcy's law is similar to Ohm's law governing the flow of electricity. Problems of ground water storage and movement are solved by measuring quantities on a model of the ground water basin constructed of electronic components. Two types of computers are available for this purpose. The passive element analog computer is the simplest one. It involves a network of resistors representing the hydraulic conductivity and capacitors representing the storage coefficient. The other type, the active element computer, replaces the simple components with electronic amplifiers which react in essentially the same manner but are readily controllable, very stable, and highly accurate. Each type of computer requires an array of supplemental equipment of a complex nature to provide input and initial operating conditions and to measure outputs.

The active-element computer was selected for studies of the Coastal Plain of Los Angeles County by the California Department of Water Resources. Basic data necessary as inputs to the computer included boundaries of the ground water basin, geologic structures within the ground water basin that affect ground water movement, and physical characteristics such as hydraulic conductivities and storage coefficients. The Coastal Plain of Los Angeles County has an area of about 480 square miles. Study of some 5 thousand drillers' logs of water and oil wells throughout the area served as the

basis for delineating the aquifers. All water-bearing sediments were assigned values of specific yield and hydraulic conductivity. As a simplification it was necessary to assume that neither specific yields nor hydraulic conductivities changed with time or with ground level fluctuations. With this given information the study area was divided into 82 unit areas, each represented by a control node point, or junction point, in the analog model. Locations of nodes were based on geologic replenishment, extraction, hydraulic conductivity, specific yield, and ground water level data. Concentrations of nodes were in areas of rapid change in physical conditions in order to more accurately predict these changes. The general equation of ground water movement was then solved by the electrical interconnection of these nodes and by the computer formulated on this plan to solve the 82 simultaneous differential equations with changing conditions of inflow and outflow.

Historical data on replenishment of and extraction from the aquifers in the basin were applied to the analog model to determine whether the computer could actually represent the physical conditions of the aquifers and to measure the ground water flow throughout the study area. For these tests, data for an 11-year period were readily available and were given as inputs to the computer. Initial elevations of ground water levels were set on the computer using function generators to vary the current flow for net extraction at each node point in the analog model. The variation in voltage, or ground water level, with time was read from the model. This variation was compared with historical fluctuations. After some adjustment of the physical factors in specific areas, a representative model was obtained, that is, one that demonstrated water level changes throughout the basin similar to historical changes.

After the test work on the analog model it was then applied to study problems of managing the ground water basin under future conditions. Changes could be made in rates and locations of extraction and replenishment. Output data from the model indicated ground water level elevation changes with time due to these input variations. This information indicated areas in which extractions should be limited, maximum rates of artificial recharge, and where recharge should be accomplished. The computer also produced a variety of useful information. It was found, for example, that reasonable amounts of recharge in the upper areas of the Coastal Plain would not be effective in halting sea water intrusion at the coast 22 miles away. It was also ascertained that, because of the physical characteristics of the basin, an adjustment period after any change in input or output would require more than 100 years before an equilibrium condition would be reached. The information derived from the model served as a basis for preparation of alternative plans of operation which can be coordinated with available imported supplemental sources of water to reach optimum utilization of the resources of this basin. Thus, conjunctive use of local ground water sources and imported surface water supplies can only be accomplished in an optimum manner if this basin is operated under a planned management scheme. The analog computer not only assisted in these investigations but also will aid in making future

management decisions required for operation of the basin.

Current developments in the upper portion of the Indus River Basin in West Pakistan provide a good illustration of conjunctive use of surface and ground water sources. Large irrigation areas have been developed by a network of canals over the past 75 years. Seepage from these canals, however, has raised the ground water level from a distance of roughly 75 feet below ground surface up to an average of less than 10 feet below ground surface. As a result, at the present time, a large portion of the area is subject to waterlogging and salinization. Areas available for agricultural production are being decreased by the detrimental influences at a rate of approximately 100 thousand acres per year. In order to alleviate the situation it has been proposed to construct a grid of tube wells over the irrigated lands. The soil is quite permeable and will yield large quantities of water to wells approximately 200 feet deep. The pumped water will be discharged into existing irrigation canals to supplement the water available for irrigated agriculture. The tube wells, therefore, will serve a double purpose. First, they will assist in lowering the water table by the removal of excessive water in the irrigated areas. Second, these wells will provide additional water for irrigated land so that a downward movement of water through the root zone can be established to leach accumulated salts. The magnitude of pumping can be varied depending upon local conditions, especially rainfall and existing ground water levels. Initially, large ground water pumping is desirable to accelerate the lowering of the high water table. After the water table has fallen from 10 to 20 feet, however, there is no need to lower the water table from the standpoint of its impairment upon agricultural production. Any subsequent lowering would increase the cost of pumping; therefore, the magnitude of pumping should be restricted so that the ground water level will fluctuate seasonally and secularly in a range governed by the recharge to ground water. Ultimately, this recirculation system will cause an increase in salt content in the ground water. However, as the salt content tends to build up, increasing amounts of water can be pumped to waste in the rivers and discharged into the ocean. In this manner the system can be operated for an indefinite period without causing high salinity which would endanger irrigated agriculture.

Aerial Photographs

As the occurrence of ground water is related to terrain characteristics, proper interpretation of aerial photographs is often a valuable means of identifying ground water conditions. Vegetation, land form and use, drainage patterns, erosion, color, and special ground features are apparent on air photographs and indicate subsurface conditions. From studies of air-photo mosaic maps and of stereoscopic photo pairs, drainage and soil maps can be prepared.

A recent study in Indiana (5) indicated that air-photo interpretation could be employed to develop a ground water prediction map. An area was divided into zones of good, fair, and poor water yield based upon air-photo analysis. The classification indicated areas yielding more than 200 gallons per minute as good ground water areas, areas yielding 50 to 200 gallons per minute

as fair ground water areas, and those yielding less than 50 gallons per minute as poor areas. Examination of well data subsequently confirmed the analysis.

The preparation of hydrogeologic maps is also greatly facilitated from aerial photographs. The delineation of the most and least promising areas for ground water supplies can be indicated on such maps. These maps aid in selecting test drilling sites, in reducing costs of ground water investigations, and in assisting in locating industrial plants requiring large ground water supplies.

The art of air-photo interpretation has progressed to such a point that investigations of vegetation are often useful indicators of ground water. It is possible, under certain conditions, to determine from air photos alone where water may be obtained in arid and semi-arid regions, the minimum amount that is perennially available, and whether the water is of good chemical quality. Studies by Mann (6) in the Southern California desert showed that the interpretation is based on the premise that water of good quality forced to the surface in dry regions will have been preempted by phreatophytes and that the amount of water available will govern the size of the vegetated area. A familiarity with the general region and the local plant types may be necessary to interpret with maximum effectiveness. Although such hydrobotanic investigations need subsequent field investigation, it is apparent that this rapid means for identifying potential ground water sources can represent a vast savings where new water supplies are needed in large relatively undeveloped areas.

Many times the geologic conditions in a particular area, as well as the associated hydrobotanic conditions, will reveal ground water situations which can be adequately analyzed from aerial photographs alone. For example, a fault acting as a conduit will show springs where it intersects the axes of the valley. A small spring produces a spot of phreatophytes, whereas a larger spring will show a line of phreatophytes extending downstream. A fault acting as a barrier is shown by a patch of phreatophytes sharply limited by the fault on the downslope side and often a strip of dense vegetation marking the overflow. Areas of constriction in dry alluvial channels are often marked by large quantities of rising water. In closed desert basins, alluvial fans often discharge large quantities of water. Phreatophytes arranged like the spokes of a wheel around the base of an alluvial fan may indicate where ground water is rising to the surface. Indications of water quality depend upon correlations between water salinity and plant species. Although some work has been done in this field, further investigations are needed to define these relations before specific statements can be made about ground water salinity from aerial photographs alone.

Sea Water Intrusion

A common problem in ground water formations located near the coast is that of sea water intrusion. This may be defined as an increase in salinity of ground water over that normally occurring at a given location in an aquifer. It is usually the result of acts of man, primarily from concentrated extractions of ground water in localized areas. The problem is well-known along the coasts of the United States; in particular it has affected the coast lines of Long Island, Florida, Texas, and California (7). Intrusion is also known along the coasts of Europe, Israel, and Japan.

In order to control sea-water intrusion, five methods have been suggested: (a) Reduction and/or rearrangement of pattern of pumping draft, (b) Direct recharge, (c) Development of the pumping trough adjacent to the coast, (d) Maintenance of a pressure ridge above sea level along the coast, and (e) Construction of artificial subsurface barriers. Although reduction of pumping is an obvious method of control, in many locations legal restrictions and property rights prohibit government agencies from regulating pumping from privately-owned wells. Therefore, more costly procedures are necessary involving one or more of the other methods in order to control intrusion.

In recent years a comprehensive field test of the pressure ridge method has been conducted in Los Angeles County, California (8). The pressure ridge method involves building up a fresh water pressure ridge adjacent to the coast by means of a line of recharge wells. The piezometric surface along the ridge is raised sufficiently high to repel sea water, causing the recharged water to flow both seaward and landward. By proper control of the height of the ridge, the amount of recharge water wasted to the ocean can be minimized. The ridge consists of a series of peaks at each well with saddles in between. The ridge should be located inland from the saline front to avoid advancing sea water further inland. This method has the advantage of not restricting the usual ground water storage capacity but has the disadvantages of high initial and operating costs and the need for supplemental water.

In the Los Angeles test a confined aquifer was selected for study that had been badly degraded by sea water. A line of recharge wells was located parallel to and about 2,000 feet inland from the ocean. The piezometric surface along the well line was 6 to 12 feet below sea level and the ground water contained 16,000 ppm chloride. Nine gravel-packed recharge wells were constructed at intervals of 500 feet to form a line 4,000 feet long. Numerous small observation wells were also drilled in the vicinity. Injection into the recharge wells with treated fresh water was begun in 1953. Immediately after recharge had begun, the ridge pressure began to develop and at the present time the ridge is still successfully being operated and maintained. The combined recharge rate for the eight wells is about 5 cfs. The amount of water flowing toward the ocean is approximately 5 percent of the total recharge water, while the remaining 95 percent flows landward for subsequent replenishment to the ground water basin. Chlorination of the recharge water has been found necessary to prevent clogging of the wells by bacterial slime. Chloride content of ground water near the recharge well line dropped rapidly to that of the fresh water content after the injection had become effective.

This investigation demonstrated the technical feasibility of maintaining a recharge line parallel to the coast for control of sea water intrusion. Subsequently economic justification of the barrier for protecting the entire ground water basin indicated that the safe yield of the basin was of such importance that the line was worth extending in both directions in order to protect the entire coastal plain of Los Angeles County. At the present time the recharge well-line is being extended and additional studies are underway for new recharge lines in nearby areas.

Artificial Recharge

Artificial recharge may be defined as the increasing of natural infiltration of precipitation or surface water into underground formations by some method of construction, by spreading of water, or by artificially changing natural conditions. The technique is well known in the United States and in Europe(9). In recent years considerable attention has been focused upon the importance of increasing rates of artificial recharge in order to provide larger ground water supplies and also as a means of management of ground water basins.

Water may be recharged underground by a variety of methods. The surface methods come under the general heading of water spreading. Water spreading may be classified as flooding, basin, ditch or furrow, natural channel, and irrigation types. In the flooding method, water is allowed to spread evenly over large, flat areas. The thin sheet of water spreads at a minimum velocity without disturbing vegetation and soil. Although the cost is minimal for this method of artificial recharge, control of the water is difficult and maximum efficiencies are difficult to obtain. More common is the basin method in which water is released into shallow basins formed by excavation or construction of dikes or small dams. Horizontal dimensions are relatively large with depths being of only a few feet. Typically, systems of basins are fed from a nearby surface-water source, allowing one basin to discharge into an adjacent lower basin after it becomes full. The basin configuration can be suited to the local topography so that a system involving many basins can be constructed near flat flood plain areas bordering surface water supplies. From the lowest basin, excess water is returned to the stream channel. In California, where recharge artificially has been practiced to the maximum extent in the United States, basins have been constructed in abandoned stream channels. Usually basins will permit water contact with 75 percent to 80 percent of the gross area involved. This method, because of its high efficiency and easy maintenance, represents the favored method of artificial recharge by spreading. The ditch or furrow method consists of construction of flat ditches paralleling the land contours. Gradients in the ditches must usually be sufficient to carry suspended material through the system; deposition of fine-grained material tends to clog soil surface openings. The method is most useful for irregular terrain where large, relatively level areas are not available for basin construction. The natural channel method consists of developing channel barriers to form basins, the primary purpose being to extend the time and area over which water is in contact with the stream channel. Small dikes may be constructed in the stream of concrete, rock, or simply of the channel material. Quite often these are of a temporary nature, requiring only bulldozer work, and may be washed out during the next high water period. Finally, irrigation method consists of spreading excess water on irrigated land. This involves no additional cost or land for the spreading system. The main requirements are availability of water and periods of application in which water will not affect the existing crops or when crops are not being grown.

In a typical water spreading operation the initial recharge rate is high and then decreases rapidly with time to a low minimum value. As the recharge rate decreases, the efficiency of the operation, and therefore the cost of recharging, increases proportionately. Considerable study has been given in recent years to field techniques for increasing the rate of water spreading. Studies by the U.S. Agricultural Research Service have indicated that recharge rates are related to the mean particle size of the soil in which the spreading is occurring. Efforts have been made to increase the soil pore openings for water passage by the addition of organic matter and chemicals as well as growing vegetation on the spreading area. Certain procedures, such as the spreading of cotton gin trash and the growing of Bermuda grass, have indicated that increased intake rates are possible. Another effective means for controlling the rate of artificial recharge involves alternate wetting and drying of the soil. It has been found that prolonged wetting of a soil exposed to the atmosphere will produce microbial growths which tend to clog the soil surface. Drying kills these growths and reopens the soil pores. Thus, in order to maintain a high recharge rate intermittent application of water may prove essential.

Another means for increasing artificial recharge is by detonation of nuclear explosives to improve subsurface conditions for artificial recharge. Two applications are possible in this particular approach. For the disposal of waste liquids, such as radioactive materials, brine, and industrial chemicals, it has been suggested that nuclear explosives could create large underground cavities into which these wastes could be disposed.

These cavities would in turn be connected to deep permeable formations such as abandoned petroleum reservoirs well below any existing ground water sources. A second application is that of fracturing near-surface impermeable zones and creation of shallow craters into which water could be disposed for subsequent infiltration and percolation into the ground. Field and laboratory research on this subject to date looks promising; in a few years perhaps it will be possible to apply this tool for beneficial purposes to supplement ground water supplies.

Radioisotopes

The availability of radioisotopes in recent years has opened up new possibilities for investigation of ground water resources. An excellent example is the use of tritium for studying the flow and age of ground water. Molecules of water containing tritium, an isotope of hydrogen, act in the same manner as water molecules. Therefore, tritium serves as an excellent tracer, which can be detected in very low concentration. In addition, because tritium produced in the atmosphere by cosmic radiation and by thermonuclear explosions is found in rainfall, it is possible by tritium measurements of ground water samples to ascertain how long water has been underground.

The U.S. Geological Survey recently completed a study in New Jersey (10) of the natural tritium in a sandy aquifer adjoining a river. Results showed that concentrations decreased from 120 tritium units at 0.6 meter below ground surface to 1 tritium unit at a depth of 30 meters. This gradient revealed that water older than 25 years existed at the lower level, while water less

than 8 months underground existed at the water table. This confirmed a hypothesis long recognized from hydraulic studies that ground water occurs and moves in layers with the youngest water in the upper layers moving the fastest. To complete the picture, measurements of the tritium content of the river, whose flow was essentially all base flow from ground water, showed concentrations almost exactly equal to the uppermost ground water values.

Injections of tritium into ground water through canals and wells enable ground water flow to be traced. Recent field tests have confirmed that tritium tracer can be used to ascertain canal seepage rates (11). The procedures in working with tritium as a tracer are identical to those for salts and dyes as tracers. Because tritium can be measured in minute concentrations, there is a greater possibility of following tritium after long distances of flow than with other previously available tracers.

The availability of radioisotopes has also produced neutron probes. These probes are recent developments now available commercially for the measurement of moisture content in soils above the water table. Neutrons, being particles having no charge and having a mass about equal to that of the hydrogen atom, are slowed by collisions with hydrogen whereas with other materials of much larger masses the collisions are essentially elastic. Collisions with hydrogen, however, reduce the rate of neutron travel up to one-half, thus fast neutrons become slow neutrons by contact with material containing hydrogen. Underground, this is chiefly water. Therefore, measurements of slow neutrons give a measure of moisture content. The neutron probe is contained in a cylinder which is lowered in a small observation hole in the ground. Radiation is emitted from a radium beryllium source of fast neutrons. The detector is a foil of stable indium-115 which by bombardment by slow neutrons becomes indium-116. This radioactive material can then be measured by means of a Geiger counter. The procedure involves lowering the neutron probe into the hole and observing the measure of radioactivity at given levels.

Important applications for neutron probes include measurement of infiltration rates from applied water and from precipitation. An especially useful benefit is the measurement of need for irrigation by determining critical soil-moisture levels in the root zone. Depths of rainfall penetration and effects of nonhomogeneous layers can also be ascertained easily for the first time.

Well-Logging

Well-logging is the investigation of subsurface conditions from wells which have been drilled into the ground. Methods of logging are numerous and in recent years improved techniques and new types of logging have extended the possibilities for investigating subsurface conditions. Electric logs which involve the measurement of resistivity of the earth and potentials within the earth's crust have become standard techniques for studying underground formations. Recently these techniques have been refined and improved so that it is now possible to ascertain more about ground water than was previously possible.

Radioactive logging can be carried out in cased or uncased holes. Two types of logging are recognized (12). The first is gamma-ray logging which measures the vertical variations of natural gamma rays in the earth. These rays originate from disintegrations of uranium, thorium, and potassium. The relative radioactivity can be used as a rough method of identifying formations and is best done with other supplemental information. Applications of gamma-ray logging include correlation studies and identifications of lithology, formation depths, and bed thicknesses. The second type of radioactive logging is neutron logging. Here neutrons released from a source within the hole can be used for identifying lithology, porosity, fluid type, and formation depths and thickness. In practice it is common to carry out the neutron log in conjunction with the gamma-ray log. Most radioactive logging has been done in the petroleum industry; application of this from oil wells to water wells is now in an early stage.

Other logging techniques now available include current meter logs for measurement of the vertical flow of water inside wells. Often such measurements are indicative of sources of water movement from one aquifer to another. Such flows are important in establishing recharge to confined formations and migrations of saline water into fresh water aquifers. Other logging techniques include caliper logs, which can be used to determine diameters of holes. Such information indicates formations which are subject to caving and in other instances can be used to locate well casings or drilling tools. With the availability of television, TV logs are now possible for the first time. In this system, portable television cameras and lights of special design are lowered into water wells. By means of a closed circuit system, the interior of the well casing can be studied in detail. Such studies assist in locating casing breaks and sources of contaminating water, in studying the condition of wells, and in ascertaining positions of lost drilling tools.

Well Drilling

The advent of rapid means of drilling deep holes has done much to stimulate ground water development. Development of the rotary drilling process in the petroleum industry was rapidly copied for ground-water purposes (13). The hydraulic rotary method operates by hollow rotating bit cutting the rock while a mixture of clay and water, or drilling mud, is forced down through the drill rod to carry the cuttings upward in the rising mud. The mud serves the additional purpose of stabilizing the wall of the well, preventing caving, and making casing unnecessary. After the drilling is completed, perforated casing is lowered into the hole and the clay lining is washed from the wall by injecting water down the drill rod. Wells can be constructed to depths of about 2,000 feet by this method and even deeper if it is worthwhile from a hydrologic standpoint. Diameters up to 18 inches are common; with reamers diameters twice as large are possible.

The reverse rotary method uses water instead of mud and operates as a suction dredging method (14). Cuttings are removed by a rotating suction pipe, while the hydrostatic pressure of water within the hole acts against fine-grained deposits to support the wall. The method is especially useful for large-diameter wells in unconsolidated materials.

Direct rotary drilling using air instead of mud or water to remove cuttings is a rapid and convenient method for small-diameter holes in consolidated and unconsolidated formations (15). The latest drilling development is a rapid procedure for drilling in hard rock formations. It involves a rotary-percussion combination with air (16). Above the rotating bit an air hammer delivers 600 to 1,000 blows per minute to the bottom of the hole. Penetration rates by this method of up to 1 foot per minute in hard rock have been reported. Thus, we are rapidly reaching the stage in which water wells can be drilled within a matter of a few hours rather than a few days or weeks as was common only a decade ago.

As an illustration, some 18 hundred new irrigation wells have recently been drilled in the Indus River Basin of West Pakistan. These were 18 to 24 inches in diameter and were drilled to an average depth of 250 feet. Drilling time for most of these was less than 24 hours by the reverse rotary technique.

Education and Manpower in Hydrology

With the advances in technology of ground water resources development a great need has developed for competent young men to carry out investigational and developmental work in ground water. The problem is so acute that universities throughout the world need to give attention to educational programs and facilities which will enable men with backgrounds in the science of hydrology to be produced. Education requires time; therefore attention needs to be given as soon as possible to means for providing educational facilities and trained manpower. A variety of procedures are possible and these will be commented upon briefly.

The availability of fellowships for studies at universities throughout the world for students in the field of hydrology would do much to encourage interest and education in hydrology. At the same time exchange of faculties from one country to another would be helpful. Men experienced in hydrology and in ground water development could lecture and supervise research at other universities which have not had personnel and facilities before in this field.

An effective intermediate means for improving the educational background of existing personnel in developing nations is by means of seminars and short courses. These have long been held by the U.S. Geological Survey as a means of indoctrination and instruction in ground water hydrology for new personnel. International seminars and conferences, such as those which have been sponsored in recent years by UNESCO and ECAFE, are effective means for bringing key personnel from developing nations together so that they will have an opportunity to become familiar with latest techniques in the field. A continuation of these programs and other forms of international cooperation in the field of ground water hydrology will do much to develop competent manpower and the benefits of adequate water supplies for mankind throughout the world.

REFERENCES

(1) Todd, D. K., *Ground Water Hydrology*, John Wiley and Sons, 336 pp., New York (1959).

(2) *Large-Scale Ground Water Development*, Water Resources Development Center, United Nations, 84 pp., New York (1960).

(3) Committee on Ground Water, *Ground Water Basin Management*, Manual of Engineering Practice No. 40, American Society of Civil Engineers, 160 pp., New York (1961).

(4) Fowler, L. C., *Electronic Analog Computers and Ground Water Basin Management*, Proceedings 1961 Biennial Conference on Ground Water Recharge (L. Schiff, editor), Agricultural Research Service, Fresno, Calif. (1962).

(5) Howe, R. H., H. R. Wilke, D. E. Bloodgood, *Application of air photo interpretation in the location of ground water*, J. American Water Works Assoc., *48*, pp. 1380–1390, New York (1956).

(6) Mann, J. F., Jr., *Estimating quantity and quality of ground water in dry regions using airphotos*, Publ. No. 44, General Assembly of Toronto, International Association of Scientific Hydrology, pp. 125–134, Gentbrugge, Belgium (1958).

(7) Todd, D. K., *Salt Water Intrusion of Coastal Aquifers in the United States*, Publ. No. 52, Assembly of Helsinki 1960, International Association of Scientific Hydrology, pp. 452–461, Gentbrugge, Belgium (1961).

(8) James, L. B., et al., *Sea-Water Intrusion in California*, Bulletin No. 63, California Department of Water Resources, 91 pp., Sacramento (1958).

(9) Todd, D. K., *Annotated Bibliography on Artificial Recharge of Ground Water Through 1954*, U.S. Geological Survey Water-Supply Paper 1477, 115 pp., Washington, D.C. (1959).

(10) Carlston, C. W., L. L. Thatcher, E. C. Rhodehamel, *Tritium as a Hydrologic Tool—The Wharton Tract Study*, Publ. No. 52, Assembly of Helsinki 1960, International Association of Scientific Hydrology, pp. 503–512, Gentbrugge, Belgium (1961).

(11) Kaufman, W. J., D. K. Todd, *Application of tritium tracer to canal seepage measurements*, Tritium in the Physical and Biological Sciences, *I*, International Atomic Energy Agency, pp. 83–94, Vienna (1962).

(12) Jones, P. H., H. E. Skibitzke, *Subsurface Geophysical Methods in Ground-Water Hydrology*, Advances in Geophysics (H. E. Landsberg, editor), *3*, Academic Press, pp. 241–300, New York (1956).

(13) *Wells*, Technical Manual No. 5-297, U.S. Department of the Army, 264 pp., Washington, D.C. (1957).

(14) Gossett, O. C., *Reverse-circulation rotary drilling*, Water Well Journal, *12*, 3, pp. 6–7, 22, 48, Urbana, Ill. (1958).

(15) Yoeman, R. A., *Direct Rotary Air Drilling*, Water Well Journal, *12*, 7, pp. 12, 32, 34, Urbana, Ill. (1958).

(16) Yellig, E. J., *Down-the-Hole Air Percussion Drilling*, Water Well Journal, *12*, no. 5, pp. 8, 22, 24, 27–28, 30, Urbana, Ill. (1958).

Hydrology and Scientific Reclamation in the Punjab, West Pakistan

D. W. GREENMAN

Chief of Party, U.S. Geological Survey Ground Water Group, West Pakistan

Introduction

Punjab means five waters, and in its geographic sense refers to the vast alluvial plain—40,000 square miles in area—traversed by the Indus River and its five major tributaries in the northern part of the Indus Plain (figure 1). Similarly, doab means two waters and refers to the interfluvial area between two rivers. Thus, the Punjab of West Pakistan comprises four doabs—Bari Doab between the Sutlej and Ravi Rivers, Rechna Doab between the Ravi and Chenab Rivers, Chaj Doab between the Chenab and Jhelum Rivers, and Thal Doab between the Jhelum and Indus Rivers.

The Punjab is essentially a flat featureless plain which slopes gently toward the southwest at an average gradient of about one and one-half feet per mile. Natural internal drainage is poorly developed. Intermittent drainage channels, called "nalas", carry monsoon runoff to the major rivers during the summer months, but they are dry throughout most of the remainder of the year.

Virtually all of the runoff of the Indus Basin is derived from snowmelt and precipitation in the Himalayas. The average annual discharge of the rivers, where they enter the plain, is over 160 million acre-feet (maf) of which more than half is contributed by the Indus. The rivers are subject to extreme seasonal variations of flow, the mean monthly discharge during the summer being about 15 to 20 times that of the winter months. In a typical year the period of low-flow extends from December to March. The rivers begin to rise during March with the melting of the Himalayan snows and reach their peak discharge in July or August during the height of the monsoon. About 60 percent of the annual discharge of the rivers is concentrated in the 3-month period, June to August.

The climate of the Punjab, typical of the low-lying interior of the Indo-Pakistan sub-continent, is characterized by large seasonal fluctuations in temperature and precipitation. It is continental, and ranges from sub-humid in the northeast to arid in the southwest. Maximum temperatures higher than 105° F are common during the summer months of May through August. Winters are relatively cold. Daytime temperatures in the sixties and seventies and night-time temperatures in the high thirties are typical of the months of December to February. The mean annual temperature ranges from about 70° F in the northeastern parts of Rechna and Chaj Doabs to about 85° F in the southern tips of Bari and Thal Doabs.

The Punjab is located on the eastern fringe of the monsoon belt. Precipitation is scanty and sporadic, and not a dependable source of crop moisture. Average annual precipitation ranges from over 30 inches in the upper reaches of Rechna and Thal Doabs near the Himalayan foothills, to about 6 inches in the southern parts of Bari and Thal Doabs. But precipitation rates diminish rather abruptly south of the foothills, and most of the Punjab receives less than 14 inches of rainfall in a typical year. The seasonal distribution of precipitation is the same for the entire area; about 70· percent of the annual precipitation occurs during the monsoon period of June through September.

The soils of the Punjab are of alluvial origin and contain high percentages of silt and fine to very fine sand. According to preliminary land classification studies, about 60 percent of the area of Rechna and Chaj Doabs is unsuitable for irrigation, chiefly as a result of salinity. But the soils are inherently fertile and well-drained, and highly responsive to conventional reclamation measures. If the salinity hazard were eliminated 90 percent or more of these lands would be classified as suitable for irrigation farming. Except for the desert area of central Thal Doab, approximately the same conditions obtain elsewhere in the Punjab.

The Punjab's economy is largely agricultural, based upon an intensive system of canal irrigation that was introduced over one hundred years ago. Rural population density is high, averaging about 5 hundred persons per square mile and exceeding 8 hundred persons per square mile in some areas. About 75 percent of the population of the Punjab is supported by agricultural activities.

There are two crop seasons—the "Kharif," which extends from April to October and includes the monsoon period; and the "Rabi," which includes the dry winter months. The principal Kharif crops are cotton, sugarcane, rice, and maize. Wheat is the chief crop during the Rabi season.

History and Problems of Irrigation

The climate of the Punjab makes irrigation a prerequisite to intensive agriculture; and the favorable combination of other natural factors such as abundant surface water, flat terrain, and inherently fertile and well-drained soils, makes irrigation feasible. Thus throughout recorded history man has contrived ways to divert water to cultivated fields.

The oldest method of irrigation in the Punjab is flood irrigation, locally known as "sailab," which is restricted to the active flood plains. Crops, mainly wheat, are planted after the recession of the summer flood waters. Lands under sailab irrigation retain their productive capacity indefinitely and the method is still employed in riverine areas, most of which are not served by canals.

Canal irrigation in the Punjab began at about the end of the 17th Century with the construction of inundation canals which draw water from rivers during periods of high stage for distribution to upland areas bordering the flood plains. The original purpose of the inundation canals was to furnish water for Moghul parks and gardens. However, some diversions for agriculture were permitted and the results were so successful that subsequent canals were constructed primarily for agricultural purposes. By the middle of the 19th Century a rather extensive network of canals was in operation with the maximum development concentrated along the Sutlej and Chenab rivers.

The inundation canals represented an advance over sailab methods because they could convey water to more remote areas and draw water through a greater range of river stage, thus maintaining irrigation deliveries for a longer period of the year. But they could only function during periods of relatively high flow, so irrigation was limited to the summer season and to a relatively narrow belt along the rivers.

The final step in the evolution of the irrigation system in the Punjab came in about the middle of the 19th Century with the introduction of so-called perennial canals. Permanent diversion works known as barrages or headworks were constructed at strategic sites on the rivers to place the inundation canals under weir control. These facilities allowed larger diversions from the rivers than were possible with the inundation canals, especially during the winter season when low flows could be exploited. Thus, irrigation was extended into the central parts of the doabs, and in many areas the canals operated throughout the year, hence the term "perennial."

The first perennial canal system in the Punjab was the Upper Bari Doab Canal which was opened in 1861. This was followed by the Lower Chenab Canal in Rechna Doab in 1896, and the Lower Jhelum Canal in 1901. In 1915, the Upper Chenab, Upper Jhelum, and Lower Bari Canals were completed as parts of the Triple Canal Project which also included an extensive system of link canals to transfer water from the Jhelum River and Chenab River to the Ravi River. Between 1915 and 1930 the inundation canals fed by the Sutlej River were converted to perennial canals, and with the completion of headworks on the Indus River at Kalabagh in 1946 and Taunsa in 1958, all of the canals serving the Punjab had been converted to weir control.

Average annual diversions through the complex of canal systems are about 26 maf which are used to irrigate about 13.5 million acres annually. This constitutes about 7 percent of the world's irrigated land, and it is probably the largest area of essentially contiguous irrigation development in the world.

As canal irrigation always involves diversion and redistribution of surface runoff, some disruption of the hydrologic regimen is inevitable. In the Punjab the hydrologic effects of perennial canal irrigation were especially marked because the same natural factors that made irrigation attractive and feasible were also the sources of serious hydrologic problems in the artificial environment. Thus the permeable soils favored canal leakage which dissipated 40 percent or more of canal diversions within the distribution system. Apart from depleting the supply available for irrigation, the seepage losses formed a new increment of groundwater recharge which, under the flat hydraulic gradients that prevail in the Punjab, can not be disposed of through subsurface drainage. Hence, throughout the Punjab, the inception of canal irrigation was followed by a period of rising ground water levels. This trend persisted until the water table rose sufficiently near land surface to establish a new equilibrium in which evaporation losses were the dominant discharge factors.

Those conditions formed a nearly ideal setting for salinity and water-logging, and these hazards were amplified by inefficient management practices. In the Punjab irrigation is operated for revenue benefits rather than for reclamation benefits. With this philosophy and with the pressure of a growing population on the land, the tendency has been to expand the irrigated acreage and adjust irrigation applications accordingly, rather than adjust the irrigated acreage according to the availability of irrigation supplies. As a result, irrigation applications are generally inadequate to satisfy the consumptive uses of the crops, not to mention leaching requirements of the soils. And the combined effects of river regimen and terrain precluded additional development of surface water to make up the deficiency in the irrigation supplies. About 70 percent of the runoff occurs in the summer months, but most of this is wasted to the sea because the flat plains do not offer favorable reservoir sites.

In this environment, characterized by deficient irrigation supplies and inadequate subsurface drainage, the economic utility of the irrigated lands has steadily depreciated. Over 8 million of the 13.7 million acres under irrigation in the Punjab are to some degree affected by salinity. Of this about 3.5 million acres are classified as seriously affected, including 1.5 million acres that are out of production. Salinity is encroaching upon new lands at the rate of about 100,000 acres a year, of which about half goes out of production. Furthermore, crop yields from unaffected lands are only a fraction of world averages owing to the inadequate application of irrigation water.

The potential hazards of inadequate subsurface drainage in the Punjab were recognized soon after the perennial canals went into operation. Beginning about 1870, observation wells were established in the irrigated areas, and a schedule of semi-annual ground water level measurements was adopted to monitor the effects of irrigation activities on the water table. The networks of observation wells were extended as new areas were brought under irrigation and now comprise several thousand wells.

Since about 1915, when salinity and water-logging began to rank as major problems, the observation-well data have been subjected to frequent study by various government commissions, officers on special duty in the irrigation service, and scientists from universities and government bureaus. Most of the studies were too limited in scope to evaluate all pertinent factors, and the findings were generally inconclusive and often misleading. On the basis of these studies various remedial measures were employed including closure of canals during the monsoon season, construction of open-ditch drains in water-logged areas, and planting of phreatophytes along canals. The most ambitious effort was the installation of about 1,600 drainage wells along major canals in Rechna and Chaj Doabs. However, none of these measures provided more than temporary or local relief, and the regional problems of salinity and water-logging continued to increase in severity. Thus, down through the years, canal leakage, water-logging, and salinity came to be regarded as undesirable, but inevitable, concomitants of irrigation, and inefficient practices were accepted as the only compromise between the opposing factors in the system.

Effects of Recent Hydrologic Investigations on Reclamation Planning

The first comprehensive study of the problem of subsurface drainage in the Punjab was made by Carlston (1953) under a United Nation's grant. He examined all available hydrologic data for Rechna Doab and concluded that leakage from the canal distribution system was the major factor involved, but he recommended further detailed studies to provide an adequate basis for planning reclamation activities. In 1954, a program of comprehensive water and soils studies was begun in the Punjab under a cooperative agreement between the U.S. Foreign Operations Administration (a predecessor of the U.S. Agency for International Development) and the Government of Pakistan. Under the terms of the agreement the Government of West Pakistan has furnished personnel, and field and office facilities. U.S. AID has provided a team of technical advisors on loan from the U.S. Geological Survey, and vehicles, drilling rigs, field and laboratory equipment, and other commodities required by the project.

The objectives of the investigations are to inventory the water and soils resources of the Punjab, and to describe the cause-and-effect relationships between irrigation activities and natural hydrologic factors and the incidence of water-logging and subsurface drainage problems which threatens the agricultural economy of the irrigated areas. The ultimate purpose of the information is to provide a scientific basis for the planning of regional reclamation and development

programs, and the design of individual projects under those programs.

Most of the basic data on the geology, and on the occurrence and quality of water in the Punjab, have been published by the West Pakistan Water and Power Development Authority (WAPDA) in a series of more than 20 preliminary reports on the investigation. In addition, a comprehensive interpretative report on the hydrology of the Punjab has been completed (Greenman and others) and is now in the process of publication. Subsequent reports will describe in greater detail certain critical aspects of the hydrology until the requirements of the reclamation and development programs are satisfied.

From the standpoint of planning water resources development in the Punjab, the significant findings of this investigation are as follows:

(a) Geologic studies show that virtually the entire Punjab is underlain to depths of 1000 feet or more by unconsolidated alluvial sediments which are saturated to within a few feet of land surface. The alluvium varies in texture from medium sand to silty clay, but the sandy sediments predominate, and large capacity wells yielding 4 cubic feet per second or more can be developed at virtually any site.

(b) Quality of water studies shows that the alluvium beneath about two-thirds of the Punjab is saturated to an average depth of 500 feet or more with water of acceptable quality for irrigation supply. The average concentration of dissolved solids in these supplies is less than 1,000 ppm; the upper limit of concentration of acceptable supplies is placed in the range of 1,800 to 2,000 ppm on the assumption that it is feasible to blend ground water with canal water at a ratio of 1:2. That limit probably is conservative. Reclamation planners now are thinking in terms of using more highly mineralized water under certain conditions. In any event, assuming an effective porosity of 25 percent for the saturated sediments, the volume of useable ground water in storage is on the order of 2 billion acre-feet.

(c) Water level studies indicate that leakage from the existing canal distribution system is the principal cause of subsurface drainage problems in the Punjab, and it is also the major component of ground water recharge. Approximately one-third of the total canal discharge is diverted to ground water storage through canal seepage.

In view of the above it is evident that the alluvial aquifer underlying the Punjab is an unexploited resource of enormous economic value—the more so because it is highly susceptible to flexible operation and scientific management. From that knowledge has evolved a new approach to reclamation which is based on working with, rather than against, the hydrologic factors. It is now recognized both by reclamation officials in Pakistan and international aid agencies abroad that scientific development and management of the ground water resources is the key to permanent irrigated agriculture in the Punjab. From the results of the ground water studies, WAPDA has prepared a long-range program for reclaiming the irrigated lands of the Punjab (WAPDA, 1961). The essential feature of the program is a network of tube-wells, located on an average density of about one per square mile. Where the ground water is of acceptable quality the wells discharge into the canal system, and the yield of each well is determined by the supplemental irrigation requirements of the land under its command. Thus, the ground water withdrawals serve the dual purpose of satisfying irrigation requirements and providing subsurface drainage. The system offers a permanent solution to the problem of the leaking canal because it both controls the effects of leakage and salvages the losses from the canals. In fact, under this kind of operation, canal leakage is an asset to the system rather than a liability because it constitutes the major component of recharge to the ground water reservoir.

In areas where the quality of ground water is unsatisfactory, the wells discharge into drainage ditches, and the yield of each well is determined by the subsurface drainage requirement of its area of influence. In these areas the tube-wells offer only a compromise solution to the problems of canal leakage. They control the effects of leakage but do not salvage the losses, hence canal leakage remains a liability and operates only to put an extra burden on the well-drainage system.

The first tube-well project under this program went into operation in 1961. It comprises nearly 2 thousand wells which serve an area of about 2 million acres in Rechna Doab (figure 1). During 1962, construction is scheduled to begin on several other projects in Chaj Doab. Future development is planned at the rate of about 15 hundred wells per year. About 25 thousand wells will be required to serve all of the irrigated areas of the Punjab.

Tube-well reclamation methods are hydrologically feasible in the Punjab. That is, with respect to drainage, the position of the water table can be controlled by pumpage; and with respect to supplemental irrigation supplies, there is sufficient ground water in storage and adequate recharge to sustain large-scale withdrawals for an indefinite period. Furthermore, ground water supplies offer some unique advantages to the irrigation system. Unlike canal supplies they are not subject to seasonal variations, and they can be developed to serve virtually any topographic situation. Thus, ground water can be used to meet seasonal deficiencies in canal supplies and to extend irrigation to areas that cannot be brought under command of canals.

Despite the feasibility and inherent advantages of tube-well reclamation methods, it is inevitable that just as superposition of the canal system on the native environment caused undesirable side-effects, the tube-well reclamation projects will again disturb the environment and introduce new problems that will require new solutions. From the standpoint of hydrology there are two distinct, but related, potential hazards which must be considered in the design and management of the tube-well projects.

Distribution of withdrawals is an obvious question of immediate concern which should be resolved before the tube-well reclamation program is far advanced. According to current estimates the ground water resources of the Punjab appear to be adequate to meet the regional requirements for supplemental irrigation supplies. But there is not a favorable relationship throughout the Punjab between the availability of ground water and the need for supplemental supplies. The ground water potential for irrigation use diminishes from north to south, or down-doab, and is nil in the southern parts of the doabs where the ground water is too highly mineralized for use. On the other hand, the demand for supplemental

irrigation supplies is more-or-less uniform but tends to increase toward the more arid southern areas. Under these conditions it is evident that the design criteria for a program of maximum exploitation of the ground water resources must be based on regional hydrologic factors, rather than on local demand factors. In short, ground water supplies must be developed where they are available and conveyed to points of use. Such a program will involve the transfer of water into the southern parts of Rechna, Chaj, and Bari Doabs, which will probably require remodeling of the existing canal system or construction of new canals. That, in turn, will amplify the problems of canal leakage and subsurface drainage in the areas where the quality of ground water is unfit for use and the leakage can not be salvaged by tube-wells. In those areas, in the interests of conservation of water and economical drainage operations, it may be feasible to inhibit canal leakage using the emulsion-type sealants that can be applied while the canals are in service. There are alternative methods of conserving water in the areas of deficient supply, such as reducing the intensity of cultivation or modifying the cropping pattern. Regardless of the details of the regional program, it is essential that individual tube-well projects be designed to accommodate the requirements of regional development. Otherwise ground water development will be unbalanced, and in some areas more serious problems may be created by over-development of the aquifer than will be solved by the reclamation activities.

Maintenance of a favorable salt balance in the ground water supply is a related problem—related in the sense that pumpage will trigger changes in the hydrologic environment that will influence the quality of water relationships in the aquifer. Several inherent factors in the tube-well systems will tend to depreciate the quality of ground water with time. Firstly, the leaching of the soil profile that will occur when full irrigation supplies are available will add appreciable amounts of salt to the ground water in storage. The effect will be most pronounced in the early years of reclamation when the residual of salts that have accumulated during the past years of irrigation will be leached from the soil. Secondly, the reduction in volume of the ground water in storage that will occur in response to pumping will cause a proportional increase in the mineral concentration of the ground water. In the cycle of recirculation of water from the aquifer to the irrigated fields and back to the aquifer, most of the salts will remain in solution whereas most of the water will be lost to evapotranspiration. Thirdly, there will be an annual increment of salts derived from canal irrigation supplies which will also be transported down to the water table. Finally, chemical reaction between the percolating recharge water and the unwatered sediments will bring more salts in solution. In addition to the above factors, which essentially involve mobilization of salts, there are the added hazards of lateral and upward migration of saline waters into fresh-water zones in response to pumping.

The effects of these factors will be mitigated somewhat by dilution with other components of recharge such as seepage from canals and rivers, and infiltration of precipitation; and by blending with ground water in storage in the aquifer. It is not even possible to estimate the changes that may occur in the quality of ground water because so many

unknown variables are involved. But considering the enormous quantity of ground water in storage in relation to the annual rate of recharge under the reclamation program it is reasonably certain that the rate of change in quality will be slow and will not present serious problems in the near future, or probably within the 40- to 50-year economic lifetime of the present group of projects. If the tube-well reclamation operations are continued indefinitely it may ultimately be necessary to provide for the removal of salts from the area of development, unless technological advances in the meantime offer a better alternative. It may also be feasible to enhance the quality of the ground water by promoting artificial recharge through canals and other structures that are designed to leak.

These and other problems and policies of water resources management will be studied under the so-called Mona pilot project which will be operated by WAPDA with the assistance of U.S. AID. The pilot project occupies an area of about 150 square miles northeast of the city of Sarghoda in Chaj Doab (figure 1). It involves the installation of 140 tube-wells having an average capacity of about 3 cubic feet per second, and related supplemental surface drainage and distribution works. Construction is scheduled to be completed in the spring of 1963 in time to begin operations in the 1963 Kharif growing season.

This area was selected because it contains most of the essential elements of the hydrology, both natural and manmade, that occur elsewhere in the Punjab. Thus, it will be possible to reproduce or simulate on an experimental scale most of the problems that are likely to arise in connection with the management and operation of the full-scale reclamation program. With the experience gained from the pilot project coupled with careful monitoring of the full-scale reclamation projects, it should be possible to anticipate major hazards and adopt appropriate counter-measures before serious problems develop.

The implications of the tube-well program go beyond the immediate irrigation problems of the Punjab. If the program is successful it may point the way to a final solution for the most vexing problem of water management in West Pakistan—that of storage. The potential for on-channel storage in West Pakistan is inadequate to provide full control of river flow, and even the most favorable reservoir sites have serious shortcomings. For example, the two major dams included in the current development program, Mangla on the Jhelum River and Tarbela on the Indus River, each have a reservoir capacity of only about 5 million acre feet. That is less than 10 percent of the discharge of the Indus Basin, and it can only be utilized once a year owing to the characteristics of the river flows. The reservoirs are remote from areas of water use and they are relatively short-lived because of the high sediment load of the rivers. Present estimates indicate that the useful reservoir life of Mangla Dam will be on the order of 50 to 60 years and of Tarbela about 40 years. There are few other feasible reservoir sites in West Pakistan and they are similarly handicapped in any event, so in the long run it probably will be necessary to develop other storage facilities for surface runoff.

Diversion of surplus surface water to ground water storage appears to offer the most favorable prospects for control of the runoff of the Indus Basin. The alluvial aquifer that underlies the Punjab is ideal for the purpose in nearly all respects. It is favorably situated with respect both to availability of recharge and to areas of use of the water, and there are no extensive geologic barriers to recharge or to circulation within the aquifer. The storage capacity of the ground water reservoir is equal to many times the annual flow of the Indus River system and the reservoir has an indefinite life, because ground water recharge is free of sediment. Thus the use of ground water storage would permit more flexible and complete control of the water resources of the Indus Basin. The ground water reservoir can be replenished according to the availability of surface water for recharge, and it can be tapped according to the demand for water without regard to seasonal or annual variations in runoff.

The major problem involved in the management of the aquifer as a reservoir is that of promoting artificial recharge at a sufficient rate to accommodate surplus surface supplies during the periods of high runoff. Although the problem is formidable, a solution probably will be found as a normal consequence of operations under the tube-well reclamation program. If the history of other areas is repeated in the Punjab, demand for ground water supplies will increase through the years and the threat of over-development will stimulate research on methods of conserving water and inducing recharge. In that manner the tube-well reclamation program may ultimately evolve into the broader water management operation simply by the process of diverting more and more of the surface runoff to ground water storage until the entire supply is allocated. If these activities are pursued aggressively it is not unlikely that the present generation of surface reservoirs will be the last for West Pakistan. By the time their reservoir capacity is depleted, their function may have been preempted by ground water storage.

REFERENCES

Carlston, C. W., *History and causes of rising ground water levels in the Rechna Doab:* United Nations, FAO Report No. 90, 1953.

West Pakistan Water Power and Development Authority, 1961, *Program for waterlogging and salinity control in the irrigated areas of West Pakistan:* West Pakistan Water and Power Development Authority, Lahore.

Government as a Dynamic Agent in Mineral Resource Development

JOHN M. KELLY

Assistant Secretary, Mineral Resources, U.S. Department of the Interior, Washington, D.C.

Introduction

For many nations the unlocking of mineral resources represents a major opportunity to stimulate progress for their peoples through the creation of economic wealth. The utilization of a nation's mineral resources can be a determinant of social and industrial progress. The income so derived can make a substantive contribution to material progress and can provide additional means for advancement of the technical skills of the people. Unused, mineral resources contribute nothing to a nation's welfare. Under any political philosophy, government initiative is integral to the maximum utilization of mineral resources in the national interest.

Government plays many roles in mineral-resource development: surveyor, scientist, landlord, proprietor, revenue collector, economic regulator, planner, protector of the public welfare, educator, negotiator in international affairs. In these activities the government has a dual responsibility to establish and maintain a stable course for its nation while, at the same time, assuring its responsiveness to changing fundamental conditions. The extent to which government dynamically creates a healthy environment for a minerals industry measures the degree to which indigenous minerals may assist in improving the national standard of living.

To raise a nation's standard of living through creation of wealth from mineral resources requires technical and professional competence and investment capital. Most important, government must stimulate and encourage mineral-resource development. While minerals are a foundation for modern industry, agriculture, and urban life, it may be noted that some nations have a high degree of economic activity and high living standards with few, if any, mines or oil fields.

In a less developed nation the government's part in resource programs is peculiarly important because the usually limited number of persons with managerial and technical talent tend to concentrate in the government, which is the locus of power. The success any less developed nation attains in creating a prosperous economy based on mineral wealth depends largely upon the intelligent planning and effective implementation of that nation's leadership.

Exploration and Assessment

It is vital for newly created or less developed nations to assess as soon as possible what mineral resources may be available. An initial step in this regard, for which there is much precedent, is the establishment of a state organization designed to foster and encourage minerals investigations. Such a national service presupposes the availability of scientific specialists and technicians sufficient in number to staff an efficient, even if limited, research agency charged with responsibility for reconnaissance and assessment of the national minerals potential.

The United States and many other nations have benefited from establishment of such minerals-research agencies. Geological surveys and mining bureaus func-tion effectively in India, Mexico, Canada, Peru, Chile, Japan, Australia, much of Europe, and elsewhere. Since World War II an outstanding contribution has been made in the Philippines where a small but effective mining bureau has been of great assistance. Such service agencies, staffed with competent personnel, have more than paid their way. Even an extensive assessment of mineral resources is only a beginning. It cannot be an absolute inventory, for despite improvements in geological techniques and instrumentation, we can only make educated guesses as to what lies beneath the ground. It is the role of such an agency to constantly improve its estimates of the minerals potential.

In many cases, development of mineral deposits and ancillary facilities requires large capital investment. In fact, foreign investment contributed much to the early development of the mineral industry of the United States. Many governments turn to foreign financing in such cases. Peru's Marcona iron deposit was known for years, but the Nation did not benefit from it until foreign financing, encouraged by the Peruvian Government, enabled its development on a large scale. Now the deposit provides a raw material for Peruvian blast furnaces, foreign exchange through exports, and, possibly most important of all, training in industrial operations for Peruvian technicians, businessmen, civil servants, and engineers. Such a "creation" of mineral resources through application of capital, technology, and labor obviously benefits the Peruvian people in many ways.

Government's Direct Interest

As landlord or proprietor the state determines the development of state-owned resources. These resources may be developed by the state, by private domestic companies on license or concession, by private foreign entities on license or concession, by private companies in cooperation with the state, and possibly in other ways or combinations of effort. The state must provide a program and an incentive for any desired private development. Government also may provide that mineral resources shall be owned and developed by the finder. In most instances the development program should be designed to maintain maximum efficient employment and production, while permitting a reasonable return on invested capital.

Regulation and Revenue Collection

The primary long-term goal of national policies affecting mineral resources should be economic betterment of the citizens, and this must be kept constantly in view. Mineral-resource development is of questionable value if it does not result in enhancement of living standards, encompassing the provision of adequate food, housing, communications, health facilities, education, and gainful occupation. The extent to which effective development takes place within a reasonable time may depend upon the laws and regulations under which the mineral industry operates. Although a seeking for political goals, without regard for economic gain, occasionally may intervene, all industry should pay its way and contribute through taxation and other means to the national welfare.

The government that encourages the accumulation of capital for research, development, and utilization of mineral commodities is taking an essential step in stimulating a sound domestic minerals industry. On the other hand, government can defeat efforts toward mineral-resource development through inequitable taxation, short-sighted tariffs, poorly devised mining laws, difficult legal requirements pertaining to labor and business structure, and a generally unsympathetic attitude.

Planning in the National Interest

No single formula applicable to all nations can be devised to encourage minerals development, and the actions any state takes will depend upon its own social, technological, and economic capabilities. Each state, however, can assure that planning of mineral resource development is coordinated with related energy, transportation, agriculture, and education programs, thus spreading costs over a wide base and extending social benefits to more people. It should be emphasized that mineral planning must be coordinated with import and export policies. Imposition of a high import tax on drilling or mining machinery, especially when such equipment is not manufactured within the nation, can inhibit mineral search and development. Export taxes on ores and concentrates should be gauged to economic levels compatible with world markets since many nations compete for trade and few have a product that is unique. Often it is impractical or impossible to process or fabricate mineral raw materials locally, and at times a mineral commodity initially cannot be used to maximum advantage in the producing country. It may be desirable to export such materials with the object of accumulating capital for subsequent industrial development when the nation's economic position warrants the installation of more complex fabricating or manufacturing units.

Government has a specific responsibility in resource development in the field of labor. Progress in industrialization requires real incentives to produce for the common welfare. For the individual worker, incentives must embrace opportunity—full opportunity to employ all his capabilities and to achieve recognition through advancement and promotion on the job, and full opportunity for better living for his family and children, including good housing, medical care and sanitation, and education. The worker must share and benefit from industrial effort. There should be recognition of this philosophy at the inception of a resource development program.

There is another point that must be emphasized. Throughout the world there is a staggering underutilization of human skills and capacities. This serious defect must be corrected whenever possible if full advantage is to be taken of industrial development. There are untapped reservoirs of human ingenuity in emerging nations, hidden or dormant creative abilities striving for recognition and use. Basic training in the use of modern tools and equipment, coupled to educational programs designed to stimulate initiative and ingenuity on the part of the individual worker, is the essential method of unlocking these latent possibilities—government must recognize and encourage such endeavor.

Inherent hazards in mining can be greatly reduced through safety training, establishment and enforcement of safety codes, and alert supervision and inspection. Also needed is the protection of the health and safety of persons in the vicinity of mining and processing operations. In seeking solutions to such problems, the experience of the United States and many other nations may be helpful.

Technological Education

Minerals development requires skilled and educated personnel competent to undertake the unusually difficult and complex assignments inherent to minerals resource investigation and technology. Such personnel will be needed both in research and in production. Most nations, particularly the less developed nations, need outside technical and scientific assistance to some degree. In these days no nation is truly self-sufficient in scientific and technical talent. Establishment or expansion of technical schools cannot be accomplished overnight, and this certainly is true where the domestic demand for such specialized skills may be limited to a relatively small annual increment of new specialists. Also, because of the need for mineral development concurrent with the strengthening of technical education, and because of the highly specialized nature of this education, it may be best that the schooling of a nation's own citizens in such professions as geology, mining, engineering, and metallurgy be undertaken outside the country. There are many ways that government can act as a dynamic force in expanding the number and improving the quality of technical and professional personnel. Among these in the United States are direct incentives such as grants and loans to students, and contracts, grants, or loans to institutions, and indirect incentives such as adjustments of the tax structure for mineral industries which support supplemental education for their employees.

Since resource research and management, be it in forestry, water, minerals, agriculture, or public health, involves extensive training at the post-graduate level, there may be substantial advantage in seeking a regional approach to these problems. Cooperative establishment of education and research centers available to more than one nation, with a faculty and facilities able to meet the requirements of the resource field, might be a satisfactory solution.

International Aspects

Governments today have the opportunity to seek assistance in resource development from international agencies and from several nations. The thoughtful and selective use of such assistance can and should provide some of the essential elements needed to initiate mineral-resource utilization. A major component of such outside aid can be the provision of assistance in resource surveys and advice on regional development along with accelerated education and training. It must be recognized, however, that technologies from developed countries may not be readily transferable to the less developed countries—adaptive innovation on the part of both nationals and foreigners will be required.

Economic mineral deposits are not evenly distributed around the earth. This uneven distribution is a major factor in stimulation of world trade, making the various parts of our world interdependent, and this, after all, should be to everyone's advantage. Government has a major role in this situation, developing import and export policies that will encourage the exchange of surplus raw materials, and their processed or manufactured products, for those in short supply domestically.

The Impetus for Development

The impetus for mineral-resource development in less developed nations may include a seeking for national prestige through industrialization. This prestige factor cannot be ignored, but it can be overweighted. An impressive industrial plant, by itself, cannot improve a nation's economic level and, in fact, may require an expenditure of money, manpower, and material far in excess of its capacity to produce economic benefits.

The establishment of a viable minerals industry may become a primary means of stimulating the growth of public utilities, such as transportation and power, and may result in large expansion in markets both for raw materials and fabricated products. But the dominant impetus for resource development should be the desire for a higher standard of living. A minerals industry can well contribute to this objective, providing full, creative opportunity for a nation's people. The extent to which these broad benefits of mineral-resource development are realized depends, in large measure, on the implementation of dynamic, practical, and farseeing policies by the government.

A Cooperative Mineral Exploration and Development Program in Pakistan*

Nur M. Khan
Director-General, Geological Survey of Pakistan

John A. Reinemund
Senior Geologic Consultant to the Geological Survey of Pakistan, U. S. Geological Survey

Introduction

Importance of mineral development in Pakistan. Pakistan is a nation of about 95 million people inhabiting two geographically separated provinces having a total area of 365,504 square miles (figure I). These provinces have few known mineral resources in the quantity or quality required for economic use. East Pakistan, which has more than half the total population but less than a sixth of the territory, is mostly an alluvial area

with very restricted possibilities for the discovery of economic minerals. West Pakistan, which has sparsely populated mountainous terrain in three-fifths of its area, contains numerous widely scattered mineral deposits, but not more than a dozen mineral raw materials are in adequate supply to meet domestic requirements (table 1) and not more than half of these are available even in modest amounts for export (1).

Because of the short supply of indigenous raw materials, Pakistan depends heavily on imported mineral products to sustain its economy, causing a

*Publication authorized by the Director-General, Geological Survey of Pakistan, and by the Director, U.S. Geological Survey.

TABLE I. *Production of mineral commodities in Pakistan, 1956–60*

(Figures in long tons, from Pakistant Bureau of Mineral Resources*)

Commodity	1956	1957	1958	1959	1960
Antimony	156	164	36	152	89
Asbestos				46	
Barite			305	508	633
Bauxite	3,000	3,317	1,979	2,139	574
Bentonite					579
Celestite	300	854	457	664	1,332
China clay					73
Chromite	22,746	16,173	24,049	16,023	18,094
Coal	644,751	514,858	596,499	732,634	817,197
Copper					134
Dolomite					151
Fire clay	6,100	11,634	11,467	14,400	16,071
Fuller's earth					98
Gypsum	36,200	44,064	66,095	84,952	89,541
Iron ore	7,012	23,223	8,097	2,250	5,421
Lead			34	331	17
Limestone	756,400	913,871	1,119,120	925,142	1,063,577
Magnesite		22		396	434
Manganese				29	292
Marble		882	553	2,796	2,245
Ochre	400	411	231	276	451
Silica sand	10,500	21,414	19,740	21,611	25,873
Soapstone	1,100	1,232	1,585	2,340	3,370
Sodium carbonate					1,458
Rock salt	160,916	155,669	177,601	161,983	180,813

*Pakistan Bureau of Mineral Resources, *Annual report of activities for the year 1960*, Government of Pakistan Press, pages 42–43, Karachi (1960).

substantial drain on available foreign exchange. Imports of mineral fuels alone have recently exceeded the equivalent of $60 million each year. Moreover, the mining industry contributes less than a tenth of one percent ($13 million equivalent out of $6,300 million equivalent in 1959–60) to Pakistan's gross national product (2).

The supply of mineral raw materials and the economic contribution of the mining industry in Pakistan need not be permanently restricted to present levels. Geological environments in many parts of the country are favorable for the discovery of additional resources. A number of potentially important mineral deposits have been found by reconnaissance-mapping in recent years and it seems likely that other significant discoveries will be made as detailed geological mapping, which presently covers only about 5 percent of the country, and geophysical surveys for minerals, which have heretofore been limited to scattered localities, are carried forward (figures I and II). Many known mineral showings and low-grade deposits may be found to be exploitable as a result of geophysical or geochemical studies to locate buried extensions of mineralization or through mineralogical studies to develop methods for the recovery of minerals from low-grade ores. Furthermore, there are good possibilities for expanded production from known deposits through geological and technological studies to improve the quantity and quality of output, and increase the efficiency of mining.

In the 16 years since Pakistan achieved independence, an increase of more than $1\frac{1}{2}$ percent per year in population and a total increase of more than 500 percent in industrial production have rapidly intensified the demand for mineral raw materials. As a result, mineral exploration and development have been stressed in both the First Five Year Plan (1955–60) and the Second Five Year Plan, now under way. For the period from 1961 to 1965, an allocation of $210 million in rupee equivalent (3) has been made to stimulate the discovery and exploitation of minerals and mineral fuels, including $6 million in rupee equivalent for expansion of the Geological Survey of Pakistan in accordance with the goal expressed by the Pakistan Planning Commission (4) as follows:

"The task before the country is to develop the proved mineral resources as rapidly as possible, and to accelerate the geological investigation of unmapped areas and of identified but unproved deposits."

History and scope of the Mineral Exploration and Development Program. To help achieve the First Five Year Plan targets for mineral production, the U.S. Geological Survey and the Geological Survey of Pakistan began a cooperative program in September 1956 to intensify

the exploration and appraisal of Pakistan's mineral resources. Initially, this program was concerned mainly with expanding, reorganizing, training, and equipping the Geological Survey of Pakistan for increased effectiveness in geological mapping and exploration. In 1961, however, to help attain the goals of the Second Five Year Plan the program was expanded to include joint geological investigations in the principal mineralized districts in Pakistan, systematic appraisal of the nation's mineral resources, and preparation of regional geological and resources maps to guide future exploration. At the same time, the U.S. Bureau of Mines began assistance in mining technology, mine-development planning, and mineral-utilization studies as an integral part of the program.

As a result of this recent expansion, the cooperative Mineral Exploration and Development Program in Pakistan, which involves all aspects of geological and mining investigations, is one of the most comprehensive efforts now being made in a newly independent nation to increase the discovery, appraisal, production, and utilization of indigenous mineral raw materials. The progressive increase in staff and funds assigned to this program by Pakistan and the United States is shown in figure III.

The scope, organization, and operating methods of the Pakistan Mineral Exploration and Development Program are, of course, adjusted to circumstances existing in Pakistan, such as the possibilities for mineral development; the structure and responsibilities of agencies concerned with mineral resources; and the capabilities of staff made available by the cooperating governments. Although the circumstances may be different in other countries, it is believed that some of the concepts and methods used in the Pakistan Program would be applicable in other newly independent nations that urgently need to increase the production of indigenous resources.

Agencies and officials directly responsible for the Program. Responsibility for the execution of the Mineral Exploration and Development Program has been assigned by the Government of Pakistan to N. M. Khan, Program Director, and by the U.S. Agency for International Development to John A. Reinemund, Senior Program Advisor. The successful operation of the Program, however, is a result of the collective efforts of the more than 1,000 Pakistani employees and the 30 United States employees assigned to the Program, and to the support given by officials of both governments.

Objectives and Functions of the Program

Major objectives and sub-programs. As now constituted, the Mineral Exploration and Development Program in Pakistan is a cooperative effort to increase the exploration, appraisal, development, and utilization of Pakistan's mineral, mineral fuel, and ground-water resources to help achieve the economic targets in the Second Five Year Plan. Major objectives of the Program are defined as follows in the agreement between Pakistan and the United States under which this Program operates:

"Through this project it is hoped to achieve a rapid increase in the production and supply of raw materials needed for the growth of industry and agriculture in Pakistan, by creating a higher rate of geologic mapping and exploration to locate new mineral and mineral fuel resources; promptly evaluating the reserves and mining possibilities of the known resources; preparing and publishing geologic and resources maps and reports needed to guide future prospecting and development; improving the mining techniques, output, and efficiency of existing mines; planning and guiding the development of major new mines; and increasing the reserves and marketing possibilities of indigenous mineral raw materials."

The Mineral Exploration and Development Program includes three closely integrated sub-programs: Geological Survey Consulting Service; Geological Exploration and Resource Appraisal; and Mining Technology and Development. Each of these has specific objectives and functions and is intended to fill a significant need in achieving maximum production and utilization of Pakistan's geological resources.

Geological Survey Consulting Service. The Geological Survey Consulting Service, which was established in 1956, is intended to help organize, train, and equip the Geological Survey of Pakistan to make it fully effective as a national geological investigations and research organization capable of performing the following functions: to explore, evaluate, and determine the development possibilities of the known mineral, mineral fuel, and ground-water resources of Pakistan; survey areas favorable for locating additional resources; investigate geological conditions and availability of construction materials at public construction projects; classify the mineral potential of leased areas; provide geological criteria for conservation rules and practices; and supply geological consultation, advice, and resources information as required by other agencies.

Increasing the size, scope, and effectiveness of the Geological Survey of Pakistan was given initial emphasis under the Mineral Exploration and Development Program, partly because an effective Geological Survey is a basic requirement for a thorough and continuing inventory of national resources and partly because an excellent start had already been made in creating a modern Survey department.

When Pakistan achieved independence in August 1947, it acquired an embryonic Geological Survey consisting of six geologists and two chemists who had been on the staff of the Geological Survey of India. Under the leadership of H. L. Crookshank, who was Director of the Geological Survey until 1955, the technical staff was increased to 30; a tradition of rigorous field investigations was created; a preliminary catalogue of economic minerals was compiled (5); and geophysical surveying was introduced as an integral part of Survey operations. Also during this period, a significant advance in reconnaissance geological mapping of West Pakistan was made by the Photographic Survey Corporation of Toronto under Canadian auspices in association with the Geological Survey of Pakistan through a Colombo Plan project (6) that covered the southwestern half of the province (figure I).

As a result of these early activities, the Geological Survey's staff and program by 1956 formed an excellent base for expansion into an organization capable of supplying Pakistan's rapidly growing requirements for geological investigations and information. Therefore, when the Geological Survey Consulting Service was started in 1956 as the first phase of the Mineral Exploration and Development Program, it was feasible to establish optimistic targets for the Survey's growth in size, scope, and effectiveness. From 1956 to 1959, under the leadership of E. R. Gee, a comprehensive expansion plan was initiated (7), a systematic field training program was started, photogeologic and drilling sections were organized, systematic publications procedures were established, and plans for constructing a new headquarters at Quetta were approved. Under the direction of N. M. Khan, who took over the direction of the Geological Survey in 1959, and with the increased emphasis given to geological investigations under the Second Five Year Plan, expansion targets for the Geological Survey were further increased and the Geological Survey Consulting Service was expanded to its present size and scope.

This part of the Program involves the services of 11 specialists from the U.S. Geological Survey (table 2) who are assigned to work with the senior staff of the Geological Survey of Pakistan in reorganization of the Geological Survey, technical and supervisory training of staff, conduct of specific demonstration projects, and development of new procedures, techniques, and facilities. It also involves training of selected members of the staff in the United States, the supply of about $1,500,000 in field and laboratory equipment from Pakistan and United States funds, and the construction of a new 12-building Geological Survey headquarters establishment at Quetta, West Pakistan, and a new building for its eastern regional office at Dacca, East Pakistan, at a total cost exceeding a million dollars in rupee equivalent.

Targets for the Geological Survey Consulting Service include expansion of the Survey to a technical staff of about 220, training of new staff adequately for independent work, organization of staff into well-defined branches and divisions, completion of at least 10 technical demonstration projects, construction of scheduled buildings in Quetta and Dacca, and installation and use of all equipment. The progress of expansion, training, demonstration, construction, and procurement in recent years has been at a rate sufficient to achieve these targets by 1965.

Geological Exploration and Resource Appraisal. In April 1961, the second part of the Program was established. Its objectives are to promote the

TABLE 2. *Specialists and technical activities of the three parts of the Pakistan Mineral Exploration and Development Program*

	Categories of activity	Type of activity	No. of U.S. specialists
Part 1. Geological Survey Consulting Service.	Geological administration Economic geology (metals) Economic geology (non-metals) Economic geology (fuels) Engineering geology Photogeology Paleontology Mineralogy Geological engineering Photography Map publication	Demonstration, consultation, and training; conduct of specific technical projects for demonstration and training purposes; introduction of new techniques and methods.	One in each category
Part 2. Geological Exploration and Resource Appraisal.	Geological resources Regional surveys Mineral surveys Map compilation Photogrammetry Paleoecology Geophysics Geochemistry Cartography Drilling Electronic equipment Programming	Technical projects in mineral investigations, mapping, and resources appraisal; consultation, demonstration, and training undertaken as supplemental activities.	1 4 2 1 2 1 1 1 1 1 1 1
Part 3. Mining Technology and Development.	Technological administration Mining technology (minerals) Mining technology (coal) Mineral dressing	Technical projects in mining technology and mineral utilization; consultation service to mining industry; demonstration and training.	One in each category

rapid discovery and appraisal of economically important mineral resources, to provide data on mineral reserves for realistic development planning, and to encourage investment in resources development. This part of the Program is intended to supplement the work of the Geological Survey of Pakistan until that agency is fully staffed, trained, and equipped, with the help of the Geological Survey Consulting Service, to independently undertake the investigations required for maximum exploration and development of resources.

At the start of the Second 5-Year Plan in 1960, it was apparent that even with the help provided by the Geological Survey Consulting Service, the Geological Survey of Pakistan would not be able to undertake the mapping, exploration, and appraisal of the Nation's resources rapidly enough to meet the requirements for economic growth during the Plan period. About half the Geological Survey's staff were newly recruited and in need of several years of specialized training before they could be important contributors to the Survey's operations. Nearly two-thirds of the total planned staff were still to be recruited, mainly because of the relatively small output of geologists from Pakistan universities prior to 1960 (table 3).

The shortage of trained staff was accompanied by an urgent need to undertake many important geological commitments. Most mineral showings and mining districts had not been thoroughly investigated, up-to-date summary maps and reports had not been prepared for most mineral resources, and compilation of a new geological map of Pakistan had not been started. Demands for Survey investigations from the Pakistan Atomic Energy Commission, Pakistan Industrial Development Corporation, other governmental agencies, and industries needing geological information were far in excess of the Geological Survey's investigational capacity.

TABLE 3. *Number of students completing courses in geology and geophysics at universities in Pakistan through 1961**

University	Course	Year											
		1950	'51	'52	'53	'54	'55	'56	'57	'58	'59	'60	'61
Karachi..........	BSc							1	4	....	8	9	14
	Geology MSc										9	3	18
Dacca............	BSc		3	5	5	6	7	8	16	19	19	19	18
	Geology MSc										6	3	7
Punjab...........	BSc						4	7	3	8	28	19	14
	Geology MSc							5	....		6	5	7
	Geophysics MSc											4	5
Sind.............	BSc									1	6	10	14
	Geology MSc												4
Totals..........	BSc		3	5	5	6	11	16	23	28	61	57	60
	Geology MSc							5	...		21	11	36
	Geophysics MSc											4	5

* Geology courses at Peshawar University were not started until 1961.

To help meet these urgent demands during the expansion period of the Geological Survey, it was necessary to provide extensive assistance in geological and related investigations. Accordingly, the Geological Exploration and Resources Appraisal subprogram was established, involving the services of 17 specialists from the U.S. Geological Survey (table 2) who work with selected staff of the Geological Survey of Pakistan on geological, geophysical, and geochemical surveys of the principal mineralized districts, systematic evaluation and appraisal of mineral deposits or showings, preparation of summary resources maps and reports, and preparation of a new geological map of Pakistan.

Targets for this part of the Program include the determination of mineral potential and significance of known deposits in the principal mineralized districts in Pakistan; detailed geological mapping of economically important parts of these mineral districts, compilation and publication of a series of four maps of Pakistan showing geology and economic resources, and preparation and publication of a series of reports describing the resources of the mineral commodities in Pakistan that are available for exploitation.

Mining Technology and Development. Beginning in June 1961, the U.S. Bureau of Mines undertook the third part of the Program, called Mining Technology and Development, which involves consultation and guidance to the Government and mining industry of Pakistan in mining engineering, mine supervision, mine planning, raw material utilization, and mineral economics. It is intended to help stimulate a rapid increase in mineral production by helping to improve existing mines, develop new mines, organize training programs in mine engineering and supervision, investigate possible uses of known mineral resources of Pakistan, and develop a Pakistani engineering staff to carry on similar activities in the future.

The Mining Technology and Development subprogram was established to help make prompt and effective use of geological information obtained through the activities of the first two parts of the Program. A rapid increase in mineral production could not be achieved unless realistic plans were made to encourage the development of newly discovered resources, improvements were achieved in existing mining methods, and markets were found for known resources not being mined. No agency existed in Pakistan to undertake such activities. The Pakistan Industrial Development Corporation (recently divided into East and West Pakistan Industrial Development Corporations) had contracted with foreign consultants and employed foreign engineers in its government-owned coal and iron mines, but there were few qualified engineers available to assist the private mining operators, and the Pakistan mining industry in general was not served by an engineering organization—either governmental or private—having staff and facilities adequate to undertake the mining technology and mineral utilization studies needed in Pakistan.

Under this part of the Program, services of three mining engineers and one metallurgist are presently supplied by the U.S. Bureau of Mines. These specialists work in close coordination with the Pakistan and United States geological staff assigned to the first 2 parts of the Program in appraising the development and utilization potential of mineral showings and deposits. They also work with mine operators in studies of principal mining districts to recommend better mining methods and plan unified development of the districts. Demonstration engineering projects have been established in selected mine areas, and a refresher course in the fundamentals of mine surveying has been organized for mine surveyors. Plans for establishment of a mineral dressing laboratory have been completed.

Targets for this subprogram include the organization of mine engineering studies, mine planning, training in mining methods, and demonstration of mining techniques in each major mining district; preparation of unified plans for development of mining districts; evaluation of mining potential of all significant undeveloped resources; creation of a mining technology and mineral research staff of at least 20 Pakistani engineers to help in the execution of this subprogram; and establishment of three regional mining technology centers—two in West Pakistan and one in East Pakistan.

Originally this part of the Mineral Exploration and Development Program was conducted in collaboration with the Pakistan Bureau of Mineral Resources—an agency of the central government that existed from 1959 to 1962 and included the Geological Survey, Department of Petroleum and Minerals, and other offices dealing with mineral leasing, statistics, and imports. Expansion of this Bureau had been planned to include a mining technology staff that would assist the United States specialists in carrying on the functions of the Program. However, in 1962 the Bureau was abolished under the new Pakistan Constitution and most of its functions, apart from the Geological Survey, were transferred to the provincial governments. Thereafter, the organization of a mining technology and mineral

research staff was rescheduled for close affiliation with the Geological Survey of Pakistan in the Ministry of Industries and Natural Resources.

Organization and Methods of the Program

Major Activities. All activities in the three parts of the Mineral Exploration and Development Program may be grouped into three categories: technical, administrative, and supervisory. The staff provided by the United States agencies serve as consultants to the Geological Survey of Pakistan in all three categories. In addition, they participate directly with Pakistani staff in technical investigations and in certain administrative and supervisory functions authorized by the program director and senior program advisor.

Technical activities in which Pakistani and United States staff are cooperatively engaged are in the fields listed in table 2; their organization and scope are described in paragraphs 36–42.

Administrative activities include budget and accounts, procurement, property control, and personnel. These are mostly handled by the administrative staff of the Geological Survey of Pakistan, except for procurement, which is mostly handled by the Pakistan Department of Supply and Development. A geologic program assistant provided by the U.S. Geological Survey helps in preparing budgets, program and training documents, specifications for equipment, and records of program activities. Property control is exclusively the responsibility of the Geological Survey of Pakistan, and personnel actions are the responsibility of the cooperating agencies of the two governments to which the staff are permanently assigned.

Supervisory activities include direct supervision of technical and administrative operations; development of operating objectives, plans, and schedules; establishment of procedures; and contacts with officials and agencies in the cooperating governments. Overall supervision of the program is the responsibility of the program director and senior program advisor, who coordinate their activities by frequent informal consultations. Immediate technical supervision is exercised by senior consultants from the United States in geology and mining technology in association with the staff in the Office of Program and Planning which is described below.

Organization of Functional Units. Technical, administrative, and supervisory activities conducted jointly by Pakistani and United States personnel are divided into functional units as shown in figure IV. Some functional units, such as those under "Economic Geology," are not organizational entities at present—they exist only as groupings of technical projects and staff. Other units, such as those under "Technical Services," now exist as branches in the Geological Survey of Pakistan, although in none of these are the internal structure, operating procedures, and functional responsibility completely defined.

Establishment of a suitable internal organization structure and appropriate operating procedures is a major goal of the Mineral Exploration and Development Program. It seems likely that this structure will be similar to that shown in figure IV, and, in fact, well-defined organization and procedures have already been established for an Office of Program and Planning and an Office of Publication and Information with the Geological Survey of Pakistan. As the technical operations of the Program become more firmly established, experienced Pakistani officers become available for key posts, and administrative procedures are developed and tested, it is planned gradually to define and establish branches and Divisions for the other functional categories. This will involve the definition of responsibilities and functions for each organizational unit, the preparation of position descriptions for each post in the unit, and the compilation of a manual of administrative and technical procedures.

Pending the establishment of a complete internal organization, the operational control of the Mineral Exploration and Development Program and the Geological Survey of Pakistan is exercised by the Office of Program and Planning. Such supervisory activities as personnel assignments, performance evaluation, and review of technical progress, which will ultimately become the responsibility of branch and Division chiefs, are presently handled jointly by Pakistani and United States personnel attached to the Office of Program and Planning.

The ultimate organizational status of the mining technology and mineral utilization functions has not as yet been determined. Whether these functions will be an integral part of the Geological Survey or a closely affiliated organization depends partly on the scope of the technical activities ultimately undertaken by the Central Government in Pakistan in support of mineral development and partly on the size of the governmental mining technology and mineral research activities that are required to support the mining industry.

Organization of Technical Activities. All technical activities of the

Mineral Exploration and Development Program are organized into technical projects staffed jointly by Pakistani and United States personnel. As of September 1, 1962, there were 52 geological projects and 5 technological projects. Additional technological projects will be started as rapidly as Pakistani engineers become available.

Each technical project is a discrete part of the Program, concerned with a selected type or area of investigation, and intended to achieve specific objectives that are necessary for the attainment of overall program goals. The importance, objectives, general methods and schedule of work, reports to be prepared, and staff to be assigned for each project are specified in a Technical Project Description and Schedule prepared by the Office of Program and Planning and approved by the program director and senior program advisor before the project is started.

At the beginning of each fiscal year (July 1), a Technical Project Operating Schedule is prepared jointly by senior Pakistani and United States staff on each project and submitted through the Office of Program and Planning to the Program Director and Senior Program Advisor for approval. This gives the detailed operating schedule for each member of the staff for the ensuing 12 months, a summary of the project accomplishments for the preceding 12 months, and a listing of the reports or maps to be prepared by the following June 30. After approval, this document serves as a guide and a commitment for the staff of the project. It is also used by the Office of Program and Planning in compiling an annual report on accomplishments and plans which is issued mainly for the guidance of governmental officials and agencies inter-

ested or involved in the operations of the Program.

It is, of course, necessary and desirable at times to change or amplify the plans given in the Technical Project Operating Schedule. Such interim changes or clarifications in project schedules are made by a Memorandum Report of Operations and Plans prepared by senior project staff personnel in consultation with the staff of the Office of Program and Planning. Copies are distributed to all who are directly or indirectly concerned with the project. Approval by the program director and senior program advisor is not required unless changes in project staff or objectives are involved.

Technical projects in geology are distributed so as to cover the principal mineralized districts and geological resources in Pakistan (figure V), to obtain data for preparing summary reports on raw material resources; and to supply lithological, stratigraphical, and structural information for use in preparing geologic, tectonic, and resource maps of the country. The staffs of these projects are expected to serve as expert consultants in the areas or fields of investigation with which the projects are concerned. For each project that involves mapping of a specified area, the project staff is responsible for initial examination of all newly reported economic mineral localities in the area and for obtaining any geological information required to fill interim requests from other agencies.

Technical projects in mining technology include studies of possibilities for improved mining methods, coordinated mine planning, increased output, better quality control, and expanded markets for principal mining districts. It is hoped to increase the number of technology projects during the next 2 years so that all mining districts will be covered and utilization studies of all major raw material resources will be started. Engineers assigned to each project are expected to serve as consultants to mine operators in the district covered by the project within the limits of available time and until the operators have access to private consultants.

A single activity titled Mineral Resources Evaluation in Pakistan, staffed jointly by Pakistani and United States geologists and engineers, comprises a project in geology and a project in technology. These projects are intended to make rapid evaluation of new mineral discoveries, prepare recommendations for exploration or initial development needed to prove the deposit, and prepare summary reports describing the major mineral resources of Pakistan and their development possibilities. The combined operating schedule for both projects is revised every 3 months to incorporate the needs for examination of new discoveries. The staff of these projects is available for consultation with, and assistance to, other projects as required for specialized mineral investigations. The projects maintain a comprehensive mineral commodity file containing data and references to all mineral showings in Pakistan, and during the year beginning July 1, 1962 they are preparing, or supervising the preparation of, national mineral maps and summary reports on the following commodities: iron, manganese, copper, lead, zinc, antimony, laterite, clay, bentonite, limestone, marble, magnesite, barite, celestite, glass sand, greensand, construction materials, gypsum, salt, sulphur, potash, and sulphate.

Methods of Technical and Supervisory Training. Training of young geologists and mining engineers is one of the most important goals of the Mineral Exploration and Development Program, as future mineral development in Pakistan will depend in large part on the vitality of the Geological Survey of Pakistan and associated agencies resulting from the capabilities and interest of the technical staffs. Moreover, owing to shortages of staff and funds, many aspects of geology and engineering are not adequately covered in the Pakistan universities and, in consequence, recruits in geology and engineering generally need intensive instructions in fundamentals as well as specialized training and experience over a period of several years in governmental service before they are ready for productive participation in technical investigations.

To expedite the training of Pakistani geologists and mining engineers, training activities are in progress at four levels, as follows:

(a) University training assistance, involving (i) lectures and short courses at five universities by about 25 senior Pakistani and United States personnel during the present year to augment the university curriculum, and (ii) arrangements for students to be assigned to field and laboratory work with the Mineral Exploration and Development Program for practical training during vacation periods.

(b) Basic training of all newly recruited Pakistani geologists and mining engineers, who are assigned to technical projects on which they will work under close supervision of senior Pakistani or United States personnel.

(c) Foreign training of technical staff at intermediate grades who have had several years of experience and have demonstrated an aptitude for specialized work. The staff are selected on the basis of proved capacity for work in the selected fields of study and they are required to take along information, maps, samples, or other material from individual investigation on Pakistan resources, to be worked into publishable reports as part of their foreign study. To date, 33 participants have been sent under this technical assistance program.

(d) Senior staff personnel from the Geological Survey of Pakistan are sent abroad for highly advanced research and study in selected fields that are of outstanding importance for future growth of the Survey. This type of training activity was inaugurated in 1959 by N. M. Khan, who undertook and helped to organize a highly successful 6-month study of geological administration with the U.S. Geological Survey.

All staff sent abroad for training are selected jointly by the program director and senior program advisor. In the United States the training is supervised and arranged by the Geological Survey and the Bureau of Mines.

Methods of Publication. One of the principal goals of the Mineral Exploration and Development Program is publication of maps and reports giving the results of the technical projects for use in resource development. Most of the technical activity of the Program produces maps and reports. The adequacy of these products and the speed of publication determine to a large extent the effectiveness of the Program. To aid in establishing a more efficient publication activity, specialists in map compilation, cartography, photography, and photo-grammetry have been added to the Program; a senior Pakistani geologist was sent to the United States in 1961–62 for study of map editing and processing techniques, and a manual was prepared giving standards for use in Geological Survey of Pakistan reports.

Five publication series have been established as follows:

(a) Administrative Series, consisting of short report for limited distribution containing economically important results of investigations on which rapid publication is essential.

(b) Geologic Investigation Series, containing interim reports covering major units of technical investigation or partial results of technical projects.

(c) Geologic Map Series, including general-purpose multicolor geologic and topographic maps covering 15-minute or 1-degree quadrangles published in a standard format with cross sections, columnar sections, and explanation on a sheet 35 x 45 inches. National and regional geological or resource maps are also to be published in this series.

(d) Records Series, containing final reports of technical projects, summary resource reports, and annual reports.

(e) Memoirs Series, containing major scientific reports and papers of a highly specialized nature.

As of September 1, 1962, 22 reports have been issued or were in press and 62 were being edited for publication in the series listed above. A bibliography of reports issued or in press is given at the end of this paper. More than 50 mimeographed file reports were also prepared, but not formally published, from 1956 to 1960.

Major Concepts of the Program

In concluding this review of the Mineral Exploration and Development Program in Pakistan, it seems appropriate to list the major concepts that have been used in organizing and guiding the program. These are as follows:

(a) Investigations in geology and mining technology in government should be concentrated in, or closely affiliated with, the Geological Survey of Pakistan. In view of the shortage of technical and supervisory staff, funds, and facilities, dispersal of geological and technological functions among several agencies is both administratively inefficient and economically unsound.

(b) The Geological Survey of Pakistan should be organized, trained, and equipped to efficiently undertake all the resource investigations required to meet the needs of other governmental agencies and to support geological resource development, and the Mineral Exploration and Development Program, and should provide the full range of technical assistance needed for this purpose.

(c) Pakistani and United States personnel should be fully integrated and work jointly on all projects to encourage cooperation, promote understanding and exchange of ideas, and make possible maximum on-the-job training.

(d) All training possible should be done in Pakistan under expert supervision, on technical projects so that the trainees can contribute to the work output of the projects. Foreign training should be limited to subjects and courses not adequately covered in Pakistan and to personnel whose potential has been demonstrated by several years of satisfactory on-the-job performance.

(e) All activities of the program should be directed toward upbuilding the permanent effectiveness of the counterpart agency and staff, as well as toward completion of specific technical projects.

REFERENCES

(1) Government of Pakistan Central Statistical Office, *Statistical pocketbook of Pakistan,* Government of Pakistan Press, p. 69, Karachi (1962).

(2) Government of Pakistan, *The Second Five Year Plan* (revised), Government of Pakistan Press, p. 61, Karachi (1961).

(3) Government of Pakistan, *The Second Five Year Plan* (revised), Government of Pakistan Press, p. 36, Karachi (1961).

(4) Government of Pakistan, *The Second Five Year Plan,* Government of Pakistan Press, p. 265, Karachi (1960).

(5) Geological Survey of Pakistan, *Directory of Economic Minerals of Pakistan,* Records of the Geological Survey of Pakistan, 7, pt. 2, 146 pp. (1955).

(6) Photographic Survey Corporation, *Reconnaissance geology of part of West Pakistan,* Government of Canada, 30 sheets, Ottawa (1958).

(7) Gee, E. R., *The role of geology and allied sciences in the economic development of Pakistan,* Pakistan Association for the Advancement of Science, 11 pp., Lahore (1958).

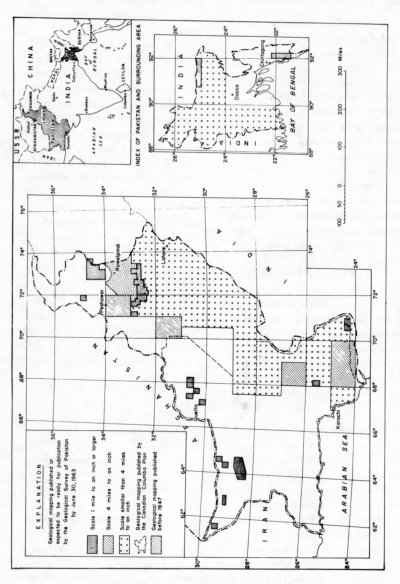

FIGURE 1. Status of geological mapping by Geological Survey of Pakistan.

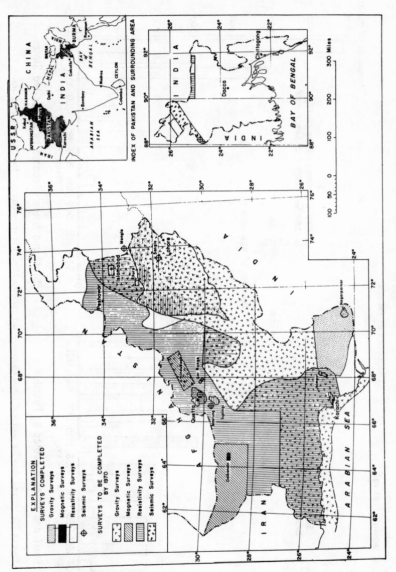

FIGURE II. Status of geophysical surveys by Geological Survey of Pakistan.

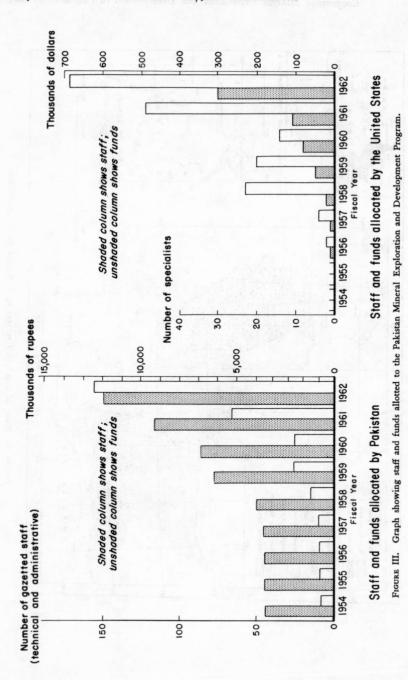

Figure III. Graph showing staff and funds allotted to the Pakistan Mineral Exploration and Development Program.

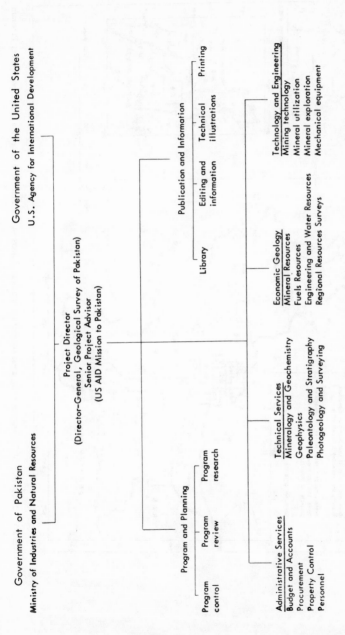

Government of Pakistan
Ministry of Industries and Natural Resources

Government of the United States
U.S. Agency for International Development

Project Director
(Director-General, Geological Survey of Pakistan)
Senior Project Advisor
(US AID Mission to Pakistan)

Program and Planning

Program
control

Program
review

Program
research

Technical Services
Mineralogy and Geochemistry
Geophysics
Paleontology and Stratigraphy
Photogeology and Surveying

Administrative Services
Budget and Accounts
Procurement
Property Control
Personnel

Economic Geology
Mineral Resources
Fuels Resources
Engineering and Water Resources
Regional Resources Surveys

Publication and Information

Library

Editing and
information

Technical
illustrations

Printing

Technology and Engineering
Mining technology
Mineral utilization
Mineral exploration
Mechanical equipment

This chart shows the relationship of activities with which the combined Pakistani and United States staffs assigned to the Mineral Exploration and Development Program are now concerned. The chart does not illustrate the structure of a particular governmental organization, but shows the relation between functional categories performed jointly by the assigned staffs from the cooperating agencies.

FIGURE IV.   Functional organization of the Pakistan Mineral Exploration and Development Program.

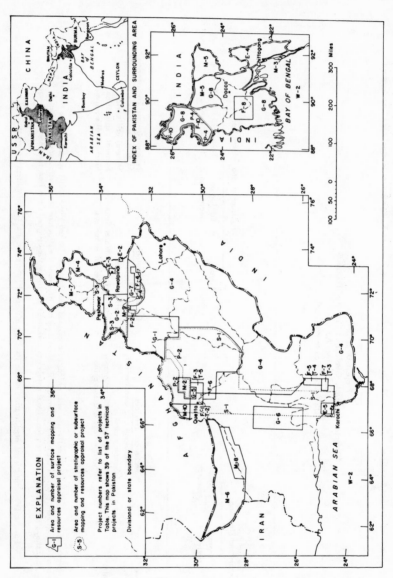

FIGURE V. Index map of Pakistan showing areas covered by technical projects of the Mineral Exploration and Development Program.

Organizing for Agricultural Development

FORREST F. HILL

Vice President, The Ford Foundation, New York

ARTHUR T. MOSHER

Executive Director, The Council on Economic and Cultural Affairs, Inc., New York

Introduction

There are two crucial points requiring attention in organizing for agricultural development. One is the individual farm or holding. The other is the wider economy as it affects agriculture.

This paper will be concerned primarily with the first point, with emphasis upon those aspects of organization that bear most immediately upon the production decisions of farm operators. Attention will be focused upon the kinds of jobs that need to be done if substantial and sustained increases in agricultural production are to be achieved, and upon the more difficult problems of organizing to do them. Scant attention will be given to forms of organization or to administration.

Back of those activities that have an immediate bearing upon farmers' production decisions are a host of supporting activities in the wider economy that are essential to agricultural development—provision of transportation networks; general and technical education; health facilities; appropriate patterns of land settlement, tenure and tenancy; irrigation facilities; appropriate tax, credit, fiscal and monetary policies; and many others. Although each of these influences agricultural development, directly or indirectly, and to a greater or less extent, because of space limitations we shall do no more in this paper than recognize their importance. We shall concentrate on what seems to us to be the central problem of organizing for agricultural development; namely, how to broaden and make attractive the alternatives available to each farm operator in the direction of increasing farm output.

Basic Considerations in Organizing for Agricultural Development

Agricultural production is not a mechanical process but one of facilitating biological growth under almost infinitely varying conditions. It is very different from factory production, in which it is possible to control within narrow limits the quality and quantity of each input and the environment in which the production process takes place in order to produce, day in and day out, a highly standardized product in predetermined amounts. Instead, agriculture is carried on in varying climates under fluctuating weather conditions, drawing upon variable supplies of plant nutrients and soil moisture, using crop varieties of differing genetic potential, and with crops and livestock subject to diseases, pests, and other hazards.

On most of the cultivated lands of the earth, there are variations in soils, available plant nutrients, soil-water relationships, and in sunlight, air and soil temperatures during the growing season, not only among regions and areas within regions but in greater or less degree from farm to farm, field to field, and even

within fields. The north and south slopes of a single hill may be best adapted to different crops or require a different set of production practices for best results. The intricate pattern of land use on individual farms in Japan illustrates close adjustment of agricultural production to microdifferences in factors affecting plant growth. Fields at different distances from villages in North India currently differ widely in soil fertility. They are planted to different crops and cultivated with different intensity.

Thus, it is characteristic of the production process in agriculture that, in technical terms, the quality and quantity of most inputs are variable, and joint costs and joint products are more characteristic than in many types of industrial production.

What this means for agricultural development is that standardized recommendations for wide areas of agricultural land are seldom if ever justified. Instead, the essence of maximizing agricultural production is to find the best use for individual fields and plots, modifying each in such ways as are necessary and economically feasible to increase the quantity and improve the quality of the product.

Although the basic process in agriculture is the management of biological growth, *agricultural production is an economic activity*. In societies in which the farm operator (whether owner, tenant, or hired manager) makes production decisions, the individual farm or holding is the unit for which costs and returns must be compared whether in monetary or nonmonetary terms. It may be that the real cost of using a new production technique is decreased leisure or lowered social status if the cultivator is considered by his neighbors to have violated his role in society by breaking a long-established tradition. An increased harvest does not constitute increased income if the cultivator is forced by social custom to share it through feasting or to support relatives instead of being allowed to sell it. Or an increased harvest, beyond family and local needs, may not represent increased returns if there is not a market for it at a remunerative price.

The key to agricultural development is to make it *possible and attractive* for the operator of each farm or holding to change practices in ways that will increase production on a sustained basis. *It is on the alternative combinations of practices available to the individual operator and the potential rewards associated with these alternatives that attention must be focused if substantial and sustained agricultural development is to be achieved.*

In organizing for agricultural development we are trying to encourage and help men and women to behave in a manner that will result in their producing more agricultural products, but at the same time we must recognize and respect the fact that few of them are interested in production for the sake of production but only as it serves ultimate values and goals held by them or by the social groups of which they are members.

In this era of national planning, we have grown accustomed to thinking in national terms and national programs. This is important and has its place. But we must never allow the national view, important as it is, to cause us to overlook those characteristics of agriculture that make imperative the use of effective local integration of efforts to increase production and the substantial adaptation of development programs to meet varying sets of local conditions.

What has been said applies almost equally in regions where agriculture is still largely *traditional,* in regions where it is in the *transitional* stage of development, and in places where agriculture has entered the *commercial* stage. In the remainder of our paper, however, we shall center our attention on organizing for agricultural development at the early transitional stage. This stage has two important characteristics: First, it is the stage in which farmers' decisions are based less and less upon tradition and more and more upon rational choice from alternatives.. Second, it is the stage when more and more purchased requisites are used in agricultural production.

If, at the early transitional stage, a program to increase agricultural production is to be successful, effective organization and follow-through are essential in three areas:

(a) First, provision must be made for developing *locally-tested* combinations of improved practices which, if adopted by farmers, will increase production on their farms;

(b) Second, production supplies and equipment of the kinds and quality farmers must have if they are to put recommended combinations of practices into effect must be locally available when needed;

(c) Third, individual farmers must be convinced that the recommended practices will in fact increase production on their farms and that it is to their advantage to adopt them.

Activities in these three areas must be carefully coordinated in a single, integrated program if sustained development at a satisfactory rate is to be achieved.

Locally Tested Combinations of Practices

Economic increases in agricultural production seldom result from the adoption of a single improved practice. Substantial and sustainable increases in agricultural production usually depend upon the use of a *combination* of improved practices including use of improved crop varieties; use of chemical fertilizers and other measures to insure an adequate and balanced supply of available plant nutrients; practices designed to provide suitable water-air relationships in the soil; and plant protection measures.

Since there are usually significant variations among farms, and even among the fields of a single farm, in soils, topography, available supplies of plant nutrients, water relations, air and soil temperature, sunlight, etc., it follows that not one but many different combinations of inputs must be used in a single community and even on different fields of a single farm if returns from land, labor, purchased requisites and other factors are to be maximized. Seldom, if ever, is a single set of recommended practices suitable for use without adjustment throughout an area of appreciable size. Such a set of "standard" recommendations is like the U.S. Army uniforms in World War I, designed to fit the "average" man with the result that they were too big for half the army and too small for the other half. There is, of course, a limit to the number of sizes of clothing it is feasible to manufacture, whether for soldiers or civilians. The individual either has to be satisfied with an approxi-

mate fit or get a local tailor to make the necessary adjustments. So it is with agricultural practices. Even the recommended practices that constitute the "best fit" for a particular farm usually require some adjustment if the best results are to be obtained, especially when economic considerations and the operator's management capabilities and financial position are taken into account.

A large body of scientific and technical knowledge exists that makes possible the development of locally-adapted practices that, if properly applied, will increase agricultural production by substantial amounts in the developing countries. Unfortunately, political leaders, government administrators and members of the public with little knowledge of agriculture sometimes fail to distinguish between this general body of knowledge and its application to specific situations. The scientific principles and the art of plant breeding are highly developed. It may still remain *to apply* the principles and the art to the development of varieties of wheat, corn or rice suited to particular conditions of soil, climate, consumer tastes, etc.

It should not be overlooked that even in countries with highly developed programs of agricultural research, while some research workers are adding their bit to the world's store of basic knowledge, by far the greater number are engaged in applying known principles to the solution of local problems. They are engaged in trying to develop improved practices that, when appropriately combined, will better meet the needs of farmers in particular situations.

Few developing countries have the necessary financial resources or trained personnel to establish a full-fledged system of central laboratories and research stations, experimental farms and demonstration fields within a short span of years. Too often in such circumstances the tendency is to establish central laboratories and research stations to which the scientific staff retreat, there to engage in long-term, station-based research when the pressing need is for field studies and diagnosis of key problems retarding agricultural development and for scientific and technical work designed to find solutions to them. Laboratory and central station research is needed in developing countries. The question, however, is not whether such research is needed but how to make the *best use* of limited scientific and technical personnel and other scarce resources in the early stages of transition from a traditional toward a more highly commercialized agriculture.

Field trials and test demonstrations supervised and evaluated by research scientists have two special advantages at this stage. First, they take research scientists into the field where they come into direct contact with production problems, members of the agricultural advisory staff, and practicing farmers. This usually proves useful all · around, particularly in providing for the kind of "feedback" to central research stations and laboratories that is necessary if successive roadblocks to increased production are to be systematically attacked as they appear. Second, observation of local field trials and test demonstations by farmers can have an important influence in their developing a rational scientific attitude toward farming. In observing local testing and field trials, farmers may learn the basic steps of observation, measurement, comparison of results and drawing of conclusions that are the fundamentals of rational thinking and science-based agriculture.

Production Requisites

Efficient and timely production and distribution of the requisites of agricultural production are a basic requirement in the shift from a traditional toward a commercial agriculture. This is too often overlooked in the early years of the transitional stage and too little effort and too few resources devoted to the manufacture (or importation) of the production supplies and equipment required by a changing agriculture. The first requirement is to get "requisites" (purchased equipment and supplies) of the required kind and quality, produced or imported. This must be followed by measures to improve distribution, reduce costs, and assure the quality of the product as it reaches the farmer.

The purchasable inputs or requisites of agricultural production fall into four principal groups: (a) improved seeds; (b) fertilizers; (c) pesticides; and (d) implements, handtools and sources of mechanical power. Seeds better than those now in use by most farmers already are available locally in many places. In traditional and early transitional agriculture, there is considerable variation in the productivity of seeds customarily sown by different farmers. In addition, few farmers systematically collect, save, and use the best of their own seed. Consequently, the first and easiest step in the provision of better seed is to find the best of the seeds already in use in each locality and to introduce more systematic seed selection and storage by individual farm operators.

Production

All production requisites other than seeds—fertilizers, pesticides, implements and tools, and sources of mechanical power—must be manufactured. They differ, however, in whether they can be manufactured locally, using present technology; whether they can be efficiently manufactured in many small, widely scattered plants using new technology; or whether they can be efficiently manufactured only in centralized plants of large capacity. Improved implements and tools often can be manufactured locally by rural artisans using present technology. Some pesticides, and many tools and implements, can be manufactured in small-scale plants using new technology. Fertilizers ordinarily require large-scale manufacture in centralized plants if the operation is to be efficient.

Only two of the four principal classes of requisites needed for increased agricultural production—namely, fertilizers and pesticides—may require substantial amounts of foreign exchange to finance imports at the beginning of a program for agricultural development. These requisites are so important to agricultural development that sufficient foreign exchange should be made available to import as much of each as farm operators are ready to buy. The great importance of fertilizers and pesticides, and the demand their importation places on available foreign exchange, requires that the establishing of fertilizer and pesticide manufacture should have high priority in plans for industrialization in every country of substantial size in which agriculture is a major industry.

The provision of improved seeds normally will make very little demand on foreign exchange. Implements, tools and sources of mechanical power can make high demands on foreign exchange if allowed to do so, but in most cases a country is better advised in the early stages of development to use the implements, tools and sources of power it can produce domestically. There are exceptions, of course, to this general statement.

Salability

Production requisites have four qualities inherent in themselves that significantly affect salability to farm operators: (a) technical effectiveness; (b) dependability as to quality; (c) availability when needed; and (d) price. When farm operators fail to purchase requisites in "planned" amounts, officials, administrators and others frequently explain the failure in terms of the "backwardness" or "conservatism" of farmers or because of "lack of credit." These factors may be involved, but before passing such judgments it is important first to examine what was offered and on what terms.

The first quality a requisite must have to be salable is *technical effectiveness*. Is the "improved" seed really better? Too often, yield per acre at the central research station has been the principal factor taken into account in recommending its use. Unless the seed has been locally tested, differences in soils, available supplies of plant nutrients, water relations and microclimates may be such that the "improved" seed yields little or no more than varieties already in common use. If the growing season is significantly different from that at the central station where the new variety was developed, its use may expose the farmer's crop to greater than normal danger of damage by frost, disease, insects or birds because it ripens at a different time from local varieties. If the crop is used chiefly for local consumption, the taste or cooking quality may be sufficiently different to make it unpopular. In the case of fertilizers, differences in local soils, unless adjusted for, may result in yields quite different from those obtained on the central experimental farm.

Whatever the causes for local differences in technical effectiveness, only carefully planned and supervised local testing can assure that requisites recommended and offered for sale really represent increased production opportunities.

A second influence affecting salability is the purchaser's *confidence in the genuineness and purity of the item offered*. Even tools and implements of inferior quality are not easily identified in the market place. For this reason, a prime requirement of widespread and repeated purchase of production requisites is sufficiently careful control of quality at all steps in the production and distribution process to insure that farm operators develop confidence in their sources of supply.

The third factor affecting the salability of requisites is *availability when needed*. If a particular crop must be sown in early April, improved seed that arrives at the local distribution center on April 20th is useless and will go unsold since farm operators already have had to make other arrangements. If the seed is to be treated before sowing to control disease, the fungicide also will go unsold. In most agricultural operations, timing within a relatively narrow range has an important effect on yields and for requisites to be useful, and therefore sal-

able to farm operators, they must be available when needed.

The fourth factor affecting salability of requisites to farm operators is *price*. It is important, but it is perhaps the least important of the four. Even a low price will not attract purchasers if the requisite is not technically effective, if its quality is uncertain, or if it is not available when needed. On the other hand, farmers have again and again demonstrated their readiness to pay premium prices for requisites that are effective, of reliable quality, and available on time.

Distribution

In a number of developing countries, arranging for the production and distribution of production requisites has proved to be a major bottleneck in programs to increase agricultural output. Even when the necessary requisites have been imported or manufactured domestically, existing facilities have not been geared to the job of distribution.

In almost every newly developing country, private commercial channels for the marketing in local areas of many articles in wide demand already are well established. However, because of the widespread, largely untested assumption that distribution through private merchants is more costly and less efficient than through governmental or cooperative agencies, the usual pattern is to set up new agencies to distribute production requisites. It would seem justifiable to recognize that the present merchants comprise a pool of experienced, trained manpower no less than do the present cultivators of land. It would appear, therefore, that advisory services in newly developing countries to help present merchants introduce the changes necessary to make the distribution of agricultural production requisites efficient and satisfactory might be worthwhile.

What is important, whether distribution is through governmental, cooperative, or private channels, is that there be no gaps in the system from importation or manufacture to village outlets within easy reach of farm operators. Manufacture, transportation, storage, and village retailing all must be articulated, whether handled by the same or by different agencies. At the village end of the supply line the amounts of various requisites stocked must be related to the recommendations of extension or other farm advisory services.

Production Credit

Even if locally-adapted combinations of improved practices are available, farmers are ready to adopt them, and the necessary requisites are at hand, the purchase of requisites still has to be financed. In some cases this can be done from savings. In others it will be necessary to borrow.

It is widely believed that new agencies to make production credit available to farmers are a necessity in the early transitional stages of agricultural development. Several recent studies have indicated that even though interest rates are high, lack of special credit facilities may not stand in the way of the purchase of production requisites provided tested practices offering attractive prospects of increased income are available, and provided that requisites of proved effectiveness are for sale at fair prices. This is not to say that improved credit facilities are not desirable and needed. It does point to the fact that the *first* requirement is for improved practices that produce results and for the requisites necessary

to put them into effect. The failure of farmers to adopt improved practices on a wide scale is often ascribed to lack of organized credit facilities when the real reasons lie deeper.

Although lack of credit on favorable terms may not be a barrier to agricultural development, it is clear that a well-organized credit system that functions effectively—whether private, cooperative, governmental or a combination of the three—greatly facilitates development. More and more credit is used and credit therefore becomes increasingly important as agriculture moves from the traditional through the transitional into the commercial stage of development.

In the early stages of development, lenders usually rely heavily upon pledged collateral or the reputation of borrowers as security for their loans. This penalizes the farmer without collateral who is progressive and capable of repaying a loan from the production of his farm. An important first step in developing an effective production credit system is to begin to make loans based on an analysis of the borrower's ability to repay his loan from increased farm income rather than by the possible liquidation of pledged collateral.

A second important step is to adjust the term of the loan to the normal production and marketing cycle. Production loans should not fall due until a reasonable period *after* the marketable product is in hand. Otherwise the borrower is placed in a position where the lender can bring pressure upon him to sell immediately at harvest time when prices are often low, perhaps to the lender or someone he designates. This works to the disadvantage of the farmer, decreases his incentive to borrow to increase production and goes counter to programs to encourage orderly marketing.

Like any other production requisite, credit must be available when needed if it is to influence farmers' production decisions. A loan applied for on March 15 and approved May 1 to finance a crop that must be planted not later than April 10 is not likely to speed the adoption of improved practices.

Cost is a factor affecting farmers' use of credit, just as cost affects their use of other production goods and services. As previously indicated, however, the cost of credit may not be the critical factor determining the extent of its use. This being the case, the question whether or not to subsidize interest rates and if so to what extent is a matter for careful analysis and consideration.

Inducing Farmers to Adopt Improved Practices [1]

In most countries the individual farm operator, whether owner, tenant or hired manager, is the key decision-maker in agriculture. If improved practices are to be adopted, he must be trained to use them and persuaded to adopt them.

Observations in a number of countries in which agriculture is in the early stages of transition suggest that, within the limits of their knowledge and the alternatives open to them, farmers in these countries are as rational in their economic decisions as farmers anywhere. They respond to price differences. They are affected by the share of the harvest they can retain. They operate within the limits of their knowledge. They also respond, of course, to the prevailing social values of the groups in which they live.

In most newly developing countries illiteracy in rural areas is high, ranging from 60 to 90 percent or even higher. A high degree of illiteracy does not mean that farmers lack intelligence. It does mean that their knowledge of underlying factors affecting plant and animal production is limited, as is their ability to calculate probable costs and returns as a basis for choosing from alternatives. A recent Indian survey reports that the number of improved practices adopted by individual farmers was directly and significantly related to levels of educational attainment. This suggests that although it may not be too difficult to get farmers to adopt a single, simple practice in areas where illiteracy is high, achieving widespread adoption of *combinations* of improved practices may prove to be slow, at least in the beginning. It will become easier and more rapid as farmers become, first, literate, and then better and better educated, and as extension and research personnel become more and more competent.

There are three important means by which change to improved farm practices can be accelerated. One of these is the type of education usually associated with the term extension education. A second way to provide greater inducements to farmers to adopt improved practices is to protect them against undue economic risks of innovation by establishing price floors for important agricultural products so that farmers need not fear disastrous price declines as production increases. A third way is to devise conditions of tenure and tenancy that assure farmers of reasonable security of tenure and a fair share of such increases in production as may result from the adoption of improved practices. At the same time, these arrangements need to be such that they will encourage land improvements and other medium- and long-term types of capital investment by landowners.

Tenant farmers who receive only 50 or 60 percent of the added yield and must pay all the added cash costs may not feel they are likely to gain enough from adopting improved practices to justify the risks involved.

Research and advisory services in developing countries may not be the kind to win the confidence of farmers. Research workers, few of whom have a farm background, spend a large part of their time in laboratories or central research stations and little time in the field. They have little first-hand knowledge of production and related economic problems confronting farmers, and they contribute little toward their solution. Advisory services are frequently understaffed, and at the village and farm level may have persons without farming experience and only the limited technical knowledge that can be gained in training courses extending over periods of six months to two years. Acting under instructions from above, they can tell farmers *what to do* but seldom can they tell them *why* or show them *how*. Few are competent to advise individual farmers *how to adjust* recommended combinations of practices to fit their particular situations or help them to develop medium- or long-term farm plans based upon estimated costs and returns from alternative possibilities. Because communication with research scientists is usually irregular and poor, members of advisory services seldom can be of help in dealing with new and unexpected problems.

Yet, despite all the handicaps confronting them, some village-level workers and farm advisers do surprisingly well. An important problem in the early stages of developing an advisory service is how to bring the performance of the many to the standards of the best, while at the same time seeking to raise the general level of technical knowledge and competence.

A Strategy for Agricultural Development

Obviously a comprehensive strategy for agricultural development in a newly developing country must be much broader than the needs discussed in this paper. Such a comprehensive strategy must include attention to optimum investment in roads and transport, improvement of arrangements for marketing farm products, measures for public health and general education, determination of appropriate patterns of land tenure and taxation, and to many other aspects of the total economy.

The burden of this paper is to highlight the activities most essential to improving managerial decision-making and husbandry practices by individual farm operators, and to urge the absolute necessity of the coordination of these *at the local level*. Far too frequently, the all-important local testing of single improved practices and of combinations of these receives little or no attention. Extension education is frequently uncoordinated with local testing, with the production and distribution of requisites, and with production credit.

We suggest that the obvious starting point in coordinating these activities in each agricultural area is in the arrangements made for local testing and for extension education. Widespread *demonstrations* of the results of local testing can be an effective addition to extension practices.

To this basic combination of local testing and extension there must be added adequate provision for the supply and financing of production requisites. These are sufficiently different from local testing and extension education that they usually are best handled by separate staffs. But close coordination between these and extension education and local testing is imperative. This coordination can be achieved within each agricultural area by making those responsible for all these activities locally responsible to a single local administrator of agricultural development.

Each newly developing country faces a seeming conflict between economic considerations on the one hand, and social and political considerations on the other, in its program for agricultural development. Economic considerations argue for concentration of scarce resources, including skilled manpower, on increasing agricultural production in those regions where both natural and cultural factors are most favorable. Social and political considerations frequently argue for spreading development resources fairly evenly over the whole rural population.

The conflict between these may be more apparent than real. For what is imperative in the first instance is to find and develop a pattern of local coordination of the activities necessary to improve managerial decision-making and husbandry practices by individual farm operators. Except, perhaps, in the case of very small countries, this cannot be done on a nationwide basis in the first instance; it must be done first in a few selected areas. In view of the economic consideration of increasing total agricultural output as rapidly as possible, these first experiments in adequately supported and coordinated local programs should be in areas where natural and cultural circumstances are most favorable. A pattern of operations, once determined, tested, and established, can then be spread, as rapidly as resources (particularly of trained manpower) will permit, to more and more regions of less and less initial agricultural potential, until the social and political considerations, which are of equal importance in the long run, are satisfied.

FOOTNOTE

[1] We have drawn extensively upon an unpublished memorandum prepared by Dorris D. Brown, Agricultural Economist, The Ford Foundation, New Delhi, in the preparation of this section.

Efficient Use of Labor, Land, and Capital for Agricultural Development of Densely Populated Areas

SHERMAN E. JOHNSON

Deputy Administrator for Foreign Economics

RAYMOND P. CHRISTENSEN

Chief of Economic Development Branch, Economic Research Service,
U.S. Department of Agriculture, Washington, D.C.

The Problem Under Review

Within the world's densely populated areas are countries that have achieved a high level of economic development as well as countries just beginning the development process. This is evident if we look at Figure I where data on arable land and income per capita have been plotted. Countries with less than .40 hectares of arable land per capita or about one acre, might be defined as densely populated. Among these countries, there are many that have high incomes per person as well as many that have low incomes.

The fact that many densely populated countries have high incomes should be encouraging to the low-income countries that are striving to improve economic conditions for their people. One of the chief differences between the high and the low-income countries is the high percentage of the population engaged in agriculture in the densely populated low-income countries. But we cannot assume that because the high-income countries are highly industrialized the low-income countries should give first priority to industrialization with emphasis on heavy industry. The fact is that improvement in agricultural productivity and adequate food supplies were important preconditions in the early stages of industrial development in the countries that today enjoy relatively high incomes.

In this paper we stress the essentiality of agricultural improvement to balanced economic development. The discussion deals primarily with agricultural development in densely populated areas that have the following characteristics:

(a) Arable land per person of .40 hectare or less.

(b) From 60 to 80 percent of the population directly dependent on agriculture.

(c) Abundance of unskilled labor.

(d) Scarcity of capital, and of managerial and technical skills.

(e) Little use of modern technology.

(f) Annual income per person of $250 or less.

Table 1 indicates that the countries with these characteristics account for about 40 percent of the world's population. Under the conditions described, from 40 to 60 percent of the national income originates in agriculture. Even though, typically, most of the population is engaged in food production, the use of primitive methods results in low yields per unit of land and other resources, and consequently in chronic food shortages.

Some less developed countries have large areas of land available for settlement. Even in these countries food-shortage problems may occur because much capital, management, and technical skill are required for exploitation of additional land resources, but they do have the possibility of developing more land. In most of the densely populated countries, however, relief from chronic food shortages will be found chiefly by substantially increasing production on the land now in cultivation. Commercial food imports would absorb scarce foreign exchange, and food aid is only a temporary and, at best, partial solution to food-shortage problems. Fortunately, higher yields per hectare are physically possible in most countries, but many obstacles need to be overcome before this is realized. These obstacles are discussed in later sections of this paper.

Adequate Food Supplies Crucial to Sustained Development

In order to bring out the crucial importance of food in a development pro-

TABLE 1. *Distribution of world population and arable land among countries grouped according to arable land and income per person* [a]

Countries grouped according to arable land and income per person [b]	Percentage of world total		Arable land per person	Percentage of labor force in agriculture	Percentage of national income from agriculture
	Population	Arable land			
	Percent	*Percent*	*Hectares*	*Percent*	*Percent*
.40 hectares or less:					
$250 or less.............	41	23	.31	67	44
Over $250..............	15	4	.17	26	10
Over .40 hectares:					
$250 or less.............	12	21	.97	64	41
Over $250..............	32	52	.95	35	11
All countries..............	100	100	.57	48	14

[a] Based on most recent data available from FAO and UN sources. Data for mainland China were not available. Estimates of percentage of labor force in agriculture and of national income from agriculture are based on incomplete data. Countries in each category are shown in Figure I.

[b] Larger countries in each group in terms of total population are as follows: Countries with .40 hectares or less and incomes of $250 or less per person—India, Indonesia, Pakistan, Philippines, Egypt, South Korea, East Germany, North Vietnam, South Vietnam, Peru, and Taiwan. Countries with .40 hectares or less and income over $250 per person—Japan, West Germany, United Kingdom, Italy, Czechoslovakia, Netherlands, Austria, Cuba, and Switzerland. Countries with over .40 hectares and $250 or less per person—Nigeria, Turkey, Thailand, Ethiopia, Burma, Iran, and Yugoslavia. Countries with over .40 hectares and over $250 income per person—U.S.S.R., United States, France, Mexico, Spain, Poland, Argentina, Rumania, and Canada.

gram, let us assume a country that gives first consideration to construction of industrial plants and improvement of transportation, communication, and other services necessary for industrialization. When such a development program gets under way, the first effects on the national economy are additional employment and increased consumer purchasing power. In countries with relative scarcity of food and insufficient diets for the working population, perhaps 60 to 70 percent of the increase in purchasing power will be spent for more food. There is actual need for more food because of greater physical activity. Since customary diets have been inadequate, the higher purchasing power results in demand for a greater quantity of food, largely of the same types that have been consumed previously.

The food demands arising from higher employment and purchasing power are added to the increase resulting from growth of population. Enough food must be available for both demands, otherwise economic growth is stopped in its tracks. In many of these countries, agriculture as presently organized may have difficulty meeting even the higher demands occasioned by population growth of 2 to 3 percent a year. Added to this, however, an annual increase of perhaps one percent may be needed to meet the increased demands resulting from higher employment and purchasing power. If these demands are not met, price inflation will be generated in the food sector, and economic development will be retarded (1).

Efficient Use of Resources in This Context

Efficient use of resources under food-shortage conditions must be viewed from the standpoint of combining the scarce resources with abundant unskilled labor for rapid achievement of maximum food output. Land and reproducible capital are scarce factors, but management and technical skills for adoption of improved technology are scarcest of all. We reach this conclusion because more capital and labor applied to the land now in cultivation by prevailing primitive methods will result in very little, if any, increase in output.

Olson found little increase in yield even from the use of hybrid maize seed in the Punjab of India if the same production methods were followed as for local varieties. On the other hand, if improved combinations of fertilizer, planting, tillage, and irrigation practices were used on both hybrid and local varieties, the yield from hybrid seed was much higher. These results illustrate the importance of adopting *combinations* of new technology rather than single practices (2). If management and technical skills are used with a limited amount of capital to develop systems of farming that involve combinations of improved technology, substantial increases in output can be expected.[1]

10. Because capital is needed for development of industry, and for overhead services, as well as of agriculture, only limited capital investment will be available for the agricultural sector. However, the allocation between agriculture and other industries should be planned to achieve balanced development, recognizing the importance of increased food output.[2]

The limited quantities of capital allocated to agriculture must be siphoned into the most productive uses, into investments that will yield the highest returns over a relatively short period of time. In this event, new land development, even where additional land is available, is likely to receive a rather low priority unless it is a part of a multipurpose project which includes power, flood control, and other objectives.

Unskilled rural labor in densely populated countries is essentially a free good in the sense that more labor applied to agricultural production with prevailing practices is likely to yield little or no increase in value product. Consequently, any different use of labor that actually will increase food production or, alternatively, improve the land base for later increases in output will constitute a productive use of unskilled labor. The key question of efficient use of resources, therefore, becomes one of maximizing the value output from a relatively fixed area of land, utilizing available management and technical skills with a limited supply of capital allocated to agriculture and using direct labor as effectively as possible.

Sometimes small areas of land can be irrigated, drained, or cleared largely with direct labor that otherwise would be unemployed. Such opportunities should be utilized as a means of adding to the capital assets by direct labor methods. But although small areas of land may be made available in this way, most of the expansion of food production will need to be obtained by increasing the yields per hectare on land already in cultivation. The physical potentials for raising output per hectare and per person usually are very great in countries relatively untouched by scientific advances in agriculture. For example, table 2 indicates that yields of cereals per hectare in the low-income countries with scarce land resources averaged less than half as high as in the higher income

countries that also had limited land resources. Also, the yield increases in the low-income countries have lagged behind those in the higher income countries in recent years.

It is physically possible to double or triple yields in many of the densely populated low-income countries. For example, cereal production per hectare in Japan averages nearly four times as much as in the less developed countries in Asia. These results are achieved by adopting suitable combinations of improved technology. Figure II shows cereal production per hectare and use of chemical fertilizer per hectare of arable land in selected countries. The countries with high yields use large quantities of fertilizer *in combination with other improved practices* to obtain the higher yields.

Low yields per hectare, produced largely with hand labor and primitive methods on small units, also represent very low production per person. Cereal production per rural person in high-income industrialized countries averages nearly seven times as high as in the less developed low-income countries.

The high yields currently realized in the industrialized countries are a phenomenon of relatively recent origin, if one looks at the long sweep of agricultural history. Figure III indicates that yields per acre of wheat in England and of rice in Japan have gone up more in the last 50 years than in the preceding 500 years. Today, farming methods in many of the less developed countries are probably similar to those that prevailed in England and Japan five or six centuries ago, when relatively little capital was employed, and land and labor were the main inputs. The promise of a solution to chronic shortages of food in the

Table 2. *Cereals: Production per hectare and percentage changes in production per hectare, area, and total production, by countries grouped according to arable land and income per person, averages 1948/49–1952/53 and 1959/60–1960/61* [a]

Countries grouped according to arable land and income per person [b]	Production per hectare		Percentage changes, 1948/49–1952/53 to 1959/60–1960/61		
	1948/49–1952/53 average	1959/60–1960/61 average	Production per hectare	Area	Production
	Metric ton	*Metric ton*	*Percent*	*Percent*	*Percent*
.40 hectares or less:					
$250 or less.............	.95	1.18	24	16	45
Over $250.............	2.24	2.86	28	−1	27
Over .40 hectares:					
$250 or less.............	.97	1.09	12	28	44
Over $250.............	1.47	1.89	29	0	29
All countries.............	1.29	1.60	24	8	34

[a] Estimates based on data reported in 1960 FAO *Yearbook of Agricultural Statistics*. Complete data for all countries were not available. Cereals included are wheat, rye, rice, barley, oats, and corn.
[b] See footnote [b] in Table 1 for countries included in each group.

densely populated, less developed countries depends chiefly upon achievement of higher yields per hectare on the land now in cultivation. This problem comes to the forefront in the next section as we discuss the achievement of increased productivity.

Achievement of Increased Productivity

Efficient achievement of higher productivity in a densely populated country requires adoption of those combinations of improved technology that will maximize output from scarce capital, management, and technical skills by utilizing the abundance of unskilled labor as productively as possible. In other words, efficient production under these conditions involves using scarce capital sparingly and making the most effective use of persons with management and technical skills in a labor-intensive agriculture.

This approach runs into head-on conflict with those who believe that the only alternative to a primitive low-productivity agriculture is a highly mechanized agriculture, organized in large-scale units. A part of the reasoning back of the urge for mechanization stems from the belief that, with rapid industrialization, the excess rural labor will find employment in industry, and in fact will be needed to man the new industries. This belief fails to distinguish between countries with much land and little labor, such as the United States and Australia, and those with much labor and little land, as Egypt and India. It also seems to ignore both the timing of the labor pull of new industries and the rapid increase in rural population, which is likely to continue for some time.

As to timing of the labor pull, most of the less developed countries have large pools of unemployed people in the cities and towns. The first expansion of the nonfarm labor force, therefore, is likely to absorb these pools of labor before drawing heavily on rural areas.

Moreover, the pull from farm areas will be felt first in those villages most accessible to the new employment. National planners frequently overlook the fact that concentration on heavy industry requires many special skills, and these industries are likely to absorb fewer unskilled laborers than smaller scale consumer goods industries.

The most important factor contributing to persistence of superabundant labor in agriculture, however, is the high birth rate and the consequent rapid growth of population. Dovring has pointed out that the agricultural population typically has increased during the early phases of industrialization in the developed countries (3).

A numerical example may bring out the problem of abundant rural labor even more forcefully. Suppose we assume a country with a population growth rate of 2.5 percent annually and with 75 percent of the population in agriculture. Then nonfarm employment would need to increase 10 percent in the first year in order to absorb the new entrants to the labor force from growth of population in both the rural and urban areas.

It is apparent that even absorption of all the new entrants to the labor force from population growth represents a staggering load for a fledgling industrial sector. Consequently, productive work must be found in rural areas, either in farm production or in improvement of rural resources, that will result in future expansion of farm production. At a later stage, when industrial activity is firmly mounted on the high-speed track of accelerated growth, the labor pull of nonfarm employment opportunities should gradually reduce the rural population. In Japan the working population in agriculture, forestry, and fishing actually increased during the first 20 years of industrialization, and remained relatively constant for about 15 more years before the beginning of a gradual decline (4).

Effective Use of Abundant Labor

Because surplus workers cannot all be absorbed in nonfarm employment in the early stages of industrialization, efficient use of resources necessitates finding productive employment in agriculture. But another controversial question arises in this connection, namely, the most efficient size of operating unit. The small size holdings in densely populated areas (frequently less than 2 hectares), and the fragmentation of each holding into several tracts, have led many people to the conclusion that efficient operation can be achieved only through consolidation of units, and some type of joint or group operation. Others contend that the peasant's hunger for land of his own is so strong that efficient production can be achieved only by directing this hunger toward means of increasing production on owner-operated family farms.

Perhaps part of the confusion can be cleared away by recognizing the need for consolidation of fragmented tracts into contiguous holdings wherever possible. This step is likely to require much strain and stress to achieve equity among different landowners, but in several countries a large number of villagers have undertaken successful tract-consolidation programs.

The size-of-unit issue would be clarified further if there were general recognition that where too many people are attempting to earn a living directly from the land, it becomes necessary to establish a minimum standard of land resources per operating family, and to prevent fragmentation below this level. Obviously, the minimum size will vary, depending upon the potential productivity of the land. Consequently, the standard must be adapted to local conditions, but it should conform to the general size of unit needed by a farm family to provide a level of living that is acceptable within the country's pattern of culture.

If minimum sizes of farm units are established in densely populated rural areas, the land resources are not likely to be sufficient to provide land for all the landless families who desire land of their own. In India, for example, some 20 to 25 million rural families have little, if any, land and are dependent primarily on wage earnings. If all available lands were distributed pro rata, the units would be too small to provide more than the barest subsistence with prevailing methods of production. Consequently, other ways must be found to utilize these superabundant labor resources. A developing economy cannot afford the waste of having a large segment of its population unemployed.

If the operators of larger farms can be persuaded to adopt labor-intensive combinations of new technology requiring increased use of manpower, they can provide productive work for some of the landless at higher than prevailing wage rates. Many landless laborers would find more secure employment at somewhat higher wages a better alternative than a parcel of land too small for subsistence. The bargaining problems involved in this alternative are mentioned later.

Because private employment in rural areas is not likely to absorb all the unemployed rural workers into productive jobs, there will be need for a rural public works program. Efficient use of public funds necessitates giving priority to projects that will result in capital for-

mation by using direct labor with a minimum of new equipment, and to activities that will increase agricultural output as rapidly as possible. Such land-improvement measures as terracing, land leveling, drainage, minor irrigation, and reclaiming of wastelands meet this requirement. Access roads and needed storage facilities are other examples of capital improvements which utilize direct labor and only local materials (5).

Decisions concerning funds for a rural public works program will need to be made in the interest of preventing the waste of large-scale unemployment as well as in the urgency of attaining rapid increase of food production.

Are there other ways to use superabundant labor productively? Some advocates of cooperative or collective farming seem to visualize such structural organization of farming as both the only road to production efficiency and a panacea for rural unemployment and underemployment.

In considering the advantages and disadvantages of group farming as compared with family farming, we need first to realize that joint operation does not make more land available. If there is too little land, neither joint nor private operation will provide adequate living for all the farm families in the village. Under such conditions, every effort must be made to utilize all available land resources as productively as possible whether the land is operated jointly or privately.

Effective Use of Scarce Land Resources

Large-scale organization of farming frequently is not the most effective way to increase land productivity in densely populated areas. In fact, much available evidence indicates that small family farms generally have higher yields per acre. This was the conclusion reached recently in a study by Dr. Harbans Singh Mann, Ludhiana University, India. Dr. Mann studied conditions leading to the establishment of cooperative farms, factors affecting their success, and the economic performance of these farms as compared with family farms in the Punjab. He obtained detailed data for ten large cooperative farms in different areas of the Punjab and for several nearby family farms in each area studied. His data show that production per acre generally was higher on small family-size farms than on the large cooperative farms (table 3). In the few instances where yields were higher on the cooperative farms, it was because the cooperative farms had obtained capital for construction of superior irrigation facilities. Government credit and subsidies made available to cooperative farms for purchasing tractors and constructing tube wells were important incentives for

establishing these farms. However, only three of the ten cooperative farms continued in existence more than a few years. Landowners decided that production and income from their land would be greater if they farmed it themselves or leased it to operators of small family-size farm units.

Results of studies made by Farm Management Research Centers in India, summarized recently by Long, also indicate that gross output per acre averages higher on small farms than on large privately operated farms. (6) Data supplied to Long by G. D. Agrawal, then employed by the Directorate of Economics, Ministry of Food and Agriculture, India, show the following gross relationships:

Size of farm in acres	Gross output per acre in rupees
0–4.9	240
5–9.9	213
10–19.9	171
20 and over	103

Some of the inverse relationship between size of farm and output per acre in the above comparisons undoubtedly was caused by the fact that the areas of lower productivity per acre tend to be characterized by larger farms. To overcome this difficulty, the frequency distributions for individual states were recombined and classified into four groups. This had the effect of holding differences between states constant in the analysis. Average results for eight states included in the study were as follows:

Farm size groups	Gross output per acre in rupees
Smallest	219
Second smallest	188
Second largest	170
Largest	159

These data show clearly that production per acre averaged highest on

TABLE 3. *Production per acre on cooperative and family farms, Punjab, India* [a]

Area	Family farms	Cooperative farms
	Rupees	*Rupees*
1	270	190
2	185	249
3	158	137
4	160	145
5	188	167
6	155	158
7	258	219
8	108	152
9	154	103
10	162	187

[a] Data are from Mann, Harbans Singh, *Cooperative Farming and Family Farming in the Punjab: A Comparative Study*; Ph. D. Thesis, Ohio State University, 1962. Data are for years centering around 1953–54.

small farms. They show quite conclusively that it cannot be assumed that reorganization of farming into larger scale units will increase production per acre or per hectare.

Larger production per acre on small farms than on large farms also prevails in the more agriculturally advanced countries. For example, data for account-keeping farms in Jutland, Denmark, for 1955–56 indicate that gross output per acre averaged 35 percent higher on farms under 20 hectares than on farms over 20 hectares (7). Value of production per acre was as follows:

Size of farm in acres	Gross output per acre in Kroner
49.4 and under.......	1, 070
49.5 and over........	706

Throughout this paper we have emphasized that in a densely populated country with chronic food shortages, the crucial test of efficiency is high production per unit of scarce land resources. The foregoing illustrations indicate that group farming frequently does not meet this test.

Another test is productive employment for unskilled labor in rural areas, with economical use of scarce capital as well as management and technical skills. In the more advanced countries larger-scale operations might economize on use of capital for buildings and machinery, but in the first transition from primitive agriculture, the need for maximum utilization of superabundant labor dictates a labor-intensive agriculture. Consequently, most capital expenditures will be confined to fertilizer, seed, and other variable inputs which directly increase production per hectare. Returns on such inputs will vary with skill and timeliness of application rather than with size of unit.

Effective Use of Scarce Managerial and Technical Skills

The one reason frequently cited as an indication of need for group farming is the lack of technical and managerial skills among operators of small farms. We must recognize, however, that if a number of small holdings are combined into one operating unit, the management problem is multiplied far beyond the experience of any one of the operators whose holdings are being merged. The question then arises whether outside managers can be obtained who have the requisite local experience, and ability to supervise a large group operation. A mistaken decision on a one-family unit will affect only the fortunes of that family, but a decision resulting in large losses on a group enterprise would mean tragedy for the entire village.

Even if capable management can be obtained, it would have to be very productive to offset the individual initiative and detailed supervision provided by family unit operation. The latter gives scope for individual accomplishment and pride of workmanship which seem to be spurs to productivity in all societies. This is indicated by the remarkable production obtained on household allotments in countries that have organized collective farms. Evidence from another source is the pride taken in ground beautification and other improvements by home owners all over the world.

We recognize the need for assistance to farm families in development of management and technical skills but, in the transition stage at least, these services can be provided more effectively to individual families than to group farming units. Trained management assistance can be assigned by public agencies to work with individual families in helping them to adopt improved systems of farming. The management problem is greatly simplified on small units. Such management and technical assistance could be combined with other activities of multipurpose cooperatives, which also would provide credit, production supplies, and storage and marketing facilities. In this way, most of the economies of scale would be obtained without taking away the initiative and the incentives of individual operation.

A third test of group farming is whether it will provide higher incomes, better living, and more security for a larger number of farm families. Unless higher production per unit of land can be obtained from group farming, it is unlikely that higher incomes can be obtained. In the study made by Mann in the Punjab, the adjoining family farms had a higher output-input ratio than the cooperative farms in 7 out of 10 communities.

As for security, a parcel of land represents the only security known to a family living in a relatively primitive agricultural society. The pressure for land reform stems from the need felt for security of tenure. We know of no examples of peasants voluntarily giving up individual use of land that they customarily have operated. On the other hand, where the agrarian reform has brought about increased owner-cultivation and establishment of farmer cooperatives and other services, it has contributed greatly to improvement of agricultural productivity.

A recent report on land reform in Egypt, for example, states that "Agrarian reform is based on respect for private ownership linked to membership of the cooperative established in the local village" (8). This report points out that,

"It is not enough to assign to the farmer a plot of land leaving him to himself, he should learn the best methods of cultivation and should be offered technical and material help." It goes on to say that "The benefits which the farmer reaps from using modern farming methods to contribute to improved production are not only material. There is also the psychological satisfaction of being able to keep for himself the fruit of his own labors, and this in turn is a strong incentive to additional efforts" (9). Field surveys conducted in land reform areas of Egypt indicate that quality as well as quantity of farm production increased substantially from 1957 to 1960 when land was distributed to cultivators, and the operations of individual cultivators were supported by service cooperatives.

In Taiwan, where total agricultural output has nearly doubled since 1950, the land reform programs under which rents were reduced and many tenants became owner-cultivators have contributed greatly to increased productivity in agriculture. However, farmer associations and cooperatives which supply essential production requisites, assist in the marketing of farm products, provide credit on reasonable terms, and help farmers learn improved production methods, also have been necessary for the rapid rate of agricultural progress.[3] Land reform also has been an important factor in bringing about increased productivity of agricultural land in Japan in recent years (10).

Overcoming Resistance to Change

Improvement of agriculture involves the changing of rural attitudes and of institutions that have been built up over many generations. It requires a break in the closed circle of village culture that has grown up to protect the community against external exploitation. Accomplishment of a breakthrough will require agricultural leadership of a high order. The three requisites for overcoming resistance to change are (a) knowledge, (b) incentives, and (c) means— (K I M).

Knowledge. In a static agriculture each new generation learns from its elders the production practices of the community. Adoption of new technology, however, will require drastic changes and the learning of new skills and management techniques from outside teachers. Therefore, even the venturesome will require convincing evidence that substantial benefits will accrue from the change. To begin with, only a few families in a village will be sufficiently courageous to try new methods. Perhaps even these families will need guarantees that no losses will be incurred by the change. Once they have agreed to adoption of new farming plans, they will need technical and management assistance for carrying out the improved farming program, and, as indicated later, they will need also credit and supplies.

Accomplishing the first breakthrough will be difficult in villages where most of the people are illiterate, but a dedicated worker will find ways of overcoming this obstacle. However, it emphasizes the great need of elementary education for improved farming and for successful functioning of cooperatives as well as for other advances. In a frantic search for quick results, we frequently forget that a new generation enters the labor force each year, and that neglect of the education of 10-year-old children means that they will become unskilled laborers in five or six years. A simple economical program of elementary education undertaken by dedicated teachers is the beginning of training for youth to become the skilled workers of the next generation.

Incentives. Village people often fear that if they increase production for the market, prices will be reduced and they will get lower rather than higher incomes. Assured markets, storage facilities, and stable prices are among the incentives needed to induce producers to shift from subsistence farming to production for commercial markets.

If some of the larger farms are employing wage labor, those who work the land should have an opportunity to share in the rewards from increased output. If high production has been achieved on some of the large-scale farms, distribution of the land to hired workers may result in temporary reduction of output. In this situation, equity considerations may conflict with the national need for larger output. An alternative to land distribution may be a program of assistance to workers in bargaining for better wages, housing, garden allotments, and provision of health and educational services.

Means. Even when the benefits from improved farming are known, and land reform and other incentives are provided, the means for carrying out the new farming program may well be lacking. Supplies of chemical fertilizer, pesticides, better seed, and simple tools will be needed, also assistance on how to use them. Availability of supplies requires either arrangement for importation or manufacture within the country. In many countries this means that priority must be given to industries that provide agricultural supplies and that process farm products if the food barrier is to be broken sufficiently to facilitate economic growth.

Because most farm operators will not have either cash or credit to buy the necessary supplies, new credit institutions may have to be established to supply credit on the basis of farm plans that promise increases in output and incomes. Local storage and marketing facilities will also be needed to handle the expanded production. In many countries this requires establishment of a new marketing system which may have to be provided through publicly sponsored cooperatives. Public works programs for underemployed workers can be organized to provide storage facilities, access roads, and other rural improvements that will be needed to increase farm output and to transport the products to market.

Feasibility of Suggested Approach

Our suggestions for overcoming resistance to change may seem quite unrealistic because they require case work with individual families. Even if the possibility is recognized of startling increases in output from farm plans that include combinations of new technology, the question is still unanswered whether it is feasible to provide such assistance to all the farm families in a country. Obviously, competent assistants will not be available to work with *all families* in the beginning of such a program. How-

ever, we are convinced that there is no other way of accomplishing a breakthrough that eventually will result in large increases in productivity. Consequently, a solution must be found to the dilemma of the necessity of working with individual operators and the inability of doing case work on a large scale (11).

It seems sensible to begin with this type of program in the most promising villages—those where improvements seem feasible in the shortest time. When many of the villagers have adopted improved farming programs, they can serve as examples to other families. It should then be possible to shift the assistance personnel to other villages. In the process of carrying out the intensive phase of the program, new personnel should be trained to undertake independent assistance in other areas. These apprentices would later be qualified to undertake independent work in other villages. The principle of "Each one teach one" would need to be carried out on a large scale, and eventually the "spread effect" would become nationwide.

The suggested approach is not a panacea that will work miracles in two or three years, but we believe that it holds the promise of achieving eventually a more efficient agriculture, and better living for farm people in densely populated areas.

FOOTNOTES

[1] See also paper for this Conference by Charles E. Kellogg, *Interactions in Agricultural Development*.

[2] See paper for this Conference by Rufus B. Hughes and Erven J. Long, *Complementarity Between Agricultural and Industrial Development*.

[3] See also paper for this Conference by Kenneth H. Parsons, *The Tenure of Farms, Motivation, and Productivity*.

REFERENCES

(1) Cochrane, W. W. *The World Food Budget: A Forward Look to 2000 and Beyond.* Address at the World Food Forum, Centennial observance of the United States Department of Agriculture, Washington, D.C. (May 15–17, 1962).

Nicholls, W. H. *The Importance of an Agricultural Surplus in Underdeveloped Countries.* Presented as the J. S. McLean Memorial Lecture at Ontario Agricultural College, Guelph, Ontario, Canada (January 1962).

(2) Olson, R. O. *Economics of Hybrid Maize Production in Punjab.* Group Leader of Ohio State University Team, U.S. Technical Cooperation Mission to India (December 1958.)

(3) Dovring, F. *The share of agriculture in a growing population.* Monthly Bulletin of Agricultural Economics and Statistics, Food and Agriculture Organization of the United Nations, Rome. *8,* No. 8/9, (August/September 1959).

(4) Ranis, G. *Factor proportions in Japanese economic development.* The American Economic Review, *47,* No. 5 (September 1957).

(5) *Report on India's Food Crisis & Steps to Meet It,* by the Agricultural Production Team sponsored by The Ford Foundation. Issued by The Government of India, Ministry of Food and Agriculture and Ministry of Community Development and Cooperation (April 1959).

(6) Long, E. J. *Economic basis of land reform in underdeveloped economies.* Land Economics, *37,* No. 2 (May 1961).

(7) Data from Jydske Husmandsforenings regnskaber, 1956, quoted from Lomme-Handbog for konsulenter og landbrigslaerere, *3,* part 16.

(8) *Replies to United Nations Questionnaire on Agrarian Reform in the Egyptian Region.* Public Relations department, Agrarian Reform General Organization, Cairo, p. 39. (April 1961).

(9) *Op. cit.,* p. 38.

(10) Tang, H. S. and S. C. Hsieh. *Land Reform and Agricultural Development in Taiwan.* Rural Economics Division, Joint Commission for Rural Construction, Taiwan. Mimeograph Report (1959).

(11) Johnson, S. E. *Management assistance in farming.* The Indian Journal of Agricultural Economics, *14,* No. 4 (October-December 1959).

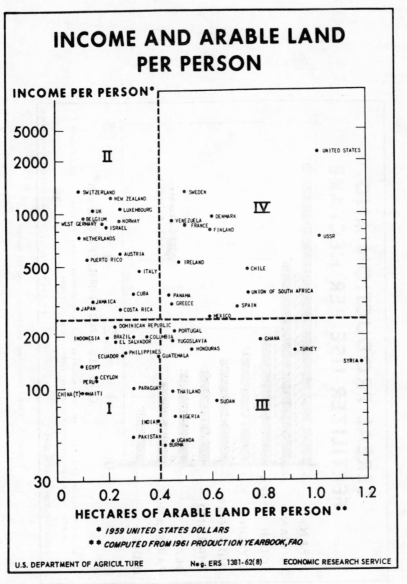

FIGURE I. Income and arable land per person

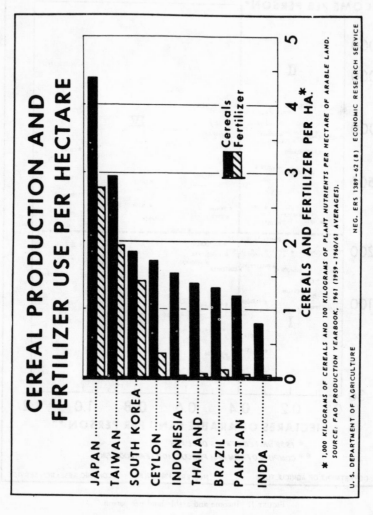

FIGURE II. Cereal production and fertilizer use per hectare

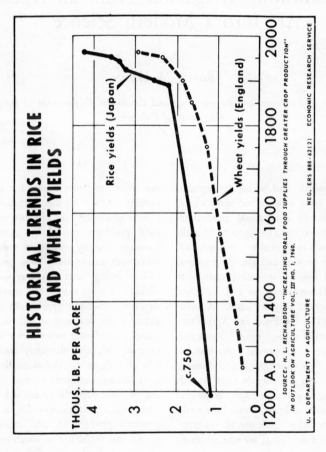

FIGURE III. Historical trends in rice and wheat yields

Transforming Irrigation From an Age-Old Art Into a Modern Science

ROBERT M. HAGAN

*Professor of Irrigation and Engineering, and Chairman, Department of Irrigation,
University of California
Davis, California*

Economic and social development of many areas is dependent upon achieving increased agricultural production. This often requires the opening of additional lands to agriculture through new irrigation projects and also the improvement of existing irrigation systems to insure efficient water use and continued productivity of irrigated lands. A recent report (1) of the Food and Agriculture Organization of the United Nations suggests that: ". . . improved water management (including irrigation and drainage practices) can probably do more towards increasing food supplies and agricultural income in the irrigated areas of the world than any other agricultural practice." Science and technology are now advanced enough, if properly integrated and summarized, to transform irrigation from an age-old art into a modern science capable of providing the basis for productive irrigation projects.

Irrigation was extensively practiced by the earliest civilization known. Remnants of dams, canals and other structures testify to the extensive practice of the art of irrigation among the ancient peoples. Much of this irrigated agriculture ultimately failed because of technical problems created by incomplete planning and by misuse of watershed areas, soils and water. These problems include failing water supply, erosion and siltation of water storage and conveyance structures, excessive applications of irrigation water, leaching of soil nutrients, rising groundwater tables and waterlogging of soil, and ultimately accumulation of toxic salts. Unfortunately these same problems continue to cause the failure of some recently established irrigation projects, reduce crop yields far below potential productivity, and create economic and social unrest which so often accompany slowly developing and unproductive irrigation projects. In some areas food production lost through deterioration of irrigated lands is estimated to offset production from additional lands being brought into production under new irrigation schemes.

The development of water supplies may involve construction of impressive and ultra-modern engineering structures, but the developed water is often conveyed through inefficient distribution systems to farmers who continue to irrigate in accordance with age-old practices and traditions little influenced by modern science and technology. Actually, new or improved irrigation projects should not be considered as complete until scientifically sound and well-engineered provisions have been made to apply water efficiently to the last crop row on the last farm and adequate arrangements made to remove any surplus water wherever necessary. Intelligent application of today's knowledge of irrigation science and technology would accelerate the effective utilization of water and soil resources in developing areas, achieve maximum crop production from available water supplies, insure an abundant and permanently successful irrigation agriculture, and reclaim many previously productive lands now waterlogged and often salinized.

The modern science of irrigation, in a broad sense, must seek to increase the efficiency of converting rain or other precipitation into useable water and to reduce all losses in utilizing this water. Figures I and II illustrate some of the elements in the water-supply and water-utilization systems and some of the sources of water loss. Each loss represents a challenge to the irrigation scientist and engineer to seek economic means for its reduction or elimination.

Since modern science and technology are now generally employed in construction of water supply projects, this paper will concentrate on opportunities to use present knowledge for increasing the effectiveness of man's utilization of developed water supplies. This requires the skillful combination of accumulated knowledge in many professional fields including engineering, soil science, plant science, and agricultural economics. Difficulties in obtaining and coordinating the knowledge from the many professional disciplines involved contribute to serious problems encountered in planning and operating many irrigation schemes.

Irrigation needs and practices vary widely. This complicates the planning of new irrigation projects and also the operation of existing irrigation systems and irrigated farms. One important aspect of science is the ability to predict what results can be expected in given situations. Mankind in general, and particularly the less developed countries, can ill-afford the time-wasting, resource-depleting, and disappointing process of trial and error and inadequately planned local trials. With the gradual development of modern irrigation science, basic irrigation principles are emerging which can serve as valuable guides in predicting irrigation requirements and potential problems. Now available in both the developed and developing countries are much knowledge and methodology for evaluating irrigation sites, determining the suitability of proposed irrigation waters, estimating irrigation requirements of crops, predicting the effects of specific irrigation practices and related farm operations on given crops under prevailing site conditions, diagnosing drainage needs, and estimating leaching requirements to maintain favorable salt balances. Considerable information is also available on the tremendously important interrelations between irrigation, fertilization, tillage, and other crop production practices.

The success of any agriculture, especially an irrigated agriculture, is dependent upon the soil. Modern methods of soil survey and land classification provide an essential inventory and summary of soil characteristics. Soil investigations should include textural and structural conditions of soil profile, infiltration and hydraulic conductivity, water retention characteristics, nutrient status, salinity, etc. Such modern instrumentation as pressure plate and pressure membrane apparatus, flame photometers, pH-meters, and electrical conductivity meters are available to aid in quickly appraising soil properties. Although there is great need for further development of such measurements, present knowledge and instrumentation permit reasonably accurate prediction of soil behavior under irrigation and should avoid the economic and social tragedies arising from developing and settling people on lands unsuited to irrigation farms.

Investigations of water supplies to be used for irrigation should include considerations of both quantity and quality (content of dissolved or suspended materials). Research by the U.S. Salinity Laboratory (2) and other agencies provide valuable guidance in predicting the effects of given waters on soil properties and ultimately on crop production. Methods and instruments developed by the Salinity Laboratory are now used in many countries for water analysis and prediction of irrigation suitability. However, for accurate prediction, information on climatic conditions of the area (evaporation and rainfall), soil properties (including clay minerals), irrigation method, drainage conditions, and crops to be grown must also be considered in addition to water analysis data. Water quality considerations will become increasingly important as more complete utilization is made of available water supplies.

Vital for planning, operations, and the ultimate success of an irrigation project is reliable information on consumptive use of water by different crops as well as the seasonal and annual variations in these requirements. Such data provide the basis for selection, construction, and operation of storage structures, conveyance and distribution networks, and irrigation systems. Consumptive use should also be a major factor in selecting crops to be grown in water-deficient areas. It has become a highly important factor in arbitration of controversies over river systems both within and between nations.

Consumptive use is difficult to measure directly. Research in the United States and Europe has developed methods for utilizing climatic data for estimating consumptive use. Formulae proposed by Penman, Thornthwaite, Turc, Lowry-Johnson, and Blaney-Criddle are widely used and, unfortunately, sometimes misused. The simpler, but more empirical formulae, are satisfactory only if the local correction factors, which are substantial, are known. The extensive investigations correlating water evaporation from standard pans with consumptive use may be useful, but they also require knowledge of required correction factors. Although much more research is needed, present knowledge intelligently applied could provide the basis for wise selection of crops and more efficient planning and operation of irrigation projects and systems.

The gross effects of deficient and of excessive soil water on plant growth are well known, but there has been much controversy about specific irrigation practices required to produce a desired level of crop production. Some irrigation specialists have advocated relatively infrequent irrigation, while others have favored keeping the soil quite wet. Many agriculturalists, knowing that water is essential for crop growth, assume that the more irrigation water applied, the higher the crop yield obtained. This belief leads many farmers to irrigate with unnecessary frequency and with a great waste of water—thus leaching plant nutrients and aggravating drainage problems.

Since water, especially in the arid regions, is a limiting and usually a costly resource, it is generally desirable to plan irrigation programs for "efficiency" in terms of maximizing crop yield per unit of water applied. In some cases it may be preferable to maximize crop yield per unit of irrigated land or per unit of initial investment in land preparation or irrigation distribution system. Thus the most desirable irrigation practice will vary with the situation and depend upon proper integration of all factors involved. Efforts (3, 4), are now being made to formulate some general irrigation principles useful in determining irrigation practices. The practices to be recommended should be based on sound irrigation principles and should be designed specifically in accordance with prevailing soil, crop, climate, management and economic factors. Irrigation practices should not be merely copied from irrigation practices reported as successful elsewhere without carefully comparing all factors involved. It should be emphasized that a permanently successful irrigation agriculture requires that the irrigation, fertilization and other cultural practices be adjusted carefully to match local conditions.

Detailed research on the effects of irrigation on the physiology of the cotton plant (carried out at the Cotton Research Station at Shafter, California by scientists of the U.S. Department of Agriculture and the University of California) may help answer some baffling problems encountered with irrigated cotton in developing countries. For example, recent investigations (5) made by a scientist from California, while serving as an expert with FAO, suggest that much of the severe loss of cotton production experienced in the United Arab Republic (Egypt) in 1961, which gravely affected the financial position of that country, was likely caused by irrigation practices which, although traditional, were not favorable to the cotton plant under the climatic conditions of this year. He believes adverse irrigation practices and resultant unfavorable drainage were more responsible for the crop loss than the so-called "reddening" disease or insect infestations. It is estimated that application of recent research on cotton irrigation could increase U.A.R.'s cotton yield nearly 50 percent or about $250 million per year at today's prices while at the same time permitting substantial savings in irrigation water and reducing drainage requirements.

Research on crop irrigation reveals many opportunities to influence the development of crop plants so as to best serve man's needs. Studies in the United States showing possibilities for increasing the percentage of sugar in maturing sugar-beets by withholding irrigation are now being successfully applied in Israel with important savings of water in this arid country. Research demonstrating the critical periods in the water relations of maize, when combined with better varieties and improved cultural practices, now permits this grain to augment the food resources of Central and South America, Africa and India.

To take full advantage of available

research on irrigation of crops, water must be conveyed to the farmers' fields and spread in accordance with the water requirements of the crop and soil characteristics. Many countries are tolerating appalling wastes of water in conveyance, distribution, and application losses. Leached soils, high groundwater tables, and salinity are the unfortunate consequences of such losses. The poorly controlled application of irrigation water to appropriate land is unfortunately still a common sight in both developed and less-developed countries. On the other hand where there is neatly graded contour furrows it should permit much more efficient irrigation with less labor.

The irrigation method to be used should be carefully selected in accordance with topography, soil, rate of water delivery, drainage hazards, the crop and its consumptive use, water quality, salinity, and other considerations. If conditions favor use of sprinkler systems, they must be designed correctly and used under the conditions for which they were designed. If conditions favor surface irrigation—either border, furrow, corrugations, basins, or controlled flooding—the land must be topographically surveyed, graded, and the correctly computed size of head ditch or pipeline determined. The proper length of run, width of border, or size of basin must be selected, but this is most difficult. Because of variability in rates of water intake into soils and other factors, the irrigation engineer must still depend partially on local experience and trial-and-error methods. However, the engineer's art is now being supplemented by scientific research which is providing methods for more accurate prediction of irrigation system performance. Considerable information is available on land grading

and on selecting, designing, and operating different irrigation systems in publications issued by the U.S. Department of Agriculture and University Agricultural Experiment Stations. A pamphlet on grading land for surface irrigation (6) prepared in California has now been reprinted by other countries in French, Greek and Spanish and is extensively used by developing countries.

Very efficient, but expensive machines are now available to grade land for irrigation. In many cases these large and costly machines are not suitable for use in developing countries. The activities of an U.S. Agency for International Development irrigation specialist working in India, Mr. George C. Knierim, demonstrate the successful application of sound principles of irrigation system design simplified to meet local conditions and carried out using very simple and inexpensive land grading tools made by a village blacksmith or the farmer himself from local materials. Buck scrapers, ridgers, corrugators, furrowers, and cultivators have been built by adapting tools used by the Mormon and other pioneers in the American West. It is estimated that some 60 percent of all water supplied for irrigation in India is lost. Water lost on improperly prepared fields constitutes a major loss. With graded contours, Mr. Knierim and his Indian associates are now able to grade fields for efficient irrigation and drainage, even on difficult soils and terrain, thus boosting the productivity of the land often by as much as four- or six-fold. With improved water management, salinity hazards are greatly reduced. His advice: sound principles, simple methods, and simple tools. This work illustrates that the conversion of irrigation from art into a science need not be dependent upon costly imported equipment.

Modern technology now produces an array of materials and equipment to control seepage, possibly reduce evaporation, and regulate flow in canals, distributaries, and on fields. Although some materials and equipment are relatively expensive, their use by less developed countries to conserve water, stimulate crop production, and avoid water-logging should be seriously considered. Some water control equipment can be produced inexpensively from local materials. For example, an inexpensive and locally made canvas dam is being used in India to hold water in irrigation ditches, and in another case simple spiles employed in Jordan do control effectively the flow of water from a forebay into furrows. Very satisfactory spiles can be easily cut from bamboo in many tropical countries.

Siphons are now often used to deliver water from a supply ditch over its bank and onto the land. They permit easy control of water, eliminate cutting ditch banks, greatly facilitate ditch maintenance, and provide much more accurate control of quantities of water being applied. They can be easily constructed out of metal, plastic or rubber. Flow tables for different siphon sizes and operating heads are readily available and have been reproduced in many countries.

An age-old practice in Egypt, improved by modern scientific analysis at the U.S. Salinity Laboratory (7), now provides a clever means of reducing salt damage to germinating seedlings. By special shaping of seedbeds and furrows causing salt to accumulate away from seed rows, salt concentration around germinating seeds may be greatly reduced, permitting emergence of a good stand even in the presence of saline soils and irrigation waters.

No irrigation project should be conceived or operated without attention to possible drainage requirements. Although the art of drainage is probably as old as agriculture itself, the need for drainage is still frequently overlooked. Painstaking research by mathematicians, soil physicists, and engineers has produced in the last 20 years effective means for analyzing the causes of drainage problems, predicting required capacities, and selecting the optimum depth and spacing of drains. Soil chemists have developed guides for computing the amount of water which should pass through soils to leach salts and maintain favorable salt balances. Thus engineers now have a valuable body of scientific knowledge to guide them in drainage system design and operations.

The irrigated plains of the Indus River and its tributaries in West Pakistan constitute one of the most difficult irrigation and drainage problem areas of the world. Today, waterlogging and salinity are causing approximately one hundred thousand acres to go out of agricultural production each year. Additional large areas are partially affected by inadequate drainage and salts which have together reduced crops yields to levels of only 30 to 50 percent of those in comparable well-drained non-saline soils.

The attack now being made on this enormous problem by a special United States team of scientists and engineers (8), working under agreements with the Republic of Pakistan, provide a striking example of the application of modern science and technology to the solution of complex and vast irrigation and drainage problems. This team is employing mathematical model techniques and high-speed digital computers to study the feasibility of using tubewells to drain the

Indus area and provide a water management program which will permit restora-
tion of a productive agriculture. More
specifically, they seek: (a) to evaluate
choices between water management designs involving different combinations of
tubewells, surface drains, subsurface
drains, and canal lining with sealants; (b)
to determine the optimal number, spacing and depth of tubewells for irrigation
project areas, and to identify the optimal
schedule of pumping water for crops or
to drains during the year to maximize
agricultural productivity and to control
the salinity of the irrigation water; and
(c) to study the mechanism of the salt
balance including leaching from root
zones, movement of salts in the ground
water, interactions between adjacent regions arising from discharge of brine to
the waterways, and the magnitude of the
salt accumulation in aquifers during the
next 50 years. Another general objective
is to test and demonstrate the use of
modern techniques of systems analysis
and electronic computers for economic
and engineering analysis, as a basis for
planning and design of irrigation and
drainage systems.

Many irrigation specialists who
have studied the problems of the Indus
Plain over the past 20 years assumed that
the waterlogging and salinity problems
were caused by canal seepage and over-
irrigation. Accordingly, most specialists
have suggested lining canals and reducing excessive irrigation. By using a fresh
scientific approach to an old and difficult problem, new solutions have been
proposed. In brief, these new techniques
indicate *for this area* that: (a) tubewell
systems can effectively eliminate water-
logging and salinity in large areas of
West Pakistan although several test well
projects during the past 15 years have

not been encouraging; (b) tubewells can
provide an important supplemental water
supply for increasing agricultural production on the Indus Plain; and (c) the
lining of canals to retard seepage cannot
be justified under present costs in this
area. The computer also provides data on
optimal spacing and depth of wells and
on pumping programs for wells to maintain salinity within tolerable limits.

As illustrated by this Pakistan
study, mathematical models, digital computers, and other techniques under development can give the irrigation scientist and engineer powerful new tools to
hasten the progress of irrigation from an
art into a fully modern science. These
new techniques permit rapid and accurate
consideration of a vast spread of hydro-
agronomic conditions and of technological
possibilities in order to formulate corresponding responses corrected, as necessary, for "feed-back" relations. These
techniques are not merely *problem-solv-
ing* tools; they are perhaps even more useful as *problem-identification* tools. By
synthesizing the best available data in a
theoretical construct, even though incomplete, it is possible with error analysis
to show quantitatively the effect upon
practical conclusions of the inadequacy
of certain planning data and also the cost
of having to base decisions on poor rather
than good data. With the multiplicity of
variables and inter-actions involved in
irrigation and drainage projects, the simulated results yield a rational basis for
evaluating the relative importance of
variables and of types of data obtainable
from field and laboratory observations.
This permits problem-identification. It
also provides the irrigation specialist with
valuable guidance for selecting data to
be collected as the basis for planning, op-

erations, and long range predictions. Such techniques add much to the modern science of irrigation.

Man has within his grasp the means to insure a highly productive and permanently successful agriculture, if full advantage is taken of opportunities now available to transform the art of irrigation into a modern science. Useful aids in doing this are Monographs on Irrigation (10) (in preparation), Drainage (10), and Salinity (11) which summarize research in these subject areas. An FAO–UNESCO Sourcebook (12) is also being written. These detailed Monographs and the more general Sourcebook should provide irrigation scientists and engineers with valuable guidance. Man's goals of more favorable living standards in this increasingly populous world can be met much more quickly both by increased utilization of the world's science and technology and by more effective cooperation between engineers, soil and crop scientists, and other professional groups whose combined efforts are needed to attain an abundant and permanently successful irrigation agriculture.

REFERENCES

(1) Houston, C. E., *Recommendations for Improved Water Management Programs*, Food and Agriculture Organization, Rome, unnumbered mimeo. (1962).

(2) Richards, L. A. (editor), *Diagnosis and Improvement of Saline and Alkali Soils*, U.S. Department of Agriculture, Agric. Handbook No. 60. (1954).

(3) Israelsen, O. W. and V. E. Hansen, *Irrigation Principles and Practices*, John Wiley and Sons, New York-London. (1962).

(4) Hagan, R. M. and Y. Vaadia, *Principles of irrigated cropping*, UNESCO Arid Zone Research Proceedings, Plant-Water Relations Symposium, Madrid, p. 215–225. (1959).

(5) Walhood, B. T., *Report to Government of U.A.R. on Physiologic Problems in Cotton*, FAO, Division of Plant Production, Mimeo. (in press).

(6) Marr, J. C., *Grading Land for Surface Irrigation*, University of California Agricultural Experiment Station and Extension Service, Circular 438 (1957).

(7) Bernstein, L., M. Fireman, and R. C. Reeves, *Control of salinity in the Imperial Valley, California*, U.S. Dept. of Agriculture, ARS–41–4 (1955).

(8) Information on West Pakistan project from preliminary statement by Professor Harold A. Thomas, Jr. for later inclusion in Draft Report of White House-Interior Panel on Waterlogging and Salinity of West Pakistan. For more complete discussion of these techniques, see Maass, A. et al, *Design of Water Resource Systems*, Harvard University Press, Cambridge, Massachusetts. (1962).

(9) Hagan, R. M., H. R. Haise, and T. W. Edminster (editors), *Irrigation of Agricultural Lands*, American Society of Agronomy Monograph Series (in preparation).

(10) Luthin, J. N. (editor), *Drainage of Agricultural Lands*, American Society of Agronomy Monographs, 7, Madison, Wisconsin (1957).

(11) Richards, L. A. (editor), *Diagnosis and Improvement of Saline and Alkali Soils*, U.S. Department of Agriculture, Agric. Handbook No. 60 (1954). Note: a revised edition is in preparation.

(12) Kovda, V., R. M. Hagan, and C. van den Berg (editors), *FAO–UNESCO International Sourcebook on Irrigation and Drainage of Arid Lands in Relation to Salinity and Alkali* (in preparation; to be published by FAO and UNESCO).

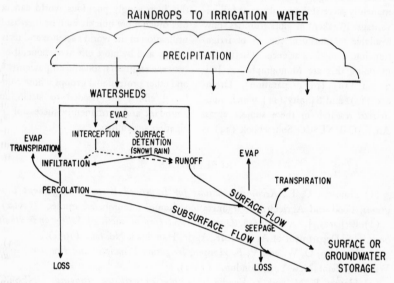

FIGURE I. Sources of losses in converting precipitation to irrigation water.

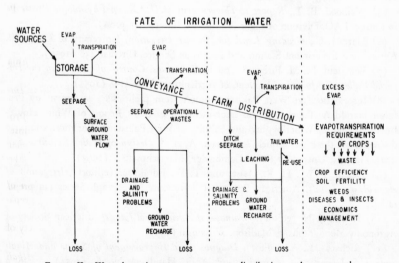

FIGURE II. Water losses in storage, conveyance, distribution, and crop growth.

Principles of Plant Genetics and Their Use in Increasing Food Production

W. M. MYERS

Professor and Head, Department of Agronomy and Plant Genetics,
University of Minnesota
St. Paul, Minnesota

Introduction

Applied genetics or plant breeding has been one of the most effective sciences for increasing productivity of crop plants. Improved varieties, developed by application of genetic principles, provide increases in total yield of food, feed or fiber; reduce production losses caused by diseases, insects and other hazards; improve nutritive and industrial values of the crops; facilitate introduction of the crop into new areas; and reduce production costs through greater efficiency of fertilizer usage, easier culture and harvest and adaptation to mechanization. Plant breeding provides short term results from use of superior local seed sources or introduced varieties and long term results through development of varieties specifically designed for local soil conditions, climate, and use. In less developed countries, improved varieties have the advantage of requiring, after the variety is developed, little capital outlay by the farmers. Furthermore, experience has shown that improved varieties lead the way to other improvements by the farmers in cultural practices, irrigation, fertilization, and disease and pest control.[1]

Testing Indigenous Materials and Introductions

The first step in a plant breeding program is evaluation of already existing materials. These include such indigenous materials as local varieties, farmers' seed lots and natural stands, as well as varieties and collections from other areas of the world. Trials of these materials can and frequently do enable the plant breeder to identify varieties that can be increased and distributed without further breeding work. Furthermore, they enable the plant breeder to assess more precisely the characteristics of the crop which are most in need of improvement. Thus, they are useful to him in defining the objectives of his breeding program and identifying the most useful parental materials.

Collecting and Testing Indigenous Materials

In any area in which a crop has been grown for many years and in which there has not been an active seed improvement program, large differences among seed lots in different villages and among farmers' lots in the same village may be expected. As Love (28) pointed out, seed lots bearing the same variety name may be strikingly different while, conversely, lots having different names may be the same. Some of these farmers' seed lots may be much superior to others or to the average of all others used by the farmers. A collecting and testing program to identify the best seed lots for each region and the subsequent increase and distribution of the best as varieties can have an important impact, within a short time, on food or fiber production in the country.

There are a great many examples of improved varieties identified by this procedure. Mere listing of them would require far more space than is available. Only a single example will be given as illustrative of the scope of the program and the potentialities of the method. For more than thirty years prior to 1950, the Ministry of Agriculture of Thailand had conducted breeding programs and varietal trials with rice, the principal food crop. A number of varieties had been identified as government standard varieties. In 1950, the program was greatly enlarged and, through an arrangement with an agency of the U.S. Government, Dr. H. H. Love, plant breeder from Cornell University, joined forces with the Thai rice workers.

The Thai varieties available from the earlier program were tested at several locations in 1951–54. A striking discovery was that one government standard variety produced up to 80 percent more yield in certain areas than another, the poorest government standard (28).

6. Recognizing t h a t the varieties among farmers' seed lots offered potential wealth, and that the approximately 40 varieties in official trials were only a small sample, the investigators collected 3,000 from various parts of Thailand. Of these about 1,000 were grown in observation plots in 1951 and an additional 1,000 were grown in such plots in 1952. Selections among lots were made from observations in these years, and part of the lines were again grown for preliminary evaluation in 1953. In 1954, 368 varieties were grown in replicated plots at one location and 407 at another location. With further discarding, there were 192 and 163 varieties to be grown in replicated plots at the two locations, respectively, in 1955. The value of this

program is indicated by the fact that the best collected seed lots exceeded the superior government standard variety, used as a check, by 16 to 40 percent at one location (28).

Introductions from Foreign Countries

Another important potential source of "ready made" varieties which quickly can be put to use in the developing country is the plant introduction from other areas of the world. Agro-climatic analogues exist between various countries (see Nuttonson, 31, and preceding papers) and varieties adapted in one country may in general be expected to be adapted in another country with similar ecological conditions. Plant introduction has been essential for many countries like the United States, where few of the important crops were indigenous. The first varieties of cereal crops, clovers, alfalfa, soybeans and many other crops in the United States were direct introductions from Europe, the Near East and East Asia. Most of the earliest introductions were made by immigrants who brought seed with them from their home lands, but by the mid-19th century organized programs of introduction had begun. The varieties used at one time in the United States, which were introductions from other countries, are too numerous to mention. The interested reader is referred to the U.S. Department of Agriculture Yearbooks of Agriculture for 1936 and 1937, as a source of information on this subject (1, 2).

In more recent times, introductions have been important in filling the gap with useful varieties in many countries while the somewhat slower formal breeding programs were developing specifically adapted, superior varieties. Here again,

only a few examples from among many can be cited.

The first conference of European maize breeders was held in Bergamo, Italy, in the summer of 1947. In the following year, under the guidance of M. T. Jenkins and with the help of FAO, the first extensive cooperative trials of U.S. corn belt hybrids were conducted (3). Certain U.S. hybrids were strikingly superior in yielding ability in these and subsequent trials, and the European hybrid corn production program began, on the foundation of these hybrids, several years before it could have been based on hybrids specifically bred for the various European conditions.

In a like manner, U.S. maize hybrids were found to be superior in yield to desai corn in parts of India. They were unsuitable, however, for Indian conditions because of the difficulty of maintaining the inbreds and producing the single crosses and because they were dent types. Nevertheless, their superiority helped to pave the way for the Indian Coordinated Maize Breeding Scheme, a cooperative undertaking of the Indian Council of Agricultural Research and the Rockefeller Foundation. Here again, plant introduction played a key early role. In addition to the U.S. dent inbred lines already available, large numbers of hybrids and inbreds were introduced from the Mexican, Colombian and Central American breeding programs. The first four double cross hybrids, now being introduced only four years later, are from crosses involving, in various combinations, three inbreds of Indian origin, three from U.S. germplasm, and four of South American origin. These four hybrids produce yields of 122, 142, 151 and 153 percent of the best local strains in the areas for which they are released (9).

Other examples include Guatemalan flint maize varieties which have expanded maize production in Thailand (6); Nebred wheat, Buffalo alfalfa and numerous vegetable varieties in Afghanistan; yellow flint corns of the Caribbean, Hawaiian sweet corn, U.S. peanut varieties and varieties of several other crops in Cambodia (26); Gabo wheat in Jordan; Kenaf varieties in Guatemala, Colombia and Viet Nam (14); Bourbon coffee which yields 40 percent more than common *arabica* types and has now largely replaced them in Central and South America[2]; several varieties of wheat, barley and other crops in Libya (32); and many others.

12. The plant breeder in the developing country may obtain introductions from foreign sources by (a) correspondence with other plant breeders, (b) exchanges of collections by individuals or organizations in the respective countries, and (c) organized collecting expeditions.

The last method usually requires more time and resources than the developing country can afford. There have been extensive organized collecting expeditions carried out in many areas of the world by the USSR (39), the British Commonwealth Nations, Japan, the United States and other countries. As a result of these expeditions and of other efforts to assemble samples of the world's germ plasm, large collections are available from various sources.

In the United States, so-called "World Collections" of wheat, oats, barley, corn, rice, soybeans, flax, alfalfa, and several other crops are maintained on a systematic basis. The Regional Plant Introduction Stations in each of the four experiment station regions of the United States maintain viable seed stocks of most recent plant introductions. The National Seed Storage Facility, often called the National Germplasm Bank, at Fort Collins, Colorado, has facilities for long time storage of many thousands of seed lots. An effort is currently being made to place in storage at this facility seed of every variety or collection, domestic or foreign, which is not currently being used in plant breeding programs in the U.S. or being maintained by the Regional Plant Introduction Stations, and which, therefore, is in danger of being lost.

The plant breeder in a developing nation can tap this resource of germ plasm by applying to the New Crops Branch, Agricultural Research Service, U.S. Department of Agriculture, Beltsville, Maryland, or by addressing a request for seed lots to the Investigations Leader for the particular crop, Crops Division, Agricultural Research Service, U.S. Department of Agriculture, Beltsville, Maryland.

The Food and Agriculture Organization also can be helpful to the plant breeder by providing names of breeders of his crop in other countries of the world and by suggesting sources of varietal collections of the crop.

A plant breeding program should not be initiated until there has been some systematic evaluation of varieties that are available already as indigenous materials or as introductions from other countries. Evaluations of additional indigenous and introduced materials should continue, of course, after the formal breeding program is initiated.

Plant Breeding Procedures

Once suitable breeding materials have been identified, the breeding objectives clarified, and, if possible, progress made on increasing and distributing stop-gap varieties, a more formal plant breeding program can be initiated. From this program, varieties specifically adapted to the environmental and use conditions of local areas of the country can be expected. These should be considerably superior, usually, to the best indigenous or introduced varieties. For example, work in the coastal regions of Guatemala showed that some locally bred maize hybrids exceeded by 15 to 25 percent other hybrids in trials (4). However, several years are required before the varieties are developed, tested, and ready for distribution. Hopefully, the indigenous or introduced varieties will provide for some improvement and will be suitable for interim use until the locally bred varieties are available.

There are three basic steps in plant breeding; namely, (a) finding or developing suitable populations within which effective selection can be practiced; (b) selection, including evaluation of the selections; and (c) use of the selections to produce varieties for distribution to the farmers.

Finding or Developing Populations for Selection

A suitable population for selection is one which has sufficient genetic variability and within which the genes desired in the new variety occur in high enough frequency to permit the recovery of combinations of them in populations of feasible size. The plant breeder is, limited in general, to the genes that are available in the populations which he has. Furthermore, frequencies of the desirable genes are important in the effectiveness with which the plant breeder can select for combinations of them. For illustration, if each of two desirable alleles, A and B, has a frequency of 0.5, more than half of the plants (56.2 percent) in a freely interbreeding population would carry both favorable alleles. If, however, the frequency of each were 0.1, only 4.4 percent of the plants in such a population would carry both favorable alleles.

In the early stages of the breeding program, farmers' seed lots, indigenous varieties and introductions p r o v i d e abundant sources of suitable populations within which effective selection is possible. Most of the varieties developed by selection in the United States during the first quarter of the twentieth century were from populations of this kind. All varieties of seed flax grown in the United States in 1936 were developed in this manner (19). Hayes, Immer and Smith (19) have summarized some results in the self-pollinated crops of individual plant selection from such populations. For more detailed information, the reader may consult the Yearbooks of Agriculture, 1936 and 1937 (1, 2).

Many examples of successful selection from existing populations can be cited from plant breeding programs in developing countries. A few may suffice for illustration. A number of years ago, U.S. technicians working on the Cooperative Fiber Commission in Cuba were faced with near destruction of the kenaf crop by a disease caused by *Colletotrichum hibiscii*. One composite variety, *Salvadorian,* proved to be a mixture of types, some highly resistant to the disease. By selection, a new resistant variety was developed in a short time.[3]

The selection program with rice in Thailand (28) serves to illustrate the scope of work and potentiality for improvement when locally grown varieties and seed lots are used as the source pop-

ulations. From individual heads collected in many parts of the country, 114,079
individual head progenies were grown
in 1951. By observation, the numbers
of lines were reduced to 22,652 for evaluation in 1952, 10,062 in 1953, and 3,902
in 1954. The lines that appeared most
promising were grown in three-row plots
in 6 replications. A total of 683 lines
were tested in this way. Among lines in
such tests in 1952–54, some yielded 10
to 40 percent more than the standard
checks as an average of the three years.

Although much progress can be
made by selection in existing populations,
particularly in the early stages of the
breeding program, the plant breeder can
expect to make greatest ultimate progress
by developing populations which have
the combinations of genes and gene frequencies leading to most effective progress by selection. A number of breeding
methods or mating systems are available.
These include hybridization, inbreeding,
backcrossing, recurrent selection, and
reciprocal recurrent selection. These
methods are treated in some detail in
recent plant breeding textbooks, including Hayes, Immer and Smith (19), Elliott (16), Poehlman (33) and Allard
(11). From these books original references can be found for more intensive study by the interested student.
Only some general comments will be
made here regarding these methods.

Hybridization is the most power-
ful tool available for creating source populations. The segregation and recombination that occur following hybridization result in extensive genetic variability, a prerequisite to successful selection.
Furthermore, by selection of the parents
used, populations can be produced in
which the genes desired in improved
varieties occur.

Controlled hybridization between
parents of known performance has been
used extensively in the more advanced
breeding programs with the self-pollinated crops. In cross-pollinated crops,
where genetic variability in natural populations is very high, controlled hybridization has been less essential. Nevertheless, hybridization between selected
inbred lines of maize has been an effective means of producing new populations
from which superior inbreds can be extracted (18, 19). Intervarietal hybrids
and crosses between non-inbred clones
have also been used in alfalfa, *Hevea*,
cacao, fruit crops and other cross polli-
nators.

Inbreeding results in rapid increase
in homozygosity and segregation of the
population into lines with varying degrees of relationship to one another.

In the naturally self-pollinated
species, in which inbreeding by selfing
occurs normally, unless prevented by the
plant breeder, populations which develop
following hybridization consist, after a
few generations, of predominantly homozygous plants. In F_4 or later generations,
there are F_2 sub-populations within F_1
populations, F_3 sub-populations within
F_2 sub-populations, F_4 sub-populations
within F_3 sub-populations, etc. (20).
Since the varieties of commerce in the
self-pollinated crops are relatively homozygous lines or mixtures of them, inbreeding is allowed to occur in such
species following controlled hybridization. A practical level of homozygosity
is reached by the F_5 to F_8 generations.

Breeders of the self-pollinated
species differ regarding steps to follow
between hybridization and the point of
relative homozygosity. Proponents of the
pedigree method use visual selection of
individual plants in each generation and

of the progenies of these selected individuals in each succeeding generation. By the F_5 to F_6 generation, the remaining lines are but a small sample of the total genetic recombinations that would be found in a corresponding unselected population. Hopefully, this selected sample will have a substantially higher frequency of favorable genes than the unselected population.

Proponents of the bulk method apply no artificial selection pressure on the population during the several generations between hybridization and the time of relative homozygosity. Shifts in gene frequency in such populations are the results of drift or natural selection. Selection by the plant breeder is started in F_6, F_7 or F_8.

Between the extremes of the pedigree and bulk methods, there are various combinations of the two. Much has been written regarding the relative merits of these methods, and a review of this extensive literature is not attempted here. It is sufficient to say that neither method is clearly superior in all circumstances. Choice of the time at which selection pressure should be applied depends upon a number of factors, including mode of inheritance of the most important characters, the facilities available to the plant breeder, and his knowledge and skill.

Inbreeding, usually by enforced self-pollination, is commonly used in the naturally cross-pollinated crops. The objectives are (a) to speed up increase in frequency of desirable genes and (b) to develop lines that can be reproduced from seed through successive generations of evaluation and subsequent use in the breeding program.

Where favorable genes can be selected for effectiveness on the basis of the individual plant or selfed progeny, inbreeding by selfing provides the most rapid method of obtaining lines that are homozygous for such genes. Success of this method has been amply demonstrated in corn by the development of lines and, subsequently, hybrids with good smut resistance, stalk lodging and breaking resistance, ear shape, ear placement, suitable maturity and other characteristics of economic importance.

On the other hand, there is evidence that inbreeding with visual selection is relatively ineffective in raising the average frequencies of desirable genes for such characters as combining ability for yield (21, 35, 41, 17). Because of the urgency for producing improved maize varieties as rapidly as possible, the first hybrids distributed by the Officina de Estudios Especiales in Mexico were produced from four S_1 lines. Use of lines inbred for additional generations has resulted in more uniform hybrids, but little improvement in yield over the hybrids was made from S_1 lines (40). Although there may be advantages in more inbreeding, such as the greater uniformity noted by Wellhausen (40) and the greater ease of maintaining the lines without significant genetic shift, the lesson from these results for the maize breeders of developing countries seems obvious—improved maize yields that can come from hybrids should not be delayed by the years taken for a long inbreeding program.

Backcrossing results in a rapid and predictable shift of gene frequencies in the population, following hybridization, toward the genotype of the recurrent parent (11, 19). When continued for sufficient generations, all plants of the population theoretically will have the same genotype as the recurrent parent, except for genes from the non-recurrent parent retained in the population by deliberate selection.

Backcrossing is an appropriate tool when one of the parents used in hybridization is superior in a number of characteristics while the other parent is deficient in most. With each generation of backcrossing, the frequency of genes from the recurrent parent is increased, thus enhancing the possibility of obtaining selections which combine most of these genes. The primary limitation of backcrossing for breeding programs in developing countries is the necessity, if it is to be an effective tool, of having a variety or varieties that are generally superior. Such superior varieties usually will not be available until after years of intensive breeding.

Results with rice breeding in Colombia indicate, however, that backcrossing may be expeditious in producing adapted varieties with resistance to the hoja blanca disease. Certain introduced varieties, including Bluebonnet 50, have proved to be superior varieties for use as recurrent parents (8).

Recurrent and reciprocal recurrent selection are effective methods of increasing desirable gene frequencies in populations while retaining a high level of heterozygosity and genetic variability. In this respect, these methods contrast with inbreeding where, through rapid progress to homozygosity, genetic variability and, hence, further progress through selection are rapidly reduced.

The success of these procedures in maize breeding, in which they have been investigated most extensively, is indicated by results of numerous experiments, including recent ones reported by Comstock and Robinson (13), Sprague and Russell (36), Sprague, et al (37), Lonnquist and McGill (27), Thomas and Gris-

som (38), and Douglas, et al (15). Impressive results have been reported in yellow sweet clover (*Melilotus officinalis*) by Johnson (22) and Johnson and El Banna (23) and in *Lolium perenne* by Beddows (12).

A major potentiality of recurrent selection for use in developing countries is that the new population developed at the end of each cycle may, if desired, be increased as a synthetic variety. Such a procedure is being used successfully in Colombia in development of improved synthetic varieties of maize (7, 8). First cycle synthetics, from certain varieties have exceeded the original variety in yield by 10 to 22 percent. In other varieties, however, little improvement in yield has resulted from the first cycle of selection.

Selection

Success in plant breeding, once suitable source populations are available, is dependent upon the effectiveness of selection. Genetic progress is a function of the selection index and of heritability (25).

Heritability is an expression of the proportion of total phenotypic variation which is attributable to genetic effects. Obviously, the genotype, in selection of which the plant breeder is really interested, is best estimated by the phenotype when variances, due to genotype, are very large and those due to environment are very small. In order to maximize the effectiveness of selection, the plant breeder must seek to reduce the differential environmental effects to a minimum, relative to the genetic differences in the population. He has several means for doing this including (a) special measures for control of the environment and for insuring as nearly as possible uniform environments for all plants in the population, (b) appropriate experimental designs to reveal differences, control and measure error, and to provide a valid estimate of significance of the differences, and (c) use of selection units appropriate for the characters for which selections are made.

One of the simplest and frequently neglected methods for controlling or reducing environmental effects is by good cultural practices, good stands, and uniform fertilization. These are inexpensive practices that are within the grasp of any plant breeder. The breeder of a crop cannot hope to be successful until he has learned how to grow the crop. Other steps to reduce environmental effects include special disease nurseries, and controlled insect infestation in which uniform disease or insect distribution is fostered by various techniques. Finally, the breeder may find use for special facilities for control of photoperiod, light intensity, humidity, and temperature in greenhouses or environment control rooms. Since much progress can be made in breeding by less expensive equipment, the plant breeder in the developing country usually will not require such equipment, at least for a number of years. In any case, money should not be invested in it until it can be assured that the equipment is really needed and that there are staff members who are capable of operating and maintaining it.

In determining the best experimental design to use, it should be remembered (a) that the simplest design to serve the purpose may be the best and (b) that no experimental design or statistical analysis of the data will overcome the problems introduced by poor cultural practices, uneven stands, and other faulty experimental techniques.

The selection unit to be used will depend on the kind of characters for which the breeder is selecting. For characters of high heritability, effective progress can be made by phenotypic selection; i.e. by selection of individual plants, clones or lines. Conversely, for characters of low heritability, selection must be based upon a progeny test if it is to be effective.

In the self-pollinated crops, in which the relatively homozygous selections are increased to become the varieties of commerce, the selection unit is normally the plant itself or its selfed progeny. In the cross-pollinated crops, on the other hand, the selections normally are used for development of synthetic or hybrid varieties. Since the selections are to be used in hybrid combinations, they usually may be evaluated most effectively in some kind of hybrid combination. These include top crosses or polycrosses for evaluation of general combining ability and diallel crosses and crosses with specific lines or clones for assessment of specific combining ability and identification of the best specific combinations.

The usefulness of tests for general and specific combining ability, the efficacy of early versus delayed testing, the most efficient tester parents to use, and other problems related to evaluation of selections are dealt with extensively in the plant breeding literature. The interested reader is referred to such books as Hayes, Immer and Smith (19) and to many recent journal articles on these subjects.

Use of Selections

Use of selections is dictated, to a large extent, by the kind of crop and particularly the mode of pollination and the method of reproduction in the agricultural use of the crop. In the naturally self-pollinated crops selections usually are increased through successive generations to become the varieties of commerce. Exception to this is found in some crops, tomatoes for example, in which ease of producing hybrid seed and the relatively small amount of seed required make the use of F_1 hybrids feasible.

In vegetatively propagated species, such as potatoes and sugar cane, the varieties used commercially are clones of the original selections.

Selections, either families, inbred lines or clones, of the normally cross-pollinated crops are used in the development of synthetic varieties or as parents of single, three-way or double-cross hybrid varieties.

The striking success of hybrid maize in the United States has focused attention of plant breeders on the potentialities of using maize hybrids in other areas of the world and of using hybrid varieties of other crops as well. Maize hybrids were introduced soon after the war in Europe, and much European maize production is now based on hybrids. Maize hybrids also have been developed and distributed for use in Mexico, Colombia, India, and several other countries. In Mexico, in 1960, a new maize hybrid, H–507, was released which yields 20 percent more than the previously recommended hybrid, H–503, and about 35 percent more than the best open-pollinated native varieties in the area (8). Yield increases of similar magnitude are being obtained from new maize hybrids in Colombia and in India (8, 9).

Although the best hybrid varieties will yield more than the best synthetic varieties that can be produced, difficulties are encountered frequently in adequate scale production of hybrid seed. This is especially true in some developing countries where neither private nor public institutions are available for an orderly process of seed increase and distribution. In such situations synthetic varieties of maize may prove to be an acceptable solution at least until the procedures for hybrid seed production on an adequate scale can be developed. In other crops, where hybrid seed is not readily produced, synthetic varieties are likewise the means for using selections.

Much of the improved maize seed used in Mexico is advanced generations of double cross hybrids. These synthetics have approximately one-half the yield superiority over open-pollinated varieties that the hybrids have. Extensive breeding programs are in progress in Mexico and Colombia on the development of superior synthetics by combinations of several inbred lines and by recurrent selection (8).

The development of synthetics in forage grasses and legumes has been discussed in several papers (30).

An interesting application of controlled hybridization between non-inbred clones is found in rubber tree (*Hevea braziliensis*) and cacao breeding. As a result of extensive breeding investigations, centered at Turrialba, Costa Rica, but with cooperative work in several Central and South American countries, *Hevea* clones were developed which combine high resistence to South American leaf blight with the high levels of rubber production of the susceptible "Eastern" clones (34). Plantings in Brazil, Guatemala, Colombia, Peru and Costa Rica now are made almost exclusively with these clones. From extensive progeny tests, however, certain parental combinations are now known from which seedlings can be used for commercial planting with only the precaution of selecting for South American leaf blight resistance in the seedling nursery.[4]

Likewise, in Cacao so-called clonal seedlings are now being used for commercial propagation. These are seedlings from controlled crosses of parents which are known to have superior specific combining ability. Work of this kind is in progress in Ecuador and Brazil.[5]

Cooperation in Plant Breeding

Cooperation is one of the most important essentials of a successful plant breeding program. This includes cooperation among scientists of different disciplines within the same organization and among scientists of the same discipline in different organizations, stations and countries.

Dr. H. K. Hayes, Emeritus Professor of Agronomy and Plant Genetics, University of Minnesota, has helped with development of plant breeding programs in China, Chile and the Philippines. In each case he gave major emphasis to the development of cooperation among research workers, and it is probable that this was the most permanent of the many contributions he made. The remarkable agricultural progress in Taiwan is attributable, at least in part, to excellent cooperative and coordinated research and development programs (6). This cooperation may well be a legacy of the understandings which Hayes helped the Chinese scientists reach on the mainland almost 30 years ago.

Recognizing that cooperation among scientists, which is now accepted as the normal condition, did not always exist in the United States, Dr. Hayes has stated, "As I see changes in agricultural research, say from 1915 to the present, it seems to me that this type of coordinated effort, free exchange of ideas and materials without inhibiting individual initiative, is the most important accomplishment that I know of in our own country".[6]

Seed Production and Distribution

A plant breeding program, no matter how successful, has not made a contribution to increased food production until seeds of the improved varieties are generally available for use by the farmers. Experience in many countries, including the United States, has shown that seed increase and distribution do not take care of themselves. When small lots of seed of a new variety are distributed by the plant breeder, and there is no organized effort to guide further increases, the variety is soon lost or the seed becomes mixed with other types.

The procedures and organizations for orderly increase and distribution of seed of improved varieties vary considerably among countries (5, 6, 24), and even among states in the United States. Under programs of certification, which are found in many countries, different classes of seed are recognized. In the United States these are called breeder, foundation, registered and certified. Various names for analogous classes are used in different countries. For varieties developed by public agencies, the usual procedure is for a government agency, frequently the plant breeding station, to maintain the breeder seed and to produce the foundation. From this stage, procedures vary between the extremes of (a) having all seed of subsequent classes, which will be used by farmers for commercial planting, produced by private seed growers and (b) having all seed of the subsequent classes produced and distributed by government seed farms.

Economic conditions, social structures, previous practices and other factors vary so much from country to country that no one system will be best for all situations. Instead, the system used must be fitted to the needs and conditions of the country. Nevertheless, the writer's experience suggests the following principles as guides in devising the seed production and distribution system:

(a) The breeder seed can best be maintained under the close supervision of the plant breeder who developed the variety.

(b) Reliable planting stock (foundation and registered seed) must be available in sufficient quantities for production of the seed that the farmer plants for his commercial crop. This requires some kind of organized program, either public or private.

(c) For production of large quantities of certified seed, private producers are usually more efficient than government seed farms.

(d) Government subsidy of the price of seed of improved varieties does not, in the long run, result in as good farmer acceptance of the improved varieties as when he must pay a premium price for the seed.

(e) There is need for certification program, by government or private agency, to insure maintenance of varietal identity and purity.

Special Methods of Breeding

Numerous special methods of breeding are available, including transfer of genes from related species, chromosome doubling, use of monosomic and nullisomics, and induction of mutations by radiation.

Use of ionizing radiations and other mutagens has attracted the attention of plant breeders as a new tool. Enthusiasm has been particularly high in areas where conventional plant breeding is less well developed and where needs for increased food production are great. Mutation breeding has been approached as a sort of magic bridge by which the plant breeder can hope to span, in a few years, the development by conventional plant breeding in other areas during half a century. The potentialities and limitations of mutation breeding have been examined in recent symposia (10, 29). It is perhaps appropriate here to quote a statement which applies particularly to the use of mutation breeding in developing countries:

"As a general rule, the plant breeder cannot afford to adopt it today as a breeding method. To do so will result in wasting the time and facilities so used. The plant breeder who studies mutation breeding must do so primarily to evaluate and develop the tool. Unless he has more than sufficient resources for plant breeding by conventional methods, he cannot afford to divert part of his resources to mutation breeding" (29).

The same conclusion seems appropriate in general for other highly specialized tools of breeding. There is so much to be done and such rich potentials for development by conventional plant breeding procedures that efforts in the developing countries should be concentrated primarily on them.

FOOTNOTES

[1] The author is indebted to Drs. Elton G. Nelson, William H. Cowgill, Clement Orrben, Munroe McCown, Lawrence Kapp and other staff members of the Agency for International Development for information on some plant breeding accomplishments in US/AID programs.

[2] Personal communication, Dr. William H. Cowgill.

[3] Personal communication, Dr. Elton G. Nelson.

[4] Personal communication, Dr. William H. Cowgill.

[5] Personal communication, Dr. William H. Cowgill.

[6] Personal communication, Dr. H. K. Hayes.

REFERENCES

(1) Anon. *Yearbook of Agriculture.* United States Department of Agriculture, Washington, D.C. (1936).

(2) Anon. *Yearbook of Agriculture.* United States Department of Agriculture, Washington, D.C. (1937).

(3) Anon. *Results of Cooperative Hybrid Maize Tests in Europe—1949.* F.A.O. Development Paper No. 7, Washington, D.C. (1950).

(4) Anon. *Maiz para Guatemala.* Reporte Annual para 1956. Servicio Cooperativo Interamericano de Agricultura. Guatemala (1956).

(5) Anon. *Proceedings of the Far East Seed Improvement Conference.* Republic of China and United States of America. Taipei, Taiwan (1956).

(6) Anon. *Seed Improvement in the Far East.* Proc. of Second Far East Seed Improvement Work Shop. Tokyo, Japan (1959).

(7) Anon. *Program in the Agricultural Sciences, Annual Report 1959–1960.* The Rockefeller Foundation, New York (1960).

(8) Anon. *Program in the Agricultural Sciences, Annual Report 1960–1961.* The Rockefeller Foundation, New York (1961).

(9) Anon. *Co-ordinated Maize Breeding Scheme. Progress report.* Indian Council of Agricultural Research and The Rockefeller Foundation, New Delhi, India (1961).

(10) Anon. *Symposium on Mutation and Plant Breeding.* NAS–NRC Publ. 891. Washington, D.C. (1961).

(11) Allard, R. W., *Principles of Plant Breeding.* John Wiley & Sons, Inc., New York (1960).

(12) Beddows, A. R., *Grass Breeding.* Rept. of Welsh Pl. Br. Station, Univ. College of Wales, Aberystwyth 1950–56, pp. 11–35 (1958).

(13) Comstock, R. E. and H. F. Robinson, *Findings Relative to Reciprocal Recurrent Selection.* Proc. Intern. Genetics Symposia 1956, pp. 461–464 (1956).

(14) Dempsey, J. M., *Survey of Indonesia for Long Vegetable Fiber Production.* Processed USOM/Saigon, Viet-Nam (1961).

(15) Douglas, A. G., Collier, J. W., El-Ebrasy, M. F., and J. S. Rogers, *An evaluation of three cycles of reciprocal recurrent selection in a corn improvement program.* Crop Science, *1,* 157–161 (1961).

(16) Elliott, F. C., *Plant Breeding and Cytogenetics.* McGraw-Hill Book Co., Inc., New York (1958).

(17) Hanson, A. A., Myers, W. M. and R. J. Garber, *The general combining ability of orchardgrass selections and their I_4 progenies.* Agron. Jour., *44*, 84–87 (1952).

(18) Hayes, H. K., and I. J. Johnson, *The breeding of improved selfed lines of corn.* Jour. Amer. Soc. Agron., *31*, 710–724 (1939).

(19) Hayes, H. K., Immer, F. R., and D. C. Smith, *Methods of Plant Breeding.* McGraw-Hill Book Co., Inc., New York (1955).

(20) Horner, T. W., Comstock, R. E., and H. F. Robinson, *Non-allelic Gene Interactions and the Interpretation of Quantitative Genetic Data.* North Car. Agr. Exp. Sta. Tech. Bull. 118 (1955).

(21) Jenkins, M. T., *The effect of inbreeding and of selection within inbred lines of maize upon the hybrids made after successive generations of selfing.* Iowa State Jour. of Sci., *9*, 429–450 (1935).

(22) Johnson, I. J., *Further progress in recurrent selection for general combining ability in sweetclover.* Agron. Jour., *48*, 242–243 (1956).

(23) Johnson, I. J. and A. S. El Banna, *Effectiveness of successive cycles of phenotypic recurrent selection in sweetclover.* Agron. Jour., *49*, 120–125 (1957).

(24) Julen, G., and A. Kjaer, *Seed Certification Schemes for Rice in Various Countries.* International Rice Commission Newsletter, 9, 1–16 (1960).

(25) Lerner, I. M., *The Genetic Basis of Selections.* John Wiley and Sons, Inc., New York (1958).

(26) Litzenberger, S. C., *Agronomy Development. Aid to Cambodia.* End of Tour Report, International Cooperation Administration, Washington, D.C. (1960).

(27) Lonnquist, J. H., and D. P. McGill, *Performance of corn synthetics in advanced generations of synthesis and after two cycles of recurrent selection.* Agron. Jour., *48*, 249–253 (1956).

(28) Love, H. H., *Report of Rice Investigations, 1950–54.* Agr. Division, United States Operations Mission and Ministry of Agr., Government of Thailand (1955).

(29) Myers, W. M., *Some limitations of radiation genetics and plant breeding.* Ind. Jour. Gen. and Pl. Breed., *20*, 89–92 (1960).

(30) Myers, W. M., *New Developments in Forage Crop Breeding.* Proc. Eighth Intern. Grassland Cong., pp. 11–15 (1960).

(31) Nuttonson, M. Y., *Ecological Crop Geography and Field Practises of the Ryukyu Islands, Natural Vegetation of the Ryukyus and Agro-Climatic Analogues in the Northern Hemisphere.* Amer. Inst. Crop. Ecol. Wash. (1952).

(32) Oram, P. A., *Crop Agronomy and Improvement in Tripolitania.* Report to Government of Libya. Food and Agriculture Organization, No. 1144 (1959).

(33) Poehlman, J. M., *Breeding Field Crops.* Henry Holt and Co., Inc., New York (1959).

(34) Rands, R. D., and T. G. Polhamus, *Progress Report on the Cooperative Hevea Rubber Development Program in Latin America.* U.S. Dept. of Agr. Circ. 976 (1955).

(35) Sprague, G. F., and P. A. Miller, *The influence of visual selection during inbreeding on combining ability in corn.* Agron. Jour., *44*, 258–262 (1952).

(36) Sprague, G. F., and W. A. Russell, *Some Evidence on Type of Gene Action Involved in Yield Heterosis in Maize*. Proc. Intern. Genetics Symposia, Tokyo, Japan, 1956, 522–526 (1957).

(37) Sprague, G. F., Russell, W. A., and T. H. Penny, *Recurrent selection for specific combining ability and type of gene action involved in yield heterosis in corn.* Agron. Jour., *51*, 392–394 (1959).

(38) Thomas, W. I., and D. B. Grissom, *Cycle evaluation of reciprocal recurrent selection for popping volume, grain yield, and resistance to root lodging in popcorn.* Crop Science *1*, 197–200 (1961).

(39) Vavilov, N. I., *World Resources of Cereals, Grain, Leguminous Crops and Flax and Their Utilization in Plant Breeding. Agroecological Survey of the Principal Field Crops.* Izdatel stvo Akademii Nauk SSSR Moskva—Leningrad, p. 462 (1957). (Extensive review in Pl. Br. Abs. 28, 3576: 1958).

(40) Wellhausen, E. J., *Modern corn breeding and production in Mexico.* Phytopathology, *44*, 391–395 (1954).

(41) Wellhausen, E. J., and T. S. Wortman, *Combining ability of S_1 and derived S_3 lines of corn.* Agron. Jour., *46*, 86–89 (1954).

Animal Improvement and Adaptation

JAY L. LUSH

Iowa State University,
Iowa City, Iowa

JORGE DE ALBA,

Instituto Interamericano de Ciencias
Agricolas de la OEA,
Turrialba, Costa Rica

What is Ideal?

The first step in an animal improvement program is to define what kind of animal is best for the purposes of the people in the country concerned. That definition must encompass not only the human needs for the products of these animals, but also the qualities of the animal itself which will promote its own well-being. Even religious or other cultural values may bear importantly on whether surplus animals or those of little merit can be killed and whether animals have values as symbols of their owner's social status or wealth. Usually, only a local person or at least one who has lived in the country for several decades can know the culture of the people well enough to realize the true value of livestock in that society, but this value may seriously modify the objectives of an improvement program. Human needs include such things as milk, meat and eggs for human food, work, wool, hides, etc. The animal's well-being can depend to some extent on its tolerance to heat, cold or rain, its ability to withstand inadequate nutrition during certain seasons, its resistance to diseases and to insect pests, etc.

Individual Merit

Measurement or appraisal of an animal's merit merely expresses how closely that animal conforms to the ideal. Merit may be defined either phenotypically or genetically. The former involves only the animal's own observed qualities. The latter concerns the kinds of offspring and other descendants the animal is likely to have. An animal's genetic merit can be estimated only indirectly by considering its own phenotypic merit and also the phenotypic merits of its available relatives. In considering all of these phenotypes the effects of variations in the environment should be discounted as much as possible.

The simplest definition of individual merit may be merely a verbal description. A score card is a somewhat more quantified description. A selection index is a score card modified still further by such knowledge as we have of heritability and genetic and phenotypic correlations among the constituent qualities. The selection index is intended to rank the animals according to their value for breeding purposes (i.e., according to their genetic merit); whereas the ordinary score card ranks them only phenotypically according to their own appearance or performance.

The individual merit that concerns the modern breeder is in productivity, rather than in bodily form. The measurements of productivity should be as direct as possible, such as: Weights of fleece or of milk produced, weights of young reared to weaning, growth rates in general, longevity, lifetime production, etc. Although such measures do not show an animal's real and complete productivity with perfect accuracy, they are so much more accurate than the easily observable external "sign characters" such as color, shape or size of horns, shape of head, size of skeletal frame, conformation of legs, etc., that the latter have only faint utility. The wide popularity of sign characters can be laid mainly to human nature and to the ease of observing such signs.

Practical merit involves many characters, several of them important, but the whole animal is the smallest unit that can be selected or rejected. Therefore, one simply *must* add (or combine in some other way) an animal's high merit in one quality, medium merit in another, and low merit or defectiveness in others, to decide whether to keep or cull the animal. This combination we call "net merit," realizing, of course, that in some cases net merit can be for breeding. The measurement of merit *must* be kept simple for practical reasons, but it is com-

plicated by the fact that many qualities enter into it, some of which are of minor importance. The following procedure seems to work best: Measure as directly and simply as possible the two, three or five most important aspects of productivity and allot to them about 60 to 80 points. Then group together all the remaining characters which contribute enough to merit to be worth considering, calling this group by some such term as "general appearance" or "other qualities." Allot to this group the remaining 40 to 20 points on the score card. More detail and refinement of records and their use will be worthwhile, only if the accuracy of choices is increased enough to be worth more than the costs of the extra work. However, this is not likely to be feasible in the first programs in the less developed countries, but that is a matter for local decisions and ingenuity.

What one actually will do at a given moment, on the basis of these ratings of merit, is simple. Either one culls the animal or keeps it for breeding purposes. If one keeps it, one may also need to decide whether to keep its sons as well as its daughters, or to keep only the daughters. For the animals which are retained, decisions may need to be made again next year when new information has become available.

Improvement by Breeding

The basic principle is that the animals closest to the ideal in their genetic merit should be used most extensively for breeding, while those furthest from the ideal should be culled at the earliest opportunity. Performance testing is done to measure phenotypic merit. Progeny testing, as well as information on parents and collateral relatives, comes into the picture only to help to correct some of the mistakes which would be made if decisions about each animal were made entirely on its own phenotypic merit. Artificial insemination comes into the picture only as it permits more intense selection among the males thought to be best. It does not change at all the kinds of genes the chosen sires transmit. Also, it can make importation less expensive by getting more offspring per imported sire. With artificial insemination, therefore, the importance of deciding correctly *which* males are really best for breeding use is increased, since fewer males are used and any mistakes made in choosing one of them will affect more individuals in the next generation.

Improvement in animal breeding can follow two different roads. These have some things in common but are mutually exclusive in others.

The first road, the traditional one, is to select the best and cull the worst in the hope of improving the whole stock more or less steadily. The ultimate goal is to produce a stock which is fully as perfect as any cross which could be made from it. In genetic terms, this is hoping to make a stock homozygous for all the "good" genes and free from all hereditary defects. To this end, attention to ancestors, collateral relatives, and progeny is merely a check for making selection more accurate and therefore hastening progress. On this road, line-breeding is used as a holding action, whenever an unusually good animal appears, and for profiting from some of the epistatic effects by bringing together repeatedly in favorable combinations those genes which in other combinations are unfavorable. Otherwise, all forms of inbreeding are avoided. If this road really is traversible, it is the simpler of the two.

The second road leads toward a situation in which seedstocks are bred separately from each other but are outcrossed, in one way or another, to produce animals for use. This can be called breeding for heterosis. This road may be the better when, in many pairs of genes, the heterozygote is individually preferable to both homozygotes. This may happen for a variety of genetic reasons, which will be mentioned briefly later. Since the seedstock animals are to be crossed on those from a different seedstock, the practical test of their individual breeding merit is the average merit of the crossbred progeny they produce *with that other stock*. This road relies more on the progeny test and much less on individual merit of the animals in the seedstock than does the other road. The important thing is that the progeny by which an animal's breeding value is judged shall be out of crosses with the same kind of stock as that on which it is expected to be used when producing animals for use. The pure seedstock is to be improved not in its own individual merit, but in its ability to produce good crosses.

This second road, if ultimately successful, would lead to pure seedstocks which are only mediocre or less in individual merit but cross with each other to produce individuals which average better than any purebred population which could possibly be produced by traveling the other road. This second road is currently being used in the United States in producing hybrid maize and in practically all of the poultry breeding. The methods of forming the various seedstocks may be simple intense inbreeding, which is the usual one in maize, or more complicated systems, such as reciprocal recurrent selection, may be used.

Crossbreeding is a way to travel this second road, a method widely practiced with some farm animals in some parts of the world. Instead of starting by making new seedstocks especially well adapted to crossing with each other, one merely finds which of the already existing breeds, or other genetically separate stocks, cross well with each other and then proceeds to use those at once. Formerly it was recommended that all the crossbreds, both males and females, be sold and none of them saved for breeding. The generally successful work on crisscrossing at the Minnesota Station and elsewhere, which began to be published in the 1930's, casts doubt on this recommendation. The experiments with 3-breed and 4-breed rotation crossbreeding, which began late in the 1920's, have tended to confirm the conclusion that the replacement females can come profitably from the crossbred stock. This also agrees with the extensive experiments of the maize breeders and, as far as they go, with the experience of the poultry breeders.

All that remains important is that the males shall be purebreds from breeds which cross well with the breeds from which the sire (and preferably also the maternal grandsire) of the females come. Even crossbred sires may be used, provided *both* are breeds which were crossed to produce the sires and maternal grandsires of the females on which these crossbred sires are to be used. Naturally, this last condition is rarely met. The use of an actually crossbred sire is still regarded generally with disfavor by animal breeders, although it is standard practice in the breeding of maize and of some chickens, particularly among the egg-producing crosses.

Such crisscrossing or rotation cross-breeding could begin at once in the less developed countries if one or more breeds can be found and imported which cross well with each other and with the native stock. The native stock are likely to furnish some useful local adaptability. In a crisscrossing system in which the natives constitute one of the stocks, the percentage of native blood will vary from 33 to 67 after the system gets well under way. In a regular 3-breed rotation, it would vary from one-seventh to four-sevenths. The producer need not buy females. It is important, however, that someone in the country continue to breed enough pure native stock to furnish the native sires needed at one step in the rotation.

Trying to travel this second road without using the existing stocks or breeds at the very beginning would be unwise for any of the less developed countries. Making new and relatively pure lines would be expensive and would require several generations, whether they were made by inbreeding or by selecting on progeny tests for cross-combining ability. Much expensive and detailed progeny testing and other recordkeeping would be necessary. This may not be feasible in such lands, and waiting so many years to harvest the increased productivity may be impossible. Even in the countries where animal breeding is highly developed, it is not certain that making seed-stocks expressly for their increased cross-combining ability will ever be feasible for types of animals that are less prolific and which have longer generation intervals than swine. Even with swine the practicality of this road is still in doubt.

Crosses often have higher average individual merit than either parent race. This is generally called "heterosis". It is rather frequent, but it does not occur for all characters nor in all crosses. To gain the benefits of heterosis is the chief reason for using breeding plans which are more complicated than simply finding and breeding the best individuals, while culling the worst as opportunity offers. To see how the gain from breeding for heterosis might be large, consider a case of simple over-dominance where AA averages 100 on the scale of merit; Aa averages 110; and aa averages 70. If these contribute offspring to the next generation in proportion to their own merit, the population will reach a ceiling where it consists of .64 AA: 32 Aa: .04 aa and its average merit is 102. Selection cannot increase its average merit further, so long as the individuals interbreed freely. To select more intensely for the $Aa's$ would lower average merit by making the $aa's$ more frequent, while selecting more intensely for the $AA's$ would lower merit by making the $Aa's$ rarer. The constant presence of 4 percent of definitely inferior aa individuals in the population is the price paid for raising the average merit of the population to 102, instead of leaving it at 100 where it would be if the population were homozygous for the "best" gene; i.e., were pure AA. If, on the other hand, one could make and keep two separate pure seedstocks, one aa and the other AA, and could cross these to produce the animals for use, this crossbred population would average 110 in merit. The cost of securing this gain from 102 to 110 would be the costs of making and maintaining the two pure seedstocks which, in their own merit, would average only 70 and 100, respectively.

Heterosis in net merit can occur everywhere the cross does not exceed the better of the two parent races in any character. All that is necessary is for the one parent race to be superior in some respects and the other in other respects, while the cross tends to be nearer the better parent in each case. This is illustrated schematically by the following figures where equal weight is given each character.

		Race	
	A	Cross	B
Merit in character No. 1.	100	98	80
Merit in character No. 2.	90	96	100
Average merit.....	95	97	90

This is a rather common situation in crossbreeding. Usually, a breed will be chosen for a cross only if it has some characteristics in which it excels, and, since it is not perfect, it will fall behind the other breed in some other qualities. If several characters are involved and if the cross is nearer to the better parent in each, the cross is likely to excel both parents in *net* merit, even though it may not excel the better parent in any one character considered singly.

Several genetically different mechanisms or situations can cause heterosis. They include such diverse things as the following:

a. Each parent race having some of the desired characters which the other lacks (discussed above).

b. Simple overdominance in one or more pairs of genes (the order of merit is Aa-AA-aa).

c. Year-to-year or place-to-place variations in the environment, whereby sometimes one and sometimes the other parent has the higher merit. This is partly the same as (a).

d. The heterozygote is better buffered against the environmental changes than the homozygotes are. This is partly the same as (c).

e. The population is not entirely at linkage equilibrium.

f. Pleiotropy whereby each gene has several effects, some good and some bad. This may be the main cause of (b).

g. Some of the desired characters may be partially antagonistic to each other genetically. This partly overlaps (a) and (f).

h. Epistatic effects in general. (The simplest case is where two non-allelic genes together produce desirable effects although their average separate efforts are undesirable.)

All these causes of heterosis require some dominance. Most of the immediate and observable consequences are the same as if the heterosis were all caused by (b), although the results can become different in later generations, especially if (a), (e), or (h), cause much of the heterosis.

The amount of heterosis expected in the first cross between two stocks each of which have been breeding within themselves depends mainly on the degree of dominance and the genetic diversity of the two stocks. Each pair of genes contributes to the heterosis $(k-1)(q_1 - q_2)^2 x$; where k is the degree of dominance on a scale from 1 for no dominance, through 2 for complete dominance, to more than 2 for overdominance; q_1 and q_2 are the respective frequencies of that gene in the parent stocks; and $2x$ is the average difference between the phenotypes of aa and AA. Half of this is permanent; the rest disappears at once and entirely from the offspring when first crosses are mated together—somewhat more than half of it disappears if 19(h) is a major cause of heterosis. A little of the half of heterosis which is temporary can be retained by continuing to outbreed, as by backcrossing, crisscrossing, mating those from the most unrelated families, etc. The $(q_1 - q_2)^2$ term, which measures the genetic diversity, indicates roughly how much can be retained in this way.

In a system of rotation crossbreeding where the females are always mated to males with a percentage of blood as different from theirs as is available, the percentage of heterozygotes remains higher than it would in a pure breed made from any of those crosses. This is the basic genetic reason for using a rotation crossbreeding system wherever the heterosis is large and the economics of the case and the kinds of animals available will permit.

· The following actual data from the Inter-American Agricultural Institute in Costa Rica illustrate marked heterosis in daily gains and practically no heteorsis in muscle area.

Breed or Cross	Daily gain (grams) (corrected for sex)	Muscle area (cm.²) (males only)
Brahman (Zebu)	602	64
Criollo	495	80
Criollo X Brahman	495	80
Brahman X Criollo	622	78

In daily gain the two crosses exceed the average of their parental races by 73 and 142 grams, respectively. In muscle area the two crosses differ little, either from each other or from the average of the parental races.

Deception by Heterosis

When the first cross offspring of imported males and x native females seem definitely superior to the native stock, it would be only human to credit all this improvement to the imported sires, especially if purebreds of the imported race are not available for comparison. This, however, may not be valid. The crosses also may be superior to what the pure imported stock would be if grown under the same conditions.

In the example of cattle gains in Costa Rica, if we had data only on the Criollos and the cross of Brahman bull and Criollo cow, we might infer that the Brahmans were vastly better genetically than the Criollos. If, however, data were available only on the pure Brahmans and on the cross of Criollo bull and Brahman cow, it would have been inferred that the Criollo was better than the Brahman. With data from all four of these combinations we conclude correctly that the Brahmans do gain somewhat more rapidly than the Criollos, but that the crossbreeding effect itself is tremendously larger than this difference. This is a measure of what is called heterosis. By contrast, in muscle area, the Criollos have definitely larger muscles than the Brahmans and the heterosis seems small.

If we know only one pure breed and one pure cross, we can be vastly misled in inferring the merit of the other pure breed. For example, if we know the rate of gain only for the Criollos and for the cross of Brahman bull on Criollo cows, we might infer that the favorable results were due to the general merit of the Brahman breed. Then we might think that the rate of gain of the pure Brahman would be 887 (i.e., $691 + (691 - 495)$), plus or minus whatever allowance we thought proper for the data being few! We would estimate that if we made a second cross to the Brahman, the ¾ Brahmans would average 789 (i.e., $691 + (691 - 495)/2$) whereas, if we know the data for all four kinds of breeding and allow for loss of heterosis, we will expect only 629 (i.e., half of

$(691 + 622)/2 + 602$) for the ¾ Brahmans.

As another example in which, however, only one of the reciprocal crosses is present, consider the following data from the same station for average 4% fat-corrected milk production of stablemates in kilograms during each of the first four months of the first lactations.

Breed or Cross	Month			
	1st	2d	3d	4th
Criollo	266	230	224	189
Jersey	237	226	202	178
Criollo ♂ X ♀ Jersey	273	248	245	254

Heterosis is nearly 9 percent in the first two months, 15 percent in the third and 38 percent in the fourth. This is the evidence on the amount of heterosis in this character in this cross, although one may wonder whether reciprocal crosses would show any differences such as might be caused by sex-linkage or by maternal effects.

Heterosis should be estimated early in the process of planning to improve the native stock by using sires imported from some supposedly superior breed. The amount of heterosis might alter decisions on such important matters as whether: a) to continue grading the native stock to an imported breed, b) to follow a plan of rotation crossing, or c) to try to make a new breed, moderately stabilized at some fraction of imported and native blood. The larger the heterosis, the more important a practical plan for b) becomes.

Importing

As soon as one has decided what kind of stock would really be ideal for his purposes, he seeks the breeding stock which already is nearest that ideal. The native stock should be considered first, as it is the most available, almost always the cheapest, and already usually has considerably more adaptability to local conditions than any stock which could be imported. Although well adapted to survival under the local conditions, they are likely to be slow maturing, thinly muscled, and not likely to produce large quantities of milk or wool, or other of the products which a developing country needs. However, before deciding that the native stock is not suitable, it may pay to visit all the possible places where such native stock has been improved by the better local breeders. Some of these local efforts may show definitely that the local stock contains many advantageous qualities which are hidden now but which will come to light when the animals are given better care and are selected for more production. One cannot thus estimate the ultimate to which the stock might be improved, but, if even a few breeders have already made obvious improvement, it is likely that those limits are still far off. At least, one may infer that the local stock has enough obvious or hidden merit that it should not be replaced entirely but should be retained as one of the stocks to be used in a rotational crossbreeding program or as part of a foundation from which a new breed is to be made.

Improvement by breeding is a slow process. Hence, it might be quicker to import an already improved stock if a productive one can be found which is adaptable to the local husbandry. Whether such stock exists is difficult to determine. The excellence of an improved stock in its native land may be due largely to the good nutrition and other

excellent environment given it there. One of our colleagues active in extension work in dairy cattle breeding in the United States has often said: "No bull was ever good enough to transmit to his daughters good pastures and leafy green alfalfa hay." How the imported breed will perform in the importing country can be learned only by trying it there. This, however, is costly in time and money. Some of that often can be saved by visiting other countries, somewhat similar in climate and other environmental conditions, to see how any breeds they have imported have actually thrived. Verbal testimony about performance may need discounting, since at least a few enthusiasts about almost any breed usually can be found.

An imported breed is rarely suited perfectly to the local needs. Occasionally a breed may fit the local needs well enough that the wisest course is to import the breed and use the males to grade the local stock continuously toward that breed. In such a case, importing also a few females might be wise for two reasons. First would be to learn how well the females of that pure breed perform under local conditions. If the native stock is graded continually toward this imported breed, the resulting high grades will eventually be much like the imported purebred females genetically. If the purebred females are ill-adapted to the environment in any important aspects of their performance, that should be discovered before the grading goes far. Second, the sons of the imported females could be used for continuing the grading process. This would reduce the amount of importation necessary for replacing the initial purebred males. Using sons and grandsons from such a nucleus herd need not lead inevitably to high-breeding. As long as the breed continues to exist in its native land and occasional importation, perhaps at considerable expense, of fresh stock to be used on the nucleus herd would cancel at once the inbreeding accumlated up to that time.

The native stock should be very nearly equivalent to the imported stock by the time it has been graded up to contain seven-eighths or more of the imported blood, unless improvement in the native land of the breed continues much more rapidly than in the importing land. In such a case, which is rather unlikely but not utterly impossible, continuing indefinitely into the future to import a few animals from the original home of the breed at frequent intervals may be advisable.

More frequently, it will be found that no breed exists which is already this well adapted. Each of many breeds which might be imported may be desirable in some characteristics such as ability to produce milk, wool, or meat when properly fed; and very undesirable in others, such as adaptability to extreme heat or cold, or susceptibility to parasites or diseases, or to other environmental influences different from those in their native land. Desirable characteristics tend to be partially dominant. Some heterosis often occurs when strains very unlike in their racial origins are crossed. Hence, the first crosses of imported stock on the native stock often appear more desirable than the natives and also more desirable than the pure imported stock would be. Continuing to grade toward the imported stock, generation after generation, will then cause a decline in average merit, partly because the animals are losing the adaptability of the natives and partly because they are losing heterosis.

Two very divergent roads to meet this situation are imaginable. One is to try to make a new breed out of the first crosses, or perhaps out of a mixture of first crosses and back crosses, hoping to form a new breed which will be more than halfway toward the qualities of the better breed in each respect. The other road is to adopt and continue some form of rotation crossing, first, toward the one parent stock and then toward the other. This requires maintaining both of the parent stocks in a usably pure condition. If successful it maintains more heterosis than if all of these animals were mated at random.

Making New Breeds from Crosses

When no existing breed comes close to the ideal but each of two or more have some different desirable characters and some of these crosses are known to be promising and heterosis seems not to be large when each character is considered by itself, trying to blend them into a single new breed may sometimes be wise, although this will require so much time that its advisability in a less developed country may be questioned.

The first step is to decide what crosses one should make and in what proportions. Naturally, the breeder would want to use enough breeds to introduce all the qualities he thinks he will need eventually. Of course, he also would want to use a larger fraction of blood from the races which had several desirable traits and were nearer to his ideal than from races which had only one or two desirable characters which the other races lacked. At least two generations are required to bring together the inheritance from three to four different races. At least three generations are necessary if five or more are to be brought together.

The second step is to discount the effects of heterosis. Unless this is done, one will be unduly disappointed in the generation when all the temporary heterosis first disappears. That will be the first generation produced by mating together males and females which have the same percentage composition of blood. Then for the first time one sees the average phenotypic merit of the population with which one is really starting to make a new breed.

A third important part of the plan is to keep the genetic base broad. Neglecting this appears to have been the major cause of failure in most of the past attempts to form new breeds which were successful initially. To keep the genetic base broad, present knowledge of genetics suggests that every generation of animals saved for breeding should include the offspring of four or five widely used males. This might mean starting 10 or 12 males in service each generation or it might mean starting as few as five or six, depending on how many of the males that were first tried were later culled on the basis of progeny tests, along with most of their offspring. This should keep the genetic base broad enough that no trouble would arise from this source, at least within the next 6 or 10 generations of animals.

Failure to keep the genetic base broad is most likely to arise through not using enough different sires in each generation. For instance, if only one sire is used, or if four are used but one of these does so much better that all four of the sires saved for the next generation are sons of this one, it will soon happen that any mating which can be made and still remain the limits of the new breed will involve more inbreeding than is safe. Most of the bad consequences of such inbreeding, especially those from numerous genes with individually small and harmful effects, can then be repaired only by a wide outcross. Such a wide outcross would also undo most of the favorable progress already made.

When trying to make a new breed, the pedigrees should be planned roughly for the next two or three generations. That means choosing now the group of females from which are to come the males to be used in the next generation, and choosing a somewhat larger group from among whose daughters are to come the sires to be used in the second and third generations. Mendelian segregation introduces enough chance and uncertainty that one is usually wasting time if one plans today the exact pedigree of an individual sire one intends to use two generations from now.

If the new breed is to be used commercially as nearly pure for its own qualities, rather than to be used in a rotation crossbreeding scheme, the new breed would be made as a single large population with only slight subdivision into families. Such subdivision would be for line breeding or progeny-testing purposes and with the intention of top-crossing the best families on all the rest of the stock as soon as the best ones are identified. If, on the contrary, this new breed is being made for use i rotation crossbreeding plan, one would want to produce at least one other stock to be rotated with it in that crossbreeding and would want to keep these two or more stocks genetically as unrelated to each other as possible.

Other practical considerations enter the problem, such as the fact that the females of the native race may be better grazers or otherwise better adapted to the local environment, so that the cross made one way may give better results than the reciprocal cross. Factors such as difference in mothering ability and the probability that the imported race and the native race were not equally far from the goal initially, make it sometimes advisable to choose a level of one-fourth imported blood, or of three-fourths imported blood, or some fraction other than one-half as the best percentage of blood around which to make a new breed or around which to oscillate in a criss-crossing plan. The question of what is ideal in this respect may well have different answers for differing breeds and different crosses in different countries. Being familiar with the country and with the actual average performance of different mixtures is of the utmost importance for making correct decisions on points like this.

Individual Adaptation

An animal taken from its native country to a land with a distinctly different climate may require many months to adjust its own individual physiology in the new environment. If the animal is mature when imported, it may never complete this adaptation. For example, beef bulls reared in the cornbelt in the United States until they are two years old and then taken to the harsher range country are mostly too old then to learn how to make a living on the open range. They would have learned if they had spent their calfhood there. The reproductive cycle may be upset when animals are taken from the Northern to the Southern Hemisphere or the reverse. Usually they adjust within a year or so. Similar upsets may occur when they are moved suddenly from a temperate climate to the tropics or from low to extremely high altitudes.

These practical and important facts are already moderately well known to stockmen and herdsmen who have made or accompanied importations of animals from one climate to a distinctly different one, This individual adaptation has little or no genetic implication, except insofar as ability to adapt is itself partly conditioned by the animal's genotype.

Fitting the Plans to the Country

Animal improvement plans should be fitted to the present state of husbandry in the area under consideration, or to what seems likely to be the state of husbandry there in the near future. Because improvement by breeding comes slowly, one really should be breeding animals adapted to the conditions which will prevail at least two or three animal generations later, as far as one can estimate now what these conditions will be.

Conditions of husbandry may sometimes change rapidly. Resistance to disease and to insect damage may be highly important initially but they will become unimportant if and when cheap and effective methods of disease and insect control are put into use. Perhaps pastures and feed production may be improved so much that, in a generation or two, different qualities in the animals will be wanted, such as earlier maturity, and less value may be attached to their ability to survive well through periods of submaintenance nutrition. Perhaps such nutritional improvement will not come?

Such changes in husbandry or changes in market demand occur, even in the highly developed countries. Robert Bakewell's achievements in animal breeding two centuries ago consisted largely in breeding animals to be fatter at early ages than animals had ever been before. New edible fats of vegetable origin have become far more abundant than in Bakewell's time, and pigs and even cattle are being bred with less fat and more lean.

Consequently, the men who guide the animal improvement need to know the local conditions well. A man from the outside cannot go in and guide the animal improvement schemes effectively. The plans for performance testing and progeny testing need to include provision for training local personnel to operate these plans, and especially to push the extension phases of the plans. These men need access to experiment stations where they can obtain answers to some of the simpler questions and can measure the individual performance and adaptability of at least those animals in the nucleus breeding herds. First-hand familiarity with the reproductive rates, rearing percentages, and other vital statistics of the species in that region is almost a prerequisite for a man to help wisely in planning animal improvement.

Some of the devices for improving animals genetically require keeping individual pedigrees. Sometimes this is not possible. Fencing may be too expensive or other reasons may prevent knowing which male was the sire of each animal. If individual pedigrees are not known, no progeny testing of males is possible and the progeny testing of females is very limited. This will slow down the possible rate of improvement but does not stop it altogether. When the sires are unknown, most of the selection must be done on individual qualities. One can perhaps separate the males and females which seem to be the very best into a top stud flock from which will come the sires to be used in the next generation

and keep that stud flock isolated. In this way, even without knowing the individual sires, one can get some (but not all) of the advantages of selection on pedigree.

If individual production cannot be measured, the possible rate of animal improvement is much reduced. Then one can only fall back on "eye-ball" judgment, which is reasonably good for some characters but notoriously ineffective for improving others, especially for those aspects of production which are complex and rest more largely on physiological than anatomical differences.

The main considerations for long-time progress are assurance of economic stability, reasonable expectation of law and order, and that the owner or local manager of the herd have incentive to use his own initiative and to take some risks. If the local manager is blamed when things turn out wrong but does not receive a special reward when they turn out well, he will generally try to take as few risks as possible. If this condition is extreme, he may do little except execute written orders scrupulously, so as not to be blamed. This is more serious in animal breeding than in many other branches of human endeavor, because the actual outcome of animal breeding efforts, especially in herds of small or moderate size, is greatly affected by chance events. Mendelian segregation and recombination keep restoring and introducing individual variability in breeding values. With the finitely small number of sires chosen on any one farm, the man who does the choosing will often be wrong in individual cases, even though he works diligently and intelligently. Knowledge of genetics has reached the stage where one can predict with high accuracy the average result of choosing

1000 sires by method A rather than by method B, but one cannot yet, nor is there any prospect that one ever can predict closely the outcome for each such individual sire. Operationally, animal breeding

is much like aiming a shotgun and not at all like aiming a rifle! This may not be entirely a disfavor; any sensible hunter would choose a shotgun for some kinds of game and a rifle for others!

Forestry's Contribution to a Permanent Agriculture

TOM GILL

President, International Society of Tropical Foresters
Washington, D.C.

Introduction

In a world where hunger remains an unsolved problem, and where the need for assured food production becomes more insistent with the passing years, few nations can neglect whatever measures may contribute to a permanently productive agriculture and to adequate living standards for their rural population.

The fate of a nation's agriculture is seldom decided in the croplands alone. Factors far removed from the farm may play a major role. Thus, the condition and permanence of an agricultural economy may, in very large degree, be governed by the protection afforded to the often-distant upland soils. Erosion, destructive floods, loss of top soil, and water failure may have to be dealt with in establishing a permanent agricultural economy. These age-old enemies are still an ever-present menace to food production, but they can be curbed by a vegetative cover of grass or trees. Grass provides valuable protection against the erosive effects of rain and wind but has the disadvantage of being susceptible to fire and to destruction by grazing animals. Forests are generally the more effective and, throughout history, have proven to be staunch allies of agriculture in many diverse ways.

In a nation's use of land, forestry and agriculture share the same objective—the most efficient management of the soil for human good. Only when the two are seen as interlocking, mutually-sustaining measures can land use be envisaged as a whole, or can the richest returns from agriculture be hoped for. Forestry and agriculture combine to form an essential way of transforming soil fertility into the raw materials which man requires. Their techniques and time factors may differ widely, but both agriculture and forestry are concerned with growing crops, and both play primary roles in man's dealing with the soil. The very term "farm forest" implies this integration.

A planned relationship between agriculture and forestry increases their mutual effectiveness and helps to advance the prosperity of the farmer who, in many countries, is both a forest worker and forest owner.

The critical importance of forests to agriculture is still far from recognized by all agricultural planners. As a consequence, thousands of farms have failed to maintain or even reach satisfactory productive standards and thousands of hectares of once-irrigated croplands have been lost to the invading desert.

This paper is an effort to point out the intimate relationship that forests bear to a balanced agriculture. It is intended to suggest how their protective influences may be enhanced and how their economic potential may contribute to the living standards of a nation's rural population. It is directed primarily to countries formulating or expanding their agricultural programs to the end that forestry may bring to a farm economy the stability that can best come from an integrated use of agricultural and forest soils.

Protection Forests

Forests serve agriculture in two ways—as a protection of soils and crops and as a permanent source of many farm essentials. For this reason they have been designated "protection forests" and "production forests" depending on their function, although actually most forests serve both purposes. However, when one objective clearly outweighs the other, forest management is directed toward the major goal.

Protection against erosion and destructive waterflow is usually the chief function of the forests in the higher regions where shallow soil and steep slopes make the land unstable. Through the centuries, these forests have attained an equilibrium that enables them to endure and hold the soil in place, but this equilibrium is extremely delicate and any disturbing force—such as fire or widespread cutting—can easily destroy its protective value. Once destroyed, it may never be regained.

Where agriculture depends on irrigation, the need to stabilize the upland soil is even more critical. Vast funds have been wasted on the construction of costly irrigation reservoirs and canals which were soon rendered useless by the deposit of silt. The best insurance for permanence of these installations and for a continued supply of water is a forest cover to hold the soil in place, to check the destructive violence of storms, and to conserve every available drop of moisture for use in the croplands below.

Forests and Floods. No responsible forester would say that forests can prevent floods. If sustained rainfall is heavy enough, neither trees nor grass nor any vegetative cover can absorb all the water, and in that event floods may result. Forests can, however, absorb vast quantities of water and greatly reduce both flood volume and destructiveness. Peak flows from forested areas rarely exceed 60 second-feet per square mile, while from denuded or eroded land they often exceed 1,000 feet.

A forest cover not only increases the power of the soil to absorb large quantities of water, but it reduces debris and sediment and the vast amounts of silt which augment a flood's volume and violence. It is hard to conceive of the amount of solid material that can be carried by floodwaters rushing down bare or denuded hillsides. Sixty percent or more of the flood's total volume may be composed of solid substances and it is this material which, if deposited on arable lands, can destroy them. Eliminate this, and the destructiveness of the flood will be vastly reduced and its menace to croplands minimized. There is this dual protection, then, which forests provide to agriculture—reducing the volume of floodwaters and curtailing the accumulation of sediment and debris. From a farmer's standpoint, the deposit of mud and debris may be far more destructive than the water itself.

Forests and Farm Water Supply. The effect of trees upon the conservation of water supplies has been too completely documented to need any lengthy discussion. It is well known that waters emerging from forested areas are usually clear and that the flow of water itself tends to be equalized, avoiding both wasteful peak periods and periods of water failure.

No matter what tree species compose it, a forest stores a greater amount of precipitation than any other vegetative cover. The litter of leaves, twigs, and branches that collect on the forest floor vastly increases the permeability of the soil and allows greater amounts of water to soak in than than does a bare earth surface. This water, sinking into the soil, later takes the form of ground water or becomes the source of springs and is not lost in swift and often-destructive surface flow. Forests, then, increase underground storage water much more than a bare surface or one scantily covered with vegetation. Forests, in a word, tend to maintain a steady flow of water in the streams and to increase the reservoirs of ground water, without which many agricultural communities would find it difficult to endure.

Windbreaks and Shelterbelts. Trees are more than protectors of agricultural soil and guardians of agriculture's water supply. From very early times, they have been found effective in shielding crops and farm animals against the hot, drying winds of summer and the freezing gales of winter. Thousands of hectares have been planted to trees for these purely agricultural purposes and such planting usually takes the form of windbreaks or shelterbelts.

The broad function of both is the same—protection against the wind. The "windbreaks" usually refer to one, two, or three rows of trees whose purpose is the local protection of farm crops from soil movement and the drying effects of wind. Shelterbelts are wider and often of great length, and their establishment is ordinarily beyond the resources of the individual farmer and requires the assistance of government. Governmental action and support made possible the thousands of miles of shelterbelts that today protect millions of acres of Russian farmlands. The mile after mile of tree strips in Jutland, without which farming would be impossible, was a governmental enterprise. In Rumania the protection afforded by trees in the farmers' battle against erosion and drought is largely responsible for the continuous production of agricultural crops and for maintaining the living standards of the population. In parts of the United States it is almost useless to grow fruit without windbreaks, and both the quality and quantity of fruits and vegetables have greatly increased when protected by trees. Added to all this are the very tangible benefits of reduced fuel costs and of making the farm homestead more livable, both winter and summer.

Establishing windbreaks in agricultural communities is not difficult, but three steps are essential: (a) adequate preparation of the site to be planted; (b) careful planting of hardy tree species, preferably of local origin or proven to be locally successful; and (c) thorough cultivation in the early stages.

Production Forests

Added to the purely protective values of forests is their value as perpetual sources of materials required in an agricultural economy. Here, forests are essential to continuous wood production, and it is here, too, that forestry and agriculture are interdependent economically and are mutually self-sustaining. Work in the woods helps many a farm community financially, and these farm communities in turn create markets for wood industries and provide manpower for logging operations. Work in the forests enables a farmer to utilize his time profitably during seasons of slack agricultural activity and constitutes an important contribution to the stability and standards of rural living.

When farm communities have ready access to woodlands, the entire pattern of life is in striking contrast to that of communities living under a chronic regime of wood famine. It is not generally recognized that firewood is one of the world's most important agricultural crops; yet fuel is indispensable, and where wood cannot be obtained, as in the Upper Ganges Plain of India, the farmer is forced to burn cattle dung and agricultural refuse which should go to maintain soil fertility. The time and effort consumed in gathering fuelwood from distant woodlands represents a staggering loss of agricultural manpower—a loss that could be eliminated by devoting the less fertile, non-agricultural portion of the farm to trees.

Wood is not only a sparetime crop. It is a "poor-land" crop, growing on soils too rugged or too sterile for raising food. Farm woodlands, while still exercising a protective function, may make profitable the use of land which a farmer cannot gainfully cultivate for crops. From them he realizes needed products and often a cash income. Fuel, fence posts, material for houses and barns, food for livestock— all these offer the farmer direct opportunities for cash savings. In times of crop failure, the merchantable material in a farm woodland may prove a welcome buffer against financial disaster.

In parts of England, where agricultural work alone, or forest work alone, may not suffice to support a family, planned coordination between forestry and farming has made settlement possible and brought about a stabilized prosperous existence. Again, in the semi-desert area of southwest India, where land has been placed under irrigation, sections are specifically set aside for forest plantations to meet the need of the farmer for woods.

This integration of agriculture and forestry in many parts of the world has brought a stability and abundance to human living that neither agriculture nor forestry alone could achieve. But it does require planning, and often it requires governmental leadership. Certainly, a basic function of government lies in raising the living standards of its people, and in an agricultural community the integrated use of a nation's arable and forest soils is a definite step toward that goal.

Developing Farm Forest Values

In planning an agricultural economy, many nations have found that to include a definite policy for their forest lands helps to insure permanent foodcrop production and creates a source of steadily increasing values on their non-arable soils.

No country can be said to have a comprehensive land-use policy until it has decided what part its forests and forest soils can play in both agricultural and industrial development. Thus, in seeking a balanced economy, a nation may be faced with the need to convert part of its tree-covered land to agriculture or, on the other hand, to establish tree plantations and increase its forested areas in the interests of soil protection and wood production. In any case, a national policy should direct itself to decisions as to the functions of that nation's forests and forest soils in the major categories of production and protection.

Specific requirements will dictate which objective is paramount. In critical areas, the need for soil protection may be so urgent that little or no tree-cutting is advisable. In other situations, the forest may be managed purely to provide

the maximum amount of fuel or other wood products. In any case, intelligent planning demands that the lands of a nation be broadly classified as to their suitability for agricultural use and forest use and, where the forest contains extensive commercial values, that an inventory be made of its contents.

Land Classification. In many regions, there exists a profound misconception of what constitutes true agricultural soil, and the world is dotted with abandoned hectares following attempts to force non-agricultural lands to produce permanent food crops. In North and South America, millions of hectares of once cultivated land have been ruined by erosion because they were not adaptable to agriculture. In the Philippines any patch of earth capable of producing two or three meager crops is considered agricultural by the "pioneer" farmer, and thousands of hectares have been denuded of forests in misguided attempts to convert the land to agriculture, only to have it found unfit for any growth but trees.

The fact that an area may support heavy, luxuriant forests but be valueless for food crops is one of the most costly paradoxes in the history of agriculture. These soils appear so abundantly fertile that it is difficult to believe they may be inhospitable to any form of vegetation but trees. Actually, the fertility that sustains the forests lies in the tree itself. The soil is often little more than a foothold for roots and a passageway for nutrients. The fertility derives from the rapid decomposition of leaves and forest litter, returning to the living tree in a kind of closed cycle. When the land is cleared for agriculture, in only a short while the soil is totally unfit for food crops. After brief cultivation, the land is abandoned, the soil having lost what little vitality it once possessed. Some tropical soils are particularly fragile. Once the forest cover is destroyed, the baking sun soon converts the earth's surface to a hard, brick-like substance incapable of supporting even the scantiest vegetation.

Farm Forests. In many parts of the world, farm forests comprise the largest area and represent the highest values of a nation's timberlands; yet the average farmer falls far short of bringing to the management of his woodlands the same degree of skill that he brings to his food crops, and, when he sells the products of his farm forest, he seldom receives their full value. It is in this dual field of forest management and merchandising that governments can be of practical aid by furnishing the farmer with information and technical assistance. Many countries employ a specialized type of forester known as the "farm forester," trained in the management and the merchandising of farm woodlands. He works directly with the farmer, recommending the proper protective and cutting methods, assisting in selecting trees to be cut, and advising on marketing methods.

Forest Research and the Farmer. With a nation's development, the position of the farmer as a forest owner becomes progressively more important. His forests are usually more accessible and occupy more fertile soils than industrial forests, and hence good management yields rich returns. To develop improved practices can be a major objective of any agricultural program where the potential value of farm forests is a significant factor.

These improved practices may be arrived at by the slow and often costly road of trial and error, but a far better way lies in research which is planned directly toward the solution of farm-forest problems and toward increasing their productive and protective values. Pilot tests, for example, can provide the farmer with established facts before he spends time and money on ventures of questionable value. Tests will tell him what tree species are most desirable from the standpoint of survival and rapidity of growth. They will tell him what species are best for special needs.

Investigations of this type are usually beyond the financial means of the individual farmer, and it becomes a responsibility of government to assume leadership in this rewarding field. Tests of exotic species that promise to be well-adapted to farm needs, tests of structural characteristics, tests of species most suitable for windbreaks, soil retention, and a host of other purposes, can best be made by government. In the United States it is a joint Federal-State responsibility to see that the benefits of scientific advancement in forest management and utilization are made available to the small woodland owner. Funds devoted to research of this kind have proven to be among the best investments a government can make in seeking a stable and permanent agriculture.

Improvement of Production and Preservation Methods in an Underdeveloped Fishery

Charles Butler, H. B. Allen and Lee Alverson

Bureau of Commercial Fisheries
U.S. Department of the Interior
Washington, D.C.

Introduction

Acre for acre, the seas are potentially as productive as arable land, but only about one percent of the food consumed by man is derived from the oceans. Estimates place the potential sustained annual yield of the seas at around 500 billion pounds, but only about 16 percent of this potential is harvested now. More important, of the world's harvest of 32 million metric tons of fish in 1958, not over 5 or 6 million metric tons were taken by the less developed nations. While millions of people in such nations suffer the wasting of tissue and the failure of growth associated with the often fatal protein deficiency diseases, just off shore lie vast resources of animal protein, self-reproducing and almost wholly unexploited.

This industrial and nutritional imbalance in the use of the world's fishery resources and in the diets of its people can be redressed. It will require high priority national programs, developed with the assistance of experts, and courageously implemented over a period of years, to provide the skills and supporting facilities necessary to the operation of a sophisticated deep-water fishery. Fishery programs designed to supply either domestic food requirements or the capital necessary for industrialization must visualize the entire fishing industry and its supporting services as a unit. The harvesting of fish, its delivery to port, its processing and ultimate delivery to the consumer, domestic or foreign, must be considered as an integrated system, having one major objective: the feeding of man from a wisely managed, self-reproducing resource. The need for many supporting skills and services, ranging from net-mending, engine repair, and vessel construction to processing facilities and distribution systems, must be foreseen. The initial support facilties should be provided at a level of development consistent with the technological awareness of the nation and its contemporary fishing industry. Plans should provide for a systematic upgrading of these skills and facilities as market demands for fish increase in size and complexity.

A clear understanding of the relative priorities of the national needs, whether protein food for the domestic population or procurement of capital for industrialization through export of fisheries products, must underlie the national fisheries program. The latter goal is most easily and rapidly reached through contractual agreements with industry representatives of the advanced fishing nations, whereby the entire harvesting, processing and distribution system is planned, developed and operated for the sole purpose of exportation of its products at a profit to industry and to the state. Such systems have been developed for the new tunafisheries of Ghana and of the Ivory Coast. This paper, however, concerns itself with the plans of a nation determined to use its off-shore resources primarily as a source of food for its own population and then gradually to achieve export nation status as a natural consequence of this internal growth. The paper will consider a hypothetical, nonindustrialized coastal nation to which a wide variety of marine resources are available for exploitation. These resources would include demersal (bottom-living) fish, pelagic (surface-swimming) fish, and shellfish.

The initial level of development of a planned food fish delivery system must be based upon knowledge of the distribution and movements of the fishery resource, on the availability of trained manpower, processing and distribution systems, on consumer demand for the products and on the domestic availability of investment funds. The appropriateness of one or more of the many different types of fishing gear is contingent upon these considerations.

Improved Production Methods

Methods that may be considered for improving fish harvest include (a) increasing the efficiency of existing gear by better design and materials, (b) increasing the effective range of craft through incorporating power into vessels, (c) introducing new types of fishing gear which are more effective for harvesting now untapped resources, (d) increasing catch through better fishing tactics, and (e) increasing the number of units employed.

In the initial stage of development, let us assume that the nation involved has little more than canoes or other small craft to conduct fishing operations, that capital for investment is small, and that shore facilities for maintenance of larger craft are practically nonexistent. In a situation of this sort it is important not to upgrade the methods and craft more rapidly than the other equally important facilities are improved. Thus, simplicity in gear, vessel and deck machinery in the initial stage is important.

We would recommend for the first five years of development: (a) That existing gear used to harvest fishes be upgraded through better design and the use of better materials. (b) That fishermen be educated in the best specialized use and tactics for gear with which they are familiar. Employment of a fishing expert familiar with many types of gear would be advisable during this phase, to educate the fisherman in the care and use of these and of the more sophisticated gear to be introduced in the second phase of the program. (c) That all possible efforts be made to increase the number of vessels in the fishery to a point limited only by the demand for their products. (d) That gear for gathering marine animals which remain more or less fixed in their environment, such as oysters, clams, and abalone, be introduced. Simple devices would include shovels, tongs, and rakes. The simple dredge which is effective for harvesting oysters or scallops also could be employed. (e) That the smaller round-haul type nets such as the lampara, purse seine, or ring net, be employed from existing small craft. The lampara nets similar to those used in the California bait catching operations for tuna can be operated from small vessels or open boats and handled manually, and yet they are relatively effective in harvesting the smaller school fishes. Gill nets currently are used in most of the world and represent an effective and simple device for harvesting both fresh-water and marine fish. Some increase in efficiency in this type of gear may be achieved through improvement of materials and use of mesh sizes appropriate to local stocks.

In the middle part of the first five-year phase small outboard engines could be introduced. Initially these should be of rugged and simple design to preclude the repeated failures and to eliminate the bulk of the more complicated types. Fuel tanks, remote starting, remote control, and reversible propellers are not necessary for this phase of the program.

Within this same period concurrent training in basic skills and services and in the operation and maintenance of larger craft (inboard engines, net-fabrication and principles of navigation and seamanship) should be initiated. The number of fishermen and repair men brought under such training need not be large, but if the program is to be effective, attempts should be made to include talented persons who could pass on their knowledge to their fellow workers.

Eventually, as progress is made in processing, marketing and transportation, in development of shore facilities, and as general economic development in the country warrants, the program should be expanded to include more sophisticated fisheries operations. In our hypothetical example exploitation of latent marine resources would require development of craft suitable to operate in offshore waters. Such craft need not be large or complicated, but should be seaworthy, and the engines, the Swedish semi-diesel for example, should be simple and dependable with a minimum of moving parts. The development of inboard small craft which could operate several days at sea would require the additional skills in seamanship, maintenance, and construction. Availability of such craft and skills would be the first step in bringing a large variety of marine resources within reach of the coastal nation.

Expansion of fishing out over the Continental Shelf to exploit demersal and pelagic fishes and shellfishes would require modification of the simple nets used hitherto. The introduction of the specialized net called the otter trawl or of the similar two-boat trawl should be considered in this phase. Trawl nets need not be as large as those used in North Atlantic fisheries; they can be sized to the capacity of the vessels available.

It is suggested that in the initial stage the utmost simplicity be employed in winch types and in deck layouts designed to handle trawl cables. Obviously, some trawling in the shallower waters can be accomplished even without the use of winches. The construction of trawls is simple, and although they vary in complexity throughout the world, a common design theme prevails. Use of trawls does not require extensive training, and the skills of local fisherman could quickly be adapted to their use.

Further development in the coastal fisheries would be geared to more advanced use of longline gear, both pelagic and ground gear, and to systematic gillnetting or driftnetting in coastal waters. With both types, some mechanization of handling would be desirable but is not essential. The training of fishermen should be expanded now to include visits to foreign areas where operation of craft similar to those being introduced could be observed. This would provide the fishermen with an understanding of the diversification and mechanization possible in fisheries. It would, in the long run, enhance their capabilities to bring about maximum exploitation of their coastal waters.

It should not be overlooked that the most effective means of bulk production of pelagic fish have been through the use of purse seines or other round-haul nets. Consequently, during the latter phases of development, the skills, knowledge, and actual use of modern gears of this type must be mastered. The introduction to active fishing with these nets need not be with large complicated gear such as are used in the California tuna seine fisheries. A wide variety of smaller encircling nets is available. The introduction and use of encircling gear will provide the basic training in fishing tactics for the harvesting of schooling fishes such as herring, mackerel, cod, hake, etc.

If all phases of the fisheries (production, processing, and distribution) advance in a coordinated manner, and the program achieves some success, then sufficient capital may well have accrued to initiate ocean fishery activities. These would involve large complex craft such as the modern tuna seiner, tuna longliners, or distant-water trawlers. Operation of vessels and gear of this type would require highly developed seamanship and fishing tactics, and skilled operation of vessel machinery, including refrigeration installations. Because ocean fishing involves distant-water operations and considerable knowledge of mechanics and electronic devices, one might expect that expansion into these more complex operations would go beyond the humanitarian aspect of providing protein for the nation involved, to that of providing raw material for export in the world markets.

Construction and design of gear probably would not be a major problem, as skills in their operation would have been gained through operating similar units of a smaller size. The advance into the more complex fisheries, however, will require greater assistance from outside technicians than any other phase. This is essentially the period when the local fishermen must master the problems involved in mechanization and the logistics of large vessel operations and when processors must master the most complex problems of worldwide distribution of their products.

During this phase the basic vessel design should be given considerable thought, with emphasis on such factors as geographical operating ranges; species to be sought; flexibility of use (multipurpose vessels); refrigeration requirements; and the possibilities of fleet-operated factory vessels. This kind of planning requires a degree of fishing sophistication comparable to that of the advanced fishing nations of the world. The new fisheries, however, need not develop to this degree to be satisfactory. Extremely successful small-boat operations of a local nature may be achieved, and with these, a considerable portion of the protein needs of the nation can be supplied.

Improvements in Preservation Methods and Sanitary Procedures

In developing a schedule by which the latent fishery resources of a small coastal nation can best be developed and utilized for the benefit of the people of that nation, it must again be remembered that any increases in the processing and distribution of fish must be coordinated with other aspects of the nation's overall economic improvement effort. If the nation has a wide variety of fish and shellfish available for local exploitation by small boats, the processing problems during the initial five year period may be expected to be associated with maintaining the quality of the fresh fish on the vessel and during delivery to the market place. Two principal factors, time and temperature, are always involved in the spoilage of fresh fish. In the less developed fishing countries of the world, only one of these factors can be controlled practically. This factor is the duration of time the fish are held before being delivered to processors. If both supplies of ice and the facilities to store and use ice on the fishing boats during the initial period are lacking, there is little hope of controlling the second factor by reducing temperature of fresh-caught fish.

Sanitation and improvement of quality will require: (a) evisceration of the fish at sea, (b) rinsing of the fish with salt water and (c) the use of wet canvas, spread over the freshly caught fish in the bottom of open boats to protect the fish from the hot drying effects of the sun. It is vital that at first fish should be taken as close to shore as possible so that they can be handled quickly.

The lack of adequate marketing and distribution techniques is the basic obstacle encountered when a fishery has developed sufficiently, through the use of outboards or improved vessels, to supply more fish than is demanded by the consumers in the immediate neighborhood of the fishing port. Retail facilities generally consist of an itinerant peddler, or at best, of a small makeshift store, usually in unsanitary surroundings. Early attention should be given to construction of simple covered structures, consisting of from 80 to 100 stalls. Such structures, costing approximately U.S. $10,000, would provide retailers, including those handling fishery products, with clean, organized facilities. Each structure should have an adequate water supply, counter space, roof protection, concrete floors and toilet accommodations. Maintenance of sanitation should be enforced through periodic inspections by regulatory officials. Such structures would form the base for a local retail market and for the distribution of the product into the hinterlands. Screened or closed trucks or motor launches, also inspected periodically for sanitation procedures, would serve to transport products from the markets to consumers in the surrounding countryside. As soon as it is technologically feasible, fish must be iced down, both in the market and throughout the distribution system.

More complex systems for distribution of fish to increasingly distant markets cannot be accomplished by utilizing strictly fresh fish without refrigeration, as may be done in the seaport area. Therefore, beginning with the sixth year, product preservation through drying, smoking, and salting techniques must be undertaken on a commercial scale in coastal processing plants. The simplest preservation techniques, such as sun drying, should be developed as a commercial enterprise first since they require little or no fuel or chemicals. As fish supplies increase, and the economic situation improves, it will be possible to process fish meal and smoked fish and salted fish for shipment to the hinterlands.

Although many of these fish preservation techniques may now be known and in use on a small scale, considerable training and effort will be necessary to adapt them to a commercial processing plant stage. Structures capable of handling several tons of fish per day must be built. Large commercial supplies of fish and salt must be obtained. Practical information about inventory control and sanitation techniques for small plants must be imparted to local workers through training courses in order to step up these operations from the customary family level of effort to the commercial level. To assist in this transformation, it is recommended that technical experts from developed countries be brought in to demonstrate to the local operators the fundamental principles of these processes. This can be done best by constructing demonstration processing plants and employing selected personnel to operate the plants on a training basis under the guidance of the visiting experts. These trainees would be encouraged to apply this knowledge by building and operating similar plants in other regions.

As these small plants are established and become productive, and as supplies of fish are increased through the use of more efficient catching equipment such as fishing trawlers, the construction of fish canning and freezing factories should begin. In training of personnel to operate these factories, experts can be brought in again from developed countries, and local plant managers can be sent abroad to study existing plant practices. The prospects for foreign investment are great

at this stage because of the opportunity for developing profitable export products. Domestic markets, especially for canned fish, also should be vastly improved as local transportation and distribution channels are developed and more people become familiar with the products.

Summary

In summary, techniques for the production and preservation of fish in emerging nations must be developed step by step. Introduction of these new techniques will take considerable time since old and established but inefficient catching, processing and marketing methods must be replaced with new and improved methods. Consideration must first be given to simple improvements such as the increased use of outboard motors and more efficient methods of salting and drying of fish. Later, as other segments of the national economy are improved, additional changes such as the use of motorized trawlers and the construction of fish canning and freezing plants can be considered. At this point, exports of more valuable products such as shrimp and lobsters can provide a significant boost to the economy of the nation.

Ideally, the first phase (five years) of a national program for industrial development of the fisheries should include, as a minimum, the following steps:

(a) Improving existing fishing gear through better design and use of better materials.

(b) Educating fishermen in best uses and tactics of contemporary fishing gear.

(c) Training of net-manufacturing and vessel-repair teams and of other supporting services.

(d) Obtaining, by charter, an exploratory deep-water fishing vessel of advanced design to develop an inventory of domestic marine resources, the ship to be operated by foreign nationals.

(e) Planning for construction of shore facilities for processing and distribution of products of 2nd phase of fisheries program.

(f) Training of cadres in outboard motor maintenance and in transom-stern boat construction.

(g) Educating fishermen in primitive preservation and sanitation techniques for use on existing vessels and products.

(h) Training of the most promising young men for administration of the 2nd phase fisheries, with the help of fisheries colleges and government laboratories of advanced fishing nations.

(i) Developing sources of international assistance in financing 2nd phase plant and vessel construction and in procurement of processing and distribution equipment.

A general plan as suggested here may provide one key to successful development of a fishing industry. Obviously, the actual course of events of fisheries development in a nation cannot follow any standard pattern, and the technical advisors must adapt their programs to local customs, sources of material, existing economic situations, and even political factors. In any event, the upgrading of fishing techniques should be paralleled by improvements in processing and distribution facilities. The success of such a program would depend on the capacity and quality of the technicians involved and on the national effort expended rather than on the specific suggested scheme of attack.

PART FOUR

The Challenge in Developing Industry

WHILE the agricultural sector predominates in most underdeveloped economies, this alone is unable to provide adequate job opportunities for the rapidly growing work forces. What industries can or should be promoted and how, therefore, are prime questions for the economic developer. The articles in Part Four proceed from the general to the particular in dealing with this key area of endeavor.

That developing industry needs focus and centralized guidance is the burden of Bryce's message. The less-developed country should have an industrial development center to make studies, give advice, and organize investment channels and development banks, in order to create the climate for high expectations.

The image of the United States is often that of a country run by the giant corporation. In terms of production and employment, there is much to the image. Yet, 90 per cent of the manufacturing establishments in this country have fewer than one hundred employees. Staley stresses the need to develop small operations in underdeveloped countries, giving special care to cultivate those already existing. Such firms serve as a nursery for entrepreneurial talent, check monopoly, and foster local rather than foreign investment.

Marketing problems are rampant in the underdeveloped country. Gallagher describes, with pointed examples, how an established distributor—in this case, Sears, Roebuck and Company—has been utilized to generate local production, train hundreds in marketing for local business, and trim use of scarce foreign exchange for imports.

The remaining four articles by Sandbach, Wickersham, Heritage, and Williams explore the possibilities of creating specific industries—steel, food processing, forest products, and textiles—all basic or representative and often first in line of consideration in the list of feasibilities produced by indigenous development boards. Given the basic resources, what does a successful steel operation need? With so much emphasis on increasing farm output, should not food processing units be available to handle the expanding yields? How can an underdeveloped country eliminate the great waste in its present forest product usage? In many countries textile imports constitute a staggering drain on foreign currency needed for important development projects. Williams marks the pitfalls as well as the hurdles encountered in establishing a textile industry. Knowledge in these instances may provide clues to problems met in developing other industries.

Creating a Practical Industrial Development Program

Senior Development Economist, Arthur D. Little, Inc., Cambridge, Massachusetts

If reasonably favorable economic and political conditions exist, some industrial growth will take place in a developing country without organized stimulus. Experience has shown that a sound and aggressive campaign for industrial development will bring about much more industrial growth. An industrial-development effort can be organized like a war effort, to mobilize resources, stir the imagination and spirit of the people, and advance according to carefully planned strategy. While the techniques of forcing the pace are still in the early stages of evolution, enough has been learned to enable countries seeking industry to profit from the experiences of others.

Conditions for an Industrial Development Program

The creation of a practical industrial-development program should start with an understanding of the prerequisites for industrial growth, and, by defining the functions which make up an organized effort, to force the pace of industrial growth. Only after this foundation is laid is it time to set up institutions and get the program under way. This is not to suggest that everything in the environment must be just right for industry before a start can be made. If this were the situation, special efforts to speed up industrial development probably would not be needed. However, unless some minimum conditions by way of industrial environment are in order or at least in the process of being put in order, even a well-organized industrial program will have little hope of producing worthwhile results.

Basic Industrial Development Concepts

Industrial Development Can Be Accelerated. Basic to the whole idea of an industrial-development program is the belief that a dynamic and well-organized effort can bring about more industrial development of an economically sound nature than would otherwise occur. The concept of active industrial development is rooted in the conviction that there is much that a country can do to remove barriers to the growth of industry, and to create positive incentives for the development of industrial technology. There is a task for the country itself to perform in finding industrial opportunities, developing them, and attracting the interest of those who can supply the industrial capital, equipment, and skills which the country needs. This is not to imply that the government must become the industrialist, although occasionally this may be necessary. More often in the mixed economy of today, the government will be involved intimately in decisions and actions which determine whether or not an industry is established, and it will look to those with more industrial and commercial experience to establish and operate the new industries.

Industrial Development Means Importing Technology. Experience has shown that rapid industrial development in a non-industrial economy is almost entirely a matter of bringing about a large inflow of technology, in the form of equipment and skills, from industrialized countries. This is the basic concept on which an industrial-development program needs to be built. Almost all the needed processes and equipment exist in the industrial countries as a result of hundreds of years of research and evolution. The odds are long that the problem will be one of transfer, not of creating something new.

In the nationalistic atmosphere of much of the world today some developing countries may find it difficult to accept the necessity of importing industry at the start. The alternative to a massive inflow of foreign technology may be no industrial development, or unacceptably slow growth in an unnecessary repetition of the century-long process by which industry grew in Europe. The political task is to find ways to gain public support for the import of industry, then to create conditions which will stimulate the industrial inflow while safeguarding the legitimate interests of both the country and the foreign suppliers of industrial finance and knowledge. Foreign investors must have confidence that capital can be brought in safely, profitably employed, and withdrawn at will. They must be free of worry about expropriation, discrimination, unreasonable controls, and capricious acts. Tax holidays, infant-industry protection, import-duty relief, and direct subsidies already have proved their value as incentives to development of non-industrialized countries. Alternatively, industrial technology can be imported by purchasing equipment and hiring people with skills to operate it and to train nationals in its operation. Whichever way technology is imported, it must be brought by people who can impart their skills. A growing influx of technical personnel is therefore not something a developing country should tolerate, but something it must stimulate as a temporary means to get industry going and to train its people in the skills needed.

Industries Vary Greatly in their Value to a Country. The greatest illusion in industrial development is the belief that any industry is worth having at almost any price. In reality there is a vast range in the value of industrial projects to a country. The best may have all the advantages claimed for industrialization itself. The worst will be a perpetual drain on the economy, which, one way or another, will have to subsidize them. If countries seeking industry offered no tariff protection and no subsidies or other incentives, there would be some validity to the common idea that any profitable industry is worth having. But without some protection or incentives, few new industries would be established. The measurement of the value of projects to the economy, as distinct from their commercial profitability, provides the way to determine what subsidy a country can afford to pay for an industry. It will be discussed in the next section of this paper.

Functions and Methods of Industrial Development

The Industrial Development Functions. A program to speed up the industrial development of a country consists of several different but related functions. A country may have development agencies performing one or more of these functions, but the program as a whole may not be successful because some of the important tasks are not being undertaken. There are eight core functions which should be carried on in any country which is setting out to force the pace of industrial development:

(a) Improving the investment climate.

(b) Identifying industrial opportunities.

(c) Evaluating the feasibility of projects.

(d) Attracting investment.

(e) Assisting investors.

(f) Financing projects.

(g) Improving industrial productivity.

(h) Performing applied industrial research.

The creation of a practical industrial-development program means getting work on these functions started. There are, of course, other related functions such as technical education, economic planning, and building the infrastructure, but they will not be discussed here. The last three items, financing projects, improving productivity, and applied research, will also be omitted because they are being covered in other papers, and

they generally should be made the responsibility of three separate and specialized institutions: an *industrial development bank, a productivity center,* and an *applied research institute.* The five basic functions listed first fit together well as the work of a single institution which we shall call an *industrial development center* (IDC) and which will be the main agency to organize and push the industrial development drive. Its functions will constitute the industrial-development program.

Improving the Industrial Climate. The rate of industrial growth in any country is greatly influenced by what is often called the "industrial investment climate," a term encompassing all environmental factors affecting the ability of industry to operate successfully. These include:

(a) The attitudes and policies of government toward private business, foreign capital and personnel, and industrial problems generally.

(b) Taxation, including rates, exemptions and procedures.

(c) Import and tariff policies, such as protection for new industries, import duty relief on capital goods and materials.

(d) Foreign-exchange controls affecting imports and repatriation of capital and earnings.

(e) Immigration rules affecting the inflow of skilled personnel.

(f) Financing, its availability and cost.

(g) Labor, its availability, skills and costs, laws affecting employment of labor, and the position and attitude of labor itself.

(h) The infrastructure of power, fuel, transport, water, and communication facilities, and their pricing.

(i) The availability of suitable plant sites and their cost.

(j) The availability of services needed by industry.

Systematic efforts to better these elements are known as investment-climate improvement work, a vital part of an industrial-development program. If well-done, this work can reduce the risks of new industries, thus increasing the numbers started and enhancing considerably their chances of success and their contribution to the economy. It should be noted that every climate factor listed is subject to great influence by laws, regulations, government budgets, or the attitude of people, and all can be changed if the need for changes is accepted.

How is industrial climate improvement work done? First, the problems encountered by those seeking to establish or operate industries must be identified clearly. This can be done by investigating how and why projects have been delayed or killed or hampered by unsatisfactory climate factors. Documented case studies are needed. The remedial action required in regard to each major problem should be developed in detail. The strategy for getting action on each problem must be prepared thoroughly to mobilize support for new policies or laws. Item by item, the IDC should attempt to get the industrial climate improved by every method of persuasion and pressure it can muster. The work of improving the climate is a continuous task requiring follow-up on old problems and attention to new difficulties as they arise.

Identifying Industrial Opportunities. It is a well-recognized fact that one of the greatest barriers to industrial development is the lack of industrial entrepreneurs—men who can see a potential industrial opportunity, who can measure its soundness, and who can put together a project in a way to attract financing, and who can do all that is necessary to get a new industry into operation. In a highly developed society, private businessmen are continually looking for new industrial opportunities, and rarely is a really good possibility neglected for long. In a less developed country, good industrial opportunities may go unnoticed indefinitely unless people with sufficient knowledge of business and specific industries recognize the possible project and do something about making it into a business. To make up for the shortage of entrepreneurs is one of the prime functions of the IDC. It must do at least part of the job of discovering industrial opportunities so that, if the projects turn out to be feasible, necessary financing and management can be attracted.

How can the IDC discover industrial opportunities? It can proceed in a systematic, scientific way to examine areas of possible opportunity. This may be done by making studies of broad sectors of industry such as textiles, chemicals, wood products, and food processing. The industry studies should be made by or with the help of specialists intimately familiar with the technology and economics of each industry being examined. Through a study of raw materials, labor skills, markets, comparative production costs, and interrelationships in the industry, capable industry employers can identify the missing links and the logical next steps in development.

Another useful technique is to examine in a preliminary way the feasibility of producing any product which is being imported in significant quantities, and of upgrading any major product being exported in unprocessed form. Additional ideas to test may be obtained by listing industrial operations being carried on in other developing countries. Ideas may also be stimulated by using a standard industrial classification as a guide and by analyzing inter-industry relationships. The product of screening is a preliminary list of possible opportunities which seem sufficiently promising to warrant more thorough feasibility study. The screening process should go through several stages—a rough listing of ideas which may total a hundred or more, a series of refinements in which the list is narrowed down by critical examination to perhaps 1 or 2 dozen possibilities which seem to justify high priority for detailed study. Through this process, new possibilities are continually added, and some are advanced to the feasibility study stage, while others are dropped or relegated to low priority until more is learned of the probable technical or economic merits.

Measuring the Feasibility of Industrial Projects. The examination of project feasibility, one of the most important functions of an IDC, determines the soundness of industrial opportunity ideas which have originated in the IDC, or passes upon the merits of projects which have been prepared by a prospective investor or machinery seller. In either case three different kinds of feasibility need to be evaluated.

The first is technical feasibility. The proposed project must have the right selection of machinery and processes so it can make what it is supposed to make, and produce it competitively. It must have access to suitable materials, power, fuel, water, transport, and other requisites on a reliable basis and at acceptable prices. It must be able to obtain the labor it needs, either skilled or trainable. The right location which maximizes the

project's advantages must be found. Making such studies usually requires the assistance of highly specialized engineers who are knowledgeable about the industry, its technology, and its technical requirements. If the project design has not been developed, the IDC may have to determine the appropriate size, the process to be used, the machinery and buildings needed, and the location.

The second kind of feasibility that must be evaluated is commercial viability—the prospective soundness of the project as an investment, either of private or public funds. This analysis requires the application of normal accounting techniques to the technical requirements and local cost data. For the proposed volume of production, the amount of needed material, supplies, labor, power, and fuel is computed to arrive at direct manufacturing costs. When depreciation, management, selling, and other overhead expenses are included, the annual operating costs can be derived and compared to projected revenues obtained by multiplying the expected volume by the estimated sales price. These calculations will show the probable profit before taxes of the proposed project, and, when the amount of investment needed is taken into account, the return on total investment. This is the commercial profitability which is the measure of the probable value of the project to its owners.

The third kind of feasibility, and the only one which justifies public subsidy of one kind or another, is the prospective value of the project to the national economy, the gain which it should produce in the national income. This kind of feasibility is often not thought of, much less measured, thanks to the erroneous but common idea that any industry which can be profitable must be good for the country. Only when the IDC has measured the national economic profitability of a project can it advise soundly what subsidy, if any, is needed to make the project investible, and what national value the project will have to justify the subsidy.

Measuring the national economic profitability requires that the cost of production in the project be recalculated on the basis of the real cost to the economy of each item. This means eliminating taxes, pricing foreign exchange realistically, and calculating labor and materials at their best alternative value to the economy (if any). The value of the product to the economy is what the goods could be purchased for on the world market and brought to the country, before duty is levied. This is the "make or buy" concept, for a country always has the choice—import the product, or attempt to manufacture it. If the figures show the real economic costs of making the product are lower than the cost of importing it, the project has positive value to the economy. If not, the IDC should attempt to calculate whether unmeasurable benefits, such as training and influence on further industrialization, are enough to justify the amount of subsidy needed to make the project commercially profitable.

Attracting Investment. The successful discovery of an industrial opportunity and the detailed examination of its feasibility will contribute nothing to the development of the country unless capital and management are attracted to the project and unless they set it up as an operating industry. Attracting investment is the marketing phase of industrial development, and perhaps the most important part of the work of the IDC. In at least one of the most successful industrial-development programs in the world,

Puerto Rico's investment promotion constituted more than half of the total effort.

To most countries seeking industrial investment, the promotion of such investments has consisted of little more than publicity in capital-exporting countries about the investment climate and the general nature of industrial-growth possibilities in the developing country concerned. Such efforts are basic and desirable and can create an image that the country is progressive and welcomes foreign capital and industrial knowledge, but a serious investment-attraction program must involve much more than this "shotgun" approach aimed at investors in general. What is needed is a "rifle" approach in which specific investors are identified as being likely prospects for a specific industrial project which has been prepared sufficiently to be ready to attract investor interest. Using this technique, the IDC should develop projects to the point where their value to the economy is established and to the point where possible private investors will do the remaining work of investigation and plant design and actually make the investment. The degree to which projects should be carried by an IDC naturally varies considerably. In some cases a preliminary feasibility study is enough to establish the value of the economy of the project and attract a potential investor to make his own detailed feasibility study. In other instances, the IDC must develop the project through the stages of detailed feasibility study, site selection, plant design, and then publish a detailed technical-economic prospectus which a potential investor merely needs to review to determine whether to invest.

When the IDC has made a thorough feasibility study prior to any potential investor's expressing active interest in the project, the strategy of promotion needs to be carefully planned. Investors can be placed in two broad groups: manufacturers and financial institutions. The first have a reason to be interested in a project because of their experience in manufacturing and marketing the product. These are the investors of highest value, for their contribution of technical and management experience, marketing connections, and possibly accepted brand names, patents, and licenses, may be much more valuable to the country than the mere money they invest. Financial institutions such as banks or generalized investment companies with no specialized industry knowledge or connections are often highly desirable in completing the financing for a project, but rarely will they sponsor the project in the first instance and supply the vital elements of management and market connections.

Identifying the potential primary investors is a major part of investment promotion work. It is readily possible to identify the major companies in the world which own or participate in the operation of plants in the same industry in foreign countries and those producing the product in their own countries, but not operating elsewhere. Companies producing the product abroad for export to the country seeking the investment should be identified as very important targets because of their natural desire to protect the markets they have developed.

The other kind of investors, who do not operate manufacturing plants directly but who participate in the financing, usually have no strong preference for one kind of manufacturing compared to another. Generally, they do not want to become involved in the management of industries, preferring to play the role of investment bankers while satisfying themselves that the projects are feasible and that management is in the hands of others who are technically and commercially competent. This type of financial institution makes an ideal partner in a project, supplying either loans or share capital or both. Some investment companies of this kind are branches of commercial banks, some are industrial-investment companies which are offshoots of wealthy individuals or corporations, others are international financing institutions started with capital from governments.

How should an IDC make contact with potential investors and interest them in considering investments? Some will "walk in the door" and express interest in hearing about investment opportunities; others will initiate contact by correspondence. With those who take the initiative the job of the IDC is simple: maintain the contact, and develop it. To generate new prospects requires IDC initiative. Partly it can be done by mail. When a feasibility study is prepared it can be sent to all firms which have been identified as potentially interested. Other promotional material such as news of industrial development, lists of possible new industries, and background material on investment climate, can be sent to large mailing lists of firms known to be concerned with international investment. The most productive type of prospect development, however, is direct contact in which a representative of the IDC calls on top officials of companies which are potential investors, and places before them the project prospectus and offers to supply any additional information desired. Any country with a serious investment attraction program needs to have energetic and personable promotion officers resident in Europe and North America continually calling on investors. In this work, and in the identification of the prospective investors, developing countries often benefit from assistance of industrial consultants and public relations counsels.

Developing contact with the financial institutions is another part of the work of investment promotion officers resident in the capital exporting countries. As there is a limited number of these investment institutions, the IDC should know them well, and continually refer projects to them. They are always looking for good, well-prepared projects. They may also be able to suggest other companies which might participate in the financing or management of projects.

Assisting Prospective Investors. Any country with industrial opportunities, a good investment climate, and an active industrial-development and investment-attraction program will soon have a steady flow of potential visitors coming in person to see for themselves. Others will be writing with questions relating to projects. An important part of the work of the IDC is to serve these potential investors in a variety of ways. Their questions must be answered promptly and fully. This may involve supplying an item of readily available information or it may involve extensive investigation and analysis which may even constitute a complete private feasibility study. Such help may include market research, obtaining local cost data, finding legal or architectural help, or investigating alternative sites. Performing this type of consulting research work free for one potential investor on an exclusive and private basis should not be regarded as inappropriate. A prospective investor who has taken the initiative to seek help in preparing or evaluating his project idea is already half

committed and is much more likely to end up making the investment than prospects who are approached "cold" by investment-promotion personnel. If the inquirer for whom special research has been done fails, within a reasonable time, to take action on the investment project, the IDC should retain the right to take the material to other investors who might be interested.

A different kind of service to potential investors consists of helping them break through the obstacles standing between them and their proposed investments. They may arrive in the country as strangers without contacts or even the names of the people they should see. It is the work of the IDC to act as guides and advisers to such visitors, making sure they have the opportunity to meet the officials and businessmen who can help them, and ensuring that they get the access to the information they are seeking. They should be shown a selection of successful enterprises and be introduced to the managers who can give them direct observations on the problems of starting a new industry in the country. The IDC should be prepared to set up a program which will make the best use of the visiting investor's time. When the project moves past the stage of feasibility inquiry, the IDC should be ready to help the investor obtain any necessary government approvals, guarantees, incentive benefits, subsidies, or concessions, which he is entitled to, and which the IDC, as a result of its analysis, considers it in the public interest for the new industry to have. Throughout the whole process of project investigation, analysis, and finalization, the IDC in effect acts as an adviser and consultant to the prospective investor, and an intermediary between him and the government to whatever extent he wishes to use the service.

Once the investor has made a commitment to go ahead with his project the work of the IDC is not ended. It should continue in the closest cooperation with the investor until his factory is in successful operation. He may need help in finding key local staff, in setting up a training program, in getting title to land, in selecting a contractor, in establishing a marketing system, in expediting customs clearance on machinery, and a hundred and one other details. The IDC, being intimately familiar with both government and business in the country, is in the ideal position to help the newcomer solve the problems which stand in the way of success for his new industry.

Organization for Industrial Development

Institutions to Perform the Industrial Development Functions. The functions which make up the Industrial Development Program will be performed by people working in and through the organized framework of institutions. The five functions discussed in detail may well be assigned to the single institution, the Industrial Development Center.

Because the functions of the IDC represent activities of an official nature mainly designed to assist and encourage the development of industries which will be privately owned and managed, the IDC occupies a position somewhere in between the government and the private sector. The IDC, representing as it does official policy toward industry, and using government funds for its work, is basically a government agency. The need for it to occupy middle ground between gov-

ernment and private business argues that it should be somewhat outside of the regular ministerial machinery of government. Such a position should help insulate it from the pressures of politics and help to keep its work on an objective and technical basis. It should also help it to operate more along commercial lines through avoiding some of the restrictions of governmental system. This quasi-official status may be obtained by establishing the IDC as an independent, public-service corporation with a board of directors representing both government and business. Such a board, if composed of influential and public spirited citizens, should be able to create for the IDC a role of importance in such matters as improving the industrial climate. A joint government-business board should serve as a bridge between the public and the private sector, and help make industrial development the national campaign in the public interest which it should be. The board should concern itself only with the policies to be followed by the IDC, and with the efficiency with which the institution carries out its work. The day-to-day operation of the IDC should be delegated completely to its director.

The director of the IDC should be a leader of such stature and prominence in the country that he personally can impart to the organization some of the status it needs to be effective. The director must be a dynamic organizer, capable of attracting highly qualified personnel, and building them into a strong and active organization. He must have the confidence of top government leaders so he can influence the changes in official policy needed to improve the industrial climate. He must have the confidence of investors and industrialists so they will be serious about investment projects brought forward by the IDC. While it is naturally desirable for the director of the IDC to be a man with technical knowledge of industry, this is not nearly as important as his talent for organizing and promoting. The director must be well supported by his technical staff, but he must have the capability himself to attract various and often divergent interests to work together to invest in new industries.

The Organization and Staffing of an Industrial Development Center. The responsibilities which have been described for the Industrial Development Center could be distributed in various ways within the organization, but the different nature of the various functions suggests that the IDC should be composed of several units, each performing one of the functions. Thus the IDC might well be set up as shown in this chart:

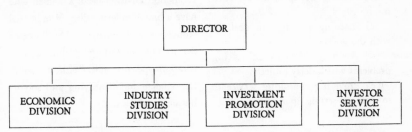

The "Economics Division" should be responsible for work not strictly related to only one specific industrial project. Its areas of work should include:

(a) Industrial planning.

(b) Advisory services to government on industrial policy questions.

(c) Investment climate improvement work.

(d) Preliminary screening for industrial opportunities.

(e) Infrastructure studies (transport, power, etc.).

(f) Industrial land availability work.

(g) Background studies (labor, incentives).

(h) Development of industrial statistics.

(i) Evaluation of industrial progress.

The "Industry Studies Division" should be responsible for the development and evaluation of specific projects. Its work should include:

(a) Preliminary evaluation of project ideas.

(b) Industrial-p r o j e c t feasibility studies (all aspects, including engineering, commercial prospects, economic value to country).

(c) Market research related to projects.

(d) Evaluations of alternative locations and sites.

(c) Plant design or evaluation, and costing.

(f) Financial estimates.

(g) Preparation of prospectuses.

The "Investment Promotion Division" should be the marketing arm of the IDC with responsibility for finding the prospective investors. Its work should include:

(a) Identification of potential investors for specific projects.

(b) Preparation of promotional material, both general and project.

(c) Distribution of promotional material to prospective investors.

(d) Correspondence with potential investors.

(e) Direct contact with potential investors.

The "Investor Service Division" should have the responsibility to do all things possible to help potential investors make their investigations, arrive at investment commitments, and get their projects started. Its work should include:

(a) Obtaining information requested by investors.

(b) Making arrangements for visiting investors.

(c) Assisting investors in dealings with the government.

(d) Assisting investors in solving problems which delay projects.

(e) Providing consulting service to investors in setting up operations.

The quite different nature of the work of the several divisions suggests that different kinds of people are required to do their work well. The Economics Division requires mainly industrial economists, preferably at least one with legal training. The Industry Studies Division needs engineers and economists with a broad knowledge of industry, and also of finance and economics. The Investment Promotion Division needs salesmen who have a broad understanding of industrial economics and finance. The Investor Service Division requires business-administration-type personnel with a consultant's talent for identifying and solving business problems.

The Place of Small and Medium Industry in Development

EUGENE STALEY

Director of Basic Research, International Development Center of Stanford Research Institute, Menlo Park, California

Large factories are a characteristic feature of the modern industrial economy, but they are not the whole of it. Despite the well-known "economies of scale," manufacturing is not always and everywhere more economical in large than in small establishments. This is true even in the highly industrialized countries. It is still more true in newly industrializing countries where markets are smaller; systems of transport, communication, and product distribution are less developed; and there is less experience with large-scale organization. A country will achieve the most productive industrial structure by developing a well-chosen combination of large and small manufacturing units, the place of each determined on the basis of economic efficiency.

Often, in countries striving to industrialize, small-scale manufacturing has been regarded as an inevitably backward and lagging part of the economy, perhaps to be aided for social reasons and in a rather defensive or protective spirit, but not as a promising opportunity for development. In most industrialization programs, too little attention has been paid to the benefits to be gained by helping existing small industry to modernize

and by stimulating the growth of new, modern small industry. A latent resource has thus been overlooked and neglected.

Characteristics of Small and Medium Industry

Small industry means manufacturing carried on in relatively small establishments. Before giving a quantitative interpretation to "relatively small," however, it will be useful to note some non-quantitative functional characteristics which distinguish small from large industry. These are the characteristics which justify separate discussion of the role of small industry in development and the adoption of special-development programs for small industry. (Medium industry, of course, stands between small and large industry with respect to these characteristics.)

Most important is (a) the relative lack of specialization in management. The small manufacturing firm characteristically depends on "one-man management," generally by an owner-manager, perhaps with a few assistants. The very large firm, by contrast, can have a vice-president for production, a vice president for sales, a vice-president for finance, and a vice-president for research. Other characteristics are (b) lack of access to capital through the organized securities market and handicaps in obtaining capital and credit through other channels, (c) no special bargaining strength in buying or selling in a major market, and (d) often, though not always, a relatively close integration with the local community through local ownership and management and dependence on nearby markets and sources of supply.

These characteristics give the small manufacturing firm certain disadvantages and certain special needs for types of advice and aid that are not so much needed by large firms. They also confer some advantages, chief of which is flexibility. The close personal contact which "one-man" management makes possible between the manager, workers, customers, and suppliers can be, if the manager is a good one, a source of strength in many ways. This goes far to explain why, and in what kinds of manufacturing, modern, well-managed small industry can compete successfully with large industry—as will be seen below.

Use of Terms

One obstacle to clear thinking about the role of small and medium industry in economic development is the confusion over use of terms. A United Nations report on *The Development of Manufacturing Industry in Egypt, Israel, and Turkey* (1958) refers to manufacturing establishments employing 10 or more persons as "medium-scale and large-scale," thus limiting the term "small-scale" to establishments with fewer than 10 persons. A Working Group of the Economic Commission for Asia and the Far East some years ago suggested that small industry be defined for statistical purposes as establishments with no more than 20 employees when using motive power or 50 when not using power.

Governments which offer special assistance to smaller manufacturing firms use diverse administrative definitions. In India until 1960 the Government's small-industry program was directed to establishments having no more than 50 employees with power or 100 without power and no more than Rs. 500,000 (about US$100,000) of fixed capital. Now there is no limitation on number of employees; only the capital limitation applies. In Japan, various laws for assisting "smaller enterprises" recognize an upper limit in manufacturing of 300 employees, sometimes with a capital limitation of 10 million yen (about $28,000). In the United States, a manufacturing firm is officially a "small business" for purposes of government financial and other assistance if it has fewer than 250 employees, and large if it has more than 1,000, but within the 250–1,000 range it may be classified either small or large, depending on size standards set for different industries. Obviously, discussion of small and medium industry may proceed at cross-purposes unless we take care to define what we mean.

The most serious confusion results from a tendency to identify smallness with certain other characteristics. Thus, "small industry" and "village industry" are sometimes lumped together, which is unfortunate because small-scale manufacturing goes on not only in villages—that is, in rural areas—but in urban areas as well. More important, smallness and outmoded techniques are often treated as inseparable. The *Economic Survey of Europe, 1959*, in its illuminating chapters on "Development Problems in Southern Europe and Ireland," refers several times to the "modern" as contrasted with the "small-scale" industrial sector. At present it is undoubtedly true that the great majority of small-scale manufacturers in the less industrialized countries have backward technology, inefficient management, and low productivity. But these are not inevitable characteristics of small industry. There are modern, efficient, small manufacturing enterprises in many countries, and in some of the highly industrialized countries the average labor productivity in small plants is not very far below that in large plants.

Any definition of "small" or "small and medium" industry in measurable terms, as required for statistical studies and for administration of special kinds of aid, cannot avoid a certain arbitrariness. It is like defining "hot" water. And just as the concept of "hot" water depends on whether one is thinking of shaving or of running a steam turbine, so definitions of small and medium industry can reasonably be different in countries at different stages of development and for different purposes. However, it is important to be clear, and it would be advantageous to achieve a fairly consistent international use of terms.

There is no single satisfactory way of measuring the size of an industrial establishment. Besides number of employees, other possible measures are capital investment, output, amount of energy used, and relative position in the industry. All of these are relevant in any complete characterization. Number of employees is, however, the most widely available, the most convenient, the most readily comparable internationally, and on the whole probably the least objectionable for general purposes. At Stanford Research Institute, where for some years we have been engaged in basic research and field work on the role of small industry in development, we have decided for the purpose of statistical comparisons (recognizing the arbitrariness of all such decisions) to call manufacturing establishments with fewer than 100 workers "small industry"; those with 100–249 workers (or thereabouts, where census data break differently), "medium"; and establishments with 250 or more, "large." Within the "small industry" group, we find it wise to separate out, where possible, establishments with fewer than 10 employees. We label them "very small." Those with 10 to 49 employees, we label "the central group," and those from 50 to 99 "small-to-medium." However, one of our field teams which recently worked with the Banco Popular in Colombia on a joint study leading to special measures for small- and medium-industry development found that in Colombian conditions the most appropriate definitions, both for analytical and program purposes, were: small factory, 10 or more persons engaged and gross assets below 500,000 pesos (about US$50,000); medium factory, fewer than 100 persons engaged and gross assets from 500,000 to 2 million pesos (about US$50,000 to US$200,000).

Prospects for Different Types of Small Industry

It is essential to distinguish a number of types of small industry, for these different types have very different prospects as a country transforms itself from a traditional, pre-industrial into a modern, industrial economy.

One important distinction is that between traditional small industry and modern small industry—the latter defined as manufacturing units in which reasonably good application is made of the best science and technology currently available. It is *modern* small industry, or movement toward it, which holds promise for newly developing countries.

It is also important to distinguish between household industry, artisan industry, and small factories.

Household industry is manufacturing carried on in or near the home, mainly by family labor. It is sometimes called cottage industry, though more properly this term might be reserved for rural household industry. This is the oldest form of manufacturing, and it is still important in many countries that are striving to modernize. Undoubtedly it will continue to be important in these transitional economies for a long time. Well-planned measures to improve and regulate household industry will be needed. But the long-term trend in developing countries will be, and on economic and social grounds ought to be, for household industry to disappear, save for special functions. Among such special functions are providing work for the handicapped and for dwellers in isolated places, part-time supplementation of seasonal incomes of farmers in some situations, and production of handicrafts of an artistic and quasi-hobby sort. For ordinary production of manufactured goods, household industry is inefficient and is subject to social abuses that are practically impossible to control, such as extremely low rates of pay, long hours, and child labor. Development planners in newly industrializing countries will do well to regard their household industries as a temporary form, to be supplanted over the long-term by small and medium factories, artisan workshops located outside the home, and large factories.

Artisan industry is manufacture carried on in workshops by craftsmen working singly or with a few hired helpers or apprentices and without extensive division of labor. The craftsman (artisan) is central, and articles are produced for the most part one at a time with individual variations, often to the requirements of a particular customer. The potters, weavers, blacksmiths, shoemakers, bakers, and other ancient crafts are examples of "old line" artisan industry. As a country moves from traditional towards modern economy, some of the old crafts will decline, as a result of competition with factory goods and changes in tastes. Still more crafts will undergo readjustments by which they will become "service trades" and in this form will supplement rather than compete with factory goods. "New line" artisan activities will arise, such as automobile repairing, installation and repair of electrical equipment, and photographic work. Artistic handicrafts, and craftsmanship in the design, decoration, and individualization of factory goods, will find increasing markets. Readjustments such as these, especially the growth of service trades, have belied predictions which were common a half-century ago in the then industrializing countries of Europe that factory competition would lead to the disappearance of the artisan. The highly industrialized economies of today seem, on the contrary, to be using increasing numbers of artisans whose functions have undergone a transformation from the making of manufactured goods to their installation, servicing, and repair. Often these functions are combined with retail trade.

The long-term problem of the newly industrializing countries with respect to artisans is to help them readjust in a changing environment which presents both new opportunities and new competition. The transitional adjustments will not be easy. But the basic strategy must be to help the artisans in one of two ways: (a) Some can be helped to adapt their skills to the rising modern demands, forsaking the declining traditional demands. This means village blacksmiths learning to install and repair irrigation pumps and diesel engines, skilled weavers concentrating on designs and qualities not readily reproducible by machine, shoemakers turning to shoe repairing. (b) Others must be guided into entirely new occupations, preferably occupations for which the demand is rising as development takes place.

The small factory is distinguished from artisan industry by its greater division of labor and the consequent need for planning and coordination. The manager rather than the craftsman is the central figure. In larger factories management itself has to be subdivided, and specialists handle such tasks as production management, product design, sales management, personnel management, and financial management. The small factory has much less division of labor in management, and the medium factory an intermediate amount. As already noted, this is a source both of weakness and of strength in the smaller scale units. If there is right choice of product lines and skilled management, small units can emphasize their areas of strength and avoid those in which they are too greatly handicapped.

The outlook for modern, progressively managed small and medium factories in newly industrializing countries is therefore favorable. Well-conceived programs designed to foster this sector can be important tools of development. However, the utility of such programs will depend on the kinds of small manufacturing industry that are encouraged and how they are encouraged. An economically sound program for small and medium industry development is one that fosters *selectivity* in the choice of product lines and *efficiency* in production and business operations.

The benefits which an industrializing economy can gain by intelligent promotion of this sector may be summarized as follows:

(a) Small and medium firms serve as a nursery for entrepreneurial talent, for growth in some cases into large industry.

(b) Alert owner-managers in intimate contact with market needs and possessing practical technical competence are important sources of product innovation and adaptation.

(c) The limited size of the home market in many newly industrializing countries makes production on the scale that is usual in the major industrialized countries unfeasible. Smaller plants may be able to produce quantities required by the smaller market at reasonable cost, if provided information on current-product opportunities and if given technical and managerial guidance and stimulus to efficient performance.

(d) Efficient and forward-looking firms, even though of modest size, can contribute to development of export trade, especially if market exploration is undertaken cooperatively and with government help.

(e) Vigorous small and medium factories help to check monopoly, improving prices and services to consumers.

(f) Small and medium manufacturers are usually local entrepreneurs, and the healthy growth of their firms helps to balance the importation of foreign capital and the growth of foreign-owned enterprises.

(g) Small and medium enterprises add to employment opportunities.

(h) Such enterprises tap sources of capital (especially from family savings and, if the enterprise is successful, from plowed-back profits) which would not otherwise contribute to the country's capital formation.

(i) Small and medium factories can be important in local and regional development and in promoting a more decentralized pattern of industrial growth.

(j) Vigorous small and medium industry helps to create an active tradition of independent initiative by alert individuals and a strong middle class, which in turn is important as underpinning for political democracy.

The Economic Basis for Modern Small Factories

It is sometimes asked, "Will not the large manufacturing firms drive out the smaller ones? Can the small enterprise, lacking a staff of specialists and with limited access to capital, compete against large, highly organized, highly capitalized firms?" The answer is that while many small factories can and do compete successfully, others do not compete directly with large factories but rather serve as a complement to them. That many small manufacturing establishments do in fact manage to compete or to coexist, even in the most highly industrialized environment, is shown in table 1.

In the United States in 1958, as the table shows, more than 90 percent of all manufacturing establishments had fewer than 100 employees. These establishments employed 27 percent of all manu-

TABLE 1. *Role of manufacturing establishments having fewer than 100 employees*

Country	Year	Percent of all manufacturing establishments	Percent of all manufacturing employees*	Percent of all manufacturing output**
United States............................	1958	91	27	23
West Germany..........................	1953	89	27	23
United Kingdom.......................	1954	95	33	n.a.
Puerto Rico.............................	1954	91	41	38
Australia................................	1955	97	50	n.a.
Japan.....................................	1952	99	59	37

n.a. Not available.

* United Kingdom, percent of workers.

** United States and Puerto Rico, value added by manufacture; West Germany, turnover excluding goods purchased and resold without processing; Japan, value of shipments.

Sources: United States—Bureau of the Census, *Census of Manufactures*, 1958. West Germany—Statistisches Bundesamt, *Statistisches Jahrbuch für die Bundesrepublik Deutschland*, 1955. United Kingdom—Annual Report of the Chief Inspector of Factories for the year 1954. Puerto Rico—Puerto Rico Planning Board, *Statistical Yearbook, Puerto Rico*, 1957. Australia—Australia Commonwealth Bureau of Census and Statistics, *Official Year Book of the Commonwealth of Australia*, 1957. Japan—Office of the Prime Minister, Bureau of Statistics, *Japan Statistical Yearbook*, 1954.

facturing employees and produced 23 percent of the total value added by manufacture. Incidentally, the fact that these smaller factories accounted for not very much less in proportion of value added than their proportion of employment shows that their average labor productivity is not very greatly below that of the larger factories. The relative importance of small factories is as great or greater in West Germany and the United Kingdom, and considerably greater in Puerto Rico, Australia, and Japan.

Here are some of the factors which enable small and medium factories to compete or to coexist successfully with large industry:

(a) Economies of scale are less important in some lines of production than in others. In blast furnaces and cement kilns there are great engineering advantages and cost advantages in using big pieces of equipment to handle large amounts of materials, so that these are not undertakings suitable for small units. But in the manufacture of garments or certain kinds of machine tools the advantages of scale are much less significant, and a moderate sized plant may be just as efficient as, or even more efficient than, a large one.

(b) Small units have an advantage where shipping costs are high or the product is perishable. Thus, bricks and tiles and fresh baked goods can be produced more economically by relatively small, local establishments than by great central factories.

(c) Small manufacturing establishments have an advantage in meeting highly specialized or individualized demands or in catering to a small-volume market or one requiring frequent quick readjustments because of style changes or for other reasons. They compete very well in certain kinds of precision instruments, some types of specialized machinery, some types of surgical equipment, women's wear, and so on. Here the flexibility of the small firm stands it in good stead. Large enterprises are handicapped by their bureaucratic procedures and their relatively large overhead expenses. It does not pay for them to produce short "runs" of a non-standard item, but the small factory can often do so at a profit.

(d) Where labor and social laws are applied more stringently to large than to small plants, as is often the case in newly industrializing countries, this may be a factor (whether or not a desirable one) in the competitive ability of small plants.

(e) The small factory can "fill the cracks" between the large-volume, standardized outputs of large factories. Many small manufacturers produce specialized sizes or styles or slightly different products for which the demand is not great enough to justify large-scale production but still large enough to provide an attractive market for them. For example, a very successful small-cycle manufacturer near Madras, India, produces junior-size bicycles, also tricycles and tricycle-mounted delivery carts, thus supplementing rather than competing with a major bicycle factory in his immediate vicinity.

(f) The small factory can produce components and supplies for large factories. Much of Japanese small industry works on contract for large industry. One of the reasons for the efficiency of industry in the United States is that large plants characteristically buy many specialized parts from hundreds or even thousands of other plants, both large and small. A small enterprise supplying a specialized item to several large firms may have greater economies of scale on that item than any of the large firms could obtain. Also, small industry often performs job shop operations for large industry.

(g) The small factory often serves to initiate new products, and sometimes grows large with growth of the market for the product. Henry Ford and other pioneer automobile manufacturers started on a very small scale. The electronics industry today is bursting with small firms, as well as large ones, hopefully exploiting new ideas. In countries where industrial diversification is at an early stage, small-scale manufacturers can discover opportunities to introduce products that are new to the country though not necessarily new in the world.

Policy Implications

The policy implications of the preceding analysis may now be summarized.

(a) First, development leaders in countries striving to accelerate the rate of industrial advancement will do well to give attention to the constructive possibilities in modernization and growth of small and medium industry.

(b) Second, as a country moves through the transitional stage from a traditional toward a modern economy, the outlook is for household industry to be replaced, for artisan industry to be transformed, and for the small but modern factory to be developed and to increase in importance.

(c) Third, these shifts can be made much more productive if they are properly guided. Some product lines and some situations offer opportunities for efficient small-scale manufacturing and others do not. Conditions vary from country to country, from region to region in the same country, and from time to time as a country develops. Therefore, continuous research to provide up-to-date analysis of changing markets, production methods, costs, and other economic and technical factors is advisable in a program of small- and medium-industry development. It will also be necessary to have some type of communication system, such as an industrial advisory service or industrial extension service, to carry to existing or potential entrepreneurs the information on which they can base sound investment decisions.

(d) Fourth, much depends on improving the efficiency of management in small-scale enterprises and on introducing improved production technology. This again suggests the need for some type of industrial advisory service. Among its functions would be to encourage a progressive outlook among small entrepreneurs and to keep feeding them improved ideas on the economic, technological, and management problems of their enterprises. These ideas should be based on the best modern techniques of production and management, suitably adapted to smaller scale operations.

(e) This last point has a direct bearing on the application of science and technology for the benefit of less developed areas. Significant help could be given in the advancement of the newly developing economies by devoting more scientific and technological effort to the search for methods of increasing the efficiency of comparatively small-scale production units.

Designing a Development Program for Small and Medium Industry

What types of practical development aids should be considered in designing a positive program to improve the efficiency and promote the growth of small and medium industry? The following checklist is offered:

(a) *Industrial Advisory or Counseling Services.* Some of the principles and techniques that have made agricultural extension services valuable instruments of agricultural improvement are now being applied for small-industry development in a number of countries. A small-industry advisory service or industrial extension service should give counsel on two kinds of problems: (i) economic and business management problems, including the choice of promising lines of manufacture, marketing, costing, financing, and personnel management, and (ii) technical production problems, such as plant layout and better use of machines and materials. An industry advisory service needs a trained staff, closely linked with and backed by industrial training services, research services, financing services, and all the other developmental aids.

(b) *Industrial Training Services.* For effective development of modern small industry, training programs are needed for: (i) managers, (ii) supervisors and foremen, (iii) technicians, and (iv) skilled workers.

(c) *Industrial Research Services.* Applied research is constantly needed in order to adapt the best available science and technology to the special needs of existing or potential industries and, through the counseling service, to make the results available to small industrial-

ists. Two kinds of research are important: (i) research on problems of economics and business management affecting the prospects and operations of small industry, and (ii) research on technical production problems.

(d) *Measures to Improve Small Industry Financing.* Small industry generally needs financial counseling. Also, special institutional devices are necessary to cope with the problems and risks peculiar to the financing of this sector of the economy.

(e) *Industrial Estates.* An industrial estate is a tract of land on which industrial utilities are installed (roads, water, electricity, etc.) and on which standard-type factory buildings are erected for lease or sale to manufacturing firms or on which firms may build their own buildings in conformity with designs approved by the estate. This greatly aids small and medium enterprises, for they are able to have suitable premises and utilities without the burdensome tasks of acquiring land, obtaining all necessary permits, and obtaining access roads and electric-power connections. The offer of factory premises on a rental or installment-purchase basis is also a good way of making financial help available to promising small industrial enterprises. Industrial estates are likewise an important tool for city planning and the control of urban growth.

(f) *Marketing Aids.* The small industrialist, especially if he enters manufacturing from the craftsman or engineering side, oftentimes fails to do an adequate job of marketing. He can be helped in a number of ways. One of the most important aids is marketing information, based on economic investigations and market surveys which small firms are not in a position to undertake themselves. Trade fairs, expositions, trade directories, and special assistance in making export contacts are helpful devices. Larger firms can be encouraged to contract with smaller firms for component parts and supplies. In some countries a deliberate effort is made to channel suitable portions of government purchases to smaller manufacturers.

(g) *Aid in Procurement of Materials and Equipment.* The small manufacturer suffers handicaps in purchasing as well as marketing. Therefore, development programs sometimes promote bulk-purchasing arrangements for groups of small enterprises, through purchasing cooperatives or governmental agencies. Where important supplies, domestic or imported, are subject to allocation and control, it is highly advisable to establish special, simplified procedures adapted to the needs of small manufacturers.

(h) *Fostering Interfirm Assistance and Industrial Self-Help.* In some countries, such as the northern countries of Europe, trade associations or associations of small industrialists have proved themselves capable of carrying on advisory services, training services, research services, and financial services for their members—often with the aid of government subsidies. Large manufacturing firms can also be an important source of technical assistance for the many small firms among their customers and suppliers. The exchange of ideas and information at trade meetings and conventions, through trade periodicals and in other ways, can be an important factor in industrial progress. Small-industry development may well include efforts to

stimulate constructive activities of these various types.

A development program for small and medium industry need not, of course, include every type of measure on the foregoing checklist. It should, however, be reasonably comprehensive. Usually it does little good merely to set up an institution for making capital and credit more readily available to small industry without, for example, doing anything to improve techniques of production and management. An action program, to be effective, must push outward simultaneously on a considerable number of limiting factors. Which factors are most strategic in the circumstances of a particular country should be determined by a preliminary survey. Usually the limiting factors so revealed will be multiple, and the action program will need to be a broad, integrated one, so that each kind of assistance reinforces the other kinds and is reinforced by them.

Each country requires a set of measures tailormade in general approach and in detail to its own situation. Valuable ideas can, however, be had by studying the experience of other countries. Among the less industrialized countries, India has by all odds the largest, most comprehensive, and the best planned program for small-industry development. At a further stage of industrialization, Japan has evolved a wide array of measures which well merit study. The United States has an active "Small Business Administration" which aids small and medium manufacturers and other types of small business, supplementing many aids provided through other public institutions and through the private-business system. The Scandinavian countries, the Netherlands, Germany, the United Kingdom, France, Italy, and other European countries, also some of the Provinces of Canada, have adopted a variety of measures with different emphases, sometimes focussing on the financial needs of small manufacturing units, sometimes on technological and managerial training and productivity improvement, sometimes on product design and marketing. In Puerto Rico there is an active industrial-development program in which a large proportion of the enterprises that have been started are small units, and a number of other Latin American countries—Mexico, Brazil, Colombia, and others—have special banking institutions designed to stimulate small industry, as well as industrial development centers, industrial research institutes, productivity centers, and the like.

Indonesia, Burma, Pakistan, and the Philippines are using various techniques of small industry promotion, and the Federation of Malaya is strengthening its Rural and Industrial Development Authority. In Africa, Nigeria has been experimenting with industrial estates and other measures and is considering a more comprehensive small-industry program.

It should be stressed, however, that no system worked out in one country can be recommended in its entirety for another. Rather, the development officials of each country must analyze their particular country's small-industry problems and opportunities, then borrow some ideas and invent others, in order to act creatively and practically in their specific situation.

Markets as a Basis for Industrial Development

John F. Gallagher
Vice President, Sears, Roebuck and Co., Chicago, Illinois

The market for consumer goods is a basic factor in an economy. Clothes; furnishings for the home; kitchen utensils; appliances for cooking, for refrigeration, for washing—all these are fundamental to personal well-being.

Of equal importance is the provision of adequate distribution facilities to supply the consumer with his requirements.

Developing countries are ideally situated for small manufacturing plants which make use of raw materials obtainable locally. Efficient marketing of the products they produce must follow if the consumer and the economy are to benefit fully. This efficiency can be achieved by the establishment of a mass-distribution system where the large distributor purchases the product he sells from a large number of small manufacturers.

The very fact that the mass-distribution system exists will in itself give impetus to the development and improvement of local industry, in addition to providing an outlet for the goods produced.

The mass distributor is able to have buyers, trained in market analysis, with detailed knowledge of the products they are buying, who are able to advise the small manufacturer on the use of new engineering and production techniques.

Also, they are able to pass on to him the results of extensive research and testing which will enable him to improve his product, and to give him guidance on the financial aspects of his operations. The end result will be more efficient production, improved product development, lower selling prices, expanded markets, and enhancement of the local economy.

The paper will show, through a case study of Sears Roebuck and Co. in Latin America, that an efficient system of distribution, where emphasis is placed on merchandising techniques, source development, personnel training, and community participation, is as essential to the expansion and growth of an economy as are the extraction of mineral wealth, agriculture, power, transportation, or heavy industry.

Sears entered the Latin American retail market late in 1942 when it opened a store of medium size in Havana, Cuba. However, the real plunge into significant investment abroad began in February 1947 when a complete department store was opened in Mexico City.

Encouraged by initial success in Mexico and the post-war recuperation of Cuba, expansion southward continued at a rapid pace. By 1949, three stores formed the Mexican Corporation, and stores in Sao Paulo and Rio de Janeiro were the beginning of the Brazilian Corporation. Venezuela with a store in Caracas became a host country in 1950, and Colombia in 1953. Peru, Panama, and Costa Rica were added in 1955. Today, Sears has 64 retail outlets in nine countries.

The expansion was not without many problems; Sears learned its greatest lesson between 1947 and 1949. The initial concept was to build or rent and furnish stores similar to stores in the United States, to staff the key positions with qualified North Americans, teach U.S. merchandising methods and sell U.S. merchandise.

In 1948, however, the dollar exchange acquired during the war by Latin America as a whole was exhausted. The major nations with major appetites did not have the dollar resources to feed those appetites with dollar goods, with the single exception of Venezuela. Sears had to find local factories and train them to manufacture to its design, specifications, and assortment. Qualified buyers with years of buying and technical experience in the United States had to be moved into Latin America. Their job was to acquire quality merchandise at competitive prices and to train local personnel in merchandising and buying methods. It was at this point that Sears began contributing to the development of local industry. In 1962, Sears has separate buying organizations established in Brazil, Colombia, Mexico, Panama (for Central America), Peru, Venezuela, and Puerto Rico.

The majority of the North Americans who aided in setting up these offices returned long since to the United States, their places taken by nationals trained in buying techniques and methods. These buyers, in 1962, are purchasing quality merchandise from 7,540 local sources. The ratios of local purchases to total merchandise requirements are:

Brazil	98.01 perecnt
Colombia	98.82 percent
Mexico	97.45 percent
Peru	74.96 percent
Venezuela	50.75 percent
Central America	25.00 percent

Operations in Peru

The operation in Peru [1] will illustrate the pattern of development. In 1955, when Sears entered the Peruvian market, it immediately established a buying office to: (a) train local personnel in its buying methods, (b) develop local merchandise to its specifications, and (c) develop local sources. This was done despite the fact that all goods could have been imported and that the competition was following this method of acquisition. The buying office in Lima followed a program taken from the U.S. company and known as the basic buying program.

Basic buying involves purchasing merchandise at known cost, over an extended period of time, from large numbers of small efficient factories, located as close to customers as possible. Buying at known cost is based on a careful analysis of a factory's production capacity, the price and availability of raw materials, the employment picture in the community where the factory is located, and the anticipated volume of purchases over a specified period of time.[2]

The buyer is trained to think in terms of product development, of engineering and manufacturing procedure, and of production costs. He must be familiar with the most recent developments that influence the marketing of his product, from raw materials and synthetics to current sales figures. The company feels that since it deals directly with the customer, it is in a better position than a manufacturer to decide what the shopper wants in quality, style, and price.[3]

What aspects of basic buying are useful in stimulating industrial development in Peru? To answer this question, we shall set out six goals which are necessary but not complete conditions for the industrial growth of the country:[4]

(a) To promote the formation of domestic capital.

(b) To increase the local source for commodities hitherto imported, in order that more foreign exchange can be devoted to the purchase of capital goods; in other words, to foster import substitution.

(c) To reduce the income-elasticity of demand for imports through a "Buy Peruvian" policy; to establish confidence in domestic manufacturers and thus reduce the marginal tendency to import as national income rises.

(d) To increase employment opportunities to absorb the great amount of manpower that will appear on the labor market.

(e) To increase the product-capital ratio in industry.

(f) To channel production by artisans into the manufacturing sector proper.

There are a number of barriers impeding the mobilization of domestic Peruvian capital.[5] A related problem is how to channel available capital funds into profitable undertakings. During the preparation of this report, a group of Lima's businessmen engaged in manufacturing on small and medium scales was interviewed. There was common agreement that of all the conditions they faced, two were outstanding: Lack of access to market information (i.e., knowledge of future demand) and tight-credit conditions which were manifested in a 90-day waiting period for payment of invoices on goods delivered to the customer.

Sears has dealt with these conditions by supplying sources with concise, well-spaced orders. The corporation's buyers are, in this respect, drawing on a basic buying practice: In line with all Sears buying, demand is projected in terms of a year or, at least, of a season. The buyers generally do not go out and buy 10,000 units. Instead, they buy on a rate of production determined by their earlier projections, which rate is based on records of previous sales, with additions or cutbacks based on developing market trends. A source usually knows pretty well at the outset what the size of his orders will be. Further, Sears likes to point out that "outset" is so timed that the manufacturer is enabled to schedule the part of his production that is to go to Sears at times when he would otherwise experience a slack season. The source is thereby helped to achieve steady, year-round production instead of slack periods alternating with rushes of peak activity.[6]

With his production figures in hand, the source is able to estimate the amount of profits he can plough back into his operations for purposes of expansion. Given the going interest rate of 18 percent on loans from commercial banks, such procedure represents a considerable saving to the source on capital cost. Thus, Sears fills the missing link in Peru between manufacturer and consumer.

19. The Peruvian corporation makes prompt payment for goods delivered. It is standard practice in just about every other retail store in Peru to pay invoices

in 90 days. Thus, the manufacturer is forced to finance the retailer, who hopes to dispose of most of the goods during the 3 months he withholds payment. If the goods do not move, some retailers simply return the remaining stock to the factory and cancel the outstanding amount on unsold items. Sears, on the other hand, pledges to buy the entire order even though the goods may not be turning over well.

The Sears operation has reduced importation of consumer goods. Within the San Isidro store, 20 percent of the 1955 inventory was manufactured locally, while a scant 6 years later the figure had climbed to 75 percent. To achieve this, Sears, Roebuck del Peru, S.A., helped to establish Peru's first suit factory, water-heater plant, and refrigerator manufacturer—among many other businesses. It helped local manufacturers to increase both quality as well as output, and lower costs not only to Sears, but also to other stores. Further, when potential sources lacked the working capital to produce the desired goods, Sears helped them to get started by making loans or giving advances against future deliveries.

The intensification of demand for domestic goods—Industria Peruana—is an incentive to domestic capital formation: One possible mechanism for inducing a higher rate of plough-back into production investment is a rapid expansion in the effective demand for domestically manufactured consumer's goods, which would direct into the hands of vigorous entrepreneurs an increasing proportion of income flows under circumstances which would lead them to expand their own capacity and to increase their requirements for industrial raw materials and semi-manufactured components.[7]

Sears' reliance on local suppliers is stimulating a growing respect for domestic consumer goods. Not only is this taking place through loans and technical assistance supplied to sources, but also by informing the people that, "*Lo que el Peru hace, hace al Peru*"—"This which Peru makes, makes Peru." Thus the concept of economic development is linked in the public's mind to an increased demand for national products.

Source development and the related "Buy Peruvian" campaign have created more jobs. The suit factory which Sears helped to establish employs over 100. A transformer manufacturer now has 22 people working for him. Before, he worked alone. These are but 2 of the 375 firms, small and large, that supply Sears. Their total employment stands at nearly 20,000. Though many were founded before the corporation, their production has grown with Sears sales, which in turn reflect an increased confidence in domestic products as well as normal growth.

Some Case Studies in Source Development

Home Furnishings

Before Sears went to Lima, the manufacturers commonly supplied the consumer directly. Small and medium-size shops produced on a custom-made basis for their clients, who would work out price agreements on what they ordered. When Sears began searching for sources of home furnishings, the buyer found he had to convince the manufacturer that he could make better use of his skills and more profit by abandoning custom-made furniture production, and working with Sears on exclusive designs.

Interiores Modernos. In 1955, all quality mattresses in Peru were imported.

The entire Sears line had to be shipped in through the port of Callao. Then a young Cuban immigrant presented himself in the buying office, shortly before the September opening, to inquire whether there was an interest in purchasing a local product of good quality.

This young entrepreneur had three great assets that the corporation fully appreciated: good business sense; a thorough knowledge of production techniques and the problems raised in a limited market; and capital to invest in the proposed enterprise. In a matter of months, he was turning out the first good-quality Peruvian mattress. He began working in cramped rooms in an old building in Lima. But as production grew, he invested in a site in the industrial area of Callao. Gradually, his work expanded to encompass six basic types of mattresses, each being made in three sizes.

Within 6 months after the Sears opening, this concern, Interiores Modernos, was supplying Sears' entire mattress line, and the corporation happily stopped ordering the more expensive imports. The firm uses almost exclusively Peruvian materials in its production. The major exception is the spring steel, which must come from the United States as there is no local source. Foam rubber and polyester, cloth for the coverings, bed pads and plastic covers are bought from national industry.

In 1957, the buyer of home furnishings found he no longer could rely on his source for upholstered furniture. The material being used for living-room pieces was subquality. Fortunately, Interiores Modernos was familiar with the problem and had enough capital to invest in the equipment necessary to begin working in another line. Over the years, a close working relationship has developed between this firm and the buying office. New designs are now discussed at least once a month. Interiores Modernos has begun selling from its own showroom, carefully avoiding any conflict with its design and production agreement with Sears.

The Sears' buyer emphasizes that the corporation does not want its sources totally dependent upon the store's purchases. In the first place, this could seriously affect the prosperity of a manufacturer and his employes should consumer tastes change and the source's product no longer be marketable. More important, selling to several retailers helps to keep production going and to spread fixed costs to goods being made for other customers. Thus, when Interiores Modernos' percentage of total output taken by the store dropped from 85 percent to 60 percent in 1959–1960, Sears was delighted.

Clisa. When Sears began its business in Peru, there was but one rug factory. The Clisa firm still claims this distinction. Clisa had an excellent reputation in Peru when the corporation turned to it for floor coverings and Clisa's management exemplifies a dynamic sense of entrepreneurship. Clisa had been in business for 5 years by 1955. Beginning on a small scale in Callao, the three partners moved the factory to Arequipa, Peru's second largest city, situated at 9,000 feet in the southern Andes. Employing roughly 100 workers, the firm took advantage of the new site to purchase raw materials at a lower cost, for Arequipa, the "White City," is the center of the wool and alpaca market of the country. Finished rugs and blankets, produced in a modern, efficient plant, were shipped to a sales office in Lima.

Clisa provided Sears with an already established source for a high-quality product. The firm possessed a plant equipped for cleaning and combing, spinning, dyeing, and weaving. When Clisa approached Sears in 1955, the buyer had little to do but develop a number of exclusive patterns and designs, and settle on a price agreement. During their 6 years as partners, Clisa and Sears, Roebuck del Peru, S.A., have become firm friends. Sears now takes about 30 percent of the Arequipa output for its sales. Other Lima stores do business with them, but they do not work as closely with the firm as the corporation and do not obtain exclusive designs. Clisa, in turn, has expanded manufacturing, and now employs 260 workers. Its products enjoy an excellent reputation and are exported to agents in the United States.

Appliances

There was no local source for appliances when Sears began selling in Lima. The market simply would not support the production necessary to justify a major capital investment. Gradually, as income rose, Sears began developing local suppliers, starting with smaller items. Sewing-machine cabinets and water heaters, transformers for imported appliances, television cabinets and kitchen furnishings were imported and assembled. When the corporation began bringing Japanese sewing machines through Callao by way of the New Orleans Free Port, a demand for wooden cabinets was established.

Sears' buyer used his technical background to solve a number of production difficulties. For example, when a manufacturer of medicine cabinets refused to use stainless steel for the metal band about the mirror because of the difficulty in working the material, the buyer experimented for 6 months to find a more malleable stainless import to substitute for the nickle-plated brass the source insisted upon using. Having found the material, the buyer designed a 20-ton hydraulic press to shape the strips.

Industrias Reunidas. On July 13, 1961, Sears sold the first refrigerator made in Peru. This event and its background provide an excellent example of the corporation's efforts to build supply sources and substitute local manufacturers for imports as rapidly as possible. It reflects the improved economic conditions that have developed in Peru during the past 6 years. And the introduction of the new product, made by Industria Peruana, provides a good illustration of how the Sears team works.

In 1959, the Lima firm of Industrias Reunidas, S.A., approached Sears to inquire whether the corporation would be interested in marketing a national refrigerator. The idea met with approval for several reasons. The smallest Coldspot refrigerator that the buyer had to offer was the 10.8-cu.-ft. model, and its list price after transportation and import taxes was $2\frac{1}{2}$ times list price in the United States. The local demand for such an expensive refrigerator was limited. Too, there was the problem of projecting inventory requirements over the coming months, complicated by the time consumed in shipping from the United States and the damage incurred in transit. An added inducement came from the background of success Sears had in marketing national refrigerators in Mexico, Colombia, and Brazil.

Industrias Reunidas began putting its proposal into action by commissioning a firm of consulting engineers to make a study of the economics of the project. The report submitted to Industrias Reunidas affirmed that a national refrigerator could be produced at a lower cost than an import could be landed. The study suggested a number of North American firms that might be approached in order to secure a license under which Industrias Reunidas could produce. Most favorable terms were obtained from the Whirlpool International Corporation with the help of Sears; Whirlpool was also manufacturing for Sears in Colombia, Brazil, and Mexico.

On the basis of prior research and the financial reputation of the firm, a $250,000 loan was obtained from the International Finance Corporation of Panama. Thereafter, the project developed rapidly. Contracts were let for capital equipment recommended by Whirlpool representatives who visited the site during construction. Meanwhile, the Industrias Reunidas plant engineer visited factories in the United States, Mexico, and Colombia, all Sears sources, to observe production techniques. He returned from Bogota with a refrigerator that Sears was selling in its Colombian corporation, using it to train assembly line workers.

At the same time, Sears U.S.A., which had been instrumental in obtaining the Whirlpool International, Inc. franchise, sent to Lima a buyer and factory-management expert to advise the buyer how to deal with his new source with regard to contracts, quality standards, and general working relations.

The plant was constructed rapidly. Building of the assembly line had begun in August of 1959. The first unit was completed in June 1961, a record for setting up production of a major appliance in Latin America. Just before presses and ovens began functioning in Lima,

shipments of motors and coils arrived from Italy, while the plastic inner door was delivered by another Sears source. The integrated operations commenced without delay with the labor force of 50 workers.

To assist the source in keeping its production costs as low as possible, Sears has supplied the firm with a breakdown of monthly figures of expected demand for the first year of manufacturing. In addition, the corporation has suggested that Industrias Reunidas open its own retail outlet in Lima Centro—in direct competition with Sears—to help boost sales and lower unit-production costs.

The manufacturer is enthusiastic because he now has a refrigerator that sells for 2,000 soles less than the 10.8-cu.-ft. Coldspot import. He feels that in time he will be able to reach a much greater percentage of the consumer market with the lower price. Further, he is thinking of plans for a 7-cu.-ft. model that would be even less costly.

Dry Goods

Sears has achieved its greatest success in stimulating local manufacturing in the dry-goods industries. Whereas roughly 75 percent of the appliances sold by the corporation are imported, over 95 percent of the dry goods are being made in small factories and shops scattered about the Lima-Callao area.

Compas. As Sears moved into Mexico, Brazil, Colombia, and Venezuela, many long-established attitudes changed. Latin American men wore custom-made suits, trousers, and sport jackets. Low prices, good quality, and fast alterations induced the switch to ready-to-wear. Thus, some time before the first customers were fitted in the Lima clothing departments, the corporation began searching for someone to make ready-to-wear.

The owners of Compas, a small trouser factory—the only such firm in Lima—were approached by Sears in 1954. The Sears buyer for dry goods, accompanied by two Chicago executives from the Sears research laboratory, offered financial and technical aid to assist the firm in producing ready-to-wear suits and jackets. When the partners agreed, patterns were brought down from Chicago. The first order was filled by mid-1955.

To assist in the coming expansion, Sears arranged for partners of Compas to visit U.S. suit factories. Following an intensive examination of these operations, the two purchased necessary production machinery from U.S. makers. On their return to Lima, the partners passed through Colombia, where Sears had established a similar factory. Later, a Compas technician returned to Colombia for a 6-week training visit. Sears arranged for him to study production and design techniques. The corporation advanced funds to Compas against future deliveries. This practice continued for 2 years, until the plant was able to support itself. By 1957, Compas had substituted its boys' and men's suits for the store's imports. As the popularity of ready-to-wear grew, demand for Compas products grew rapidly. In 1956, the partners had a one-story building. Three years later, production required an added floor. A payroll of 30 grew to 250 by 1960.

Last year, Sears bought over 5,000 men's suits. In addition, the corporation ordered sport jackets, boys' suits, and slacks. Yet in total, the Lima buying office took less than 50 percent of Compas' production. Other local clothing stores

have copied Sears by joining the shift from tailor-made clothing, and have become customers of Peru's only fully integrated suit factory. Excluding Sears, Compas deals with 14 stores throughout the country. The company has found that the advice of Sears Peruvian buyers has helped it to improve production. The corporation's orders are seasonally spaced, and each payment is made promptly upon delivery. Compas draws on Sears quota figures to estimate its needs for other customers. Thus, it ties up less working capital in inventory, and turns over its stock regularly.

Compas' production line represents a mixture of U.S. planning adapted to local tastes. Components of each garment are numbered so that the finished product will be of uniform size. This technique was brought down from the United States. At the same time, suits are made with extra-heavy linings, for Peruvians are not accustomed to wearing overcoats.

Last year, Sears introduced washable fabrics in Lima, which Compas used to make up a small volume of coats and slacks. An excellent consumer response has prompted the firm to make this type of garment part of regular production. Other stores are following the Sears lead by placing orders for washables.

Conclusions

Volumes could be written about the progress and profits Sears, Roebuck del Peru has shared with its sources. The examples given illustrate outstanding characteristics of the cooperation between retail store and manufacturer:

(a) A vital link between producer and consumer, scarcely existent in Peru prior to 1955, has been created. By projecting demand over relatively long periods of time, the corporation has helped its sources to improve quality, lower costs, and increase production.

(b) In many countries, technical and financial assistance that has fostered import substitution has been provided.

(c) Often the dynamic character of the local supplier, coupled with a fast-growing market, has been more of a stimulus to greater productivity than the Sears buyer.

(d) Experience in other Latin American countries has given a pattern for building local sources.

(e) National saving in Peru has been promoted through investment in capital goods by Sears' sources.

In Peru, Brazil, Colombia, Mexico, Venezuela, and to a lesser degree Panama, Costa Rica, and El Salvador, the establishment of a mass distributor has made possible more efficient production, improved product development, lower selling prices, expanded markets, and enhancement of the local economy.

FOOTNOTES

[1] Much of what follows is taken from *Progress and Profits*—The Sears, Roebuck Story in Peru by William R. Fritsch. Published in 1962 by the Action Committee for International Development, Inc.

[2] From *The Story of Sears in America*, a company publication for its employes. Chapter III, "Partners", p. 4.

[3] The *Story of Sears, Roebuck and Co.* (New York: Fairchild Publications, Inc., c. 1961.)

[4] The Industrial Development of Peru, which also considers the reform of banking institutions, government monetary, fiscal policy, etc.

[5] ". . . most of the capital available for investment is owned by a comparatively small group of wealthy persons.

". . . small and medium-sized investors who are not members of the existing financial groups do not feel safe or welcome in investing in industrial ventures. It is clear that in Peru there is no protection for minority shareholders at the present time. There is no effective requirement that companies whose shares are sold to the public must provide adequately detailed or even correct financial statements. There is no control over the financial practices of corporations, and it is clear that certain groups of shareholders may be favored at the expense of others." Arthur D. Little Report, p. 26.

[6] *Catalogues and Counters*, p. 399.

[7] Rostow, W. W., *The Stages of Economic Growth*. (Cambridge: The Cambridge University Press, 1960.)

The Iron and Steel Industry in a Developing Economy

Vice President, Koppers International, C.A.
Pittsburgh, Pennsylvania

Introduction

The establishment of an integrated iron and steel industry in a developing economy creates a great new driving force which experience demonstrates provides the basis for rapid economic, industrial, and social growth, and the decision by a developing nation to create an iron and steel industry begins a long chain of events which require the most careful and professional planning in a large number of fields.

Before a decision of this magnitude is made, responsible officials need to weigh carefully the many considerations involved. This paper is intended to be of assistance in this regard and is divided into three parts: First, prerequisites for building an iron and steel plant; second, the benefits which accrue to the economy when a basic iron and steel industry is established; and third, the step-by-step evolution of such a project.

Prerequisites for Building an Iron and Steel Plant

Despite the attractiveness of the idea of creating an iron and steel facility, there are definite prerequisites which must be fulfilled before any steel-mill project can be wisely undertaken. This cannot be overemphasized.

Whether or not these prerequisites can be fulfilled, however, can be determined only through a very careful survey and analysis by specialists in a number of key areas. These prerequisites are:

(a) Adequate markets—based on present consumption and predictable growth to support a minimum economic-sized plant.

(b) Adequate raw materials at reasonable cost.

(c) Adequate transportation at reasonable cost for raw materials and finished products.

(d) Good site location accessible to raw materials (including water), markets, and labor supply.

(e) A satisfactory financial plan for construction and operation of the plant.

Adequate Markets

None of the benefits of an iron and steel industry is possible, unless there is a sufficient internal market for steel products to support an economically sized steel-producing facility. Therefore, the first step to be taken to determine the economic feasibility of establishing a steel industry is to undertake a well-planned market survey. Quantities of iron and steel imported in the past serve as a convenient starting point.

If the statistics available in the country are inadequate to establish this point, then this information can be obtained from the records of importers of these products. To predict the future growth is sometimes difficult because, in a rapidly developing economy, previous economic history is not indicative of future growth after steel products become available locally at steady prices. Prediction of future trends depends upon a study of conventional indices, such as the Gross National Product, population growth, and combinations of statistical facts which may seem reasonable and relevant in the light of present conditions. Of special significance, here, is the use of information on trends in other developing nations comparing what has happened before and after the building of the steel plant.

Once total steel consumption has been established, it is necessary to spell out the various end-uses of the products. These end-uses include such things as reinforcing rod for concrete construction, round rods for wire and nails, small angles and channels for construction, pig iron for independent foundries, structural shapes for construction of buildings and machinery, flat sheets for siding and roofing, utensils and hollow enamelware, containers, and tinplate.

The quantity of each of the products which the mill is to make must then be carefully estimated. This information is used to determine the size of mill to be designed to satisfy the markets immediately available and as projected for the immediate future. It is important to understand that it is seldom practical to propose a plant that will make all of the sizes or all of the types of steel products that have been imported in the past. It would not be economic to make a small quantity of a given product, particularly if the market forecast for this product were also small. Therefore, it is necessary to design the plant to produce the greatest number of those products which it can make most economically.

It is interesting to note that in steel-plant projects in developing economies there is a pattern of growth which usually begins with the production of merchant products required for construction applications, such as concrete reinforcing bars and angles, and then proceeds eventually to flat steel products necessary to a more highly industrialized economy.

Consideration of all these factors will result in an estimate, by classification of products and individual sizes, of the total iron and steel requirements for the next 10 years which is about as far ahead as one can make a reasonable prediction.

Raw Materials

Accessibility of adequate raw materials at a reasonable cost is vital to the development of the plant. And, as it will be necessary that proven reserves, or assured sources, of the various raw materials shall be available to serve the plant for a period of 20 to 25 years, a scientific program of drilling and testing under competent supervision must therefore be undertaken. This program must prove not only the quantity of the raw materials available, but also their physical and chemical characteristics. The costs of mining and transporting these raw materials to the plant site must also be established, and these costs *must* be reasonable or the economic soundness of the entire project may be jeopardized. If insufficient quantities are available, or poor qualities of raw materials are encountered, it may be necessary to consider importing such materials, or at least importing a portion of the total requirements, if the economics justify doing so.

A firm commitment for adequate supplies of these materials must be obtained at definite prices on which to base the economic viability and financial projection of the project.

Transportation

Next comes accessibility and transportability of raw materials at a reasonable cost. Also, consideration must be given simultaneously to the cost of moving the finished products of the plant to consuming markets. Excessive costs here, even with all other factors favorable, could defeat the project.

The most desirable and cheapest form of transport is by water (river, lake, or ocean). Other methods of transport are railroad, aerial ropeway, and highway. Each method has its own pros and cons as compared with the others. Hence, it is necessary to make a thorough investigation of the cost of transport of materials to and from the various plant sites selected for investigation.

Plant Location

Plant location can often make the difference between profit and loss in steel-plant operation. In addition to the obvious factors of accessibility to raw materials and markets, and the cost of transportation, the land must be obtainable at a reasonable cost. The land must also have good soil-bearing conditions to carry the heavy loads and not require extensive piling or other site-preparation costs. In addition, the site must provide adequate supplies of potable and process water, and be situated so that it will be easily served by good housing, schools, hospitals, utilities, and other facilities for workers and their families. Highways, roads, airports, waterways, and transportation service into the plant are also required for a well-located plant.

In the event that it is necessary to locate the plant in an undeveloped part of the country, it may be necessary to construct a complete town site at that location and provide all the necessities of a town or village. When this happens, it adds to the economic burden of the steel-plant project if the cost of these facilities must be charged to it. Experience indicates, however, that local governments are often willing to subsidize the town-site development in order to make the project possible, to decentralize their industries, and to bring about the development of a new portion of the country. In this event, the iron and steel plant is relieved of this financial and administrative burden.

Financial Plan

Sufficient funds must be provided on reasonable terms to finance the construction and initial operation of the plant. The loans must be on a long-enough term and at low-enough interest rates to permit the plant to be economically viable.

With satisfactory answers to these five prerequisites, possible benefits may now be evaluated and the characteristics of the project determined in terms of plant design, capital cost, financing, and plan of operation.

Benefits

It is well known that the consumption of iron and steel products is a barometer of economic, technical, and social growth. Examples could be cited showing that the advent of an iron and steel plant in some of the recently developing nations resulted in economic advancement. In addition, the development of an iron and steel industry promotes certain other immediate benefits which include local availability of steel products as compared with imports, large-scale employment of local labor, and conservation of foreign exchange.

While the primary benefits created by the introduction of an iron and steel industry are of great importance, the other benefits which are in turn created play a very significant role in spurring economic growth. For instance, it has been learned by experience that for each individual employed directly in an iron and steel mill approximately 8 to 10 persons will find employment in supporting industries such as the mining of iron ore, coal and limestone, and in the trans-

portation services associated with the plant. A tertiary effect is the generation of other smaller servicing businesses that find their mainstay of support in the industries created. In addition to this, as a result of local availability of steel at steady prices, a wide variety of consuming industries come into being for converting the steel-mill products into finished and semifinished goods. The local steel mill provides a basis for confidence among people who desire to go into business because they are assured of a steady supply of these steel products.

Because of their need to import a large number of finished products, many developing countries find themselves with a major problem of conserving foreign exchange. Hence the introduction of an iron and steel industry and the substantial reduction of iron and steel imports which this brings about make it possible to conserve foreign exchange and bring the economy of the country into better balance. The full realization of this saving is made possible when the raw materials for the production of steel are indigenous. Quite obviously, if a steel mill were built on the premise of importing some or most of its raw materials, the advantage which would accrue to the country would be correspondingly reduced.

Because the greatest quantity of products needed initially by a developing economy follows a pattern, it can be stated that even a small steel plant with a capacity of only 150,000 metric tons per year, producing only a partial range of steel products well-selected according to local market demand, may be able to supply a very large percentage of the total finished steel requirements.

Thus we find that in most cases the creation of an iron and steel industry in a developing country introduces a dynamic, driving force that provides a real basis for rapid economic, industrial, and social growth.

Evolution of an Iron and Steel Plant

Size of Plant

Using the information furnished in the market survey, it is possible to determine the size of plant which should be built to satisfy the market for the various products required by the economy. It may be that the required quantities of one product are insufficient to justify expenditure of huge sums for the specialized equipment necessary for its production. For example, if a country had a market for a small quantity of high-quality tinplate for its canning industry, say 20,000 tons of electrolytic grade, and had no use for other flat products, it would be impractical—cost-wise—to build a good flat product mill to produce such small tonnages of this high-quality product. The same would be true if a small quantity (say 5,000 tons) of large structural members or a small quantity of railroad rails were required, provided the facilities for such small-scale production would increase costs beyond the point of economic feasibility.

It is necessary, therefore, to decide on a plant of such size as to produce economically the greatest possible number of products required by the growing economy.

The Iron-Making Process

Once the size of plant has been determined, and the raw material costs and availability established, it then becomes necessary to select the iron-making process best suited to that size of plant and those raw materials. In some developing countries, the selection of a suitable iron-making process is much more complex than in the highly industrialized nations of the world due, generally, to the small plant capacity required, coupled with the lack of one or more of the basic materials in the quality and quantity usually considered acceptable. Subject to the availability of raw materials and the planned size of plant, any of the following processes may be adopted:

(a) *Blast Furnace.* The conventional blast furnace normally operates with high grade, lump iron ore (or sintered or pelletized iron ore) which is low in contaminants such as titanium, zinc, nickel, chrome, copper, and the like. A good grade of metallurigical coke must be used. This type of furnace is highly efficient and is preferred when the capacity required is sufficiently high, and when high grades of iron ore and coking coals are available. It is ideally suited to continuous operation at larger tonnages. If smaller tonnages are required, however, and if good grades of iron ore and coking coal are available, and electric power can be furnished at reasonable rates, then consideration might be given to the iron-making process described below.

(b) *Submerged Arc Electric Smelting.* The submerged-arc electric-smelting furnace may be built for capacities as low as 100 metric tons of pig iron per day. The advantages of this furnace over the blast furnace described above are that it can give acceptable economies at smaller tonnages, and it uses electricity which may be available and cheaper than other sources of heat. The major disadvantage is that, in the larger sizes, it costs more to produce pig iron by this method than by the blast furnace under normal conditions.

(c) *Electric Reduction Processes.* The need for a process that can treat off-grade iron ores, or can use non-coking coals with low- or high-grade iron ores, has been evident for many years. During the past few years a number of such electrical reduction processes (often referred to as direct reduction processes) offering certain technical and economic advantages have evolved. After an exhaustive study of those developed in the past 10 years, Koppers Co. decided that the Strategic-Udy process is the best of these processes applicable to the above conditions. The Strategic-Udy iron-making process heats and partially reduces the iron ore, coal, and limestone in a rotary kiln. This heated and partially reduced mixture is then introduced as a free-flowing sinter into an electric furnace where the final reduction takes place. It is not able to compete with the blast furnace when tonnages are large and other conditions are proper for that type of operation. However, if the capacity of the plant is small, if the available iron ore contains copper, nickel, chrome, titanium, or the like in substantial quantities, or if only non-coking coal, anthracite, or lignite is available, the Strategic-Udy process can produce pig iron under these conditions which are technically and/or economically unsuitable for the blast furnace or the submerged-arc electric furnace. The significant advantage to a developing economy of using the Strategic-Udy process is that it may use the locally available source of non-coking coals and off-grades of iron ore. The same coals (whether lignite, anthracite, or non-coking bituminous) may be used also to produce comparatively low-cost electric power. Especially significant to the developing nations is the fact that this process, operating at a capacity of approximately 100,000 metric tons per year, can produce pig iron cheaper than the conventional processes operating at this capacity. In addition, this process can make full use of fine iron ores without sintering.

(d) *Scrap melting.* Still another alternative exists for the developing nation, namely, the melting of available scrap. However, a scrap-melting operation generally serves as only the beginning of a steel plant since such an installation is dependent upon the continued availability of scrap. In some nations there exists initially sufficient scrap to support such a facility but the scrap gradually disappears and imports of scrap are required, depleting the foreign exchange which most developing nations are attempting to conserve. The process unit in which the scrap-melting can take place depends upon many factors, the most important being the source of heat. A cold-charge, open-hearth furnace may be used, fired either by oil or gas. If there is reasonably priced electric power an electric melting furnace is ideal, followed by the usual metal-processing facilities as dictated by economics. If electric power is not readily available in sufficient quantities, then the hot-blast cupola offers certain advantages for the production of pig iron. The hot-blast cupola, however, requires the use of metallurgical grade coke. In some of the developing nations, pending development of a market sufficiently large to support an integrated steel plant, it may be advantageous to start with a scrap-melting operation to be expanded later to include more basic metal-producing facilities. However, because of the need to furnish scrap iron from local sources on a continuing basis, the plant would have to be small in size and would, therefore, be capable of producing only a limited line of products. If the initial requirements were small enough, however, this initial plant could be designed for later expansion into an integrated iron and steel plant.

Steel-Making Process

The selection of the process for converting the pig iron or molten iron to steel is also a vital decision. It is dependent on the type of iron produced from the raw materials and the capacity of the installation under consideration. Each of the various available processes has unique advantages and disadvantages.

About 60 years ago, most steel manufactured in the world was made by the so-called "Bessemer Process," which consisted of blowing air through the bottom of a refractory-lined vessel containing molten iron. In the United States, Bessemer steel was all made in acid or siliceous refractory-lined vessels and it was necessary that the molten iron be low in contaminants, such as phosphorus and sulphur, since neither was removed in the process. In some parts of Europe a similar pneumatic process became widely used with vessels having a basic refractory lining which was necessary because of large amounts of phosphorus in the molten iron which had to be removed by means of a basic flux such as lime. The process of making steel by this method from high-phosphorus iron came to be known as the "Thomas Process." Both

of these pneumatic processes produced steels limited in their useful application since they are relatively high in nitrogen which was picked up from the air blast.

About 1870, the open-hearth steel-making process was invented by Siemens. Adoption of this process in the United States was very rapid and, by 1905, about half of all steel ingots produced in the United States were made by this method. Use of the process continued to spread and, by 1951, it accounted for approximately 87 percent of the steel-producing capacity of the United States. This process permits a wider range of quality steels than the Bessemer process.

Some years ago steel manufacturers began using relatively pure oxygen as the oxidizing agent, the iron being contained in a vessel similar to a Bessemer shell. Oxygen at high pressure was applied to the molten iron by means of a top lance. This process has gained increasing favor in the past 10 years because it makes steel of as high a grade as the open hearth and because, for a new installation, the initial capital investment is likely to be lower.

If reasonably priced electric power is available, electric refining furnaces may be economical to use due to their inherent flexibility and adaptability to comparatively low capacities.

There are other generally accepted and widely used methods of refining pig iron into steel, but, for the purposes of this paper, the discussion has been narrowed to the better known and more widely used processes.

Billets and Slabs

The selection of a method for the production of billets and slabs is of vital significance. Billets are normally square bars varying in size from 2 in. x 2 in. to

8 in. x 8 in. from which merchant products are made.

34. Slabs, rolled to produce flat products such as sheets and plate, vary in thickness up to 12 in. and in width up to 75 in. The type of process used to produce these billets and slabs has a direct bearing on the cost of producing the finished products as well as on the initial capital investment.

In small-size plants where large capital investment cannot be supported, a method of producing billets and slabs directly from the molten steel has been developed—the continuous casting process. In such a process, the slabs and billets are continuously cast and cut into desired lengths by means of an oxygen-acetylene torch.

By eliminating the need for ingot molds, soaking pits, blooming and slabbing mills, and billet mills, initial capital investment and production costs are reduced. It is probable that the continuous casting process would be more appropriate for a developing nation whose market is in process of expanding.

Rolling Mills

It is necessary to determine which combination of rolling mills will most economically produce the immediate requirements and, at the same time, have excess inherent capacity to take care of the future demand predicted by the market study. Normally in a developing economy smaller merchant products such as rods for concrete reinforcing, small angles and channels for building construction, and round rods for wire and nails constitute the bulk of initial demand. These items can be produced economically, if nothing more is needed, in a smaller merchant mill. Next, the economy begins to demand larger steel sections and shapes. However, a much larger capital investment is required and a greater demand for these products is necessary to justify the additional facilities.

As the economy continues to develop a market is created for flat products—sheets and plate. The market study will have determined current and future demand of the types of flat products required. Many countries embarking on an industrialization program have need for a small quantity of flat products—sheets and plate for corrugated roofing and siding; black sheet for hollow enamelware, for barrels and cans, and for tinplate. This need may amount to only 40,000 or 50,000 metric tons and, therefore, a large reversing hot-strip mill or the even larger capacity continuous hot-strip mill could not be justified.

A possible solution to this situation and one that has been used in many countries is the hand-sheet mill which, as its name implies, uses more manual labor in its application and less highly automated machinery. The hand-sheet mill has the advantage of a lower economic break-even point and consequently is well-suited to fulfill the requirements of a smaller market.

Unit cost of production of the hand sheet mill will be higher than that of a continuous hot-strip mill producing above its break-even point but the unit cost could be far less than that of the larger mill if the latter were producing only 40,000 to 50,000 tons of product.

It is necessary, therefore, to design the rolling mills to take care of the immediate needs of the market, as projected to the end of the first 5 years of operation (this will normally be 8 to 10 years after it has been decided to build the plant)—so as to produce the most product for the least capital and operating cost.

Source of Electric Power

The source and cost of electric power is important to the steel-making facility whether it is based on the conventional iron-and-steel-making processes, or based on electrical reduction and refining processes. In the latter cases, it is more important and forms a larger part of the iron-and-steel-making cost—supplanting the coal or coke in part. But whatever the iron-and-steel-making processes, the cost of electric power is important to the operation of the rolling mills and the multitude of auxiliaries used throughout the plant. In many nations, sufficient local power exists in the form of hydro-electric or thermal plants. The use of these particular sources are, to a large part, dependent upon the availability of power in adequate quantities and dependability of the supply.

In many instances, due to the unusually large demands and an already overloaded grid, it has been found both practical and economical to construct captive-power plants. This has the added advantage of giving complete control of the power source to the steel-plant management and is not subject to power interruptions due to breakdowns in the distribution system outside the plant boundaries.

General Facilities

Provision must be made within the plant boundaries for other utilities such as potable and process water, electric lighting and power, sewage, etc., as well as for roads, railroad, repair shops, warehouses, first-aid stations, and the like. If the steel plant is located in a remote area, it may be necessary to build shops capable of repairing almost any of the equipment in use in the plant. This will necessitate the establishment of the following maintenance departments:

(a) Mechanical.
(b) Electrical.
(c) Mason.
(d) Blacksmith and Welding.
(e) Carpentry.
(f) Instrument Repair.
(g) Locomotive and Car Repair.
(h) Auto and Truck Garage.

The Utility Department controls the supply of water, power, steam, oxygen, compressed air, etc. It is responsible for the maintenance of all potable and process water lines as well as fire lines; for the operation and maintenance of power generation and distribution facilities as well as tie-ins with other utilities.

Adequacy of Infrastructure

In selecting the location for a steel plant consideration must be given to the availability (or lack thereof) of all facilities (the infrastructure) needed to support such a plant. In general, these facilities may be divided into those required for the people working in the plant and those required to support the plant itself. The workers and their families need housing, schools, churches, hospitals, stores, water, lights, sewage, transportation, and other facilities.

The plant requires developed highways, railroads, and/or waterways for low-cost transport of raw materials and supplies to the plant, and finished products to the consuming market. Potable and process water must be brought to the plant and effluent taken from it. Electric power, fuel oil, natural gas, or other power sources must be made available.

Before any plan can be finalized for the construction of a steel plant, all of the infrastructure problems must be solved—who will furnish the services, or the money to supply them. Wherever possible, it is highly desirable that all supporting facilities (the infrastructure) be supplied to the steel plant so that it is not burdened with the cost of the facilities or their administration. The steel plant is then left to its primary task of making steel.

Profitability

Because of the heavy initial investment required for a steel plant, large capital loans are needed to finance the construction and operation of the plant. These loans, obtained from private and public financing institutions, must be repaid with interest. In addition, shareholders will demand that they be given a fair return on their investment. Therefore, the steel plant must be designed to hold all costs to the minimum so as to make it a profitable operation.

Private enterprise, working in cooperation with government, mindful of its duties to produce efficiently and for profit, should be the goal for the majority ownership of the steel plant. Many governments have stated their intention of supporting private enterprise by agreeing to sell their interests to the private sector as private investment capital becomes available.

Profit, of course, is the difference between income (which is the total value of the steel products sold) and cost (which is the sum of the direct operating cost, the overhead expense, and the financing charges). Therefore, the selling prices of steel products which create income deserve our consideration. In most instances, it has been found that prices being paid for steel by non-steel-producing countries are high enough to justify construction of local steel plants (provided raw materials, power and other necessities are available). If the plant is small, steel products cannot be provided as cheaply

as they can be produced in the huge mills in Europe or America. It may require, therefore, that the new small plant be given a modicum of protection by its government during its formative years. It normally will not be necessary to raise tariffs, but it may be necessary to continue existing tariffs for a period of years. In addition, provision may have to be made to prevent the sale of steel products in the local market at exceptionally low prices during periods of over-production in the larger mills abroad. This protection may take the form of a program of import licensing for the products produced by the new local steel mill.

It is, therefore, essential to the economic viability of a project that decisions as to raw materials, location of the plant, source and cost of electric power, and methods of transport be made strictly on the basis of economics. This is true because a small new mill, with its high-capital charges, newly trained operating and management personnel, newly developed sources of raw materials and services, must be given every possible assistance to stand on its own feet without subsidy—and to make a profit for its owners, public or private, so that it may grow and expand, and assist in the industrialization of the nation.

Corporate and Capital Structure

The corporate structure of the steel plant will depend on the source of capital and the policy of the government. In most developing countries there are insufficient funds in the private sector to finance the development of a steel mill, and the local government may furnish some or all of the funds. In such cases, the local government may pledge itself either to take a subordinate position to private owners, or offer to sell its shareholdings to private owners in the future. The capital required to build and operate the plant normally comes from two sources: the shareholders or owners of the business, and long-term loans from private and public lending institutions.

Although steel is a basic industry, it is not one in which high profits can be expected. At the same time it is an industry in which capital requirements are high. It is desirable, therefore, that loans provide a substantial part of the capital required to build the plant, that these loans be long-term, and that the interest rate be reasonably low.

A medium-size steel plant producing an adequate mixture of steel products has an excellent chance of success provided the following conditions exist:

(a) Adequate market for its output.

(b) Suitable long-term debt financing.

(c) Reasonably established sales prices for its products.

(d) Adequate raw materials and power reasonably priced.

(e) A mutual determination by government and business for its success.

An important source of long-term loan capital has been the various lending institutions in Europe and the United States, both public and private.

Another source of financial assistance has been the equipment suppliers who have been willing to extend long-term credits for the purchase of their equipment. In some instances these suppliers have assumed a financial interest in the operation by purchasing shares of stock in the company.

The raising of capital within the borders of the nation through the sale of stock to insurance companies, banks and other lending institutions, and the general public is recommended since this ensures active participation by those most affected by the results of the steel plant.

At the same time, it helps to develop the private sector as a moving force in developing the industrial strength of the nation.

Technical and Management Assistance

The management and operation of a steel plant is a complex task requiring many highly trained specialists in many different fields. It is not to be expected that all of these qualified specialists will be available in a developing country and it will, therefore, be necessary to import additional specialists. The number of such imported technicians and managers will depend on the local availability of skilled technicians and managers and the number of local employees who can be trained during the period of plant construction. However, specialists have to be imported at the start to inaugurate an interim program for training local personnel immediately—training in all phases of plant operation and maintenance, as well as training in management and administration not only on-the-job but also abroad. The president, sales manager, plant manager, plant superintendent, safety director, superintendents of the various departments, the chief of the laboratory, the operators of furnaces and rolling mills, the superintendents of electrical and mechanical maintenance must be trained to assume their responsibilities. As soon as they are qualified the imported specialists are released.

It is vitally important, therefore, that the company selected to furnish the technical and management assistance to the new steel plant be one with a background and history of achievement in this field where unusual technical ability and previous experience are so vital.

The objectives of the technical and management assistance group must be to obtain the most efficient and economical operation of the steel plant and to complete the training of the local employees of the plant at the earliest possible date so that they themselves can progressively assume in the shortest possible time all the management, administrative, and technical positions in the plant.

If competent personnel are available for the management, administrative, and supervisory positions in the office and in the plant, then the technical-assistance group will furnish only advice and guidance in the execution of their duties. If, on the other hand, such personnel are not available locally, then the technical-assistance group will help the steel plant recruit adequate talent from abroad and supervise the training of local personnel to take over these responsibilities after a period of training. It is necessary that the technical- and management-assistance group align themselves with the steel plant on a longterm, continuing basis because it takes many years to bring a steel plant into full and efficient operation. When that point has been reached, the plant will undoubtedly have to be expanded to take care of the market for steel products which has been growing rapidly because of the availability of locally produced products at steady prices.

Conclusion

It will be seen, therefore, as emphasized at the opening of the discussion, when a developing country has economically and technically usable raw materials and a sufficient market for steel-plant products, building its own iron and steel industry will usually benefit its entire economy, expand its industrial base, and accelerate its social progress.

Food Processing and the Developing Society

JAMES E. WICKERSHAM

President, International Operations, Foremost Dairies, Inc., San Francisco, California

Introduction

For years man has been engaged in finding ways of increasing agricultural output. He has developed dependable and stable sources of food to provide for better living standards. Those countries which have achieved a high level of technological development in food processing have benefited from tremendous economies in food production, conservation, and distribution. Throughout this paper, I will attempt to illustrate these technological, social, and economic benefits that have accrued to countries which have developed food-processing industries and to relate these experiences to the particular needs and conditions in developing countries.

The first section of this paper is a brief discussion of food processing, recent innovations in food technologies, and an appraisal of the function this industry has in the United States and in other food-processing countries. The second part is concerned with food processing in the less developed countries and in particular with a few countries which have been the beneficiaries of new technologies introduced by private foreign sources. The experience of our firm in the dairy industry both in the United States and in the less developed areas where we have plants will illustrate how specific technologies have been made to work. My final interest is to suggest some practical opportunities that specific new technologies could afford for solving some of the basic problems.

Food Processing Description

Some of the objectives of food processing are: (a) To overcome dependence on seasonal or annual crop production and the concomitant feast or famine; (b) to minimize deterioration, spoilage, and resulting waste; and (c) to retain palatability and nutritional qualities of the food.

Foods are made available for longer periods of time by the use of: (a) *elevated temperatures* for the heat treatment required for pasteurization, and sterilization as in canning; (b) *lowered temperatures* for cooling—as in the ordinary "ice box" or refrigerator, cold storage—from $-18°C$ to $-23°C$, and freezing—$-23°C$ or lower; (c) *removal of moisture* by one or more methods such as spray, or drum drying, and baking; and (d) *harmless additives* (formerly and often still called preservatives) such a propionates in bread, sorbic acid in cheese, salting and brining, and pickling (vinegar).

All of these methods succeed in inhibiting or destroying microorganisms, the major spoilage agents in food. The principal food processes—canning, freezing, and dehydration—are designed to keep food in one or more of its usable forms. These methods are most efficient when raw foods of high quality are processed.

New Processes

New processes which are being developed may have considerable impact on the future use of older methods. Briefly, these processes include:

(a) *Liquid nitrogen freezing.* Raw or precooked food is precooled with a spray of liquid nitrogen, then passed through an immersion bath of liquefied gas. The product is frozen to $-18°$ C or lower in less than 5 minutes. Small pieces of food are frozen almost instantaneously. Rapidity of freezing is the distinctive advantage of liquid nitrogen over the conventional methods of freezing. There is promise too of new-product development through ability to freeze foods which have defied successful freezing by any other method. Unless there is a low-priced source of liquid nitrogen available, the process is not economical. Byproduct liquid nitrogen is obtained usually from the manufacture of liquid oxygen.

(b) *Irradiation of foods.* Food irradiation is a method which employs ionizing radiations to reduce or completely destroy the micro-organisms responsible for most food spoilage. Electron beams (from linear accelerators, for example) and gamma rays (from radium, cobalt-60, or cesium-137) are used as sources of radiation. Irradiation of foods is still very much in

the experimental stage. Progress is being made. However, we must remember that a complex technological innovation may require 15 to 20 years or more to go through its development period and reach general acceptance. The simple innovation of frozen foods took 15 years to get started. Considering historical precedents, food irradiation may not be off schedule. Among the several potential uses of irradiation for food processing are:

(i) Surface pasteurization of fresh foods in flexible packages. Shelf-life of fruits, vegetables, and meats is extended even under the usual handling conditions. Refrigeration of these irradiated foods further extends the shelf-life. The low doses of energy used have little effect on the food's taste or physical makeup.

(ii) Sterilization of foods by use of high-radiation dosage is not as promising as the pasteurization. Undesirable changes in color, taste, odor, and texture must be overcome.

(iii) Other uses of irradiation that have been investigated include: inhibition of sprouting in stored potatoes and onions; destruction of direct infestation in stored grains, spices, dried fruits, and vegetables. As techniques for irradiating food are perfected, highly seasonal perishables will be protected through pasteurization. Sterilization of foods by radiation eventually will become more important than pasteurization. Sterilized foods would be grocery-shelf items along with conventional canned goods.

(c) *Freeze-drying.* The food to be dried is quick frozen. Drying is then carried out in a high vacuum, the process permitting rapid conversion of the water from the frozen into the vapor state without going through the liquid phase. Moisture is lost from the surface of the food leaving a porous product which greatly facilitates rehydration when the food is prepared for consumption. Drying foods at low temperatures minimizes bacterial growth, enzyme activity, and undesirable chemical changes. Damage to color, flavor, and texture is low. The reconstituted food is superior in these respects to conventionally dried or concentrated products and generally equal to frozen foods. Freeze-dried foods need no refrigerated storage, weigh less because of the loss of moisture, and are easier to handle than foods processed by other methods. Freeze-dried foods do not have to thaw but merely be rehydrated before cooking or serving. Before this process becomes widespread, cost of processing equipment must be reduced, freezing rates determined to improve rehydration, and drying times reduced.

(d) *Dehydro-freezing.* The method consists of partial dehydration followed by freezing of the food. Food is dried in a hot-air stream to aproximately 50 percent of its original weight, then quick-frozen. Storage requires deepfreeze temperatures. Rehydration is needed at the time of use. Conventional dried fruits and vegetables, while the least costly, suffer serious quality losses in drying and storage. Frozen foods have excellent quality but also high costs. The combination of these two processes into dehydro-freezing has several distinct advantages: less bulk, weight, drip, and better moisture control in remanufacturing than frozen products; easier and more complete rehydration; better color, flavor, texture;

and lower sulfite levels than dried products. The method is applicable to a number of foods. Currently it is applied commercially to apple slices, peas, and the major citrus juices.

(e) *Foam-mat drying.* This method involves making a stiff foam by whipping air or an inert gas into a concentrated foodstuff in the presence of an edible foam stabilizer. The stabilized foam is deposited as a uniform layer onto perforated trays; the trays pass over an air blast to perforate the foam and thus greatly increase the surface available for heat transfer and evaporation of water. This perforated mat of foamed-food concentrate then passes through a dryer which decreases product moisture to 2 to 2.5 percent. Materials that have been foam-mat dried include water infusions of tea and coffee, fruit purees, and extracts of beef and chicken. Flavor and color of these foam-mat products are reported to be superior to those dried by other methods. The process obviously is limited to liquids and concentrates as foaming is required. It is not suited to products sensitive to oxygen in the drying air. Volume and weight reduction of the dried food is approximately the same as with spray and drum-dried foods.

(f) *Aseptic canning.* This treatment of foods that have been sterilized by a high-temperature, short-time process is receiving a great deal of attention in several countries. The high-temperature, short-time sterilizing process in conjunction with aseptic canning minimizes the heat damage that accompanies traditional long-time processing of food. The new method retains more of the desirable properties of foods. In addition, large containers—

we have used 210 liter drums—can be sterilized and filled aseptically. Foremost Dairies has pioneered in the research and commercial application of these processes. Milk, evaporated milk, processed cheese, fruit juices, and similar products processed by this method provide a more natural tasting and more nutritious product than the same foods processed by conventional canning methods.

The Value of the Food Processing Industry to a Country

In the countries of Western Europe, North America, Oceania, and Japan, the food-processing industry (through technical progress) has brought many benefits, in addition to plentiful and wholesome food. A smaller proportion of the population is engaged in producing foodstuffs on the farm. Basically, food processing and the allied technologies required to keep it efficient prevent the loss of the food that is produced. Thus, the efforts of more members of a well-fed population can be directed to providing manufactured products and services. These are the material things that lead to what is called a better standard of living.

The improved nutrition and resulting better health and well-being of the people have brought pronounced increases in the productivity of labor, technical achievement, and economic activity. Table 1 lists a few characteristics of the food-processing countries. Table 2 gives the output of processed food in various countries.

In considering the dietary (or nutritional) status observed in the technologically less developed countries, the relationship and importance of food and food processing to man's well-being becomes more clearly defined. The acceptance of initial technical help from outside sources can be the catalyst to a continuing and expanding technological achievement in the developing country.

Direct Application of Food Technology to Developing Countries

I would like to discuss the part our industry, the dairy industry, has played in improving the well-being of people in developing countries. A study of the dietary needs of these countries shows that additional protein and vitamins would be of material benefit in two ways: (a) preventing and eliminating clinical symptoms of protein and vitamin deficiency, and (b) maintaining a better nutritional status in the well person. Milk is widely considered one of the best of foods. The biological value of its protein is seldom equalled in any other food. It is unique in its variety of minerals. With its complement of carbohydrate, fat, and vitamins, one can see why milk is referred to as "nature's most nearly perfect food."

The approach needed in establishing modern dairy facilities in a developing country depends to a great extent on local conditions:

(a) *No appreciable dairying.* Establish a plant for "recombined whole milk" and milk products.

(b) *Small amount of dairying.* Establish a plant for recombined milk, and as dairy herds increase in size integrate the use of the fresh and recombined milks.

(c) *Developed dairying.* Here, the local supply of fresh milk is processed. The ingredients for recombined milk, if economical to use in comparison to local milk, are used in milk products other than fluid milk.

TABLE 1. *Economic characteristics of principal food processors*

Indicator	Unit	Year	United States	Canada	United Kingdom	France	Germany	Italy	Netherlands	Japan
National Income—per capita [1]		1960	2,297	1,540	1,084	961	967	509	804	341
Personal Consumption Expenditure—Proportion of GNP [2]	Percent	1960	64	65	66	65	n.a.	63	56	54
Food Expenditures as Portion of Personal Consumption Expenditures [3]	Percent	1960	21	20.7	32.7	37.8	33.6	46.5	33.7	47
Labor Force—Agriculture [4]	Percent	1961	7.6	23.4	4.3	27.6	16.2	40.4	20.7	40.1
Labor Force—Manufacturing	Percent	1961	32.8	35.1	47.6	36.1	47.7	37.1	35.7	24.0
Labor Force—Services	Percent	1961	59.6	51.5	48.1	36.3	36.1	32.5	43.6	35.9
Fertilizer Consumption per septia [5]	Kilograms	1959	38.1	15.8	24.4	43.1	44.2	17.3	36.8	166.8
Tractors in Use [6]	Number	1959	4,770,000	399,686	433,870	626,500	778,003	225,224	64,200	650
Caloric Consumption—per capita, per day [7]	Number	1959–60	3,130	3,150	3,290	2,940	2,890	2,710	2,970	2,210
Protein Consumption—per capita, per day	Grams	1959–60	93	96	87	98	78	79	80	68
Animal Protein—per capita, per day	Grams	1959–60	66	64	52	52	46	27	45	18
Food Supplies Available for Consumption: [8]										
Cereals	Percent	1959–60	9.4	10.7	13.1	15.5	13.8	25.6	13.0	40.0
Starchy roots	Percent	1959–60	6.7	9.6	13.8	14.5	22.6	9.5	13.7	17.5
Sugar	Percent	1959–60	5.8	6.8	7.9	4.6	4.4	3.6	6.0	3.7
Pulses	Percent	1959–60	.9	.8		1.6	.7	2.3	.6	4.8
Vegetables	Percent	1959–60	13.8	11.7	9.2	18.6	6.5	24.9	9.4	19.0
Meat	Percent	1959–60	13.4	12.4	11.0	10.7	8.8	4.9	6.7	1.6
Eggs	Percent	1959–60	2.8	2.9	2.3	1.6	2.1	1.7	1.8	1.1
Fish	Percent	1959–60	1.1	1.1	1.6	1.1	1.1	1.7	.8	6.1
Milk [9]	Percent	1959–60	43.6	41.6	36.7	30.1	35.8	24.1	44.1	5.3
Fats	Percent	1959–60	3.0	3.0	3.4	2.5	4.7	2.9	3.8	1.1

[1] United Nations Statistical Yearbook, 1961. Estimates derived from official population and national income data of respective countries.
[2] Ibid.
[3] United Nations, Yearbook of National Accounts Statistics, 1961.
[4] United Nations Statistical Yearbook, 1961.
[5] Foreign Agriculture Organization, *Production Yearbook*, Vol. 14, 1960.
[6] Ibid.
[7] Food and Agriculture Organization of the United Nations. The State of Food & Agriculture, 1961 United States and Japan data for 1959.
[8] Ibid. United States and Japan data for 1959.
[9] Milk and milk products estimated in terms of liquid milk.

TABLE 2. *World output of processed foods (output in thousand metric tons)*

	Whole milk equivalent per capita consumption lbs.[2]	Fluid milk	Condensed evaporated milk[3]	Nonfat dry milk	Butter	Cheese	Meat	Wine	Beer	Wheat flour	Sugar	Margarine	Olive oil	Canned deciduous fruit 000 cases 24/2½'s	Canned fish	Salted fish	Animal feeds
World (Output)[1]		335,600	2,282	1,369	4,776	1,943	55,900	239,000	381,000	47,387	49,223	3,480	1,250	88,718	1,010	1,309	2,316
		Percent of total	*Percent of total*	*Percent of total*	*Percent of total*	*Percent of total*	*Percent of total*	*Percent of total*	*Percent of total*	*Percent of total*	*Percent of total*	*Percent of total*	*Percent of total*	*Percent of total*	*Percent of total*	*Percent of total*	*Percent of total*
North America	n.a.	19					23	5	34	29	27	23		72	25	5	36
South America	n.a.	6					9	9	5	10	12				3	3	
Europe	n.a.	38					25	72	49	49	22	60	78	3	32	38	15
Asia and Near East	n.a.	12					2		3	8	16	19	7		15	15	26
Africa	n.a.	3					2	11	1	2	6				9		12
Oceania	n.a.	4					4		3	3	5	1		3			9
Selected Countries																	
United States	653	17	42.8	66.5	14.0	37.4	22	4	28	24	5	21		72	22	4	36
Canada	894	3	6.7	6.9	3.3	2.7	1		3	4		2		3	3	1	
United Kingdom	835	6	8.1	4.7	1.6	5.8	3		11	8	2	10		3	8		5
France	853	3	8.5		4.6	17.2	4	25	5		2	3					
Germany	803	6	16.9	6.0	8.9		4	2	12	7	3	17			10	4	
Italy	449	2						28			3		23	3	2	2	
Netherlands	725	2	17.6	4.6	2.0	10.3	4		2	1	1	7			1	3	3
Japan	32		2.4						2	5		1			10	10	12
Argentina	n.a.	1					4	7	2		2						
Brazil	n.a.	1	3.0				3		3		6	1					
Australia	966	2		2.8	4.0	2.7				5	2			3	2		
New Zealand	1,320	2		3.1	4.5	5.1											
Mexico	207	4															
Venezuela	310	6															
India	130	2															
Pakistan	103																

Source: Food Engineering, July 1962. Data for year 1959. Percentages are rounded; less than 1% not given. World total includes some countries not included in specified regions.

[1] Excludes U.S.S.R.

[2] National Dairy Council, *How Americans Use Their Dairy Foods*, 1962. Japan—U.S.D.A. Impact of U.S. Nonfat Dry Milk in Japan 1948–59, June 1960, p. 9.

[3] All other data on dairy products taken from U.S. Department of Agriculture, *Foreign Agricultural Circular*, May 1962.

Since 1946, recombined milk has been used to supply fresh-tasting fluid milk and milk products to areas lacking an adequate supply of dairy foods. Fresh whole milk is separated. The skim milk is dried. The milk fat is dehydrated to practically 100 percent milk fat. These two parts of milk are processed and packaged separately and therefore have an excellent storage life. At destination the two parts of milk are recombined with purified water, homogenized, pasteurized, and filled into bottles or cartons. Distribution is carried out in the usual manner.

Fortunately, as development of the local dairy herds progresses, it is relatively simple to adapt the recombined milk plant to a fresh-milk operation. The majority of the equipment is the same in both type plants. Fresh-milk handling requires only the addition of incoming milk-holding and -cooling tanks.

Thailand

Our experience in Thailand is an excellent example of cooperative achievement by a private foreign company, the Thai government, and local interests. In 1956, when our company entered this project, fresh milk was not consumed in Thailand and no local dairy industry existed. There were, however, considerable quantities of sweetened condensed milk imported into the country.

In the intervening years, this project has been successful in making available a broad range of dairy products. The infant dairy industry is supplying its first fresh milk and shows every indication of healthy growth. There is an increasing consumption of fluid milk and ice cream in Bangkok. In reflecting on this progress in Thailand, it becomes obvious that the country is realizing a better nutritional status, an expansion of technical skills in several fields, a broadened perspective and economic goals. Other than a few of our industry's technicians, all of the employees in the dairy project are Thai citizens.

This partnership effort is aided significantly by the Thai government, which provides a climate for enterprise and individual incentive. Recently the Thai government has approved construction of other dairy plants which will utilize locally produced sugar and other materials.

Japan

In 1947, milk drinking in Japan was not popular—especially among men. Our company's primary job in Japan was to supply the Americans living there with recombined milk products. In our plants, the personnel were Japanese citizens whom we trained in dairy technology. Also, we provided technical assistance to the established dairy processors. The stimulus has resulted in the establishment of the Japan Dairy Council. This group is carrying out an educational program on the nutritive value of milk. In a 10-year period, imports of dried skim milk increased 1200 percent. Their own domestic milk production increased over 700 percent. The net result of these operations has been a tremendous increase in the consumption of milk by the Japanese, a betterment of the nutritional status of the people, and a growth in their dairy industry.

Venezuela

In those countries where milk and milk products are an established part of the dietary habits of the people, the fresh-fluid and powdered-milk industries can be developed further within the country. This has happened in a spectacular manner in Venezuela through the combined efforts of: (a) a private foreign dairy company supplying the technology, (b) local interests, and (c) well-planned help to the dairy farmers by the Venezuelan government.

In 1949, when our firm, in conjunction with the International Basic Economy Corporation and Venezuelan farmer investors, began operations, fluid-milk consumption was less than ten million liters per year. Today this project has grown to six plants across the country. Fresh-milk consumption has reached over three hundred million liters and is still increasing. Dried-milk production, which has been encouraged by other private foreign companies and ourselves, has risen from three million pounds in 1945 to thirty million pounds in 1960.

India

The "Bombay milk project" is an excellent example of well-managed efforts by: (a) the state and city government of Bombay, and (b) international resources. The project is well-deserving of the publicity given it. At the time it was started, none of the milk available to Bombay consumers was subject to modern processing.

The overall operation centralized and coordinated the production, processing, distribution, and pricing of milk and milk products. In spite of the growth of the project and increase in processing facilities, the supply of milk did not meet consumers' needs. To help meet this need, and meet it economically, the project introduced "toned" milk—a form of recombined milk.

Buffalo milk (7.5 percent fat; 9.3 percent solids not-fat) is recombined with skimmed milk solids and water to provide a fluid milk of 3.5 percent fat and 9 percent solids not-fat. The project has assured a safe source of wholesome and nutritious milk for a sizeable number of Bombay consumers.

Thus the "toned" milk provides a method of distributing the high-fat buffalo milk into a nutritionally more balanced product.

Conclusions

From the several examples of successful efforts between private outside technical resources, local government, and local industrial interests that have been discussed, the time-tested and practical method for bringing food technologies and related skills to an interested country is through a partnership working arrangement between: (a) the government of the interested country creating incentives and assisting in promotion of private industrial development, (b) local resources and local initiative of individuals of the interested country, and (c) a private outside source of talent thoroughly versed and knowledgeable in the desired technology.

The Significance of the Forest Products Industry in Economic Development

CLARK C. HERITAGE
Consulting Engineer,
Tacoma, Washington

The occurrence of forest cover of some kind is almost universal. It is now recognized that the precise species available is not of major importance. Because of the great variety of possible products and the wide choice of process steps, almost any species can be put to profitable use.

There are some who fear that the use of wood is declining and that it may come to an ignominious end in the not distant future. What they are really thinking about are some contemporary products made of wood, not wood itself. Some products decline, others taking their places, grow. But the commodity, wood, is used in ever-increasing volume. There is no evidence to support the fear that wood use will decline.

The tree-farm concept of sustained yield and crop harvest in perpetuity rescued the forest-products industry from an existence strongly flavored with expediency, and gave it instead long-range planning, orderly development, and a favorable climate for investment.

The objective of this presentation is to make clear and convincing the unique contribution which any forest can make to the economic development of a community, large or small, and to define certain guidelines which are essential to the success of this development, particularly in the area of complete and integrated utilization of the forest crop.

Multiple Uses of Forest Products

The most important broad uses that are made of manufactured forest products are in:

(a) Serving construction, both structural, functional, and decorative.

(b) Serving transportation, from the irreplaceable railroad tie at one extreme to the decking of ships at the other.

(c) Providing the necessities of living: the millwork, the cabinets, the counters, the wardrobes, the closets, and so on.

(d) Providing the comforts of living: the paneling, the furniture, the flooring, the insulation, the sound deadening, and so on.

(e) Serving communication: the spoken, written, and printed word.

(f) Providing shipping containers and their accessories of all kinds from the little egg carton of perfect performance to the huge modular transferrable crates or bins.

(g) Providing the pleasures of living from the gun stock of the sportsman to the grand piano of the artist.

(h) Providing the paper products for healthful living.

(i) Contributing to the great areas of films, filaments, textiles, finishes, explosives, soil mulches, concrete additives, well drilling aids, adhesive extenders, and others.

Diversity of the Forest-Products Industry

Only when one attempts to list all the markets for and the uses made of forest products, does one realize how greatly diversified the industry is. This diversity, however, can be broken down into three major categories of forest products: solid wood, fibers, and chemicals.

Solid wood takes many forms: round piles, poles, and posts; sawed lumber of many varieties; sawed timbers larger and heavier than lumber; millwork engineered to specific uses; laminated lumber as structural members; plywood serving an entire panel-using world of its own; sawed or split shingles and shakes; and finally subdivided whole wood running the gamut from wood wool through shavings and flakes to sawdust and wood flour.

Fibers, from whole wood to all-cellulose, also take many forms, their variety being such as to force one to be arbitrary in attempting any all-inclusive classification. Wood fibers cannot be prevented from felting and their great utility depends upon this felting action. Among these fiber products now on the

market, exclusive of paper or paperboard, are low density mats and blankets for packing, padding, deadening sound and restricting heat transmission; insulation boards providing decorative and acoustical ceilings; sheathing, roof decking, and sidings; and finally hardboard, which is currently undergoing a change from commodity to engineered product reaching for additional markets through improved hardness, smoothness, durability, and visual appeal.

With respect to the ramifications of paper and paperboard, the differentiation between the two is largely a matter of thickness. The variety of materials used runs the full range from reclaimed waste paper through mechanical pulps or groundwoods, high-yield chemical pulps to full chemical pulps unbleached, bleached and purified. There are papers well-standardized in appearance and performance, e.g., newsprint containing a high percentage of mechanical pulp, and such strong all-chemical pulp papers as kraft liner, kraft bag, and kraft wrapper. Huge investments are required for this aspect of the paper industry since these products serve big tonnage uses and their producing mills are large and of high cost per daily ton of capacity.

The more than a million tons of chemical cellulose produced annually for conversion to filaments, films, lacquers, and explosives is the oustanding commercial accomplishment in chemicals from wood. Although this is over-simplification, we may take wood apart gently, or we may break it up by rough treatment into chemical pieces. Broadly, we may attempt this in four different ways: The first is fractionation or extraction, an ideal method to employ in which the severity of treatment is kept to the minimum required to accomplish the separations.

The second may be called cleavage, whereby the lignin is rendered soluble by delignification, leaving the cellulose insoluble; or the cellulose is made soluble by conversion to sugars by hydrolysis, leaving the lignin insoluble. The third approach makes almost everything soluble by hydrogenation. The fourth approach produces a mixture of solids, liquids, and gases by pyrolysis. All four of these techniques continue under development in the United States and no doubt in other countries also.

Sound economics require that chemical use be centered in conversion of all of a given raw material into valuable products. Those who continue to discard a substantial portion of their raw material as waste are not showing sound judgment.

Establishment of a Forest-Products Industry

In planning for the establishment of a forest-products industry there are a number of factors that need to be taken into consideration. First consideration should be given to the possible markets for the products, the availability of raw materials, and the requirements of use. If these appear favorable, then consideration should be given to such matters as practical technology, sound economics, capital, right timing, and provisions for renewing the forest resource.

Any specific business originates in the markets and the uses it serves. These govern the nature of its products, the products in turn control their production, and the process steps and corresponding equipment are chosen to convert economically the available raw material to the product desired. Hence, choice of market, uses, and products come first;

second is choice of raw material, depending on the forest inventory, sustained yield and delivered cost species by species; third, choice of the process steps to connect the raw material to the product; and fourth, the choice of equipment to execute the process steps.

The choice of the raw materials to be used depends to a great extent on taking advantage of unique superiorities exhibited by some one of the species, both product- and process-wise. The scope of practical technology encompasses both the process steps and the equipment to carry them out.

Both industry and government have paid much too little attention to the requirements of use. The requirements of use control the property values of the product; they control its satisfactory performance in use, and thereby its price level, both absolute and relative to competition; and, finally, its very business existence. Therefore, before we plunge into commercialization, the facts of performance must be developed. These are some suggested steps:

(a) Record the use requirements involved in ordinary nontechnical terms; this describes what the product must do.

(b) Select the corresponding product properties.

(c) Establish adequate methods of test for each property.

(d) Prepare an ideal specification.

(e) Modify the ideal to a technically and economically practical specification.

(f) Measure product performance; this describes what the product must be.

We therefore observe that there are two performance yardsticks—one absolute based on use, the other relative based on competition. The foregoing sequence is called the use-requirements technique, and before it is attempted a thorough market survey should be made.

The technology to be practical must either have been practiced elsewhere or have gone through pilot-plant studies successfully. It must not be too complicated, yet adequate for the job to be done. It should provide ease of control. It should lend itself to the application of continuity of manufacture, and should be amenable to developing manufacturing costs which allow production to reach its profit objective.

The most often encountered stumbling block to successful commercialization is that of sound economics. One cannot help but marvel at the number of projects going into commercialization without any serious attempt at an operating forecast. This forecast merely determines net earnings after taxes by subtracting all expense from net sales income in as simple and logical a manner as possible.

A definition of sound economics in this instance might include the following: Enough volume of goods bringing a sufficient price in the competitive marketplace to furnish a profitable income; to provide workers with the necessities and some of the luxuries of living; to pay direct and indirect manufacturing costs, including those for replacement of equipment priced at more than the depreciation reserve; to provide for normal company growth; and to finance a fair share of governmental functions while still maintaining enough earnings to pay as much for use of the funds invested in the enterprise as could be obtained otherwise on an equal risk basis.

In connection with the capital requirements per unit of production capacity, there is great leeway in the case of wood to choose the extent to which the traditional simplicity of process steps and equipment shall be enjoyed as compared with the more complicated contemporary techniques.

Right timing is often overlooked. It is a hard lesson to learn. Regardless of how attractive the market may be, how practical the technology, or how sound the economics are, there must be good justification for attempting commercialization—justification which has its genesis usually in a real need. One often hears of the inventor who was ahead of his time. His timing was wrong. The semi-chemical pulping process went into the first pulp mill about 1930. The process slept peacefully until 1945 when it was suddenly awakened owing to the realization that it would permit cheaper species to be used for pulp and paper. Advent of the compression barker was inadvertently timed perfectly, since a great need existed for a barker of low capital and operating cost.

The Tree Farm Program

The fact that forests are a renewable resource should be recognized, of course, in planning for a forest products industry, and the whole program should be structured on this important asset.

It has now been recognized that forest cover is not an inexhaustible resource and that nature alone cannot be expected to replace the timber that man has harvested. Nature can supply the seeds but, unfortunately, as in the case of the conifers, rodents find these very tasty and, when the relatively small number of seeds that survive produce seedlings, the ruminants come in to feast on the succulent plants. Electrical and wind storms, likewise, take their toll. Thus, man's help is needed.

The tree-farm concept came into being as a means of helping nature replace the trees that are harvested or destroyed, and thereby insuring an adequate future supply of lumber. Basically, it involves a series of measures which when properly applied provide the reforestation required. One of such measures is to coat the tree seeds with a repellant that is distasteful to rodents. The coated seeds are then spread over a denuded area by helicopter. Another is to establish large tree nurseries to grow seedlings for transplanting. Different practices are followed for the various species. In the case of ponderosa pine, for example, the modern practice is to harvest the tree crop by a thinning-out process and then to replace the cut trees with seedlings. The result is a whole forest of trees at various stages of growth. The douglas fir seedling, on the other hand, is not able to survive under such conditions since it does not thrive in the shade, and the accepted practice, therefore, is to completely clear the various plots where the trees have reached maturity, and then spread seeds over the area by helicopter or transplant seedlings. In any case, the young seedlings require careful attention so that those damaged by ruminants, or by other means, can be replaced. Also, the whole forest area must be inspected periodically for diseased trees and these should be promptly removed to avoid having the disease spread and ruin the forest.

Integrated Utilization of the Forest Crop

If we are to enjoy the unique opportunity wood gives us to benefit by integration, then we should plan against a background of complete utilization of the tree farm crop. This in turn means building an industrial complex, gradually certainly, starting modestly, and proceeding soundly as the integration expands.

In forest products, our first concern is to utilize the whole log and when this has been accomplished, then the whole tree harvest and finally the whole tree farm crop. Common sense tells us to give highest priority to the integrated utilization of the whole log as brought to the mill.

It is axiomatic that whole log use can be successful only to the extent that markets and uses consume huge quantities of products. That any such markets could be found for mixtures of such different materials as wood and bark is certainly remote. Then, regardless of the ultimate products, these two constituents must be cleanly separated, wasting neither one. Until 1950, saw-log users had been unconcerned about the barking process; plywood producers chewed the bark off of their so-called peeler blocks along with a substantial percentage of clear sapwood.

The pulp makers for years had accomplished their barking of small logs by manual woods peeling or by the use of huge drums at the mill. Later they employed hydraulic barkers for both small and large logs giving bark-free wood, but not wood-free bark. These hydraulic barkers were so expensive in first cost and operating cost that their use in any but the largest operations could not be justified. This was the situation which demanded an answer, especially one within the ability of the small operator to finance. A number of approaches to an answer to this question have been attempted in the last decade, and the answer now seems definitely in hand, namely, continuous mechanical barking at the mill.

Sparked by the desire to achieve bark-free logs and in turn, if possible, convert wood-free bark by a dry process to useful products, the Weyerhaeuser Company began to explore the possibilities of dry-log barking in 1945, at that time for application to peeler logs. The first barker of this type was put into successful operation in 1947 in the then new plywood plant of Weyerhaeuser and furnished "as is" bark to a new bark utilization plant which went into operation that same year. Since that time this basic principle of compression and shearing at the cambium layer has been employed in many designs of log barkers, with a cost well within the resources of the smaller log processors. This technique of compression barking is probably the greatest factor in accelerating integrated whole log use in the United States.

Now, assuming we have bark-free wood in log form ready for processing, what key product will do most to reach whole log utilization? Since the manufacture of fiber or chemicals starts with wood in relatively small pieces, it would appear logical that solid wood products of substantial dimensions should be our first choice. This means, of course, lumber and plywood. Will lumber manufacture be a sufficiently stable and profitable business to justify the close relationship that is involved in future raw material integration?

The storage and handling of huge tonnages of raw material are economically accomplished even with species whose logs do not float. Fifty tons of coniferous wood is fed to the mill per hour, or a ton a minute, for the sawing of 100,000 FLS in 8 hours. The reduction of the log to lumber is continuous, proc-

essing temperatures and pressures are atmospheric, no other raw materials of any consequence are required, the equipment is reliable, the performance dependable and reproducible. Labor and plant investment per unit of output are low, and annual net income per capital dollar invested is attractive. These are the details which provide a stable successful basis for integration.

The manufacture of lumber and plywood has a unique opportunity to bring raw material integration into being. Certain it is that no cheaper hardboard, softboard, particleboard, or pulp or paper can be made than that provided by integration with the manufacture of lumber and plywood. It is believed that these solid wood products constitute the best foundation for whole-log use.

Integration other than that of raw material depends on the details of the specific case so far as process steps and supporting equipment type and arrangement are concerned. The harvesting of marginal logs and their transportation require little change in techniques. Chipping, flaking, and screening operations are new, but the handling of masses of bulk materials is old. The servicing of the integrated operation, both from the standpoint of producing and distributing the utilities, and supplying all the administrative functions, involves merely enlarging the staff and facilities, with the opportunity to improve performance by so doing.

Our discussion thus far has been limited, at least by inference, to mill residuals of chippable shape and size. There are, however, many other kinds of residuals. The following listing includes all types commonly encountered:

(a) *Mill residuals*—concentrated at the mill:

Lumber—
Bark; chippable—slabs, edgings and trim; shavings—green and dry; and sawdust—green and dry.
Plywood—
"Lilly pads"; bark; cores; broken and discarded veneer—green and dry; panel trim; and sander flour.

(b) *Logging residuals*—on the ground:
Tops; branches; chunks,—large diameter short length pieces; tooth-picks,—small diameter shatter and knocked down saplings; and marginal logs,—crook, decay, shake and so on from felled merchantable trees, sometimes called "wood logs."

(c) *Forest residuals*—standing:
Cull trees, producing "cull logs" if felled—those of poor form and large defects; small trees, including thinnings; unwanted or unpopular species; and inaccessible trees, too costly to secure.

The chippable residuals have as chips many uses in the fiber field, which is well understood and widely practiced in the United States. The shavings find their outlet primarily in particleboard, although some go along with the chips. We now find it convenient to differentiate between coarse and fine sawdust, the former being usable to a modest extent in certain fibrous products. Tonnage use of fine sawdust is still a problem with the answer probably to be found in chemicals manufacture. Bark is being converted in many ways to usable commodities through both mechanical and chemical processing. Ten percent of the incoming logs cannot be wasted indefinitely, especially in view of the unique constituents it contains. In the plywood picture, lily pads, cores, and discarded veneer are chippable re-

siduals. Volume uses for sander flour are still to be found.

As the mill residuals earn a profit, the easiest-to-get logging residuals begin to come in with the good logs and, since these do not appear in any timber cruise, they cost only what it takes to bring them in. It is clear that the cost increases as the pieces are smaller, shorter and farther away. So the complete integrated utilization which we seek depends not only on efficient conversion and marketing, but on less costly techniques of harvesting and transportation. As an example of the advantages of integrated use, the yield per acre from an old but heavy stand of douglas fir was increased over a period of some 15 years from about 40,000 feet log-scale to 80,000 feet.

Typical Commercial Integrations

A listing of some of the common practiced simple integrations is as follows:

(a) Softwood lumber production with the production of industrial wood parts, glued-up panels, prefabricated timber members, laminated structural members ("glu-lam"), chips, veneer, plywood, softboard, hardboard, particleboard, and various pulps.

(b) Plywood production with production of industrial wood part, prefabricated panels and structural members, chips, softboard, hardboard, various pulps, paper overlays, and hardboard overlays.

(c) Softboard, hardboard production with hardboard overlays, paper overlays; and particleboard production with veneer overlays and paper overlays.

A listing of some of the unusual integrations is as follows:

(a) Lumber production with the production of whole wood fiber, wet pulp molding, bark products, and carbohydrate gum.

(b) Plywood production with the production of bark products, paper overlaid veneer—(2 faces), and facings of pulp.

(c) Particleboard with facings of pulp.

There are many complex integrations in the largest operations in the United States, one of which for example, based on lumber and plywood, includes lumber panelization, glue laminated members, prefabricated timber members, bark products both mechanical and chemical, sulfite, semi-chemical and sulfate pulps, and various grades of paper from food board to glassine.

Smallest Practical Manufacturing Capabilities for Various Forest Products

Approximate guidelines frequently asked for by those contemplating entering some phase of the forest-products industry, usually as part of an integration are: What is the smallest practical manufacturing capacity, and what is the fixed capital investment likely to be?

The principal problem, even in generalizing, is to rationalize the wide differences in prices, costs, climate, availability of services, site quality, product variety, and extent of finishing operations. There are a number of well-known factors which put a ceiling o plant size. There are also others which are used to determine the minimum size, e.g., to avoid unsound economics, a size too small to integrate or a size controlled by the maximum operating capacity of a key piece of equipment.

It is customary in the United States to express plant capacities in short air-dried tons per day, and capital cost in dollars per daily short ton, because of the variety of units of measurement of production encountered with different products. The following table is self-explanatory.

Lumber has been omitted from the tabulation because of the terrific variety of mill designs and sizes extending from as little as 1 million feet board measure (FBM) annually to as much as 200 million in certain places on the West Coast of the United States. The principal matter of interest here is the minimum size finished kiln dry lumber-mill to support integrated utilization. We may assume roughly that half of the actual volume of solid wood going into such a mill turns up as residuals and half of these are suitable for chips or flakes. One thousand FBM of U.S. West Coast douglas fir lumber shows an actual volume of about 70 cubic feet. This, at 30 lbs. per cu. ft., is equal roughly to a ton of wood. Hence for every 2 tons dry going into the mill, one-half ton turns up as chips or flakes.

To tie the figures of table 1 into the required size of a lumber or plywood mill to be the sole source of usable residuals requires knowledge of such details as usage of nonchippable residuals as well as chips for raw material; the actual distribution of incoming wood and most important weight yields from residual to finished integrated product; and days per year the mill is operated.

It should be emphasized that all the foregoing figures are for the purpose of initial project orientation and it is hoped they will be useful in crystallizing a course of action. They must not be used to arrive at firm and final decisions without adequate confirmation. Also, all the figures apply to the North American conifers.

Table 1

(1) Product	(2) Minimum daily production capacity	(3) Expressed in units thus	(4) Days per operating year	(5) Shifts per operating day	(6) Capacity limited by	(7) Factor to convert 2 to short air dry tons	(8) Minimum daily production capacity tons*	(9) Basic fixed investment dollars per short ton
Structural plywood	220,000	Sq. ft. ⅜ in. 30 lbs. pcf	240	2	1 Hot press	0.00047	100	35,000
Softboard	330,000	Sq. ft. ½ in. 20 lbs. pcf	340	3	1 Wet forming machine	0.00042	140	45,000
Hardboard	275,000	Sq. ft. ⅛ in. 64 lbs. pcf	340	3	1 Dry forming machine	0.00033	90	35,000
Particle-board	45,000	Sq. ft. ¾ in. 40 lbs. pcf	240	3	1 Single opening press 8 by 16 ft.	0.00125	50	20,000
Semi-chemical pulp	100	Short AD tons	340	3	Defibering and economics	1.00	100	25,000
Unbleached Kraft pulp and paper.	200	Short AD tons	340	3	Economics	1.00	200	40,000

*Figures rounded off.

Organization of a Textile Industry—Costs and Benefits to the Economy

SIMON WILLIAMS

Senior Industrial Development Adviser
Arthur D. Little, Inc., Cambridge, Massachusetts

In every country where industrialization is a basic part of economic planning, the establishment of textile and related industries—e.g., apparel manufacture—is likely to be given high priority. This is the natural result of a variety of factors:

(a) Textile imports are relatively high in general, resulting in a significant outflow of scarce foreign exchange.

(b) The internal market often seems large enough to support local production on an import-substitution basis.

(c) Often the potential exists for producing or increasing existing production of raw textile fiber from vegetable, animal, or chemically derived sources, e.g., cellulose from wood for rayon, as part of long-range agricultural plans. Logic would seem to dictate that abundant local sources of fiber would generate significant savings in an industry where raw-material costs are a high percentage of total manufacturing costs.

(d) Sometimes a glance at less favored neighboring countries raises the hope of an export market within a regional-trade framework.

(e) Textile manufacturing is sufficiently labor-intensive that the benefits to the economy of the resultant employment and training are important considerations to both planners and politicians.

(f) Throughout the world there is a vast capacity to produce textile machines. Further, technical obsolescence in the advanced countries plus an abundance of excess capacity has created a huge warehouse of used machinery. These circumstances are manifested in a steady sales pressure, replete with the lure of easy credit, on the less developed countries to venture into textile production.

(g) There is a long history of international relations in the textile industry. A manufacturer in one country is likely to be familiar with production, financial, labor, political, and trade problems in other countries.

It is not surprising, in view of the foregoing, that textile manufacturing has advanced rapidly in the less developed countries. Taking cotton as an example, while world production of cotton fibers almost doubled between 1912 and 1958, world imports of cotton remained at about the same level and world imports of cotton fabric dropped to less than one-half their earlier volume. Analysis of these data clearly reflects the internal consumption of locally grown cotton by domestic mills in the low-income countries (1).

What has been learned as a result of this growth in textile and allied industry throughout the world? What procedures must be followed if further growth is to be on economically sound ground?

One thing is eminently clear. The start-up of a textile manufacturing enterprise requires the same kind of careful economic and technical feasibility analysis, prior to the commitment of capital, as does any other industry. Such feasibility studies covering textiles present no unique problems. The nature and size of the internal market and the means whereby the market is being served are readily determined, as are trends of consumption. The technology relevant to the manufacture of any kind of yarn, fabric, or derived product is well-known and the details covering machine costs, building costs to house machines, the cost of water and power and fuel, the cost of transportation and other items affecting production costs, are also readily derived from local sources or from experienced consultants. Whether or not suitable land is available at reasonable prices on which to site a plant can quickly be assessed. The availability of labor, its level of skill, its relative efficiency, the cost and duration of training and related aspects of staffing (e.g., the cost of resident foreign technicians and management) can also be estimated based on the experience of other manufacturers (whether or not in the textile field) and from the experience of educators in the technical, commercial, and management-training institutions. The impact of tariffs, tax laws, and other government regulations can be calculated directly; the cost of sales may be a subtle estimate, but it too is one that can

be made in light of existing trading patterns in the country.

There is no need to labor the point. If every new textile factory were to come into existence solely on its ability to compete on a straight commercial basis with imports, there would be no need for articles such as this one. The elements of a good feasibility study are well-known, and there are competent people who can be retained to conduct such studies anywhere in the world on any phase of textile industrial development from fiber production to finished consumer product. Promoters, machine salesmen, and experienced textile manufacturers know this, and a government can rest assured that if private capital only is to be involved such studies will be made. Too, if governments are to participate in textile ventures, with equity or loan capital or through industrial incentives provided at some cost to the economy, they too need only to ensure as a matter of policy that comprehensive feasibility studies precede a final decision to move ahead with a project, assuming that feasibilty in a commercial sense, that is, the yield of profit on the original investment, is to be the keystone of textile development policy.

However, it is known and accepted that industrial development in the low-income countries does not depend wholly on purely commercial considerations. Private investors will not be interested unless profit is possible, but within a developing country social and political forces accelerating industrial growth often transcend the current economics of a given manufacturing project and, even where a feasibility study demonstrates that commercial profit is possible only through some form of subsidy, a judgment is often reached to pay this price for technological advance.

The price of progress in textile manufacturing may be particularly high, and it is here that a problem is defined which is deserving of far more critical attention throughout the world than has been true heretofore; namely, is it possible on the one hand to calculate the balance between the cost to a national economy of providing industrial incentives to encourage new textile manufacturing investment and, on the other hand, the benefits to the economy derived from the existence of a textile mill or an integrated textile industry? Unless there is a net gain, the value of this type of industrialization is illusory.

There can be no doubt that the problem is real and significant. It would be difficult, if not impossible, to find a major textile project in a less developed country wherein textile manufacturing has come into existence during the past decade which is not subsidized in some way through tariff protection, or duty relief on imported machinery and materials, or tax holidays, or import control, or some combination of these and other devices such as exchange control. This situation is the result of a number of factors which must be faced realistically:

(a) Production units have tended to be relatively small and not able to provide some of the economies of size characterizing the textile mills of India, Japan, Hong Kong, the United States, and the exporting countries of Europe which compete most intensely for the market in the less developed countries.

(b) Certain segments of the textile industry, even when relatively small, e.g., spinning, weaving, and finishing flat goods, still require more capital than is generally available locally. In turn, risk capital from abroad requires a higher rate of return than is normal to textile manufacturing in the major exporting countries.

(c) In these major textile-exporting countries, the industry plays a large and vital role in the economy. Full production, full employment, and an expanding overseas market have become both economically and politically important and are heavily subsidized when the need arises.

(d) In the less developed countries, there is little, if any, background in industrial-textile production. No pool of skilled labor, supervisory personnel, or management generally exists. Hence labor efficiency is low, negatively affecting quality and increasing labor costs. Training costs are high. The overhead burden of foreign technicians and managers, including as it does salaries at a premium level, housing, leave-time and paid travel to and from the home country, may also be excessively high.

(e) All textile machinery is imported into the developing countries. This requires a large inventory of spare parts. Coincident with this is a general lack of skilled mechanical and electrical services. Maintenance costs and the cost of idle machinery tend to run higher in these countries than in the older textile centers of the world.

(f) Most basic chemicals used in textile manufacturing must be imported into the less developed countries, usually at a price disadvantage despite duty relief.

(g) Power, water, transport, and often fuel costs are generally high and also penalize the local manufacturer.

9. While all of the foregoing factors influencing the cost of production may be transient in their effect, no one can predict with assurance or with precision

how many years it will take for local production in a given less developed country to become fully competitive with imports. To be realistic, therefore, any country wishing to encourage the growth of textile manufacturing must offer incentives to ensure commercial profitability and to attract the required capital. *In so far as these incentives keep the price of textile products in the local market artificially high or reduce government revenue (actual or potential), they constitute a cost to the economy.* In effect, such incentives are a subsidy provided by the public at the expense of purchasing power and available government services.

Whether or not the benefits to an economy more than offset the cost of incentives to textile manufacture is a difficult question to answer without equivocation. Some incentives such as tariff protection and duty relief have direct effects which are readily quantified. Other incentives such as tax holidays and the freedom to repatriate profits are more complex in their effect and are more difficult to rationalize into trustworthy numerical terms. Similarly, benefits range over quantitative and qualitative results. Foreign-exchange savings, for example, related to the real value of such exchange vis-a-vis the value of local currency, are specific and readily identified. On the other hand, converting the value of training the unskilled or employing the unemployed in industry to an equivalent sum of money calls for certain assumptions always subject to question.

Nonetheless, the development of a textile industry worth having depends upon making the best estimates possible of the cost of incentives and the value to be placed on benefits. That this is not an impossible task may be indicated by the following examples.

The cost of tariff protection lies in the higher price paid by the ultimate consumer than would be true if no tariff were imposed on the competitive import. This cost can be reduced to quantitative terms.

Illustration: This proposal for a cotton-fabric printing mill states that, because there has been no prior experience in the country, labor inefficiency and difficulties in operation would increase production costs far above world average. To compete on the local market, therefore, request is made for an increase in tariff of 7 cents per yard on all imports which could in any way be competitive (2). Although mill capacity is planned at 20 million yards annually, the imports affected cover almost 270 million yards, thus raising the price to the consuming public by \$18.9 million (or decreasing purchasing power by this much if the total sale of this type of fabric remained unchanged).

The cost of duty relief is the loss of revenue to the government which either would be recovered by other taxes or would result in reduced government services. These costs become particularly significant when import duties constitute a significant portion of government revenue. Whether or not a loss of revenue is actually the result of duty relief depends upon prevailing conditions.

Illustration (a): If the material for which duty relief is granted does not replace another import which yields duty revenue, there is no real cost to the government in the sense that no prior revenue is lost. Potential revenue might not be forthcoming, but this cannot be treated as a loss in calculating the cost of industrial development.

Illustration (b): If duty relief is granted on a material not heretofore imported but which tends to replace a prior import, a real loss of revenue is incurred equal to the duty on what is replaced. A printing mill is proposed which requests duty relief on 20 million yards of greige goods a year. Without this plant these goods would not be imported. With this operation locally the net result will be a decrease in imports of 20 million yards of printed fabric on which the duty equals 16 cents per yard. This equals a revenue loss of $3.2 million.

Illustration (c): If duty relief is granted on a material which would continue to be imported even if the relief were not granted, the loss in revenue is directly related to the relief granted. A shirt factory has started up within a given framework of import duties affecting shirting and affecting finished shirts. Experience indicates that while a certain limited line of shirts can be made under these conditions, profit is discouragingly small and expansion out of the question. Request is made to grant duty relief on shirting used by this factory. One hundred thousand yards of shirting a year is now consumed, involving a loss of revenue of $16,000. The request indicates that with this relief production could be quadrupled and employees doubled from 40 to 80 workers. Shirting imported above and beyond the original 100,000 yards consumed would involve no real loss to the economy since this situation would reflect that described in Illustration 13(a) above.

Tax holidays, if used only as an incentive to the establishment of new competitive production facilities, do not generate a cost to the economy. Rather receipt of new income taxes is merely deferred for a period of years in order to ensure the formation of additional national wealth. However, when granting or withholding a tax holiday is used to control production rather than to stimulate it, a loss to the economy may be incurred.

Illustration: Two manufacturers of yarn and thread had been given a tax holiday for a period to cover their infant-industry status. After getting into production and in light of shifting patterns in the textile marketplace, each mill decided to expand into knitting of tubular interlock fabric for sale to indigenous cutters and sewers. Upon application to the government, the tax holiday benefits were denied to two applicants wishing to knit the same types of tubular interlock fabric, both to produce from imported yarn. One of the two withdrew, eliminating an investment of roughly $500,000 which could have resulted in employment for several hundred people. The other proceeded into partial production in the hope of obtaining an early and favored position in the market; this objective was achieved but only because the output concentrated on very inexpensive styles, yielding low profit. Long-range plans to expand have been curtailed and consideration is being given to selling out and leaving the country.

Calculating the net effect of the repatriation of income in the form of foreign exchange involves a number of considerations. Surely, if the profit earned by a textile mill was wholly retained and distributed locally, the economy would benefit directly. Purchasing power would grow, savings would increase, investment capital would be formed, and its use encouraged. To the extent that money which might be so used is taken out of a country, there is a net loss equal to the amount of money withdrawn or even greater if foreign exchange is scarce and in reality more valuable than the exchange rate would indicate.

On the other hand, unless there is a liberal repatriation policy, foreign investors, often necessary to the development of a textile industry in the low-income countries, are unlikely to risk their capital. As with all incentives, the question is whether the price paid to attract these investors, e.g., the outflow of foreign exchange in this instance, yields a sufficient return.

Pursuing the lines of thinking and analysis set out above in paragraphs 12 through 16, and adding in a valuation of the major benefits resulting from a textile mill operation, a reasonable balance can be struck.

Illustration: This proposed cotton-textile mill, to spin, weave, and dye in one operation and in a separate plant to print imported greige goods, calls for an investment of roughly $5 million, $4 million to come from foreign sources, and the balance from the government. In full operation, duty relief requested would result in a revenue loss of $3.2 million a year. Imports would require an outflow of foreign exchange of approximately $5.4 million a year. The final product would replace imports currently valued at about $5 million. Operations of the spinning and weaving section would require the diversion of domestic raw cotton normally exported with a foreign-exchange yield of roughly $800,000. A tax holiday to last 5 years is requested in line with government policy and existing legislation to encourage pioneer industries if the letter of law is followed. Repatriation of an undefined amount of income for debt service, management fees and profit is a basic requirement of the foreign investors. The impact on the economy of having this come into existence may be calculated as follows:

(a) Direct cost to the economy, assuming that revenue losses will be made up from other sources, will be $3.7 million resulting from the duty relief requested; this is the revenue which would be collected on the goods to be replaced by the product of the mill.

(b) Foreign exchange net deficit would amount to $3 million resulting from these elements:

(i) Outflow for fabric, chemicals, and other materials exceeds the value of import substitution by $400,000.

(ii) Debt service at 10 percent of total foreign loan capital equals $250,000.

(iii) Management fees payable to the technical partner set at $500,000.

(iv) Repatriation of 50 percent of estimated profit equals $500,000.

(v) One-half of the estimated salaries of foreign technicians would be $175,000.

(vi) One-half of estimated depreciation allowance repatriated as a means of recovering capital invested would be $250,000.

(vii) Miscellaneous foreign exchange costs might come to $150,000.

(viii) This mill will consume domestic cotton normally exported. This diversion will eliminate approximately $800,000 per year in foreign exchange earnings.

(c) Benefits to the economy would accrue in a variety of ways:

(i) One thousand native employees, not heretofore gainfully occupied, would receive a payroll of roughly $325,000 a year.

(ii) One thousand untrained people would be taught operating and maintenance skills. Assuming 20 percent turnover a year, over 5 years an average of 360 people would be trained each year. In this particular country, the cost to the government of training (exclusive of capital costs) is roughly $560 a year per student. Using this figure to calculate the value of training in this textile mill to the economy, 360 × $560 per year equals $201,600.

(iii) Estimated purchases for fuel, water, rent, power, transportation, and miscellaneous services amount to $800,000 per year. In total, this may be thought to strengthen and perhaps contribute to the growth of these vital supporting elements in an economic-development program.

(d) In summary:

(i) Direct costs, e.g., loss in government revenue, $3,700,000.

(ii) Net foreign-exchange deficit, $3,000,000.

(iii) Value of benefits, $1,325,000.

Is the mill proposed in the illustration above worth having? For some years to come, while the debt is being paid off, while a large volume of imported materials is required, until efficiency develops, making the product more competitive with imports, and if the foreign investors require a substantial and immediate return on their risk capital, the value of having this mill in the country may be seriously questioned.

Does this mean that this proposal should be rejected? At this point the decision passes out of the technical realm into the area of broader economic, social, and political considerations. Is industrial development so fundamental to economic development that pioneer industry must be sponsored even at very high cost? Must industrial-development planning be well advanced before a given industry is

permitted to develop so that there is a clearer view of which industries are more economically viable than others? Is industry necessary for internal security?

The purpose of this paper is not to answer these questions but rather to point to the need of knowing better than has been true in the past the cost of the value of claimed benefits of any industrial project. The textile industry has served to illustrate a method of closely approximating what the costs and benefits are and what they add up to as they take effect. Whatever the final decision of the governments of less developed countries to subsidize their infant industries, there are ways to quantify the impact of a given manufacturing enterprise on the national economy. This calculation should always go hand in hand with the analysis of commercial profitability upon which an investor makes his decision.

In conclusion, the foregoing illustrations and calculations are not at all inclusive. They do cover the most significant elements of cost and benefits deriving from a new industrial operation. They do carry beyond textiles to any other kind of manufacturing. Other factors may come into play and may be rationalized by the same system of thought. For example, anti-dumping legislation may be sought as well as import controls or limiting competition by prohibiting new manufacturers in given fields of production. In some way, each of these actions, if taken, will affect the price in the marketplace. It may affect the quality of goods sold; it may affect the rate of inflow of investment capital in a negative way. Conversely, this paper has not reflected the nonrecurring benefits of new industry, such as payments and employment resulting from initial construction. Nor has this paper put a value on the stimulation generated by one going manufacturer to investment by others in the field. This is particularly a factor to reckon with in the textile industry which is so varied in nature and so highly interrelated. Similarly, existing industry is a living symbol of the investment climate of a country and by demonstration does far more than speeches and promises to prove the role of government in matters such as taxes, freedom from controls, and other matters of critical concern to those who risk their capital and those who come to operate and train.

Despite these limitations, it is felt that by applying the methods of analysis suggested above, governments and their advisors have a powerful tool with which to cut directly to the realities of proposed textile (and other industry) projects, including schemes to grow new fiber crops and tie agriculture and industry closer together.

REFERENCES

(1) FAO Commodity Review. Special Supplement, *Agricultural Commodities Projections for 1970*. Food and Agricultural Organization of the United Nations. Rome (1962).

(2) In all illustrations, which are taken from actual cases, money value has been converted to the equivalent in U.S. currency for convenience.

PART FIVE

The Challenge in Developing Infrastructure

THESE seven essays deal with a familiar but critical field of economic development. Without infrastructure, "take-off" would be impossible, the "big push" would succeed only in creating bottlenecks, and "vicious circles" would perpetuate frustrating effort without noticeable gain. Power, transport, and communications are often the key to dramatic breakthrough in the complex struggle.

Seymour compares power programs in Greece, El Salvador, Puerto Rico, and Iran with the TVA scheme in the United States, illustrating how foreign aid from various sources—Agency for International Development, International Bank for Reconstruction and Development, U.S. Department of Agriculture, and Atomic Energy Commission—and numerous private foreign companies have assisted in initiating power projects in these countries. He provides a helpful series of generalized solutions to the problems posed by these case histories.

Low-rank or noncommercial power and fuels, as Guyol shows for India, produce as much horsepower as and more heat than all other energy sources combined in the underdeveloped countries. Modernization and utilization of every source of fuel available are greatly needed. Large quantities of low-rank coal remain unused, often for lack of some of the know-how described in the Landers article.

Guyol has long experimented with energy balance as a basis for forecasting petroleum consumption. Here he exhibits some of the virtues of a complete energy balance in planning for the underdeveloped country.

In the next three articles the authors outline the strategy and some practical problems of developing transportation facilities in less-developed areas. What impact will a boldly conceived and executed transport system have? Will labor mobility increase? Is this what is wanted? Will pressures increase on the urban centers? Should not the causes of demand for increased mobility be eliminated to keep transport construction costs within bounds? Meyerson probes these questions.

To deal rationally with the ubiquitous pressures for railroad building, Keller proposes a study group system to focus on specific aspects of railroad installation.

For other countries, improved or developed waterways and port facilities are outlets for pent-up potentials. While Frater, Dodge, and Philip warn that such facilities are seldom self-supporting, such infrastructure may establish the groundwork for future advances on many fronts.

Two-thirds, or more than 2 billion, of the world's people lack the barest means of learning what is going on even in their own countries. Vast rural areas are without any means of communication beyond the confines of field and village. The last article in Part Five attests to the vital role of communication in economic development. The key may well lie in the search for what Schramm and Winfield remind us about Hirschman's "binding agent"—that common strand among all the myriad elements in the development psychoses that instills into men's minds a "growth perspective" or an "ideological fervour" for economic progress. Thus, these authors do not confine themselves to the mechanical problems of communication, but allude to its potential as a catalyst for growth.

Typical Problems in the Development of Modern Power Supply in Less Developed Areas *

WALTON SEYMOUR

*Vice President for Industrial Development,
Development and Resources Corporation,
New York City*

It is the purpose of this paper to describe, in terms of some specific areas concerning which the writer has personal and professional knowledge, the situation of electric-power supply before and after major development efforts. In each case a new institution was established which undertook to expedite a process of change as one of its major functions. Of these institutions, each has a framework of major characteristics which is of interest. The specific problems with which these new agencies dealt are set forth, and the actual solutions that were adopted are stated. The present status of power supply and prospects for the future are also summarized.

The cases include the areas served by the Tennessee Valley Authority (TVA); Greece, which is served by the Public Power Corporation (PPC); El Salvador, where increments of power supply are the responsibility of the Comision Ejecutiva Hidroelectrica del Rio Lempa (CEL); Puerto Rico, served by the Puerto Rico Water Resources Authority (PRWRA); and the Khuzestan region

of Iran, where a modern power system is under development by the Khuzestan Water and Power Authority (KWPA).

The final portion of the paper summarizes some conclusions, based upon the experience in these five areas, which are of potential significance in other areas facing somewhat similar problems in providing modern power supply for their homes, farms, commercial establishments, and factories. Especially to be noted are the common elements in the individual solutions developed in each of the areas. These common elements may well be significant for other areas because they can be clearly identified in the five cases, and because, in all five, modern electric-power supply has been or is being achieved in areas where electric service had previously not met modern standards of adequacy, reliability, and reasonableness of cost.

The Cases

The TVA Area. In 1933, during the early days of the administration of

President Roosevelt, the law was passed which established the Tennessee Valley Authority. The TVA Act was the conclusion of a series of preceding but unsuccessful efforts to establish an agency for development of the resources of the Tennessee River and the region through which it flows. Key policies for electric power included the following:

(a) The TVA power system was to be self-supporting and self-liquidating; it was to be able to use its revenues for power-system purposes.

(b) Power was to bear its share of the costs of facilities used also for TVA's primary purposes of flood control and navigation.

(c) TVA power was to be conceived as being available primarily for the benefit of the people of the section as a whole, with preference for the domestic and rural consumers, and the sale of power to industry was to be a secondary purpose, primarily to secure a high system-load factor and to improve revenue returns; TVA was to seek the application of electric power to the fuller and better balanced development of the resources of the region.

(d) The Act clearly implied that TVA was to sell power primarily on a wholesale basis, giving preference to public and cooperative agencies not doing business for a profit.

(e) In lieu of taxation, TVA was to pay a percentage of its revenues from the sale of power to the States within which it operates, a part of these payments to be paid to local agencies of government which suffered loss of tax revenues due to TVA's acquisition of properties formerly in private ownership. This is now 5 percent.

Some of TVA's other key policies applying to all of its operations are these:

(a) It was to have much of the flexibility of a private enterprise; for example, its employees were to be appointed without any political tests and were to be employed under a merit system with salary classification established by TVA, independent of the U.S. Civil Service system.

(b) Its Board was to consist of three members, chosen by the President with the consent of the Senate, responsible to the President and with staggered terms, ultimately 9 years each to assure continuity through changes in national administrations.

(c) Its accounts were to be kept in accordance with the Federal Power Commission system of accounts.

(d) It was given the power of eminent domain.

(e) It was to have authority to take necessary action to carry out these policies.

By 1933, in the Tennessee Valley region power supply was, in most cases, available from large central-station sources only in the major centers of population. There were a number of isolated municipal systems, usually depending on diesel-electric generators. Rural electrification extended to only 3 percent of the farms. Average residential use was 600 kwh per year, about the same as the national average. Total regional electrical energy requirements were about 1½ billion kwh. In hearings about TVA legislation and appropriations, representatives of existing power systems testified that the future market for power in the region was limited and the capacity planned for installation by TVA was not required.

One of TVA's statutory tasks was to develop a comprehensive plan for integrated development of the Tennessee River and its tributaries. This was completed in 1936 and guided future development.

TVA, located in an area which was predominantly agricultural, began its operations with a labor force in which modern industrial skills were limited. Training of foremen, accountants, managers, and skilled workers was an essential element of its early program.

In order to develop the region's power supply on the most economical basis, an integrated generation, transmission, and distribution system was required. This was accomplished largely through the acquisition by TVA of the existing bulk-supply (generation and transmission) facilities, and through acquisition of the existing distribution facilities by local public agencies, and by cooperatives, which became the distributors of TVA power. Acquisitions were negotiated at prices agreed upon between buyers and sellers. The acquisition program was completed in 1945 and included properties for which sales prices totalled about $125 million. The facilities thus acquired were interconnected with newly constructed facilities owned by TVA and by the municipal and cooperative distributors of TVA power.

TVA's financing has come primarily from direct Congressional appropriations and from its own earnings. The early acquisition program was financed in part by the issuance of bonds which were purchased by the U.S. Treasury. Within the past few years, TVA has been authorized, by amendment of the Act, to issue up to $750 million in revenue bonds for sale to the public to finance the further expansion of its power system within its existing service area. Some $100 million of such bonds have since been issued.

TVA now supplies power throughout an area of some 80,000 square miles, with a population of some 5 million and with about 1½ million consumers of electricity. Total requirements for electrical energy have reached 60 billion kwh, or about 40 times their level of 30 years ago. Almost half of these requirements are for national-defense purposes, including atomic energy. Ninety-eight percent of the farms in the region have electric service. A high proportion of all new homes are heated with electricity. Average residential consumption is almost 10,000 kwh per consumer per year, or about 2½ times the national average. The average rate for this service in the TVA area is a little less than 1 cent per kwh, or about 40 percent of the national average. With total-system generating capacity of over 12 million kw, TVA ranks as one of the largest integrated power systems in the world. Having practically exhausted the economical hydroelectric power in its region, it will, in the future, depend largely upon thermal sources to meet its continued growth requirements. It now uses about 20 million tons of coal per year. TVA has a cooperative understanding with the Atomic Energy Commission for work on an experimental gas-cooled reactor for power purposes.

Greece. When fighting ceased in Greece in 1949, it was recognized that electric-power supply should have a high priority in the work of reconstruction and expansion which needed to be done. A survey of power requirements and some of the principal power resources was made by a firm of consulting engineers, Ebasco Services, Inc., of New York, financed by U.S. aid funds. Following the completion of this survey, the U.S. and Greek Governments agreed that electric-power development would be one of the major programs during the period of reconstruction, to be financed in part by Marshall Plan funds, in part by Italian reparations, and in part by Greek resources.

In 1950, the Greek Parliament enacted legislation to establish the PPC to own and operate the new power system, and Ebasco was employed for a term of 5 years to manage the affairs of the PPC, to train its personnel, and to supervise the contractors engaged in developing the new power facilities. Ebasco was responsible to the Greek Board of Directors of PPC for its work.

Before PPC came into being, the only modern electric system in Greece, with electricity in reasonably adequate supply at reasonable cost, was that belonging to the Athens-Piraeus Electricity Company (APECO), largely owned by British interests, and serving the metropolitan area of the capital. In the second city of Greece, Salonika, the urban electric system was partly alternating and partly direct current, and service was inadequate and costly. In 1950, a portion of that city's power supply came from small naval vessels moored at the quay and connected to the electric-distribution system. Salonika's entire system had to be extensively rebuilt and expanded. A few other urban centers had electric service but only on an inadequate and high-cost basis.

By 1954–55, PPC completed the first stage of a new nationwide system which included three hydroelectric plants, a large thermal-electric station, a 150 kv transmission system, and primary distribution networks at 15 kv. Service began to be extended to the villages of

Greece. Inadequate urban systems were replaced. Further power expansion was undertaken by PPC after the completion of the first program. In 1960, PPC acquired the APECO system. Today, PPC is responsible for power supply throughout Greece, including the Greek islands. Only a few local systems remain in their previous ownership, the largest being that of Patras.

In 1950, total generating capacity in Greece was less than 200,000 kw. By 1955, with the completion of the initial expansion program financed in part by U.S. aid, total capacity had doubled. The second expansion program now completed or under construction will bring the total generating capacity to about a million kw, or over five times the capacity in 1950. Further substantial expansion of the PPC system is now under design. Since 1955, development has been largely financed by earnings and by internal and external loans and equipment credits.

PPC's initial policies were set forth in its original enabling legislation, adopted in 1950, and in its subsequent amendments. It was to be an autonomous agency, responsible to the Greek State through the Ministry of Industry. Members of the Board of Directors were to be appointed by the Government on the Minister's recommendation. The members of the seven- (later changed to nine-) man Board were to have 5-year terms of office, for staggered periods. Power was to be supplied by PPC on a basis which would assure its availability at the cheapest possible cost to the consumer, while PPC covered its costs of service. There was to be no unreasonable discrimination in the sale of power between regions of the country or between customers of the same class. For its key personnel, PPC was to be exempt from

Civil Service rules and regulations. It was to be able to act as though it were a commercial enterprise. Its accounts were to be kept in accordance with best modern public-utility accounting practice. There was to be a representative assembly, consisting of representatives of government, labor, banks, industry, the principal municipalities, professional societies, trade associations, etc., with responsibility for general annual or special review of PPC's operations.

It was intended that the resources used by PPC for power supply were to consist primarily of those indigenous to Greece—water power and lignite. Before 1950, except for emergency use in wartime, these resources were practically undeveloped. PPC has been instrumental since that time in opening up a large lignite deposit at Aliveri, on the island of Euboea, to fuel a power plant at that location, and a very large deposit at Ptolemais in the north, to fuel another power plant and to provide raw material for industrial development. A 150-kv interconnection has been established with Yugoslavia.

Most of the villages on the mainland of Greece and many on the islands have been electrified under the PPC program. A standard set of rate schedules is applied throughout the PPC service area, including the islands, except in the capital region, where APECO's rate structure has been maintained by PPC, the new owner. The levels of average rates for the various clases of consumers are not significantly different in these two parts of the PPC territory.

PPC's rate of growth has averaged 10 to 12 percent per year, the growth being more rapid outside than inside the capital area. Total use of electrical energy was 538 million kwh in 1950, of which 451 million kwh were used in the Athens-Piraeus area. Total use in 1961 was 2156 million kwh, of which 1445 million were used in the capital area. Plans for new power sources are under active consideration to meet future needs including the provision of a new large thermal-power station in the Peloponnesus at Megalopolis, which will tap large lignite deposits in that area.

The hydroelectric development of the Acheloos River in Western Greece, which is to be interconnected with the national network, is the base for quite an industrial complex, including an aluminum smelter being erected by a combination of French and American interests.

Since 1955, PPC has been managed and operated by its Greek organization. The Ebasco management group was entirely withdrawn after expiration of its original 5-year contract, and consulting services have since been of a more technical and traditional character.

El Salvador. El Salvador, a Central American republic, has a population of about 2½ million, and an area of some 8,000 square miles.

In 1945–46, it was decided by the Government that a large increment of electric power was needed, and a hydroelectric development at Chorrera del Guayabo, on the Lempa River, with associated transmission facilities, was undertaken, after detailed investigations. In 1948, the IBRD undertook the financing of the foreign-exchange portion of the costs of this project. Harza Engineering Company of Chicago, Illinois, were the consulting engineers, and were responsible for design and supervision of the construction of the project. The dam is now known as the Fifth of November.

Before 1948, the only fairly large electric system was that in the capital, San Salvador (CAESS), which also served the surrounding towns. It is owned by a Canadian group. The same group owns the much smaller system serving San Miguel, in the eastern portion of the country. Another smaller system served Santa Ana in the west, and there were small scattered systems in other towns, most of them privately owned. In 1953, total generating capacity in the country was about 20,000 kw.

With the decision to move ahead with the Lempa development, the Government of El Salvador established, through legislation and executive action, CEL, a public entity owned by the Government. Initially established by decree to make the necessary preliminary studies and investigations, CEL was later (1948) given a legislative charter. CEL had a seven-man board of directors (with staggered 4-year terms), four of whom were designated as individuals by the Government (acting through four cabinet offices). Of the other three, one was selected by the banks; one from a list provided jointly by the local agricultural, commercial, and industrial associations; and one by the local bondholders (other than the Government). For each board member, an alternate was appointed by the same procedure.

The Lempa project includes four generating units of 15,000 kw each, two of which were installed by 1954, one in 1957, and the fourth in 1961. A second hydro-project, Guajoyo, is almost completed. It will control and utilize the outflow from Lake Guija, which lies athwart the border of El Salvador and Guatemala.

CEL's legislative charter gives it irrigation as well as power responsibilities. It is exempt from civil service rules and regulations. It is to operate as an autonomous nonprofit public service enterprise. It is directed to give preference to the sale of power at wholesale to public or private agencies. Rates and charges are to be reasonable and adequate to cover costs, including debt service. CEL can borrow money in its own name, with Government approval. It has the right of eminent domain. Employees are to be chosen solely on the basis of merit and efficiency, without any political test. CEL and its contractors are exempt from customs duties, for imports necessary for its work, and from local taxation.

In 1953–54, CEL negotiated a wholesale power contract with CAESS, which specified wholesale and retail rates, and the maximum rate of return on investment which the company was to be permitted. This contract gives CEL the opportunity to assure that the benefits from the availability of CEL power are shared on a reasonable basis between the consumers and the owners of the company. Since return has recently exceeded the contractual allowance, retail rates were reduced in 1961.

Since 1953, the year before the Fifth of November project began operating, generating capacity in El Salvador has been quadrupled and requirements have risen equally rapidly. CEL now supplies over four-fifths of the country's electrical energy needs. Over 80,000 consumers are using CEL power. Service has been extended to most of the main urban centers from the CEL system, and contracts similar to that with CAESS have been negotiated with the distributors in other areas.

Puerto Rico. Puerto Rico, an island about a thousand miles south and east of Miami, Florida, bounded by the

Atlantic and the Caribbean, has an area of about 3,500 square miles. Its population is approaching 2,500,000. It is a Commonwealth within the United States, with a unique constitution established in 1952 by compact.

In 1942, legislation was enacted by the Puerto Rican territorial legislature establishing the PRWRA, an entity owned by the people of Puerto Rico. Its purposes were to produce and supply electricity, which it now does throughout the island, being responsible for serving all but a few of the ultimate consumers. It also had some irrigation responsibilities.

In 1942, PRWRA acquired the properties of the Canadian-owned company serving the San Juan capital area, and of the company serving the third largest urban center, Mayaguez. The privately owned system serving Ponce, the second largest town, had been acquired previously by the public agency which was the predecessor of PRWRA.

In 1941, the year before PRWRA was established, the total production of electrical energy for public use in Puerto Rico was about 192 million kwh; and 113,000 consumers were being served. Twenty years later, in 1961, total production was about 2,300,000,000 kwh, or a multiplication in two decades by twelve times. In 1961, over 400,000 consumers received service.

The legislative charter of PRWRA provided for the establishment of a three-man Board of Directors, the members to serve ex-officio, including the Governor, who was the chairman of the Board, and two members of his cabinet. Responsibility for managing the affairs of the agency was placed in the executive director, who was to be chosen by the Board. The PRWRA Act provides that charges for electric service fixed by PRWRA

shall be reasonable and adequate to cover costs, including obligations to the holders of the agency's bonds. It may borrow money in its own name and pledge its revenues for its debt service. It appoints its own officers and employees, and fixes their rates of compensation. It has the power of eminent domain, in the name of the people of Puerto Rico. In lieu of all other taxes, PRWRA pays 5 percent of its power revenues to the Commonwealth Treasury, and 6 percent is divided among the municipalities within which it operates.

The PRWRA system was in part acquired from its predecessor public agency (which was called Utilization of Water Resources, an office of the Insular Government), in part built with grants from the United States, and in part acquired or constructed with funds obtained through the sale of revenue bonds on the New York market. The most recent bond sale, in 1962, was in the amount of $22 million, at an average annual interest rate of about 3.6 percent.

About 110,000 kw of PRWRA's generating capacity is hydroelectric. Since practically all of the economical hydro sites have been utilized, increments since 1956 have been thermal-electric. The thermal plants are fueled with oil, largely consisting of the heavy residuals available from the two oil refineries now in operation on the island, one in the north and one in the south. Total PRWRA generating capacity at June 30, 1962 was about 700,000 kw.

The expansion of rural electrification throughout the rather mountainous terrain has been rapid. The work is carried out under a program financed by the Rural Electrification Administration of the U.S. Department of Agriculture which buys some of PRWRA's bonds each year, with an annual interest cost of 2 percent. Rural electrification is also supported by annual payment from the Commonwealth Treasury, in order to enhance its economic feasibility for PRWRA.

PRWRA is staffed almost 100 percent by Puerto Ricans. Many have had training in the continental United States. It retains Jackson & Moreland of Boston as its consulting engineers. Development and Resources Corporation is also retained for consultation and advice, especially in the fields of power economics and management policy. PRWRA, in cooperation with the U.S. Atomic Energy Commission, is constructing a 16,000-kw nuclear power plant (BONUS) in the western portion of the island. This plant will have the advanced feature of integral nuclear superheat with a boiling-water reactor.

Puerto Rico has for the past 10 years been engaged in what has become known as Operation Bootstrap, an intensive program of economic development. As a result, several hundred new industrial enterprises have been established on the island, transportation and communication have been improved, modern water-supply and sewerage systems have been built, and the standard of living has been significantly raised. Income from industrial activity now exceeds by a significant margin agricultural income, which had been the predominant income source throughout the island's recent history. One of the prominent factors in support of this development program has been the availability, thru PRWRA, of an adequate supply of electric power at reasonable cost. PRWRA's rates for electricity are comparable with those of electric utilities serving the Atlantic seaboard of the United States. They lie roughly in the middle of the range of these schedules between the high and low extremes. PRWRA is now the second largest non-Federal publicly owned electric system in the United States and its territories.

The Khuzestan Region of Iran. In southwestern Iran, bordering the head of the Persian Gulf, lies the region known as Khuzestan. It comprises an area of about 58,000 square miles, with a population of about 2½ million. It includes a broad desert plain, very flat, extending from the Gulf to the Zagros or Bakhtiari Mountains to the north and east. In the foothills of these mountains lie most of the producing oil fields of Iran.

The plain is drained by five rivers. On one of these, the Dez, there is rising toward early completion a thin-arch concrete dam, sixth highest in the world, which will have initial generating capacity, in two units, of 130,000 kw, and ultimately an eight-unit capacity of 520,-000 kw. It will be placed in operation in early 1963.

In 1956, Development and Resources Corporation was asked by the Government of Iran to assist in devising a plan for the economic development of Khuzestan, the region which, for many centuries, was the source of the economic power of ancient Persia. After receiving and approving the recommendations, the Government asked the firm to assume responsibility for helping to execute them. The firm completed and delivered to Plan Organization a unified program for development of Khuzestan. This program included a total of some 6 million kilowatts of hydroelectric capacity in fourteen projects, and water supply for a million hectares of agricultural land.

In 1957–58, electric-power supply in Khuzestan was primitive. The only partial exception was Abadan, where the oil companies have one of the largest of the world's refineries. There the companies were supplying their own employees, who constitute the majority of the electricity consumers of the town. In the other urban centers, there were various combinations of public and private systems, with no control or regulation. Service was unreliable and otherwise inadequate, connection charges were exorbitant, and rates were not such as to encourage the use of the service.

As part of the development program, in 1959, a 132-kv transmission line was placed in service between Abadan and Ahwaz, the capital of Khuzestan province. This was used to deliver to Ahwaz power purchased from the oil companies at Abadan. The Ahwaz distribution system was rehabilitated and expanded. The number of consumers served has grown from 7,000 in 1958 to 18,000 in June, 1962. Included in the Ahwaz service area are about 10 surrounding villages previously without electric service of any kind. Power demand on the Ahwaz system quadrupled in 3 years.

As a basis for system rehabilitation and expansion in Ahwaz, D&R negotiated on behalf of the Government the acquisition of the privately owned system in the town and integrated it with the municipal system under the ownership of the newly formed company owned by the municipality. D&R is assisting the Government in managing the affairs of this company and training its organization. A wholesale power contract, which establishes retail rates and terms of sale, was made effective. A similar series of steps is in progress in the four other urban centers of Khuzestan to which Dez power will initially be made available.

As part of the plan, in 1960, the Government established the Khuzestan Water and Power Authority to carry on the development program, and gradually to assume D&R's responsibilities. KWPA has its own legislative charter, which places primary responsibility for its affairs upon the Deputy Prime Minister and head of the Government's Plan Organization. The Deputy Prime Minister can delegate his powers to the managing director of KWPA whom he also recommends for appointment by the Prime Minister. Such a delegation has been made. KWPA, under its charter, may use its revenues to finance its operations, may appoint its own officers and employees and fix the levels of their compensation. It establishes rates for the sale of electricity and charges for irrigation water. It maintains its own system of accounts, and, while wholly owned by the Government, it is intended to have sufficient autonomy to operate as an independent enterprise. KWPA is to conduct development operations for irrigation and power associated with the waters of the five Khuzestan rivers.

D&R has already transferred, and KWPA has accepted, full responsibility for power operations and for general services, although the firm's staff and contractors continue to assist KWPA in carrying out this work. In power operations, the firm entered into a contract on behalf of KWPA with the Hydroelectric Power Commission of Ontario to operate and maintain the Dez hydroelectric project and to train a staff of Iranians later to assume these responsibilities. The Ontario Hydro group serves as part of the organization of KWPA's Power Division, which is headed by an Iranian engineer. Reporting to him is the technical director of the Power Division, through whom the various elements of the organization now report. He is a D&R employee and also serves as a consultant and advisor to the chief of the Power Division and to other members of KWPA's management. By 1965, it is anticipated that the power operations of KWPA can be entirely handled by its Iranian organization, with the training it will have received.

D&R assisted the Government of Iran in its negotiations with the International Bank for Reconstruction and Development, which agreed to lend $42 million to Iran for the Khuzestan program. The balance of the funds required are being supplied by Plan Organization, from Iran's oil revenues. The total cost of the present KWPA program is estimated at $150 million. Included are Dez Dam, transmission lines and substations, a pilot-irrigation project, a sugarcane plantation and factory, and rehabilitation and expansion of five electric distribution systems in and near the principal load centers. The loan agreement with IBRD includes provisions for maintenance of rate levels for power and the establishment of KWPA.

With the availability, for the first time, of modern reliable electric service, in adequate supply and at reasonable cost, power requirements in Khuzestan have been demonstrated to be capable of rapid growth. The third Dez generating unit is scheduled for installation in 1965–66, and will be needed by then. The fourth is scheduled for 1968. Its actual date of installation can be adjusted to meet any changes from the rate of growth of power needs which is now foreseen.

Conclusions

Securing modern electric-power supply for a particular less developed area requires the solution of many problems which are peculiar to that area. The technical nature of the facilities to be provided, the type of primary energy sources which are available, the existing power systems and their integration, these and more need to be approached for each such area so that their solutions can be tailored to meet the area's needs. In the five cases which have been reviewed, however, there were some problems of significance for the solution of which common avenues were pursued. These common avenues may be of special interest as holding promise for other less developed areas. These problems and their solutions were as follows:

The problem. To establish an agency with power to exercise sufficient responsibility to carry out the necessary work. No private agency has accomplished this, and no existing agency of Government is set up with the necessary skills and authority.

The solution. By formal governmental action, usually including actual legislation, to establish key policies and new institutions, separate from the regular administrative departments, although by various methods, responsible to and through the existing structure of Government at some fixed point. There are some especially significant policies for these institutions which appear with frequency:

(a) They resemble the corporate rather than the governmental form.

(b) They are intended to be largely autonomous.

(c) They are to have wide flexibility of action and decision.

(d) They are to be largely independent of the regular civil service.

(e) Accountability is assured by prescription of modern accounting practices and regular reporting.

(f) Administration and personnel are intended to be nonpolitical.

(g) They are intended to be financially self-supporting, and to charge the users of their services enough to cover their costs.

(h) They are to be nonprofit.

(i) They are to be exempt from regular taxation, with provision in some cases for payments in lieu of taxes under a specified formula. Except for such payments, none of the agencies can serve as a channel for contributions by electric consumers to the general funds of the owning Government.

The problem. To finance the cost of construction of the modern electricity supply facilities.

The solution. With initial contributions from the sponsor or owning Government of cash and property, the new institution finances its costs through (a) its income, (b) its own internal and external borrowings, and (c) through borrowing made or guaranteed by the sponsor Government. In each case, the sponsor Government is in the position of the owner of the equity in the new institution, the new institution being responsible directly or indirectly for defraying the debt service costs. The return on the owner's equity is not ordinarily to be in cash terms, but in terms of benefit to the general welfare.

The problem. How can the necessary higher skills be acquired rapidly in order to utilize and apply the advanced technologies involved in providing and operating a modern electric power system?

The solution. Each case, in its own way, has involved the importation into a geographical area of management, engineering, and labor skills not indigenous to the area. Training programs are then depended upon to bridge the gap between (a) the early organization using foreign skills and (b) the ultimate organization made up largely of local people. Continuing availability of high-level technical and management assistance is obtained through appropriate contractual arrangements.

The problem. How to integrate existing electric systems into the newly constructed system in such a way as to make optimum use of existing properties and organizations, while moving ahead toward the integrated system with its inherent economies.

The solution. Most common among the five cases has been the negotiated purchase of existing privately owned systems, and the absorption of existing publicly owned systems, if any, into the new one. Existing organizations are absorbed, to the extent that they can be useful to the new institution, either directly or by retraining. Wholesale power contracts are also used as the vehicles through which the new institution's policies are adopted by local agencies distributing power supplied from the new system. They control retail rates and customer service and accounting policies. This is, of course, not necessary in cases such as PPC and PRWRA, which serve all, or practically all, ultimate consumers in their service areas.

The problem. How to develop internal and external sources of financing for the large investments necessary to supplement its own and its owning Government's resources to provide for a modern electricity supply system?

The solution. In each case the new institution has the power to borrow money in its own name, and has used this power or the borrowing power of its owning Government to secure a portion of the funds required. In each case, also, the new institution has the right to dispose of its revenues for power purposes. The electric-power business can be depended upon to yield revenues adequate to cover its costs. Investors will be willing to advance funds for it at reasonable cost if they are assured that the institutional arrangements will preserve the financial integrity of the business; if, in other words, the credit of the new institution is established and maintained, if it is proven as a "good risk." The private capital markets, within the country or in the outside world are depended upon in some of the cases, others have so far limited themselves to public agencies, still others have used a combination of private and public sources. Supplier credits have also been utilized.

The problem. How can the magnitude of future requirements be measured, in order to determine goals for the development of the new electric system?

The solution. The records of actual growth for the five cases throw some light on this question. In each case there was a clean break from past records, when the institutions went into operation. With new objectives as to adequacy of electricity supply, levels of rates, etc., the increases in level of use were far greater than many expected. The most important step was the establishment and implementation of the new objectives.

Then, the provision of new capacity to meet changing future needs could be geared to provide adequate margins. If growth is less rapid than expected, planned expansion can be postponed, if growth is more rapid new facilities can be accelerated. Plans should be made for power-system development which are geared to probable future levels of needs with certain specified timing assumptions. Changes of timing can then readily be accomplished as the facts of future requirements and their rates of growth become available. Initial market predictions can take into consideration basic economic considerations such as population and its growth, and specific industrial development possibilities, as well as experience in other areas when adequate power supply becomes available. The experience in the five cases shows that high rates of growth are probable, and that doubling every 5 years or so can be maintained for extended periods.

The problem. Determining what role in electric-power supply should be played by indigenous primary energy sources.

The solution. Emphasis was first placed in all cases upon development of indigenous energy sources, especially water power. Then, as requirements continue to increase, local coal and oil refinery product resources enter the energy supply for the power system. Foreign exchange needs for oil purchases place a premium on the use of other primary sources which may encourage their development, even at somewhat higher economic cost. However, the premium thus paid by consumers of electricity as their contribution toward preserving their nation's foreign exchange balances should be continuously examined with a critical eye to assure that it does not become so large as to interfere with the accomplishment of the objectives of power-system development. Electricity is a highly flexible form of energy. Technology now has advanced to the point that it can be produced economically through the use of a wide range of primary sources, including, in addition to water power, coal of practically all grades, natural gas, and many grades of petroleum products, ranging from crude oil, through light products to residual fuel oil (Bunker C) and even to refinery pitch which is used by PRWRA directly from the refinery and which is quite economical.

With the establishment of public sources of financing such as the IBRD and its affiliates, International Finance Corporation and International Development Agency, the Inter-American Development Bank, the U.S. Agency for International Development, and its counterparts among other Western nations, opportunities have greatly multiplied for less developed areas to secure assistance in financing modern electric-power systems. Consulting and advisory services are widely offered by private and public agencies. And experience in other areas such as the five cases described here is accumulating rapidly.

Metallurgical, Domestic, and Industrial Utilization of Low-Rank Coals

W. S. LANDERS

Chief, Denver Coal Research Laboratory, Division of Bituminous Coal, Bureau of Mines, U.S. Department of the Interior, Denver, Colorado

The proper utilization of coal resources is an important, and possibly essential, step in the advancement of less developed areas of the world. Coal is a widely distributed mineral, usually comprising a significant potential source of energy and chemicals where the reserves of coal are adequate and where it can be economically mined. The low-rank coals of the world are widely distributed; but their utilization, particularly in expanding economies of the less developed areas, has been restricted, because of their chemical and physical properties. Low-rank coals for the present purpose include brown coals, lignites, and subbituminous coals, corresponding to classes 10 through 15 of the International System for classifying brown coals and lignites. They are all characterized by high-moisture content, a relatively low heating value, high-oxygen content, inability to fuse to produce coke, and high susceptibility to spontaneous combustion during transportation or storage.

In less developed areas of the world, the major historical use of low-rank coals has been as fuel for local consumption. Even this restricted use, however, has

been difficult in many areas because these coals cannot be burned successfully and easily in equipment used with wood, charcoal, and other traditional fuels. The purpose of this paper is to present and discuss techniques applicable in these areas that would permit the extension of the use of such coals as technologic and industrial development progresses. Within the space limitations of this paper, it will not be possible to do more than suggest or mention many of the possible areas and techniques of utilization. It is my intent, however, to show that widespread application can be made of such fuels through the use of technologies and information now available.

Coal utilization may be discussed best under several general categories. I have chosen to emphasize the application of low-rank coals to iron-ore reduction because of the widespread international importance of metallurgy and the projected expansion of the steel industry in the less developed areas of the world.

Since prehistoric times, metallurgical operations have used charcoal or anthracite as a source of heat and as a chemical reducing agent. These fuels, however, are too costly or do not possess the proper physical or chemical properties for use in modern, large-scale metallurgical operations. As the need for stronger, cheaper, and more uniform fuels developed for these applications, the metallurgical industry concentrated in those areas of the world having coking coals. Small local metallurgical industries persist to this day in countries not so fortunately endowed, but such installations are not adequate to serve the needs of an expanded industrial economy.

The most intriguing, useful, and desirable metallurgical application of coal in our present economy is in the production of pig iron. The blast furnace is used almost universally, in one way or another, to produce this material. Because of the requirements of the blast furnace, the fuel supplied to modern units is a strong, hard coke, containing low concentrations of water and volatile matter. Low-rank coals do not possess the property of directly fusing in the coke oven to form such a coke. If they are charged in their natural state as a coke substitute, the blast furnace cannot function because the coals, in addition to having a high-volatile-matter content, will crumble and clog the passage of the air blast. However, recent developments have demonstrated two processes by which pig iron can be produced with noncoking coals. The first of these is the modification, through suitable processing, of the low-rank coals to form a synthetic coke that can be charged as part of the burden in conventional or modified blast furnaces. The second approach is the utilization of metallurgical techniques not requiring the use of the blast furnace. It is not the purpose of this paper to discuss the relative merits of these two

techniques, as the choice between them transcends technologic consideration.

The production of synthetic coke by modification of low-rank coals consists basically in changing the chemical structure of the coal to reduce its moisture, oxygen, and volatile-matter contents, to increase its fixed-carbon content and heating value, and to consolidate the modified coal into a strong, dense agglomerate. The FMC Corporation and the U.S. Steel Corporation, both of the United States, have recently developed and announced a process to accomplish these results. This process, generally known as the "FMC Process", consists of the following steps:

(a) Stage crushing of the coal to less than $1/8$ in. (3.2 mm).

(b) Preprocessing of the crushed coal by controlled oxidation at a relatively low temperature in a fluidized bed in order to modify both chemical and physical nature of the coal.

(c) Carbonization of the modified coal in a fluidized bed to produce a low-temperature char (semicoke) and sufficient condensable tar for use in the subsequent briquetting operation.

(d) Production of a low-volatile char by recarbonization of the low-temperature char at high temperatures in a fluidized bed.

(e) Briquetting of the high-temperature char with the entire output of low-temperature tar in conventional, high-pressure, opposed-roll presses.

(f) Controlled oxidation at moderate temperatures in a shaft furnace to modify the chemical nature of the tar binder.

(g) Recarbonization of the modified briquets at high temperatures to produce a strong, low-volatile matter briquet suitable for blast furnace and other metallurgical applications.

A comparison of the physical properties of large-size FMC Process briquets and similar properties of conventional foundry coke is given in table 1. The FMC briquets may be made in any size, and it has been indicated that reactivity and other properties of the briquets can be controlled by selection of temperature, residence time, and other operating variables.

TABLE 1. *Physical and chemical properties of FMC Process and foundry cokes* [1]

	Coke from FMC process	Foundry coke
Shape	Uniform pillow blocks	Random.
Size ..... inches.	As desired, up to 3½ x 4	Random, up to 4 x 8.
Moisture ..... percent	1–2	1–2
Drop shatter index	92+	92+
Tumbler index	92+	92+
Crushing resistance ..... psi	3,000–6,000 [2]	2,000–4,000 [3]
Apparent specific gravity	1.0–1.05	0.95
True specific gravity	1.95	1.95
Bulk density ..... lb ft [3]	38–42	28–32
Proximate analysis, moisture-free basis, percent:	([4])	([4])
Volatile matter	2–3	1–2
Fixed carbon	92–95	88–93
Ash	3–6	5–10
Sulfur	0.5–0.8	0.5–1.0

[1] Data supplied by the FMC Corporation, New York, N.Y., U.S.A.
[2] Based on cylinders of one-square-inch cross sectional area.
[3] Based on ½-inch cubes.
[4] Analyses shown are typical. Actual values depend upon ash and sulfur content of the coal used.

Brown coal and lignite have effectively been converted in various parts of the world to materials suitable for use in low-shaft furnaces. Many of these low-rank coals are briquettable in high-pressure equipment without the use of binders. This technique, where applicable, requires crushing and drying of the high-moisture lignite or brown coal to a preestablished optimum moisture content, briquetting in high-pressure equipment, and carbonization of the briquets to high temperatures to produce a low-volatile coke. The heating schedule for the carbonization is critical, but an excellent product can be obtained by this technique. For those lignites and brown coals not briquettable without a binder, briquets can be produced from either the dried or carbonized coal using pitch or other binders. Such briquets are usually carbonized to produce a low-volatile, hard coke. If high-density fuels are not required, it is possible to pelletize coal with suitable binders and to carbonize the pellets by a carefully controlled heating schedule in a stream of hot natural gas or methane. This treatment sets the aggregate into a strong coke-like structure.

The other major approach to the utilization of low-rank fuels in the production of pig iron involves the use of techniques not requiring the blast furnace. There are a variety of such "direct reduction" processes that have either been tried or suggested, but most of them make use of an inclined rotary kiln into which a burden of ore, flux, and solid fuel is charged. As the burden moves through the kiln, some of the fuel burns in the air blast introduced at the discharge end to produce the heat required for the reactions; the remainder of the fuel then acts as a chemical reducing agent to produce metallic iron (or partially reduced iron oxides) from the oxide ores. There are many variations possible in this approach. For example, some processes produce a molten slag of vitreous material in which the iron particles are suspended. The slag issuing from the kiln is quenched and crushed, and the iron particles are collected by gravity separation or by magnetic means. In other processes, the kiln is operated under nonslagging conditions producing either finely divided metallic iron distributed throughout the nonfused product, partially reduced iron ore, or a mixture of the two. It has been successfully demonstrated that char or semicoke made by the carbonization of low-rank coals is a satisfactory fuel for use in direct reduction kilns. These chars, generally produced in entrained or fluidized beds, are highly reactive, and if formed at the proper temperature, they do not produce any objectionable tars or liquids that could affect the operation of the necessary dust-collecting apparatus used at the gas-discharge end of the kiln. It has also been demonstrated that raw lignite can be used efficiently as the reducing agent in at least one of the direct-reduction operations. It is likely that, through suitable modification of operating techniques, raw, dried, or carbonized lignite, brown coals, and subbituminous coals can

be used in a variety of the direct-reduction processes.

The use of low-rank coals in the production of pig iron can be accomplished, then, through either the radical modification of the coal to produce a synthetic cokelike material that can be used in the blast furnace or the application of direct-reduction kilns with either raw or modified noncoking coals as the fuel. The choice between these two approaches is an extremely complex one, depending upon quality and physical structure of the ore, as well as upon economic and other technological considerations.

Other metallurgical processes, such as scrap melting, slag reprocessing, and reduction of nonferrous metals, can utilize the coke substitutes prepared from the low-rank coals. These coke substitutes can also replace coke in other industries; for example, FMC Process briquets have been used in electric furnaces producing elemental phosphorus.

Sources of adequate fuel for domestic heating and cooking are becoming increasingly important problems in many of the less developed areas of the world. The fuels frequently used in these areas are wood, charcoal, and dried dung. The source of wood and charcoal has been the forests contiguous to centers of population, and a natural balance has been effected over the centuries between the use of the wood and the rate of growth of the forests. In recent years, however, such balances have been upset in many places by the rapidly increasing population. The forests are being depleted, the source of wood is receding from the population centers, and the cost of wood or charcoal is increasing rapidly. Raw low-rank coals can be used effectively for cooking and heating; however, it is necessary to have stoves and furnaces specifically adapted to the burning of high moisture solid fuels. Such equipment is not readily available in the less developed areas of the world. In addition, there are established techniques of cooking and heating based upon the traditional fuels available in these areas. Eventually, it might be possible to modify the habits of the inhabitants of these areas so that the coals can be burned directly in proper stoves and furnaces, but this will be a slow process. The better solution, and one more likely of immediate acceptance, is to modify the low-rank coals by processing so that the resulting products can be burned in braziers and other existing equipment in the traditional manner.

Let us examine the properties of the traditional fuels and compare them with the equivalent properties of the low-rank coals. Wood is an easily stored, easily ignited fuel requiring no special equipment for its handling or use. When it burns, however, it produces a smoky flame with an acrid odor. As a consequence of this smokiness, the practice has developed in many villages and towns of burning charcoal. Charcoal is also an easily ignited, handled, and stored fuel. It burns without odor or smoke and is well suited for use in populated areas and in kitchen stoves not equipped with flues or smoke stacks. Dried cow- or water-buffalo-dung is easily stored and ignited. While it burns with a distinctive odor, it does give a smokeless flame and is an extensively used fuel. All three of these fuels are easily handled and consist of relatively large-size particles that can be burned in simple equipment with little difficulty in providing adequate draft. When the immediate use is complete, the remaining fuel can be extinguished with water, allowed to sun dry, and later re-

ignited and used until it is completely consumed.

The low-rank coals, on the other hand, are characterized by high moisture content. Lump low-rank coal will slack and degrade to fine sizes or powder as the natural moisture in the coal evaporates if it is stored by simply piling or stacking. The resulting powder, or dust, is not suitable for burning in braziers. If the coal lumps are charged while they are fresh, that is, with their full moisture content, they are very difficult, if not impossible, to ignite in such equipment. As the lumps become heated in the fire, they dry and disintegrate, producing powder which chokes the fuel bed and prevents combustion. It is almost impossible to quench and recover unburned lumps from a fuel bed prepared from low-rank coals.

The problem, then, is to convert the coal into materials having properties as similar as possible to the preferred fuels. The general approach is to briquet the coal. Some of the low-rank coals can be crushed, dried to an optimum moisture content of about 10 to 16 percent, and briquetted without binder in high-pressure extrusion presses. The resultant briquets are then carbonized, converting the coal into a smokeless, easily ignited, free-burning char or semicoke briquet. The carbonized briquets are relatively porous and are reactive enough to be ignited by the same procedure used by the housewife for igniting charcoal.

If the coal cannot be briquetted without binder, an additive must be used to provide the cohesiveness necessary to form briquets. Such coals are carbonized to eliminate moisture and reduce the volatile-matter content, and the char is briquetted with a suitable binder. Starch, molasses, kraft paper waste, portland cement, clay, and other binders have successfully been used for this purpose. Excellent binders are pitches and asphalts. These latter materials coke when heated and form an extremely strong matrix, giving coherence to the briquet in the fuel bed. However, they burn with a smoky flame, and it is generally preferable to recarbonize these briquets before use in open domestic appliances. The problem of odor occurring during the burning of carbonized coal briquets made from char and tar has become important in the United States because of the use of such briquets for outdoor cooking. One of the major producers of carbonized coal briquets in the United States has effectively eliminated such odor through proper cooling of the char and briquets, and by the addition of small quantities of additives and catalysts. These briquets are finding wide acceptance as a premium domestic fuel.

One of the largest and most important uses of coal in the less developed areas of the world will probably be in thermal power plants. It has been adequately demonstrated that any of the low-rank coals can be burned efficiently in modern equipment, and the use of coal is primarily determined on the basis of economics. Small power plants can burn the coal on spreader or traveling-grate stokers, or the coal may even be hand-fired. Larger plants will probably use pulverized fuel burners. High-moisture coal must either be partially dried or very finely ground before it enters the pulverized fuel burners. The modern approach is to partially dry the coal, either by using hot-gas-swept pulverizing mills or by predrying the coal before pulverizing. Large power-generating plants in the United States using lignite with 35- to 45-percent moisture as the

fuel are operating successfully with each of these drying schemes. Pulverized-fuel burning is also successfully employed on brown coal and peat in other parts of the world. Processes and techniques for drying the low-rank coals to any predetermined moisture content are well developed and are available in any capacity.

The coal-burning gas turbine offers another route by which the low-rank coals can be used for power generation. Extensive pilot plant research is being conducted in several laboratories on the development of this technique. The coal-burning gas turbine will be able to generate power with the consumption of far less water than is required for the conventional thermal-electric plant, a feature of tremendous importance in arid areas. It should be kept in mind, however, that the coal-burning gas turbine is still in the process of development. The main problem yet to be solved is the development of a unit that will perform for long periods of time between outages for other than routine maintenance. The research being conducted in this field should prove productive, and it is believed that an extremely reliable unit will be developed. When this is an accomplished fact, it will be possible to make a rational economic analysis of the application of the coal-burning turbine for a particular installation. It should be pointed out that factors other than the savings in water are of significance in the selection of power-generating equipment.

New developments in the transportation of energy may influence the location of coal-burning thermal-electric plants and the economics of their operation. While these developments will probably be discussed in detail by the specialists on power generation, it is felt that attention should be called to suggested techniques that could extend the economical utilization of coal. These include pipeline transportation of coal-in-water or coal-in-oil slurries, improved and more efficient equipment and procedures for rail transportation of coal, and extra high-voltage (over 400 kv ac or about 375 kv dc) transmission of power. The cost of delivering the coal to the power plant and of delivering power to the distribution center are significant factors in determining the economic position of coal-burning thermal-electric plants.

In many parts of the world, coal historically was the main source of railroad fuel. In recent years it has been supplanted to a large extent by diesel fuel. This change in fuel supply has been dictated almost entirely by economic reasons. In those countries having adequate reserves of cheap, low-rank fuels, and where coal can be produced at a lower energy cost than diesel fuel, a definite area of application for railroad use exists. Because of the properties of low-rank coals, it is usually unsatisfactory to charge raw high-moisture coal to the firebox of a locomotive. With the high-temperature and high-draft conditions found in the firebox, the high-moisture coals break down into small particles and a large percentage of the fuel is lost up the stack. This obviously presents serious problems of economy and nuisance. It has been found, however, that briquets made from such coal are very satisfactory for railroad use. The type of briquet used is determined by the properties of the coal. For example, some high-moisture coals can be partially dried to 10- to 16-percent moisture content and briquetted without binder. Such briquets are excellent fuel. For this application it is not necessary to produce a smokeless briquet as was the case for domestic cooking, because the draft conditions in the firebox will burn most of the volatile matter. If a binder is required, satisfactory briquets for railroad use can be made by briquetting the dried or carbonized coal with a pitch or asphaltic binder. When such briquets are charged into the firebox, the hydrocarbon binder decomposes and forms a coke matrix, binding the coal fines into a lump-like structure.

Low-rank coals can be used in a variety of special industrial applications. Possibly the most significant of these to the less developed areas is the use of such fuels for cement burning. In order to efficiently burn cement clinker, it is necessary to develop a temperature of at least $3,000°$ F ($1,650°$ C) in the kiln. Because of the heat required to evaporate water from high-moisture low-rank coals, it is not possible to develop the necessary temperature with these coals unless costly and complicated airpreheating devices are used. If these coals, however, are dried before being pulverized and charged to the burner in the kiln, a flame temperature high enough to burn clinker can be obtained. This technique permits the substitution of low-rank coal for higher rank coal or other fuels for this very important application. The drying of coal in the large quantities required for cement burning can be accomplished economically, in existing equipment. The upgrading of low-rank fuels for cement burning and other industrial applications requiring high temperature could well prove to be one of the most significant uses of the high-moisture coals in the less developed areas. Extraction of montan wax and the production of low-ash material suitable for carbon-electrode manufacture are among the possible minor industrial applications of selected low-rank coals having the right chemical properties.

It is well-known that any rank of coal can serve as the basis for the production of a variety of organic chemicals. Coal supplies the necessary building blocks of carbon and hydrogen, and these can be formed into practically any synthetic organic compound. Carbonization, hydrogenation, gasification, and catalytic treatment are some of the major techniques used. The possibilities for such treatment are only mentioned within the context of this paper. Economic analyses have demonstrated that the production of chemicals by these techniques is competitive only when conducted on a very large scale. Such analyses have shown conclusively that there must be almost complete utilization of the fuel and of the byproducts in order to be economically attractive. Both of these considerations require that a well-developed industrial complex be established in order to use the quantity and variety of products that must be produced if such chemical processing is to be economical. By definition, the less developed areas do not yet have such complexes. I believe that it is premature to consider specific chemicals that can be made from the low-rank coals, but some of the major types of products that can be made from these fuels are solvents, protective coatings for pipe, rubber plasticizers, phenolic compounds for plastic manufacture, dye stuffs, fertilizers, and pharmaceuticals.

There are, however, two general areas of chemical utilization of the coal that might be considered; namely, synthetic liquid fuel and fertilizer production. Synthetic liquid fuels can be produced by complete hydrogenation of coal at high pressure and temperature and with suitable catalysts, or by the catalytic conversion of "synthesis gas", a mixture of carbon monoxide and hydrogen, obtained from the controlled gasification of the coal. The general use of these techniques for producing liquid fuels is well-known, although specific application to any given coal would have to be studied through laboratory investigations. Each of these processing schemes results in relatively complete conversion of the coal. Low-rank coal may be carbonized in an entrained or fluidized carbonizer to produce tar for hydrogenation to liquid fuels. The difficulty, however, with this process is that about 65 percent of the potential heat in the coal remains in the char residue and uses must be found for this fuel. Large quantities of char will be produced and must be consumed if an economically sized plant is constructed. The major application for the char in large quantity would be for power generation, since char is an excellent fuel and can be efficiently utilized in properly designed power plants. It should be kept in mind that, if this latter application is considered, a large power-generating industry is required to maintain a balance in the utilization of the two major products.

Nitrogen-containing fertilizers are of extreme importance to the less developed areas of the world. Atmospheric nitrogen is fixed by combining it with hydrogen at elevated temperatures and pressures. Low-rank coals provide a source of the hydrogen through either carbonization or gasification. Carbonization requires that uses be found for the char and tar produced concurrently with the hydrogen and again an integrated, balanced, industrial complex is necessary. Gasification, on the other hand, results in reasonably complete conversion of the coal to hydrogen and carbon monoxide, and these two products can be readily separated. The carbon monoxide can be utilized as a low-quality gaseous fuel even if no specific chemical application is available. Fluidized techniques are attractive for gasification, but conventional vertical shaft retorts using the briquetted fuel will probably prove more economical for carbonization. Fertilizer production must be conducted on a large scale to be economical, and large quantities of power are required. Such an industry should, therefore, be integrated with an adequate power generating installation.

Naturally oxidized lignites, such as leonardite, can be used as soil conditioners. They contain large percentages of naturally produced humates that are beneficial to the soil because of their ability to hold water and loosen the soil. Oxidized lignite generally occurs as outcrops or in beds under shallow, porous cover. The natural process of oxidation occurring over long periods of time can be approximated by chemical oxidation. Humates can then be extracted from the converted coal, or the entire mass of oxidized materials can be used as a soil conditioner. Oxidized coals, because of the water-holding power of the humates, are being used as additives to mud used in well drilling.

Any of the low-rank coals can be used for general industrial heating. They can be handfired or charged with a variety of mechanical stokers such as underfeed, traveling grate, or spreader. For such purposes it is not necessary to preprocess the coal, although care must be taken in selecting equipment designed to handle the type of ash found in the particular coal. For example, if the ash in a given coal has a high fusion temperature, the coal cannot be used in equipment requiring clinkering of the ash,

and accordingly, a low-fusion ash coal must be used in equipment providing for clinker removal. Most handfired units require lump material, but the fines can be briquetted as described before to make lumplike material suitable for handfiring.

Specialty carbons can be made from a wide variety of the low-rank coals, particularly those with low-ash contents. Some uses, such as electrodes for electrochemical applications, would not be of immediate interest in the less developed areas. The use of activated carbon produced from low-rank coals for water purification could be profitable. It is possible to convert lignite and other high-moisture coals to excellent activated carbons by carbonization in simple devices. For example, such carbons have been made in large quantity in externally heated rotary kilns, with no byproduct recovery.

Storage is a very important factor in the utilization of low-rank (high-moisture) coals. These coals become extremely reactive as they lose moisture. As the moisture evaporates from the capillaries in the coal, new internal surfaces are produced. In addition, the coal slacks or crumbles, also creating new surfaces. These new surfaces are extremely reactive, and any appreciable lot of low-rank coals merely heaped on the ground is susceptible to spontaneous combustion. This tendency towards firing has been a deterrent to the large-scale use of low-rank coals in many parts of the world. Storage is important because it is usually not possible to intergrate mining and transportation of coal with utilization in order to prevent the necessity for storage. For example, climatic conditions may make it necessary for mining to be practiced only during a portion of the year.

It may be too cold or too wet to operate the mines and to transport the coal during some seasons. If the coal cannot be properly stored, usually at point of use, it becomes necessary to restrict coal use to those industries operated on a seasonal basis. Seasonal operation would not be attractive to the power industry, where production is required throughout the year.

As mentioned earlier, the difficulty in storing low-rank coals arises from the drying of the coal and its subsequent oxidation and heating. This heat escapes slowly and the temperature rises, increasing both the rate of drying and the rate of oxidation. This spiral continues until the coal pile ignites. The proper technique of storage, therefore, is one which will prevent these effects. The best approach is to build the pile in layers. The coal is spread in a layer to reduce size segregation and is packed to a high-bulk density before the next layer is formed. By increasing the bulk density of the coal in the pile, circulation of air through the pile is minimized. This technique has proven more effective than either ventilating the piles or covering them with thin layers of sealing materials. The packing technique has proven effective on large storage piles, each containing as much as 1,000,000 tons of lignite. Another deterrent to the stocking of high-moisture coals is their tendency to freeze in the cars when they are shipped by rail in extremely cold weather. When this occurs, it is necessary to break up the coal or thaw it before the car can be unloaded. It has recently been demonstrated that freezing can be prevented by mixing a relatively small proportion of thermally dried coal with raw coal before loading.

The logical assignment of coals for specific uses requires at least some testing or research. It is to this phase of coal utilization that I would like to direct a few remarks. I have observed that in some areas where there is little or no experience in coal utilization, the need for pretesting the coal to establish its properties and amenability to a specific use has not been recognized. It cannot be emphasized too strongly that even though we speak of coals in terms of large classes, each coal has certain individual characteristics that cannot be predicted. It is necessary in our present state of knowledge to treat such coals as individuals and to determine their specific capabilities. It is certainly possible for an experienced coal technician to block out the general areas of application from only a cursory examination, perhaps by only a visual examination, but selection of the specific equipment and optimum operating conditions requires testing and analysis of the coal.

If it is accepted that some competent examination of the coal should be made before utilization processes are finalized, the question arises as to how and where such studies should be made. Laboratory and research facilities should be established in each coal-producing country, but it is necessary that selected local personnel be trained in a country having an established coal industry and adequate research facilities. This training can then be utilized in the orderly establishment of the local research facilities. Parallel to this training of laboratory personnel, specific initial coal-utilization problems of the less developed area should be studied in existing laboratories in the more developed areas. By obtaining research data and design suggestions from established industrial countries, coal production and utilization can be initiated in an efficient and reasonable manner. The existence of even a nucleus of a coal industry then provides the impetus for the development of the local laboratory and research facilities. It is very difficult to maintain continued interest and support in a laboratory being established in a country without the support of an operating industry in the same field.

A realistic approach to coal research must be maintained in development of the new facilities. The distinction must be recognized between fundamental and applied research, and the proper distribution of effort made in the research organization between these two lines. I believe that the most effective approach to the establishment of a coal research organization is to emphasize studies on applied technology. If the local laboratory can demonstrate the application of an existing technique or the development of a new technique that will result in production and utilization of a local coal, continuing financial and political support for this laboratory will be easier to obtain; the laboratory can then expand its fundamental studies.

Techniques for Appraising the Energy Economy and Outlook in Less Developed Countries

NATHANIEL B. GUYOL

Senior Staff Economist, Standard Oil Company of California, San Francisco, California

The purpose of this paper is to outline one approach to energy planning and forecasting and discuss its applicability to the less developed countries of the world.

The approach consists mainly of the construction of a complete energy balance for the country under consideration; appraisal of the influence of various physical, economic and institutional factors upon this balance; and application of the understandings thereby gained to the problems of planning and forecasting.

The energy balance is a device that has proven particularly useful in the collection and organization of data on the physical aspects of the energy economy. It is in fact nothing more or less than a consolidated account for all sources of energy, in which the several sources used in a particular area during a stipulated period of time are expressed in a common unit and brought together in a single table or graph. Fully developed, the energy balance traces each source of energy from origin to effective use, showing at each stage in this flow the physical and functional interrelationships of the several energy sources.

This analytical tool has come into rather wide use during the past decade, but mainly for countries that get most of their energy from sources that enter normal trade channels and are duly recorded—that is, the so-called commercial sources of energy. Among these countries are Austria (1), Belgium (2), Bulgaria (3), Canada (4), Germany (5), Italy (6), the Netherlands (7), Spain (8), and the United States (9).

There is at least one case, however, in which an energy balance has been constructed for a country that depends primarily upon non-commercial sources of energy. This case is India, whose energy balance is shown graphically in figure I, and statistically in table 1 (10).

The chart and the table demonstrate the importance of noncommercial sources of energy, including even draft animals, in less developed countries. In this particular case, it should be noted that draft cattle provide nearly as much *power* as all other sources of energy combined, and noncommercial fuels, such as firewood and dung, more *heat* than all other sources of energy combined.

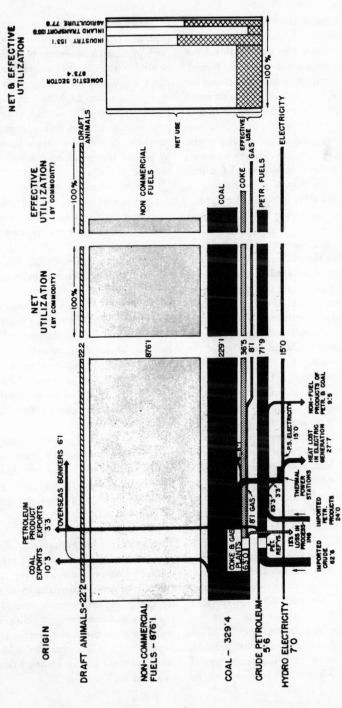

FIGURE I. Origin and utilization of energy in India—1959. (Data in million megawatt-hours, electricity equivalent.)

The main point in presenting the chart, however, is to demonstrate that energy balances *can* be constructed for less developed countries when needed. So far as commercial sources of energy are concerned, it is, in fact, somewhat easier to prepare accounts for less developed than for developed countries. The volumes to be accounted for are smaller; the flow from production or imports to end-use is ordinarily simpler, and the pattern of distribution is usually less diverse.

On the other hand, balances for less developed countries are complicated somewhat by the necessity of including noncommercial sources of energy, especially when the work output of draft animals must also be taken into account. This is not as difficult as it may seem, for supply and demand of energy from these sources can be estimated, with accuracy that suffices for most purposes, by methods developed in the Statistical Office of the United Nations (11) and the U.S. Department of State (12).

The most difficult problem that arises, in both developed and less developed countries, is that of estimating the quantities of energy *effectively* used—that is, the amount of energy converted to useful heat, light or power. The importance of this calculation cannot be over-emphasized, because the real costs of energy are determined as much by efficiency of use as they are by prices. Diesel oil, for example, is far more expensive per unit of contained energy than is coal, but as a locomotive fuel it costs less than coal per unit of work performed because of the relatively high efficiency with which it is used.

Reasonable approximations of effective use, satisfactory for most purposes, can be obtained by the application of standard efficiency factors to data on energy supplied to various consumer groups. The efficiency factors needed can be obtained from any one of a number of studies such as the United Nations paper on World Energy Requirements in 1975 and 2000 (13), and the papers previously referred to in (2), (6), and (9). Standard factors such as these can sometimes be improved upon, however, by special surveys of combustion practices and results (14).

National energy balances such as those described above provide most of the data needed concerning physical aspects of the energy economy, especially where the country dealt with is small. In large countries such as India, these can be usefully supplemented by *regional* energy accounts, especially when patterns of energy supply and demand vary significantly from one region to another.

The usefulness of both national and regional accounts is considerably enhanced when they can be repeated for a series of years, thus affording a basis for computing historical rates of growth in production, consumption, or other phases of supply and demand.

For planning purposes, data on energy reserves are needed, especially data on the location of mineral fuel deposits and water power sites that are readily accessible to domestic markets and can be developed at relatively low cost.

Energy balances provide a useful panorama of the energy situation. When repeated for a series of years and supplemented by data on energy reserves, they also provide some understanding of why the energy economy operates as it does. For a more complete understanding, it is necessary to consider also certain other factors which affect the energy economy—*economic* and *institutional* factors in particular.

Costs are among the factors to which particular attention must be given—mainly costs to consumers, but also costs to the economy as a whole and costs to the country in foreign exchange.

Data on costs appear to be relatively rare, but a surprising volume of such data can be assembled through systematic research within the area under study. In India, for example, it was found possible to obtain data on the costs of energy to industrial establishments, railways, power systems, households, airlines, gas works, and motor-vehicle operators. It was also found possible to obtain data on pithead prices of coal, on prices of petroleum products at refineries and distribution depots, on costs as well as charges for moving coal by rail, on charges for moving fuels by ship, on the aggregate values of fuels imported and exported, and on taxes on petroleum products and coal. Altogether, enough data were available to reveal the structure of energy costs in each sector of the economy and each major portion of India.

Institutional factors that affect the energy economy include the *agencies* responsible for managing portions of the energy economy, the *instruments* through which control is exercised, such as price controls, taxes, and subsidies; and the *will* of the government and the people to develop the national economy.

Data on institutional factors are not sought through separate research, but are accumulated in the course of normal research on physical and economic aspects of the energy economy. Some, such as taxes and subsidies, are brought to light through studies of the structure of prices or costs. Others are indicated simply by deviations of the supply-demand pattern from its expected course. As a rule, institutional factors tend to stand out in the publicly operated branches of the energy economy, and to fade into the background under private enterprise.

With data on the physical, economic, and institutional aspects of the energy economy in hand, an analysis of the energy situation becomes possible. This appraisal can be addressed initially to the single question: are consumers getting the energy they require? If they are not, there is need for immediate action to find out why not and what can be done to see that they get what they need practically *regardless of cost*. The penalty paid for any energy shortage normally exceeds by far, in terms of production, the costs of energy itself.

As a rule, it is fairly easy to find out whether consumers are getting the energy they require. Shortages, when they occur, have rather dramatic consequences, such as the closing down of industrial establishments, rationing, load shedding, and rapidly rising prices. They are therefore likely to be given considerable prominence in the press and other news media.

Attention must also be focussed on the costs of energy to consumers, to the economy as a whole, and to the country. Costs to the economy as a whole may be defined as consumer costs adjusted upwards to correct for subsidies and downwards to correct for taxes. Costs to the country may be defined as the net gains or losses in foreign exchange that result from the purchase of energy from foreign sources.

It is *relative* costs that are important to consumers and to the economy as a whole. The real question is one of whether energy is being made available to the two groups at as low a cost as possible, taking into account relative efficiencies of use as well as relative prices of the several

TABLE I. *India's energy balance, 1959*

[In Million MWH Electricity or Equivalent]

	Coal	Coke	Coal gas	Crude oil	LPG	Avgas	Jet fuel	Mogas	Kero.	Dist. F/O	Resid. F/O	Ref. fuel & loss	Nonfuel products	P.S. elect.	All comm. sources	Noncomm. fuels	Inanimate sources	Draft power sources	All sources
Primary Production	329.4			5.6											342.0	876.1	1,218.1	22.2	1,240.3
Secondary Production		42.5	8.1		0.1	1.1	1.8	12.2	9.5	17.7	19.9	4.0	4.3	7.0	126.3		126.3		126.3
Net Import	-9.7	-0.5		63.1		1.1	1.8	-1.8	14.7	2.8	-1.5		3.7	8.0	73.7		73.7		73.7
Gross Consumption	319.7	-0.5	8.1	68.7		1.1	1.8	-1.8	14.7	2.8	-1.5	4.0	3.7	7.0	415.7	876.1	1,291.8	22.2	1,314.0
Overseas Bunkers	1.0					0.3	0.3			0.3	4.3				6.2		6.2		6.2
Gross Inland Consumption	318.7	-0.5	8.1	68.7		0.8	1.5	-1.8	14.7	2.5	-5.8		3.7	7.0	409.5	876.1	1,285.6	22.2	1,307.8
Processed In—																			
Coke Ovens	43.3														43.3		43.3		43.3
Gas Works	1.3														1.3		1.3		1.3
Soft Coke Works	18.7														18.7		18.7		18.7
Petr. Refineries				68.7											68.7		68.7		68.7
P.S. Elect. Works	32.2									1.3	2.1				35.6		35.6		35.6
Total	95.5			68.7						1.3	2.1				167.6		167.6		167.6
Net Inland Consumption	[1]229.1	[2]36.5	8.1		0.1	0.8	1.5	10.4	24.2	18.9	12.0	4.0	8.0	15.0	368.7	876.1	1,244.8	22.2	1,267.0
Utilization (Input):																			
Transportation	108.8	21.9	7.8			0.8	1.5	10.4		13.3	0.8			0.5	136.1		136.1	1.0	137.1
Industry	95.3	13.1	0.3		0.1				23.7	2.9	10.7	4.0		9.0	151.6	1.5	153.1		153.1
Domestic Sector	4.8								0.5					2.7	44.7	828.7	873.4		873.4
Agriculture	6.4									2.7	0.6			0.7	10.9	45.9	56.8	21.2	78.0
Nonfuel		1.4											8.0		9.4		9.4		9.4
Lost and Not Accounted	13.8	0.1												2.1	16.0		16.0		16.0
Total	229.1	36.5	8.1		0.1	0.8	1.5	10.4	24.2	[3]20.2	[4]14.1	4.0	8.0	15.0	[5]372.0	876.1	1,244.8	22.2	[5]1,270.3
Utilization (Output):																			
Transportation	6.8					0.1	0.2	1.0		1.8	1.0			0.5	11.4		11.4	1.0	12.4
Industry	52.4	12.0	6.2							0.9	6.4	2.4		-2.0	78.3	0.6	78.9		78.9
Domestic Sector	1.4	3.9	0.2		0.1				1.6					1.4	8.6	124.3	132.9		132.9
Agriculture	2.5								0.1	0.5	0.3			0.7	4.1	13.8	17.9	21.2	39.1

Total	63.1	15.9	6.4	---	0.1	0.1	0.2	1.0	1.7	3.2	7.7	2.4	---	0.6	102.4	138.7	241.1	22.2	263.3
Heat	58.0	15.9	6.4	---	0.1	---	---	---	1.2	---	6.7	2.4	---	-13.8	76.9	138.7	215.6	---	215.6
Power and Light	5.1	---	---	---	0.1	0.2	1.0	0.5	3.2	1.0	---	---	14.4	25.5	---	25.5	22.2	47.7

1 Including 5.6 from oven coke and 0.4 accounting difference.
2 Excluding 6.3 transferred to coal/soft coke; including 0.7 transferred from oven coke.
3 Including 1.3 converted to electricity.
4 Including 2.0 converted to electricity.
5 Including 3.3 converted to electricity.

LPG = Liquefied Petroleum Gas	Avgas = Aviation Gasoline
Mogas = Motor Gasoline	Kero. = Kerosene
Dist. F/O = Distillate Fuel Oil	Resid. F/O = Residual Fuel Oil
Ref. Fuel & Loss = Refinery Fuel & Loss	P.S. Elect. = Public Supply Electricity
All Comm. Sources = All Commercial Sources	Non-Comm. Fuels = Non-Commercial Fuels

Source: National Council of Applied Economic Research.

energy sources. As previously indicated, the importance of taking efficiencies of use into account cannot be overemphasized.

The appraisals described above will have brought to light many of the problems and opportunities facing the energy economy. They will thereby have created a sound basis for energy planning, the objective of which is to maximize the contribution of energy to the development of less developed areas.

A somewhat different approach is needed for forecasting, because forecasting is concerned with things as they are *likely* to be rather than things as they *should* be.

One basis for forecasting is provided by data on historical trends in demand or supply of energy. The value of such data is extremely limited, however, because of potential changes in the fuels used and in the efficiency with which they are used. As a rule, the main value of trend data is in indicating probable upper and lower limits to the development of supply or demand.

Forecasts of national product also provide a basis for estimating future needs and supplies of energy, but only on the basis of the historical relationship of energy to national product. The results obtained by this device are no more satisfactory than simple projections of the energy curves.

To get really satisfactory forecasts it is necessary to take into account, in addition to historical trends, various economic and institutional factors that influence energy demand and supply. The real problem is to ascertain how much weight should be given to each of the factors affecting demand or supply. In private-enterprise economies, where economic forces have relatively free play, the pendulum is likely to swing toward economic factors. In public enterprise economies, institutional factors are more likely to dominate. But there is no hard-and-fast rule to guide the forecaster. He must, finally, weigh intuitively that which he cannot weigh mathematically.

REFERENCES

(1) Austria. Bundesministerium für Verkehr und Wiederaufbau, *Osterreichische Energiebilanz für das Jahr, 1953,* Vienna (1955).

(2) Marchal, G. H., *Bilan énergétique de la Belgique,* Annales des mines de Belgique, Brussels. (Annual)

(3) Georgiev, D. A., B. St. Kostov, *d'ánergie complet de la R. P. de Bulgarie pour les années 1956–57,* Sofia (1961).

(4) Davis, J., *Canadian energy prospects,* Royal Commission on Canada's Economic Prospects, Ottawa (1957).

(5) Arbeitsgemeinschaft deutscher wirtschaftswissenschaftlicher Forschungs-institute e. V., *Untersuchung über die Entwicklung der gegenwartigen und zukünftigen Struktur von Angebot und Nachfrage in der Energiewirtschaft der Bundesrepublik unter besonderer Berücksichtigung des Steinkohlenbergbaus. Juni 1959,* Duncker & Humblot, Berlin (1962).

(6) Società Edison, *Il bilancio energetico Italiano nel 1960,* Quaderni di studi e notizie, 343, Milan (16 July, 1961).

(7) Netherlands. Centraal Planbureau, *Production and consumption of energy in the Netherlands in 1947,* The Hague. (Chart.)

(8) Spain. Ministerio de Industria, *Balance y estructura de la produccion y el consumo de energia en España,* Madrid (1956).

(9) Barnett, H. J. *Energy Uses and Supplies: 1939, 1947, 1965.* Washington: GPO, 1950. Department of the Interior, Bureau of Mines, Information Circular 7582.

(10) The chart and table are based on studies prepared in 1961 by the National Council of Applied Economic Research, New Delhi.

(11) United Nations. Statistical Office, *World energy supplies in selected years, 1929–1950,* Statistical papers, J–1, New York (September, 1952).

(12) U.S. Department of State, *Energy resources of the world,* U.S. Government Printing Office, Washington (1949).

(13) United Nations. Department of Economic and Social Affairs, *World energy requirements in 1975 and 2000,* International Conference on the Peaceful Uses of Atomic Energy: Proceedings, *I,* New York (1956).

(14) A good example of such surveys is the survey of household fuel efficiencies conducted for the National Council of Applied Economic Research in India and reported upon in *Domestic fuels in India.*

Strategy Planning for Transportation and Economic Development

MARTIN MEYERSON

Director, Joint Center for Urban Studies, Massachusetts Institute of Technology and Harvard University, Cambridge, Massachusetts

An effective transportation system is a prerequisite for extensive economic growth. As a result, transportation takes a huge share of the technical assistance programs, national development plans, and capital loans in the developing countries. The World Bank, for example, loaned 475 million dollars (U.S.) for transportation in Africa, well over half of all its loans on that continent up to June 1961. In Asia, transportation loans were slightly more than 40 percent of the total, and in Latin America, slightly less than 40 percent (1). In Thailand, over 40 percent of all public investment was spent on transport and communication during the years 1952–56, and the amount rose to about 50 percent during 1957 and 1958 (2). In the Middle East, transportation improvement took at least 25 percent of governmental expenditures for development in the postwar years (3). Most countries with economic plans allocate a fifth or more of their public investment to transportation.

Since transportation receives such a high proportion of public investment, the developing countries are under pressure to plan transportation improvements so that they will maximize the objectives they are intended to serve with the lowest possible capital and operating cost. A strategy for transportation should therefore consider transportation from a functional point of view, rather than from a facility point of view.

Goal Clarification, a First Essential

Transportation and other movement is rarely desired for its own sake; it is valued as an instrument to achieve other objectives. The character of transportation and communications networks will differ markedly according to the principal and subordinate services they will be called upon to perform. Developing countries may have many objectives and may want simultaneously to exploit natural resources, increase agricultural productivity, increase industrialization, improve internal protection, and raise urban amenities; some kind of hierarchy of objectives or best combination of objectives and actions must be determined before investment takes place in transportation and communication systems, if for no other reason than the lack of sufficient resources to maximize all objectives. The best combination approach will undoubtedly mean that some elements of the combination will receive less than maximum attention. But it is the combination that should be optimized, not the separate elements. And certainly, it is that combination which best provides for economic development within the country that should be sought (4).

It is no simple task to work out the best combination of objectives and actions to stimulate economic development. It is possible, for example, that the leaders of a nation set a high value on political unification. To help achieve this, they would spread transportation expenditures thinly but extensively through the country. These expenditures might be regarded as uneconomic: that is, they will not produce the direct results of concentrated transportation improvements for specific industries. (Fishing vessels, for example, and a fishing port would promote the fishing industry.) Yet, political unification might turn out to be a more successful means of spurring economic growth than the development of a specific industry. Once the people of the nation are brought in contact with each other, even by relatively primitive transportation means, trade and specialized production might be stimulated. Indeed, there are usually some benefits which result from almost any extension of transportation into a previously unserved territory, or from any investment in transportation facilities (e.g., one common unintended consequence of road improvement in developing countries is the reduction of road accidents) (5). Policy makers should try to anticipate as many of the unintended as well as the intended results of a transportation proposal when judging alternatives. (Will labor mobility be increased? Will residential densities along transportation routes be altered? Will people usurp road margins for additional living and commercial space, as they do in Japan, reducing the effectiveness of the highway?)

The major transportation investment choices include (a) The amount to be invested in transportation compared to that which is invested directly in industrial facilities, agriculture, or other parts of the productive sysem; (b) the amount invested in movement for productive purposes compared to that invested in transportation for purposes which are not directly productive (the convenience or safety of the users), and (c) the locus of the investment and whether it favors capital city development, is concentrated in urban or metropolitan areas generally, or is diffused over regional or national areas.

In making these choices, the ratios between transportation and other economic investments (a) which are appropriate at one point will have to be revised over time and should be so planned. However, only some transportation investments can be incremental or gradual; many must be constructed in a technically complete and therefore expensive unit. A main stretch of railroad track must connect origin and destination; one spur will not do. Therefore, except for feeder roads which might be "self-help" projects (6) most transportation facilities require the kind of "big push" which Paul Rosenstein-Rodan suggests for economic development (7).

Most developing countries will put little importance on non-productive purposes of transportation (b). The Soviet Union, by having a simple basic rail service, with few concessions to special preferences, has had extremely high utilization of its plant, with almost no weekly or seasonal peaks (8). A main exception should be the conservation of the time of skilled personnel, a scarce resource in developing countries.

The locus of transportation investment (c) will have to be determined in conjunction with policies which favor concentration or decentralization of industry. Most observers tend to agree with Holland Hunter that the "speed of industrial development and geographic dispersion of economic activity appear to be inversely related. If rapid growth of industry is a major objective, it is likely to foster the expansion of established industrial centers or to concentrate them into new centers" (9).

Therefore, advocates of decentralization usually have claimed social and political advantages, rather than economic ones; the least disorganization of the social structure and great potential growth of political responsibility and leadership have been expected to accompany smaller-scale, gradual industrialization. However, some have claimed economic advantage as well. For example, Eugene Staley notes, "There is good reason for thinking, however, that in many situations, decentralization and diffusion of industry may also be justified on strict grounds of economic efficiency, when account is taken of the social overhead costs of moving people to central cities, housing them, and providing utilities" (10). Small plants and cottage industries in rural areas may be recommended temporarily because they "require less capital per worker than most large-scale industries and can use local labour during slack periods for agriculture without diminishing food production" (11). This would clearly be an intermediary step in economic development since production would not be so standardized to require a uniform product and the tendencies would be to minimize con-

sumption rather than to increase it as a spur to added production.

If a concentrated industrial policy were followed, transportation outlays would have to be made for internal circulation of goods and persons in densely settled and congested areas and some kind of mass transportation would be inevitable. Greater emphasis would have to be placed, if a decentralized industrial policy were followed, on the multiple interconnections of the smaller scattered specialized places of production. Staley points out that the latter course is more feasible now that reliance no longer need be placed on rail or water transport: "Some of the most recent trends in technology help to make smaller, diffused manufacturing operations more viable— for example, cheap electric power, automatic transport, improved communications." Louis Lefeber, warns however against irrational freight rates when, as in India, each province feels that it should have its share of industry and transportation (12).

The Imperative to Cost Minimization: Reduction of Demand

The transportation system must be planned on a cost-minimizing principle to conserve capital. The traditional means of conserving capital should, of course, be explored, but should not be accepted automatically as being economic in the long run. In surplus labor areas it may be wise to rely temporarily on human power instead of mechanical power to build roads or to load freight. But it may be even wiser to purchase the latest labor saving devices, skipping intermediate and less efficient transportation means, and channeling the labor instead into other productive enterprises. (Indeed, it may be wise to try to automate as many operations as possible—automatic marshalling yards, for example, or automatic loading facilities—to minimize the possibilities for human error in countries where skilled personnel are scare and the opportunities for breakdown are many.) In like manner, water transportation should not be regarded as necessarily cheaper than motor, rail or even air transport unless all the cost factors are calculated. These would include the speed of movement, labor consumed, transfer charges, traffic volumes, seasonal availability, and the linkage of strategic points.

Minimization of cost can also be achieved through dealing with transportation from a functional vantage point. Present patterns of traffic flow—or the typical Western ones—need not be accepted as bases for future decisions. It may be possible, for example, to reduce the demand for transportation through land use planning, through substitution or through organization. It may also be possible to minimize transportation cost through rationalizing the transportation system.

Minimization of The Need for Movement Through Land Use Planning. If related land uses can be grouped together geographically, much of the crosshaul and traffic movement among these interdependent activities can be eliminated. By clustering industries which are linked to each other, associating commercial establishments, or giving workers ready access to their employment, the transportation network can be simplified. Many ports, for example, have set aside land for port-related industries, thus reducing the need for transhipment of imported materials. Food processing plants built close to sources of production can

reduce the need for speedy handling of perishables; warehousing at terminal points can even out peak demands for transportation.

Minimizing transportation needs through placing related activities in physical proximity is most feasible when an area is being newly developed. It may be far more costly in a built-up area, for example, to relocate industrial, commercial and residential facilities than to link them with transportation facilities. However, spot relocation may effect important transportation economies. When an area is newly developed, enough land must be reserved to accommodate future expansion. If workers' housing completely surrounds an industrial district, for example, there will be no room for growth of the existing industries or for the introduction of ancillary services or complementary industries.

Minimization of the Need for Movement Through Substitution. Transportation should be regarded as only one of the means for linking persons and things which are spatially separated. Economies may be secured through the judicious use of modern communications or utilities. For example, it may be cheaper to burn coal at its source (or at another location) and transmit electric power over poles and wires to industry than to transport the coal over a highway or railroad which has to be constructed almost exclusively for the purpose of carrying fuel. In the United States oil and gas pipelines have largely replaced the long-haul of coal. Dieselization or electrification of trains reduces the need for freight traffic sharply; the railroads are prime consumers of the coal they carry.

Transportation may be avoided through extensive use of television or radio where personal services rather than goods are involved. In Australia, for example, patients explain symptoms and get advice on how to treat their ailments by radio, when they are in spots so distant or inaccessible that a physician cannot readily travel to them. Emergency service by airplane supplements the radio communication. Two-way television could be extremely useful in health and education services, minimizing the actual physical transporting of the consumer to the professional or vice versa. In developing countries, improving the telephone system would be of enormous assistance in spurring economic growth. If entrepreneurs could talk to each other and to government officials by telephone instead of in person, not only a great deal of personal travel could be cut down but a great deal of time and energy saved. Radiotelephony, with very high frequency to cross areas where pole and line equipment is impractical, Telex and private teleprinter circuits (the latter permit exchange of information for airline and railroad traffic bookings, and thus more rational use of these forms of transportation) would all help speed messages—and spur economic growth.

In general, it does not appear that nearly enough emphasis is being put on the development of communications as a substitute for or a supplement to other kinds of movement. Allocations are usually only a fraction of that for rail or highway or other transportation.

Minimization of the Need for Additional Capacity Through Organization. Transportation and communication systems frequently have peak loads which˙ strain the capacities of facilities. Rather than add new capacity, it may be possible to adjust the conditions creating the peak demand. For example, in western cities, the pattern of employment is such that the work day is approximately uniform in the commercial and other central business district activities. Congestion just before 9 o'clock in the morning and just after 5 o'clock in the evening is strangling. Various kinds of alleviating measures may be introduced ranging from converting streets normally in two-way use to one-way rush hour use, to trying to obtain flexibility in the work day by getting some firms to open earlier than others, some to close later than others. Staggering the hours of employment could result in evening the traffic load; such programs were attempted during wartime. Richard Meier suggests that in high density areas, schools, shops, factories and offices could go on shift operations around the clock, keeping the transportation system in full use (13). Regulating the price system to stimulate use during off-peak hours (and to discourage peak hour use) is another method for equalizing demand and obviating an increase in capacity. This has been done for mass transit lines and telephone calls to distant points.

Another way to circumvent transporation capacity is to encourage stockpiling at individual plants or in warehouses. This is a questionable policy since it is more economic in productive terms to keep inventories as low as possbile, and the possibility is suggested as an emergency measure only.

The Imperative to Cost Minimization: Rationalization of Movement Systems

Many of the technical assistance programs are striving to rationalize and mechanize transportation, with considerable success. Standardized parts, standardization of terminology, methods and signals, basic training programs, specialization of personnel and equipment—these are a few of the ways in which efficient operations of transportation and communication systems may be secured.

Because great emphasis is currently being placed both privately and governmentally on the rationalization and increased efficiency of movement, only three points will be briefly noted: (a) the necessity for coordination and integration of movement, (b) the necessity for consideration of maintenance and operation in choices for transportation and communications, and (c) the necessity for land reservation for future needs.

Coordination and Integration of Movement. Duplication of facilities must be avoided, both to minimize capital investment and to insure the high traffic volume necessary to efficient service. To achieve maximum efficiency, coordination must be on two levels: (a) division of roles assigned to different forms of movement and (b) the integration of the various forms of movement. The less glamorous forms of transportation, for example, can play an important part in small distance travel: animal carts, bicycles, walking. Division of responsibility between long-haul and short-haul trips, between bulk and small package goods, between high-value and low-value, and between freight and passenger service are a few of the kinds of specialization which might take place. Yet specialization is not desirable in itself, and ways of combining movement as well as separating it are needed. Thus, for example, within urban areas passengers might be carried during the day on streetcars, and freight distributed at night over the same tracks. The same division of traffic might occur on railroads, conserving trackage. Motor vehicles traveling in rural areas

might haul passengers and high value goods in the same vehicle.

Coordination implies administrative cooperation and agreement. In order to have a free flow of vehicles from one jurisdiction to another there must be a number of uniformities established by agreement (for example, uniform gauges for railroads, uniform weight for trucks, uniform traffic devices for signalling). Although feeder lines are an obvious component of coordinated movement, transfer of goods from one kind of vehicle to another should be minimized wherever possible. The costs of transshipment are frequently overlooked and are high even when the transfer is mechanized.

Maintenance and Operation as Considerations. Maintenance and operating costs enter into calculation of movement expense as much as do initial capital costs. The difficulty of replacing parts, the fuel consumed, the speed of amortization, are among the more obvious cost considerations. But human behavior must be considered in addition to mechanical performance and the geographic and other physical conditions under which the machines will function. That is to say, if vandalism is likely to occur, pipelines will not be satisfactory since they are too long and costly to be policed. If skilled drivers or mechanics are not available to drive and repair motor vehicles, the vehicles will be abused, will consume excess fuel and tires, and will otherwise be wastefully operated and only have a short life-span. If the telephone is used to amuse the baby, the system may be put out of order. These are short-term considerations—such behavior is subject to change.

While maintenance and operation should be considered at each point in the system of movement, the facilities for linking one kind of movement to another should be particularly examined for potential break-down and for high costs. Transfer, as mentioned above, is frequently undercalculated in time loss and in labor expense. Technological innovations at these weak points or organizational innovations might strengthen a system that might otherwise bog down. For example, cargo handling might be eliminated if water transport could accommodate loaded truck-trailers which just needed to be hitched to a cab and driven off; "piggy-back" operations have been tried successfully by both rail and water carriers. Containerization also promises to cut the labor costs in cargo handling.

Land Reservation for Future Needs. One of the most costly lessons the developed countries have learned is that highway or railroad land acquisition can be extremely expensive, once the land has been built upon. If the developing countries initially set aside additional land along the rights of way of roads and railroads for later expansion to a two track system, or a four-lane highway, or other additional capacity, they will conserve much capital and human energy.

The Potentialities of New Technology

There have always been arguments in developing countries over the wisdom of high capital expenditures when labor surpluses exist. Most of the new technological developments are of high capital cost, many are still in the experimental stages. Developing countries may not want to bear the costs of early experimentation; yet, if they are sensitive to the possibilities of technological advances, they may profit from costly investment in intermediate facilities and may anticipate the kinds of patterns which might come about by harnessing new technology at a time when costs are reduced.

For example, developing countries are expanding industrially, are urbanizing and are improving their systems of movement in a period of fossil fuel shortage. Not only do the developing countries frequently lack such fuels, but the existing world supplies are in great demand by the already developed countries. Fortunately, nuclear energy is emerging as a source of electric power; although costs presently are not comparable to electric power produced by more traditional means, the time may be foreseen when nuclear energy will be able to provide electric power for areas which do not have large supplies of fossil fuels. Moreover, nuclear power will not place great demands on the limited transportation facilities of a country as do the transporting of coal and oil.

Furthermore, it seems probable that nuclear power can be effectively employed in the reduction of ores, permitting metallurgical industries to locate near the source of the ore rather than in an elaborate locational relationship which must take the source and transshipment of fuel into account as well.

This prospect has particular significance in developing countries because so many of them have low-grade ore deposits requiring a very high ratio of weight of ore to weight of resulting metal. Transportation could be greatly minimized if nuclear energy enabled metal extraction at the source of the ore supply.

If nuclear energy does become relatively inexpensive in the coming years, electrification of main-line movements where industrial activities are intense and population is dense would seem advantageous. Electric pumps to propel large volumes of gaseous liquids or crushed and emulsified solids through pipe lines would become economical as would conveyor belts for sand and other bulky items. Solar energy, sonic energy, wind power and possibly tidal power may also be effective substitutes for fossil fuels.

Other technological possibilities may reduce the demand for transportation and otherwise be economical to a developing country. For example, certain kinds of intensive food production—hydroponics, fish farming and very intensive gardening such as already in Japan—may mean that most of the bulk perishable foodstuffs could be produced on the outskirts of metropolitan areas.

Technological improvements in transportation and communications instruments themselves are constantly occurring. The greatest potential probably lies in communications as more and more transmission of messages and storing of messages become automatic. Within air, water, motor and rail technology, innovations have led to carrying bigger volumes, more specialized cargo handling, conservation of fuel. Perhaps innovations will come in the crossing of traditional divisions of flow—e.g. the diesel-electric rubber tired train which can run over any territory which has a path; the piggy-back transport of truck trailer bodies on ships or flat cars, the amphibious vessel which can go on land or water on its own power.

These are just a few examples of the possibilities of new technology to reduce and ease the frictions of space which must be bridged by intricate systems of movement if economic development is to occur.

REFERENCES

(1) International Bank For Reconstruction and Development, Washington, D.C., *The World Bank in Africa*, (July 1961), p. 1; *The World Bank in Asia*, (October 1960), p. 2; *The World Bank and IDA in the Americas*, p. 2, (January 1962).

(2) The International Bank for Reconstruction and Development, *A Public Development Program for Thailand*, John Hopkins Press, Baltimore, p. 121, (1959).

(3) Grunwald, K., & J. O. Ronall, *Industrialization in the Middle East*, Council for Middle Eastern Affairs Press, New York, p. 82, (1960).

(4) Chenery, H.B., *Comparative advantage and development policy*, The American Economic Review, 51 No. 1, 18–51, (March 1961).

(5) Hawkins, E. K., *Investment in roads in underdeveloped countries*, Bulletin of the Oxford University Institute of Statistics, 22, No. 4, p. 361, (November 1960).

(6) Checci, V., and Associates, *Honduras; A Problem in Economic Development*, Twentieth Century Fund, New York, p. 157, (1959).

(7) Rosenstein-Rodan, P. N., *Notes on the theory of the "Big Push"*, in Howard S. Ellis (ed) *Economic Development for Latin America*, Macmillan & Co., London, 57–67, (1961).

(8) Williams, E. W., Jr., *Freight Transportation in the Soviet Union*, National Bureau of Economic Research, Princeton University Press, Princeton, p. 135, (1962).

(9) Hunter, H., *Soviet Transportation Policy*, Harvard University Press, Cambridge, p. 27, (1957).

(10) Staley, E., *The Future of Underdeveloped Countries,* Council on Foreign Relations, Harper Bros., New York, (1954).

(11) *Asia and the Far East, Seminar on Population,* Bandung, (21 Nov. to 3 Dec. 1955), United Nations, New York, (1957).

(12) Lefeber, L., M. Dutta Chandhuri, *Transportation Policy in India,* typescript, (1961).

(13) Meier, R. L., *Relations of Technology to the Design of Very Large Cities,* in Roy Turner, (ed) *India's Urban Future,* University of California Press, 299–323, (1962).

Phase Building of Railroads and Equipment for Less Developed Countries

W. M. KELLER

Vice President-Research, Association of American Railroads,
Chicago, Illinois

It is assumed in this paper that either oil or central plant electricity will be used as the primary power source, that diesel or electric locomotives will be used, and that highway transport will be auxiliary to the main transport system. No consideration will be given to the use of steam locomotives because of their poor thermal cycle. The steam locomotive operates at an overall thermal efficiency of about 6 percent, whereas the diesel locomotive has a comparable efficiency of 25 percent. This paper recommends railroad transportation for less developed countries where traffic exceeds 500,000 tons annually because the unit cost per ton-mile is less than that for alternative modes of transport.

Units cost per ton-mile	
Mode of transport	*(Railroad=1.0)*
Railroad	1.0
Highway truck	4.5
Airplane	16.3
Barge (waterway)	0.29
Pipeline	0.21

Where the traffic will be less than 500,000 tons annually, an examination of the specific conditions should be made to determine if the capital investment in the railroad is justified. If the traffic load is less than one-half million tons annually but a large passenger potential exists, it is considered advantageous to provide railroad facilities.

Laying Out the Route

In establishing the route to be followed by the railroad, two basic considerations are involved: (a) The area to be served, and (b) the terrain over which the railroad will operate. Major cities on the railroad generally should be connected by rail lines even though this may entail indirect routes. As an example, if a rail line is to be constructed between cities "A" and "B" and there is an important city "C" off a straight connecting line, consideration should be given to laying out the railroad so that the intermediate city "C" is connected by the rail line, even though the distance between cities "A" and "B" is increased substantially. If the terrain is such that grades of over 2 percent and curves of 6 degrees must be used too extensively, it may be better to build a straight line between cities "A" and "B" and connect the straight line with a branch line to city "C". Each individual case must be studied separately, but the philosophy of connecting as many towns and cities as can be conveniently accomplished without undue construction costs should be followed.

In the layout of a railroad, studies of the terrain should be made to establish grades of 1 percent or less. On 1 percent maximum grades the use of helper locomotives for tonnage trains is largely eliminated. Curves should be restricted to 6 degrees unless extenuating circumstances are introduced, but curves should never exceed 10 degrees in mainline track. In locating the railroad, photogrammetry should be employed as the first step in the problem. The use of this technique will expedite construction work and permit initial planning to be completed at an early date.

Potential Industrial Developments

In considering the type of railroad track to be constructed a thorough survey should be made of the less developed country with respect to possible future development of natural resources. This survey should include a comprehensive investigation by competent geologists to determine what mineral resources may be in existence such as gold, tin, silver, antimony, lead, zinc, molybdenum, manganese, aluminum, coal, iron ore, etc. The possibility of oil resources also should be determined. Certain areas may be well suited to agricultural use either as they exist or with the aid of irrigation and fertilization. Any substantial timber resources should be determined as well as likely sources of power from natural waterfalls, or from generating plants if water and coal supplies are plentiful. If potentialities for generating substantial amounts of electric power exist, manufacturing centers and perhaps even refining plants may be started depending upon available types of metallic ores. This possibility may also influence a decision to provide electric traction for the railroad.

Right-of-Way

The right-of-way should be obtained after the line has been located. Aside from the fundamental requirements of obtaining sufficient width of right-of-way to accommodate the heights of fills, cuts, passing tracks, yard facilities, etc., it would be well to obtain additional right-of-way in areas where there appear to be possibilities for future industrial development. Of considerable aid to the future growth of the railroad and expansion of railway traffic would be the acquisition of land adjoining the railroad that could be offered at a reasonable price to encourage the establishment of new industries on the railroad.

Gage of Track

Selection of the gage of railway track may be quite important in future years and should be given careful consideration. If the railway line of a given country will connect at one or both of its terminals with that of another country, it would probably be desirable to construct the track of a similar gage in order to facilitate interchange of equipment. Unless there are such compelling reasons, it would seem preferable to use the 4 ft. $8\frac{1}{2}$ in. gage which is the most commonly used throughout the world. This gage is adjudged quite adequate for handling any type of traffic that needs to be moved by rail and has the important advantage of facilitating interchange of equipment. Its wide use also makes it possible to purchase rolling stock and track accessories less expensively. Compared with narrow gage track, the additional cost involved in widening cuts and fills the relatively small amount required to accommodate the 4 ft. 8½ in. gage is not a big item in the construction cost of the railway.

Track Structure

The preliminary survey made of the resources in the less developed country can have a major bearing on decisions regarding the details of the railway construction. If the survey for example, indicates that traffic will be relatively light initially, but that in future years there is good expectation of a considerable increase in traffic, it would be well to decide upon a track which is practical in first cost, but which lends itself to upgrading for handling heavier traffic later by merely adding to the existing construction and not having to tear it down and completely rebuild it to the upgraded type. Even if the traffic is anticipated to be low initially with little expectation of a substantial increase, this plan would be advisable.

It is suggested that as Step 1 in the construction of a railroad, a large scale map of the territory be used as a preliminary guide. On this map should be located the population centers, the point of origin of any resources such as minerals, manufactured goods, foodstuffs, etc., as well as the maximum points of consumption. The lines connecting these various resources with existing cities and seaports can then be drawn on the map to indicate the tentative rail system. Following the completion of this map, the lines indicated should be used in a photogrammetric survey. A second trial map can then be made with necessary line changes to indicate the exact location for the survey for building the track. Upon completion of this work, the builders of the rail system will then be in position to study the type of equipment needed for the particular traffic that will be handled. Three study groups should be set up to handle the following categories: (a) Track and Fixed Structures, (b) Locomotives, Freight and Passenger Cars, and (c) Shops and Special Equipment.

Each of these study groups should take into consideration the optimum method of producing an expandable system at a nominal cost that would not interrupt traffic flow once the original system is built. The intention of this analysis would be to provide a basic railroad that would not require major rebuilding of either tracks or equipment in order to accommodate greatly increased tonnage and passenger miles at a later date. The system, however, would be built without providing unneeded facilities for heavy traffic during early years of light traffic service.

Study Group 1 on Track and Fixed Structures

Under this assignment a study group would consider first the track. A clearance diagram should be adopted that will permit large equipment to move without restriction. The subgrade of the railroad should be prepared by providing proper drainage. Where earth fills are used, analysis of the earth should be made to determine if slides or soft spots will be experienced. Poor drainage can result in expensive maintenance costs that would far offset the original cost of providing a proper sub-base at the time the railroad is built.

Roadway. One of the first considerations in the design of the roadbed itself is the width to be provided on the top of fills and the side slope, and the width to be provided in cuts and the side slope. Obviously the greater the width provided for fills and cuts, the greater will be the grading costs. This increased cost, however, must be weighed against future maintenance expenses because an adequate width of fill is necessary to hold the ballast and the cuts should be wide enough to provide both good drainage ditches and room for washdown from the side slopes without requiring frequent cleanings. Soil characteristics will determine the slopes to be used. In general, a $1\frac{1}{2}$ to 1 slope will be found satisfactory for fills and a 1 to 1 slope on cuts, but some types of soil require flatter slopes than this on both fills and cuts to be stable. If the excavation is rock the slopes may be made much steeper.

Because maintenance and construction costs are higher for tunnels, it is desirable to lay out the line to avoid tunnel construction where possible. In general, it is preferable to have very deep cuts rather than build tunnels, but if the cuts run more than 150 ft. deep, cost studies should be made to determine whether the first cost and added maintenance costs of a tunnel would exceed the construction cost for the depth of cut required.

Establishing the width of roadway for fills and cuts with proper slopes is not too serious a matter in a new line because inadequacies can be corrected at a later date without too great an additional cost. It is important, however, in constructing the roadbed that material be properly selected and compacted on fills with optimum moisture content in order to reduce subsequent maintenance costs. Rock excavated from cuts for making fills should be used with discretion, particularly if the fills are quite high. The rock can be placed advantageously in the lower portion of the fill, but if used in the upper portion the fill may become too heavy and tend to slide during rainy weather.

Ballast. Ballast applied over the roadbed is important from the standpoint of drainage and tie support. While it is sometimes difficult to obtain the ballast best suited to the track conditions, it is preferable to avoid economy in the use of this important material. Good ditching is not a complete substitute for proper ballast, but proper drainage will make some inferior forms of ballast reasonably acceptable. Crushed limestone, granite, cinders, gravel and crushed slag have all been used for ballast with acceptable results. In certain communities there may be other materials that will be satisfactory. Where ballast has the tendency to break down and become foul with dust and dirt, it prevents proper drainage from the track. Also the matter of ballast hardening by working under the ties at the center of the track introduces a condition generally termed "center binding". When the center of the ballast supports the tie to a greater degree than at the ends, as occurs when center binding is present, the tie supports the load on the rails in a manner similar to that described as a simple beam. This condition has a tendency to stress the tie unduly, introducing cracks and early fatigue.

Proper selection of ballast is quite important in providing a track structure for economical maintenance. As a minimum requirement, it would be desirable to have a 6 in. depth of sub-ballast consisting of hard, sharp particles of one-half inch maximum size, graded with a considerable portion of fines to keep the subgrade from working up into the top ballast. As a further minimum, at least a 6 in. depth under the ties of top ballast should be used with the cribs well filled in between the ties and a suitable shoulder at the ends of the ties. Many different materials give very satisfactory performance as ballast and any suitable type of available material involving minimum cost of processing and hauling should be selected. In building a railroad in a less developed region, it is probable that the type of ballast material most readily available would be crushed rock or gravel. Some gravel ballast that contains a high percentage of sand and hard parties that do not wear or disintegrate gives very satisfactory track performance. If the available gravel supply needs to be washed and processed by screening to prevent a large percentage of sand or fine particles, it should be crushed sufficiently to ensure a breakup of the round particles that would prevent particles or pebbles toward rolling or being displaced under the vibration of traffic. If the available gravel supply consists of a large percentage of soft or chalky materials, or even limestone, consideration should be given to finding a more suitable source of ballast supply.

Crushed rock makes a very satisfactory ballast if it is hard and will not disintegrate or powder under the vibrating action of traffic. If a suitable hard rock is available for crushing into ballast, crushing and gradation should be made to give a maximum size that would pass a $1\frac{1}{2}$ in. screen to ensure that the ballast will form a compact bed with relatively few voids to collect and hold dirt or other foreign materials.

Cross Ties. Here again the selection of the materials to be used will depend to a large extent upon availability. Experience in the United States has been quite satisfactory with treated wood ties of hardwoods that lend themselves to preservative treatment as well as certain softwoods such as pine and fir. The hardwoods are preferred because they are less susceptible to gage widening on curves and to tie plate cutting. If softwood ties are used it is necessary to have an adequate number of spikes in the plate to hold gage with a large enough area of tie plate to prevent cutting.

If wood ties are used, it is important that they be treated with preservative to give a long life. Experience in the United States has been most favorable with a preservative treatment of either creosote and petroleum or creosote and coal tar. In general the creosote and petroleum mixture is preferred in arid regions because there is less tendency for the tie to dry out and split in the hot dry weather. The cross section size of the tie and spacing will depend upon the weight of wheel loads to be carried. With axle loads of approximately 65,000 lbs., United States experience has shown a tie spacing of 22 to 23 in., center to center, satisfactory for light traffic lines. A spacing of 20 in. is preferred for heavy and very heavy traffic density lines with a tie size of 7 in. deep by 9 in. wide. If the initial traffic is relatively light it would, of course, be possible to use smaller size ties with increased spacing. This is not recommended, however, if there are reasonable prospects of increases in traffic because it is expensive to change tie spacing. Additionally, ties with proper preservative treatment should last from 25 to 30 years and it would be wasteful to replace smaller ties with larger ones at a shorter tie life than this.

The length of tie will depend upon the gage of track used. Long ties are beneficial in distributing pressure over more of the subgrade, in reducing maintenance costs, and the tendency of the track to become center bound. As a general proposition, it is believed that a selection of a length of 8 ft. 6 in. for a track gage of 4 ft. 8½ in. would be preferable for the reasons stated.

In countries where suitable wood ties may not be readily available, the expense of purchasing and importing them might make consideration of pre-stressed concrete ties desirable. Although prestressed concrete ties have been used for several years in European countries, the service performance experienced with them has not been long enough to determine useful life. The added weight and firmer fastening of the rail to the prestressed concrete tie is an advantage if continuous welded rail is to be used. The inherent inability of concrete to absorb impact, particularly that resulting from derailments, is another distinct disadvantage. These factors should be weighted together with the first cost of the prestressed concrete tie in comparison with treated wood. Where wood ties are used, gum, oak, walnut, fir and pine are all acceptable materials as previously stated. With the softer woods, however, the maximum size tie plate between the rail and the tie should be used. Depending upon the kind of wood, consideration should be given to the application of anti-splitting dowels. There are varying practices with regard to the doweling of ties and it appears that for an extended life, it is economical to use two dowels in the end of each tie before they are creosoted and regardless of whether the ties are split. The wood tie also has certain other advantages such as convenience in applying fastening devices, reclamation of used ties, and economy of first cost.

Steel ties are infrequently used. The advantage of steel ties, however, is that they provide a certain convenience in attaching rails and are not subject to any serious splitting or cracking. They are subject to corrosion, and because of their smaller section do not imbed themselves in the ballast to provide as much holding power as other types of ties.

Tie Plates. Tie plates are a relatively expensive item in the track structure but are of value in holding gage and reducing mechanical cutting of the tie. It is an item that can be dispensed with if traffic is initially light for they can be added at a later date without an appreciable economic penalty. If wood ties are used, it would seem desirable to use tie plates initially, even with light traffic, on curves of two degrees or more, but plates could be dispensed with on tangent track. It should be pointed out that tie plates should be provided initially if feasible economically because of the advantages in holding gage and the rail to the proper cant, considered to be 1 : 40 for conditions in the United States. The size of the tie plate is determined primarily by the amount of traffic density and the species of wood used in the ties. If the initial or anticipated traffic density is moderate to heavy for axle loadings approximating 65,000 lb., United States experience has indicated that a 7¾x12x14 in. plate is economical. The size of the tie plate also will depend upon the size of rail selected.

Rail. Rail is the most important component in the track structure from the standpoint of safety of operation and economical maintenance. Every effort should be made initially to use as large and strong a rail section as possible. The life of rail is long and benefits in track maintenance costs make the flexural stiffness and strength of the heavier rail sections an attractive investment. The strength of rail must be adequate to support the axle loadings for the equipment to be handled. In general it might be stated that the use of a rail of less than 90 lbs. per yard would be very questionable, even for light traffic density lines that have little expectation of future increases in traffic. If the traffic initially will be moderate to heavy, or there is expectation of increases in traffic density, then 115 or 132 lb. rail sizes should be considered depending upon the wheel loading and traffic density to be handled.

The selection of the rail section is also important. A design that will give maximum flexural stiffness and strength for the amount of metal used is important. Modern designs of rail provide a top contour that is adapted to fit the average contour to which car wheels will wear, with the upper web fillets providing adequate strength against the development of head and web separations.

The question of whether rail should be laid jointed or welded should be considered. For track that is expected to handle moderate to heavy traffic the rail should be welded on tangent and curves up to two degrees. For curves beyond two degrees, regular standard rail lengths joined with conventional joint bars should be used to facilitate changing rails when they become curve worn, excessively flowed, or corrugated.

Main Track and Sidings. It would be very unusual if the contemplated railway traffic for a line built into a less developed country could not be handled with a single track railway with adequate passing tracks, particularly with the increased traffic handling potential that is afforded by centralized traffic control. Centralized traffic control could be applied at any future time without incurring economic penalties. Assuming that the initial traffic will be relatively light, passing tracks could be spaced at sufficiently close intervals to accommodate anticipated traffic without undue train delays. The length of the passing track should be such as to accommodate the train tonnages selected. In general passing tracks should be located not further than 10 miles apart and should be at least 1 mile long. The switches provided at passing tracks should be of a sufficiently large frog number to permit train operation at reasonably fast speeds. Number 10 frogs and 19 ft. 6 in. switch points will permit satisfactory train operation at speeds up to 25 miles per hour, considered adequate for most operations. Here again no serious penalty would be incurred if at some later date increases in traffic density and speed requirements indicate the desirability of changing the turnouts to have smaller frog angles and longer switch points. The selection of the type of turnout frog is worthy of consideration. For initial construction a bolted rail or spring rail frog is the least expensive in first cost, whereas a railbound manganese frog, while more expensive in first cost, affords cheaper maintenance cost. Assuming that initial traffic density will be light and operating speeds moderate, bolted rail or spring rail frogs might well be used with no serious problems involved in changing to the more expensive rail-bound manganese frogs at a later date.

Bridges, Trestles and Culverts.

Provisions for spanning necessary drainage openings is important in the cost of construction of a new railway. In general, it is desirable to provide openings by using suitable culvert pipes, even the large sizes if clearance between the track height and flow height permit. Either corrugated steel suitably protected against corrosion by galvanizing or reinforced concrete pipe or boxes may be used depending upon the relative cost of the drainage opening that must be provided. Where open spans are required, it is desirable to establish a number of standard span lengths and designs to make the initial cost of construction economical and to facilitate later maintenance and repair work. If treated timber is available, a timber trestle span of any desired length and reasonable height makes a good structure from the standpoint of long life and economical maintenance. One of the biggest disadvantages of treated timber trestles is the fire hazard and treated timber may not be readily available in many areas and therefore expensive to obtain. In some areas species of wood may be available in abundance that are naturally resistant to decay and should be given consideration for use in constructing openings of timber trestles.

The use of concrete spans, either reinforced concrete arch, prestressed concrete slabs or girders, or post tensioned prestressed concrete arches, may be considered in cost comparisons with steel spans. Decisions made will depend to a large extent upon the availability of these materials at the location where the railway is being constructed. Reinforced concrete and prestressed concrete have the advantage of lower maintenance costs compared to steel. Steel I-beams, gird-ers, arches and truss spans are entirely satisfactory for all locations and perhaps one of the most serious objections to the use of steel spans is the necessity for cleaning and painting them at periodic intervals. Even this may be a minor expense if the construction is in arid locations where there is no unusual corrosion environment such as brine or acid fumes in the atmosphere.

Signaling and Grade Crossing Protection. It is probable that the amount of traffic to be handled initially in most less developed areas would not require the installation of block signals. It is further unlikely that flasher light or automatic gate protection would need to be provided at many, if any, highway grade crossings. Fortunately signaling does not offer a serious problem as there is no penalty incurred in deferring the installation of automatic block signals, train control or centralized traffic control, and grade crossing signal protection until such time as traffic conditions warrant their use.

Study Group 2 on Locomotives, Freight and Passenger Cars

Locomotives. The selection of motive power is based on a number of factors which include type of fuel, speed of operation, profile of the railroad, and size of trains. With the use of diesel engines it is preferable to hold passenger train speeds to that of freight trains so that motive power can be used interchangeably. Modern freight trains travel at speeds that do not present problems to schedules, permitting a greater flexibility of locomotive use and reducing slightly the number of locomotives required for a given operation.

It is possible to build general purpose diesel locomotives weighing approximately 120 tons which can be used interchangeably for freight, passenger and switching service to provide maximum flexibility. Diesel locomotives of this type can be equipped with one-half of the normal propulsion equipment required and used in this manner for light trains until the other half of the equipment can be provided. It is preferable to purchase full-sized locomotives that can be converted later to full horsepower output by the addition of an engine, generator and two truck motors rather than purchase smaller locomotives which would be replaced eventually with larger locomotives.

In selecting motive power, it is preferable to employ one standard type of locomotive in order to minimize repair costs and reduce repair parts inventory that must be carried for replacement parts. The use of a standard type locomotive also minimizes the problem of training operating and maintenance personnel. Once familiarity is established with a certain design of locomotive and its parts, complication of working on another locomotive with quite different design of parts will not be introduced. One set of drawings and maintenance manuals is all that is required when a standard type locomotive is used. Diesel locomotives can be built with both electric and hydraulic propulsion systems. The hydraulic drive locomotive has advantages in a less developed territory because the maintenance equipment used does not need to include equipment for rewiring coils, armatures and electrical repairs of this general type. The hydraulic drive is purely mechanical and only a minimal staff of trained electricians need be employed for maintenance purposes. Should

it be decided to convert a section of the railroad to electric propulsion, the replacement of the diesel engine by electric motor is all that is required to convert an electric drive diesel locomotive to a motor-generator electric unit. With the hydraulic drive, the trucks and cab portion of the locomotive would have to be extensively modified for the accommodation of electrical equipment needed for the drive.

The straight electric locomotive has the inherent advantage of being capable of working in excess of its continuous rating for short periods of time. When electric locomotives are used, the horsepower output can be doubled at certain speeds by merely working the locomotive at a higher rate. Since the power in a diesel locomotive is limited by the maximum output of the diesel engine, this same condition cannot be obtained. Electric locomotives can use hydro- or coal-fired steam power plant energy which is desirable under certain circumstances.

In areas where traffic loads of 40 million tons or more are not hauled annually, the added investment for transmission, catenary and trolley wires is difficult to justify. The 40-million ton volume necessarily is an arbitrary figure, and unusual circumstances may justify electrification. If in a short period of time, such as a 5-year period, it is predicted that the line will eventually carry sufficient volume to justify electrification, it is preferable to select electrification at the outset.

Many designs of electric locomotives have been built. The present tendency is to build electric locomotives with truck-mounted motors and swiveling trucks following the general practice used for diesel-electric locomotives. The use of a body-mounted motor requires either a jack shaft with side rods or a quill drive. Quill drives, however, are expensive to maintain, somewhat more expensive to build, and have been eliminated in modern electric locomotives.

The use of driving wheels with tires should be avoided. The integral wrought steel wheel requires no tightening of tires or inspection of spokes and is somewhat more economical in first cost. The availability of wheels of this type is so general throughout the world that the ease of obtaining such a wheel in a less developed country should result in its adoption if there were no other advantages present.

The stresses in the underframe of a locomotive should be kept at the minimum since failure of a main frame or sub-base of a locomotive would require complicated repair facilities that probably do not exist. The use of cast steel trucks should be employed, as they seldom fail, are free of extensive repair requirements, and cracks in their frames can be repaired by welding followed by stress relieving.

In selecting the number of locomotives to be used, it is essential to determine the average horsepower per ton of train weight moved. This requires a study of considerable intricacy if it does not follow train schedules and power units for reserve. The best way to determine horsepower requirements without using train schedules is to develop a mathematic regression which takes into account the speed of trains, their tonnage, grades, curves and other permanent slow downs, number of stops, and any other operating data that affect tonnage per train hour. These data may then be processed through a computer to obtain horsepower per train. For an ordinary railroad with average grade and curve conditions a figure of 2.5 h.p. per ton of train weight is considered satisfactory. This figure, however, is subject to wide adjustment to cover speed and steep grades as well as traffic density. It has been shown on a 117 mile division that a 5,000 h.p. diesel locomotive will be able to move a 2,000 ton train (2.5 h.p. per ton) in 2 hours, 39 minutes, but will require 3.5 hours to move a 5,000 ton train (1.0 h.p. per ton) the same distance.

Freight Cars. The future requirements of a country should be the primary factor in the design of freight cars. If, for example, 40-ton cars were adequate for the initial traffic volume but the question is whether or not the 40-ton car would be adequate in 3 to 5 years, it is preferable to build the cars with 50 or 70-ton trucks and with an underframe designed to handle the increased load. The difference in cost between a 40-ton truck and a 70-ton truck is relatively small, but replacement of the lighter capacity trucks with those of 70-ton capacity would approximately double the cost. It is possible to modify the brake of a 70-ton car which is used in light tonnage service by replacing the original cylinder with a larger brake cylinder when the cars are converted to heavy tonnage service. Automatic couplers and automatic air brakes should be used on all cars. The automatic coupler can be of the AAR knuckle type or the Willison type coupler. Draft gears should be of high capacity with a minimum 75,000 ft. lb. per gear. A draft gear travel of approximately 4½ in. will be satisfactory for any general requirements in a less developed country.

The question of car journal bearings should be given consideration. With a stabilized journal assembly and using lubricator pads, the present AAR plain journal bearing assembly is satisfactory.

The plain journal bearing box is simple to maintain and requires less technical attention than does the roller bearing box. When difficulty is experienced with journal bearings enroute, the plain bearing assembly can be given simple repairs to permit bringing the car into the next terminal.

Hopper and Gondola Cars. If mineral products are a large percentage of the total traffic, a study of the handling facilities that will be used at the point of origin and destination should be made so as to determine the extent of the need for, and the appropriate design of, the hopper car. High side gondolas can be used as a substitute for hopper cars if a rotary dumper is used at destinations.

Flat Cars. Flat cars lengths should accommodate two of the average-size motor trucks used in a country. These flat cars should be of general purpose design to permit hauling agricultural implements, rolling mill machinery, and power plant equipment such as turbines, transformers and generators. If there is any question about volume of traffic that may ultimately be available for flat cars, they can be designed to permit the addition of sides and ends for conversion to gondola cars at a later date.

Tank Cars. Tank cars should be provided to permit transport of all liquid chemicals, petroleum products and possibly, in some areas, drinking water. Tank cars used for such products as blackstrap molasses or heavy residual oils should be provided with interior heating coils. These heating coils may be either steam or electrically activated depending upon the availability of primary power. The heating coils need not be used if the tank car traffic is in climates that are above 50° F. Tank cars should be constructed sufficiently heavy to permit conversion to pressure cars at a later date. Properly designed drain and safety valves should also be provided.

Stock Cars. Stock cars in sufficient quantity to provide for the movement of cattle should be in the equipment register of the railroad. Stock cars should be constructed of steel with interior wood protection to prevent injury to the animals in transit. If smaller animals are transported, the stock car should have double-deck construction to increase hauling capacity.

Refrigerator Cars. The problem of locating ice at stations along the railroad in isolated territory presents such problems that it is preferable to use mechanical refrigeration for cars. The insulation in refrigerator cars should have a thermal conductivity of not over 0.27 Btu's per inch of thickness per square foot per degree fahrenheit differential per hour at 70° F. The thickness of the insulation in sides and ends should be 4 in. and in floor and roof, 4½ in. The interior of the car should be lined with smooth tongue and groove plywood. The refrigeration equipment should be diesel operated since diesel fuel is readily available and does not introduce serious fire hazards. Thermostats should be installed to control the inside temperatures at any desired level from 0° F. for frozen foods to 60° F. for such shipments as tomatoes. In addition to the refrigeration equipment, the car should be provided with ventilation facilities to permit the handling of such commodities as citrus and potatoes without use of refrigeration.

Box Cars. These cars should be designed to haul all kinds of miscellaneous freight. The doors of the cars should be 8 ft. wide and of the plug type to permit grain-tight opening for carriage of grains such as wheat, barley, oats, rice, etc. These cars should be equipped with lading anchor devices to block lading, and special devices when assigned to specific services. The floors of box cars should be not less than 2¼ in. thick. If the cars are to be used for mechanical loading where lift trucks are employed, a protective plate should be used in the door.

General. All freight cars should be equipped with geared hand brakes for controlling their movement during flat yard switching operations and for parking cars on industrial sidings or at warehouses. The use of running boards should be omitted since they have no advantage and are an avoidable expense. Since running boards would not be used, ladders are unnecessary at the corners of the car to gain access to the roof. The use of these ladders invites the curious to climb up on the car roof, particularly dangerous in an electrified territory where an inexperienced individual might touch a high voltage overhead wire and be electrocuted.

Passenger Cars. The design of passenger cars is governed by the length of the run and area climate. For short runs in moderate temperatures simple coaches without air conditioning can be used. The use of reclining seats requires a reduction in capacity of the car. For short runs, the reclining seat is an unnecessary luxury. The so-called "walkover" or reversible seat can be placed upon 35½ in. seat centers whereas the minimum seat center spacing for the rotating reclining seat is 41½ in. If rubber upholstery is used, a very comfortable walkover type seat on 35½ in. centers is possible. Unless cars are operated in areas

with temperatures of 85° F. or higher, the use of air conditioning should be avoided. To adequately air condition a passenger coach, an 8-ton refrigeration capacity is required. These systems involve repair problems that should be avoided in a less developed country.

The use of fluorescent lights in coaches should also be avoided. This type of lighting requires alternating current, lamp starters, and ballast, expenses that can be avoided if incandescent lighting is used. The flush-mounted enclosed incandescent light fixture is practical and requires little maintenance. For vestibule lights, toilet room lights and hallway areas, the open incandescent lamp in a reflector is sufficient to provide satisfactory lighting.

Trucks for passenger cars should be of the cast steel type to minimize repairs. The bolster and equalizer springs should be of the helical type to provide proper cushioning even when subjected to rust and corrosion. When elliptical or leaf springs are used, any rust between the leaves will cause the spring to operate in such a manner as to impair its riding qualities. Unless broken or bent seriously, coil springs provide good cushioning.

Study Group 3 on Shops and Special Equipment

Part of this group's work should include a study of the needs for station buildings, car dumpers, unloading ramps, shops, terminal servicing facilities, offices, communications and all related facilities and equipment. It should also examine the equipment needed for clearing derailments such as derricks and cars fitted with jacks, cables, blocking, etc.

Shops. These should be constructed in expandable units. A diesel shop unit should be 22 ft. wide and 185 ft. long, dimensions that allow a space around the track for a platform. The track in this shop should be built on an elevation to permit examinations, inspection and repairs to be easily made on the trucks and underframe. As additional shop units are required, they may be built alongside the first unit in 22 ft. wide additions. Where it is anticipated that a shop will be enlarged in a few years, the first unit should be built with three permanent sides and one temporary side which can be removed when the second unit is built.

One end of this shop should be built with 14 ft. wide 16 ft. high motorized lift doors to permit the entrance of diesel units. The opposite end should be built with a 10 ft. wide doorway leading into a room 22 ft. wide and 75 ft. long. These rooms built at the end of each diesel shop should provide space for a parts cleaning room, machine shop, electric shop, air brake shop, and storeroom. Not all of these facilities can be housed in a 22 x 75 ft. room and the first diesel shop unit built should include at least two end rooms to provide space for other shop facilities.

If truck wheels and traction gear work are required, a separate shop unit 44 x 75 ft. should be provided. When diesel wheel treads are reconditioned in a pit-mounted machine that permits restoring the contour of wheeltreads without removing them from the truck, this facility can be located outside the shop building by installing a concrete platform with a canopy roof for weather protection. The location for the facility should be selected to avoid blocking the movement of tracks while the wheel truing device is in use. This requires that a separate track near the shop be selected equipped with a winch to permit movement of the locomotive when its own propulsion equipment is inoperable.

The machine shop should be equipped with an engine lathe, metal shaper, drill press, pedestal grinder, valve grinder, and milling machine. Complete sets of socket and open-end wrenches with torque measuring equipment, a cylinder honer, portable hydraulic jacks of 50-ton capacity, welding machine, pneumatic or electric hand drills, and a complete complement of small hand tools should be provided.

The shop should be equipped with pneumatic air lines supplied from a central reservoir. The compressed air can be provided by the use of a diesel locomotive air compressor driven by an electric motor. For auxiliary compressed air supply the central reservoir can be connected to the air brake system of a diesel locomotive. This method, however, should be supplementary to the regular compressor in order not to immobilize locomotives for extended periods of time.

A diesel engine generator set should be provided for shops located at points that do not have an electric supply. The diesel engine may be the standard locomotive engine but a special generator having a 110 or 220 v. output also should be provided.

Each shop and terminal will require a tank storage for water, sand, engine fuel and lubricating oil. The fuel oil storage should be in tanks elevated about 12 ft. to permit gravity flow into locomotive reservoirs. Their capacity should be not less than 20,000 gallons. Lubricating oil storage of about 1,000 gallons is sufficient until large numbers of locomotives are handled requiring increased fuel and lubricating oil capacity. Water for cooling systems must be provided with proper treatment to prevent scale or corrosion. Storage of fuel oil, lubricating oil and water can be made in tank cars where the shop or terminal tank capacity is limited.

Sand for increasing traction should be kept dry and stored in elevated tanks. Piping to the locomotive should be arranged to permit replenishing sand at the time units are refueled.

Stations and Buildings. Stations and other buildings should be functional with minimum structural features arranged to provide weather protection for the particular area. Only a shell is necessary for buildings in tropical climates, whereas substantial buildings equipped with good insulation are necessary in cold weather areas.

Freight stations should be kept to minimum in both size and construction permanence. Portable sheet-metal buildings are adequate for small stations, and corrugated sheet metal on wood framing is generally acceptable for larger stations. Where traffic permits, team tracks should be used as a substitute for station buildings.

General

Study groups 1, 2 and 3 should maintain continual liaison for proper exchange of pertinent information. It may be preferable to assign one member of each group as the liaison member of the committe to permit a more effective concentration of team effort in any one area.

Harbors, Marine Terminals, and Waterways for Less Developed Areas

Thomas J. Fratar
Partner

Eric D. Dodge
Chief Economist

Nicholas W. Philip
Associate

Tippetts-Abbett-McCarthy-Stratton, Engineers and Architects,
New York, New York

Introduction

Inland waterway or ocean transportation, or both, have been important elements in the growth of nearly all nations. In some areas, the use of inland waterways from the earliest times has been the prime if not the only means of moving people and goods. The almost universal importance of water transportation in some form is due to its serviceability in a natural state through use of naturally protected seacoast harbors and major rivers.

In many less developed areas, the improvement of facilities for ocean and waterway transportation is requisite to further growth. Characteristically, such improvements should be made at existing natural port sites and on inland waterways which previously have not been developed to a very high degree. They can include the provision of more modern terminals at ocean ports to handle rising volumes of commerce, the straightening and deepening of existing waterways, and the provision of waterway terminals for more efficient service to traffic, especially bulk cargoes. Construction of new ocean ports may be required, sometimes at sites requiring artificial harbor protection, to serve regions where economic development is being encouraged. These improvements represent major civil works and necessitate the expenditure of relatively large capital sums. Their planning and construction call for careful staging of work to meet budgetary limits to maintain balance in the overall development program of the nation.

The modern ocean port is a gateway for the export of a nation's natural resources which can provide necessary foreign exchange, and for the import of materials and manufactured goods essential to local industrial development. The function of the port is the transfer of cargo between water and land transport, or between deep-water ocean transportation and shallow-draft inland waterway transportation. A typical port is a complex of diversified elements. For shipments by water, the port ideally provides deep sheltered channels, anchorages, turning basins, and individual berths or moorings. The actual point of cargo transfer is the marine terminal for the collection, distribution, temporary storage, and sometimes the processing and classification of cargo in transit. For movement by land, the port must be connected to inland agricultural and industrial centers by adequate highways, railroads and waterways.

Waterways may be compared to railways and highways in function and service. They are often maintained along coastlines and behind barrier beaches and islands, and may extend many miles up rivers to inland commercial centers. In areas fortunate enough to have deep-water rivers, inland waterway transportation can be established with only a modest investment. If natural limitations exist such as slope alignment or periodic deficiency in stream flow, it is often practicable to develop waterways through canalization to serve the needs of inland navigation, a task that can only be accomplished at great cost.

Because waterway transportation is relatively inexpensive per ton-mile of cargo carried, it often makes possible the savings necessary to render mineral, agricultural and forest resources competitive in world markets. Waterway transportation can supply many of the consumer needs of a region at lower costs than other transport modes and, in many cases, permit the use of goods which would otherwise be prohibitively costly.

Associated with ocean ports and inland water transportation systems are various types of waterfront industries which rely on the proximity of water transportation for receipt of essential raw materials and the shipment of their products. The development of these industries stimulates the use of local natural resources with secondary benefits accruing to the region through the growth of associated industries and services.

Planning an Area's Water Transportation System

In some less developed areas, planning for the development of ocean ports, inland waterways, and terminals commonly takes place as an element in a coordinated national development program. Size, location, type of facility, and timing of improvements are requirements that may be governed by other elements in the program, requiring close coordination with the development of other transport media. The desirable objective is the establishment of an integrated system of transportation for the country or region as a whole, or the strengthening of an existing system to advance economic growth in the area. The failure to consider other essential components of a nation's transportation system can result in poorly located facilities, or the improvements of existing facilities which have no viable means for service to the expanding economy.

In some areas it may be necessary to consider the development of ocean ports or waterways that transcend national service or boundaries. The joint use of a single port by two nations may prove advantageous to both, although the principal advantage probably will accrue to the nation which lacks adequate access to deep water. While the less developed nations often place great importance on the independent development of port and waterway facilities, there are some situations where international cooperation in the development or operation of transportation systems will be of advantage to all nations concerned. The Republic of El Salvador, for example, has no seacoast on the Caribbean Sea, but now ships and receives cargo by Guatemala's Caribbean ports of Puerto Barrios and Santo Tomas. While there has been no international port development, El Salvador has joined with its neighbors in a customs union and common market agreement that simplifies the common use of port facilities. Thus El Salvador is expected to use Honduras' Caribbean port of Puerto Cortes upon completion of a new trans-Isthmian highway across Honduras and El Salvador.

Forecasts of Commerce and Utilization of Facilities. The probable future volumes of commerce prospective to port and waterway facilities depend on the economic development of the entire area which may be linked to the port, both physically by various forms of transportation and economically by the interdependence of local industrial and agricultural production and the movement of natural resources. Economic studies should be directed to the identification of characteristics affecting the generation of waterborne commerce in this tributary area, including geography, topography, climate, resources, population, income, employment, agriculture, forestry, mining and manufacturing.

The limits of the tributary areas to be served depend largely on type and cost of inland transportation to and from port, plus ocean transportation to the ultimate destination. The limits of the tributary area also are affected by competitive relationships between existing ports which include frequency of sailings, adequacy of facilities and services, and cargo handling costs. Allowances for the competitive aspects of port and waterway development should be extended beyond a nation's borders when there are reasonable opportunities for the use of these facilities for certain cargoes in neighboring countries. Where local industries are being established, it also may be necessary to allow for local production of commodities formerly imported. These import substitutions have occurred, or are expected to occur, for such basic commodities as cement, paint, fertilizer, glass and sometimes steel.

Estimates of the potential volumes of commerce and other indices of utilization should be made for appropriate future time periods. Frequently, a guide to a useful date for estimating will be the expected staging of some other corollary activity which is related to ports or waterways, such as construction of a connecting highway.

It is desirable to make fairly short-range estimates of 5 to 10 years for determining immediate needs and longer-range estimates of 15 or 25 years to establish the scope of future construction. Estimates for periods less than 5 years are too short for practical use, since approximately 3 years will probably be needed for financing, design and construction, followed by several years to establish the new transportation pattern.

Evaluation of Existing Facilities and Operations. A detailed evaluation is required of the conditions and characteristics of existing port, terminal or waterway facilities and operations. These investigations include surveys of the condition of structures and equipment, and the collection of hydrographic, meteorological and topographic data. A thorough understanding of existing operational characteristics is essential to the planning of improvements. There will almost certainly be aspects of existing methods of operation that are distinctive to each of the less developed areas, and in many cases these methods are valuable guides to the organization of operations at new facilities. The presence of an abundant labor supply, for example, may influence the degree of mechanical equipment provided at new facilities, or the successful use of storage buildings with open sides may suggest economies in future construction. Recognition of such local characteristics will avoid imposing conventional solutions which may be unwarranted.

Similarly, existing methods of regulating and administering facilities may influence planning. Excessively detailed customs inspection procedure, for example, may render impractical the movement of some materials in pre-palletized lots or in containers, a common situation in Central American ports. An understanding of the policies which strongly influence existing methods of operations will suggest the need for study and recommendation of more advanced administrative guides, since purely engineering and operational solutions may not be sufficiently comprehensive.

Site and Facility Planning. In planning ocean and inland waterway transportation for less developed areas, improvements must provide a level of performance appropriate both to the needs of estimated commerce and traffic and the ability of the nation to finance, maintain and operate the facilities provided.

There are few departures possible from accepted design standards from the standpoint of service to modern vessels. In planning for terminal operations, however, it may be possible in some cases to provide initially for minimum facilities with enlargement at a later time. This is characteristic of past port and waterway development in the United States. In less developed areas today, these conditions are intensified. Where such under-building or improvising takes place, terminal structures and navigation improvements generally should be designed to permit economic enlargement in the future to meet modern standards. Piers, for example, must be designed to withstand the ultimate dredged depth; port areas must be arranged to permit easy enlargement of ancillary facilities such as warehouses and transit sheds; and suitable space must be reserved for the future lengthening of wharfs.

The function that the port or waterway is to perform in the less developed area will influence its physical planning in at least three general categories:

(a) One of the more common situations in less developed areas is the need for ocean port facilities devoted exclusively to the extraction and export of a single natural resource such as ore, oil, or bananas. The facilities required will necessarily be highly specialized, involving terminals and handling equipment of unique design. Designed to meet the economic needs of a single industry, the facilities cannot readily handle more diversified cargoes and there is little latitude in varying their basic design criteria. The most important requirement is the safe accommodation and efficient loading of large specialized vessels such as tankers and bulk ore carriers. Deep, well-protected anchorages, berths, or moorings, are essential and the handling equipment is usually highly mechanized. The selection of a site generally is a compromise between areas affording the best natural harbor conditions and those with proximity to commodity sources.

(b) As part of national programs, water transportation development in less developed areas is often undertaken to stimulate the economic growth of a country or region. The success of such undertakings will depend both on the presence of such advantages as natural deep harbors or navigable rivers to permit development of waterway service and marine terminals at minimum capital cost, and the economic potential of the tributary area. In the first stage of construction, it may be practicable to provide the most rudimentary piers and wharfs with provision for later expansion. To obviate the need for initial waterfront construction, landing craft have been used in some areas to transport heavy construction equipment.

(c) Many water transportation projects involve the provision of additional facilities to provide for the handling of larger volumes of cargo or greater variety of cargo types. Such projects are more likely to be undertaken during the later stages of an area's economic growth. The reduction of terminal operating costs and vessel time in port through faster, more efficient cargo handling is important in facility planning. Additionally, the ability of the port to compete with other ports may be a factor in undertaking improvements of this nature. Generally, the facilities provided must conform to modern standards for berth length and depth, open storage space and working areas, in transit covered storage space, dockside cranes, rail and highway connections, and other supporting services.

The arrangement, size, and number of the principal components of an ocean port such as ship berths, transit sheds and warehouse are related mainly to the capacity desired and expected operating practices. New techniques in Operations Research have been developed to relate the capacity and rate of utilization of new construction to the size, numbers and arrangement of individual facilities. It is possible, for example, to predict quite accurately the maximum occupancy which may be expected at marine terminal berths through theoretical frequency distribution functions. Similar techniques may be extended to determine the most efficient size of transit shed or warehouse or the numbers of dockside cranes which can be efficiently utilized.

Alternative Types of Port Facilities and Operations

Harbors. Favorable natural side conditions permit the greatest economies in harbor development. A protected harbor with a safe approach, good holding ground for ships' anchors, and deep water close to shore is desired to permit economical wharf construction with minimum dredging. Where natural harbor protection is lacking, the site can be protected artificially by jetties or breakwaters, but the expense of such work is difficult to justify in less developed areas. Lightering of cargo from a ship anchored in an open roadstead may be more feasible for early stage operations, and fixed moorings can be provided where good anchor holding ground is lacking.

Ocean Port Terminals. A terminal for general cargo operations has requirements that cannot readily be changed. For transfer of sufficient volumes of cargo to justify the large investment in such a facility ($2 million to $3 million per berth), the terminal must provide berths of sufficient depth to handle modern vessels. Ample storage and working spaces should be adjacent to the vessel, and the terminal should be served by adequate highway and railway connections.

For bulk cargoes such as ore, coal and oil, many terminal requirement features are relatively simple, although mechanical cargo handling devices are needed. Due to the highly automated nature of bulk cargo transfer, large clear working platforms and wharf decks adjacent to the berth are not always necessary. For example a pier for oil tankers often consists mainly of a series of pile clusters against which the ship rests. A simple small working space in the center is provided for handling of hose connections.

In bulk cargo trades ocean vessels are being built to increasingly larger dimensions. Oil tankers with lengths. approaching 1000 ft. and fully loaded drafts of over 50 ft., and large ore carriers with lengths of nearly 800 ft. and drafts of 40 ft. pose new problems in the safe accommodation of vessels for loading or discharging cargo. For conventional berthing arrangements, these vessels require complicated pier structures and elaborate fending systems. The longer, deeper draft vessels force the construction of terminals in deep water with direct, easily negotiable channel approaches, but oftentimes in areas where natural shelter

from wind, sea and swell is less than would be desired, or in river estuaries where silt deposits complicate substructure design and the maintenance of adequate water depth.

It is expected that there will be increased requirements for construction of offshore moorings and submarine pipeline terminals. The offshore mooring avoids expensive structures and takes advantage of the greater stability of the larger ships. For handling of products with multiple pipelines and for packaged cargo, the offshore submarine berth is not usually satisfactory.

Inland Waterway Terminals. The requirements for inland waterway terminals are much simpler than those of ocean port terminals. Since waterway terminals serve barges and river boats, shallow depths of water at the wharfs are acceptable, and the terminals are relatively simple and inexpensive without complicated substructural problems. A small transit shed and wharf arranged parallel to the shore is usually sufficient for passenger and general cargo services. If the terminal is located in an estuary, the wharf may actually consist of a floating deck (an old barge can be used for this purpose) for ready adjustment of deck level during periods of river flood or high tide.

Many waterway terminals are used in bulk cargo trades, particularly those of petroleum products or grain. For these services, it is suitable to provide pile mooring clusters to which barges may be secured with a small platform for handling either hoses or dry bulk loading and unloading machinery. The terminal should be positioned to avoid obstructing waterway traffic, and to take advantage of slack water where possible.

Ocean Port Operations. Port operations should be arranged to meet appropriate levels of technological advance and financial practicality. The use of lighters, for example, may be a means of reducing major capital investment in fixed installations, and the organization of a lighterage system may be practicable if a local wooden boat building industry is present with experienced manpower available to operate and load lighters. Manual cargo handling may be planned for in initial stages of a terminal operation, supplemented in due course by such mechanical equipment as wharf cranes, tractor-trailers, and fork lift trucks.

Among the several new types of shipping methods in use today, cargo movement in containers has promise for operations in less developed areas. Containers have been used for a number of years for the assembly and shipment of small packages of high-value general cargo of common destination. Containers now range in size up to 25 ton capacity (1800 cu. ft.) and special ship designs and conversions have evolved that are devoted exclusively to ocean carriage of containers. While the all-container vessel may be limited to those major trade routes that generate a sufficiently large volume of container cargo, the use of containers carried on general cargo vessels is expected to grow at smaller ports. Containers have advantages of lower handling costs with protection against pilferage and damage due to improper packing and adverse weather.

In North America and the Caribbean, loaded motor trucks and loaded railroad cars are carried by special ships on some trade routes. Trucks and railroad cars are either rolled or lifted into the ships. Although existing terminal facilities can be adapted for these special operations without great expense, the need for large regular movements of cargo and for adequate truck fleet and rail distribution facilities at each end of the trip, plus the relatively complex scheduling and operating techniques required, makes the establishment of these types of services in less developed areas unlikely in the foreseeable future.

Administration of Ocean Ports

The administration of ocean ports involves a complex range of services and responsibilities. Some of the key activities are:

(a) Customs (inspection, collection of duty, supervision of storage).

(b) Operations (assignment of berths and anchorages, cargo handling, supervision of truck and rail traffic).

(c) Rates and Charges (administration of public port tariffs and charges).

(d) Traffic (maintain commercial statistics).

(e) Maintenance (wharfs, warehouses, channels, navigation aids).

(f) Security and Control (policing, approval of waterfront construction).

(g) Other (hydrographic surveys, port planning, general port administration).

At most ports in less developed areas, some or all of these services are assumed by various combinations of local government agencies. This is especially true of the customs administration, since in many areas the collection of customs duties is an important source of revenue. In some areas, the responsibility for some of these services is assumed by major companies which have established the ports and maintain terminals for export of natural resources or agricultural products.

Other services may be performed by national or private railroad companies that are active in port areas.

Maximum use should be made of existing agencies, both non-governmental and governmental, supplemented as required by trained personnel in such fields as terminal cargo handling operations, maintenance of mechanical equipment, and establishment of tariffs and charges. It is desirable to assign the overall responsibility for coordinating port development, operations and administration to a single agency. Figure I shows an administrative organization for management and development of several outports in Burma.

Economic Evaluation of Marine Terminals, Ports, and Waterways

Waterways and ports, taken as a whole to include channels, navigation aids, protective works, and terminals, are rarely self-supporting. Their direct revenues from operations are generally insufficient to cover all capital charges, maintenance and operating costs. Some type of public subsidy is therefore necessary, either in the form of tax abatement or favorable interest rates and amortization terms, or more frequently in the form of direct cash payments. Economic evaluation of the total project requires a measurement of the total project costs against total economic benefits in order to obtain cost-benefit ratios. Terminals, when separated from other elements of the waterway or port complex, may afford opportunities to apply conventional techniques of financial analysis involving comparisons of annual costs and revenues to determine financial feasibility.

Financial Analysis of Terminals.

The annual costs of an individual terminal include capital charges, and costs for maintenance, utilities, cargo handling, insurance, and administration. Costs of such general port improvements as channels, turning basins, navigation aids and breakwaters would not be included. Marine terminal revenues are usually obtained from two types of charges: one for handling of cargo, including stevedoring, checking, separation, and rail car or truck loading or unloading; and the other for the use of a terminal or occupancy of space, including dockage, wharfage, demurrage and storage. The comparison of annual costs and annual revenues on these bases will indicate the net profit or loss and the ability to meet capital charges or debt service.

Cost-Benefit Ratios for Ports and Waterways. Major port and waterway projects considered in their entirety must be evaluated by a comparison of total costs with total benefits. The evaluation is made from the public view to determine if the improvements permit transportation at lower total expense than would obtain if the improvements were not made.

Costs are capital costs of construction plus maintenance and operating expenses. Cost factors may be converted to an annual cost basis or to an equivalent present worth. Generally, in making economic evaluations of projects in the United States, low public interest rates and relatively long amortization periods are used.

Many of the economic benefits resulting from construction of ports and waterways may be evaluated in monetary terms. They are principally transportation savings due to the provision of more economical transportation and improved

operating conditions for existing navigation. For ports they may include:

(a) Savings in cost of sea transport
by making ports and terminals accessible to larger, deeper draft vessels.

(b) Savings in cost of ship delay and
elimination of costs of tug service by
removal of obstructions to navigation
and providing shorter access channels
from the open sea.

(c) Savings in cost of cargo handling by provision of modern terminal
facilities capable of faster cargo transfer.

(d) Savings in cost of vessel operation by reduction of waiting time for
assignment to berth through provision
of an adequate number of berths and
by reduction of time at berth through
improved cargo handling.

(e) Reduction in losses of cargo due
to damage and pilferage at modern
terminals.

Transportation savings generated
by waterways include:

(a) Savings in cost of inland transportation per ton-mile of cargo by use
of low cost barge transportation in
place of other methods.

(b) Savings in vessel operation costs
through channel straightening and re-
alignment, removal of obstructions, and
deepening to permit use of larger
barges.

(c) Savings in cargo handling costs
through provision of efficient waterway
terminals.

A comparison of the total project
costs with the net benefits is made, with
the project considered economically justified if the benefit-cost ratio is 1.0, or
greater.

There are other kinds of economic
benefits which are also weighed in determining the justification of ports or inland
waterways, although they may not readily
be converted to actual savings. The economic and social benefits resulting from
opening new areas for development and
the stimulation of industrial and agricultural production are of principal importance. Direct income benefits arising
from the construction and operation of
ports and waterways are also claimed.
This income enters almost every phase of
an area's economy, and the circulation of
these funds stimulates local business, giving rise to additional, indirect benefits.
The indirect benefits to an area from the
development of a new activity are in the
order of twice the magnitude of the direct income which that activity generates.

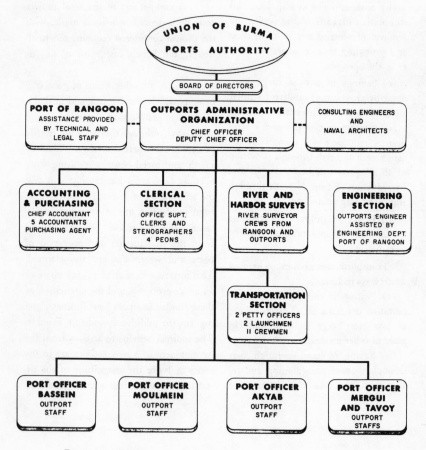

FIGURE 1. Typical ports authority organization chart—outports of Burma.

New Uses of Mass Communication for the Promotion of Economic and Social Development*

WILBUR SCHRAMM

Director, Institute for Communication Research, Stanford University, Stanford, California

GERALD F. WINFIELD

Chief, Communications Resources Division, U.S. Agency for International Development, Washington, D.C.

Introduction

Communication, as used in this paper, refers to the circulation of knowledge and ideas in human society. It is thus conceived of as a social process, rather than as machines, vehicles, roads, or electronics. By *national development* we mean the economic and social changes that take place in a nation as it moves from a traditional to a modernized pattern of society: changes associated with division of labor, growth of industry, urbanization, growth in per capita incomes,

and preparation of citizens—by literacy, education, and information—to participate broadly in national affairs. Our intent is to outline some of the relationships between the development of effective communication and the progress of national development, and in particular to suggest ways in which the new knowledge and new technology of communication can help to speed economic and social growth.

We intend to discuss these relationships in such a way as not to restrict our argument to any one economic or political system. The development of effective communication seems to be an essential of national development regardless of the political auspices and the economic model. It has appeared to play very much the *same* part even in very different systems. Therefore, we are going to try to talk about aspects of communication development that are not systembound for,

*This paper was written with the generous help and advice of UNESCO and was on the conference agenda as a UNESCO paper. However, it expresses the viewpoints of individuals, which may not necessarily in every case be identical with, and should therefore not be assumed to be, the official point of view of UNESCO, nor of the Agency for International Development.

if nations can share communication experiences with each other, then the new states need not repeat the mistakes of the older countries, and new communication systems and policies can rise on systems and policies that have gone before.

Communication's Part in National Development

Social and psychological factors have been assumed in most models of national development. These models have usually taken for granted such elements as "the will to develop," thrift, the rapid flow of knowledge, and the ability to make cooperative plans and decisions. But during recent years, planners and scholars have looked more explicitly toward the "human factors" that would help them to understand, plan for, and stimulate the pace and pattern of economic development.

They have been seeking what Albert Hirschman (1), called a "binding agent,"—something to organize and achieve cooperation among the many factors, resources, and abilities needed for successful development, and they have looked for such an agent chiefly in the minds of men. "The course and rate of politico-economic development in a country," said J. J. Spengler, "depend largely upon the contents or elements present in the minds of such country's inhabitants, and above all, on the contents of the minds of the elite" (2). Max Weber found it helpful to relate rapid economic progress to social norms and ideology (3). Hirschman found his "binding agent" in a kind of "growth perspective." An American psychologist, D. C. McClelland, looked into the motivational

patterns of economic development, and wrote in a tone reminiscent of some of the things Lenin said on the same topic: "There is no substitute for ideological fervour. A country or at least a significant portion of its elite has got to want economic achievement badly enough to give it priority over other desires" (4).

If economic development depends on "the content of minds," "a growth perspective," "ideological fervour," and the like, then it must also depend on communication, because these states of mind must be communicated to people who do not have them. Indeed, a whole set of attitudes, understandings, and skills, appropriate to economic development and social change, must be communicated over a developing country, and in many cases to people who are ignorant of them, uninterested, or resistant. If a nation, rather than merely an advanced society, is to be built, then the necessary knowledge of public affairs, the concepts of national loyalty, and empathy for fellow citizens must also be communicated so that people will be able to take part in national affairs. Furthermore, if a nation is to play a significant part internationally, communication must weave the new state to other states, and the necessary understandings of international events and relationships must be communicated to the people. Thus it is clear that national development involves serious and significant communication problems, which we shall now look at in more detail.

The Uses of Communication in Development (5)

In the early stages of national development, there are likely to be great crevasses in public knowledge and attitude that must be bridged by communication. Some of the largest of these lie between the elite and the mass of people. The elite tend to be cosmopolitan; many of them have been educated in advanced countries, and they have absorbed modern ideas and concepts of change. The mass, on the other hand, are likely to live in an unchanging world of tradition and local interest; they are largely illiterate, versed in lore rather than theory, unaccustomed to learn systematically, unfamiliar with modern technology, in fact hardly touched by modern life. In many cultures the people believe it is inappropriate for them to have political ideas and opinions. In some cultures work is not a valued activity; the idea is to do as little of it as possible. We do not mean to imply that the elite are always a force for change, and that the mass are always resistant to change. In many developing countries, once the possibility of change has been widely communicated, the chief impetus to change lies within the mass of people. In any case, however, there is likely to be different understandings of change, and different concepts of a desirable change, within different groups of the population, and communication must bridge these differences.

The task of a developing nation is to transport over the crevasse skills, attitudes, and concepts which will enable the people of the country to move out of a traditional society and to participate effectively in the modern world. Both the leaders and the people must travel across the gaps until they are joined into a nation.

There are other essential uses of communication in the process of national development. The elite themselves are likely to be far from agreement. In a new state, the period just before independence is likely to be one of great unity among the leaders. Once the common goal of independence is gained, however, centrifugal forces are released, as they were, for example, in India, in the Congo, and in Algeria. If the country is to remain united, if development is to proceed efficiently, there must be institutions and programmes of communication for reaching consensus.

We are not going to elaborate on the consensus function of communication, nor of certain other functions which the communication system of the new country must be developed to perform. But it does seem necessary to refer to the function of communication in balancing off the disintegrative forces of economic and social development. As an Italian labor leader once said, "there is likely to be great danger when the hopeless begin to hope" (6). The very idea of change, introduced into a country where for centuries people have felt themselves controlled by inheritance, tradition, and fate, is likely to be a shock. Intelligent and skillful communication must smooth out the levels of strain, soothe impatience without destroying hope, maintain a "growth perspective" that will accommodate a long-term future orientation and withstand temporary disappointments.

Communication Resources in Developing Countries

In a modern society, much of the burden on communication is borne by the educational system, the mass media, and the social organizations. In many of the developing countries, however, these institutions are themselves undeveloped.

About half of the people in the world, and well over half the people in developing countries, are not literate. Less than half of the children of primary school age in developing countries are in school; and only a tiny fraction of those beyond primary age are able to go to secondary school or to a university. In Nigeria for example (where educational opportunities are better than in many developing countries), over 70 percent of the 93,000 teachers in primary, secondary, and teacher training schools are untrained (7). In a series of continental conferences, UNESCO has been assessing the world-wide cost of training the teachers, building and equipping the schools, furnishing the teaching materials, and operating the educational systems which economic advancement calls for in the developing countries. The cost is staggering. It has been calculated, for example, that merely to achieve universal primary education in Ethiopia would require three times the present total national budget (8). The cost of the present 5-year plan for raising the primary school enrollments in Africa from 40 to 51 percent, and the secondary enrollments from 3 to 9 percent, is estimated at $4,150 million of which more than $1,300 million must come from outside Africa. The needs for Asia, Latin America, and the Middle East are comparable.

UNESCO has suggested that a minimum standard of mass media growth for developing countries might be to provide for every 100 of their inhabitants:

Ten copies of daily newspapers, five radio receivers, two cinema seats, two television receivers.

This is a modest objective. It is far below the achievements of well developed countries. In the United Kingdom, for example, the circulation of newspapers is 58 per 100 people; in the United States, there are nearly as many radios as people. But 100 States and territories in Asia, Africa, and Latin America fall below even the "minimum" standard suggested by UNESCO. These counties have a combined population of nearly 2,000 millions, so two-thirds of the people of the world lack, as UNESCO says in its report to the United Nations, even "the barest means of being informed of developments at home, let alone in other countries. In point of fact the actual situation is even worse because the above criteria do not take into account the distribution of facilities within countries. In many less developed countries, over 60 percent of the population live in rural districts, whereas the facilities for information are concentrated in a relatively few urban areas (9)." At least 40 sovereign states in the less developed areas have no national news agencies, and must rely on the five world agencies both to bring them news and carry away news of them. All the developing countries together use less than 20 percent of the world's annual consumption of newsprint.

The effect of underdeveloped information channels is to isolate a population so its members are hardly aware of the outside world, and inadequately informed of the problems and policies of their own country. In a careful study conducted recently in a Latin American country (10), it was found that over one-half of the rural adults could name neither the outgoing nor the newly elected president. About 95 percent could not name Eisenhower or Castro. The "big issues" of the day—the cold war, the nuclear bomb, developments in Cuba, and the like—brought response from only a very few. A study conducted in a South Asian country, measured the diffusion of modern ideas through villages at different distances from a metropolis (11). In the farthest village no one except the head man knew who was the ruler of the nation. Except in the two closest villages, no one knew anything about other countries, about such ideologies as communism, socialism, or capitalism, about important recent international events, or who were the nation's friends or enemies. In each village, at least some of the people knew that the country was no longer a colony, but the recent partition of the country was unknown in two of the seven villages and known by only a few in two others. Some people in six of the seven villages knew of the 5-year plan, but thereafter knowledge of new policies trailed off rapidly. People in only four villages knew anything about community development projects. This is not to suggest that there are no good reasons, in geography and economics, why these people are less well informed than we should like to see them; but merely that, until these people have a great deal more information than now, they can hardly be mobilized for a grand effort toward national development.

To build up these information channels, the mass media, like the schools, will require a great amount of construction, equipment, materials, and training. UNESCO has estimated, very roughly, that an additional $3,400 million, spent between 1962 and 1975, would be required to bring the media of the developing countries up to the minimum levels mentioned above.

Figures on the growth of social organizations—such as political parties, professional and business groups, adult education organizations, labor unions,

youth organizations, women's groups, and so forth—in the developing countries are not so readily available as figures on the schools and the mass media. Nevertheless it is clear that these, also, are much less fully organized than in the advanced countries.

Relation of Communication Development to Economic Development

There is a striking correlation between the level of economic advance, on the one hand, and the level of education and mass media, on the other. The higher the per capita income, the higher is the level of literacy, the percentage of school age children in school, and the circulation of mass media to the public. This relationship may be illustrated by comparing Tanganyika, which is relatively underdeveloped (per capita income under 100 dollars, industrialization low) with Australia (which is well advanced, with per capita income over 800 dollars, and considerable industry) (12). The two countries have about the same population, but Australia has nearly 900 times as much newspaper circulation, and perhaps 750 times as many radio receivers as Tanganyika. In Southeast Asia, as it is defined by the Economic Commission for Asia and the Far East to include the 28 countries between Iran and Korea, there is but one country in which communication is relatively advanced. This is Japan. But Japan has 77 percent of all the newspaper circulation in those 28 countries, 73 percent of all the radio receivers, and 97 percent of all the television receivers.

Correlation, of course, does not prove causality. The fact that income, industrialization, and urbanization all rise with literacy, education, and mass media development, does not prove that one group *causes* the other to rise. On the contrary, it is quite clear that an *interaction* goes on between them. Until a large number of people learn to read, there is an insufficient market for newspapers; but until newspapers and other reading material are easy to get and rewarding to read there is not likely to be a significant increase in literacy. A literate man is able to acquire more complex skills, earn more money, purchase more communication. More money in circulation and larger potential markets make it possible to expand the mass communication system, buy more printing presses and more newsprint, train more editors and printers, bring in more wire service news, teach more people to read.

In both communication development and economic development it is hard to take the first steps (13). There is a critical point at which the enormously powerful interaction of communication and economic development begins to take hold. The question, of course, is whether the nation can make the hard climb to that point. Both in economics and in communication, the first part of the path looks pretty hopeless. On the economic side, the risks are too great to attract the entrepreneur. The labor force is not trained. Capital is lacking. The population is increasing faster than productivity. Most of the population may be a relatively inert mass, neither informed about nor of a mind to cooperate with the national development plan. On the communication side there is the equally difficult outlook described so eloquently at UNESCO's Bangkok Conference by the Indian editor A R Bhat (14). Low literacy greatly reduces the potential audience. Low industrialization reduces to

almost nothing the potential advertising support. The resultant low income reduces the ability of the newspaper to buy newsprint, to bring in wire news, to obtain better presses, or to hire better qualified reporters. To break out of such a self-maintaining set of limits is not easy.

The Advantage of Coming Late— The Availability of Research and Development in the Industrialized Countries

Even with the best will and the greatest determination, developing countries find it difficult to assemble and allocate all the resources they need to develop adequately the channels of communication within their society. They are short of everything—teachers and the facilities to train them; mass media, technicians and production staffs to operate them, and equipment to make them effective; teaching and informational materials. Therefore, anything they could do to *multiply* these scarce resources and make them more widely useful, would be advantageous and important in a degree that industrialized countries might find it hard to appreciate.

In this respect, it is by no means a disadvantage not to be the first nation to develop economically. Each generation of nations builds on the experience of the generation before it. The younger nations can avoid some of the mistakes of the older ones. They can short-cut many of the painful steps of industrial and engineering development. Their goal can be, not to do as well as the nations before them, but rather to do *better;* for they can choose what they want from the storehouse of international experience, and use their creative energies, not for developing the same thing over again, but for adapting it and improving on it.

It is not necessary to choose between the older and the newer technology. Just as a developing country has uses for the wagon and the automobile even after it acquires airplanes, so it will have use for the more traditional methods of communicating even after it acquires the newest and most sophisticated methods. But it need not restrict itself to the more traditional methods when new and efficient ones exist. And in the field of human communication, the new nations can draw on two kinds of new and promising developments from the advanced countries, which have the possibility of providing "multipliers." These are, an advanced technology for printing and electronic communication, and a group of "new media" for education.

Advanced Technology of Mass Communication: Offset Printing

A quiet revolution brought about by offset printing has been taking place in some of the printing plants of industrialized countries. The idea of offset printing is not new. For more than a century it was used only for specialized tasks because the machine to compose the image, and print it at high speed, had not been invented. In the last two decades, however, composing machines have been developed that are as easy to use as a typewriter, and faster offset presses have become available. A number of small newspapers and small printing plants have gone to offset, and found that, for their particular needs, it is less expensive and demands less skilled labor. For many suburban and rural newspapers, where the runs are comparatively small and the income modest, offset has made

the difference between being able and not being able to publish.

The method is thus particularly promising for developing countries. It will print copy prepared by any source from a ball-point pen to a phototypesetting machine. It prints pictures and advertisements very sharply, requires no engraving, and for this reason offset printers can afford to use many more pictures than they could with letterpress. The most important advantage of offset printing for developing countries, however, is its cost. It permits a small paper or printing establishment to start in business with a few thousand dollars instead of much larger capital.

The Transistor

The transistor is a tiny electronic element which does the work of a radio or television vacuum tube, and requires much less current and much less space. It has made possible, in the industrialized countries, a great variety of miniaturized electronic devices, and in particular has made pocket radios practicable, and is beginning to be used for portable television receivers.

For developing countries the transistor is a particularly important advance because its low requirement in electric current makes battery-operated radio and television receivers feasible, and thus permits broadcasting to reach far beyond existing power lines. Transistorized radios now run for many hours on dry cells. Television receivers suitable for group reception are being designed to run on somewhat larger dry cells, or on wind-driven or charcoal-burning generators. It appears that the problems of supplying power to remote broadcast receivers, and thus jumping the barriers both of illiteracy and of power lines, may be well on the way to being solved.

These developments bring within reach the five-dollar radio, which has long been a goal of UNESCO. If a rugged and dependable receiving set, powered by long-life batteries, can be built to sell in the neighborhood of five dollars, then almost any developing country can afford to place these receivers in its villages.

The Communication Satellite

As this is written, the Telstar satellite is demonstrating its ability to relay television, radio, and telephone messages between continents. Telstar is only the first stage of a development which will bring all the countries of the earth closer together, so far as communication can do that, and in its later stages will offer some challenging opportunities for widespread education (15).

The present generation of communication satellites is able only to transmit messages from one ground station to another. Probably within 10 years, however, satellites will be able to transmit to home television receivers. A satellite in orbit will perhaps be able to transmit an educational television program to an entire nation. It hardly needs to be pointed out that this development, when it comes, will present problems as well as opportunities. There will be problems of ownership and control, of curriculum and language, of scheduling and programming, and of broadcast frequencies. But if these problems can be solved, then the communication satellite may contribute strikingly to the information, the education, and the binding together of the people of a nation (16).

The "New Media" of Education

The "new media" has become a common term in some advanced countries, but it is not an exact phrase, and we shall try to say what we mean when we use it (17).

Educational media are any devices that carry learning experiences to an audience. We might say that the teacher is the oldest and still the best of the "educational media." But as technology has developed, a series of devices has been produced to represent and aid the teacher in providing experiences from which students can learn efficiently. There were a number of such devices even before print, but the printed textbook was the first educational medium that permitted the teacher to multiply his efforts and provide learning experiences for many more students than he could teach personally. Several hundred years after the textbook was introduced, technology gave teachers the ability to extend educational experiences by projecting films, slides, and other teaching materials. Mockups and models became available. Educational radio and television made it possible to circulate lectures and classroom demonstrations very widely. And in the last few years, programmed instruction has made it possible to bring an efficient tutorial experience to a very large number of students.

Thus, the "new" educational media are different at different times and at different places. The textbook was the "new" educational medium 300 years ago. Films and projected materials were new 50 years ago; educational radio, 35 years ago; educational television, 10 years ago; and now programmed instruction is new. This is the timetable for the most advanced countries. In many developing countries, educational radio is still new, and educational television and programmed instruction are yet to be discovered. When educators speak of the "new educational media" at the present time, they usually refer to educational television and programmed instruction, supported by the slightly older media of radio, films and projected materials, and print.

In one sense, however, the use of the term "media" is not the same for programmed instruction as for the other devices we have called educational media. Television, films, radio, and print are simply channels to carry any kind and method of teaching or information. Programmed instruction, on the other hand, is itself a method of teaching, and must be carried by one of the other channels—by print in the form of programmed books, by films in teaching machines, or by the use of programmed methods in television. For the most part programmed instruction today takes the form of a special kind of workbook which has the ability to multiply the teaching of the tutor and offer a highly efficient learning experience; and in this respect it is a true educational medium.

The educational media, extensively used and tested in the more advanced countries, are particularly important to developing countries because they hold out the opportunity of multiplying teachers and classrooms, speeding up education, spreading information more widely, and thereby increasing the pace of national development. Indeed, these media may be the only way that the traditionally slow rhythm of educational growth may be sufficiently hurried and the benefits of knowledge and skill shared with millions of people in this generation who otherwise would never have an opportunity to be educated, or to participate as informed citizens in the development of their nations.

Questions of Effectiveness

How effective are these media? It is hardly necessary to cite evidence that the textbook is an effective device (see the proceedings of UNESCO's Geneva conference on Improving the Textbook (1961)). Likewise, films have proved for a long time that their pictorial qualities and their ability to combine sight and sound are powerful stimulants to learning. In general, experiments show that students learn at least as much from television as from sound films, and as much from either as from an average teacher teaching the same subject for the same amount of time in the classroom. Four hundred carefully controlled experiments comparing educational television with conventional classroom were recently summarized. In 65 percent of the comparisons there was no significant difference between what was learned from television and from the conventional method; in 14 percent, the conventional method came out on top; and in 21 percent, the television class learned more than the conventional one (18).

This is not the same as saying that television or sound films are adequate substitutes for a teacher. They are not. The research in advanced countries shows, rather, that television and films *plus* a teacher, make a uniquely powerful combination. If a qualified teacher is not available, then a discussion leader with opportunity to discuss what has been seen, and practice what has been taught, will add considerably to the effectiveness of television or films alone. And if neither a teacher nor a leader is available, then there will still be considerable learning from television or films alone. In the United States, for example, persons who are home-bound and unable to go to school have been taught with great success by television, supplemented with readings and practice exercises.

But the great promise of the audiovisual media for the developing countries is that, in situations where not all teachers are well trained, they can share the most expert teaching; in situations where a teacher is not qualified to teach a given subject, that course may still be made available by television or films; and in countries where many teachers need further training, making expert teaching available on the media is a kind of inservice training which will enable teachers to improve their own work. The importance of television teaching as inservice training for less well qualified teachers has been demonstrated impressively in advanced countries, and would seem to be a particularly important consideration for developing countries where the need is so great for upgrading the level of teaching. Thus the effect of the new media on education will not be to replace the teacher, but rather to give him a chance to teach better, by permitting him to observe expert teaching and to delegate certain important tasks—demonstrations, and teaching of specialized topics—to television and films, as he now delegates certain important teaching tasks to textbooks.

This is particularly important in developing countries because of their need to maintain flexibility in curriculum. In many of these countries drastic changes are being made to meet needs and cover subjects not presently represented in the curriculum. Neither qualified teachers nor materials are likely to be available in sufficient numbers and quantities to meet the requirements of these changes. Therefore new media like television, radio, and film can be especially useful in supplementing and guiding teachers, and making materials quickly available.

Television has certain advantages and certain disadvantages as compared with radio and films. Unlike radio, it can bring the visual element to teaching; but radio has greater range than television, and is cheaper to install and operate especially where electrical power is not yet readily available. For many years to come, radio will doubtless continue to be highly important in the communication plans of developing countries. Compared to films, television has the advantages of liveness and portability; but films can be controlled locally, scheduled, and repeated as needed. Films are and will continue to be an important part of educational television (19). And there are situations in which less sophisticated media are clearly preferable. For example, when it is desired that a class should look long and carefully at a picture, a slide is obviously more economical than television or moving pictures. There is a place for all the educational media, and the more advanced countries have learned to use them as a system, choosing whatever combination of teacher and media seems most suitable for a given learning experience.

But of the new media, it is television that is presently most intriguing as a multiplier for teaching and informational resources. It may seem incongruous to think of using a sophisticated and expensive medium like television to carry some of the burden of teaching in less developed countries. But television does not seem sophisticated to the person viewing a program, and its cost is a relative matter. Television has been used effectively to teach almost all subjects that can be taught by classroom lecture and demonstration. When accurate accounts of its cost as a teaching device were kept in the United States, it was found that it was cheaper to teach large numbers by television than in classrooms. If the costs of suitable receivers can be brought down, as seems likely; if rugged transistorized models can be built, as now seems almost certain; if efficient ways can be found to replace the batteries or provide other current-producing devices—then television may very well turn out to be the cheapest way of providing first-rate education in many developing countries, and perhaps the *only way* in which good teaching can be brought in this generation to large numbers of people in some of these countries.

Programmed instruction, being so new, may require a few words of explanation. It is essentially a tutorial method put into such form that a student "teaches himself." As we know, learning is an active process. One learns by responding. A "program," in programmed instruction, is essentially a series of stimuli to which a student responds. More specifically it is a series of questions which the student answers, or a series of statements with blanks for him to fill. But these have certain special characteristics.

(a) They begin with knowledge a student has, and lead him by *short steps* and *logical pathways* through the knowledge he is supposed to master.

(b) Because the steps between items are short, he makes few mistakes and therefore practices almost entirely *correct* responses.

(c) As soon as he has responded he is able to find out whether his response is correct. Thus, if he makes mostly correct responses, it is correct responses that are *reinforced* by this immediate knowledge of results.

(d) Review is built into the sequence.

(e) Using this method, the student can move at his own best pace. The quick learner will not be bored; the slow learner will not be left behind the class.

This is a brief and inadequate picture of a rather sophisticated technique of teaching, but let us point out two further advantages of this method. In the first place, before a program can be made, the desired outcome in knowledge must be defined very clearly; this often has an extremely salutory effect on curriculum and teaching generally. In the second place, when programs are being made they are tried out on individuals of the level for which they are intended. They are revised repeatedly until they are relatively flawless, and then they are tried on a large group. Thus, unlike most teaching instruments, programmed instruction can practically be guaranteed to "work" when it is released for use (20).

Programmed instruction is so new that no such body of evaluative research exists on it as on television. Yet the record of successful use is a remarkable one, considering that the first experimental programs became available only 5 years ago. It has been used successfully by children of every level and by adults, by slow learners and superior students; in school, in industry, and in the home; to teach behaviors as different as rote learning, paired associate learning, concept formation, the application of formulas, constructing logical proofs, learning to read a foreign language, "trouble shooting" in radio hookups, instrument flying, reading a radar screen, and operating an electronic digital computer. In the relatively few instances where it has been compared directly with conventional instruction, programmed instruction has more often come out ahead than behind. It has proved a useful device for individual study, home work, and remedial work. Furthermore, the method of programmed instruction has increasingly been used in teaching groups, face to face or by television and in textbooks, and programming methods promise to increase the effectiveness of those media.

Of course, programmed instruction has had less testing than the other media, and at this time only 200 to 300 programs are available, as compared to many thousands of textbooks, films, and other audiovisual materials. In particular, programmed instruction has never yet been tested in a developing country, and it is not known how much adaptation of existing materials would be required for developing cultures, or what differences in form or use might be required of programs made especially for developing cultures. The first trials in developing countries should therefore be watched very carefully.

But, noting this caveat, it seems reasonable to lay aside at this moment the question of whether students learn from the new media. So far as experiment and field tests in the advanced countries answer the question, they do learn. They learn a great deal. The useful questions are: What are the conditions of effective use in developing cultures? When does it make sense to use them as multipliers? For what kinds of uses, what kinds of topics, what kinds of students are they most effective? For what kinds of teaching, under what kinds of conditions, under what kinds of cost considerations, are they to be preferred to other channels of teaching or to no channels? We are beginning to get answers to such questions and some of them will be suggested in the following section of this paper.

The Communication Media in Developing Countries

To what extent can we trust the communication research findings of advanced countries as a guide to using the new communication techniques in developing cultures? It is quite right to be cautious about applying research results across cultures, and yet people are often more alike than their cultures, and learn in about the same ways regardless of latitude and longitude. It is probable that any materials and methods transplanted from an advanced country to a developing one would have to undergo adaptation before they could be used effectively in the new culture; and developing countries should keep this in mind before deciding to purchase teaching materials from elsewhere. On the other hand, if an effective system can be made using television and group meetings in an advanced culture, an effective system using the same ingredients can probably be made for developing countries. Whenever programs can be tailored to the needs of a developing country, programmed instruction can probably be used as effectively there as in advanced countries. Developing countries now have a number of years of experience on which to base their ideas of what kinds of communication will work, and what will not, in their cultures.

In selecting a few examples of how the new communication media have been used in the developing countries, we are going to take for granted the most common of all these uses, namely, to inform the public, to arouse their awareness of national policies and problems, to make participating citizens rather than mere residents, and in particular to enlist them in the program of economic and social development. (We shall not have space here to discuss the obvious importance of a free flow of news in relation to these objectives.) No country that has ever modernized has done so without performing this basic communication task, and every developing country is now doing it to the best of its ability, making use of the mass media, face to face contacts, and organization. Let us turn to some other uses of the new media.

Literacy Teaching

In a statement at the beginning of 1962, the Director-General of UNESCO said that in 10 years illiteracy could be wiped off the earth, if mankind wishes to do so. The pattern by which this could be accomplished is becoming clearer. It would require, in each country where illiteracy is a problem, a careful and extensive organization of teachers (volunteer or professional) to conduct literacy classes; if these teachers were not experienced in literacy training they would have to be taught the method. It would also require social pressure to make illiterates want to learn to read. It would require extensive help from the mass media both to motivate the prospective learners and to extend expert teaching where it is not readily available. And finally, it would require some special reading material to

keep up the interest of the new literate until he is able to read ordinary materials. This is approximately the way that Poland, for example, organized itself to do away with illiteracy (21).

In certain other countries, experiments have placed a larger part of the burden on the mass media. Television has been used, where it is available, even more successfully than radio. Some of the best records of television as a channel for literacy teaching come from the more developed countries. In Italy, for example, as late as 1960 there were still two million illiterates, most of them rural people in the southern part of the country. Illiterate adults in a modernized country are likely to be even more resistant than in a developing country. The appeal of being able to watch television was a great aid in persuading these people to join viewing groups around a central receiver (22).

The Italians found it desirable to station a trained teacher at each of these viewing points, to guide the students' drill and supplement the teaching they got from television. In making programs, they discovered that methods for teaching adults to read and write have to be quite different from those used for children. It is necessary not to offend adult pride by making him feel that he is being sent to "school" or being taught by "playing games." It is important to keep him aware that he is learning something useful but, at the same time, to leaven the experience with a certain amount of humor. Every student who followed this course to its end learned to read and write.

Television has also been used successfully to teach elementary reading and writing to adults in several places in the

United States. Viewers met in groups, under the leadership of a volunteer teacher or viewed the program in their homes (23). The television lesson was supplemented by reading and drill materials.

One important conclusion has been reached by every adult literacy program. This is that special easy-reading materials are urgently required, lest the student forget his newly won skill. UNESCO has issued several monographs on this problem (24). Easy-reading materials also offer a unique opportunity for a country to disseminate useful information about the state and its development plans, about better agricultural practices, health, sanitation, and other high priority subjects. In different places, this has been accomplished in different ways, but always with the requirement that the materials should present adult ideas in simple writing, that they should not talk down to their readers, and, above all, that they should be interesting and useful.

In Puerto Rico, four books and several booklets, four issues of a poster newspaper, and 8 to 10 posters are issued for this purpose each year. In Liberia a multilith monthly *New Day,* written with the 1,200-word basic vocabulary of the literacy course, is sold for three cents a copy. In Northern Nigeria a group of tabloid news sheets, each eight pages in size, are issued for new literates. Literacy House, in Lucknow, India, assembles village libraries of books with very simple vocabularies, publishes books suitable for new readers, and issues a fortnightly family magazine. Every copy, the editor reports, is read by about 20 persons.

In many countries this has proved to be an especially important function of the local press. Newspapers published once a week or once a fortnight can provide material which, through its intrinsic interest, compels attention and develops the reading habit. These papers can furnish news as well as information designed to help raise living standards, and create an understanding of community objectives and a civic consciousness. Thus they can both educate and inform at the same time as they provide practice in the useful skill of reading.

Developing countries can therefore be quite confident that both the electronic and the printed media, if used skillfully in viewing groups with group leaders, can be used to speed and extend the process of literacy training.

The New Media in the School

The printed media, slides, filmstrips, and teaching films have long been used in the schools of developing countries. The use of television, however, is relatively new. If television can be used as effectively to teach in the developing countries as it has been in some of the more advanced countries, then, it will have certain special advantages. For one thing, it will enable a country where highly trained teachers are scarce to share its best teachers very widely. Where few teachers are trained to teach certain subjects, it will make it possible for those subjects to be taught even where no resident teachers are available. Where projectors and films are scarce, television can be a "big projector" for hundreds of schools at the same time. And, television will be a powerful tool of inservice training and improvement for teachers.

In Turkey, rather than trying to develop a new television course in physics, Istanbul educators adapted for use of Turkish school children the 162 half hour lessons of the Harvey White physics course which has been used successfully on television both in America and in England (25). They also adapted the accompanying textbook, teachers guides, and unit tests. One of the problems of Turkey is the shortage of well qualified teachers for subjects like physics. Therefore, the experiment was designed so as to compare what lycee students would learn (a) if taught by experienced teachers with the aid of the filmed programs; (b) if taught by inexperienced teachers with the films; (c) if taught by correspondence but still given a chance to view the films; and all these compared with (d) what the best teachers could accomplish without the films; and (e) what the average teachers could accomplish without the films. It was found that students taught by the best teachers, using what teaching aids they wished but without the television films, scored slightly better than the students who saw films. This may be a comment on the success of the adaptation. But the other results were more significant. There was no significant difference between the test scores of students taught by experienced and by inexperienced teachers, if the films were used. There was no significant difference between the scores of correspondence students (with the films) and the scores of students taught by experienced teachers using the films. But students taught either by inexperienced teachers or by correspondence, using the films, did significantly better than students in another city taught by average teachers without the films. This seems to be very good evidence that television or films can be used in developing countries to bring the benefits of good teaching to schools where experienced teachers are not available, and even to students who must study without a classroom teacher.

Educational television has been under trial in the schools of New Delhi, India, with over 30,000 students receiving instruction in Hindi, English, and science. The results are encouraging. First reports indicate improved performance by students, increase in enthusiasm for science, and, perhaps most important, an enthusiastic response on the part of both teachers and administrators to the inservice training opportunities involved. Not only do the teachers see expert teaching procedures, but also they have a chance to refresh their knowledge of subject matter. Both teachers and administrators were quoted as saying that the Hindi lessons, in particular, provided as much learning for the teachers as for the students (26).

Iran used educational television successfully as a 6-week summer makeup course for students who had failed the course in physics during the winter term. Of the students who took the summer course, 72 percent received passing grades when they retook the course examination in the fall (27).

Western Nigeria has now been broadcasting school television for two years. It has faced many of the problems that are likely to recur in any school television program newly established in a developing country: the need to train competent producers and technicians, the time required to put good teaching on television, the difficulty of ordering suitable educational films, at long distance, for broadcast, and, especially, the difficulty of keeping school television receivers in repair. Nevertheless, the evaluation of results has been generally favorable, and the production record has been better than anticipated (28).

It must be concluded that, as a means of sharing good teaching, multiplying opportunities for students to learn, and providing inservice training for teachers, educational television in developing countries is potentially most promising.

Integrating Useful Information With Action

Every developing nation faces the need to supply its people with information on scientific agriculture, health practices, sanitation, and community development, and insure that the information is acted upon. This task is more difficult because of the high rate of illiteracy and the lack of power lines and communication channels.

A number of countries have found mobile audiovisual vans useful for this purpose. These are built on trucks and carry their own power generators. They also carry projection screens, projectors, loud speakers, microphones, and other audiovisual tools as needed.

The Philippines have been operating 22 such units, using them to show films illustrating better agricultural practices, village government organization, health and sanitation, and so forth. After the film showing, the microphones of the mobile van are frequently used for discussing the topic further. These vans commonly show to audiences of 500 to 3,000 people, and go to a different community each day. Thus, in the course of a year millions of viewers can be reached.

Radio has probably been used more often than any other medium for the dissemination of useful information as well

as news. Radio has no trouble leaping the literacy barrier and can reach into remote regions without the help of roads.

In Jordan, for example, the broadcasting station in Amman broadcasts an agricultural extension program every morning at 6:15. The broadcast is made up chiefly of answers to questions. About 300 questions come in each week. "How do I treat the sickness that makes my cow have a calf before her time?" or "What do I do about the insects that make the bark of my orchard trees fall off?" The broadcaster, who has himself been an extension agent, selects the most urgent of the questions and, when necessary, takes them to the Ministry of Agriculture and discusses them with specialists. Then, in a conversational manner, he answers the questions for his radio listeners. The number of questions he gets is a testimony to listeners' valuation of the program (29).

In South Korea, an ingenious use has been made of a limited number of battery-powered radios in an area where both radios and power lines are scarce. Twenty such receiving sets were obtained at a cost of less than $14 each, and a 50-watt transmitter was built at the cost of a few hundred dollars. For a pilot test, an area was selected where the principal health problems were tuberculosis, typhoid fever, and intestinal parasites. Using tape recorders, but also providing for a large proportion of live transmission, a 3-hour program was prepared for broadcast. It featured information on the health problems but also contained entertainment and local features such as a singing contest, music by local bands, and "man on the street" interviews. The program was broadcast three times a day— 6 to 9 a.m., 11 a.m. to 2 p.m., and 7 to 10 p.m. After each broadcast, volunteers from the girls' high school moved the sets to another community. Thus, within 3 days, the broadcast was heard in 180 different locations (30).

Not only was the broadcast a popular success; it also taught the desired information. Records were obtained from a sample of viewers before and after the 3 test days. After the 3 days, less than half as many people believed any longer that tuberculosis was hereditary, almost everyone had learned how encephalitis is transmitted, and 50 percent more than previously knew the source of typhoid fever.

Mobilizing Rural Communities

The combination of radio or television with group discussion has been found to be especially effective for informing and mobilizing rural people to play their part in national development.

68. The first outstanding model for this pattern was the Farm Radio Forum, which was started in Canada in 1941. It won an established place for itself and in its 10th year UNESCO invited its sponsors to evaluate it as an instrument of adult education. This evaluation found that the forums had been especially successful in establishing a "sense of community," in encouraging cooperation among the farmers, and in developing leadership (31).

Some of the lessons of the Canadian Farm Radio Forum were applied in France (32) and later in Japan (33), in organizing tele-clubs—viewing and discussion groups organized around television programs. The French tele-clubs were carefully evaluated and were found to carry information to their members and to encourage desirable attitude change. They appeared to be more effective when the broadcast topics were

selected and the programs planned in close cooperation with prospective viewers.

In Japan, the great appeal of television drew large numbers into the viewing groups, and these groups developed into social centers of the rural communities. "Though it was cold midwinter," said the evaluation report, "the villagers, old and young, heads of households, wives and children, came to the community hall every Thursday evening .... (They) began to take an interest in more serious subjects rather than in gossip and idle chatter. Television helped the farmers to open their mouths, to express their thoughts and to learn that it is not, after all, such a difficult thing to talk in the presence of other people. Moreover, after expressing their thoughts, they had a sense of satisfaction." One of the measures of the success of the Japanese tele-clubs is that, when the experimental subsidy from UNESCO came to an end, the Japanese government decided to continue the clubs under its own support.

The greatest success of the broadcast and discussion pattern was gained in India (34). India used radio to provide the broadcast, and organized Farm Forums somewhat on the Canadian model. So popular and successful were these forums that a pilot project in 150 villages soon spread to 3,000 Radio Forums throughout the country, and now Radio Forums, under the terms of the 5-year plan, are to be added at the rate of 5,000 per year.

As an agent for transmission of ideas, the forums proved to be "a success beyond expectation. Increase in knowledge in the forum villages . . . was spectacular, whereas in the nonforum villages it was negligible." Beyond that, however, the forums became a nucleus for democratic action on the local level.

Says the official report: "Forums developed rapidly into decision-making bodies capable of speeding up common pursuits of the village faster than the elected *panchayat.* Frequently they took on functions half way between those of a panchayat and a town meeting . . . . The forums thus became an important instrument of village democracy, and enabled many more people to partake in the decision-making process in the village . . . . The demand that (forums) be made a permanent feature was practically unanimous."

Thus, the experience of developing countries again confirms the principle, first stated on the basis of research in the more advanced countries, that mass media and related face to face discussion make a uniquely powerful combination.

Conclusion

In the first part of this paper, (paragraphs 3–17) we outlined some of the tasks which communication must perform in national development. In the second (18–42) and third (43–72) parts, we have been talking about what contributions the mass media, and especially the newer media, might make to simplifying and speeding these gigantic communication tasks. On the whole, the conclusions should be highly encouraging to the developing nations, for the research in advanced countries testifies to the potency of these media, and trials in developing countries confirm these research results and indicate that the media may be used effectively for multiplying communication resources, sharing good teaching and

upgrading untrained teachers, extending information to remote places, aiding in the teaching of literacy, and mobilizing all citizens, but especially the rural people, for the great effort of national development.

For reasons unique to their situations, some developing countries may find it desirable now to make much use, others to make little use, of the media for purposes like these. And in many countries it will not be easy to assemble the necessary resources, human and monetary, to use the new media and to make the necessary adaptations. But the challenge and the opportunity are there. And it seems a singularly fortuitous coincidence that just at the moment when efficient and widespread communication is so much needed in the developing countries, a series of significant events in communication research and development should bring forth these potent new tools and methods, to help the new countries in what Julius Nyerere called the "terrible ascent" to modernity (35).

It is now generally accepted that this "terrible ascent" requires careful planning and preparation. The import of this paper is that the communication elements should be present in the development plan from the beginning, and that trained communication skills and communication budgets should be provided even though these seem to contribute only indirectly to the growth of industry or the formation of capital. For the overwhelming evidence is that such an investment in human resources will immensely increase the value of all other developmental investments and greatly speed the nation along its desired path of development.

REFERENCES

(1) Hirschman, A. O., *The Strategy of Economic Development*, Yale University Press, New Haven, Conn., p. 10, ff. (1958).

(2) Spengler, J. J., *Theory, idealogy, non-economic values, and politico-economic development*, in Braibanti, R., and J. J. Spengler, eds. *Tradition, Values, and Socioeconomic Development*. Duke University Press, Durham, N.C., p. 52 (1961).

(3) Weber, M., *The Protestant Ethic and the Spirit of Capitalism.* Translated by T. Parsons, Scribner, New York (1930). Also, Weber, M., *The Theory of Social and Economic Organization,* Translated by A. M. Henderson and T. Parsons, Oxford Press, New York (1947).

(4) McClelland, D. C., *The Achieving Society,* Van Nostrand, Princeton, N.J. (1961).

(5) The discussion in the next two pages has gained from the cogent treatment of the topic in Richard Fagen, *Politics and Communication in the New States,* Ph. D. dissertation, Stanford (1962).

(6) Quoted in Cantril, H., *Human Nature and Political Systems.* Rutgers University Press, New Brunswick, N.J. (1961).

(7) These figures are based largely on UNESCO sources. For the Nigeria figures, see Adams, S. C., Jr., *Nigeria where education has not kept pace with politics,* Phi Delta Kappan, *45,* 162 (1961).

(8) Greenough, R., *Africa Calls,* UNESCO, Paris (1961).

(9) *Mass Media in the Developing Countries. A UNESCO Report to the United Nations,* UNESCO, Paris (1961).

(10) Free, L. A., *Some International Implications of the Political Psychology of Brazilians.* Institute for International Social Research, Princeton, N.J. (1961).

(11) Damle, Y. B., *Communication of modern ideas and knowledge in Indian villages,* Public Opinion Quarterly, *20,* 257–70 (1956). Also Lerner, D., *The Passing of Traditional Society: Modernizing the Middle East.* The Free Press, Glencoe, Illinois (1958).

(12) For recent figures on media development, see *World Communications,* UNESCO, Paris, new edition (1962).

(13) For a theory of "critical minimum effort," see Leibenstein, H., *Economic Backwardness and Economic Growth.* Wiley, New York (1947).

(14) Bhat, A. R., *Vernacular newspapers in India,* Report to the Bangkok Conference, reprinted in Developing Mass Media in Asia, Paris; UNESCO (1960).

(15) A less sophisticated experiment in transmitting educational television over great areas has been under way in the United States for two years: an airplane carrying a television transmitter, flying in circles over a city in Indiana, serving schools in parts of five states. The signal which comes directly from the airplane to school television receivers is reported to be excellent. There have been the expected troubles with scheduling classes.

(16) While mentioning these very sophisticated and costly "media," it should also be mentioned that there are recent developments of interest at the other end of the spectrum of cost and complexity. For example, there is the sunlight filmstrip projector, developed by A.I.D., which can be made very cheaply and will project slides or strip films effectively without the use of electricity, using direct sunlight from a mirror.

(17) This discussion of the new media draws on two memoranda prepared by Dr. Schramm for UNESCO: one to the Conference of Experts on Educational Media, Paris (March 1962), and a second one prepared by request for the Director-General, July (1962).

(18) Schramm, W., *What we know about learning from instructional television.* In *Educational Television: The Next Ten Years.* Institute for Communication Research, Stanford, California, 52–76 (1962). See also Cassirer, H., *Television Teaching Today.* UNESCO, Paris (1960) for a review of television's use for teaching in seven advanced countries.

(19) For a review of research on the effectiveness of these media, see Allen, W. H., *Audio-visual communications research.* In Encyclopedia of Educational Research (1960).

(20) For an excellent brief treatment of programmed instruction, see Green, E. J., *The Learning Process and Programmed Instruction.* Holt, Rinehart and Winston, New York (1962).

(21) Report of the delegate of Poland to UNESCO Conference, January 1962.

(22) See the memorandum of Mme. Maria Grazia Puglisi, Director of School Television Course in Italy, to the UNESCO Meeting of Experts on Development and Use of New Methods and Techniques in Education (March 1962).

(23) Shevlin, A., *Opération Alphabet. Une Expérience de Télévision Educative à Philadelphie.* Télévision et Education Populaire, 5/6, 27–31 (1962).

(24) See two useful publications by UNESCO. *Publications for New Literates: Seven Case Histories,* and *Publications for New Literates: Editorial Methods,* which are, respectively, numbers 24 and 22 of Reports and Papers in Mass Communication, Paris (1957).

(25) Turkey used the television recording in the form of films. For a report of the project see Turkish Ministry of Education, Board of Education, Research and Measurement Bureau. *Istanbul Physics Film Report: Technical Report and General Report.* Ankara (1961).

(26) Personal report by Douglas Ensminger.

(27) See Hadsell, R. S. and G. K. Butts, *Educational television in Iran,* The Multiplier, 4, 2, 28–31 (1961).

(28) End of tour report by Mr. George L. Arms, to U.S. A.I.D./Nigeria.

(29) Thompson, S., *First-rate farm radio program,* The Multiplier, 3, 9, 23 (1959).

(30) Winfield, G. F. and P. Hartman, *Communications—the way to health improvement in Korea.* The Multiplier, 4, 3, 2113 (1961).

(31) Nicol, J., A. A. Shea, G. J. P. Simmins, and R. A. Sim, *Canada's Farm Radio Forum.* UNESCO, Paris (1954).

(32) Louis, R. and J. Rovan, *Television and Teleclubs in Rural Communities.* UNESCO, Paris (1955). Also Dumazedier, J., *Television and Rural Adult Education.* UNESCO, Paris (1956).

(33) UNESCO *Rural Television in Japan.* UNESCO, Paris (1960).

(34) Mathur, J. C. and P. Neurath, *An Indian Experiment in Farm Radio Clubs.* UNESCO, Paris (1959).

(35) Nyerere, J., *One-party rule.* Atlas, 3, 186 (1962).

PART SIX

Social and Cultural Challenges in Development

THIS final part deals appropriately with the social and cultural impact of the rapid environmental changes caused by increased mobility and development. What happens when traditional cultures fade and vast numbers of individuals and families are cut loose from engrained and inhibiting habits of thought and behavior? What can city life do for such people in the underdeveloped countries, or for the rural populace left behind in the migration to the metropolis?

In the first article Wallace uses the American Seneca Indians to demonstrate how a revitalization program can instill new purpose and even new ideological fervor in a race that has lost its ancient traditions and motivations. This lesson should not be lost upon economic developers who are nearly everywhere confronted with the same complex problem.

Community development can be profoundly affected by dynamic leadership. On the other hand, Frank and Ruth Young in their article develop the thesis that community growth relies more upon natural forces that permeate the fabric of society.

As against those who give to capital formation, on the one hand, or to community development, on the other, the key role in motivating and producing economic development, Tumin stresses the obvious need for both. Short-run gains in economic activity may also be misleading, since injections of large sums of aid bring quick results. Yet, in the long run, motivational and cultural factors are the key to permanent progress and self-sustaining growth.

Much attention has been given to the growing problem of the urban center, resulting from the mass migrations thereto of the past and the decades to come. Clawson looks at the other side of the picture: What impact has the urban trend upon the rural sector, including the village? What happens when the young and vigorous leave the farm, while at the same time the farm is pressed to become increasingly specialized and commercialized?

India is expected to add 55 million people to towns of 20,000 or over in the next decade. Dyckman's numerous questions relate to alternative costs of various choices in providing the social overhead capital required to meet this mass movement. He asks: "Does it pay to allocate capital to subsidize free or very cheap transportation in order to save on the social overhead costs of high density?" Real costs of transport systems to spread people, he asserts, should candidly be matched against any real gains in specialization or division of labor anticipated from urbanization.

Finally, a stimulating article on the threats and trends leading us along the road toward international cooperation and common effort is an appropriate conclusion. To expect the status quo between nation states to continue or to predict a reversion to ancient or less rational forms of nationalistic expression are both, in the larger sense, perhaps unthinkable postulates for the future. Therefore, growing internationalism is a dynamic probability in the forecast for the human race—a force made more compelling by the threat of universal destruction by nuclear power. Lasswell describes how an international culture is emerging, as evidenced in common standards of science, travel, trade, and communication and in demonstration effects, leading to common value demands and expectations.

Revitalization Movements in Development

ANTHONY F. C. WALLACE

Chairman of the Department of Anthropology, University of Pennsylvania
Philadelphia, Pennsylvania

Introduction

In the world today there are new nations, and old; the people of most of these nations are seeking ways to develop their resources and to advance in civilization. Our age, in fact, is unique in the large number of peoples who are dissatisfied with the *status quo* and who aspire to development. But, of course, merely wishing does not make it so: technical and scientific development, among other things, is required, because the industrial and scientific revolutions of the past two centuries have made it impossible for the technically unsophisticated to carry forward successful social change on any large scale. Indeed, to many highly trained personnel from heavily industrialized parts of the world, it would appear that the only serious problems in development are technical and that these are to be solved by instituting the "correct" reforms in education, in the fiscal structure, in agricultural land holdings, and so forth. Thus, a recurrent dilemma of choices in development has come into existence: technology, on the one hand, which is substantially the same wherever it is made, and which demands the subservience of all aspects of the culture to

its own iron requirements for "progress"; and the human heart, on the other, which seeks a life of dignity, of values, and of self-respect, in whatever various ways are meaningful to it, whether or not they happen to conform to the demands of technology.

In brief, then, a principal problem in development is the fact that the direction of technical, industrial, and economic advance, and the direction of popular sentiment, are not always the same direction. The technical movement and the revitalization movement may be at cross-purposes. Since the motivating energy for the technical movement must, insofar as the local population is concerned, be supplied by the revitalization movement, it is necessary to examine the phenomenon of popular movements of social reform, or revitalization movements, in more detail.

Characteristics of Revitalization Movements

Definition

Revitalization movements are deliberate, organized, conscious attempts by some or all of the members of a society to construct for themselves a more satisfying culture. Their purposes may include changes in political structure, in the organization of economic activities, in the relations among kinfolk, in patterns of warfare; but whatever are the social and technical intention of such a movement, the rationale is always either explicitly religious or politically fanatical, or both. The emotional atmosphere of such movements is therefore ecstatic, particularly in the early phases, for the goal to which the movement strives is not just rational technical improvement, but (and this is an invariable rule) an improvement in the self-respect of the people. The members of a revitalization movement are seeking to achieve new identities; they hope to be reborn, spiritually, morally, intellectually. Impelled by the vast emotional force of such a movement, a people can successfully accomplish sweeping changes in culture in a very short time; but they can also virtually commit collective suicide, if the cultural changes are ill-conceived and the chosen means are unsuited to the desired ends.

Varieties of Revitalizaiton Movements

Anthropologists have discovered and described various types of revitalization movements. In Melanesia, for instance, the "cargo cult" is one of the most common forms. In the typical cargo cult, the affected population believes that their ancestors are coming in a great ship, filled with all the material wealth of Europe; when the ship docks, the white colonists will be driven away and the natives will be left in peace to enjoy the fruits of civilization. In South America, by contrast, particularly during the colonial era, many Indian tribes sought to escape the Europeans who were over-running their country by following a shaman in a long march to a mythical terre sans mal ("land without evil").

Among North American Indians, the Ghost Dance is the most famous movement: the Indian believers hoped that their dancing would preserve them through a coming holocaust in which the white man would be driven away; in the renewed world, the Indian would be able to enjoy his ancient culture, and hunt the buffalo, in peace. In Africa, the Xosa fought the Whites under prophetic inspiration in the 19th Century, and many starved in the mistaken faith that in the new world a-coming there would be not only military victory but manna from heaven: they burned their crops and killed their cattle in anticipation. In China, the Taiping rebellion was a monumental revitalization movement which nearly succeeded in unseating the Manchu dynasty; in India, the Sikh religion originated in a revitalization effort by a prophet who wished to develop a synthesis of the divergent and sometimes clashing Muslim and Hindu traditions. In the circum-Mediterranean world, we may if we wish discern in the origins both of Christianity and of Islam the general pattern of the revitalization movement. In Europe, in later times, the revitalization process is manifest in such major efforts at social reform as those launched in the name of religion by Luther and in the name of science by Marx. In the United States, it is not difficult to recognize today the swelling of revitalization movements in the efforts, led by such leaders as Martin Luther King, to secure to the American Negro his civil rights.

Thus the revitalization process, which is undoubtedly a major potentiality both for the aid and the obstruction of technical development programs, is not only familiar in those areas—often recently colonial, which are the subject of this conference—but also in the history of those industrial states which are today technologically most highly developed.

Processual Structure

The typical revitalization process may be considered to consist of five or more or less overlapping stages: (a) Steady State, (b) Period of Increased Individual Stress, (c) Period of Cultural Distortion, (d) Period of Revitalization (during which occur the functions of cultural reformulation, communication, organization, adaptation, cultural transformation, and routinization), and, (e) New Steady State. Only the successful movement will proceed through all five stages; many abort at some point during the fourth stage. The stages are briefly described as follows:

(a) *Steady State.* When a culture is in what we call a steady state, the sanctioned techniques for satisfying human needs operate with sufficient efficiency so that chronic stress remains within tolerable limits. There may be local pockets of dissatisfaction, occasional crises for many individuals, personal disaster for a few; but the cultural system is not generally blamed by the population for such circumstances.

(b) *The Period of Increased Individual Stress.* During this period, the sanctioned ways of satisfying the human needs which are generated by the culture operate with decreasing effectiveness. More and more people are unable to do what they want to do and have been taught they should do. Frequently acculturation situations, in company with political and economic exploitation, produce such a situation; but other processes, such as progressive waste of natural resources, or excessive population increase, can lead to

the same result. The adequacy of the existing cultural system is questioned.

(c) *The Period of Cultural Distortion.* Disillusionment with the existing cultural system becomes rampant and individuals seek to find a way out, often by devious means. Some turn to what have been conventionally considered to be crimes: theft, bribery, corruption; others to such psycho-pathological avenues of escape, as drugs and alcohol may afford. Cooperative use of the traditional cultural facilities declines, with "every man for himself." The cultural fabric is rent with internal contradictions and inconsistent expectations.

(d) *The Period of Revitalization.* Inasmuch as the process of decadence and decline characteristic of Period C, will, if left unchecked, end in disaster for most of the population, efforts will be made to formulate a new culture which will satisfy existing needs more reliably than the one which, for one reason or another, has broken down. Such efforts, if seriously prosecuted, become revitalization movements. Any revitalization movement must, if it is to be successful, complete six major tasks:

(i) Cultural Reformation. Someone, whether a dogmatic political leader or party, or an inspired religious prophet, must produce a Code. This Code will, essentially, divide reality into three parts: it will define the existing state or society as evil, and explain in what respects it is evil; it will describe an ideal, or utopian, goal culture, which will truly satisfy human needs; and it will prescribe an intervening state or process, which has been termed a "vehicular" or "transfer" culture, by means of which the people may pass from the present misery into the future bliss.

(ii) Communication. This Code must be communicated to the people; in other words, it must be preached. The preaching can be done in various ways: by public exhortation; by quiet, patient instruction; by insinuation, rumor, and gossip. But preaching of the Code must continue throughout the life of the movement; in fact, it is apt to outlive the movement itself, and to survive as a sort of increasingly ancient Bible.

(iii) Organization. The movement's membership must expand and have structure. At first, it is confined to the leader or prophet: he gathers disciples; the disciples in turn attract followers to perform various tasks; and, finally, the mass of the more or less converted are brought into membership. The ideological leadership remains in the hands of the charismatic prophet; practical control, however, may rest with less well-known men.

(iv) Adaptation. Almost certainly the movement will have enemies, because it is certain to threaten various vested interests. Some of these enemies can be won over by doctrinal modifications which protect certain of their special interests. But not uncommonly the movement must be revolutionary: it must fight, by open political action, or by subversion, or by military force, to seize such organs of power as are needed to put the transfer culture into operation. In the preparation for, and course of, fighting, movements may become "sour"; the early emphasis on such ideals as the brotherhood of man fades, and loyalty, courage, and persistence in attacking the heretics become heavily valued, sometimes to the point of transforming the movement

into nothing more than a military machine.

(v) Cultural Transformation. If the problems of adaptation to local circumstances are met, then the movement can, with its access to political and other forms of power unchallenged, proceed to put into effect the cultural reforms necessary to establish the transfer culture. This transfer culture may last for only a brief transition period before the goal culture arrives; but, more commonly, the transfer culture is as much of the goal as will ever be achieved.

(vi) Routinization. Once the goal culture has been realized—or, more commonly, once the transfer culture has survived all serious challenges from dissatisfied adherents of the old order, the movement organization will tend to relax, to adopt a less censorious, less rigorous attitude, and to permit civil authorities to manage the new institutions, while the movement gradually becomes, in effect, a "church."

(e) *The New Steady State*. If the movement organization successfully routinizes and contracts, and the goal- or transfer-culture continues to prove itself viable, a new steady state can be said to exist. But, of course, the society may again fall from difficulties, from which new revitalization movements will attempt to revive it; and now, the old revitalization movement finds itself in the role of the conservative, or reactionary, regime. . . .

An Example of a Successful Revitalization Movement: The Seneca Indians— 1798–1815.

As a happy example of the revitalization process and its relation to technical-aid programs, let us consider the successful cultural reform carried out by the Seneca Indians between 1798 and about 1815. Although it is remote from us now in time, and involves a small tribe of several thousand American Indians resident in New York State, in the United States of America, the principles at work are relevant and the case may serve as a relatively nonpolitical example. The Seneca Indians, having fought on the British side during the American Revolution, shared in the British defeat. Left alone to cope with the victorious revolutionaries after the war, they rapidly lost their hunting grounds in a series of land purchases (which are still the subject of litigation in American courts, by the way), and the land on which they could hunt and farm totaled only a few hundred square miles in area. Seneca morale crumbled. In two generations, they had fallen from high estate to low: in the 1760's, after the British victory in the French and Indian War, they were no longer in a position to hold the balance of power between the French and the British, and consequently had fallen in the esteem both of the British and their own Indian allies. During the Revolution, their towns were destroyed, their people were dispersed, and their hunting grounds were lost. They faced moral crisis; they still wanted to be men and women of dignity, but they knew only the old ways to honor: for the men, the hunt, the warpath, and the council fire; for the women, the raising of corn, and the management of family and clan affairs—and these old ways now led to poverty, to contempt from arrogant frontiersmen, and to despair. To abandon the old ways meant undertaking new customs, sometimes repugnant and always uncertain of success. And so the Senecas stagnated in their shabby frontier settlements, drinking heavily when they had the chance, and fighting among themselves. Two events changed all this.

The first event involves a technical-aid program. In 1798, the Society of Friends (Quakers), encouraged by the Federal Government, sent a group of young people from Philadelphia to the Seneca Indians. This group, and their successors, remained for many years. These people were not bent upon converting the Senecas to Christianity; nor did they attempt to dictate the forms of their political, religious, or family life. Their aims were simple: to teach the Senecas the technical skills of farming, carpentry, masonry, spinning and weaving, and the other arts of rural husbandry then regarded as most effective; to give, or lend, or sell at cost, the necessary tools and other capital goods needed to establish the same technology; and to persuade them to the sobriety which their own leaders had been recommending.

The second event was a revitalization movement. In 1799, into the moral chaos which still surrounded the early Quaker efforts, the revelations of the prophet Handsome Lake sped like a golden arrow, dispelling darkness and despair. He said, that unless he and his people became new men, they were doomed to be annihilated in an apocalyptic world destruction. They must confess past sins; abandon drunkenness, fighting, and witchcraft; and henceforth lead upright lives. He went on, in successive revelations (some of which were recorded by Quaker scribes on the scene), to prescribe the new way of life. Some of his instructions concerned purely theological and ritual matters; but a large part of his Code was directed toward the resolution of moral issues presented by the new social and economic situation of reservation life, and by the technical improvements suggested by the Quaker mission. He told the Senecas to adopt new techniques of agriculture, which required that men plough the fields (hitherto the Seneca women were the agriculturists); he advised that some learn to read and write; he counseled them to emphasize the integrity of the married pair's household, rather than the old matrilineal lineage.

In sum, as a spiritual leader, he incorporated into his own recommendations many of the technological improvements suggested by the Quakers; and the Quakers, on their part, conceded that his religion, although different from their own, certainly had much merit. The collective reform met with an astounding success. The Senecas became widely known for their sobriety; the new pattern of agricultural living, with its associated emphasis on the individual farm family, quickly became the norm rather than the exception; and the Code of Handsome Lake itself gradually became a force to maintain the successes accomplished during the period of enthusiasm. The Handsome Lake religion is still followed today by hundreds of Senecas.

Origins of Revitalization Movements

The social and cultural conditions predisposing to revitalization movements can most succinctly be characterized as those which maximize discrepancy between a population's aspirations and its confidence in the suitability of the presently existing social and cultural system for realizing those aspirations. No doubt a moderate degree of tension between aspiration and confidence is, at least in urban industrial civilization, both normal

and a stimulus to progress. The tension can produce disorganization, however, if as a result of internal or external factors, the discrepancy widens to a point where despair and disillusionment become widespread. Theoretically, such a situation could result from the operation of purely internal processes, such as population pressure or exhaustion of natural resources. More commonly, however, at least in the past several hundred years, these situations have been produced by intergroup relations, particularly in technologically less developed areas in contact with agents of industrialized nations, where rapid and ill-coordinated acculturation (including the communication of images of a better way of life), military and political domination, and internal corruption and decadence have established extreme discrepancy between the picture of things as they are and things as they might be.

The individual corollary of these group characteristics is a lowered sense of self-esteem and a striving for the realization of an ideal personal identity. The stress engendered by this conflict can elicit both extreme personal demoralization, or, in contrast, heroic efforts to recapture self-esteem by personal resynthesis and devoted efforts to improve the society with which the individual is identified. Leaders of revitalization movements would seem to draw their charismatic glamor from the fact that they present the image of a person who has in the past suffered from the same demoralization as his compatriots, but who has successfully worked through the dilemma. He thus acts as a sort of model about which the movement grows, like a crystal growing about its seed in a supersaturated solution.

Implications for Technical and Scientific Development Programs

The very societies in which development programs are most likely to be established are also likely to contain one, or more, revitalization movements directed against the *status quo,* or to be dominated by politically successful recent revitalization movements. In large measure, the motivation to undertake a technical and scientific development program will be supplied by the emotional forces described above, and the goals to which the development is directed will be explicitly stated, or implied by, the movement's Code. The personnel in the host area who are involved in working and cooperating with this program, will include many who are leaders in, or followers of, revitalization movements. Therefore, not only the ultimate fate, but the day-to-day operations of a development program will be heavily affected by the relationship between the program and the local revitalization movement or movements.

It is consequently of great importance for the administrators of a development program to understand and to respect the values and goals of the revitalization movements in the country in which they are working. It is not a question of foreign technical personnel identifying with, and attempting to control, such movements; this is apt to be disastrous. So also would be the effort to discourage or to disparage what the members of a movement are trying to do, even when the aims appear to be impossibly utopian, and the means somewhat strange and even bizarre, to the technical personnel. If mutual respect is maintained between technical personnel and movement personnel, there is maximum likelihood for fruitful cooperation and accommodation of differences.

Development programs with "strings" which are considered to impugn the self-respect and human dignity of the "new men" which the revitalization movement is producing are certain to be resisted openly or quietly subverted. The movement is principally concerned to develop the "new man"; from its point of view, technical development is a handmaiden to this aim. But where, as the simple example of the Quakers and the Seneca Indians shows, the technical-development program respects the movement, even if it does not fully understand it or even like it in all respects, and the movement respects the technical program, with the same qualifications, then the tremendous energies of the revitalization movement can be placed at the disposal of technical development. Under such circumstances, great progress can be made in a very short time.

REFERENCES

Deardorff, M. H., *The religion of Handsome Lake.* In W. N. Fenton, ed., *Symposium on Local Diversity in Iroquois Culture.* Washington: Bureau of American Ethnology, Bulletin 149 (1951).

Goodenough, W., *Cooperation in Change.* New York: Russell Sage Foundation. In preparation.

Mead, M., *New Lives for Old.* New York: Wm. Morrow Co., Inc. (1956).

Wallace, A. F. C., *Revitalization Movements.* American Anthropologist, *58,* 264–281 (1956).

Toward a Theory of Community Development

Frank W. Young and Ruth C. Young
*Department of Rural Sociology, Cornell University,
Ithaca, New York*

At the present time our knowledge of community development consists more of rules of thumb based on trial-and-error practice than of tested generalizations unified by a consistent conceptual scheme. This predicament is not unique to community development. No new area of investigation, particularly if there is great pressure for the immediate application of such knowledge, can expect to bypass a period of empirical elaboration that outruns available theory. However, in the last few years a number of different and in many cases independent studies have converged on what may be the beginnings of a theory and empirical generalizations about community growth. This work focuses on the sequence which communities seem to follow as they develop their component institutions. Although this sequence takes diverse concrete forms in different places, it is always unidimensional, cumulative, and appears to lead in the direction of greater participation in the national social structure, regardless of the political ideology that may be present. The basis of this phenomenon seems to lie in the requirements of modernization as they apply to nations and to their component communities.

The evidence for these generalizations is not an account of particular communities described without controls or guiding theory. On the contrary, all the studies which support this formulation of community growth are comparative and were carried out systematically. Although the particular hypotheses used by the several investigators were not identical, they were similar enough to warrant synthesis and they stem from a common theoretical orientation. The methods were also similar enough to allow cross-comparison. Specifically, the evidence comes from a field study of 24 rural communities in central Mexico (1) a cross-cultural study of 54 primitive and modern communities (2), a comparative analysis of 297 New York State villages and towns, using the data available in the Dun and Bradstreet Reference Book (3), and a study of 33 Swedish communities based on other types of published data (4). Several other studies are comparable except for their use of units other than the community (5). It is not asserted, however, that the generalizations about to be outlined are in any sense proved; rather, these studies justify synthesis at this time so that the results may be subjected to more controlled study, particularly in other countries.

One point of reference is basic to the whole discussion. These findings apply to the unit of social structure that comes

455

about as families live and work together over several generations. In most parts of the world this unit is the small peasant community. However, the generalizations are proposed for cities and small hamlets too, even though the latter may be little more than one large family. All of these communities are conceived as existing in a larger structure that is concerned with control over territory, law and order in a broad sense, and defense. Usually this unit is the nation, although colonial governments or primitive states may also qualify. The point of view taken here is that it is possible to imagine an interaction between two social units, one large and the other small. What is of interest is not the problem of typing or classifying social structures, but the typical sequence taken by actual communities as they participate more completely in the national social structure.

Five Interrelated Generalizations About Community Growth

The findings about to be reviewed are all aspects of one broad generalization but they may be separated for easier communication and analysis. The first generalization may be stated: *communities develop according to a cumulative, unidimensional sequence*. The initial indication that this was true came in the course of a study of Mexican communities (6) where it was found that certain characteristics such as having a public square, an official, access to electric power, a doctor in residence, etc., formed a Guttman scale; that is, a cumulative sequence such that the presence of a given step implied the presence of all the "lower" items. Moreover, the deviations from this sequence were so few that one was

justified in concluding that only one dimension was being tapped. Despite the apparent diversity of the items in the scale, it could be inferred that they all reflected one underlying developmental course. Table 1 shows in detail the kind of pattern of attributes that must be found. Table 1 is based on a cross-cultural study of communities (7) and is used as an illustration because the data can be simplified and presented as shown. The data on the Mexican communities are presented in a more compact form in table 2. Further discussion of this technique of social measurement may be found elsewhere (8), but it is generally agreed that it provides a much sounder basis for the study of developmental sequences than other available methods.

Given the diversity of the institutional characteristics that is organized by these unidimensional scales, another inference is possible. All the institutions of the community develop together. If this were not so, and it often happened for instance that the economic institutions outstripped the organization of the family, or vice-versa, then more deviations should occur. Although the items were not systematically selected to cover all community institutions, they do include many: aspects of religion, the economy, education, communications, medical facilities and recreation appear in one or the other of the two scales shown as well as the others that have been found. If community development involved any marked disharmonies between two or more institutions, they should show up. We are discounting the one possible negative instance. In the study of New York State communities, Wakeley (9) discovered three scales of growth: one for retail trade; another for manufacturing, wholesaling, and finan-

TABLE I. *Scalogram of community-nation articulation (abbreviated data)*

Culture in which community is located	Item content (numbers correspond to key below)									
	1	2	3	4	5	6	7	8	9	10
Jivaro	1	0	0	0	0	0	0	0	0	0
Siriono	1	0	0	0	0	0	0	0	0	0
Eskimo	1	1	0	0	0	0	0	0	0	0
Kwakiutl	1	1	0	0	0	0	0	0	0	0
Pilaga	0	1	0	0	0	0	0	0	0	0
Chiricahua	1	1	1	0	0	0	0	0	0	0
Maori	1	1	1	0	0	0	0	0	0	0
Cheyenne	1	1	1	1	0	0	0	0	0	0
Timbira	1	1	1	1	-	0	0	0	0	0
Bontoc Igorot	1	1	1	1	1	0	0	0	0	0
Kwoma	1	1	1	1	1	0	0	0	0	0
Malaita	1	1	0	1	1	1	0	0	0	0
Alor	1	-	1	1	1	1	0	0	0	0
Azande	1	1	1	1	-	1	1	0	0	0
Ashanti	1	1	1	1	1	1	1	1	0	0
Cagaba	1	1	1	1	1	1	1	0	0	0
Lepcha	1	1	1	1	1	1	1	-	1	0
Araucanian	1	1	1	1	1	1	1	1	1	0
Balinese	1	1	1	1	1	1	1	1	1	0
Fiji	1	1	1	1	1	1	0	1	1	0
Hopi	1	1	1	1	1	0	1	1	1	0
Lapps	1	1	1	1	1	1	1	1	1	1
Serbs	1	1	1	1	1	1	1	1	1	1
United States	1	1	1	1	1	1	1	1	1	1

Item Content

1. Two or more bisexual gatherings per year.
2. Public area of settlement pattern.
3. Public structure.
4. Procedure for sanctions against criminals.
5. Use of money.
6. Full-time bureaucrats.
7. Full-time religious specialist.
8. Written language used.
9. Formal education for both sexes.
10. Local group speaks same language as nation.

cial strength; and a third for non-economic services. But there was a high correlation among them and the lack of common scale may reflect the kind of data that were used rather than a true disharmony. In any event, Wakeley felt justified in combining the three scales and treating them as one.

The second generalization is that *the sequence holds for communities of all sizes and in all cultures.* The fact that the communities in table I scale despite their worldwide distribution is strong evidence that the particular ideology of the community does not decisively influence the sequence. Supporting evi-

dence comes from a study by Freeman and Winch (10) which also used a sample from diverse cultures. Although these investigators were studying whole societies rather than communities, their scale was not weakened by the cultural factor. It is obvious that if a scale is to hold cross-culturally the items must be such that all communities might acquire them. Cross-cultural items tend to be broad and abstract in contrast to the more specific regional characteristics, such as are contained in the scale of Mexican communities in table 2. But this variation in the type of item does not affect the basic generalization that all commu-

TABLE 2. *Scale of community-national articulation among 24 rural Mexican villages*

Scale step#	Item content*	Proportion of 24 villages having characteristic	Scale error
1	Named and autonomous locality group	100	—
2	One or more governmentally designated official	92	0
3	One or more organizations in village	88	1
4	A church	84	3
5	A school building	80	0
	Mass said in the village more than annually	—	1
6	A functional school	76	0
7	Has access to a railroad or informant voluntarily includes railroad in list of village needs	63	0
8	Access to electric power	46	1
	6 or more streets	—	3
9	Railroad station	41	1
	4 or more bus or train trips daily	—	4
10	School has 4 or more grades	37	1
11	Village has a public square	29	0
12	Doctor	20	0
	Priest resides in village	—	1
	6 or more stores	—	1
	2 or more television sets in village	—	1
13	Has 1 or more telephones	16	0
14	40 percent or more have radios	12	0
	Settlement area 1 square mile or more	—	0
15	Secondary school	8	0

*First item was used in present scale. Others are interchangeable. Coefficient of scalability is 0.92.

nities develop according to a definite sequence of steps.

The studies so far have not been based on samples of communities ranging from very small hamlets to large cities. Therefore it is not known for sure whether a scale can be found that continues without a break from the smallest to the largest unit. However, when taken together, the available studies cover the full range of population sizes. Both the cross-cultural scale in table 1 and the Mexican scale in table 2 begin with communities of less than 100 population and extend to those of about 6,000. The scales found in New York State extend to cities of 500,000 people. It seems reasonable, therefore, to look forward to the development of a scale that will meas-

ure the level of development of communities of any size and cultural outlook.

The third finding is that *internal institutional growth is identical with external elaboration of communications.* That is, institutional differentiation has two sides: one that faces in and the other that faces outside the community. This conclusion is based both on empirical and theoretical considerations. Inspection of the items of the two scales already presented indicates that "internal" items are intermixed with "external" communications characteristics. But thinking further, does any one item not have both aspects? Even a community name assumes that outsiders accept the designation and think of the community as an entity capable of external contact. A public place such as a plaza or a dance area may seem at first glance to be confined to the village, but when we consider the people who customarily converge on these areas—and outsiders usually enter a village by way of such public areas—then it is clear that these attributes, taken in their social function, also have an external aspect. Striking confirmation of this generalization appears in Swedner's study (11) of Swedish villages. He shows that the participation of the villages surrounding a large center in the various institutional networks of that center form a scale. That is, the services of the center such as the newspaper, secondary school and dentist, etc., are used cumulatively by the villages. When the problem is considered theoretically, it is impossible to imagine an institution or a group of people existing for long in complete isolation. Even the most primitive tribes have trade relations and marriage ties. This fact is well known and perhaps well accepted. But the identity of these two aspects of institutional growth, as indicated by the evidence of the scales, has not been appreciated.

A fourth finding is that *the direction of community growth is always toward greater participation in the national social structure*. This does not mean that all communities do in fact become assimilated to the wider structure—some may be barred from such participation. But if a community grows, the scales indicate that the various component institutions become increasingly articulated with those of the nation. At first the link between village and nation takes the form of occasional traveling merchants or an official. Then specific roles, such as the tax collector, the policeman, the priest, or the railroad official appear. Although these roles are more special-

ized than before, they are still quite general in that any one of them represents the whole community to the relevant sector of the national structure. A third stage is reached when the roles are specialized to the point of mediating between a part of the national structure and a part of the community. Thus, a doctor brings knowledge to a particular clientele. Similarly the lawyer, the teacher, or the extension agent link segments of the two social systems. In highly urbanized communities modern mass communications reach particular audiences with great sensitivity. These three phases—of village autonomy, of representative contact, and urban interpenetration—show up regardless of the number and type of cities to which the village is linked, but there is indication that the linkage is hierarchical. The smaller units tie into a local center, the local centers are linked to a regional town and these in turn have contact with a city. This finding implies that community development is inseparable with national development: if community growth is always in the direction of greater articulation with the nation, then it is also true that a weak or nonexistent national structure sets upper limits on the degree to which communities may expand.

The fifth finding is that *the population size of the community increases in direct proportion to the degree of articulation*. If community growth is essentially institutional differentiation and the articulation of more subgroups with the national social structure, then it would be surprising indeed if large populations were not associated with such growth. This relationship was uncovered in all the studies. However, the absolute number associated with a given scale step may vary from country to country. In Mexico, for instance, a town of 1,000 people usually had access to a doctor. But the population cutting point may be somewhat different depending on the kind of medical service that is available.

Problems and Implications

The picture of community growth that emerges from these five generalizations is not simply a direct summary of the empirical data of the scales because in all cases the investigators proceeded with explicit hypotheses about what they would find. Deriving such scales is not accidental. Moreover, the generalizations have introduced additional theoretical considerations. Nonetheless it is still true that no comprehensive interpretation of these generalizations is yet available. Of the possible lines of explanation, only one can be sketched here. Following Durkheim (12), one might interpret the scales as measuring the division of social labor that follows from increasing population density. In this context the present studies are innovative mainly with respect to the explication and precise measurement of a time-honored body of theory. However, in certain respects, the generalizations extend this line of thought. In addition to increasing complexity, the evidence indicates an increasing articulation with wider national organization. The scales call attention to an aspect of organizational growth that seems not to have been emphasized in classical theory, but the extension is congenial with it. We are saying that as villages grow, specialize, and elaborate, their social organization, the nation of which they are a part is also developing. The large cities, which embody the national organization, must expand into the hinterland, depending upon the surrounding villages for labor, agricultural products, and consumption of urban manufactures. These requirements force the cities to extend their government, their economic organization, and standards of living into the villages. Such ramification of the urban social organization should not be seen as typically exploitive. The presence of urban structures to which the village organization may link up is necessary for the development of the smaller unit.

From this perspective, then, community growth follows a single unidimensional path because increasing involvement in the urban structure is possible only if certain organizational prerequisites have been met. We must assume that urban life everywhere involves orderly interaction of the inhabitants, motivation to work, and contact between specialists and their clients, and that no satellite community can be admitted to the urban network until it has attained some measure of these. If the community institutions that handle these problems are well developed, articulation follows. Otherwise the community is only "provisionally admitted" to the larger structure; that is, it achieves a lower level of articulation. Presumably the particular sequence taken by the community in readying itself for urban participation is also set by the larger structure. Ultimately the explanation returns to Durkheim's density, but now large cities are taken as given and the explanation emphasizes the conditions of incorporation of the smaller unit into the larger.

The theoretical problem that is left hanging is why there should exist a definite sequence of growth. It has been assumed in the foregoing discussion that the sequence reflects the necessities of organized social life, either of the national structure or of the village, or of the interaction of the two. Clarification of this problem may depend upon the development of more scales based on different samples. When these are available, the general nature of the sequence should be apparent, and an explanation may be possible. Once the abstract sequence is formulated, it will be easier to construct scales for measuring sets of communities in unstudied areas.

One promising aspect of this research is that the scales can be built with different types of data. So far investigators have successfully used existing documentary information about local business and institutions (13), ethnographic descriptions (14), census data (15), and information collected by interviewing one informant in each village (16). There is reason to believe that these scales can be constructed from the data of aerial photographs. So far, the most trustworthy information, like that obtained from multiple interviews in a sample of communities, has not been used. Such intensive study should deepen our understanding of the growth process and make measurement more precise. Another problem area involves the study of units other than the community. It is possible that national development might follow a cumulative sequence of the type discussed here. Conceptual schemes like that of W. W. Rostow (17) might be operationalized in this manner. Similarly, intermediate units such as regions or clusters of villages might show unidimensional sequences of growth (18). Investigation of family and subcommunity structures is already underway.

If the theory and technique suggested here is not rejected by future tests,

it has important implications for applied work. Up to now we have conceived of community development as the voluntary effort of residents under the guidance of an outside leader. At times he brings with him selected contributions of a national or international source. Success or failure has been unpredictable and explanation of results has been embedded in the context of the events in particular villages. The development theory outlined here contrasts with this view by calling attention to the importance of the level of community articulation at the beginning of the experiment and the sequence through which the community must pass. While voluntary efforts may speed progress or widen the scope of influence of a community within given levels, they cannot—if the theory is correct—change the general course or enable one institution to develop unilaterally relative to the others. Understanding this process will enable the extension agent to work with nature, so to speak, rather than against it. This principle has perhaps already been accepted by many community workers, but the levels of growth hypothesis helps to clarify it.

In addition to the general illumination made possible by an understanding of community growth, new applications may come about through extensions of the theory. For example, in the study of Mexican villages it was found that the number of changes in the community increased with the level of articulation. That is, the higher the level of development, the more increments will be assimilated by the community during a given period. (We avoid the term "innovation" since this implies an evaluation of newness which is in the eye of the beholder.) A second hypothesis suggested by this same study is that the community's definition of its "important problems" is a function of its level of development. The more highly developed Mexican communities were concerned about problems like unemployment, sanitation, and infant mortality, while the smaller, less-developed communities were not so concerned despite the fact that they were immeasurably worse off when assessed by objective measures. Problems such as enough water, access to electricity, and roadbuilding loomed large in their minds. The first set of problems simply did not fall within their definition of what was a problem. When community leaders are unfamiliar with urban standards of sanitation and health, they have no reason for interpreting the objective facts of their own community in these terms. Only when a community develops a certain complexity of organization do certain phenomena become a threat or a cause for action.

These are only examples of the types of predictions that might follow from this new theoretical interpretation of community development. They perhaps illustrate the possibilities of further exploration in this area. Insofar as they hold true, they embody two characteristics: an abstract formulation tends to reveal as identical many phenomena previously thought to be different. Thus, if this hypothesis is true, many different events in communities may be seen as alternatives within certain levels of development. The other characteristic is that understanding of a process is inseparable from recognition of the limits of manipulation. Medical experience illustrates how the treatment of a disease must be adapted to the normal growth process. Similarly we may find that community development can occur only if the limitations set by the initial level and the organization of the nation are overcome.

REFERENCES

(1) Young, F. W., and R. C. Young, *Two Determinants of Community Reaction to Industrialization in Rural Mexico*, Economic Development and Cultural Change, 8, 257–264 (1960). Also *Social Integration and Change in Twenty-four Mexican Villages*, ibid., 8, 366–377 (1960).

(2) Young, F. W., and R. C. Young, *The Sequence and Direction of Community Growth: A Cross-Cultural Generalization*, forthcoming in Rural Sociology.

(3) Wakeley, R. E., *Types of Rural and Urban Community Centers in Upstate New York*, Cornell University Agricultural Experiment Station, Ithaca, N.Y. (1961).

(4) Swedner, H., *Ecological Differentiation of Habits and Attitudes*, CWK Gleerup, Lund, Sweden (1960).

(5) Aurbach, H. A., *A Guttman Scale for Measuring Isolation*, Rural Sociology, 20, 142–44 (1955); Robert Carneiro, *Scale Analysis as an Instrument for the Study of Cultural Evolution*, Southwestern Journal of Anthropology, 18, 149–169 (1962); and L. O. Freeman and R. F. Winch, *Societal Complexity: An Empirical Test of a Typology of Societies*, American Journal of Sociology, 62, 461–66 (1957).

(6) Young and Young, *op. cit.* (1960).

(7) Young and Young, *The Sequence and Direction of Community Growth. . . .* This paper contains additional technical details.

(8) Carneiro, *op. cit.*, and M. Riley, et al., *Sociological Studies in Scale Analysis,* Rutgers University Press, New Brunswick, N.J. (1954).

(9) Wakeley, *op. cit.,* 20.

(10) Freeman and Winch, *op. cit.*

(11) Swedner, *op. cit.,* 144.

(12) Durkheim, E., *The Division of Labor in Society,* The Free Press, Glencoe, Ill. (1949).

(13) Wakeley, *op. cit.*

(14) Young and Young, *The Sequence and Direction of Community Growth.*

(15) Aurbach, *op. cit.*

(16) Young and Young, *op. cit.* (1960).

(17) Rostow, W. W., *The Stages of Economic Growth,* Cambridge University Press, New York (1960).

(18) Young, F. W., *Location and Reputation in a Mexican Intervillage Network,* forthcoming in Human Organization.

Social Stratification and Social Mobility in the Development Process

MELVIN M. TUMIN

Associate Professor of Sociology and Anthropology, Princeton University, Princeton, New Jersey

If the speed with which the desire to be well off has spread throughout the less-developed nations of the world is extraordinary, it is equally extraordinary how rapidly such a goal has been accepted as reasonable by those developed nations and peoples from whom most help will be required. Moreover, however much some may insinuate that the motives of the better developed nations are not the most noble or altruistic, none can deny that there has been a very healthy increase in genuine concern by the most developed nations for those people who are less well off than they. It is no longer possible anywhere in the world publicly to assert that if some are relatively very poor and others very rich, that is only as it should be. Egregious social and economic inequality are neither fashionable nor ideologically justifiable any more—at least not publicly. In itself, this constitutes a revolution in thought and social orientation. If the desire to be well off is called the revolution in rising expectations, it is perhaps proper to speak of the acceptance of the legitimacy of these expectations and the development of the feeling of obligation to assist in their achievement as the revolution of inter-national obligation. The combined impact of these two revolutions is to set the world in motion toward a less stratified, more egalitarian world order.

The agreement on the legitimacy of developmental goals and of international obligations to assist in their achievement is matched by substantial disagreement on the most effective means toward these goals. It will not do to say that this disagreement is mostly a product of the cold war. Both within the Eastern and Western blocs of nations one finds a recurrent strain between two major schools of thought.

On the one hand, there is an emphasis, and it is currently dominant, upon a so-called hardheaded economic approach to development. This approach insists on capital formation as the key criterion or instrument of national development, and tends, after making passing bows at the human resource factor, to assume some magic in capital formation. For, generally, it is enlightened neither by an understanding of the human sentiments and activities required for capital formation nor by an understanding of the social institutions required as a matrix for the successful and enduring use of capital, once formed. Within this camp one finds persons who feel that everything is after all only a matter of water supply; or maps; or roads; or iron smelters; or some other piece of hardware or supporting technology. There is little recognition that maps must be read, understood, and desired, within a larger framework of goals; or that pipes, however beautiful, will rust and rot if not handled properly by properly oriented technicians; or even that what appear to be beautifully rational irrigation schemes will go for naught if the whole complex of sentiments and traditions surrounding more primitive methods of irrigation are not adequately supplanted by a new and more fitting complex of sentiments and activities relevant to and required by modern technology.

The other school of thought that stands in strong opposition to the so-called hard headed economic-technological approach goes generally under the label of community development. In its most exaggerated formulation, it looks upon human resources not only as the sine qua non but as the *only* important factor in the development process. Its deemphasis of technological support, of capital formation, and of concrete material gains makes it appear to believe that there is magic in men, such that aggregating 10 men, none of whom has anything, will somehow produce a magical multiplier effect, and out of 10 nothings will arise something superb. In its enthusiasm for and respect of human rights and dignity, it tends to deny excessively the importance of material support for human efforts at self-improvement and the need for continuous material payoff, if human energy and will are to continue to be mustered in community efforts.

I have deliberately exaggerated these two contrasting approaches—though there are some persons who fit the exaggerated descriptions—primarily to set side by side the twofold requirements of national development, whose successful interplay and interresponsiveness at every stage of development is indispensable to the success of any developmental scheme.

The dominance at the moment of the economy-technology approach over that which stresses the human resources side is fortunately less than it has been in the past and is visibly diminishing, at least in current political pronouncements. It 10 years ago it was considered important only to involve high level elites in various countries, at least today one sees beginning signs of a concern for adequate motivation and involvement of persons at lower echelons of the labor force and of the social ladder. There has been, apparently, a growing realization that labor and talent at all levels, and whether scarce or abundant, will be required for effective continuity of development, and that hence adequate motivation to accept developmental goals and to give conscientiously of one's best abilities must be aroused not only among an elite leadership but among all levels of the population.

This growing realization is a product not so much of ideological change in the hearts of men proposing developmental schemes as of the logic of the developmental process itself. For it has become painfully evident that there is a substantial difference, a crucial difference, between short-run and long-run developmental gains.

Short-run gains are possible to achieve in a variety of ways that involve little or no change in the basic cultural patterns of the society. Such gains can be secured through temporary infusions of external capital which may be put to spectacularly impressive short-run consumption uses. Or, one can autocratically muster a shock troop from the labor force to accomplish some exigent goal of the moment. Or one can force through, at least temporarily, a redistribution of existing goods and services so that for the moment an apparency of greater equality is achieved. Or one can bargain with cold war adversaries and secure the construction of one or more public works projects that produce a temporary effusion of national morale and support but that rapidly diminish in their effectiveness for lack of institutional supports. In brief, short-run improvements can be achieved in a variety of ways, involving no particular limits of ideology, principle, or forethought and concern for the future. Though everyone is by now well aware of these facts, and can recite examples of such stillborn improvements, it is distressing to note how frequently, still, advocates of development seem willing to settle for something less than the basic requirements for long-run, continuous, cumulative economic and social development.

Long-run improvement—that leads to a greater measure of self-sufficiency—requires the mustering of the will of the given population so that the people become knowingly and voluntarily committed to the goals and purposes of their society and are willing and able to do what is required to achieve these goals. But such commitment is not easy to secure. And the greatest obstacle in the path of this achievement is the social, political, and economic inequality which pervasively characterizes most of the nations of the world.

Such inequality in education, for instance, makes it difficult, if not impossible, for substantial majorities of the populations of the world to be aware of what is transpiring in their nation and in the world. More importantly, they are unaware of what may be in store for them in their two possible futures: on the one hand, the future characterized by a continuation of the same institutions to which they have for centuries been accustomed; on the other hand, that future which involves some radical shifts from former customary ways of life to a new place in the world scene.

Such inequality in education, moreover, makes it difficult if not impossible to recruit, train, and effectively employ the labor of numerous echelons of personnel required for any developmental scheme over the long run. The absence of literacy makes communications via the printed word ineffective. The absence of elementary school skills makes scheduling, coordination, and integration of efforts very difficult to achieve.

Even at the village level of effort, poverty and the isolation induced by illiteracy and traditionalism make it difficult for villagers to rise to the notion that they are capable of helping themselves and that with effort and learned skills a number of their most pressing problems can slowly begin to yield. Perhaps most basic here is the orientation to time that one finds among villagers and peasants throughout the world. The notion of a secular future to be planned for is outside the ordinary ken. There seems to be nothing to look forward to except much of the same that has always gone on. Planning for the future thus becomes meaningless. It is no accident that the best laid plans for such indispensable achievements as limitation of birth fail precisely because that orientation to future and the rational allocation of one's resources over a limited number of people is impossible to achieve among people for whom the future holds little or no promise. Another child cannot matter very much since nothing matters very much.

Drastic inequalities in power—such as are characteristic of many societies currently seeking to profit from developmental schemes—impede the effective beginnings of such schemes. Where men have been accustomed to having their fates settled by fiat from above, and where they have had no experience in participation in decisionmaking, there is little possibility that they will readily and happily embrace a scheme which requires them to decide increasingly for themselves what they wish to do and how they wish to do it. And yet, if one does not make it possible for the underprivileged peoples of the world to learn how to make such decisions and how to implement them, there is little hope that rational use of scarce resources—such as is demanded by effective long-run development—can ever be achieved.

Inequalities in income and social status also make a great difference in a variety of ways. Perhaps most trenchant and relevant is that which has to do with a sense of significant membership in the society. In order to commit himself to a society and its goals, and to lend his efforts relevantly and effectively, a man must feel, on the one hand, that his society is worthy of such efforts, and, on the other, that his membership in the society is valued and valuable. Actually, it is not a two-sided process in the way just stated. For, in fact, commitment to a group and belief in the worthiness of group goals arises from the sense that one's membership is valued and one's efforts worthy and valuable.

Studies of industrial sociology as well as of the relations of degraded people in status-ridden societies make it evident that such people operate at the lowest level of collective effort so long as they continue to receive only the meager portion of rewards customarily allocated to them. Rewards—whether material or spiritual or both—are the symbols by which men judge how worthy their societies deem them to be, and, in turn, how worth while they feel it to give their best efforts to their societies. A good deal of effort can be secured, to be sure, for short-run efforts, through physical coercion. But such a scheme, once undertaken, must continue with ever-increasing amounts of physical coercion.

It follows from these considerations that the social, political, and economic inequalities which are evident throughout the world actively impede the development of the kind of outlook and orientation required for effective long-run development.

It must be understood by any development planner that the vast majority of the people of the world have a great deal to lose, from their point of view, from any basic social change. They will suffer the loss of the security given by their beliefs in sacred sanctions. They will be uprooted from the securities and stabilities of kin-based social relations. They will be forced to make choices where before the simple flow of customary ways was sufficient. There will be sharp discontinuities between generations instead of the smooth flow of social obligations and performances, in conformity with traditional criteria of age and generational superiority. Inconsistency in the demands of various roles they must play will be substituted for the relatively coherent and consistent role sets in which they are currently involved. Finally, the traditional set of reassurances regarding their own purpose in life and the purpose of man in general will be shattered by the questioning, the skepticism, and the comparative frame of mind that secular development necessarily brings.

Obviously, peasants and villagers and tribesmen throughout the world do not understand social change in these abstract terms. But their usual resistance to change makes it possible for the social scientist observer to discover what it is that binds them to their traditional way of life and hence to infer what is at stake in any major social transition. Such an assessment makes it crystal clear that the new and the different way of life that developmental plans have in store for them will not be readily embraced until and only if effective alteration in their basic modes of thought has been achieved. And this cannot be accomplished except as the people themselves come, however slowly and haltingly, to appreciate in positive terms that the possible gains of development are perhaps worth while even in view of the losses and prices to be paid because of the change.

There is no quick path to such alteration in basic modes of thought and perspectives on self and society. Men cannot be cheered or propagandized or coerced into believing that nature can be overcome by human efforts. They must have the experience of having done just that, even if only on a small and—from the outside—inconsequential level, such as the construction of a primitive bridge that prevents their children from drowning on their way to school, or the clearing of a bush and the building of a primitive road that makes it possible for them to

get goods to market much more easily than before. Men must do these things for themselves before they can become convinced they can do them for themselves.

Similarly, men cannot for long be propagandized or coerced or cheered into feeling they are important to their rulers and to the nation of which they are members. Speeches and flattery and flag waving are very limited in their effectiveness. Only as men see that their concrete efforts on behalf of themselves and their nations yield them satisfactory rewards which make life more pleasant and simultaneously assure them of their worthiness in the eyes of others, only as these conditions are met can men come truly to believe that they are worthy and hence their nations or villages or groups are also worthwhile to support, protect, and work for.

In seeking to reinvigorate the spirit of people at the lower levels of society, it does not matter much whether the first beginnings are made by indigenous or foreign specialists or both, so long as the specialist, whoever he is, relates himself effectively to the people where they are and in their daily rounds of work and life. Most often this means work of the kind usually termed "community development." It means, in short, that kind of upgrading of the usual estimate of the importance of villagers throughout the world such that they are seen as key instruments in national development. And this obviously can be done only directly at the village level and starting only with existing village resources.

For the high-level planner, sitting in his nation's capital, and relating himself to foreign specialists in capital cumulation and growth, the implications of community development at the village level may seem remote and inconsequential. But it becomes apparent quickly to any but the most obdurate and blind that no national developmental scheme can hope to get off the ground until the appropriate motivations and commitments have been insinuated and institutionalized, however tentatively, at the level of those men whose physical and mental efforts will be indispensable to the operation of any development scheme, whether it be roadbuilding, or plant construction, or staffing a plant, or whatever.

For we now know, from bitter past experience, that programs which do not result in palpable improvement of the literacy, the standard of living, and the conditions of work of the most depressed segments of the population are likely quickly to be defeated by the tendency to quick consumption, leaving little or no productive capital, material or psychic, from which further development can spring.

Similarly, programs of development which do not take into account the high fertility of economically depressed populations and do not provide for this contingency at every point are likely to be defeated by the rapid consumption of economic gains by the increased population, an increase which invariably results when health and sanitation are introduced in underdeveloped areas.

To secure the new orientations of mind and of habit requisite to sustain social and economic growth, it is imperative that men at all levels shall experience active discontent with their traditional ways of life, and, at the same time, shall see projected alternatives as genuinely promising in their yield of immediate as well as long-term gratifications. Programs which demand that people with the least ability to save, to be reasonable, and to be secular, shall nevertheless be reasonable, secular, and engage in saving and planning are certain to fail. Men must be given reasons to save that are meaningful, reasons to be secular and to plan that make sense in terms of their life schemes. But this can only be done as they come to experience, albeit little by little, the direct benefits which accrue to them when they behave in this new fashion.

All of this betokens a destratification or otherwise an equalization of life situation and prospects far beyond what is currently true of most societies throughout the world. It would seem a utopian dream, indeed, to contemplate such drastic social change if in fact we did not have such excellent examples of at least some societies which have chosen that path and which have succeeded in substantial measure precisely because they have chosen that path. Among the small nations or societies of the world, Israel and Puerto Rico are outstanding examples. Among the larger nations of the world, it is quite clear that voluntary and spirited participation in national development, even among the so-called better developed nations, is evoked proportionate to the extent to which the peoples of those nations feel they have a concrete stake in the fate of the nation and feel this because, as they lend their efforts, they get what they consider to be a fair return for such efforts.

However inegalitarian and relatively well off the structures of major nations may be, it is apparent that the inequalities impede the evocation of greater voluntary commitment to national goals and purposes on the part of the people at all levels. By contrast, it is the sense of significant membership, whether in a factory work group, or in a small community, or in the nation at large that impels men to given conscientiously of their best efforts and to make the compromises between self-seeking and the requirements of effective community development that are needed if the collective will is to result in anything substantial. This significant membership, it must be remembered, arises and flourishes only as men feel valued by their societies. And they come to feel valued only as they receive from their societies that kind of share in its material rewards, in its decisionmaking processes, and in its symbols of social acceptability that tells them, more effectively than all the propaganda can ever achieve, that they are worthy people and that, under the best of circumstances, they are as worthy as anyone else.

There are a variety of ways in which nations can approach the goal of distributing this sense of membership and consequently of evoking the voluntary spirit and informed participation in national and local affairs.

There are various paces and tempos by which nations can move. There are numerously different obstacles different nations have to overcome, because of their different histories. But in the long run, only as genuine social and political and economic democracy are sought and progressively achieved, can any nation, however developed or underdeveloped at the moment, hope to institutionalize those social processes indispensable to continuous, effective and generally satisfactory long-run development.

The Implications of Urbanization for the Village and Rural Sector

MARION CLAWSON

Director, Land Use and Management Studies, Resources for the Future, Washington, D.C.

Urbanization is a contemporary worldwide process. The highly developed countries of North America and of Western Europe are experiencing rapid urban growth and sometimes shrinking rural population. However, a similiar process is underway in most of the less developed countries of Asia, Africa, and Latin America. Man is profoundly redistributing himself over the face of the globe, and more particularly in relation to his fellow man. Geographically speaking, his distribution is becoming more uneven, with immense concentrations of people in relatively limited areas, with the largest areas yet comparatively lightly occupied.

Urbanization creates a host of social, economic, and political problems in every country, highly developed and less developed alike. Urbanization, or the movement of people from a rural to an urban environment, involves major changes in the mode of living. Family structure, personal standards of conduct, and group mores are subjected to new social strains, often severe in their force. Economic investments in the city must be large, employment opportunities must be available or provided for the new urban residents,

and in other ways the economic problems of urbanization are often great. The physical regrouping of people often leads to their political regrouping also; people who were isolated in their rural areas are now together in the new urban environment, and they may form new political lineups, sometimes of explosive force.

These and other emerging problems of the city, as a human institution, are dealt with in other papers at this conference, and in a growing literature elsewhere. We shall not consider them further in this paper.

The focus of this paper is different. We shall consider the impact of the growing cities upon the village and rural sectors of the national society, economy, and political life. The central thesis of this paper may be stated as follows: urbanization, including the broad economic and social movements which it feeds upon and which in turn it feeds, has a major effect upon the rural areas of the same nations. The man who moves from farm or village to the city experiences the effects of the city firsthand; but the man who stays on the farm or in the village experiences the urban effects secondhand and in the end not necessarily less powerfully than his brother who went to the city.

Development of large urban centers will require a food and fiber supply in the cities. People must eat, and be clothed. They obviously cannot produce their food and fiber in the city, but must buy it. This requires, among other things, organized wholesale and retail markets in the city. Movement of food and fiber goods, from whatever source, through the channels of trade to the places where city people can buy it, is a major undertaking in and of itself.

The original source of this food and fiber for urban people must generally be from the agriculture of the country concerned. A less-developed nation can import some agricultural commodities, especially those which it is ill-suited to produce; but except in rare instances, it cannot import its total agricultural needs or any major part thereof, for it would ordinarily lack the necessary foreign exchange to do so. For most countries, domestic supplies of agricultural commodities will be the chief reliance for the urban people; city and farm are closely linked, in this and in many other ways.

With growing urbanization, the urban market requires a marketable surplus of agricultural commodities. In a traditional rural society, even when highly productive, agricultural production is centered upon the needs of the farm family. There is often little marketable surplus over the needs of that family. In India today, it has been estimated that 70 percent of total agricultural production does not leave the rural village where it is produced. The same was probably true in the United States in 1800, and perhaps for much later also. An agricultural marketable surplus

in an urbanizing country requires, first of all, an increase in agricultural output over the level prevailing in recent years. An increased agricultural output can often be attained in various ways, or combinations thereof; another major group of papers at this conference is concerned with agricultural output, and the subject cannot be pursued further in detail here. The way most appropriate for any country will depend upon natural and economic conditions in that country. Most or all the less-developed countries are striving today to increase their agricultural output, by one means or another. For the remainder of this paper, we shall assume that somehow they are successful.

An agricultural marketable surplus, above rural village needs, must be moved from farm to city. It has no value on the farm, either to the farmer or to the urban dweller; it is most unlikely that farmers will continue to produce marketable surpluses unless they can sell them. Movement of such agricultural supplies from farm to city requires transportation, storage, often processing, and always buying and selling of the commodities concerned. These processes, which are often grouped under the general title of "marketing," involve physical, economic, and institutional processes. At each level or stage, the commodities must be physically handled in some way; often they must be bought and sold, or appraised for credit, or otherwise be the subject of some economic measurement or transaction; and institutions, such as organized markets, banks, transport companies, and many others are involved. These various processes may be in individual (including corporate) private hands, or carried out by cooperatives, or by public agencies, or some combination thereof. In most countries, these marketing processes tend to become more complex from year to year. Supplementing the commodity flows must be information flows, as to prices, volumes, qualities, transactions, and the like.

The first impact of urbanization upon the village and rural sector comes in the demand or requirement upon the farmer for the production of certain commodities. This takes the form not merely of the kind of crop—wheat, rice, cotton, etc.—but also of the variety. Moreover, the urban demand is often highly specific as to season, method of harvest, crop condition at time of harvest, kind of packaging even from the farm, and as to many other factors. Formerly, when the farmer produced primarily for the consumption of his own family, these were individual matters. Each farmer could produce the kinds of crops, of the varieties he chose, for harvest at the season he wanted them, and handle the product in the manner best suited to his own needs. Now, he must coordinate his efforts with that of other farmers, and all must be governed by the requirements of the city. The requirements of modern food processing, storage, and handling require that farmers follow relatively uniform methods.

The agricultural production methods by which farmers are going to produce more, to meet the larger needs of the growing cities, often require the use of more fertilizer, more insecticides, irrigation water, better seeds, and various other goods and services which the farmer can no longer provide for himself, but must buy. If these goods and services for the farmer are to be available, they must be provided by organizations specializing in them. Such organizations may also be private individual (including corporations), cooperative, or public agency, or some combination thereof. They may be highly specialized and technically advanced, or they may be rather unspecialized and simple; but it is axiomatic that they are off-farm, for the farmer is unable to supply these kinds of new or expanded services himself.

If a less-developed country is undergoing urbanization and if its agriculture is developing along the lines suggested, farmers are experiencing major changes in their methods of doing business. They are now selling a major part of their total output for cash, rather than consuming so much of it themselves; they are buying for cash a larger part of their total farm inputs, rather than producing so much themselves. From a largely self-sufficient economy, they are entering a commercial, money economy. They will inevitably become more "money minded," aware of the money value or price of goods they sell and supplies they buy. They will almost certainly become more concerned with the balance between cash income and cash outgo. In the words of the economist, they are likely to think more in terms of marginal cost and marginal value, and more likely to equate the two, than has been the case in the past. Their agriculture is becoming more "commercial," in this sense of greater emphasis upon cash flows in and out; it will be less traditional in its orientation. The farmers themselves are becoming more like the "economic men" of economic theory. Anthropologists and others have noted similar changes in the past, when plantation agriculture for an export market was introduced into a self-sufficient agriculture. Now, however, the driving force is coming from within the country, not from outside; and agriculture may continue to be based on the single peasant farm, rather than shift toward plantations or larger units.

Some observers, noting these changes underway or anticipating them, have decried such changes and have tended to glorify an earlier past for agriculture. It is not our purpose here either to defend or to condemn these changes taking place, or shortly to take place, in the agriculture of urbanizing countries. Regardless of one's attitude toward the past, it seems most unlikely that this type of change could be stopped, even if it were considered desirable to do so, or even that it could be materially retarded. The changes underway may, perhaps, be guided, in order to minimize the shock and frequently admitted adverse effects— adverse both to the city and to the rural area. However, success in this direction must rest upon an understanding of the processes underway.

One major economic consequence of this urbanization process, as described, will be a large-scale regionalization process in agriculture. In drawing this conclusion, it is assumed that the less-developed nation succeeds in providing transportation, processing, marketing, and other necessary services to agriculture, as urbanization proceeds apace. When the farmer produced primarily for the consumption of his family, its needs as a consuming unit largely determined his farm production plans. Their needs for food was paramount, although, as a producer, he could choose among the possible crops that combination most likely to produce the desired output. When agricultural production is primarily for sale, then comparative financial returns to the farmer are paramount. He will increasingly choose those crops, or that combination of crops, which pro-

duces the highest cash income in relation to his costs. He will now seek the greatest comparative economic advantage—or the least comparative economic disadvantage. He no longer needs to produce a wide variety of crops to meet the full demands of his family; he can specialize in those crops for which his area has the greatest advantages. The regional pattern of agricultural production, as a result, is almost certain to be strikingly different from what it was during a period of high local self-sufficiency in agriculture.

In this regionalization process, the tested theorems of regionalization, from Von Thunen to Isard, will generally apply. Products of high perishability or of large weight and bulk in proportion to value must be produced relatively near the market; products of more durability or of high value in relation to weight and bulk may be produced in more distant regions. Whole fresh milk has both high perishability and large weight in relation to value; most modern cities have a "milkshed" of large or small proportions surrounding them. Wool is a classic of the opposite type; nonperishable, of high value in proportion to weight. Physical potentialities of producing regions may greatly modify these strictly economic tendencies.

As a result of regionalization and the economic processes inherent in it, values of agricultural land may become highly differentiated also, if there exists a reasonably free land market. However, this gets into a range of considerations beyond the scope of this paper.

The process of commercialization and regional specialization can be illustrated by reference to the U.S. experience during earlier decades, when it was an economically less developed country (1). In 1800, and to a decreasing extent for 50 to 100 years later, farmers in the United States produced most of what the farm family consumed, and consumed most of what the farm produced. There always existed, it is true, some export market for tobacco, cotton, and some other specialized crops; and there was a small, though growing, market in the small cities of the nation. But the farmer spun his own thread from cotton, wool, or flax he grew; and made the thread into cloth for clothing. He made leather from his own hides, and himself made or hired made shoes for his family. His farm food production was geared to his farm family food consumption. Transportation out of rural districts was difficult and expensive, and geared to natural water channels. Most farmers grew apples, for instance, if they could, for this was a fruit which could be stored for winter consumption. Today, the American farmer typically grows for the market. He may still have a garden, and he will consume his own milk, eggs, and meat, to the extent they are available as part of his commercial farm operations. The value of food produced and consumed on the same farm has declined materially in recent years. The American farmer no longer grinds his own flour from his own wheat, makes leather from his own hides, makes cloth from his own fiber products. He not only produces for the market; he produces those commodities for which his area is best suited. As a result, farm production is localized more and more in highly specialized producing areas. Apples, for instance, once grown on a substantial proportion of all farms are now produced in a relatively few highly specialized areas. Potatoes, likewise, were once grown widely over the United States but now production is highly localized, often

aimed at meeting the demands of particular markets at particular seasons. Vegetable crops, in general, are today found in regions and districts where natural growing conditions are best; a substantial proportion of several vegetables moves clear across the nation, from producing farming area to consuming urban area. Market demand has been the strongest single force shaping agriculture in the United States over the past 100 years or more (2). While localized production generally means higher total transport costs, the gains in agricultural efficiency from this one factor alone have been more than sufficient to offset the hgher transport costs.

A somewhat similar process is likely to take place with India's agriculture in the next generation or more. Agricultural output is scheduled to increase 30 percent in the third 5-year plan alone, to meet demands of the growing urban and rural population, and further major increases will be required in later years (3). Until rather recently, India's agriculture was almost wholly self-sufficient; as noted above, it is still largely so. Farmers tend to produce what their families need for food, and to eat what their farms produce; there is a notable lack of regional specialization within the country. If population increases as rapidly as now seems probable, and if a major proportion of the net additions to population settle in cities, as seems now to be the case, then a greatly increased flow of food from farm to city will be required. The whole process as described above will be repeated— not to the same extent as in the United States, probably, but on the whole more rapidly than was the case as our nation grew. Indian agriculture is almost sure to become much more commercialized, more money minded, and more regionalized than at present; and the basic driving force will be the increased urbanization of the country.

A notable aspect of this commercialization and regionalization of agriculture has been the development of an "agribusiness," or a series of business supply, marketing, and processing industries (4). The farmer's function has become more and more highly specialized; other industries take over, in agriculturally advanced countries, what the farmer does for himself in the less developed countries. Specialized fertilizer businesses develop; so do specialized seed production enterprises; all manner of specialized marketing business firms come into being. Without these agribusiness establishments, the modern farmer in the United States could not function at all; conversely, without the farmer, these businesses would be unable to operate. There grows up a more complex and more closely interrelated economic structure involving both farm and urban business than now exists in the less developed countries. As urban population grows, and as agriculture changes to meet the larger demands of the urban market, more or less comparable agribusinesses will arise in the presently less developed countries. These may be private, cooperative, or public, or a combination thereof; unless they develop adequately, agriculture cannot be expected to meet the growing demands of the cities.

Urbanization brings social as well as economic stresses and strains to the farm village and rural sector. We have noted that migration from rural areas to cities brings severe problems within the city. The people who enter cities encounter a new social and economic environment, which often subjects them to severe personal, internal stress. Less frequently recognized but perhaps equally serious are the stresses which arise in the old rural environment, both for those who leave it and for those who remain. Migration is almost always a highly selective social process, as reflected in the age, abilities, and temperaments of those who move and of those who stay. Under most circumstances, it is the younger rather than the older members of the group who will move to a new environment; the city often attracts the personally most able, who can best make their way in the new and challenging environment; and it is the venturesome, rather than the cautious, who move as a general rule. These qualities are often randomly distributed within a local population; those who choose to move are likely to come from families and groups containing members who prefer to stay. A breaking of old ties and old patterns of life is thus involved.

A continuing social interaction between those who migrate and those who stay is likely in most countries. Migration from rural area to city within a country usually involves much shorter physical distances than does migration from one country to another; in spite of difficulties of communication, social distance is usually not too great to prevent continued social interaction. The migrant to the city acquires new consumption patterns, new modes of living, new ideas of social relationships among men and groups, which he will communicate, deliberately or unconsciously, to his relatives and friends who remained behind. In spite of living conditions which may be substandard, migrants from rural areas often find life in the city much more attractive, in many less-developed countries, than was life in the country. The continued, and sometimes accelerating, movement of people from rural area to city would seem adequate proof of this point. The tales of the new city dweller may produce serious discontents in the rural area from which he came; those who first chose to remain may now wish to move. This in turn may affect the numbers and personal characteristics of the next wave of migrants. Several less-developed countries are coping with a flood of rural migrants larger than can readily be absorbed. Bad as are living conditions for such people in many cities, they are probably better than in the rural areas from which they came, and the migrant expects or hopes for improvement, and is willing to use to this end the political power he ac-

quires by reason of his belonging to a group.

A selective and differential migration from rural area to city, and different living conditions in the city than in the rural area, might in time lead to rather serious social and personality cleavages between rural and urban people, in spite of the continued social interaction discussed above. This would seem to be more probable to the extent that the new city dwellers were able to exploit their political strength to improve their economic and social lot above that of the typical rural dweller.

We conclude with the general observation: urbanization is a powerful economic and social force working for change in the village and rural sector, as well as within the city.

REFERENCES

(1) Benedict, M. R., *Farm Policies of the United States, 1790–1950—A Study of Their Origins and Development,* Twentieth Century Fund, New York (1953).

(2) Clawson, M., R. Burnell Held, and C. H. Stoddard, *Land for the Future,* Johns Hopkins Press, Baltimore (1960).

(3) Planning Commission, *Third Five-Year Plan,* Planning Commission, Government of India, New Delhi (1961).

(4) Davis, J. H., R. A. Goldberg, *A Concept of Agribusiness,* Graduate School of Business Administration, Harvard University, Boston (957).

Capital Requirement for Urban Social Overhead

JOHN W. DYCKMAN

Director, Regional Development and Urban Economics, Arthur D. Little, Inc., San Francisco, California

The contribution of urban agglomeration and investment in urban capital to the rise of industrial economies has been documented by many historians. The urban capital which makes industrialization feasible is generated by two distinct types of demand. The first is the production requirements of industrial enterprises, and the second is the consumption requirements of the assembled urban work force. The portion of this capital which is not directly employed in the industrial enterprises is called "social overhead." Economists' attention to the firm has somewhat obscured this latter capital input, but it is at least half the total capital requirement.

In newly developing economies, needing to amass capital for an industrial breakthrough, planners are faced with competing claims on scarce capital from industrial development on the one hand, and social overhead costs of urbanization on the other. The amount of capital needed for industry depends on the technology of production and the organization of enterprises. The capital requirements of social overhead are generated by cultural standards of consumption, and by the particular relation of

the overhead to the productive technology. Urbanization supports industrialization by providing external economies of labor assembly, communications, production linkages, and markets. Expenditures on social overhead, in turn, make urbanization tolerable and attractive, and add to the productivity of the labor force. The question for the developing economy is "What is the optimum allocation of capital to social overhead for achieving the objectives of the society?"

The traditional aim of development programs has been to minimize urban overhead costs for a given level of output and urban growth. In the short run, this criterion has facilitated the accumulation of capital for industrial "takeoff." The long-run optimal strategy has favored development of human resources and seeks to avoid premature obsolence of urban plant. The competing strategies are mediated by provisional use of "standards" which set minimum acceptable levels of service, and by planning targets, developed in physical terms, and converted into capital needs. In the development of these standards, the planners typically attempt to find some

478

minimum requirements for effective performance of the work force, some minimum requirements of enterprises, and to set these as the basis for planned targets (1).

Though social overhead requirements vary with industrial technique, they do not do so proportionately. The social overhead need of a factory with $5,000 per worker investment is more than one-sixth of that in a modern plant with $30,000 per worker invested. Both the heavy industries requiring large amounts of power, water, and transport, and the light industries with much more modest requirements will share in the same electricity and water supply systems and transportation networks. Indeed, one of the strongest arguments against the isolation of heavy industry in a developing economy is the argument that the overhead requirements of that industry are likely to be so great as to require the installation of systems on which many small plants can profitably feed. If a modern plant were forced to provide its entire social overhead in isolation from such industrial complexes, the capitalized additional costs would be upwards of 40–50 percent of regular production costs. Training and assembling the labor force would add further to these costs.

The arguments against development of the large urban complex have held that consumption standards of the urban labor force are more diversified and demanding than those in rural areas, and the cultural impetus to rising standards imposes a great drain on resources needed for industrial production. The suggested alternative is development of small, nearly self-sufficient village units, contributing to production and the accumulation of capital, but isolated from the consumption patterns of urban centers, and spared the needs of many of the capital-using urban facilities. On the other hand, there is the observable tendency of economic enterprises to seek the external economies of the established centers, if left to their own devices. These centers have always been attractive to, and supportive of, industrial growth. Which force is greater? Where are real costs higher? What strategy should be employed?

Before drawing up a balance sheet, one must specify the functions of the urban complex, and the goals of economic development. The former are more easily generalized. They include: the provision of external economies of labor assembly, communication, production linkages and markets. Specifically, the assembly of enterprises in the urban industrial complex is part of a specialization and division of labor in which consumption itself is specialized. The urban center has provided an opportunity for intensive utilization of scarce capital instruments and scarce technologists. Thus, in the historic city, it has served as a key instrument in the increasing specialization of the whole economy. For example, the development of the urban complex has acted to speed the absorption of surplus rural population, permitting, where capital was available, substitution of capital for labor and improved productivity in agriculture. Where industrial skills were scarce, and teachers and scientists in short supply, it provided a center for the diffusion of ideas and information.

This assembly imposes costs. The city must supply water, disposal of excreta and other wastes, housing for the population, transportation to work, and opportunities for the training which will convert its population from a rural to an urban work force. These costs are common to all urban centers, but they are more serious in the large ones. Studies of urbanization indicate that these costs are functions of several key variables: size of city; density of occupancy and activity; layout, especially of home-work relation; timing of construction; and particular service "standards." That service costs vary with size has long been an established dictum of Western industrial cities (2). It may be, however, that the greater costs in the larger centers in Western cities result from more varied and attractive services. What would the variation in cost be, if services were held to the minimum in cities of all sizes?

To the extent that increased size means increased crowding, or overloading of existing facilities, it may impose very high marginal costs. Living costs in the large cities tend to be higher than in smaller towns. To the extent that these higher living costs result from more intensive competition for urban resources, and do not represent real gains in standard of living, they simply exert additional pressure on capital accumulation, and appear as a "surcharge" on the minimum costs of maintaining the population. Traditionally, even in Western societies, the peasant has spent a higher percentage of his income on food than the city dweller of the same general income level, and has managed to save more. The traditional problem has been one of liquidity, for much of the saving has been in kind. In the city, in contrast, one could earn money wages and achieve more liquid and disposable assets. Where the average expenditure in the city is much higher than in the country, however, some drain on capital may result (3).

The most serious effects of urban size on social overhead costs, however, result from the greater densities in large cities. In almost every nation where data

are available, cities of very high density have exhibited higher urban service costs than lower density cities (4). Increased density of development in urban centers imposes costs, but also offers savings; for while low density saves in costs of housing and sanitary facilities, and allows lower levels of services, it is more expensive for centrally-piped systems, such as water, sewage disposal, etc., and adds to total transportation costs. High density housing, though it saves on land costs, usually means much higher construction costs. Since the land costs are more directly addressable by public policy, it would seem advantageous, in many circumstances, to attempt to economize the less reducible construction costs. In the high density pattern, there is often low private expenditure by urban workers on (a) housing, and (b) transportation to work. The lower cost of housing is a reflection of the much smaller amount of housing space purchased. But to make these very high densities work at "standard" health and amenity levels, large public expenditures on sewers, water supply, health stations, etc., are needed. The argument against reducing these densities has generally been based on the greater cost of transportation and assembly of work force from longer distances. In some countries, in the early stage of industrialization, particularly in Africa, the longer journey-to-work cost has been borne by the workers themselves. This effectively adds to the working day, and undoubtedly shortens the life of the worker to the point where accumulation of capital is being achieved with the effective sacrifice of the present generation. Where higher working efficiency is needed, and higher standards for consumption are set, the question arises: "Does it pay to allocate capital to subsidize free, or very cheap, transportation in order to save on the social overhead costs of high density?"

Transportation is the most costly, and most indivisible of overhead expenditures. Even in India, where there is a well-developed rail network, it has been allotted a greater share of net investment in the 20-year plan than agriculture and rural development, and almost as much as urban housing and municipal services (5). It will place a drain on the economies in any event. It would probably pay to subsidize passenger transport only in a few situations. In most cases, the sewers, water system, and communication systems will be needed, and a high rate of utilization of the systems is desired. In these cases, compact networks are economical, and higher densities favorable. The great savings are to be realized at certain inflection points in the cost schedules at which a substantially different technology is employed. For example, there are major savings to be realized where septic tanks, composting and night-soil collection can be utilized in place of closed sewer systems. But the costs of closed sewer systems are not the highest costs of social overhead in urban communities. Piped, filtered water systems, which will be required in most areas, will be about twice as expensive as the sewerage system (in the ratio of 25 to 15). If density is so low, and living standards so minimum, that piped filtered water is not required, very great savings can be made in the overhead cost of urban settlement. Since the cost of shelter and overhead facilities have been harder to reduce than food costs, they are likely to take a larger share of the total output of the small community. Any reduction that can be made in these items is worthwhile, but one must ask at what

point the residents of these communities can contribute to modern technology without these overhead facilities.

Transportation deserves special attention, not only because of its very large share in the budget and wide range of technical possibilities, but also because of its structural importance in the pattern of settlement. Cities, regions, and the form of settlement have been directly shaped by transportation facilities. In the discussion above, it was implied that if density were held constant, increasing size of city would lead to increased transportation costs. The increased transportation cost, in turn, spared the communities some of the other costs of urban density. But the indivisibilities in the investment requirements of a major transportation system are difficult for developing economies to meet. (Historical transportation systems in the development of Western countries, like the United States, were financed by the import of capital from outside the system.) A recent 5-year plan for Delhi called for an investment of 120 million (rupees) in transportation, an amount greater than 50 percent of the capital improvement budget. Transportation is widely believed to be an instrument in reducing central cities' land costs by making possible greater dispersion of population. Cheaper transportation is potentially decentralizing and density-reducing mainly because it permits workers to achieve the same real costs of travel to work at greater distance from the job. But transportation is also potentially centralizing, because it permits the assembly of factors of production more cheaply. Thus, the centralized pattern of industry in Australia is largely the result of relatively cheap rail transport. Similarly, the enormous investment in the subway in

New York City did not reduce land values in New York, but actually raised them, for it permitted the assembly of great numbers of people at downtown offices and shopping locations. Transportation, then, seems to act to reduce central city values only in those circumstances in which the main activities are themselves decentralized, and the pattern of movement is equally good laterally and at all points in the network, rather than simply between the center and outlying points.

Because of the heavy drain which transportation investment places on the capital budgets of a developing economy, there is great pressure to find cost reductions which do not diminish output. Meyerson has indicated that cost reduction may be obtained by (a) reducing the demand for movement required for a given output, and (b) rationalizing the organization of movement (6). He suggests three methods for reducing demand:

(a) Land-use planning to minimize need for movement.

(b) Substitutions for movement.

(c) Organizing movement to stretch a given capacity.

In the early stages of economic development, transportation of goods is the most important consideration in achieving a higher standard of living. A well-developed distribution system for commodities will, unless densities are very high and population highly concentrated, require carriers in addition to rail transport. At the level of commodity distribution, the superior economies of high-capacity systems must yield to the flexibility of the lower-capacity systems, such as trucking. In the short run, the interest is to minimize this distribution expense by two devices: (a) by producing locally all the essentials of consumption, and (b)

by maintaining as high dwelling densities as are compatible with this type of consumption. But these objectives favor a less specialized, subsistence economy, and therefore sacrifice many of the potential gains of specialization and division of labor. In the early stages of development planning, the planner must adopt the rule: Set "real" prices on distribution cost, including full charges for operation, maintenance, and appreciation, so that the decisions on urban settlement will be based on the principle that the gains of specialization and division of labor are not wiped out by hidden distribution costs.

In the longer run, a less concentrated pattern of urban organization may realize economies from changing technology. Communication techniques have been advancing more rapidly than those of transportation. Recent technology promises that the transportation of people might increasingly be replaced by the transportation of messages. In industrialized countries, the transmission of television messages, for example, has already successfully replaced the assembly of people for certain functions. Technically, the possibilities of capital savings substitutions offer the opportunity for permitting a high level of living in a decentralized pattern of settlement. Unfortunately, the task of preparing the receiver for the content of a message is more difficult when a cultural barrier must be crossed. The "common culture" of urban centers is a great advantage to economical communication. By comparison, the technical problems in the communication and transportation revolution are slight. Increasingly, the transportation of energy may be substituted for the movement of persons and goods. Much progress will be made in the efficiency of transmission lines for electricity, in the use of conveyor belts, and other continuous-flow devices. In countries with well developed rail and conventional transportation networks, the capital expenditure on these new devices is not justified; but the underdeveloped area which lacks rail facilities and roads may successfully employ certain of these innovations.

The cultural barrier is more serious than the technical barrier. Much of the social overhead cost of the large urban center in a developing economy is necessary to overcome the barriers of communications and the differences in technique and skills between groups in the society, and particularly, between urban and rural people. In the cities, new migrants learn consumption as well as production skills. The competition that sets up the new demands for capital is an informal school for private consumption. Limits on consumption, both maxima and minima, may be established by planning "standards" which serve as operational allocators.

Standards play an important role in design of urban systems, for they provide restraints for the solution of the design problem. That is, a planning standard which is taken as an absolute minimum requirement, acts as a boundary condition in linear programming. For example, if one attempts to find an optimum combination of density and travel cost, he faces an enormous number of possible combinations. But if he accepts a "standard" such as "maximum allowable journey-to-work time of 45 minutes" or "one-half mile walking distance," his problem is quickly solvable. The choice of restraints, however, is arbitrary. With the exception of a few "requirements," such as water, caloric intake, etc., human standards are very flexible.

Even some of the more irreducible requirements are capable of several forms of satisfaction. The forms chosen are a result of the prescriptive norms of the planners or of the general cultural biases of the particular community, or both. Some of these cultural preferences are so strong as to be firm "requirements." Tastes in food and drink are sometimes reinforced by religious prescription. And consumer choice may reinforce the standards. Safe potable water could be provided for the urban population of industrial countries at less than half its presently delivered cost, if considerations of taste, odor and appearance could be neglected. Cultural standards are set by forces of emulation. Many industrially underdeveloped nations wish to have the most advanced or expensive services. But not every nation would be justified in building a shiny metro or monumental school buildings.

It is plain that there are few economies in the world that can afford the standards for overhead (from roads to schools) or the densities of settlement obtaining in new development in the established industrial nations. The British New Towns have higher densities and cheaper overhead costs than the typical suburban development in the United States, but these costs are beyond the reach of India. If present population forecasts are realized, India will add 55 million persons to the population of towns over 20,000 in size in this decade. At the recent British New Town overhead costs, the accommodation of this population would entail the expenditure of over 70 percent of the planned 250 billion (rupees) net investment for new urban overhead alone (housing excluded). At the levels of the American suburban "tract," overhead would far exceed the total net investment. Thus the developing economies must have both high density and decentralization of economic activity in new towns. At the same time, levels of urban overhead costs must be minimal. But if the social services in the decentralized urban settlements are not high enough to compare favorably with those in the old established centers, migration to the largest cities will continue, and decentralization efforts will fail. Social overhead in urbanization of new centers must be pushed, therefore, to a point at which it is effective in retarding the flow of people to the largest cities. If this is not possible, negative incentives, or restraints, must be used to reduce the overhead burden of new residents on the largest cities.

Any rule for substitution intended to save short-run capital must take account of the fact that social overhead decisions have consequences over a longer life, on the average, than many private investment decisions. A street layout, for example, is extremely long lived. Maintenance costs must be considered along with initial capital costs. A prudent planner would seek to follow the rule: Marginal savings in capital from selection of a cheaper alternative in the present must exceed the sum of the differences in maintenance costs between alternatives, discounted at the average marginal productivity of capital over the life of the "superior" capital good, where the life of the latter is finite and known, and the marginal productivity of capital is measured by some index, such as the interest rate. The case for using "makeshift" substitutes in developing economies is usually based on the very high marginal productivity of capital, which justifies the short-run savings of capital. But note that if "makeshift" substitutes

must be wholly replaced before the normal life spand of a standard improvement, the replacement cost is capitalized and treated as a maintenance flow. Capitalization would be charged at the rate prevailing at the time of replacement. If such a rule is followed, many cheaper substitutes would be rejected as poor investments. In the strategy of development, moreover, a nation may need to accept higher investment-output ratios in the early stages of development in order to secure the benefits of rapid growth and productivity at a later stage.

The improvisation of substitutions which save short-run capital has other advantages. For one, they minimize the risk of being caught with heavy investments in obsolete facilities where technology is changing rapidly. Examples, in addition to transportation technology discussed above, include hospitals, with medicine and drug production, education and communication. By extension, the rule above tells us that the difference in initial cost of facility (a) and facility (b) must exceed the capitalized value, over the life of the longer lived facility, of the difference in marginal productivity of the two facilities, minus the difference in maintenance costs, discounted at the average marginal productivity of capital. Certain cautions should be exercised. The outputs of the improvised facility may not be equal to those of the standard facility measured against unity inputs. Following the rule, a chance to accumulate real capital would be lost by choosing the improvisation. In practice, however, the difference in inferior output might actually be taken out of the consumption flow of the present generation. Most of the social overhead, as we have noted, is both consumption and production. The portion that is pure "output" therefore is difficult to measure. Further, for technical reasons, it may be necessary for an economy to go through certain "standard" procedures before moving to an advanced technology. Where this is the case, delay in developing the standard procedures may result in a long-term setback.

The most important form of social overhead, both in terms of the permanence of its impact, and its supplementary role in the utilization of other forms of capital, is education. If a society is organized to utilize its talents, educational investment can be a decisive force in economic growth. But it is also an important consumer good in those economies characterized by personal economic mobility. In these cases, education can be used to spearhead economic development, and to speed up the movement of resources if it is strategically allocated. Thus, placing schools in selected areas may serve to attract population in industrial locations. At first glance, a strategy of locating educational centers in the less developed regions of the country would appear to require a larger outlay of capital than would otherwise be necessary. So far as direct short-run educational outlay is concerned, this is true. Total capital outlay, however, may actually be conserved, if the difference in educational outlay is exceeded by the difference in social overhead cost of moving people to the central cities and accommodating them there. If the long-run plans of the nation call for development of the region, return movement costs are also saved.

If the newly developing countries of the world cannot afford the general housing and social overhead expenditures of the British New Town or the American suburb, they are also unable to afford

similarly high per pupil cost of school plant. In the United States, the average cost of a classroom for 30 pupils is about $30,000, or in the neighborhood of $1,000 per pupil. Such an expenditure per pupil is greater than average family income in most of the developing economies. But the American school has strict grade division, a separate teacher for each class, and makes a strong effort to control and reduce class size. These aims are unreal for the newly developing economy. The latter will typically need to use methods of the sort employed in the United States in the early days of its mass education efforts, such as the Lancastrian or "one-teach-one" methods, in which pupils were taught to teach each other. Very large class sizes, and relatively informal grade distinctions will save on costs. Education offers an outstanding opportunity for the substitution of communication for movement. Radio, and, in favorable circumstances, television can be utilized to bring the best instruction from the large city centers to outlying school locations. Development of cheap electronic components offers the possibility of bringing the cost of radio receivers below that of text books in many countries. The great defect of electronic communication thus far is that it is one-way, and puts the receiver at the mercy of the selections of the sender. Improvements in the economies of transmission and the storage of messages offer the hope of an ultimate breakthrough in this respect, but for some time electronic communication will be limited in scope and function in the mass market. But since the cost of printing equipment will not decline much further, the cost of paper will probably rise, and textbooks must be delivered at some transport cost, radio and ultimately television will need to play a rising role in education in the developing economy.

The organization of the school system is an important element in its overhead cost. In the United States, where local control of schools is an established principle, there is much duplication of administrative services, resulting in a number of diseconomies of organization. In a country where centralization is extreme, administrative diseconomies may set in. Great flexibility, therefore, must be sought in the organization of the school system. Where in the United States, the size of a neighborhood is often reckoned by reference to an elementary school population, in parts of Asia and Africa, a "town" may come to be identified by reference to the secondary school. Clusters of villages will probably need to be served by a single high school. This high school, in turn, may become a focus of the administrative and service activities for the urbanizing area. This service town or village may, in turn, like the Israeli urban service centers, become the nucleus of a distinguishable "city" or urbanized village complex. As such, it could concentrate a number of urban overhead services, and reduce duplication of these services in individual villages.

In most of the developing countries of Asia and Africa, investment in urban social overhead in the next 10 to 15 years will need to be kept below $300 per capita. This is only about one-fourth of the cost of per capita investment in urban social overhead for additional urban facilities in the United States. Some of this saving can be achieved by higher density of living in the town, i.e., by lower space consumption. But most of the saving will result from substitution of new patterns of urban living rather than reduced standards in the same pattern. True, the developing economies can scarcely afford the automobile consumption of large American cities, with its attendant high cost. Few will be able to afford as many public school buildings, with their equipment and abundance of classrooms. Subway systems, which have made possible the dense concentration in Manhattan, would probably not be economical in Asia or Africa. Urbanization Western style means great expenditure on transportation, roads, school buildings and hospitals. The pressure to economize on these facilities in countries where the race between population growth and economic growth is a close one will not allow much luxury of choice.

Some savings will be achieved by the substitution of human capital for physical capital, as in the case of the extension of visiting nurses to save on crowded hospital facilities. Teachers may be easier to develop than classrooms, and similar extension services may be applied to education. But it appears likely, despite these efforts, that a certain amount of saving will need to come from a combination of rationalization of rural services, and decentralization of employment that slows down the movement to the larger cities. The urban village complex mentioned above, made up of a half dozen or more villages of about 2,000 population each, can conceivably help to reduce the total transportation cost in the economy, at the same time affording the opportunity for a lower level of capital investment in public services in the individual villages. Not all countries would be wise to stress decentralization as a means to capital savings, for some countries can ill afford the immobility of an underemployed rural labor force. In countries, especially in Asia, in which underemployment in large cities is equally as severe as in the smaller cities and villages, due to the pull of cities outstripping the rate of economic growth, the cost of further urban agglomeration must be reduced. For once past efficient size, each increment of population adds to the real costs of carrying on business for all members of the community through congestion and overload.

The determination of capital requirements for social overhead expenditure, then, requires a careful assessment of the distribution of resources and population in the economy, and of cultural values and aspirations of the population, an estimate of the future prospects for technological change, and an evaluation of future as against present consumption. While much of the history of urban development in Western countries can be circumvented, and more advanced technology can be utilized in some cases, planning "standards" will be very modest and flexible, and geared to local conditions. Ways must be found for achieving high performance, particularly in transportation and distribution, at a fraction of the cost of existing systems in industrialized nations. Over all, the costs of urban social overhead will not be allowed to exceed about one-fourth of the level of present costs in the advanced industrial nations. Meier has shown the technical possibility of reducing costs much more than this (7), but it is doubtful if the urban villages which would result could compete with the main urban centers for population. Unless severe repressive measures were employed, or heroic national mobilization achieved, further overcrowding of the big cities could be expected. The real costs of stinting social overhead would then show up in the lowered standards of living of the larger urban population. The true capital requirement of urban social overhead, then, is that amount necessary to achieve the desired responses in a highly dynamic growth situation. It must be found afresh for each society.

REFERENCES

(1) R. L. Meier has done the most complete work on the development of minimum adequate standards based upon population-average physiological requirements. Meier's work, the basic calculations for which were done in 1949, can be found in his book, *Science and Economic Development—New Patterns of Living,* Technology Press and John Wiley, Cambridge and New York (1956), and his paper, *"Relation of Technology to the Design of Very Large Cities"* in India's Future, R. Turner, editor, University of California Press, Berkeley (1961).

(2) See especially the work of O. E. Duncan, *Optimum Size of Cities,* in Hatt and Reiss, Reader in Urban Sociology, Free Press, Glencoe, Ill.

(3) A sample survey conducted in 1953 in India by the Taxation and Inquiry Commission found average per capita monthly expenditure in cities of 50,000 to 1 million population to be 30 percent higher than that in communities of 15,000 to 50,000 while cities of 1 million and over were 40 percent higher. See Catherine B. Wurster, *Urban Living Conditions, Overhead Costs in the Development Pattern,* in R. Turner, *op. cit.*

(4) See Duncan, *op. cit.,* and W. Isard and R. Coughlin, *Municipal Costs and Revenues Resulting from Community Growth,* Chandler Davis, Wellesley, Mass. (1957).

(5) Pitamber Pant, in R. Turner, *op. cit.*

(6) Martin Meyerson, *Planning for Movement in Developing Countries,* Regional Planning, seminar held in Tokyo in August, 1958, U.N., New York, 85–93 (1959).

(7) R. L. Meier, *op. cit.*

The Emerging International Culture

HAROLD D. LASSWELL

Professor of Law and Political Science, Yale University Law School,
New Haven, Connecticut

Definitions

In broadest definition "culture" is a distinctive way of life. It is helpful to speak of "international culture" only if there are grounds for the assertion that a distinctive mode of living has become sufficiently general to justify separate study.

Most of us have no doubt, even in the absence of detailed surveys of the globe, that an international culture is in active growth. What can we expect to accomplish by inquiring into the matter further?

(a) We can obtain more inclusive and accurate knowledge of the rate and degree of spread of international culture.

(b) We can improve our knowledge of the identity and the impact of the factors that determine these trends.

(c) Assuming that present trends are not interfered with, it will be possible to estimate the probable development of international culture.

(d) If we discover common value-goals that have emerged as part of international culture, we can consider the possibility of "interfering" with the future

by clarifying—especially by specifying— these goals.

(e) In the light of clarified value outcomes, we can encourage policy innovations that bring future developments into harmony with these objectives.

The evidence that international culture is emerging falls into three categories: (a) indications of parallel patterns in national or sub-national communities (e.g., the teaching of modern science); (b) indicators of trans-national flows of people, signs (media), and things (e.g., travel, communication, trade); (c) indicators of trans-national perspectives (e.g., group identities, value demands, expectations).

Strictly speaking, not all significant "inter-cultures" are "international," although statistics are usually reported by national areas since the "nation state" became the dominant unit in world politics. In previous epochs in Europe (and in non-national periods elsewhere) key units have included empires, cities, manors, and tribal lands. Ultimately, it may serve comparative purposes (a) to identify the dominant units through history and pre-history everywhere, (b) to ascertain the presence or absence of a degree of interaction that justifies speaking of "inter-unit" culture. If, for instance, we agree with V. Gordon Childe that cities were invented in a few places around 5000 B.C., we may trace evidence of (1) inter-city culture, (2) inter-tribal (folk) culture, and (3) city-folk culture.

An additional means of keeping hypothetical possibilities in close relationship to the data of history and geography is to choose cross-sections (in time and space) as bench marks of reference. A date in the 16th Century could be used to display the situation early in the history of the nation-state system. In view of its pivotal role we might select the treaty of Westphalia, in the middle of the next century, for reference.

Limiting attention to international culture-entities, ˙distinctions must be drawn among trans-national patterns whose scope is (a) bilateral (i.e., involves two component notions), (b) regional (i.e., includes several nations or a large geographical area), and (c) universal (i.e., involves every nation or an overwhelming percentage of nations).

Trends

The following characterization of trends in international culture must, of course, be modified to fit detailed situations.

Power Values and Institutions. Although the pursuit of political power is almost universally rejected in international culture as an "end in itself," the importance of power as a base for the defense and accumulation of all values has maintained or even increased its role. The expectation of violence, joined with the application of science to military technology, has sustained a chronic, rising level of military preparation. Simulta-

neously, the destructive implications of warfare are more widely perceived than ever, and institutions of public order, though far from strong, do exist. The political elites of the world, whatever their mode of composition or ideology, continue to be unwilling to make the seeming sacrifices necessary to consolidate an effective universal system of public order.

The structure of international politics, despite great fluctuations since the 16th Century, has moved *from* a pattern in which many or a plurality of powers were dominant (multipolarity) *toward* relative bipolarity.

In terms of ideological themes, wars and revolutions in the name of "Protestantism" or "Catholicism" were succeeded by the use of justifications phrased in the language of legality and ethics ("rights of man"), economic freedom ("liberalism," "socialism"), and racism ("organism"). However, no one system has attained universality.

On matters relating to the internal structure of political power, international culture is highly unified in proclaimed norm and sharply divided along bloc lines. Power-sharing (democracy) is the principal ideal, and allegedly finds expression in mass electorates and elections, mass political parties, pressure organizations, news and propaganda networks. In "communist" or "socialist" states one party has an overwhelming position; hence, "non-communist" or "non-socialist" states deny that democracy exists there. In rejoinder, "communist" spokesmen deny that democracy coexists with "capitalism."

Enlightenment Values and Institutions. International culture assigns great weight to the gathering and dissemination of current information and to the research and scholarship required for the advancement of knowledge.

The communications revolution makes possible the building of general media networks to which mass audiences are accustomed to give attention. In relatively capitalistic economies, the content of the media is biased by commercial advertisers; in relatively socialistic societies, by party and governmental officials.

To an increasing extent, educated men everywhere share a common map of the natural order as described by science. A common map of factors that affect human personality and society is less widely shared; yet it gains definition as the social and behavioral sciences expand.

A vast structure of international associations contributes to the advancement of science and scholarship, exerting perpetual pressure to overcome barriers to the free flow of scientific information.

Wealth Values and Institutions. Contemporary international culture proclaims the pursuit of economic benefit as the main objective of political power. Levels of consumption are expected to rise in the long run even in highly centralized states that presently rely upon forced saving to speed industrialization.

The technology of production is unceasingly transformed as science discovers means of controlling new sources of energy and of synthesizing new materials. In rapid succession, technology has moved from the use of muscle, wind, and water to steam, chemical, electrical, and nuclear resources.

Economic institutions are now generally appraised in terms of gross national product, net saving and investment, productivity, levels of productive employment, consumers' goods and services, and related measures.

Well-being Values and Institutions. The world demand for health, safety, and comfort has grown more intense with the spread of expectations in regard to the capabilities of the medical sciences and of technologies that affect conditions of work.

The spread of international contact results in the sharing of risks to life, and stimulates measures to ward off epidemics and to foster public health. Contemporary technology carries distinctive threats to well-being (e.g., in transport and mining), and instigates answering provisions for precaution and care. Some mental disorders increase with the problems of transition and elicit programs of treatment and prevention.

Life expectancy rises in spite of the intermittent devastations wrought by wars of great scale and destructiveness. Improvements in infant mortality and in nutrition stimulate reproduction and contribute to the "population explosion" of which the world community is increasingly aware.

Skill Values and Institutions. The carriers of international culture are united in demanding opportunities to discover, cultivate, and exercise the capabilities latent in the nature of man. The most rudimentary call is for universal literacy; this is a prelude to demands for elementary, intermediate, advanced, and professional education.

At the same time, modern technology strips the worth from older skills and renders every contemporary specialty subject to obsolescence. Thus, programs of skill-conversion are essential to the smooth functioning of industrialized society.

The more opulent sectors of international culture are confronted for the first time by the challenge of fostering a style of life that takes for granted the universalization of leisure.

Affection Values and Institutions. In international culture the demand for affection is becoming less inhibited, especially among women, as they become emancipated from "duty marriages" and attending restrictions.

The decline of the extended family and the accompanying rise of the small family institution—in which partners choose one another—affords wider scope for affection within family life. The danger to children resulting from transition calls active programs of child care into existence.

Because of the close relationship between family systems and other traditional structures, the family is itself under attack in highly politicized and modernizing states. It cannot be said that as yet international culture has achieved a stable balance between the claims of family and friendship on the one hand and the claims of political institutions on the other.

Respect Values and Institutions. In many ways the principal trait of international culture is the "respect revolution" signalized by the revolt against caste and class privileges, and by affirmative emphasis upon the importance of receiving at least a basic minimum of respect as a human being, plus respect deserved as a matter of individual merit.

Particular "respect revolutions" have been directed against local castes or classes, or they have been aimed at elites who "colonize" indigenous peoples. The vitality of the demand for shared respect is reflected in international declarations against discrimination, and in the intensity with which internal controversies are conducted over alleged acts of discrimination.

Rectitude Values and Institutions. The demand that conduct be guided for the purpose of influencing life after death has been weakening as secular science spreads and as standards of living rise— or are thought to be capable of rising by the leverage of appropriate public policies. It is becoming more common for codes of responsible conduct to be justified, not in theological terms, but in the framework of appeals to supposed "logic," "historical necessity," or some other version of "natural law."

International culture is affected by another cross-current, which is the trend to politicize ecclesiastical institutions by subjecting them to attack in socialist-communist states, and to defense elsewhere.

Conditioning Factors

The following paragraphs identify some major factors that have conditioned the rise of international culture. Since trends influence one another, some factors mentioned above will be referred to again in a somewhat different context.

An initiating role has often been played by enlightenment and skill in accelerating the growth of the culture that we call international. Without the expansion of scientific, scholarly, and technical proficiencies, it is not easy to account for the distinctive features of the world pattern of today.

At the same time, however, it is necessary to underline the decisive impact of political factors upon the contemporary structure, especially as a result of the continuation into the modern era of the institution of war—including the expectation of violence, the assessment of social assets in terms of fighting effectiveness, and chronic preparation or prosecution of war.

Power and wealth considerations have been intricately interwoven in the rise of modern industrialism. An analysis of the accumulation of capital goods for use in further production reveals the changing balance of influence exercised by the public elites of government and by private elites of commerce, commercial agriculture, mining, manufacturing, transport, and finance. In city-states, for instance, private elites worked closely with the public elite to foster expansion and accumulation. In rising national-states, dynasties and officials encouraged public and private accumulation as a prime base of power. At later phases of growth, national-states were largely under the domination of coalitions of private interests that were concerned with accumulation. More recently, states of retarded industrialization have been ruled by party and official elites who have taken the surmounting of delay to be the major task.

By what mechanisms has the new culture spread and such social formations as the latter elites risen to power? Information about the potential of science and technology spread gradually beyond the early centers of industrialism. Intellectuals (educated or semieducated) took the initiative in arousing resentment against the indifference and contempt with which lower social formations were held. They stimulated a sense of outrage that was directed against the ruling elite of traditional society, and against contemporary imperialists (appealing to peasants, business men, and office seekers). They contributed disproportionately to the new ruling elites.

International culture has spread at different rates and therefore accentuated imbalances within the world community. Commercial activities typically expand by seeking to draw the entire population of a zone into the market. Manufacturers, on the other hand, emphasize the control of chosen centers, and subcenters from which they can assemble minerals or other raw material, or where facilities and manpower can be concentrated for processing operations.

Economics in technology favor big-scale units. Big units are also fostered by power considerations that tend to justify more control than is strictly defensible on engineering grounds. In view of the ambiguity of cost measurement, and the urge to cut down vulnerability to outside factors, scale is pressed beyond the upper limit of economic advantage. The accounting methods employed in private or state monopolies favor the primacy of power considerations by masking the facts in regard to cost. The result is to stimulate the worldwide spread of industrial culture, and at the same time to accentuate disparities of level among subcenters and zones.

Projection

In estimating the future of international culture the most important point is that, if present trends continue, disastrous wars are probable. The annihilation of mankind is no longer a *remote* contingency.

Important factors in the total context may succeed in modifying the sequence of future development. Conceding the dangers of a divided world, the principal elites of power (and of other values) may be willing to sacrifice their seeming "autonomy" for a more general solution.

The potential advantages of such a reconstruction are not only negative—in the sense that disaster is avoided—but positive, since the huge diversion of resources to war preparation can be stopped, and the advantages of modern science can be fully realized on Earth and also in the emerging arena of astro-politics.

Goal Values

Can we affirm that international culture is sufficiently united in general goal and in specific objectives to move by consent toward a more perfect system of universal public order?

In this connection we note that a high degree of verbal agreement exists among the political elites of the globe in giving deference to the dignity of man. Constitutional charters and fundamental statutes of nearly all nation-states profess to serve the inclusive interests of the whole people, rather than the special interests of classes or castes. Moreover, the political leaders of nearly all nation-states have communicated formal agreements to one another in which they commit their bodies politic to the objective in question. Many nation-states have given notice of ratification to instruments such as the Declaration of Human Rights, which add definiteness to broad aspiration. Pertinent, too, are the many transnational meetings of an official or unofficial character that have been devoted to these topics. More convincing is the dispatch of economic, propaganda, diplomatic, and even military assistance in the name of these obligations. Testimony obtained by direct interview reveals that the leaders of groups who regard themselves as oppressed are sufficiently cognizant of their identity as part of the international community to think of seek-

ing foreign aid in improving their lot.

How far does international culture go beyond verbal agreement to behavioral conformity? The data are not at hand to give an exhaustive reply to this question. It would be a mistake to ignore or to minimize the groups who flatly reject the validity of the inclusive goal of human dignity and proclaim the right to rule of racial (or other) castes.

Alternatives

Can we participate in the creative future of international culture by formulating proposed lines of action designed to expedite the realization of the proclaimed ideal?

Scientists and scholars do not have primary responsibility for public policy. As a matter of formal authority and of effective division of labor, the obligation rests upon statesmen, officials, and political leaders. At the same time, it is evident that professional intellectuals do in fact play an important part in the decision-making and executing process within nation-states and among states. The political process is itself part of international culture, and interacts with every value-institutional component of the whole.

It is possible to be more definite about the role of scientists and scholars in world decision by examining the functional phases of the decision process itself. Official or unofficial policy formation depends upon intelligence, or the function of gathering information and evolving plans. In all that touches upon basic information it is obvious that the entire scientific and scholarly community is heavily involved. The policy process includes promotional activity, and professional scholars do not necessarily engage in this sphere nor in official legislation and administration, even though academic training is in many nation-states requisite to an active career in the bureaucracy or the officer corps. Scholars and scientists cannot fail to contribute to the appraising function, however, since public-policy activities are among the conditioning factors in the historical and contemporary process that must be weighed. It is impossible to conceive of a modern body-politic whose self-examination does not draw heavily upon the knowledge—and personnel—of the sciences. The impact of legislation (prescription) calls for assessment; so, too, does the efficacy of the invocation or application of public policy declarations.

It is probable that as international culture is more widely recognized that scientists and scholars will take more vigorous initiatives intended to illuminate the goals, achievements, and failures of international life.

Index